ROUTLEDGE HANDBOOK OF MAJOR EVENTS IN ECONOMIC HISTORY

The *Routledge Handbook of Major Events in Economic History* aims to introduce readers to the important macroeconomic events of the past two hundred years. The chapters endeavour to explain what went on and why during the most significant economic epochs of the nineteenth, twentieth and early twenty-first centuries and how where we are today fits in this historical timeline. Its short chapters reflect the most up-to-date research and are written by well-known economists who are authorities on their subjects.

The book is divided into four sections. Part I presents topics from the pre-1919 period and focuses on the experiences of the First and Second Banks of the United States, the recurring financial panics and their role in the establishment of the Federal Reserve System, the long deflation of the 1870s, the great merger wave, and the functioning of the classical gold standard. It ends with a discussion of the tragedy and horror that was World War I.

Part II addresses the history of the interwar era (1919–1939) and World War II. The economics of the 1920s and the Great Depression comprise the greatest share of chapters in this section. It ends with a discussion of the tragedy and horror that was World War II

Part III looks at the post-World War II period and the transitional economic events that make up the history of 1945 to the early 2000s. The great inflation of the 1970s to the disinflation of the 1980s, the rise of China and India to the fall of Japan and the Soviet Union, the rebuilding of Europe under the Marshall Plan and the advent of globalization to the rise and fall of the Bretton Woods system and the Phillips Curve. The urban riots of the 1960s and the history of oil shocks, shocks that have played such an important role in the evolution of post-World War II business cycle disturbances, are also included.

Part IV contains topics of the contemporary era. The most recent economic issues include world hyperinflations, the emergence of mass-market merchandisers, the panic of 2008 and monetary policy responses, the Eurozone and its future, government bailouts and the economics of entitlements, debt and deficits.

The *Routledge Handbook of Major Events in Economic History* was written with the intent of presenting the professional consensus in explaining the economics driving these historical events.

Randall E. Parker is Professor of Economics at East Carolina University, USA.

Robert Whaples is Professor of Economics at Wake Forest University, USA.

ROUTLEDGE HANDBOOK OF MAJOR EVENTS IN ECONOMIC HISTORY

Edited by Randall E. Parker and Robert Whaples

Routledge
Taylor & Francis Group

LONDON AND NEW YORK

First published 2013 by Routledge

2 Park Square, Milton Park, Abingdon, Oxfordshire OX14 4RN
52 Vanderbilt Avenue, New York, NY 10017

Routledge is an imprint of the Taylor & Francis Group, an informa business

First issued in paperback 2019

British Library Cataloguing in Publication Data
A catalogue record for this book is available from the British Library

Library of Congress Cataloging in Publication Data
Routledge handbook of major events in economic history / Edited
by Randall E. Parker and Robert Whaples.
        pages cm
    1. Economics – History. I. Parker, Randall E., 1960– II. Whaples,
    Robert. III. Title: Handbook of major events in economic history.
    HB75.R6748 2013
    330.9–dc23   2012031239

ISBN: 978-0-415-67703-5 (hbk)
ISBN: 978-0-367-86620-4 (pbk)

Typeset in Bembo
by HWA Text and Data Management, London

CONTENTS

Contents

LIST OF FIGURES

LIST OF TABLES

NOTES ON CONTRIBUTORS

Harold Bierman, Jr. has been a Cornell faculty member since 1956, and formerly taught at Louisiana State University, the University of Michigan, and the University of Chicago. Professor Bierman was a recipient of the annual Dow Jones Award from the American Assembly of Collegiate Schools of Business for outstanding contributions to collegiate business education. In 1985 he served as a scholar-in-residence at the investment banking firm of Prudential Bache and in 1990 he served as Senior Academic Fellow at the Financial Accounting Standards Board. His industrial experience includes consulting with Corning Corporation, Eastman Kodak, Emerson Electric Co., IBM, AT&T, Anheuser-Busch, and Xerox Corp. His primary teaching interest is corporate financial policy. He has written twenty-six books, including *The Capital Budgeting Decision* (with Seymour Smidt) and *The Great Myths of 1929*, and more than 160 journal articles. This information was obtained and is available at http://www.world-economics-journal.com/Contents/AuthorDetails.aspx?AID=80

Loren Brandt is a Professor of Economics at the University of Toronto specializing in the Chinese economy. He has been at the University of Toronto since 1987. He is also a research fellow at the IZA (The Institute for the Study of Labor) in Bonn, Germany. He has published widely on the Chinese economy in leading economic journals, and has been involved in extensive household and enterprise survey work in both China and Vietnam. He was co-editor and major contributor to *China's Great Economic Transformation*, a landmark study that provides an integrated analysis of China's unexpected economic boom of the past three decades. Dr. Brandt was also one of the area editors for Oxford University Press's five-volume *Encyclopedia of Economic History*. His current research focuses on issues of industrial upgrading in China, inequality dynamics, and economic growth and structural change. This information was obtained and is available at http://homes.chass.utoronto.ca/~brandt/

Richard C. K. Burdekin is Professor of Economics at Claremont McKenna College. He specializes in monetary and financial economics, Chinese economy, economic history, international economics and sports economics. He has been an Editorial Board Member of *Economic Systems* and *The Open Economics Journal* since 2008. He is a member of the American

Economic Association, the Chinese Economists Society, the Economic History Association and the Western Economic Association. He has published articles in *Journal of Money, Credit, and Banking, Journal of Financial Economic Policy, Journal of Banking and Finance, Chinese Economic Review,* and elsewhere. His published books include *China's Monetary Challenges: Past Experiences and Future Prospects, Deflation: Current and Historical Perspectives* (edited with Pierre L. Siklos), *Distributional Conflict and Inflation: Theoretical and Historical Perspectives* (with Paul Burkett), *Establishing Monetary Stability in Emerging Market Economies* (edited with Thomas D. Willett, Richard J. Sweeney and Clas Wihlborg), *Confidence, Credibility and Macroeconomic Policy: Past, Present, Future* (with Farrokh K. Langdana), and *Budget Deficits and Economic Performance* (with Farrokh K. Langdana). This information was obtained and is available at http://www.claremontmckenna.edu/rdschool/cv/Burdekin_CV_Dec_2011.pdf

James L. Butkiewicz is Professor in Economics at the University of Delaware. He received his PhD in economics from the University of Virginia in 1977. His areas of specialization include the economics of the Great Depression, determinants of economic growth, monetary theory and history, and macroeconomic policy analysis. His research has been published in *Journal of Money, Credit, and Banking, Journal of Monetary Economics, Southern Economic Journal, Land Economics, Journal of Macroeconomics,* and elsewhere. His professional affiliations include the American Economic Association, Eastern Economic Association, Economic History Association and Southern Economic Association. This information was obtained and is available at http://www.lerner.udel.edu/sites/default/files/imce/pdf/Econ/20110801-Butkiewicz%20-%20Vitae.pdf

Art Carden is Assistant Professor of Economics at Samford University. He is also a Research Fellow with the Independent Institute, a Senior Research Fellow with the Institute for Faith, Work, and Economics, and a Senior Fellow with the Beacon Center of Tennessee. He is also a regular contributor to Forbes.com and the *Washington Examiner*. Before joining the faculty at Samford, he taught economics at Rhodes College.

Mark Carlson is a Senior Economist with the Board of Governors of the Federal Reserve System. His fields of interest include banking and financial institutions, economic history, and monetary policy. He received his PhD in economics from the University of California, Berkeley in 2001. His professional affiliations include the American Economics Association and the Economic History Association. He has published articles in the *B.E. Journal of Economic Analysis & Policy, Journal of Money, Credit, and Banking, Journal of Political Economy, Finance and Economics Discussion Series* with the Board of Governors of the Federal Reserve System, and elsewhere. This information was obtained and is available at http://www.federalreserve.gov/econresdata/mark-a-carlson.htm

Areendam Chanda is Associate Professor of Economics at Louisiana State University. He received his PhD in economics from Brown University in 2001. He specializes in economic growth, foreign direct investment, and consumption and savings. Some of his research has been published in *Journal of Development Economics, Economica, Cliometrica, Journal of Economic Dynamics and Control,* and elsewhere. This information was obtained and is available at http://www.bus.lsu.edu/achanda/

William J. Collins is Professor of Economics and Chair at Vanderbilt University. He received his PhD from the Harvard Graduate School of Arts and Sciences in 1998. He has published articles in *American Economic Review, American Economic Journal: Macroeconomics, Journal of Economic History, Explorations in Economic History,* and elsewhere. He is a Research Associate for the National Bureau of Economic Research and was a Senior Economist for the Council of Economic Advisers in 2006–2007. His main fields of research interest are economic history and labor economics. This information was obtained and is available at http://www.vanderbilt.edu/econ/faculty/cv/CollinsCV.pdf

Nicholas Crafts is Professor of Economics and Economic History at the University of Warwick, a post he has held since 2006. He is also Director of the ESRC Research Centre on Competitive Advantage in the Global Economy (CAGE), at Warwick. His main fields of interest are long-run economic growth, British economic performance and policy in the twentieth century, the industrial revolution, and the historical geography of industrial location. He has published many papers in academic journals and has also contributed to research by the International Monetary Fund and the World Bank. This information was obtained and is available at http://www.voxeu.org/index.php?q=node/1392

Barry Eichengreen is the George C. Pardee and Helen N. Pardee Professor of Economics and Professor of Political Science at the University of California, Berkeley, where he has taught since 1987. He is a Research Associate of the National Bureau of Economic Research and Research Fellow of the Centre for Economic Policy Research (London). Some of his most recent books include *Exorbitant Privilege: The Rise and Fall of the Dollar and the Future of the International Monetary System, Emerging Giants: China and India in the World Economy* (edited with Poonam Gupta and Ranjiv Kumar), and *Labor in the Era of Globalization* (edited with Clair Brown and Michael Reich). Professor Eichengreen was awarded the Economic History Association's Jonathan R.T. Hughes Prize for Excellence in Teaching in 2002, and the University of California at Berkeley Social Science Division's Distinguished Teaching Award in 2004. He is the recipient of a *doctor honoris causa* from the American University in Paris, and the 2010 recipient of the Schumpeter Prize from the International Schumpeter Society. He was named one of *Foreign Policy Magazine*'s 100 Leading Global Thinkers in 2011. This information was obtained and is available at http://emlab.berkeley.edu/~eichengr/biosketch.html

Jari Eloranta is Associate Professor of Economic and Business History at Appalachian State University, Department of History. His research interests include military spending in the nineteenth and twentieth centuries, corporate political action in the twentieth century, Finnish and Scandinavian economic history, long-run explanations of central government spending and the welfare state, and others. His research has been published in *Journal of Iberian and Latin American Economic History, Cambridge Economic History of Modern Europe, Essays in Economic and Business History*, and elsewhere. Jari is currently a member of the Economic and Business Historical Society (EBHS) and the Economic History Association, as well as others. This information was obtained and is available at http://www.appstate. edu/~elorantaj/

Richard E. Ericson is Professor of Economics at East Carolina University and received his PhD from the University of California, Berkeley in 1979. His primary research areas are comparative economic systems, microeconomic theory, and the economics of transition. His articles have appeared in *Econometrica, Journal of Economic Theory* and *Journal of Economic Perspectives,* among others. This information was obtained and is available at http:// www.ecu.edu/cs-educ/econ/ericsonr.cfm

Price V. Fishback is the Frank and Clara Kramer Professor of Economics at The University of Arizona and a Research Associate with the National Bureau of Economic Research. Fishback received his PhD in economics at the University of Washington in 1983. He worked with 15 of the leading economic historians in the United States to write *Government and the American Economy: A New History*, released in April 2007 from the University of Chicago Press. His 2000 book (with Shawn Kantor), *A Prelude to the Welfare State: The Origins of Workers' Compensation*, was awarded a Paul Samuelson Certificate of Excellence by the TIAA-CREF Institute, and the Lester Prize by the Industrial Relations Group at Princeton University. In 2002 he received the Cliometric Society's highest award for exceptional service. In 2006, he was elected a Trustee of the Economic History Association. This information was obtained and is available at http://www.ellermba.arizona.edu/executive/faculty/bios/pfishback.asp

Gary Gorton is a Professor of Finance at Yale School of Management, and is currently a Research Associate of the National Bureau of Economic Research. He is a former member of the Moody's Investors Services Academic Advisory Panel. He is also the former Director of the Research Program on Banks and the Economy for the Federal Deposit Insurance Corporation. He previously worked as an economist and senior economist at the Federal Reserve Bank of Philadelphia. During 1994 he was the Houblon-Norman Fellow at the Bank of England. Dr. Gorton is a member of the American Finance Association, the American Economic Association, and the Econometric Society. Dr. Gorton has consulted for the U.S. Board of Governors of the Federal Reserve System, various U.S. Federal Reserve Banks, the Bank of England, the Bank of Japan, and the Central Bank of Turkey. He has also consulted for a number of private firms. This information was obtained and is available at http://faculty. som.yale.edu/garygorton/bio.html

Teresa Gramm is Associate Professor at Rhodes College. She received her PhD from the University of North Carolina at Chapel Hill and has published articles in *Review of International Economics* and *International Trade Journal*.

James D. Hamilton is a Professor in the Economics Department at the University of California at San Diego where he has been since 1992. He had previously taught at the University of Virginia and received a PhD in economics from the University of California at Berkeley in 1983. Professor Hamilton has published articles on a wide range of topics including econometrics, business cycles, monetary policy, and energy markets. His graduate textbook on time series analysis has over 10,000 scholarly citations and has been translated into Chinese, Japanese, and Italian. Academic honors include election as a Fellow of the Econometric Society and Research Associate with the National Bureau of Economic Research. He has been a visiting scholar at the Federal Reserve Board in Washington, D.C., as well as the Federal Reserve Banks of Atlanta, Boston, New York, Richmond, and San Francisco. He has also been a consultant for the National Academy of Sciences, Commodity Futures Trading Commission and the European Central Bank, and has testified before the United States Congress. This information was obtained and is available at http://dss.ucsd. edu/~jhamilto/brief_bio.html

Steve H. Hanke is a Professor of Applied Economics and Co-Director of the Institute for Applied Economics and the Study of Business Enterprise at The Johns Hopkins University in Baltimore. In the past, Professor Hanke taught economics at the Colorado School of Mines and the University of California, Berkeley. He is currently a member of the National

Bank of Kuwait's International Advisory Board and a member of the Financial Advisory Council of the United Arab Emirates. Professor Hanke also served as a Senior Economist on President Reagan's Council of Economic Advisers in 1981–82; as a State Counselor to the Republic of Lithuania in 1994–1996 and to the Republic of Montenegro in 1999–2003; and as an Advisor to the Presidents of Bulgaria in 1997–2002, Venezuela in 1995–96 and Indonesia in 1998. He played an important role in establishing new currency regimes in Argentina, Estonia, Bulgaria, Bosnia-Herzegovina, Ecuador, Lithuania, and Montenegro. In 1998, he was named one of the twenty-five most influential people in the world by World Trade Magazine. Professor Hanke is a well-known currency and commodity trader. He currently serves as Chairman of the Richmond Group Fund Co., Ltd., a global macro hedge fund located in Richmond, Virginia. During the 1990s, he served as President of Toronto Trust Argentina in Buenos Aires, the world's best-performing emerging market mutual fund in 1995. Professor Hanke's most recent books are *Zimbabwe: Hyperinflation to Growth* and *A Blueprint for a Safe, Sound Georgian Lari*. This information was obtained and is available at http://www.cato.org/people/steve-hanke

Robert L. Hetzel received his PhD from the University of Chicago in 1975. He is a senior economist and research advisor in the Research Department at the Federal Reserve of Richmond, and has been there since 1975. His research has been published in *Cato Journal* and *Journal of Money, Credit and Banking*. Most recently, Dr. Hetzel authored two books, *The Monetary Policy of the Federal Reserve: A History* and *The Great Recession: Market Failure or Policy Failure?* This information was obtained and is available at http://www.richmondfed.org/research/economists/bios/hetzel_bio.cfm#tabview=tab1

Robert Higgs is Senior Fellow in Political Economy for The Independent Institute and Editor of the Institute's quarterly journal *The Independent Review*. He received his PhD in economics from The Johns Hopkins University. He is the recipient of numerous awards, including the Gary Schlarbaum Award for Lifetime Defense of Liberty, Thomas Szasz Award for Outstanding Contributions to the Cause of Civil Liberties, Lysander Spooner Award for Advancing the Literature of Liberty, Friedrich von Wieser Memorial Prize for Excellence in Economic Education, and Templeton Honor Rolls Award on Education in a Free Society. Dr. Higgs authored the books *Crisis and Leviathan: Critical Episodes in the Growth of American Government, Depression, War, and Cold War, Neither Liberty Nor Safety*, and *The Political Economy of Fear*, among others. His popular articles have appeared in *The Wall Street Journal, Los Angeles Times, Providence Journal, Chicago Tribune, San Francisco Examiner, San Francisco Chronicle, Society, Reason*, and many other publications and web sites. Dr. Higgs has spoken at more than 100 colleges and universities and at the meetings of such professional organizations as the Economic History Association, Western Economic Association, Population Association of America, Southern Economic Association, and others. This information was obtained and is available at http://www.independent.org/aboutus/person_detail.asp?id=489

Michael Kitson is University Senior Lecturer in global macroeconomics at the Judge Business School, University of Cambridge; Knowledge Hub Director of the UK Innovation Research Centre; Fellow of St. Catharine's College, Cambridge; and Assistant Director of the Centre for Business Research, Cambridge. His research interests include: economic policy, regional economics, corporate performance and innovation. He has published in journals such as *Cambridge Journal of Economics, Economic History Review, Economic Journal*, and contributed to *The Cambridge Economic History of Modern Britain: vol. 3: Structural Change and Growth, 1939–2000*, and wrote the chapter "Slump and recovery: the UK experience" for the book *World Economy and National Economies in the Interwar Slump*. This information was obtained and is available at http://www.jbs.cam.ac.uk/research/faculty/kitsonm.html

Arnold Kling received his PhD in economics from the Massachusetts Institute of Technology in 1980. He was an economist on the staff of the Board of Governors of the Federal Reserve System from 1980–1986. He was a senior economist at Freddie Mac from 1986–1994. In 1994, he started Homefair.com, one of the first commercial sites on the World Wide Web. (Homefair was sold in 1999 to Homestore.com.) Dr. Kling is an adjunct scholar with the Cato Institute and a member of the Financial Markets Working Group at the Mercatus Center at George Mason University. He teaches statistics and economics at the Berman Hebrew Academy in Rockville, Maryland. This information was obtained and is available at http://econlog.econlib.org/authorakling.html

Nicholas Krus is a research associate at The Johns Hopkins Institute for Applied Economics, Global Health, and the Study of Business Enterprise. He recently graduated Phi Beta Kappa from The Johns Hopkins University with a B.A. in Economics and Mathematics. Mr. Krus was a recipient of the Bela Balassa Dean's Undergraduate Research Award for his work on currency boards and was both a BB&T and a Patel Scholar.

Eric Lomazoff is Assistant Professor of Classics and Letters at the University of Oklahoma and is affiliated with the Institute for the American Constitutional Heritage. Having received his PhD in Government from Harvard in 2010, Dr. Lomazoff's dissertation *Reconstructing the Hydra-Headed Monster: The Bank of the United States and the Constitutional Politics of Change* was focused on the first and second national banks of the United States. His research interests include the constitution outside the Supreme Court, American constitutional history, mechanisms of institutional development, and contemporary fiscal and monetary politics. Recent publications include "Approval Regulation and Endogenous Consumer Confidence: Theory and Analogies to Licensing, Safety, and Financial Regulation", *Regulation & Governance*, (December 2010). This information was obtained and is available at http://millercenter.org/academic/dgs/fellowship/2009#lomazoff

W. Douglas McMillin is Mack Hornbeak Endowed Professor in Economics at E.J. Ourso College of Business at Louisiana State University. His interests include monetary economics and macroeconomics. He has published articles in *Southern Economic Journal*, *Economic Journal*, and *Journal of International Money and Finance*, among others. He is co-editor of *Journal of Macroeconomics* and has been employed by LSU since 1983. This information was obtained and is available at http://www.bus.lsu.edu/directory/intranet_directory/facultywebpage.asp?autoid=53

Allan H. Meltzer is the Allan H. Meltzer University Professor of Political Economy at Carnegie Mellon University. He is the author of *A History of the Federal Reserve, Volumes I and II*, a definitive research work on the Federal Reserve System. He has been a member of the President's Economic Policy Advisory Board, an acting member of the President's Council of Economic Advisers, and a consultant to the U.S. Treasury Department and the Board of Governors of the Federal Reserve System. In 1999 and 2000, he served as the chairman of the International Financial Institution Advisory Commission, which was appointed by Congress to review the role of the International Monetary Fund, the World Bank, and other institutions. The author of several books and numerous papers on economic theory and policy, Dr. Meltzer is also a founder of the Shadow Open Market Committee. This information was obtained and is available at http://www.aei.org/scholar/allan-h-meltzer/

Andrew Metrick joined the Yale School of Management in 2008 as a professor of finance. He has previously held faculty positions in the finance department at Wharton and the economics department at Harvard. Professor Metrick's current research and teaching is focused on financial stability, including the regulation of systemic risk, the activities of complex financial institutions, and the causes and consequences of the financial crisis of 2007–2009. His past work has been in financial intermediation more generally, with a focus on investment management and corporate governance. Professor Metrick has been honored with more than a dozen teaching awards and distinctions, including two years (2003 and 2007) as the highest-rated professor in the Wharton MBA program. In 1998, he received the highest teaching honor at Harvard College, the Joseph R. Levenson Memorial Teaching Award, and in 2005, he received the highest teaching honor at the University of Pennsylvania, the Lindback Award. This information was obtained and is available at http://faculty.som.yale.edu/andrewmetrick/index.html

Kris James Mitchener is Robert and Susan Finocchio Professor of Economics, Department of Economics, Santa Clara University, and Research Associate at the National Bureau of Economic Research. His research focuses on international economics, macroeconomics, monetary economics, and economic history. Professor Mitchener's research is published or forthcoming in *Economic Journal*, *Journal of Law and Economics*, *Journal of Economic Growth*, *Journal of International Money and Finance*, *Journal of Economic History*, *Monetary and Economic Studies*, and *Research in Economic History*. He has held visiting positions at the Bank of Japan, the St. Louis Federal Reserve Bank, UCLA, and CREi at Universitat Pompeu Fabra. He presently serves on the editorial boards of *Journal of Economic History* and *Economics*. This information was obtained and is available at http://lsb.scu.edu/~kmitchener/research/short%20bio.pdf

Anthony Patrick O'Brien is Professor of Economics at Lehigh University. His research interests include the economic history of African Americans, the international economy during the interwar years, and the historical development of nominal wage rigidity. His research has been published in *American Economic Review*, *Quarterly Journal of Economics*, *Journal of Money, Credit, and Banking*, *Journal of Economic History*, and elsewhere. He has received grants from the American Iron and Steel Institute, the Economic History Association, the Government of Canada, and the National Science Foundation. At Lehigh, he has been a Dana Faculty Fellow, Class of 1961 Professor, and was awarded the Lehigh University Award for Distinguished Teaching. This information was obtained and is available at http://www4.lehigh.edu/business/faculty/facultyprofile.aspx?Channel=%2FChannels%2FBusiness&WorkflowItemID=1679a757-ec27-4aa1-9725-67fbcad6fb41

Lee E. Ohanian is Professor of Economics, and Director of the Ettinger Family Program in Macroeconomic Research at UCLA. He received his PhD in economics from the University of Rochester in 1993, and received a BA in economics from the University of California, Santa Barbara, in 1979. He is an advisor to the Federal Reserve Bank of Minneapolis, and previously has advised other Federal Reserve Banks, foreign central banks, and the National Science Foundation. He is a research associate with the National Bureau of Economic

Research, and co-directs the NBER research group "Macroeconomics Across Time and Space." His research interests are in macroeconomics and international economics. He has lectured and published widely in the areas of economic crises, particularly the Great Depression. He previously served on the faculties of the Universities of Minnesota and Pennsylvania. This information was obtained and is available at http://www.voxeu.org/index.php?q=node/4091

Martha L. Olney is Adjunct Professor at the University of California, Berkeley. Her fields include economic history, macroeconomics, and economics of discrimination. Her research interests include consumer spending, consumer indebtedness, race and credit and saving, and the Great Depression. She is a member of the American Economic Association, Business History Conference, Cliometric Society, Economic History Association, and the Social Science History Association. She currently serves on the board of the AEA's Committee for the Status of Women in the Economics Profession and on the academic advisory board of the Financial Services Research Program of George Washington University. This information was obtained and is available at http://econ.berkeley.edu/faculty/839

Randall E. Parker is Professor of Economics at East Carolina University. He is the author of *Reflections on the Great Depression, The Economics of the Great Depression: A Twenty-First Century Look Back at the Economics of the Interwar Era* and is the editor of *The Seminal Works of the Great Depression.* He has also published research in journals such as *Economic Inquiry, Journal of Macroeconomics,* and *Journal of Money, Credit, and Banking.*

John J. Seater is Professor in the Department of Economics and Business at North Carolina State University. His research interests include economic growth, technical change, and macroeconomic dynamics. He has published articles in *The Concise Encyclopedia of Economics, Battleground: Economics and Business, Journal of Monetary Economics, Empirical Economics,* and others. He also is an associate editor for *Journal of Business and Economic Statistics.* This information was obtained and is available at http://www4.ncsu.edu/~jjseater/PDF/Vita/Vita.pdf

Etsuro Shioji received his PhD from Yale University in 1995, and is currently a Professor at the Graduate School of Economics at Hitotsubashi University in Tokyo. His research interests center on issues in macroeconomics, microeconomics and growth in Japan. He has had articles published in *Journal of the Japanese and International Economies, Seoul Journal of Economics, Journal of Money, Credit, and Banking, Review of Economics and Statistics,* and elsewhere. Currently, he is focusing his work on the impact of the 2008 financial crisis on Japanese productivity and inflation dynamics. This information was obtained and is available at http://www006.upp.so-net.ne.jp/shioji/cv_e_january2011.pdf

Pierre L. Siklos is Professor of Economics at Wilfred Laurier University in Waterloo, Ontario, Canada, and is Director at the Viessmann European Research Centre (VERC). He specializes in macroeconomics with an emphasis on the study of inflation, central banks, and financial markets. He also conducts research in applied time series analysis. His research has been published in a variety of international journals and he has been a consultant to a variety of institutions and central banks. In 2008 he was chairholder of the Bundesbank Foundation of International Monetary Economics at the Freie Universität, Berlin. In December 2008 he became a Senior Fellow at the Centre for International Governance Innovation (CIGI). In September 2009 he was appointed to a three-year term as a member of the Czech National

Bank's Research Advisory Committee. This information was obtained and is available at http://www.wlu.ca/homepage.php?grp_id=758&ct_id=626&f_id=31

Ellis W. Tallman is the Danforth-Lewis Professor of Economics at Oberlin College and has published scholarly articles in the fields of macroeconomics, economic forecasting, and historical episodes of financial crises. In his research on financial crises, Dr. Tallman has drawn attention to the United States experience during the Panic of 1907, an event that motivated the creation of the Federal Reserve System. Dr Tallman's publications have appeared in scholarly journals such as *Journal of Monetary Economics, Economic Inquiry*, and *Explorations in Economic History*. This information was obtained and is available at http://new. oberlin.edu/arts-and-sciences/departments/economics/faculty_detail.dot?id=27124

Mark Toma is Associate Professor of Economics at the University of Kentucky. He has authored two books *Competition and Monopoly in the Federal Reserve System, 1914–1951* and *Central Bankers, Bureaucratic Incentives and Monetary Policy*, and has published extensively in scholarly journals such as *Journal of Money, Credit and Banking, Journal of Monetary Economics*, and *Journal of Economic History*. This information was obtained and is available at http://gatton. uky.edu/Content.asp?PageName=FRIndProfile&ID=52

Robert Whaples is Professor and Chair of Economics at Wake Forest University. He served as Director of EH.Net (2003–08) and editor of the *Online Encyclopedia of Economic and Business History*. His research in economic history, consensus among economists and coinage has been published in the *Eastern Economic Journal, Economic Inquiry, Economists' Voice, Journal of Economic History*, and *Social Science History*.

Elmus Wicker, is Professor Emeritus of Economics, Indiana University. His published works include *Banking Panics of the Gilded Age, Banking Panics of the Great Depression, The Great Debate on Banking Reform: Nelson Aldrich and the Origins of the Fed, Federal Reserve Monetary Policy 1917–1933*, and *The Principles of Monetary Economics*. His more recent research consists of a retrospective on the Fed's efforts since 1914 to control stock market speculation. He is completing a paper on what happened in the recent financial crisis and comparing it with the banking crises of the Gilded Age and the Great Depression (with Ellis Tallman). This information was obtained and is available at http://www.indiana.edu/~econweb/faculty/ wicker.html

Robert E. Wright is the Nef Family Chair of Political Economy and Director of the Thomas Willing Institute at Augustana College in South Dakota. In addition to editing three series of primary source documents for Pickering and Chatto Publishers, Dr. Wright has authored or co-authored fourteen books, including *One Nation Under Debt: Hamilton, Jefferson and the History of What We Owe*, which explores the untold history of America's first national debt, arising from the immense sums needed to conduct the American Revolution. Another title, *Financial Founding Fathers*, is a compelling account of the nation's early finances. See his information page at http://www.amazon.com/Robert-E.-Wright/e/B001IGLMVQ

PREFACE

The *Routledge Handbook of Major Events in Economic History* aims to introduce readers to the important macroeconomic events of the past 200 years. The chapters endeavour to explain what occurred during the most significant economic epochs of the nineteenth, twentieth and early twenty-first centuries, *why* it occurred and why this matters for us today. We hope that it will serve as supplementary reading for college courses in macroeconomics and economic history as well as a reference book useful to professional practitioners, policy makers and the public. Its short chapters reflect the most up-to-date research and are written by well-known economists who are authorities on their subjects.

The *Routledge Handbook of Major Events in Economic History* is divided into four parts. Part I presents topics from the pre-1919 period and focuses on the experiences of the First and Second Banks of the United States, the recurring financial panics and their role in the establishment of the Federal Reserve System, the long deflation of the 1870s, the Great Merger Wave, and the functioning of the classical gold standard. It also contains a discussion of the tragedy and horror that was World War I.

Part II addresses the history of the interwar era (1919–1939) and World War II. The economics of the 1920s and the Great Depression comprise the greatest share of chapters in this section. It ends with a discussion of the tragedy and horror that was World War II.

Part III looks at the post-World War II period and the transitional economic events that make up the history of 1945 to the early 2000s. It covers events from the great inflation of the 1970s to the disinflation of the 1980s; from the rise of China and India to the fall of Japan and the Soviet Union; from the rebuilding of Europe under the Marshall Plan and the advent of globalization to the rise and fall of the Bretton Woods system and the Phillips Curve, from the urban riots of the 1960s to the history of oil shocks – shocks that have played an important role in the evolution of post-World War II business cycle disturbances.

Part IV contains topics of the contemporary era. The most recent economic issues include world hyperinflations, the emergence of mass market merchandisers, the panic of 2008 and monetary policy responses, government bailouts and the economics of entitlements, debt and deficits.

The *Routledge Handbook of Major Events in Economic History* is written with the intent of presenting the professional consensus in explaining the economics driving these historical events.

PART I

World War I and the pre-World War I era

1

SYMMETRY AND REPETITION

Patterns in the history of the Bank of the United States

Eric Lomazoff

Introduction

For those who wish to explore the dense historical forest that is national banking in the early American Republic, past scholarly visitors have cleared and marked multiple trails. One might, for example, pleasantly venture forth using *personalities* as guideposts. Biographers have chronicled how figures large and small in American history imagined, made, sheltered, managed, and ultimately destroyed the Bank of the United States (Chernow 2004, Govan 1959, Newmyer 2001, Wright 1996, Remini 1984, 1998). Institutional *purposes* offer a second set of markers for navigating the historical terrain. Economic historians have repeatedly noted that while the "First" Bank was chartered to serve as a fiscal auxiliary to the federal government, the "Second" Bank was created to realize a mixture of fiscal and monetary goals (Redlich 1947, Hammond 1957, Womack 1978).[1] Constitutional *principles* offer a third way to tour the site and provide the way which is potentially the most straightforward. Scholars of American constitutionalism have portrayed the Bank as the focal point of a recurring two-sided dispute over the meaning of the Necessary and Proper Clause (Brest, Levinson, Balkin, and Amar 2000: 7–70, Gillman, Graber, and Whittington 2013: 123–37 and 201–6, O'Brien 2003: 60–62 and 497–500).

   This chapter is not designed to suggest that scholars need to draw yet another trail on the already crowded forest map. In other words, though the Bank's history might also be explored via two additional routes – the *parties* it helped to shape (Holt 1999, Leonard 2002, Marshall 2000: 353–54) and the *places* where it operated (Brown 1998, Kilbourne 2006, Wright 2005) – cutting a sixth pathway is not my object. By contrast, this chapter approaches the historical forest altogether differently, eschewing any close-range examination and instead taking a panoramic view from above. When the Bank's history is viewed from afar – with personalities, purposes, principles, parties, and places as mere features of a much larger landscape – two surprising patterns become visible. What is more, the interlocking character of these patterns suggests a broader orderliness about early American banking history that has gone unappreciated for far too long.

Accordingly, the goals of this chapter are to identify and document those patterns. Of course, the successful achievement of these goals necessarily entails a specialized retelling of the Bank's story. That retelling will prioritize patterns of *symmetry* and *repetition* in post-ratification American economic history. *Symmetry* invokes the image of identical shapes on opposite sides of a dividing line. Two gradual changes in the Bank, both of which commenced soon after its chartering in 1791, laid the groundwork for a two-track institutional existence. More importantly, those tracks came to mirror one another in important respects; both changes generated new sources of antagonism toward the institution and (at slightly different junctures) novel claims about its legitimacy. *Repetition* refers to recurrence over time or space. Both emergent sources of antagonism toward the Bank gained prominence periodically, manifesting themselves at multiple junctures in the institution's history. Repetition along tracks that mirror one another underwrites the claim that these patterns are interlocking.

The First Bank: in search of a fiscal auxiliary

The national bank bill that Alexander Hamilton proposed, the First Congress passed, and President Washington signed – all between December 1790 and February 1791 – created an "auxiliary to the fiscal operations" of the young federal government (Timberlake 1993: 6). This is a simple yet crucial fact that captures much about the institution's origins *and* its subsequent development. While change during the life of the First Bank (1791–1811) is treated at length below, the circumstances of its birth also warrant some discussion.

Hamilton's first years as Treasury Secretary were marked by repeated efforts to right the nation's fiscal ship, which had all but capsized following the long and costly Revolutionary War (Ferguson 1961, Bruchey 1990: 118–19). The foundation for Hamilton's efforts was the newly-ratified Constitution, which empowered Congress to both "lay and collect Taxes" and "pay the Debts ... of the United States" (Edling 2008). Congress flexed some of these new muscles almost immediately, passing two revenue-raising measures in July 1789 (Cowen 2000: 9). The Treasury Secretary soon argued that these new income streams had utility far beyond "pay[ing] the current expenses of the government"; they could be used to demonstrate the nation's creditworthiness (Beard 1915: 161, Razaghian 2002). His January 1790 *Report on the Public Credit* proposed both the consolidation of existing debts and the use of federal revenue to pay regular interest on them (Hamilton 2001: 531–74). Both the publication of Hamilton's report and its subsequent adoption by Congress signaled a serious national commitment to debt management, and "public credit" (as revealed through the price of federal bonds) improved accordingly (Sylla, Wright, and Cowen 2009: 70).

The successful push to consolidate and fund existing public debt places Hamilton's next move in its proper context. In December 1790, the Treasury Secretary submitted a second report to Congress, conventionally known as the *Report on a National Bank* (Hamilton 2001: 575). The institutional design sketched therein became the basis for the first Bank of the United States. The submission, however, was actually called the *Second Report on the Further Provision Necessary for Establishing Public Credit* (Hamilton 1963: 236). This distinction is important because it calls attention to the myriad ways in which Hamilton's brainchild was designed to support the aforementioned "fiscal operations" of the federal government.

Some of those ways are captured by the Treasury Secretary's suggestion that a national bank "is an Institution of primary importance to the prosperous administration of the Finances" (Hamilton 2001: 575). The proposed bank would provide a number of services to the federal government: it would lend money in times of public need, serve as a depository for revenue, transfer deposited funds elsewhere in the Union upon request and without charge, and make payments from those funds to public creditors (Cowen 2000: 14). These fiscal supports for the government were important, but they fail to explain Hamilton's rationale for naming the report as he did. The answer here lies in the claim that a national bank would also "be of the greatest utility in the operations connected with the support of the Public Credit" (Hamilton 2001: 575). How could the institution offer additional support to the "Public Credit"? In short, by increasing demand for the newly-funded debt. Under Hamilton's plan, shares in the proposed bank would be purchased partially with specie and partially with these government securities. Capitalizing the institution in this manner – in essence, making investors pay for bank stock with interest-bearing federal bonds – would work to support the market for (and price of) these instruments. All told, the bank might render specific fiscal services to the government, but the latter's ability to finance its operations would also be significantly enhanced by the design of the institution.

The bill modeled on Hamilton's bank proposal famously encountered constitutional opposition, first within the House of Representatives and then the executive branch (Clarke and Hall 1832: 37–114, Dellinger and Powell 1994). Some students of the episode, citing Southern anxieties concerning (a) the effect of a Philadelphia-based bank upon a compromise plan to move the nation's capital south of the Potomac River, and/or (b) the power-concentrating effect of banks more generally, have claimed that much of this opposition was insincere (Bowling 1972, Klubes 1990). The veracity of these claims is less important here than the constitutional positions staked out by the opposing sides.

The premise of the constitutional debate was not complicated. No one contended that the Constitution explicitly authorized Congress to charter a national bank. Congress was, however, empowered to make "all Laws which shall be necessary and proper for carrying into Execution [its] foregoing Powers[,]" which included laying and collecting taxes, paying debts, borrowing money, and regulating interstate commerce. Moreover, there was broad agreement that a national bank might prove "incidental, useful, or conducive to" the execution of these powers (Hamilton 2001: 618). The question, simply put, was whether mere utility or conduciveness squared with the constitutional term "Necessary." Bank advocates urged an affirmative answer here. Their opponents disagreed, fearing the scope of federal power under such a construction and offering a more exacting standard in its place (Lawson, Miller, Natelson, and Seidman 2010: 114–19). In signing the Bank bill (after its passage by Congress), President Washington at least implicitly endorsed the more permissive construction.

Institutional change, 1791–1811

The charter granted to the Bank of the United States in February 1791 ran for just twenty years, ensuring that future federal lawmakers would need to revisit the economic, political, and constitutional dimensions of the institution. This the Eleventh Congress did in late 1810 and early 1811, debating a bill to extend the Bank's charter (Clarke and Hall 1832: 115ff). In doing so, however, they encountered an altogether different institution – one that had been slowly transformed, and twice over at that. While persistent growth in the number of state-chartered banks between 1791 and 1811 slowly altered the national bank's position within the American financial order, an evolving relationship between the former and the latter over the same period rendered the Bank of the United States more than just a financial institution. In addition, these twin changes in the Bank over a two-decade period represent the starting points for the longer-term patterns of symmetry and repetition invoked above.

The legislatures of Pennsylvania and Massachusetts chartered commercial banks in the early 1780s (Gras 1937, Rappaport 1996), and their behavior was imitated in 1790 and 1791 by the governments of Maryland, Rhode Island, and New York.[2] These five institutions represented the entirety of the nascent American banking "industry" in late 1791, as the newly-organized Bank of the United States was preparing to open its doors. The combined capital of these institutions was approximately $4.6 million (Fenstermaker 1965: 111), meaning that a fully-capitalized national bank ($10 million) would immediately tower over the sparse landscape of competing commercial banks. In other words, the Bank of the United States was effectively born into a position of industry dominance.

The institutional landscape would not remain sparse for long, however. Over the next two decades, the number of state-chartered banks "grew at an exponential rate" (Mihm 2007: 108). The causes of this growth are myriad, including quests for profitable investment vehicles, efforts to solve credit access problems, and reactions to the emergence of the national bank (Bodenhorn 2003: 12, Sylla, Legler, and Wallis 1987, Lamoreaux 1994, Stokes 1902: 2, Crothers 1999: 14). The calendar year 1792 alone saw the number of state banks double to ten, and that number doubled again by the end of 1796. The fortieth state bank in the country was chartered sometime in 1803, and the eightieth at some point in 1807. By the time debate over a bill to extend the charter of the Bank of the United States commenced in early 1811, just over one hundred banks authorized by state governments occupied the nation's terrain (Weber 2006: 449).

Because the authorized capital of the Bank was never enlarged between 1791 and 1811, the steady proliferation of state-chartered institutions also happened to exert a steady downward pull on its industry share. The Bank of the United States represented 68 percent of all authorized banking capital at the close of 1791. From here, the national bank's share declined to 34 percent by December 1801, and then to just over 15 percent as the recharter debate commenced in early 1811 (Fenstermaker 1965: 111). Otherwise put, state bank growth gradually compromised the Bank's initial status as a dominant financial institution.

No contact between the Bank of the United States and its state-chartered peers was required in order for the latter to gradually and collectively erode the former's status within the banking industry. These institutions *did* interact, however. More importantly, they did so in ways that produced a second change in the national bank between 1791 and 1811: its transformation from a purely fiscal instrument to one that performed both fiscal and monetary functions within the American economy. The multiplication of state banks played a role in this development, but administrative decisions by (a) the national bank's board of directors, and (b) officials at the Treasury Department loomed especially large.

The Bank's development into a monetary institution – one that regulated the supply of credit circulated by state banks – grew in part from an early decision by its board of directors to establish "Office[s] of Discount & Deposit," or branches (Cowen 2000: 55). Alexander Hamilton wrote in his national bank report that the size of the United States "naturally inspire[d] a wish" for branches, but also expressed reservations owing to limited domestic expertise in commercial bank management (Hamilton 2001: 599–600). Scholars have suggested that Hamilton harbored two additional objections to branches, the first rooted in a desire to centralize the Bank's capital for use by the federal government and the second grounded in concerns over the "feasibility of [hosting] two or more commercial banks … in a single market" (Perkins 1994: 243, Schwartz 1947). Personal objection(s) notwithstanding, the Bank's charter offered discretion on this point to the stockholder-elected board of directors. It exercised that discretion almost immediately, voting in November 1791 to establish branches in New York, Boston, Baltimore, and Charleston (Wettereau 1937: 272).

The decision to establish branches was important because it made contact with state-chartered institutions almost inescapable. In New York, Boston, and Baltimore – not to mention Philadelphia, home of the main Bank office – state banks would henceforth operate *alongside* the national institution. In 1791, there was no domestic precedent for hosting two banks in one city, let alone two banks authorized by different governments; a 1784 effort to establish a second state bank in Philadelphia had been abandoned in favor of enlarging the existing institution (Schwartz 1947). The national and state institutions, however, quickly learned to operate within this novel environment. Each bank issued its own paper, meaning that a national bank branch and its local rival would frequently come into possession of each other's notes and checks. As such, they established procedures for dealing with this reality, including the routine exchange of accumulated paper (Gras 1937: 73). The opening of four additional Bank branches between 1800 and 1805, coupled with the proliferation of state banks in some proximity to those sites, only multiplied the contact between national and state institutions.[3]

Not only did the Bank establish regular contact with state institutions across a host of sites, but it routinely emerged as their *creditor*. That is, the national bank tended to accumulate more local notes and checks than it needed to reclaim its own paper (as acquired by state banks). This tendency resulted from several factors, including exchange operations (individuals trading local paper for Bank paper in order to facilitate transactions at a remote site) and the patronage of large-scale private parties (who would collect state bank paper in the course of business and then deposit it) (Hoffmann 2001: 41). A public variant of the latter factor was especially crucial: the patronage of the Treasury Department. Because the federal government employed the Bank as its depository, and the Treasury elected to accept state bank paper for tax purposes, revenue deposits nourished the institution with a steady diet of rivals' notes and checks (Hammond 1957: 198, Broz 1997: 233). Regardless of how the Bank acquired this surplus paper, whenever it demanded payment in specie (i.e., reserves), state banks were forced to contract lending by some multiple of the requested amount. The national bank's evolution into a monetary authority was complete when its officers, wary of "extensive credits" being "incautiously granted" nationwide, began to purposefully accumulate and redeem paper in order to induce downward modifications in state bank lending (Lomazoff 2012).

The consequences of change I: new antagonisms

The Bank's stockholders, wholly cognizant that the charter granted in February 1791 would expire in March 1811, began petitioning Congress for a charter extension in early 1808 (American State Papers 1998: 301). Extended debate on a recharter bill, however, did not begin until nearly the last moment, in January 1811 (Clarke and Hall 1832: 137). Though some cries from the 1791 battle were heard again two decades later, the sounds emanating from the halls of the Eleventh Congress were largely distinct. Both of the aforementioned changes in the Bank of the United States – the erosion of its financial dominance, and its emergence as a monetary force – inspired novel expressions of antagonism toward the institution. Almost an afterthought in 1791, state banks became the story in 1811.

The recharter bill narrowly failed in both the House and the Senate, forcing the Bank to shut its doors. The institution's demise has repeatedly been chalked up to (a) jealousy over its "dominance of U.S. government deposits" and (b) resentment over its emerging "regulatory hand" (Hoffmann 2001: 43, Broz 1997: 236–37). These twin sources of opposition – neither of which appeared in the 1791 dispute, and both of which reflected state bank interests – track the two changes outlined above.

Because state banks were so numerous by 1811, with at least one in every state, many members of Congress claimed that a network of these institutions could easily displace the Bank of the United States as the federal government's fiscal service provider. These banks might not be able to support the "Public Credit," as Hamilton had tried to do with his capitalization scheme, but they could make loans to the government, store its funds, transfer the same, and pay public creditors. As recharter advocates noted, this was hardly an altruistic offer of service from state banks; receiving a portion of the government's deposits – a "slice of the 'loaves and fishes'" as New York representative John Nicholson put it – would enable increased lending and larger profits for state bank shareholders (Clarke and Hall 1832: 260). Proponents of this arrangement, in turn, tried to justify their preference for state banks; they accused the Federalist-dominated national bank of partisan discrimination in lending decisions and suggested that Treasury funds ought to be held in banks owned and controlled by American citizens (Clarke and Hall 1832: 202 and 376). At the time, foreigners owned approximately two-thirds of all Bank stock (Atwater 1810: 3–4). Warring claims aside, the underlying point here deserves reassertion: the sustained proliferation of state banks created the institutional context for novel anti-Bank arguments.

Recharter opponents also proffered another set of arguments with roots in recent institutional change, in this case the Bank's emergence as a regulatory power. One member of the House claimed that its capacity to restrict lending by state institutions rendered it an "object of dread" among them (Clarke and Hall 1832: 221). State banks might be expected to resent an institution with the power to curb their primary profit-generating activity, but this particular brand of economic regulation also represented (for others) a significant *political* threat. The Constitution laid out a specific division of power between the federal government and the states, but the Bank's oversight of peer institutions effectively "extend[ed] the jurisdiction of the United States Government to subjects purely local." That is, the national bank's monitoring of local lending represented an affront to American federalism. Senator Henry Clay of Kentucky echoed this argument when he claimed that it was "worse than usurpation" to establish the Bank "for a lawful object, and then extend it to other objects, which are not lawful" (Clarke and Hall 1832: 142 and 355). Meanwhile, recharter advocates fully embraced the Bank's functional evolution, trumpeting its ability to force state banks "to observe some proportion between their loans and [their] actual funds" (Clarke and Hall 1832: 158).

The consequences of change II: new constitutional claims

The symmetry outlined above – two changes in the Bank between 1791 and 1811, each leading to a novel expression of institutional antagonism in Congress – extends still further, to new claims about the underlying *legitimacy* of the institution. In short, these two changes also led members of Congress to twice reconstruct the national bank's constitutional foundations (or lack thereof), albeit at slightly different historical junctures.

It was state bank proliferation, and the national bank's attending slide from financial dominance, that drove the first episode of new constitutional thinking. During the 1811 recharter battle, some Bank antagonists tried to question its constitutionality anew while simultaneously moving away from the traditional lines of debate. To recall, members of the First Congress had argued over whether a national bank was "Necessary" for the federal government's exercise of enumerated fiscal powers. Charter opponents had argued, contra Hamilton, that utility alone did not meet this standard. Twenty years later, state bank growth permitted recharter critics to make a slightly different argument. Even *if* "all agree[d] that banks [were] necessary" for conducting the nation's fiscal affairs – essentially conceding the 1791 opposition claim – the Bank of the United States was not, "since these operations can be … performed for the General Government, by the State banks" (Clarke and Hall 1832: 165). State bank growth, this argument suggested, had gradually undermined whatever constitutionality the national institution once possessed. This novel claim, of course, dovetailed with others presented in favor of state banks.

The Bank's emergence as a monetary institution also inspired new thinking about its constitutionality, though it came half a decade after the failed recharter push. A second war with Britain commenced in June 1812, and (newly) unable to avail itself of the Bank's assistance, the federal government financed the affair through a mixture of state bank loans and both long- and short-term bond sales (Perkins 1994: 324–48, Hickey 1989: 100–25). Patchwork financing aside, the War of 1812 also brought domestic monetary strife. Starting in late August 1814, state banks south and west of New England suspended the payment of specie for their notes and checks. The paper of these institutions consequently depreciated from face value, forcing many Americans to pay higher prices for goods and services (Gardiner 1815, Lawrence 1831: 546). Peace in 1815 brought expectations of a general return to specie payments, but those expectations were soon disappointed by state banks (Clarke and Hall 1832: 647). As a result, members of the postwar Fourteenth Congress sought to bring these institutions to heel by reviving an instrument with a past record of state bank regulation: the Bank of the United States.

Republicans enjoyed control of the Fourteenth Congress, and most party members ("Old Republicans" or "Tertium Quids" excepted) supported revival of the national bank as a tool of monetary reform (Risjord 1965). The party also represented, inconveniently, the institution's traditional source of constitutional opposition. Perhaps to avoid an uncomfortable about-face on the meaning of the Necessary and Proper Clause, leading Republicans – including Treasury Secretary Alexander Dallas and recharter bill sponsor John C. Calhoun – "discovered" a distinct textual anchor for the Bank: the Article I power to "coin Money, regulate the Value thereof[.]" In principle, Secretary Dallas claimed, Congress was exercising this express power to regulate the value of money by creating an institution that would force the restoration of specie payments by state banks and thus end currency depreciation (Dallas 1871: 292). Similarly, Representative Calhoun argued that Congress was merely retaking what the state banks had effectively stolen – the federal power "to regulate the money of the country" (Clarke and Hall 1832: 631). This novel reading of "regulate the Value" – it was originally understood to empower those who "strike money…to [also] set its value" (Natelson 2008: 1060) – represents a longer-term consequence of the Bank's functional development.

The Second Bank: new life fraught with old perils

The postwar effort to revive the Bank of the United States was successful – a second twenty-year charter was secured in 1816 – and state banks soon restored the payment of specie. The Bank actually proved less than a silver bullet in achieving the resumption of payments; the task was only completed once (a) Congress voted to stop receiving the paper of recalcitrant state banks for tax purposes, and (b) substantial concessions were made to those institutions in face-to-face negotiations with both the Treasury and the national bank (Smith 1953: 102–3, Catterall 1903: 24). This important postscript to recharter aside, the Bank's second life is largely a story that must be told from the perspective of its second death.

Two post-recharter developments are especially important for understanding the national bank's protracted (and final) demise between 1829 and 1836: state efforts to tax branches of the institution between 1817 and 1819, and Nicholas Biddle's presidency of the Bank after 1823. Though some scholars have suggested that state legislatures taxed the Bank in response to the Panic of 1819 – "the 'monster' bank was blamed for the collapse" (Smith 1996: 441, Howe 2007: 144) – several states, including Maryland, levied their taxes *before* the Panic's onset (Ellis 2007: 68, Killenbeck 2006: 68–9). The inspiration for various state taxes aside, the cashier of the Bank's branch in Baltimore challenged the constitutionality of Maryland's tax. When the case was argued before the United States Supreme Court in February 1819, counsel on both sides addressed not simply the tax, but also the constitutionality of the Bank itself. Chief Justice John Marshall authored the Court's decision in *McCulloch v. Maryland*, which held that Congress was empowered to create the Bank but states were not permitted to tax it. The status of *McCulloch*'s holding would become a source of controversy in the 1832 recharter fight.

Though the revived national bank struggled in its early years – state taxation was one among multiple challenges (Redlich 1947: 106–9, Perkins 1983) – the institution enjoyed a brief "Golden Age" during the early years of Nicholas Biddle's stewardship (Smith 1953: 134). Biddle managed the Bank from its main office in Philadelphia, maintaining regular correspondence with numerous branch officials and instructing them from afar (Biddle 1966). This correspondence, most of which remains unpublished, offers a "lucid running commentary" on institutional and national affairs in the Early Republic (Hammond 1957: 324–5). Many of these letters address the Bank's relationship with state institutions; Biddle saw the "great object" of the national bank as "keep[ing] the State banks within proper limits … mak[ing] them shape their business according to their means" (Womack 1978: 375). In other words, the maintenance of a "sound currency" via state bank regulation remained a critical institutional objective long after the restoration of that currency to soundness (Biddle 1966: 108). This influence over state banks, twice already (1811 and 1816) a lead actor on the stage of recharter politics, would also star in the 1832 revival.

Andrew Jackson's triumph in the 1828 presidential election had immediate repercussions for the Bank of the United States. Even before Old Hickory took the oath of office, his affiliates sought to "fetch [the Bank] within the party pale as spoils of victory" (Hammond 1957: 369); one wrote to Biddle that partisan balancing should henceforth guide the selection of national bank directors. The Bank's president politely rejected the suggestion, noting that "independence & knowledge of business" were the only requisite qualifications for the post, but another written expression of Jacksonian views concerning the "proper management" of the institution followed several months later (Biddle 1966: 63–5 and 69–71, Catterall 1903: 175). Biddle's determination to keep the Jacksonians at arm's length endured, and he later wrote of the Bank's "intractable spirit" as an irritant for the new and ambitious administration.

Not long after the Bank privately signaled its unwillingness to accommodate Jacksonian desires, the president shone a bright public light on the institution. Jackson's first annual message to Congress, delivered in December 1829, explicitly predicted that national bank stockholders would soon apply for an extension of their 1816 charter. More importantly, the president boldly added that "[b]oth the constitutionality and the expediency" of the Bank were "well questioned" by many Americans (Jackson 1908: 462). Jackson's prophecy concerning the stockholders proved self-fulfilling; his charges inspired a protracted campaign on behalf of the Bank – led by Nicholas Biddle and prominent sympathizers both in and out of Congress – that culminated in the institution's decision to pursue a charter extension in early 1832 (Clarke and Hall 1832: 734–72, Gallatin 1831, Lawrence 1831).

It is at this historical juncture – the 1832 recharter battle in Congress – that a pattern of repetition in the Bank's history becomes visible. To recall, a pair of pre-1811 developments – the multiplication of state banks and the functional expansion of the national bank – produced a novel pair of justifications for discontinuing the institution. State banks claimed that they could collectively service the federal government, and that they were collectively being oppressed by the Bank of the United States. Twenty-one years later, those same sources of change-inspired animus toward recharter *reappeared* in Bank politics; though many state banks now supported recharter, those opposed to it (a) sought to profit as substitute fiscal service providers for the federal government, and (b) resented the Bank's regulatory activity (Wilburn 1967, Broz 1997: 240–1, Bruchey 1990: 190). Congressional history did not repeat itself, however, as the Bank's supporters managed to pass the recharter bill in early July.

Countless volumes have been written concerning the next (and final) four years of the Bank's history, and these events neither extend nor break the patterns outlined above. President Jackson vetoed the recharter bill of 1832, and in an attending message both rejected claims that Marshall's decision in *McCulloch* had settled the constitutional question in favor of the Bank and explicitly fretted over the immense economic power – fiscal and monetary – possessed by a small set of "citizen stockholders" (Jackson 1949: 11–12). Congress proved unable to override the veto, and the Bank was thus set to die a "natural" death in March 1836. However, Jackson sought to slay the Bank – a "hydra of corruption" he considered "only scotched [by the veto], not dead" – in advance of that date (Remini 1984: 52). Perceiving the national bank to be an impediment to public debt retirement – institutional funds were insufficient to accommodate an aggressive Treasury Department repayment schedule – in September 1833 Jackson ordered the removal of federal deposits from the Bank and their placement in numerous state banks (Catterall 1903: 268–73, Timberlake 1993: 43–44). By scholarly tradition, deposit removal marks the beginning of the "Bank War," a colorful political affair that saw Democrats and nascent Whigs trade claims over whose behavior – that of Jackson, or that of the Bank – posed the greater threat to American constitutionalism (Schlesinger 1946: 97ff., Govan 1959: 236–74, Remini 1984: 93–151). Those deposits – partially composed of state bank paper, and thus representing a crucial resource for the regulation of local institutions – were never restored to the national bank, rendering its subsequent closure a mere formality.

Conclusion

Eschewing myriad specialized approaches to the national bank's history – stories told with reference to crucial personalities, institutional purposes, constitutional principles, political parties, or geographic places – this chapter has sought to identify and trace multiple (and to this point unappreciated) patterns in that history. The Bank's long, tortured, and discontinuous life between 1791 and 1836 displays first and foremost a pattern of symmetry; two early changes in the institution each (a) remade its place within the economic order, (b) generated novel arguments against its recharter, and (c) led to new claims about constitutional meaning. A final point of symmetry between these two tracks also reveals the second pattern in the Bank's history, that of repetition. During the institution's second lease on life, opponents of extending its charter (d) revived the (formerly) novel arguments for putting the Bank down.

Thinking about an institution like the Bank of the United States as an "event" may seem like an oddity. An oddity is not an impossibility, however. Students of the Bank need only remember that as an "event," it was driven far less by the giants associated with its birth and death (Alexander Hamilton and Andrew Jackson, respectively) and far more by a pair of institutional transformations (state bank growth and the development of monetary power) that took place between the appearance of those men.

Notes

1 On the historiographic origin of the "First" and "Second" labels, see Wettereau (1953: 70).
2 The Bank of New York, chartered in 1791, had been operating informally since 1784 (Domett 1884).
3 These were Norfolk (1800), Washington (1801), Savannah (1802), and New Orleans (1805).

References

American State Papers (1998) *Finance*, vol. 2, Buffalo, CO: Hein and Co.

Atwater, J. (1810) *Considerations, on the Approaching Dissolution, of the United States Bank*, New Haven, CT: Sidney's Press.

Beard, C. (1915) *Economic Origins of Jeffersonian Democracy*, New York: Macmillan.

Biddle, N. (1966) *The Correspondence of Nicholas Biddle Dealing with National Affairs, 1807–1844*, ed. R.C. McGrane, Boston, MA: J.S. Canner and Company.

Bodenhorn, H. (2003) *State Banking in Early America: A New Economic History*, New York: Oxford University Press.

Bowling, K. (1972) 'The bank bill, the capital city and president Washington', *Capitol Studies*, 1: 59–71.

Brest, P., Levinson, S., Balkin, J., and Amar, A.R. (2000) *Processes of Constitutional Decisionmaking: Cases and Materials*, 4th edn., New York: Aspen Law and Business.

Brown, M. (1998) *The Second Bank of the United States and Ohio (1803–1860): A Collision of Interests*, Lewiston, NY: Edwin Mellen Press.

Broz, L. (1997) *The International Origins of the Federal Reserve System*, Ithaca, NY: Cornell University Press.

Bruchey, S. (1990) *Enterprise: The Dynamic Economy of a Free People*, Cambridge, MA: Harvard University Press.

Catterall, R. (1903) *The Second Bank of the United States*, Chicago, IL: University of Chicago Press.

Chernow, R. (2004) *Alexander Hamilton*, New York: Penguin Books.

Clarke, M. and Hall, D. (1832) *Legislative and Documentary History of the Bank of the United States, Including the Original Bank of North America*, Washington, DC: Gales and Seaton.

Cowen, D. (2000) *The Origins and Economic Impact of the First Bank of the United States, 1791–1797*, New York: Garland Publishing.

Crothers, A.G. (1999) 'Banks and economic development in post-revolutionary northern Virginia, 1790–1812', *Business History Review*, 73: 1–39.

Dallas, G. (1871) *The Life and Writings of Alexander James Dallas*, Philadelphia, PA: J.B. Lippincott.

Dellinger, W. and Powell, H.J. (1994) 'The constitutionality of the bank bill: the attorney general's first constitutional law opinions', *Duke Law Journal*, 44: 110–33.

Domett, H. (1884) *A History of the Bank of New York, 1784–1884*, New York: G.P. Putnam's Sons.

Edling, M. (2008) *A Revolution in Favor of Government: Origins of the U.S. Constitution and the Making of the American State*, New York: Oxford University Press.

Ellis, R. (2007) *Aggressive Nationalism: McCulloch v. Maryland and the Foundation of Federal Authority in the Young Republic*, New York: Oxford University Press.

Fenstermaker, J. (1965) *The Development of American Commercial Banking: 1782–1837*, Kent, OH: Bureau of Economic and Business Research.

Ferguson, J. (1961) *The Power of the Purse: A History of American Public Finance, 1776–1790*, Chapel Hill, NC: University of North Carolina Press.

Gallatin, A. (1831) *Considerations on the Currency and Banking System of the United States*, Philadelphia, PA: Carey and Lea.

Gardiner, B. (1815) 'Current Money', *Rhode-Island American*, 25 August.

Gillman, H., Graber, M., and Whittington, K. (2013) *American Constitutionalism, Volume 1, Structures of Government*, New York: Oxford University Press.

Govan, T. (1959) *Nicholas Biddle: Nationalist and Public Banker, 1786–1844*, Chicago, IL: University of Chicago Press.

Gras, N. (1937) *The Massachusetts First National Bank of Boston, 1784–1934*, Cambridge, MA: Harvard University Press.

Hamilton, A. (1963) *The Papers of Alexander Hamilton*, Volume 7, ed. H. Syrett and J. Cooke, New York: Columbia University Press.

Hamilton, A. (2001) *Hamilton: Writings*, ed. J. Freeman, New York: Library of America.

Hammond, B. (1957) *Banks and Politics in America: From the Revolution to the Civil War*, Princeton, NJ: Princeton University Press.

Hickey, D. (1989) *The War of 1812: A Forgotten Conflict*, Urbana, IL: University of Illinois Press.

Hoffmann, S. (2001) *Politics and Banking: Ideas, Public Policy, and the Creation of Financial Institutions*, Baltimore, MD: Johns Hopkins University Press.

Holt, M. (1999) *The Rise and Fall of the American Whig Party: Jacksonian Politics and the Onset of the Civil War*, New York: Oxford University Press.

Howe, D. (2007) *What Hath God Wrought: The Transformation of America, 1815–1848*, New York: Oxford University Press.

Jackson, A. (1908) 'First annual message', in J. Richardson (ed.) *A Compilation of the Messages and Papers of the Presidents, 1789–1907*, vol. 2, New York: Bureau of National Literature and Art.

Jackson, A. (1949) 'Veto message', in G. Taylor (ed.) *Jackson versus Biddle: The Struggle over the Second Bank of the United States*, Boston, MA: D.C. Heath and Company.

Kilbourne, R. (2006) *Slave Agriculture and Financial Markets in Antebellum America: The Bank of the United States in Mississippi, 1831–1852*, London: Pickering and Chatto.

Killenbeck, M. (2006) *M'Culloch v. Maryland: Securing a Nation*, Lawrence, KS: University Press of Kansas.

Klubes, B. (1990) 'The first federal congress and the first national bank: a case study in constitutional interpretation', *Journal of the Early Republic*, 10: 19–41.

Lamoreaux, N. (1994) *Insider Lending: Banks, Personal Connections, and Economic Development in Industrial New England*, Cambridge: Cambridge University Press.

Lawrence, W. (1831) 'Bank of the United States', *North American Review*, 32: 524–63.

Lawson, G., Miller, G., Natelson, R., and Seidman, G. (2010) *The Origins of the Necessary and Proper Clause*, Cambridge: Cambridge University Press.

Leonard, G. (2002) *The Invention of Party Politics: Federalism, Popular Sovereignty, and Constitutional Development in Jacksonian Illinois*, Chapel Hill, NC: University of North Carolina Press.

Lomazoff, E. (2012) 'Turning (into) "The great regulating wheel": the conversion of the bank of the United States, 1791–1811', *Studies in American Political Development*, 26: 1–23.

Marshall, J. (2000) *The Life of George Washington*, Indianapolis, IN: Liberty Fund.

Mihm, S. (2007) *A Nation of Counterfeiters: Capitalists, Con Men, and the Making of the United States*, Cambridge, MA: Harvard University Press.

Natelson, R. (2008) 'Paper money and the original understanding of the coinage clause', *Harvard Journal of Law and Public Policy*, 31: 1017–81.

Newmyer, K. (2001) *John Marshall and the Heroic Age of the Supreme Court*, Baton Rouge, LA: Louisiana State University Press.

O'Brien, D. (2003) *Constitutional Law and Politics, Volume 1, Struggles for Power and Governmental Accountability*, 5th edn., New York: W.W. Norton.

Perkins, E. (1983) 'Langdon Cheves and the panic of 1819: a reassessment', *Journal of Economic History*, 44: 455–61.

Perkins, E. (1994) *American Public Finance and Financial Services, 1700–1815*, Columbus, OH: Ohio State University Press.

Rappaport, G. (1996) *Stability and Change in Revolutionary Pennsylvania: Banking, Politics, and Social Structure*, University Park, PA: Pennsylvania State University Press.

Razaghian, R. (2002) 'Establishing Financial Credibility in the United States, 1789–1860', unpublished thesis, Columbia University.

Redlich, F. (1947) *The Molding of American Banking: Men and Ideas, Part I, 1781–1840*, New York: Hafner Publishing Company.

Remini, R. (1984) *Andrew Jackson: The Course of American Democracy, 1833–1845*, New York: Harper and Row.

Remini, R. (1998) *Andrew Jackson: The Course of American Freedom, 1822–1832*, New York: History Book Club.

Risjord, N. (1965) *The Old Republicans: Southern Conservatism in the Age of Jefferson*, New York: Columbia University Press.

Schwartz, A. (1947) 'The beginning of competitive banking in Philadelphia, 1782–1809', *Journal of Political Economy*, 55: 417–31.

Smith, J. (1996) *John Marshall: Definer of a Nation*, New York: Henry Holt.

Smith, W. (1953) *Economic Aspects of the Second Bank of the United States*, Cambridge, MA: Harvard University Press.

Stokes, H. (1902) *Chartered Banking in Rhode Island, 1791–1900*, Providence, RI: Prestor and Rounds.

Sylla, R., Legler, J., and Wallis, J. (1987) 'Banks and state public finance in the new republic: the United States, 1790–1860', *Journal of Economic History*, 47: 391–403.

Sylla, R., Wright, R.E., and Cowen, D. (2009) 'Alexander Hamilton, central banker: crisis management during the U.S. financial panic of 1792', *Business History Review*, 83: 61–86.

Timberlake, R. (1993) *Monetary Policy in the United States: An Intellectual and Institutional History*, Chicago, IL: University of Chicago Press.

Weber, W. (2006) 'Early state banks in the United States: how many were there and when did they exist?', *Journal of Economic History*, 66: 433–55.

Wettereau, J. (1937) 'New light on the first bank of the United States', *Pennsylvanian Magazine of History and Biography*, 61: 263–85.

Wettereau, J. (1953) 'The oldest bank building in the United States', *Transactions of the American Philosophical Society*, 43: 70–9.

Womack, R. (1978) *An Analysis of the Credit Controls of the Second Bank of the United States*, New York: Arno Press.

Wright, R.E. (1996) 'Thomas Willing (1731–1821): Philadelphia financier and forgotten founding father', *Pennsylvania History*, 63: 525–60.

Wright, R.E. (2005) *The First Wall Street: Chestnut Street, Philadelphia, and the Birth of American Finance*, Chicago, IL: University of Chicago Press.

2

THE BANKING PANIC OF 1873

Elmus Wicker

The 1873 panic was a watershed in U.S. financial history whose historical significance resided in the prompt response of the New York Clearing House (NYCH)[1]. The NYCH had a coherent strategy for responding to the banking panics of 1860 and 1873. The strategy called for the issue of clearing house certificates to meet local reserve drains, and the pooling or equalization of reserves to meet the external drains to the interior parts of the country. To conserve the supply of legal tender reserves among the member banks, the NYCH was authorized to issue clearing house certificates during emergencies to petitioning banks who submitted the requisite collateral for the purpose of meeting their deficits at the clearing house. To meet cash withdrawals for out-of-town banks it also had the power to pool or equalize the reserves of the associated banks; that is, the reserves of the stronger banks could be put at the disposal of the weaker. By treating the reserves of the NYCH as a common pool, the NYCH was effectively converted temporarily into a central bank, like the Bank of England, with reserve power greater than that of any European central bank. It was successful in forestalling the suspension of cash payments in 1860, and as it shall be argued, suspension in 1873 was unnecessary. Just at the point that success was imminent there was a failure of will. Reserves at the Clearing House had fallen to a low that undermined the courage of officials, and cash payment was suspended. Nevertheless, the NYCH continued to pay out cash to the interior thereby moderating the anticipated effects of the panic on the interior.

Shortly after the panic had ended, the NYCH issued a report—the Coe Report (New York Clearing House 1873)—that clearly recognized the responsibility of the NYCH in the absence of a central bank for achieving banking stability. The report made a persuasive case that the NYCH had the knowledge, the power, and the instruments to prevent banking panics. Sprague (1910) called the report the most important financial document in U.S. financial history. Sprague's mentor Charles Francis Dunbar, professor at Harvard from 1871 to 1900, had described the use of reserve pooling by the NYCH in response to a panic that occurred in 1860 (Dunbar 1904). In the succeeding panics of 1893 and 1907, however, the fifty or so banks in the Clearing House could not reach agreement to equalize reserves and the bold experiment initiated in 1860 was abandoned.

Panic vocabulary

Although the term panic had been used for all major banking crises of the nineteenth century, the meaning remains ambiguous. As used originally, it referred specifically to an identifiable kind of emotional behavior, i.e. the behavior of depositors engaged in a run on the banks, behavior dominated by fear and anxiety in contrast to behavior guided by reason. Webster captured its ordinary meaning:

> as widespread fear of the collapse of the financial system, resulting in unreasoned attempts to turn property into cash, withdrawing money et cet.

The keyword is unreasoned. The evidence for such behavior of depositors seeking to withdraw cash—a bank run—is contained in the accounts of journalists in local newspapers and national financial journals. There are vivid and detailed descriptions of depositor behavior, sometimes resulting in disorder requiring police intervention.

Revisionists, for example Kaufman (2003) and Gorton (2010), have been at work in the past decade redefining what happened during a banking panic. They reject the traditional view that bank panics were an irrational depositor response, that is, that depositor behavior was dictated by extreme fear and anxiety. They argue, to the contrary, that bank runs were a rational response of depositors and were information based. Rational economic agents are presumably maximizers and pursue behaviors that are best for them. Depositors engaged in runs on banks were simply attempting to retrieve their deposits for cash to avoid the threat of loss in the event of bank suspensions in accord with the principle of maximizing their own self interest. Gorton (2010: 31) redefined a banking panic as a situation where the banking system is insolvent, unable to convert deposits into cash. Depositors run on banks "en masse." Fear and anxiety play only a minor role. There were no banking panics in the original sense. The only evidence Gorton advances, however, is the allegation that small denominational clearing house certificates traded initially at a discount from which he inferred that the clearing house was insolvent (unable to convert deposits into cash). That was not the case in 1873.

Number of bank suspensions

There are no official estimates of total bank suspension during the month of September 1873. My estimates have been constructed from two principal sources: contemporary newspaper accounts and financial journals including *Bradstreet's* and the *Commercial and Financial Chronicle*. I make no claim that my estimates account for all failures during the panic month of September. Every effort was made however to check and crosscheck claims that specific banks had shut down, if only temporarily.

Table 2.1 shows the number of suspensions in New York and the interior for September 1873 classified by type of bank organization. Private banks include brokerage houses as well. Two things stand out prominently: the small number of closures (excluding brokerage houses) in New York City—one national bank and two trust companies—and the high percentage of brokerage houses (60 percent). For the interior the percentage is much smaller, of which one half were in Philadelphia. Bank suspensions other than brokerage houses could easily be exaggerated in September 1873. Just as 1907 was described as a trust company panic, 1873 could equally well be labeled a brokerage house panic.

The geographical incidence of bank failures is revealed in Table 2.2. The highest concentration was in three states: New York, Pennsylvania and Virginia had over 70 percent of all bank suspensions. The middle Atlantic region accounted for 60 percent, due almost

Table 2.1 Bank suspensions in New York and interior by type of bank organization, September 1873

	National	State	Savings	Private	Trust	Unclassified	Total
New York	1			34	2		37
Interior	15	11	7	25	2	4	64
Total	16	11	7	59	4	4	101

Source: Author's estimates

Table 2.2 Bank suspensions by state and grouped by region, September 1873

Middle Atlantic

New York	37
Pennsylvania	22

Southern

Virginia	10
Washington, D.C.	2
Georgia }	
Alabama }	7
Tennessee }	

Midwest

Illinois	8
Ohio	4
Wisconsin }	
Iowa }	7
Michigan }	
Other regions	4
Total	101

Source: Author's estimates

entirely to the collapse of 45 brokerage houses in New York and Philadelphia. The Southern and Midwestern regions each accounted for 20 percent. City-wide bank runs were serious in Augusta and Savannah, Georgia; Louisville, Kentucky; Charleston, South Carolina; Memphis, Nashville and Knoxville, Tennessee; and Petersburg and Richmond, Virginia.

Origins

The panic had its origins in the failure of Jay Cooke and Company on September 18, 1873. The Philadelphia branch had made a $15 million advance to the Northern Pacific railroad for construction credit. First National Bank in Philadelphia, wholly owned by Cooke, suspended; and the First National Bank of Washington, D.C., also a Cooke company, did likewise. Jay Cooke and Company was one of the most prestigious banking houses in the U.S. Its closing was a surprise and changed the character of the 1873 crisis. Although it was not the first of the private banks in New York to fail, it generated the most attention. These failures brought pandemonium to Wall Street and stock prices tumbled followed by a veritable wave of insolvencies including more than thirty brokerage houses.

According to Henrietta Larson (1968: 410), Cooke's biographer, the firm was overloaded with investments and advances made to specific railroads including the Northern Pacific. Credit stringency made it impossible to obtain funds to tide it over. She maintained that the failure of Jay Cooke marked the close of an important phase of American business, that is, the speculative promotion of railroads beyond a reasonable expectation of satisfactory returns under post-Civil War conditions. Frenzied railroad building ahead of demand encouraged speculative excess and was an important contributor to the 1873 panic.

Following Cooke's failure runs began on several New York City banks. On September 20 the Stock Market closed for ten days for the first time in the city's history. The same day the NYCH authorized the issue of clearing house certificates. The Clearing House had also voted to equalize the reserves of the member banks; it gave the NYCH the authority to redistribute currency reserves of the individual banks, a measure that could have avoided the suspension of cash payment.

From September 18 to September 25, banking unrest spread down the eastern seaboard from New York, Philadelphia and Washington, D.C. to Petersburg and Richmond, Virginia, and then on to Augusta and Savannah, Georgia and Charleston, South Carolina. Simultaneously, banking disturbances erupted in the middle of the country: Chicago, Memphis, Indianapolis and Louisville. The residue of so much banking turmoil was bank runs and bank closings. On September 24, the NYCH suspended cash payment.

I conclude (Wicker 2000) that suspension of cash payment was unnecessary. The behavior of legal tender reserves of NYCH banks from September 20 to October 24 is shown in Table 2.3. Since specie did not circulate, the relevant component of total reserves was legal tender. Between September 20, the date of the issue of clearing house certificates, and September 24, when cash payment was suspended, the NYCH banks lost $18 million in reserves. The clearing house continued to pay out cash to the out-of-town banks even after suspension. Legal tender fell from $15.8 million on September 24 to $5.8 million on October 15. Considering that the NYCH was prepared to continue to pay out cash after suspension, we can well wonder why cash payment was suspended. It was the pooling of reserves that made possible the ultra-liberal policy that made the continuation of payment of cash to the interior. Since the suspension of cash payment was always accompanied by the hoarding of cash, the actual level of legal tender understates what reserves would have been in its absence. There was really no need for suspension. Had payment not been suspended legal tender reserves would not have fallen so precipitously and there would have been less reason for interior banks to have withdrawn their New York balances.

Sprague (1910: 54) concluded, however, that "the bankers were clearly at the end of their reserves, and the step taken on September 24 seems amply justified." Bagehot (1887: 199) would have counseled otherwise: "The only safe plan for the Bank of England is the brave plan, to lend in a panic on every kind of security, or on every sort on which money ordinarily and usually lent. Their policy may not save the Bank; but if it does not, nothing will save it." According to Bagehot no constraint whatsoever should be placed on the paying out freely of the reserve.

Causation

The consensus among financial historians is that at the deepest level certain structural weaknesses of the National Banking Act increased the vulnerability of the U.S. banking

Table 2.3 Legal tender reserves of New York Clearing House banks, September 20 to October 24, 1873 (in millions of dollars)

September	20	33.8	October	10	6.6
	24	15.8		11	6.5
	25	14.9		13	6.0
	26	14.1		14	5.8
	27	12.3		15	6.2
	29	10.1		16	6.1
	30	9.3		17	6.6
October	1	8.3		18	7.0
	2	7.7		20	6.8
	3	7.2		21	7.7
	4	6.9		22	8.4
	7	5.9		23	9.4
	8	6.5		54	9.9
	9	6.8			

Source: New York Clearing House Loan Committee, Minutes, December 2, 1861 to January 8, 1874, p. 24

system to panics. There are three weaknesses that have received the most attention: (1) the inelasticity of the national bank note currency, (2) the pyramiding of reserves in New York, and (3) the fixed and invariant reserve requirements. The currency stock was composed of specie, a fixed quantity of greenbacks issued to finance the Civil War, national bank notes, and, before 1866 when they were taxed out of existence, state bank notes. There was no incentive to expand the money stock seasonally nor during emergencies. National bank notes could only be expanded with the purchase by the national banks of government securities, the amount being limited to 90 percent of the par or market value, whichever was lower. Therefore the supply of national bank notes depended on the bond market. When government bonds could be purchased at below par it was profitable to issue notes. As the market value rose relative to their par value the incentive disappeared. There was no assurance that the note issue would expand during a financial crisis. Reserves were pyramided in New York and were largely fictitious. There were three separate reserve classifications with reserve requirements: for country banks 15 percent, reserve city banks and central reserve city 25 percent, some of which could be held as cash in vault, and the rest in the next highest reserve classification as deposits, a large part of which was not available in emergencies.

It is not at all clear that the National Banking Act made the banking system more prone to panics. At a more fundamental level legislation prohibiting statewide branch banking may also have been important.

At another level was the extraordinary expansion of railroad mileage in the immediate post-Civil War decade. A veritable transportation revolution was underway and one of its objectives was to link the developed East with the undeveloped West. Railroad mileage doubled between 1865 and 1873, the focal point being the completion of the first transcontinental route to Ogden, Utah, in 1869.

The expansion of railroad mileage encouraged speculation by creating expectations of generous future returns. Mileage was expanded beyond the capacity to generate supporting revenue. Some banks and brokerage houses overextended themselves to accommodate the long line of eager borrowers. The whole process was accelerated by grants of free land to the railroads and outright dollar grants of government assistance. As noted above, more than 60 percent of bank closures were brokerage houses in the two cities of New York and Philadelphia. Brokerage houses succumbed not because of banks runs but because of insolvency.

Financial effects

The financial effects of the panic are fairly easy to identify. Sprague enumerated at least three: (1) disruption of the domestic exchanges, (2) delays in the transshipment of commodities to the East, and (3) payroll difficulties. But he provided no estimate or quantitative measure by which to judge their significance. Transaction costs simply increased.

Friedman and Schwartz's (1963) annual estimates (February 1873 to February 1874) of M1 (currency and demand deposits) and M2 (currency, demand deposits and time deposits) reveal a 1.8 percent decline in M1 and an increase of 1.3 percent in M2. It seems to be quite clear that bank failures in 1873 did not cause a serious contraction of the money stock because of the fewness in number. Nor do we have any direct estimates of the amount of hoarding, a predominant characteristic of the Great Depression. We might have expected an increase in hoarding with the restriction of cash payment. The currency premium, however, reflected a scramble for currency. Between September 12 and October 13, legal tender notes held by national banks declined by more than 25 percent. By November one-half of that loss had been recovered. Sprague (1910: 70) conjectured that no considerable amount of money lost by the banks was being hoarded by depositors because of the normal seasonal increase due to the crop-moving season.

The extent of money market stringency is apparent in Table 2.4 which shows monthly commercial paper rates in New York. Rates soared in August and October by over 10 percent. Call money rates suffered even wilder gyrations.

Table 2.4 Prime commercial paper rates in New York, 1873

January	9.40
February	9.15
March	10.10
April	10.75
May	8.20
June	6.80
July	6.50
August	7.20
September	12.50
October	17.00
November	13.85
December	10.15

Source: Crum (1923)

Another indicator of the financial panic is revealed in the change in loans and discounts, total deposits and legal tender currency between 1871 and 1873. Both loan and deposit contraction was substantial in 1873 relative to comparable call dates in the two prior years. Country and reserve city banks responded to the panic by drawing down reserves by $242 million. There was a substantial flow of funds from New York banks to the interior (outside New York). The New York banks shipped $14.5 million of legal tender currency notes. Interior banks reduced their deposits in New York by $134 million. Although the number of suspensions in the interior was not large and was region-specific, there still was substantial flow from New York to the interior measured solely by national bank balance sheets. After October currency, began to flow back to New York. Flows of currency were short-lived.

Real effects

An information deficit complicates any serious attempt to measure the real effects on output and employment, We have two separate annual estimates of real GNP, one by Romer (1989) and the other by Balke and Gordon (1989), but no annual estimate for unemployment. Lebergott's estimates for unemployment begin in 1890, as do Romer's.

According to business cycle annals a serious cyclical contraction followed the panic in September 1873. The National Bureau of Economic Research identified a cyclical peak in October 1873. Fels (1959: 98) opted for September but he did not rule out the possibility that the expansion may have leveled off before the panic. Without reliable estimates of unemployment there is no way to assess the basis for the alleged perception of unrelieved gloom or any comparison with the depression of the 1890s and the 1930s. Annual estimates for real GNP do not support a claim of a serious depression. There is no decline in Romer's estimate (see Table 2.5) in the post-panic year 1874 when real GNP increased by 1.4 percent and a less than one percent decline in the Balke–Gordon estimate. There is, however, a basis for gloom in the agricultural sector where persistently falling commodity prices increased

Table 2.5 Romer and Balke–Gordon real GNP and price deflator estimates, 1869–1879

	Real GNP (1982 = 100)		Price deflator (1982 = 100)	
	Romer	Balke–Gordon	Romer	Balke–Gordon
1869	75.609	78.2	10.244	10.49
1870	76.464	84.2	9.661	9.98
1871	76.952	88.1	9.769	9.86
1872	89.605	91.7	9.423	9.60
1873	94.863	96.3	9.329	9.51
1874	96.205	95.7	9.169	9.25
1875	97.684	100.7	8.945	8.85
1876	104.628	101.9	8.539	8.51
1877	110.797	105.2	8.207	8.38
1878	118.906	109.6	7.627	7.87
1879	127.675	123.1	7.378	7.64

Sources: Romer (1989: 22) and Balke and Gordon (1989: 84), Real GNP in billions

the burden of mortgage indebtedness and freight rates did not fall as rapidly as the price of the major crops, thereby creating a cost-price squeeze. Farmer unrest is attested by the growth of pressure groups such as the Grange. Increased political activity was evidenced by the formation of the Greenback Party in 1875 whose main objective was currency expansion.

The Coe Report

In November 1873, shortly after the end of the panic, the NYCH issued a report (New York Clearing House 1873) that was acclaimed by Sprague (1910: 90) as "the ablest document which has ever appeared in the course of our banking history." The Chairman of the Committee was George C. Coe, president of the American Exchange Bank, who was one the ablest bankers in the U.S. at the time, if not the ablest. Redlich (1968: 424–38), in his brief biographical sketch, attributed to Coe the origin of the clearing house loan certificate. He may very well have been responsible for reserve equalization. Coe fervently believed that the NYCH banks possessed the knowledge, the power and the instruments to prevent banking panics in the U.S. A purely voluntary association of New York banks working through the NYCH and who recognized their responsibility for the maintenance of banking stability was a feasible solution to the banking panic problem. The Coe Report made the case that banking panics could be averted if the NYCH exercised bold leadership by exercising its power and instruments to achieve that objective.

The Report clearly stated that in the absence of a central bank, such as existed in other countries, the NYCH banks were the last resort in time of emergency. In a speech delivered to the Clearing House in June 1884, he made the point explicit that the New York banks, like the Bank of England, were holders of the country's banking reserve. The report denied the right of any bank to conduct its affairs in defiance of the best interest of all the clearing house banks. There could be no stronger statement of the collective responsibility of all the banks.

The main problem during panics was not the insufficiency of reserves but their unequal distribution. The report stated: "An expedient was found by which the stronger banks placed themselves under an unequal burden and equalized the pressure of gathering in their reserves and placing them at the disposal of the weaker who were thus furnished with the means to meet the demands of their depositors to save themselves … from ruin."

Moreover, the NYCH requested the authority from Congress to relax the reserve requirements and the cessation of interest payments on interbank balances. Not only was the nation's banking reserve concentrated in New York, but it was concentrated among a few banks. Of the approximately 60 members of the Clearing House at least 15 held almost all of the bankers' balances of the New York banks. According to Sprague (1910: 233) seven of these banks controlled 30 percent of total reserves, one-third of the loans, and two-fifths of the cash reserve. The size of these reserves was greater than that held by any one of Europe's central banks.

In subsequent years, opposition within the Clearing House to reserve equalization was so strong that it was abandoned in future panics.

Conclusions

The restriction of cash payment by the NYCH was not inevitable. The Clearing House continued to pay out currency to the interior thereby moderating the effects of the panic. What made that possible was the Clearing House policy of equalizing the reserves of the member banks by an assessment levied on the strong banks who supplied reserves to the weaker banks. The continued pay out of currency to the interior would have dispelled any doubts of interior banks about the ability of the NYCH banks to remain liquid and solvent thereby reducing the demands of interior banks for cash. The 1873 experience with pooling reserves was not repeated in 1893 and 1907. The opposition was too strong. A majority probably favored the policy. A few banks, however, were simply opposed to sharing their reserves in times of emergency, contrary to the decisions of the NYCH in 1860 and 1873.

The number of bank suspensions (101) was relatively small in contrast to the over 500 suspensions in 1893. Brokerage houses (private banks) made up a large percentage of the total. Insolvency, not banks runs, accounts for the closure of so many brokerage houses. Bank runs were confined to the eastern seaboard and the Midwest.

The extraordinary expansion of railway mileage contributed to heightened expectations of generous future returns. Mileage was simply expanded beyond the capacity to generate the necessary revenue.

The lesson we should have learned from the 1873 panic is that the continued payout of reserves through a policy of reserve equalization was a solution to the bank panic problem within the context of voluntary association of banks organized as the NYCH. A European central bank was an option, not a necessity. In the debate on banking reform prior to the establishment of the Federal Reserve no thought whatsoever was given to the reserve pooling arrangement (Wicker 2005).

Note

1   I have drawn heavily from my book: *Banking Panics of the Gilded Age* (2000).

References

Bagehot, W. (1887) *Lombard Street: A Description of the Money Market*, New York: C. Scribner's Sons.

Balke, N.S. and Gordon, R. (1989) 'The estimation of pre-war gross national product: methodology and new evidence', *Journal of Political Economy*, 97: 38–92.

Crum, W.L. (1923) 'Cycles of rates on commercial paper', *Review of Economics and Statistics,* 5: 28.

Dunbar, C.F. (1904) 'The crisis of 1860', in O.M.W. Sprague (ed.), *Economic Essays,* New York: Macmillan.

Fels, R. (1959) *American Business Cycles 1865–1897*, Chapel Hill, NC: University of North Carolina Press.

Friedman, M. and Schwartz, A. J. (1963) *A Monetary History of the United States, 1867–1960*, Princeton, NJ: Princeton University Press.

Gorton, G. (2010) *Slapped by the Invisible Hand: The Panic of 2007*, New York: Oxford University Press.

Kaufman, G. and Scott K.E. (2003) 'What is systemic risk, and do bank regulators retard or contribute to it?', *The Independent Review*, 7: 379–80.

Larson, H. (1968) *Jay Cooke, Private Banker*, Reprint, New York: Greenwood Press.

New York Clearing House (1873) The Coe Report, reproduced in Sprague, O.M.W (1910) *History of Crises under the National Banking System*, Washington, DC: Government Printing Office.

Redlich, F. (1968) *The Molding of American Banking: Men and Ideas*, New York: Johnson Reprint Corporation.

Romer, C. (1989) 'The prewar business cycle reconsidered: new estimates of gross national product', *Journal of Political Economy*, 97: 1–37.

Sprague, O.M.W. (1910) *History of Crises under the National Banking System*, Washington, DC: Government Printing Office.

Wicker, E. (2000) *Banking Panics of the Gilded Age*, Cambridge: Cambridge University Press.

Wicker, E. (2005) *The Great Debate on Banking Reform: Nelson Aldrich and the Origins of the Fed*, Columbus, OH: Ohio State University Press.

3

GOLD RESUMPTION AND THE DEFLATION OF THE 1870S

Richard C. K. Burdekin and Pierre L. Siklos

The great fall in prices ... fell with especial severity upon the agricultural classes and other producers of raw material ... One class of persons in the United States has been unaffected by the fall in prices, that is the office holders ... Grover Cleveland has been getting $50,000 annually, but in view of the appreciation of the gold dollars, paid him quarterly, now $100,000. With this appreciated dollar he can and has bought real estate at the present depreciated price; result, when elected president a poor man, now a millionaire.

(Fox 1897: 145–6)

Introduction

The deflation experienced by the United States after the Civil War is notable not only for its long duration but also the controversy attached to the decision to resume specie payments only in gold, thereby abandoning the pre-war bimetallic system that had allowed for free coinage into both gold and silver. As gold's scarcity rose with country after country abandoning silver in favor of the yellow metal in the 1870s, its command over goods and services had to rise. Under the gold standard, the value of the currency is fixed in terms of gold and so the only way for gold to command more goods and services is for the aggregate price level to fall. Under a bimetallic system, however, the scope for coining silver makes monetary expansion possible even when gold's value is on the rise. The United States effectively demonetized silver in 1873, ensuring that when specie payments resumed in 1879 the dollar's value was fixed to gold and gold became the only universally acceptable metallic money. Repeated calls for restoring the monetary role of silver were made by those who felt that the abandonment of silver was responsible for the persistent deflationary pressures and the associated hardship experienced by debtors in general, and farmers and commodity producers in particular. Friedman (1992) and others suggest that the deflation could indeed have been mitigated, or even avoided altogether, if the 1879 resumption had not been preceded by the so-called "Crime of 1873" that demonetized silver. A brief listing of the major events leading up to the 1879 resumption follows in Table 3.1.

Table 3.1 Chronology of key events, 1861–1879

December 31, 1861	Bimetallic standard abandoned as banks suspend specie payments in the face of the U.S. Civil War
February 25, 1862	Legal Tender Act signed into law by President Abraham Lincoln providing for new fiat currency issues that became known as "greenbacks"
April 9, 1865	General Robert E. Lee's surrender to General Ulysses S. Grant at Appomattox Court House effectively ends the Civil War
March 18, 1869	Act to Strengthen the Public Credit pledges the government's faith to make provision at the earliest practicable period for the redemption of all outstanding notes in specie
February 12, 1873	Coinage Act signed into law by President Ulysses S. Grant makes gold the only metallic standard in the United States and demonetizes silver
January 14, 1875	Congress passes the Resumption Act Calling for all legal-tender notes to be redeemed in specie beginning January 1, 1879
January 1, 1879	Specie payments in gold resume with silver demonetized

Price-level determination under the gold standard

Under the gold standard, any increase in gold demand not matched by a similar increase in supply causes gold to be valued more highly in terms of other items in the economy. This, in turn, requires goods prices to fall as the aggregate price level is itself simply the inverse of the price of gold. This leaves a gold standard economy susceptible to deflation whenever there is upward pressure on gold prices. Prior to the Civil War, the United States' exposure to such deflationary effects was limited by the operation of a bimetallic monetary standard, whereby the mint stood ready to coin both silver and gold under a 16:1 ratio. Any increased scarcity of gold would cause its relative market value to rise and make an ounce of gold worth more than the sixteen ounces of silver at which it was valued by the U.S. mint. Although gold holders would be unlikely to take their holdings to the mint under these circumstances, holders of silver would find the mint's valuation attractive, and increased coining of silver would tend to offset any deflationary impetus arising from higher gold prices. This bimetallic standard was abandoned under the Coinage Act of 1873, however, which laid the foundation for a purely gold standard and, in turn, the accompanying deflation that continued until the mid-1890s. The Resumption Act of January 1875 formally laid down the terms of the new gold standard with redemption in gold to commence in 1879.

Although actual specie payments were postponed until January 1, 1879, increased gold accumulation in preparation for this resumption plus the boost to gold demand stemming from the outright demonetization of silver around the world was reflected in a rising market price for gold and ongoing deflationary pressures. The American move to demonetize silver was, in fact, part of a worldwide trend that began with Germany's decision to abandon silver in 1871. Oppers (1996) suggests that the ensuing scarcity of gold was not due to any prior shortage of gold or surplus of silver but rather triggered by the silver demonetization itself. Moreover,

> much of the deflation in the gold-standard countries in the 1870s … could have been avoided by continued free silver coinage in only two countries: France and Belgium.
>
> (Oppers 1996: 158)

Flandreau (1996) goes so far as to label the French move to limit silver coinage the "French Crime of 1873," with the *coup de grâce* following in 1876 when the Banque de France imposed a bill entirely suspending silver coinage in the country.

Anticipation of the pending resumption in the United States was reflected in a rising price of gold expressed in "greenback" paper currency, while the spread between U.S. gold railroad bonds and British consols declined by as much as 200 basis points between 1875 and 1879 (Obstfeld and Taylor 2003). Expectations of greenback appreciation may actually have set in even earlier with the Public Credit Act of March 18, 1869, guaranteeing eventual redemption and principal in gold (Calomiris 1988). Just as the greenback's value steadily rose against gold, the aggregate price level steadily declined through the 1870s such that the old pre-Civil War price level had already been achieved by the time that formal resumption was implemented in 1879 (Bayoumi and Bordo 1998). This overall price decline also reflected the monetary contraction that began right after the conclusion of the Civil War, with the money stock declining at a rate of approximately seven percent per year between 1865 and 1868 while prices fell by eight percent or more per year (Timberlake 1964). Outright declines in the money stock ended in February 1868 with a Congressional bill prohibiting any further immediate retirement of outstanding greenbacks. Even though this did not end the deflation, the rate of price decline moderated considerably after this.

The persistent deflationary trend

The average rate of price decline between 1869 and 1879 was 3.8 percent per year. As shown in Table 3.2, this reflected modest money supply growth of 2.7 percent per year that was outweighed by stronger growth in output such that too little money was chasing too many goods.[1] Note that this nineteenth-century experience of an economy growing amidst deflation contrasts sharply with modern-day concerns sometimes expressed over the negative consequences of any deflation (Bernanke 2002). For example, many observers have repeatedly lamented the "lost decade" of deflation in Japan (Krugman 2009) where, incidentally, deflation was milder than in the United States over the 1870s period shown in Table 3.2 and Japanese output still grew – albeit at a slower pace than during the 1870s. As noted by Bordo and Filardo (2005), deflationary experiences are by no means all the same and there has been a wide spectrum of "good," "bad," and "ugly" deflations.

Returning to the decade of the 1870s, with money demand growing in conjunction with rising real output and income levels, money growth lagging behind output growth

Table 3.2 Money, prices and output, 1869 vs. 1879

	1869	*1879*	*Annualized Rate of Change*
Money Stock ($billion)	1.298	1.698	2.7%
Price Index (1929=100)	79.1	54.3	−3.8%
Real Output ($billion, 1929 prices)	7.36	14.52	6.8%
Real Output per Capita (1929 prices)	188	295	4.5%

Note: Money stock is valued in greenbacks at the mid-point of each year and real output is measured by net national product.

Source: Friedman and Schwarz (1963: 37)

implied also that money supply lagged behind money demand. In the 1870s, therefore, the shortage of money growth relative to the growth in output inevitably gave rise to deflationary pressures that reflected the ongoing monetary scarcity. Whereas such an outcome is possible under any monetary standard, we discuss below how the scope for monetary expansion to escape this denouement would generally be much greater under the pre-Civil War bimetallic standard than under the post-Civil War gold standard.

The continuing deflation after 1879 reflected a global pattern of rising gold scarcity that automatically produced falling aggregate prices in any nations that tied the value of their currency exclusively to gold. This deflationary trend continued until the mid-1890s, when new discoveries in South Africa, Western Australia and Alaska boosted gold supply just as the invention of the cyanide process was allowing for increased gold production out of existing reserves. There were numerous calls for a return to free coinage of silver throughout the deflationary episode, stemming not only from the silver-producing states in the western United States but also agrarian interests aggrieved at the burden of the deflation on farmers facing higher real debt burdens if prices fell while their obligations remained fixed in nominal terms. There was even a Greenback Party seeking a return to the unbacked fiat currency issues of the Civil War. The agitation for a move away from the rigidities of the gold standard fueled the presidential campaign of William Jennings Bryan, who advocated a return to bimetallism but was defeated in 1896 just as expanding gold production finally helped to reverse the longstanding deflationary trend.

Had the bimetallic standard been resumed after the Civil War, rather than being eliminated in 1873, increased minting of silver likely would have significantly reduced, perhaps even eliminated, the ensuing deflationary trend (see for example, Drake 1985, Friedman 1992, Velde 2002). Under a bimetallic standard, such stabilizing effects emerge as shifts in demand and supply that cause one metal to appreciate automatically trigger increased minting of the other (Dowd 1996).[2] As noted by Friedman (1992: 71), the U.S. deflation caused particular hardship in the agricultural sector because farmers are generally net debtors. Furthermore, agricultural prices fell more than in proportion with the aggregate price level. Although the U.S. aggregate price level declined by approximately 1.7 percent per year from 1875–1896, the wholesale prices of agricultural commodities are estimated to have fallen by as much as 3 percent per year (Friedman 1992: 70). The populist concerns expressed in many of the repeated congressional arguments for a return to bimetallism are exemplified in the remarks of Representative John H. Reagen of Texas on December 30, 1891:

> The passage of the act demonetizing silver caused a reduction in values of all property and products of about 33 per cent; it took from the people the use of about one-half of the metal money of the world; and it increased the burdens of all indebtedness from one-third to one-half.[3]

Another issue garnering support for the Free Silver movement was the shortage of small denomination coins. Gramm and Gramm (2004: 1127) note that

> at least part of the debt burden of farmers in the South and West was debt on account accumulated because of a shortage of denominations of money valued at a half a day's wages and less ... Paradoxically [they] were then, to some degree, debtors because of the dearth of silver coins and not advocates of silver coinage because they were debtors.

Was resumption in gold inevitable?

Notwithstanding the importance attached to the 1873 Coinage Act today, it seemed to very much catch people off guard at the time. Not only was the demonetization of silver largely unknown until a year or two after the Act's passage but also many of those voting on the bill later claimed that they were unaware of its game-changing implications.[4] Confusion as to the implications of the 1873 Act is reflected in the fact that, nearly eight months after signing it into law, President Ulysses S. Grant seemingly alluded to the scope for resuming specie payments not in gold but in silver in a letter dated October 6, 1873:

> The panic [of 1873] has brought greenbacks about to a par with silver. I wonder that silver is not already coming into the market to supply the deficiency in our circulating medium. When it does come – and I predict that it will soon – we will have made a rapid stride toward specie payments. Currency will never go below silver after that.[5]

Silver had suddenly come into focus in the fall of 1873 owing to a shortage of greenback notes that were being hoarded in the midst of the financial panic in late September. There were even newspaper reports of workers in Pennsylvania and Ohio being paid in specie at this time on the grounds that it was easier to obtain than greenbacks. Greenback scarcity pushed up the currency's purchasing power to the extent that a dollar in silver would buy two percent less gold than a greenback dollar (see Anderson 1939: 305). Silver's relative cheapness made resumption in silver seemingly both feasible and expedient at this time and Anderson (1939) lays out multiple contemporary news reports that anticipated the U.S. Treasury paying out silver for greenbacks on a dollar-for-dollar basis. While inconsistent with the Coinage Act of 1873, this nevertheless suggests that the resumption of specie payments in gold was not inevitable and that silver continued to be viewed by many as a viable option.

Even after the 1875 passage of the Resumption Act, numerous Congressional bills seeking to restore silver's monetary role continued apace until, during the 1877–1878 Congressional session, the House passed a bill sponsored by Representative Richard P. Bland of Missouri providing not only for the re-monetization of silver but also free coinage of silver (Walker 1893). There seems little doubt that Bland was motivated not just by an interest in silver but also by a more basic desire to find some way to engineer monetary expansion. Among his February 21, 1878, remarks on the House floor, Bland stated: "If we cannot [get free coinage of silver] I am in favor of issuing paper money enough to stuff down the bondholders until they are sick."[6] Although Bland's free coinage provision did not pass the Senate, the resultant Bland–Allison Bill became the first of several measures providing for limited silver purchases that added to the circulating medium.

The 1870s deflation in perspective

Consistent with the post-1870 U.S. deflation being a product of the rising price of gold, the United Kingdom similarly faced aggregate price declines averaging approximately 1 percent per year between 1873 and 1896. As with the U.S. case, real output continued to grow in spite of the persistent deflation. Capie and Wood (2004) also find that British price and interest rate series were relatively predictable over this period and that there was a close relationship between actual inflation and the inflation rate predicted by a simple autoregressive process. On the other hand, like most other gold bloc countries, the growth rates enjoyed by the United Kingdom and the United States accelerated after the deflation ended in 1896. Much debate has focused upon whether such step-ups in growth were coincidental or rather reflected the shedding of negative effects associated with the prior deflation. Although Bordo and Redish (2004) point to supply shocks being of greater importance to output than monetary shocks over the 1870–1913 period in both the United States and Canada, aggregate data do not, of course, enable us to assess the possible distributional effects of the deflation that seemed to fuel much of the unrest in the United States in the late nineteenth century. Important regional disparities surfaced at this time, with agricultural and commodity-producing states in the south and west suffering while other parts of the country thrived.

Concerns with price fluctuations under the gold standard certainly outlasted the nineteenth century deflation, with Irving Fisher (1913a, 1913b), for example, subsequently calling for an adjustable commodity-based dollar that would automatically offset any upward or downward pressure on its purchasing power. Whenever aggregate prices fell below target by one percent, for example, the dollar value of the resource unit would be raised by one percent – at the same time automatically lowering the number of resource units in the dollar. In case of deflation under the gold standard, a policy of setting the official gold price above the prevailing market level would be used to induce the public to exchange gold for currency and boost the money in circulation. Although Fisher envisaged stabilizing the price of a broad basket of commodities, Burdekin, Mitchener and Weidenmier (2012) show that simply stabilizing the price of silver may have been sufficient to stabilize the price level under this scheme.[7]

Conclusions

Had the United States simply reverted to the pre-Civil War bimetallic monetary standard, the course of monetary history would have been very different. Instead of facing the same deflationary pressures experienced by all the members of the gold bloc in the late nineteenth century, the United States could have enjoyed more rapid monetary expansion arising from coining silver as the cheaper metal. This might have allowed the United States to escape deflation altogether. The implications for overall economic performance are less clear because the counterfactual case would require us to take a stand not only on the types of economic shocks that would follow a different set of policy choices but also on the question of whether other countries would also have made different monetary policy choices during this period (Siklos 2010). Although it appears that resumption in silver was more than just an academic possibility, and received serious consideration by the government in 1873, reversion to silver became increasingly unlikely over time as gold became the accepted international standard in all the major European economies by the end of the 1870s. This did not stop calls for free coinage of silver persisting for as long as the deflation endured, however, remaining a key component of the 1896 presidential race and the ultimately unsuccessful campaign of William Jennings Bryan.[8] Even though the economy continued to grow under deflation, the strains on at least certain parts of the economy seem undisputable and it is astonishing how much impact was had by a seemingly obscure Coinage Act that had initially largely escaped notice even by those involved in passing it. The story of the 1870s contains a theme that has often been repeated in economic history, namely that ideology is often a poor substitute for good judgment. This truism applies equally to the choice of monetary regimes.

Notes

1 Alternative estimates by Friedman and Schwartz (1963: 39) suggest lower real output growth of 4.4 percent per year (2.0 percent for real output growth per capita) over this same period but still imply that money growth lagged behind.
2 A perennial criticism of bimetallism remains the problem that, unless these relative market values remain very close to the ratios laid down by the mint, it will not be possible for both metals to be widely in use at the same time, however (see for example, Laughlin 1901, Redish 2000). In practice, the old bimetallic system also appears to have relied upon monetary arrangements between the Bank of England and the Banque de France (Diebolt and Parent 2008). While agitation for silver did not lead to the restoration of a bimetallic standard, it did subsequently spur the adoption of a series of major silver purchase programs in the United States. The Bland–Allison Act of 1878 was followed by the Sherman Act of July 1890 that called for a doubling of the limited silver purchases undertaken under the 1878 Act.
3 Quoted in Barnett (1964: 179).
4 Walker (1893: 171*n*) adds that he was not aware of silver's demonetization despite lecturing on money at Yale University when the 1873 Act was passed and being in frequent touch with the banking community in New York.
5 Quoted in Anderson (1939: 305).
6 Quoted in Timberlake (1964: 29).
7 Other commodity-price targeting proposals and policies are reviewed in Burdekin (2007), along with the effects of the series of silver purchase acts enacted in the United States from the 1870s through the 1930s.
8 William Jennings Bryan may himself have been represented by the Cowardly Lion in the *Wizard of Oz*, joining Dorothy's group only after the western farmers (represented by the Scarecrow) and the workingman (represented by the Tin Woodman) already had the silver movement well underway (Rockoff 1990). Just 36 years old at the time of his 1896 defeat, Bryan continued on as a presidential candidate in both the 1900 and 1908 elections.

References

Anderson, G.L. (1939) 'The proposed resumption of silver payments in 1873', *Pacific Historical Review*, 8: 301–16.

Barnett, P. (1964) 'The crime of 1873 re-examined', *Agricultural History*, 38: 178–81.

Bayoumi, T. and Bordo, M.D. (1998) 'Getting pegged: comparing the 1879 and 1925 gold resumptions', *Oxford Economic Papers*, 50: 122–49.

Bernanke, B.S. (2002) 'Deflation: making sure "It" doesn't happen here', remarks before the National Economists Club, Washington, DC, November 21, available at http://www.federalreserve.gov/boarddocs/speeches/2002/20021121/default.htm

Bordo, M.D. and Filardo, A. (2005) 'Deflation and monetary policy in historical perspective: remembering the past or being condemned to repeat it?' *Economic Policy*, 20: 799–844.

Bordo, M.D. and Redish, A. (2004) 'Is deflation depressing? evidence from the classical gold standard', in R.C.K. Burdekin and P.L. Siklos (eds.) *Deflation: Current and Historical Perspectives*, New York: Cambridge University Press.

Burdekin, R.C.K. (2007) 'Nontraditional monetary policy options and commodity-based stabilization policy', *International Economics and Finance Journal*, 2: 1–18.

Burdekin, R.C.K., Mitchener, K.S., and Weidenmier, M.D. (2012) 'Irving Fisher and price-level targeting in Austria: was silver the answer?' *Journal of Money, Credit, and Banking*, 44(4): 733–50.

Calomiris, C. (1988) 'Price and exchange rate determination during the greenback suspension', *Oxford Economic Papers*, 39: 189–220.

Capie, F. and Wood, G. (2004) 'Price change, financial stability, and the British economy, 1870–1939', in R.C.K. Burdekin and P.L. Siklos (eds.) *Deflation: Current and Historical Perspectives*, New York: Cambridge University Press.

Diebolt, C. and Parent, A. (2008) 'Bimetallism: the "rules of the game"', *Explorations in Economic History*, 45: 288–302.

Dowd, K. (1996) 'The analytics of bimetallism', *Manchester School of Economic and Social Studies*, 64: 281–97.

Drake, L.S. (1985) 'Reconstruction of a bimetallic price level', *Explorations in Economic History*, 22: 194–219.

Fisher, I. (1913a) 'A compensated dollar', *Quarterly Journal of Economics*, 27: 213–35.

Fisher, I. (1913b) *The Purchasing Power of Money: Its Determination and Relation to Credit, Interest and Crises*, New and Revised Edition (assisted by Harry G. Brown), New York: Macmillan.

Flandreau, M. (1996) 'The French crime of 1873: an essay on the emergence of the international gold standard, 1870–1880', *Journal of Economic History*, 56: 862–97.

Fox, D.M. (1897) *The Silver Side, 1900 Campaign Text-Book*, Chicago, IL: W. B. Conkey.

Friedman, M. (1992) *Money Mischief: Episodes in Monetary History*, New York: Harcourt Brace Jovanovich.

Friedman, M. and Schwartz, A.J. (1963) *A Monetary History of the United States, 1867–1960*, Princeton, NJ: Princeton University Press.

Gramm, M. and Gramm, P. (2004) 'The free silver movement in America: a reinterpretation', *Journal of Economic History*, 64: 1108–29.

Krugman, P. (2009) *The Return of Depression Era Economics and the Crisis of 2008*, New York: W.W. Norton.

Laughlin, J.L. (1901) *The History of Bimetallism in the United States*, 4th edn., New York: D. Appleton.

Obstfeld, M. and Taylor, A.M. (2003) 'Sovereign risk, credibility and the gold standard: 1870–1913 versus 1925–31', *Economic Journal*, 113: 241–75.

Oppers, S.E. (1996) 'Was the worldwide shift to gold inevitable? An analysis of the end of bimetallism', *Journal of Monetary Economics*, 37: 143–62.

Redish, A. (2000) *Bimetallism: An Economic and Historical Analysis*, New York: Cambridge University Press.

Rockoff, H. (1990) 'The "Wizard of Oz" as a monetary allegory', *Journal of Political Economy*, 98: 739–60.

Siklos, P.L. (2010) 'Deflation', in R. Whaples (ed.) *EH.Net Encyclopedia*, http://eh.net/encyclopedia/article/siklos.deflation

Timberlake, R.H. (1964) 'Ideological factors in specie resumption and Treasury policy', *Journal of Economic History*: 24: 29–52.

Velde, F.R. (2002) 'The crime of 1873: back to the scene', Working Paper 2002–29, Federal Reserve Bank of Chicago, Chicago, IL.

Walker, F.A. (1893) 'The free coinage of silver', *Journal of Political Economy*, 1: 163–78.

4

THE GREAT
MERGER WAVE

Anthony Patrick O'Brien

Technological changes, court rulings and the growth of large firms in the late 1800s

The Great Merger Wave of 1898–1902 had its roots in structural changes in American industry during the previous decades. Beginning in the 1870s and accelerating in the 1880s, a number of manufacturing industries became dominated by large, vertically integrated firms. Standard Oil, the American Tobacco Company, the Campbell Soup Company, Proctor and Gamble, General Electric, and many other large industrial firms had their origins during this period. Industries such as food processing, chemicals, petroleum refining, primary metals, machinery, and transportation equipment came to be dominated by a few large firms.

Several factors paved the way for the growth of large firms in many industries. First, the extension of the railroad system in the years after the Civil War reduced transportation costs sufficiently to make selling in a national market feasible. The development of the compound marine engine in the 1880s reduced the costs of shipping across the Atlantic, opening the European market to U.S. exports, which was particularly important in some industries, such as oil refining. The elaboration of the telegraph system and the invention of the telephone in the 1880s allowed for the improved communication necessary for coordinating a national organization. The development of trading in industrial securities on the New York Stock Exchange provided a means of both financing large-scale enterprises and of capitalizing the gains from the profits made possible by the market power attained by these large firms. Electrification combined with technological breakthroughs in a number of industries greatly increased economies of scale. To take a striking example, in the early 1880s, a worker could produce 3,000 cigarettes per day by hand. In 1882, James Bonsack patented a cigarette-making machine that could produce 120,000 cigarettes per day (Chandler 1978: 249).

Technological innovations occurring during the 1870s and 1880s that allowed for the development of high-volume, continuous process production techniques included (Chandler 1978, Clark 1929, George 1982, Williamson and Daum 1959, O'Brien 1988): the roller mill in the processing of oatmeal and flour, refrigerated cars in meatpacking, the pneumatic malting process and temperature-controlled tank cars in brewing, and food preparation and can-sealing machinery in the production of canned meat, vegetables, fish, and soups. During the 1880s, the chemical industry saw the introduction first of the Solvay process and then the electrolytic processes in the production of alkalis, and the discovery of the process of producing acetic acid and acetates as byproducts of charcoal production. In the petroleum industry, John Merril's development of the seamless wrought-iron or steel-bottomed still allowed for a sharp increase in plant size between 1867 and 1873. The 1870s saw the development of the long-distance crude oil pipeline and the steel tank car. In the 1870s and 1880s the Bessemer and open-hearth processes were widely adopted in steel making. In the mid-1880s, new developments in electro-metallurgy made commercial mass production of aluminum possible. During the same period, a large number of mechanical and chemical innovations were devised that greatly facilitated the process of refining and working various metals. The development, beginning in 1880, of improved metalworking machinery based on the use of high-speed-tool steel allowed for the production of a wide variety of better machines with finer tolerances. The typewriter, invented in the late 1870s, was mass produced during the 1880s. The electrical street railway car came into widespread use during the late 1880s. Innovations in marketing and distribution, including national advertising of branded products such as cigarettes and breakfast cereals also played an important role in some industries.

Finally, a series of court decisions were needed to confirm the legal basis of firms operating across state lines. The commerce clause in the U.S. Constitution reserved to Congress the right to regulate interstate commerce. Up to the 1870s, however, states were largely free to regulate imports of goods from other states provided that they did not levy tariffs on them. One scholar has described the situation prior to 1875 (McCurdy 1978: 635):

> State and local officials prescribed marketing practices, enacted discriminatory schemes of mercantile licensing and taxation, proscribed the entry of unfavored articles of commerce, and devised inspection laws to improve the competitive position of their citizens relative to producers in other states.

The large firms selling on a national scale that arose in the 1870s and 1880s had the incentive and the financial resources to launch challenges in the federal court system to these laws and regulations. The first important challenge came from I.M. Singer, the sewing machine company. In the United States, before the 1870s most manufactured goods were sold to wholesalers who in turn distributed them to local retailers. Singer believed that it needed to operate its own stores in order to properly demonstrate its sewing machines, have adequate stocks of accessories, provide repair services, and provide customers with credit. Singer set up a system of more than 500 company-owned stores. Several states placed licensing restrictions or taxes on the stores. Singer brought a suit against a license fee levied by Missouri on Singer's stores in that state. In *Welton v. Missouri*, decided in 1876, the U.S. Supreme Court struck down the Missouri law. In another case involving state restrictions on Singer's stores, *Webber v. Virginia*, decided in 1880, the Supreme Court handed down a more definitive ruling. In his majority decision, Justice Stephen Field wrote (quoted in McCurdy 1978: 642):

> It was against legislation of this discriminating kind that the framers of the Constitution intended to guard, when they vested in Congress the power to regulate commerce among the several states.

The question remained open as to whether states could regulate imports from other states on the grounds of health or safety. As meatpackers, such as Armour and Swift, began to operate large plants primarily in Chicago and ship beef in refrigerated railcars, several states enacted restrictions on the sale of imported beef on the basis that the animals had not been subject to local inspection before being slaughtered. The Supreme Court struck these laws down in the case of *Minnesota v. Baber*, decided in 1890.

With the legal basis for a national market largely secured, firms in a number of industries became large through exploiting economies of scale. Among other industries, railroads, oil refining, meatpacking, flour milling, agricultural machinery, cigarettes, beer, chemicals, and steel came to be dominated by a handful of firms. Historians have sometimes exaggerated the extent to which the oligopolies in these industries meant reduced competition. Prior to 1870, high transportation costs, slow communication, and legal barriers to operating across state lines meant that one or a few firms had dominated sales of a particular product in many local markets. Although these firms were much smaller than the firms that came to dominate these industries nationally by the end of the nineteenth century, the lack of effective competition meant they possessed substantial economic power to charge prices well above their costs. Hence, the rise of oligopolies at the end of the nineteenth century in no sense disrupted a golden age of perfect competition because none had ever existed.

Business attempts to restrain "ruinous price competition"

The heavy capital investment required by the railroads, oil refineries, steel mills, and other large firms meant that these firms had high fixed costs but low marginal costs. Once an oil refinery or a railroad line had been built, the additional cost of producing one more barrel of oil or of hauling one more ton of freight was quite low. Because of this cost structure, the owners and managers of these firms believed that unrestrained competition – "ruinous price competition" as they thought of it – would cause prices to be pushed down to the marginal cost of production. Their high fixed costs meant that such low prices would lead to losses and eventually force them into bankruptcy. The result during the 1870s and 1880s was attempts to restrain price competition through collusive agreements among firms in the same industry. At that time there was no statutory prohibition against such agreements. There was, however, a common law prohibition against "conspiracies in restraint of trade." The result was that courts typically did not consider agreements among firms to fix prices as illegal per se, but were unwilling to enforce such agreements. So, as with the OPEC oil cartel of recent decades, large firms in the 1870s and 1880s could negotiate price fixing agreements, but had no legal means to enforce them, relying instead on voluntary compliance. And just as with OPEC, the parties to such agreements frequently cheated on them. For instance, in the 1870s, John D. Rockefeller helped form the National Refiners Association with the main objective of controlling the prices of kerosene and other refined oil products. Members of the association frequently cheated on the agreements, however, forcing Rockefeller eventually to conclude that the agreements were "ropes of sand" (Chandler 1978: 321).

In 1882, Rockefeller's lawyer, Samuel C.T. Dobb hit on a novel approach to maintaining price fixing agreements among what had been competing firms in the oil refining industry. Legal trusts had existed for centuries in English common law as a means to allow one or more trustees to control assets on behalf of a beneficiary, often a minor who had received the assets as an inheritance. Rockefeller realized that a trust could be used to reorganize the oil industry in a way that would ensure the maintenance of price fixing agreements. Executives from his Standard Oil Company served as trustees, holding the stock of the several dozen firms who had agreed to join the trust. Initially, the Standard Oil executives allowed the firms in the trust to operate independently except with respect to setting prices. Eventually, however, the trust began to operate as a single, centralized firm controlled from a new headquarters established in New York in 1885.

The Sherman Antitrust Act and subsequent Supreme Court rulings

Publicity given to the Standard Oil trust and similar arrangements in other industries led to a strong public outcry. Prior to the late nineteenth century, public concern with "monopolies" had often centered on the role of government in granting exclusive rights to private firms, as had happened at all levels of government with turnpikes, canals, and railroads and at the federal level with the charters granted to the First and Second Banks of the United States. The rise of trusts redirected this concern to the actions taken by large firms, such as Standard Oil, the American Tobacco Company, and Swift and Company, to raise prices and suppress competition. Agitation against trusts culminated in Congressional passage of the Sherman Antitrust Act in 1890. Section 1 of the Sherman Act states that:

> Every contract, combination in the form of trust or otherwise, or conspiracy, in restraint of trade or commerce among the several States, or with foreign nations, is hereby declared to be illegal.

Section 2 states that:

> Every person who shall monopolize, or attempt to monopolize, or combine or conspire with any other person or persons, to monopolize any part of the trade or commerce among the several States, or with foreign nations, shall be deemed guilty of a misdemeanor.

There is some debate as to whether Congress's motivation in passing the Sherman Act was primarily to increase consumer welfare by eliminating price fixing or to protect the interests of small firms that saw themselves unable to compete against the trusts and other large firms (Bork 1966, Grandy 1993). Werner Troesken has noted that stock prices rose as the bill made its way through Congress, suggesting that investors may have seen the Sherman Act as replacing what had been reasonably effective state antitrust enforcement with weaker federal antitrust enforcement (Troesken 2000).

Whatever the intent of Congress may have been, passage of the Sherman Act eliminated the trust as a legal means of coordinating the activities of otherwise independent firms. It also appeared to eliminate price fixing and other collusive practices among firms. But did it preclude mergers among firms in the same industry – what became known as horizontal mergers? Mergers intended to suppress price competition would seem to be combinations in restraint of trade, which were outlawed under Section 1 of the Sherman Act, but in fact the Supreme Court ruled otherwise in the *United States v. E.C. Knight Company*, which was decided in 1895. In that case, an 8–1 majority of the court rejected the attempt by the administration of President Grover Cleveland to block the American Sugar Refinery Company's acquisition of E.C. Knight, even though the acquisition gave American Sugar a 98 percent share of sugar refining capacity in the United States. The court's majority reasoned that manufacturing was a local activity not covered by the commerce clause to the Constitution and, therefore, not subject to federal regulation under the Sherman Act.

In the case of *United States v. Addyston Pipe*, decided in 1898, the Supreme Court made clear that price fixing was illegal per se. There was a sharp increase in horizontal mergers beginning in 1898 and lasting through 1902. According to one estimate, more than 1,800 firms were involved in these mergers, representing as much as one-half of the manufacturing capacity of the United States. Naomi Lamoreaux has carried out the most comprehensive study of the merger wave and finds that of the 93 mergers for which data on market shares is available, 72 ended up controlling at least 40 percent of their industry's production and 42 controlled at least 70 percent (Lamoreaux 1985: 2).

Differing interpretations of the causes of the Merger Wave

Did the Great Merger Wave result from the passage of the Sherman Act taken together with Supreme Court decisions establishing that price fixing was illegal but mergers were not? The severe economic recession that began in 1893 would appear to have increased the incentive for firms in many manufacturing industries to find a means of restraining price competition. With many firms producing well below capacity into the late 1890s and the Sherman Act having foreclosed reliance on collusive agreements, firms may have turned to mergers for relief from competitive pressures. It is possible, though, that if firms believed mergers to be a lower-cost way of reducing price competition than was collusion, the merger wave would have happened even if the Sherman Act had not been passed (Bittlingmayer 1985). If, on the other hand, in the absence of legislation, firms would have preferred collusion to mergers, then the Sherman Act may have led them to undertake mergers that they would not otherwise have entered into.

Although the timing of the Great Merger Wave leads to the inference that its main goal was to suppress price competition, it is possible that the mergers of that period are better seen as a way in which firms could exploit the economies of scale that arose from the technological and organizational innovations of previous decades. Several economists have made this argument. For instance, Ralph Nelson has claimed that the rise of large-scale enterprises dates from this period (Nelson 1959: 5):

> [The merger wave] transformed many industries, formerly characterized by many small and medium-sized firms, into those in which one or a few large enterprises occupied leading positions.

Yale Brozen argues that the Great Merger Wave allowed firms to exploit economies, thereby benefiting the economy (Brozen 1982: 11, 65 emphasis in original):

> Concentrated industries become concentrated (and some firms become and remain "dominant") because that is the road to greater efficiency and lower costs *in those industries*. ... The increased concentration brought about by substantial horizontal mergers [early in the twentieth century] lowered prices relative to those in industries where concentration was not increased by mergers.

There are reasons to be skeptical, however, that the Great Merger Wave was important in the advent of large firms in U.S. manufacturing. To begin with, as we have already seen, large, integrated firms had already appeared during the 1880s in many industries. There is evidence that the economies of scale resulting from technological progress had resulted in sharp increases in optimal factory size in many industries by 1890 (James 1983). If economies of scale had already been largely reaped by 1890, they could not have caused the merger wave.

One way to gauge the importance of economies of scale in explaining the Great Merger Wave is to look at increases in the size of factories during the late nineteenth and early twentieth centuries. The main source of data for this period is the Census of Manufacturing conducted by the federal government every ten years in the late nineteenth century and every five years in the early twentieth century. The conventional measure of a factory's size is its level of output when producing at normal capacity. The census data on production, though, are dollar values rather than units of output, so using them would require difficult corrections for changes in the price level. An alternative is to measure factory size in terms of employment per factory. There are 171 manufacturing industries for which it is possible to calculate consistent data on employment per factory from 1869 to 1929. These data indicate that about two-thirds of the increase in factory size that was to take place between 1869 and 1929 had occurred by 1889 – nearly a decade before the beginning of the Great Merger Wave. During this period, the decades of the 1870s and 1880s experienced by far the most rapid increases in factory size. For the period right around the merger wave – census years 1899 and 1904 – the connection between merger activity and increases in factory size is weak. For instance, the primary metals product industry, which included the steel industry, experienced the most merger activity of any two-digit Standard Industrial Classification (SIC) industry but did not experience a corresponding increase in factory size. The stone, clay, and glass products industry, on the other hand, experienced a large increase in average factory size but few mergers.

Some of the best-known mergers seem to have been expressly aimed at reducing price competition rather than capturing economies of scale or other efficiencies. For instance, mergers in the steel industry during this period appear to have been spurred by a desire to reduce the price competition the industry had experienced during the 1890s. Following the formation of United States Steel in 1901, Elbert H. Gary, Charles Schwab, and other top executives were in no rush to integrate the dozens of companies that had been brought together by the merger. According to one account of the operations of the firm during its early years (McCraw and Reinhardt 1989: 596):

> Organizationally, [U.S. Steel] persisted in the form of a loose holding company, long keeping intact about 200 subsidiaries – including such giants as Carnegie Steel, Illinois Steel, American Sheet and Tin Plate, and American Steel and Wire. Many of these subsidiaries had overlapping markets and duplicate sales forces. Apparently, eliminating price competition had been sufficient reason for the U.S. Steel merger.

The long-run impact of the Great Merger Wave

The bulk of the merger wave took place during the presidency of William McKinley. His attorneys general argued that filing court cases to block mergers would be futile given the Supreme Court's decision in the E.C. Knight case. In fact, only three cases were filed during McKinley's term (Bittlingmayer 1993: 4). When Theodore Roosevelt succeeded McKinley in September 1901, he was determined to pursue a more vigorous antitrust policy. In 1902, Roosevelt's attorney general Philander C. Knox filed an antitrust suit against the Northern Securities company, which had been formed as a holding company to control the assets of the Northern Pacific, Great Northern, Union Pacific, and Burlington railroads. In a 5–4 decision handed down in 1904, the Supreme Court backed the government's position and ordered the dissolution of the holding company. The decision was interpreted as indicating that the court was willing to apply the Sherman Act to mergers, although not all mergers would necessarily violate the act. Over the next few years, Roosevelt established the Antitrust Division within the Justice Department and Knox filed suits against Standard Oil, Du Pont, American Tobacco, Otis Elevator, and the Chicago meatpackers, among other firms (Bittlingmayer 1993: 6–7). Roosevelt's vigorous prosecution of antitrust cases coincided with the petering out of the merger wave. From a high in 1899 of 63 mergers involving five or more manufacturing firms, the number of mergers fell to five in 1903 and to only three in 1904 (Lamoreaux 1985: 4).

Did the Great Merger Wave have a long-lasting effect on the industrial structure of the United States? The answer to this question is related to the motives firms had for merging. If firms merged to take advantage of economies of scale or to gain other efficiencies, then we might expect that they would have gained lasting competitive advantages. If, on the other hand, firms merged to fix prices, then their position might have been undermined by competition. Charging higher prices would increase a newly merged firm's profits in the short run, but if the firm lacked any competitive advantages, then new firms would enter the industry and firms that were already in the industry but not included in the merger would increase output. The result would be that production in the industry would increase, prices would fall, and the merged firm would undergo declining market share. (Note that such a strategy of high prices and high profits in the short run, followed by a decline in prices and profits over the longer run might have been optimal in the sense of maximizing the present discounted value of the firm (Gaskins 1971).) In other words, the effects of mergers that resulted in higher prices with no increase in efficiency would likely have been reversed by increased competition in the long run.

There is considerable evidence that, in fact, during the following decades, competition did reverse some of the effects of the merger wave. For example, U.S. Steel's share of the market for ten key steel products declined from about 62 percent in 1901 when the firm was formed to about 42 percent in 1927 (McCraw and Reinhardt 1989: 597). Moreover, many mergers during this period proved unsuccessful. Shaw Livermore compiled a list of 156 mergers from the somewhat longer period of 1890 to 1905 that "could rightfully claim to be mergers with power enough to influence markedly conditions in their industry" (Livermore 1935). According to Livermore, 63 of these mergers were financial failures, 53 entered bankruptcy within 10 years of being created, and another 17 were only "limping" successes. Similarly, George Stigler found that in a sample of 19 manufacturing industries, 14 experienced substantial decreases in concentration between 1904 and 1937, four experienced minor changes in concentration, and only the automobile industry experienced a substantial increase in concentration (Stigler 1949: 53, 62). G. Warren Nutter estimated that about 33 percent of manufacturing output in 1904 was produced in industries whose four largest firms accounted for 50 percent or more of industry sales (Nutter 1951). In 1935, the first later year for which a comparable estimate is possible, about 20 percent of manufacturing output was produced in industries whose four largest firms accounted for 50 percent or more of sales (U.S. Bureau of the Census 1938 and United States National Resources Committee 1939). This large decline in industrial concentration is another indication that the effects of the Great Merger Wave were substantially reversed in the following decades.

Some of the reversal in concentration resulted from successful antitrust prosecutions instituted by Theodore Roosevelt and his successors. Notably, in 1911, the Supreme Court ordered the dissolution of both Standard Oil and American Tobacco. Overall, though, antitrust prosecutions were infrequent and left intact many companies formed during the merger wave, conspicuously, U.S. Steel, which the Supreme Court ruled in 1920 had not violated the Sherman Act. One classic study of the effects of antitrust policy concluded that (Stigler 1966: 236): "The Sherman Antitrust Act appears to have had only a very modest effect in reducing concentration." More important were the forces of competition, which over time eroded the market power of those mergers that were not justified by increases in economic efficiency.

References

Bittlingmayer, G. (1985) 'Did antitrust policy cause the great merger wave?', *Journal of Law and Economics*, 28: 77–118.

Bittlingmayer, G. (1993) 'The stock market and early antitrust enforcement', *Journal of Law and Economics*, 36: 1–32.

Bork, R.H. (1966) 'Legislative intent and the policy of the Sherman Act', *Journal of Law and Economics*, 9: 7–48.

Brozen, Y. (1982) *Concentration, Mergers, and Public Policy*, New York: Free Press.

Chandler, A.D., Jr. (1978) *The Visible Hand: The Managerial Revolution in American Business*, Cambridge: Harvard University Press.

Clark, V.S. (1929) *History of Manufactures in the United States; Volume 2: 1860–1893*, Washington, DC: Carnegie Institution of Washington.

Gaskins, D.W., Jr. (1971) 'Dynamic limit pricing: optimal pricing under threat of entry', *Journal of Economic Theory*, 3: 306–22.

George, P.J. (1982) *The Emergence of Industrial America*, Albany, NY: State University of New York Press.

Grandy, C. (1993) 'Original intent and the Sherman Antitrust Act: a re-examination of the consumer-welfare hypothesis', *Journal of Economic History*, 53: 359–76.

James, J.A. (1983) 'Structural change in American manufacturing', *Journal of Economic History*, 43: 433–59.

Lamoreaux, N.R. (1985) *The Great Merger Movement in American Business, 1895–1904*, Cambridge: Cambridge University Press.

Livermore, S. (1935) 'The success of industrial mergers', *Quarterly Journal of Economics*, 49: 68–96.

McCraw, T.K. and Reinhardt, F. (1989) 'Losing to win: U.S. steel's pricing, investment decisions, and market share, 1901–1938', *Journal of Economic History*, 49: 593–619.

McCurdy, C.W. (1978) 'American law and the marketing structure of the large corporation, 1875–1890', *Journal of Economic History*, 38: 631–49.

Nelson, R.L. (1959) *Merger Movements in American Industry, 1895–1956*, Princeton, NJ: Princeton University Press.

Nutter, G.W. (1951) *The Extent of Enterprise Monopoly in the United States, 1899–1939: A Quantitative Study of Some Aspects of Monopoly*, Chicago, IL: University of Chicago Press.

O'Brien, A.P. (1988) 'Factory size, economies of scale, and the great merger wave of 1898–1902', *Journal of Economic History*, 48: 639–49.

Stigler, G.J. (1949) *Five Lectures on Economic Problems*, New York: Longmans, Green.

Stigler, G.J. (1966) 'The economic effects of the antitrust laws', *Journal of Law and Economics*, 9: 225–58.

Troesken, W. (2000) 'Did the trusts want a federal antitrust law: an event study of state antitrust enforcement and passage of the Sherman Act', in J. Heckelman and R. Whaples (eds.), *Public Choice Interpretations of American Economic History*, New York: Kluwer Academic Press, 2000.

United States National Resources Committee (1939) *The Structure of the American Economy, Part I, Basic Characteristics*, Washington, DC: U.S. Government Printing Office.

U.S. Bureau of the Census (1938) *Census of Manufactures: 1935*, Washington, DC: U.S. Government Printing Office.

Williamson, H.F. and Daum, A.R. (1959) *The American Petroleum Industry: The Age of Illumination, 1859–1899*, Evanston, IL: Northwestern University Press.

5

THE PANIC OF 1893

Mark Carlson[1]

The Panic of 1893 was one of the most serious banking panics of the National Banking Era.[2] Of the roughly 9,500 banks that existed in 1893, about 550 were compelled to close their doors either permanently or temporarily during the panic (*Bradstreet's* 1893). Unlike some of the other banking panics of this era which appeared to originate in the financial center of New York City, the troubles in the banking sector were first manifest in the interior of the country and spread to New York. It can be helpful to divide the panic into two parts. During the first part of the panic there were widespread runs that forced bank closures in the interior which in turn put pressure on New York banks and the money markets there. In the second part of the panic, these pressures became sufficient to cause the New York banks to sharply restrict currency shipments to interior banks. As the New York banks played a key role in banking and payment systems, the restrictions on the convertibility of interbank deposits in New York to currency represented a second shock to the banking system that further disrupted financial markets.

The panic occurred against a backdrop of rising concerns about the currency and the economy. With respect to the currency, the commitment of the United States to the gold standard was viewed as being placed in jeopardy as silver purchases by the Treasury increased outstanding Treasury notes potentially redeemable in gold even as gold reserves at the Treasury declined (Lauck 1907). The health of the economy was also deteriorating around the time of the panic as mercantile and industrial bankruptcies rose and the railroad industry came under pressure (Sprague 1910). While scholars have debated the relative importance of these factors since shortly after the crisis, it seems likely that both factors played a role.

The economic downturn that followed the panic was one of the most severe in the history of the United States. An economic contraction appears to have already been underway at the time of the panic and there may well have been a notable slowdown even in the absence of the panic. Nevertheless, a variety of anecdotal information suggests that financial disruptions associated with the panic may have exacerbated the decline.

This chapter is organized as follows: the first section reviews the economic and political developments that preceded the crisis; the second provides a narrative of the panic itself, a review of the geographic impact of the crisis, and some discussion of the immediate impacts of the panic on the broader economy; the third section briefly describes the aftermath of the panic.

Developments preceding the panic

There were two factors that likely contributed to rising concerns about the stability of the banking system. First, there was a deterioration in confidence regarding the commitment of the United States to the gold standard due to the silver purchase program by the United States government and a decline in the gold reserve held by the Treasury. Fears of a devaluation could have prompted depositors to seek to convert their dollar denominated deposits into gold. Second, a decline in economic activity and an increase in commercial bankruptcies may have caused depositors to become less confident in the solvency of the banking system. The relative importance of these factors was debated even by contemporaries with some, such as Lauck (1907) and Noyes (1909), arguing for the former and others, such as Sprague (1910), favoring the latter. This section reviews both these factors and provides a brief discussion regarding their relative importance.

Concerns about the gold underpinnings of the currency

During the 1890s the United States was on the gold standard, meaning that Treasury notes could be redeemed for a fixed amount of gold. To meet potential redemptions, the Treasury maintained a gold reserve. At the same time, the Treasury was also required to purchase silver on a regular basis. Such purchases had been mandated by law for some time, but the Sherman Silver Purchase Law of 1890 notably increased the amount of silver required to be purchased each month. These purchases were paid for in notes that legally could be redeemed for gold or silver at the discretion of the Secretary of the Treasury, but which were expected by investors to be redeemable in gold on demand.

The gold reserve maintained by the Treasury declined in the early 1890s. The decline occurred in part as the U.S. government shifted from running a budget surplus to running a deficit. The gold reserve also declined as foreign investors redeemed their holdings of American securities and demanded gold, which they then shipped abroad. In early 1893, the gold reserve had fallen to just over $100 million, down considerably from $190 million in 1890. Noyes (1909) reports that the Treasury Department was required to take some modest actions if the gold reserve fell below this level, such as suspending the issuance of gold certificates, but also that the $100 million figure had symbolic importance and was viewed by both financial market participants and elected officials as important in maintaining the U.S. commitment to the gold standard. Rising concerns about the commitment to the gold standard and the risk of a possible devaluation of the currency may have caused bank depositors to prefer to hold their wealth as gold and not as dollar denominated bank deposits.

Concerns about economic developments

Prior to the outbreak of the panic, economic activity appeared to be slowing. Davis (2004) reports that industrial production experienced a local peak in 1892 and was notably lower in 1893. Moreover, failures of non-financial companies began to accelerate. On February 26, 1893, the Philadelphia and Reading Railroad failed; Sprague (1910) reports that the immediate effects of this bankruptcy were fairly moderate, but that it did raise concerns about the health of other companies. Lauck (1907) reports that the number of mercantile and industrial failures started to climb in late 1892 and the liabilities of such failures more than doubled between the first and second quarters of 1893 (see Table 5.1).

Table 5.1 Mercantile and industrial failures

Period	Number	Liabilities ($ millions)
1892:Q1	3,384	39.3
1892:Q2	2,119	23.0
1892:Q3	1,984	18.7
1892:Q4	2,857	33.1
1893:Q1	3,202	47.3
1893:Q2	3,199	121.6
1893:Q3	4,105	82.5
1893:Q4	4,826	95.4

Source: Lauck (1907: 105). Data reported as compiled from Annual Supplement, *The Commercial and Financial Chronicle*, p. 17, *Financial Review*, 1894

The railroad industry suffered notably before and in the midst of the crisis. In addition to the failure of the Philadelphia and Reading railroad, Lauck (1907: 106) reports the collapse of a number of significant railroad corporations during this period including the Northern Pacific, the Union Pacific, the Atchison, Topeka and Santa Fe, the Erie, and the New York and New England. Markham (2002) reports that over 70 railroad companies failed, placing one quarter of American railroads in the hands of receivers.

With increased business failures, the quality of bank loan portfolios would have deteriorated.[3] Sprague (1910: 161) argues that lending standards had deteriorated in the years preceding the crisis and that by 1893 banks were "carrying a large amount of loans which should have been long since written off or at least written down." As a result, concerns about bank solvency may have increased.

Discussion of the relative importance of the factors

Both these factors likely had a role in the panic. Concerns about the commitment of the United States to the gold standard likely contributed to a reduction in foreign investment in the United States, some unsettling of financial markets in early 1893, and some stringency in money markets. However, concerns about the silver purchases and credibility of the gold standard likely played less of a role in the bank runs that occurred in the interior of the United States. Sprague (1910: 169) notes that the panic was concentrated in the western and northwestern parts of the United States where "there is no evidence that people were distrustful of silver money." Rather, deteriorating economic conditions likely mattered more for domestic depositors. Carlson (2005) finds a strong geographical association between the prevalence of business failures in 1892, which also were more prevalent in northwestern and western parts of the country, and bank suspensions during the panic. It is likely that the combination of the two factors made the crisis more severe. Indeed, Friedman and Schwartz (1963: 109, footnote 28) cite both factors as contributing importantly to an overall drain in the money supply with concerns about the gold standard causing an external drain and concerns about the solvency of Western banks causing an internal drain.

The panic

A few events related to the concerns discussed above shortly preceded the onset of stresses in the banking sector. In mid-April 1893, the gold reserve dipped below the $100 million mark. Rumors circulated that the Treasury would tender silver rather than gold in the redemption of Treasury notes. The Secretary of the Treasury issued a statement that indicated he would continue to redeem notes in gold "as long as he ha[d] gold lawfully available for that purpose" (see Noyes 1909: 186). There was considerable uncertainty around the term "lawfully available" and financial markets reacted adversely to the statement. A subsequent statement by President Grover Cleveland more solidly affirming the commitment to gold appeared to calm markets but did not completely alleviate the uncertainty.

There were also further signs of economic troubles. On May 4, another notable corporation, the National Cordage Company, was put into receivership. Demonstrating the rising concerns, the stock market, already under some pressure following the failure of the Philadelphia and Reading Railroad, dropped sharply (Sprague 1910: 164).

Timing and scope of the banking panic

With financial conditions in May becoming unsettled, especially in eastern financial markets, there were a few bank runs, but they appear to have been isolated incidents. That situation changed considerably in June and bank runs began to be reported in earnest. Wicker (2000) reports that bank runs occurred in a number of western and northwestern cities including Chicago, Omaha, Los Angeles, and Spokane. The geographic dispersion of these communities points to fairly widespread deterioration in the confidence of bank depositors. During the month of June, 126 banks suspended operations. However, this figure understates how many banks were being affected by the panic as not all affected banks were forced to suspend. Wicker (2000) notes that in Chicago a run occurred on every savings bank in the city with long lines of depositors waiting to withdraw; nevertheless, no savings bank was forced to suspend operations although one did have to invoke a thirty-day withdrawal notice.

The impact of deposit withdrawals is evident in the regulatory reports filed by the banks. National banks were required to file reports of the condition of their balance sheets with the Comptroller of the Currency from time to time. In 1893, reports were filed on May 4 and July 12. These reports show that deposits, which accounted for about half of bank liabilities, declined 12 percent in just two months.

After a brief lull in early July, bank runs increased again. The period from mid-July to mid-August marked the height of the banking panic. About 340 banks suspended during July and August. City-wide panics were reported between July 11 and July 31 in Kansas City, Denver, Louisville, Milwaukee, and Portland. Bank suspensions trailed off over the course of August and were quite limited in September.

To get a better sense of the panic it is useful to describe in more detail some of the city panics that took place in July. The panic in Denver started on July 18.[4] The panic started as three savings banks closed. The banking system in Denver had reportedly been under pressure for some time and the savings banks in particular had experienced withdrawals and imposed a 60-day notice period before withdrawals could be made; that waiting period ended on July 17 and the savings banks were unable to meet withdrawals and closed. These closures were reported by the local newspaper as precipitating concerns about the health and liquidity of other banks in the town and triggering the panic in the city.[5] The result was a reported "stampede" by smaller borrowers to withdraw while business men were reported to have stood by with equanimity (*Rocky Mountain Times,* 1893, July 19). The panic struck with substantial force and nine more banks were forced to close within the next two days. While many banks were subject to runs, the targeted banks were reported to have been generally weaker institutions. Some of the stronger banks in the city reportedly had deposit inflows as depositors moved their funds to these banks. The panic ended by July 20; there does not appear to have been any particular event that quelled the panic.

The panic in Louisville appears to have been driven more by out-of-town banks rather than local depositors.[6] The panic started as one National Bank in Louisville closed on July 22 and another one closed on July 23; there were reportedly no visible signs of runs or depositor unrest at either institution. Instead, it appears that the out-of-town banks that used these institutions as correspondents had withdrawn balances with these two banks and forced their closure.[7] Following the closure of yet another bank on July 24, small depositors started to run other banks in the city. Two more suspended shortly thereafter amid withdrawals by depositors and by correspondents. On July 26, the Louisville bank clearing house announced that they would provide assistance to banks that needed support. This indication of support appears to have eased the situation and the panic subsided shortly thereafter.

It is important to note that bank suspensions are not the same as bank failures. Many banks closed their doors temporarily but reopened subsequently (*Bradstreet's* estimated that around 30 percent of the banks that closed were able to reopen). In the city panics described above, six of the eleven banks that closed in Denver reopened, all by the end of August, and four of the five banks that closed in Louisville reopened, all but one of those by the end of August. Moreover, the widespread reopening of banks is a particularly important feature of this panic. That many banks were able to reopen after suspension indicates that solvent banks came under pressure during the panic. In some cases, suspensions may have simply been the result of currency shortages; Friedman and Schwartz (1963: 109, footnote 31) note that some of the suspensions occurred as banks ran out of cash before shipments of money from New York could reach them.[8] In other cases, banks suspended for some time to allow examiners to assess their solvency.

The geographic distribution of bank closures (failures and temporary suspensions) is shown in Table 5.2. The data, and geographical demarcations, are from *Bradstreet's.* The western and northwestern parts of the country were the most severely affected. These areas accounted for close to two-thirds of all bank closures. As noted above, business failure rates also tended to be higher in these states. There were very few bank closures in the northeast or mid-Atlantic parts of the United States. The southern and Pacific regions accounted for a modest portion of closures.

Several kinds of banks operated during this period. Most common were (1) national banks, which were commercial banks with charters from the national regulator—the Comptroller of the Currency, (2) state banks, commercial banks with charters from a state regulator, (3) savings banks, state chartered institutions that took deposits but invested in securities or mortgages rather than making commercial loans, and (4) private banks, institutions operating without a bank charter. During the crisis, the number of closures was fairly evenly spread among national, state, and private banks, with only a modest number of savings bank suspensions. However, national banks, which tended to be larger, accounted for nearly half of the liabilities of closed banks while the typically small private banks accounted for only around one-tenth of such liabilities.

Table 5.2 Location and timing of bank closures in 1893

	New England states	Middle states	Western states	North-western states	Southern states	Pacific states	Territories	Total
May	-	4	32	9	9	1	-	55
June	-	8	33	30	10	44	2	127
July	8	4	109	53	22	21	6	223
August	2	10	27	47	30	2	1	119
September	-	-	1	2	4	1	-	8
October	4	1	5	-	5	-	1	16
Total	14	27	207	141	80	69	10	548

Note: Table based on *Bradstreet's* November 11, 1893: 713–15. Regions follow *Bradstreet's* classification. Bank closures include national banks, state banks, savings banks, trust companies, and private banks.

New England: Connecticut, Maine, Massachusetts, New Hampshire, Rhode Island, and Vermont
Middle states: New York, New Jersey, Pennsylvania, and Delaware.
Western states: Ohio, Indiana, Illinois, Missouri, Michigan, Kansas, Kentucky, and Colorado
Northwestern states: Wisconsin, Minnesota, Iowa, Nebraska, North Dakota, Montana, and Wyoming
Southern states: Maryland, Virginia, West Virginia, North Carolina, South Carolina, Georgia, Florida, Alabama, Mississippi, Louisiana, Texas, Tennessee, and Arkansas
Pacific states: California, Oregon, Nevada, Washington, and Idaho
Territories: Arizona, Indian, New Mexico, Utah, Alaska, and Oklahoma
(South Dakota is not included as *Bradstreet's* was prevented from doing business there.)

Impact on the New York banks

New York City was a focal point of the banking system during this period and deserves some special mention. During the national banking era, national banks—those chartered by the Treasury—were required to hold reserves against outstanding deposits by individuals and other banks and bankers. For banks outside major cities, up to 60 percent of reserves could be held as deposits at banks in larger cities referred to as reserve cities or, in the case of New York, as central reserve cities.[9] (For banks in reserve cities, deposits in central reserve cities counted as reserves.) The remainder of reserves needed to be held as cash. Deposits at banks in New York City had a variety of advantages so banks tended to keep a notable volume of deposits there.[10] Banks chartered by the states faced differing reserve requirements, but also tended to keep deposits with New York banks as part of the payments system. However, if banks needed to satisfy withdrawal demands by depositors, they needed vault cash. Thus, one signal of concern about depositor withdrawals would be for banks to reduce balances held in New York in favor of vault cash.

One advantage of deposits in New York was that they could be used as part of the payment settlement process (see James and Weiman 2010). Payments, such as those by merchants, were often made via the issuance of a draft—a check drawn by one bank against funds deposited in another bank, typically one with which the bank issuing the draft had a correspondent relationship. Drafts circulated in areas where both the party issuing the draft and receiving the draft were likely to have a correspondent in the same city, as it would be easier for those correspondents to clear the payments. As most banks had a correspondent in New York, drafts on New York banks were accepted nationwide and were vital for interregional payments.[11]

In 1893, deposits held in New York banks generally held steady through May, despite unsettled conditions. In June, there was a sharp decline in reserves held in New York banks, presumably as banks became increasingly concerned about depositor withdrawals. As the panic wore on, reserves continued to flow out of New York and pressures in money markets became tremendous. Call loans were loans to brokers used to finance the purchase of stocks and were regarded as a relatively safe and liquid investment; the rate on these loans was generally seen as an indicator of money market conditions. During the panic, the interest rate quoted on call loans reached as high as 72 percent. Prior to the crisis, this rate had been in the neighborhood of 5 percent.

On August 3, banks in New York severely restricted the shipment of currency to the rest of the country. This action had a variety of repercussions. First, due to a reduced ability to obtain cash, many banks throughout the country limited payouts of cash to their customers. Second, amid the inability to convert deposits into money, a currency premium developed.[12] The premium was highest shortly after the curtailment of cash shipments by New York and lasted for about a month. Third, drafts on New York banks were less able to be used as part of the payments system which hindered the ability of many firms to conduct business.

New York Clearinghouse member banks authorized the issuance of clearinghouse certificates in June, when pressures were starting to mount, although actual issuance of certificates at that point was minimal. These certificates could be used by banks that were members of the New York Clearinghouse to settle payments with each other, thereby reducing the amount of cash needed to clear payments among the members and allowed them to operate with lower cash levels. Use of these clearinghouse certificates by New York banks increased sharply around the time that these banks curtailed payments to banks outside New York. Lauck (1907) reports that use of such certificates in New York peaked between the last few days of August and first few days of September.

Impact of bank suspensions and the restrictions of currency shipments

Bank suspensions had a negative impact on trade and commercial enterprise. The *Rocky Mountain Times* reported several negative impacts on the local Denver economy from bank suspensions. Some businesses were "unable to reach their money to pay their bills" (July 19). Other merchants were obliged to reduce their business, "Retail dealers were advised to reduce their business to a cash basis, buying only for immediate want and in limited quantities" (July 20: 2).

Suspensions of currency shipments by New York banks also negatively affected the business environment. *Bradstreet's* reported that, subsequent to the loss of their typical source of currency, banks in some communities were unable to meet local demands. In other communities, sufficient currency was reportedly available, but banks were reluctant to process payments that would result in currency leaving the city. As a consequence, trade suffered:

> Business at Louisville is almost at a standstill, banks declining to receive country checks even for collection, and preferring not to handle New York exchange. General trade is almost on a cash basis at Indianapolis, and reduced in volume, which is also true at Milwaukee.
>
> (*Bradstreet's*, August 12, 1893: 511)

The complete unsettlement of confidence and the derangement of our financial machinery, which made it almost impossible to obtain loans or sell domestic exchange and which put money to a premium over check, had the effect of stopping the wheels of industry and of contracting production and consumption within the narrowest limits, so that our internal trade was reduced to very small proportions—in fact, was brought almost to a standstill—and hundreds of thousands of men thrown out of employment.

(*Commercial and Financial Chronicle*, September 16, 1893: 446)

In the absence of currency, various substitutes for money were reportedly used. Warner (1895) details the variety of items used in place of the currency. The most common currency substitutes were "clearing house certificates" issued by local banks in small denominations intended to circulate as a means of exchange; often there was no official clearinghouse in the community, but the name did indicate that the local community of banks stood behind the notes. In some parts of the country, banks issued certified checks against themselves, again in denominations that allowed them to be used for transactions. In other places, paychecks, teachers' warrants, and scrip circulated as currency. Warner estimates that roughly $80 million in such emergency currency was issued, though not all of it was outstanding at any one point in time. For comparison, Friedman and Schwartz (1963) estimate that currency in the hands of the public in 1893 was $985 million.

End of the crisis

Several factors contributed to the end of the crisis. Noyes (1909) suggests that the panic ended when high interest rates and the premium for specie attracted gold from Europe and boosted domestic liquidity. He reports that gold imports during August amounted to $41 million, which was larger than any previous monthly inflow. These funds reportedly helped fill depleted bank reserves, contributed to satisfying the demand for currency, and reduced the currency premium.

Lauck (1907) argues that the passage of a bill repealing the silver purchase clause of the law of 1890 by the House of Representatives on August 28 was an important turning point. While the Senate did not pass the bill until October 30, the bill passed the House of Representatives with a significant majority. Lauck argues that this gave investors, particularly foreign investors, confidence in the bill's likely passage by the Senate and he notes that pressures in the New York money market diminished shortly after the vote by the House of Representatives.

Bank regulators appear to have played a role in helping to resolve concerns about which banks were solvent and which banks were simply illiquid. After the banks closed, the regulators examined them to determine their solvency. Banks that were solvent were allowed to reopen. In the *Annual Report*, the Comptroller of the Currency reported that:

Many banks after paying out on the one hand all the money in their vaults and failing to collect their loans on the other, suspended and passed into the hands of the Comptroller. With a full knowledge of the general solvency of these institutions and the cause which brought about their suspension, the policy was inaugurated of giving all banks, which, under general circumstances, would not have closed, and whose management had been honest, the opportunity to resume business … In no instance has any bank been permitted to resume on money borrowed.

(Annual Report of 1893: 10)

Providing a regulatory "stamp of approval" regarding bank reopening likely had a positive effect on depositor confidence regarding the health of the banks.

Following the panic

By autumn, the banking panic of 1893 had ended. Bank suspensions had stopped and most banks that would eventually be allowed to reopen had done so. The premium on currency ended in September as New York banks lifted restrictions on shipping currency to banks located in the interior. Interest rates on call loans returned to near pre-crisis levels, which suggested that pressures in New York money markets had substantially dissipated.

Nevertheless, the contraction in business activity that appears to have been underway when the panic started continued for some time. Davis (2004) estimates that industrial production contracted almost as much between 1893 and 1894 as it had between 1892 and 1893; the 15 percent drop in industrial production during this recession was one of the most severe in the nation's history. It was not until 1897 that industrial production reached the levels observed in 1892. Similarly, Balke and Gordon (1986: Appendix B) estimate that real GDP declined about 13 percent. *Historical Statistics of the United States* indicate that business failures, in terms of both number and liabilities, soared in 1893 and remained elevated for the next several years (Carter et al. 2006: series V 24 and series V 27). It is uncertain whether the financial distress associated with the panic contributed toward making the economic downturn especially severe. However, the anecdotal evidence from the period and recent economic research suggest that there is a strong likelihood that it did.

Notes

1 The views presented in this paper are solely those of the author and do not necessarily represent those of the Federal Reserve Board or its staff.
2 The term panic is used to refer to a variety of phenomena. Here, the term banking panic refers to an episode in which a large number of banks in a geographically dispersed area experience fairly sudden, coincident, and large deposit withdrawals that force widespread bank suspensions. Once the deposit withdrawals have stopped and bank suspensions have subsided, the panic is considered to have stopped. Correspondingly, a bank run is a sudden and large-scale withdrawal of deposits from a single institution.
3 The notion that cyclical downturns might trigger panics has some support in economic theory. Depositors, reasoning that banks may fail as the economy deteriorates and loans go bad, have an incentive to get their money out before the bank fails. Supporting this idea, Gorton (1987) finds that consumption-weighted deposit losses predict panics. Calomiris and Gorton (1991) also find that real economic shocks tend to be associated with more bank failures during banking panics.
4 See also Carlson (2005) for a description of the Denver episode.
5 Ironically, rather than suffering concerns about silver purchases undermining the currency, the possibility of repeal of the silver purchase law may have had a negative effect on the perceived solvency of Denver banks given the dependence of the local economy on silver mining.
6 Wicker (2000) describes this episode, as well as events in Kansas City, Denver, Milwaukee, and Portland, in more detail.
7 Banks in smaller towns often had correspondent relationships with banks in larger communities. The larger city banks would hold deposits from other banks and move these deposits between accounts as part of the payment system. This process is described further below.
8 While such suspensions likely occurred during other panics, the data on temporary suspensions in this episode are uniquely available. *Bradstreet's* published information on closing and reopening to date on November 18, 1893. *The Annual Report of the Comptroller of the Currency* for 1893 also reports suspensions and reopening for national banks. These two sources differ slightly; the

differences partly reflect reopenings that occurred between the respective publication dates but also suggest that the data quality may not be perfect.

9 Chicago and St. Louis were also central reserve cities, but were not nearly as prominent as New York. Some researchers, such as Smith (1991), argue that this pyramidal system made the system less stable and provided a mechanism for shocks in one part of the country to be transmitted to New York, which could then transmit them back to all parts of the country.

10 Sprague (1910) reports that interbank deposits constituted the bulk of the liabilities for several large New York banks.

11 For example, the bank would provide the merchant a draft indicating that the bearer of the draft could lay claim to some amount of the issuing bank's deposits in a reference bank in New York. The merchant could give that draft to a goods supplier. The goods supplier would give the draft to his bank and have his account credited and that bank would contact its correspondent in New York to have the funds from the account of the bank that had issued the draft transferred to the account of the bank that had received the draft from the goods supplier.

12 For instance, Noyes (1909) describes money-brokers willing to pay with a certified check a premium for currency (so that the certified check was being sold at a discount to its face value).

References

Balke, N. and Gordon, R. (1986) *The American Business Cycle: Continuity and Change,* Chicago, IL: University of Chicago Press.

Bradstreet's (1893) New York, various issues.

Calomiris, C. and Gorton, G. (1991) 'The origins of banking panics: models, facts, and bank regulation', in G. Hubbard (ed.), *Financial Markets and Financial Crises*, Chicago, IL: University of Chicago Press.

Carlson, M. (2005) 'Causes of bank suspensions in the panic of 1893', *Explorations in Economic History*, 42: 56–80.

Carter, S.B., Gartner, S.S., Haines, M.R., Olmstead, A.L., Sutch, R. and Wright, G. (eds.) (2006) *Historical Statistics of the United States, Earliest Times to the Present: Millennial Edition*, New York: Cambridge University Press.

Davis, J. (2004) 'An annual index of U.S. industrial production, 1790–1915', *Quarterly Journal of Economics*, 119: 1177–215.

Friedman, M. and Schwartz, A.J. (1963) *A Monetary History of the United States, 1867–1960,* Princeton, NJ: Princeton University Press.

Gorton, G. (1987) 'Bank suspension of convertibility', *Journal of Monetary Economics,* 15: 177–93.

James, J. and Weiman, D.F. (2010) 'From drafts to checks: the evolution of correspondent banking networks and the formation of the modern U.S. payments system, 1850–1914', *Journal of Money, Credit, and Banking*, 42: 237–65.

Lauck, W.J. (1907) *The Causes of the Panic of 1893*, New York: Houghton, Mifflin and Company.

Markham, J. (2002) *A Financial History of the United States,* vol. 1, Armonk, NY: M.E. Sharpe.

Noyes, A. (1909) *Forty Years of American Finance*, New York: G.P. Putnam's Sons.

Office of the Comptroller of the Currency (1893) Annual Report Volume 1, Washington, DC: Government Printing Office.

Rocky Mountain Times (1893) Denver, Colorado, May–August.

Smith, B. (1991) 'Bank panics, suspensions, and geography: some notes on the contagion of fear in banking', *Economic Inquiry,* 29: 230–48.

Sprague, O.M.W. (1910) *History of Crises under the National Banking System*, Washington, DC: United States Government Printing Office.

Warner, J.D. (1895) 'The currency famine of 1893', *Sound Currency*, 2: 337–56.

Wicker, E. (2000) *Banking Panics of the Gilded Age*, Cambridge: Cambridge University Press.

6

THE PANIC OF 1907

Ellis W. Tallman

The Banking Panic of 1907 was the final banking panic that took place during the National Banking Era (1863–1913); the most severe of these panics occurred in 1873, 1893 and 1907, whereas the episodes of financial distress in 1884 and 1890 were considered minor in comparison. A central difference between the Panic of 1907 and all the earlier panics of the National Banking Era was the type of financial intermediaries that were struck with panic-related withdrawals. During the prior panics, national banks were more notably affected by widespread withdrawal of deposits. In 1907, widespread withdrawals centered on New York City trust companies, which were state-chartered intermediaries. The aggregate assets of the trust companies were small during prior panics, but had grown rapidly in the decade prior to 1907. By that time, trust companies were second only to national banks in aggregate assets and aggregate net deposits among depository institutions within the New York City financial market.

The central role of trust companies in the panic was well recognized by contemporaries of the event as well as by present day scholars, although recent work draws stronger conclusions about how problems with the trust companies affected subsequent reforms. With specific reference to monetary reform, the Panic of 1907 holds historical distinction as the proximate catalyst for the successful political movement toward the establishment of a central bank in the form of the Federal Reserve System, which has contributed to a surge in interest surrounding the Panic of 1907.

This chapter highlights the key distinguishing factors of the financial crisis, examines its influence on subsequent financial and monetary regulation, and places the Panic of 1907 in historical context relative to the size of the associated business cycle. In addition, the chapter describes how the Panic of 1907 bears some resemblance to the Financial Crisis of 2007–2009 in the United States. Among the similarities, both crises arose among New York City financial intermediaries that were perceived as indirectly connected to the payments system – trust companies in the case of 1907 and investment banks in 2007–2009. Further, these intermediaries lacked direct access to the relevant sources of liquidity – the New York Clearing House in 1907 and the Federal Reserve System in 2007–2009.

Characteristics of nineteenth-century financial crises and banking panics

Economists contemporary to the panics, most notably Sprague (1910), Kemmerer (1910), and Laughlin (1912), attributed financial crises and banking panics to the rigid structure of the National Banking System. The modern reader may find that perspective reasonable because the structure of that monetary system seems awkward and limited. The system lacked a central banking institution that could quickly adjust the stock of high-powered money (legal tender and specie) by the sale or purchase of marketable short-term assets, that is, the system lacked a reliable institution to manage aggregate liquidity provision. The independent Treasury system tried to perform such a role when its fiscal position allowed such actions and when the Treasury Secretary was so inclined, but was not capable of performing the role consistently. As a result, the aggregate supply of liquidity was subject to shocks that were external (and largely exogenous) to the domestic monetary system.

Separately, the existing financial system had no explicit lender of last resort to whom a bank could turn for emergency loans if it was suffering widespread withdrawal of its deposits. In the role of lender or liquidity provider, the New York Clearing House (as well as the clearing houses in other important banking cities) attempted to perform the role, but again, the institution(s) lacked crucial powers to ensure success. To address liquidity demands of individual banks during crisis episodes, the clearing houses employed clearing house loan certificates as a way to increase the credit available to individual member banks during a panic. A clearing house loan certificate was a temporary debt contract (a transaction liability) that was exchangeable at par value between clearing house members and was transferable between clearing house members. The clearing house loan certificate served as an adequate substitute for legal tender and specie for the termination of a payments transaction so that clearing house loan certificates settled debit balances between member banks at the New York Clearing House. However, these certificates could not pass to intermediaries beyond clearing house members or to the general public, so they were an imperfect substitute for an increase in legal tender or specie. Still, clearing house loan certificates provided temporary credit during credit crises so membership in a clearing house was an important characteristic of any bank that was subject to rapid changes in depositor liquidity demands.

The large, national banks in New York City were the largest correspondent banks in the country, and were the most influential members of the New York Clearing House Association. These banks (referred to as the "Big Six" by Sprague 1910) were: National City, National Park, National Bank of Commerce, First National, Hanover, and Chase National. All national banks in New York City were members of the clearing house, as were many of the state banks. The member banks were associated with the clearing house because their business included a large volume of bank check clearing.

Trust companies were notably absent from the membership of the New York Clearing House. As state-chartered institutions, trust company charters were vague and allowed trusts to engage in activities that were prohibited to a number of other intermediaries. For example, trusts were able to invest in real estate and in stock equity investments directly, which were two activities specifically prohibited for national banks. Trusts competed effectively for retail deposits with national banks in New York City. Yet trusts were not considered part of the high-volume check-clearing part of the payments system, because deposits at trust companies did not turn over at rates similar to national banks. As a result, trust companies did not seek membership in the New York Clearing House when membership was offered in 1903. Trust companies eschewed membership largely because the costs of membership (primarily the 10 percent cash reserve requirement [as a share of deposits]) were perceived to be too high relative to the benefits of more efficient check clearing. Note that the cash reserve requirement requested by the New York Clearing House was less than half what was required of member national banks.

In contrast to all previous National Banking Era panics, the U.S. was officially on the gold standard during the Panic of 1907.[1] The gold standard put constraints on the financial interventions of the U.S. Treasury to affect the stock of high-powered money, credit availability, or financial conditions more generally. Specifically, the U.S. Treasury was limited by its gold reserve balances and its surplus balances. During the Panic of 1907, the U.S. Treasury added over $40 million to the stock of high-powered money, but its ability to respond was effectively exhausted by October 25, 1907, limited by the available budget surplus.

Regulatory reserve requirements of the system – lower among country banks and higher in more populous areas – encouraged a pyramid structure of reserve holdings among the national banks. Banks lower down on the pyramid could claim as reserves their deposits in reserve city banks and central reserve city banks further up on the pyramid. For example, an interior, country bank would hold deposits in a New York City national bank and those deposits would count toward the reserve requirement of the interior bank.

The correspondent banking structure contributed toward a concentration of funds in New York City in the large, clearing house member national banks. The funds arising from interior banker balances in New York City national banks were largely used to finance call money loans on the New York Stock Exchange. Call loans on stock market equity provided the "buffer" liquidity for the New York City national banks. During normal financial markets, the correspondent national banks could accommodate idiosyncratic fluctuations in banker balances and liquidity demands by liquidating (or extending) call loans because there were typically lenders (or liquidators) who would take the opposite transaction. The call market failed miserably, however, during financial crises when banks in aggregate demanded repayment of call loans. During crises, stock equity values were typically falling precipitously, thereby making the liquidation of call loan collateral both unprofitable and of uncertain value. Also, the signaling value of collateral as a "commitment to repay" declined along with the nominal value.

During the National Banking Era, the "usual suspect" as the cause of a financial panic was the banking system's lack of a reliable mechanism to expand quickly the base money supply in response to increased (seasonal) demand for cash or credit by interior banks. The proximate trigger of a banking panic was often the failure of a major financial intermediary, and the first sign of widespread financial crisis was a steep upward spike in the call loan interest rate and sharp declines in stock equity values. All these characteristics were present in 1907 and they were interrelated. For example, as stock equity values fell, banks and trust companies extended less credit to the stock market while demand for credit may not have contracted, so call money interest rates increased to exorbitant rates.

Goodhart (1969) describes how the structure of the U.S. banking system led to a fragile balance of payments between interior firms, interior banks, New York City banks, and foreign purchasers of U.S. goods. The equilibrium could be altered notably by shocks within the links of the arrangement. In related research, Miron (1986) investigates the period using this conventional description of the financial flows in which the cash demands of the interior banks drain cash balances held in New York City banks in order to finance shipments of grain during harvest season. The typical cash drain would lead to a seasonal rise in the interest rates in New York City during fall, which attracted some of the cash that flowed to the interior

Table 6.1 Time line of major events during the panic of 1907

Wednesday, Oct 16	Failure of the Heinze attempt to corner stock in United Copper sparks concerns. Bank runs begin on banks associated with Heinze forces.
Friday, Oct 18	New York Clearing House agrees to support Mercantile National Bank, the bank that Heinze controlled directly, upon resignation of its Board (including Heinze). Run on Knickerbocker Trust begins, apparently the result of rumored association of Charles Barney, President of Knickerbocker Trust, with Charles Morse.
Saturday, Oct 19	Morse (Heinze's associate) banks are struck with runs, and requests aid from the New York Clearing House Association. Newspapers infer an equivocal response on the part of the New York Clearing House.
Sunday, Oct 20	New York Clearing House agrees to support Heinze-Morse banks but requires that Heinze and Morse relinquish all banking interests in New York City.
Monday, Oct 21	Run on Knickerbocker Trust accelerates. Request by National Bank of Commerce for aid from the New York Clearing House on behalf of Knickerbocker Trust was denied. J.P. Morgan denies aid to Knickerbocker Trust as well.
Tuesday, Oct 22	Run on Knickerbocker Trust forces its closure with cash withdrawals of $8 million in one day. Run spreads to Trust Company of America, Lincoln Trust, and other trust companies in New York City.
Wednesday, Oct 23	J.P. Morgan agrees to aid Trust Company of America and coordinates the provision of cash from New York Clearing House member banks to trust companies.
Thursday, Oct 24	U.S. Treasury deposits $25 million in New York Clearing House member national banks. J.P. Morgan organizes provision of cash (money pools) to the New York Stock Exchange to maintain the provision of call money loans on the stock market floor.
Saturday, Oct 26	New York Clearing House Committee meets and agrees to establish a Clearing House Loan Committee to issue certificates. Also the Committee agrees to impose restrictions payment of cash.
Monday, Nov 4	Trust companies provide $25 million to support other trust companies that endured large-scale depositor withdrawals.

back toward New York City. In a panic, those flows toward New York City do not occur and in fact the flows were clearly reversed.

The Panic of 1907 followed closely a failed attempt to corner a copper stock (see Table 6.1). O.M.W. Sprague (1910) claims that the financial market could normally withstand such a financial market shock without much issue. Other unfavorable conditions in the fall of 1907 made the U.S. financial market vulnerable to financial stresses in addition to the perceived flaws in the U.S. banking structure in the National Banking Era described above.

Among the unfortunate circumstances in 1907, the Bank of England imposed unwritten but effective barriers to the free flow of capital to the United States by restricting the issuance of American finance bills issued in London. These bills were typically issued in anticipation of the arrival of U.S. agricultural shipments, and their issuance would thereby smooth gold flows (see Goodhart 1969: 112–17). The restrictions on American finance bills were in

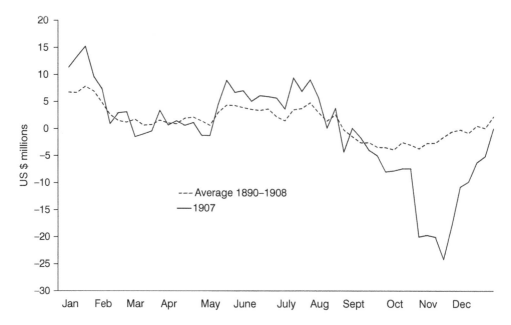

Figure 6.1 Seasonal net cash flows to New York City banks

response to gold outflows from England to the U.S. in 1906 in part prompted by Treasury Secretary Leslie Shaw's actions to subsidize gold imports to the U.S. from abroad. The subsequent gold outflows from England exacerbated an already significant gold drain from England to the U.S. as a result of insurance payments to San Francisco policy holders by Lloyds of London (see Odell and Weidenmier 2004). The 1906 drain of gold from England nearly caused a panic in London.

During the Panic of 1907, net cash flows to New York City and interest rates in New York City deviated substantially from the seasonal patterns of net cash flows and interest rates observed over the period 1890–1908. In Figure 6.1, the substantial net flow of cash out of New York City in October and November in 1907 plummeted sharply away from the seasonal average. Figure 6.2 shows how the call money interest rate in New York City spiked upward during several weeks in October and November of 1907. In comparison to the seasonal averages, the precipitous decline in cash inflows to New York City banks – indicating a large and unusual cash outflow – accords with the sharp upward spike in the call money interest rate; both series clearly display aberrant yet mutually consistent deviations from the seasonal norms.

Banking crises can exacerbate an economic contraction. Banking (or financial) panic is defined here as the widespread withdrawal of deposits from intermediaries (a run on deposits) observed along with an increase in perceived risk across a broad array of assets. But it is unlike a bank run that focuses on specific institutions. In a bank run, a depositor may redeposit his or her funds in another bank that is perceived to be stable and solvent. In contrast, a run on deposits is a withdrawal of deposits from the banking system marked by a sudden shift in the components of the money supply. In a banking panic, the public holds a larger proportion of the money supply in cash instead of in the form of intermediated deposits. In a fractional reserve banking system such as the national banking system, runs on deposits force contractions in bank balance sheets, which may involve contracting the

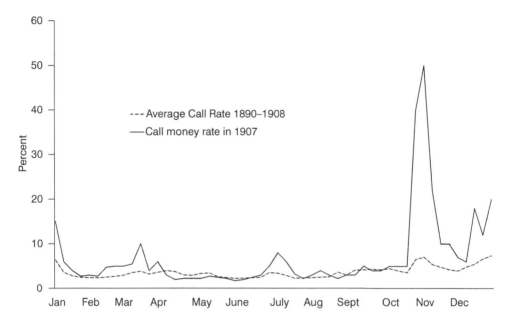

Figure 6.2 Seasonal average call money interest rate versus the path in 1907

volume of loans outstanding. Reductions in credit outstanding can impose real costs on the economy by forcing the premature termination of profitable, positive net present value loans. During financial panics, banks would try to preserve the credit extension (e.g., loans) when the loans were viable but illiquid (that is, hard to sell without taking a large percentage capital loss). The New York Clearing House used several methods to combat the panic that were direct attempts to prevent a contraction in credit. Hoarding cash – removing cash from the banking system – forced a contraction in the money supply. However, the closure of banks and trust companies during the National Banking Era financial panics also led to a (temporary in some cases) contraction in the money supply because the deposits of failed banks are unavailable to depositors. There were fewer than 75 bank suspensions as a result of the Panic of 1907, and there were 13 suspensions among New York City intermediaries (Wicker 2000: 4–5). In contrast, there were over 500 bank failures in 1893 and only three among New York City financial institutions.

The New York City nexus of the Panic of 1907 is notable particularly because nationwide problems – like, for example, the imposition of partial restrictions on cash withdrawals from banks – arose from the initial depositor withdrawals from New York City trust companies; four of the thirteen institutions that failed in New York City were trust companies. The failure of just one trust company – the Knickerbocker Trust – reduced New York City deposits by over two percent ($48.8 million in deposits over $2,116.5 million in the aggregate of national, state and trust company deposits in New York City, August 22, 1907). More importantly, the failure of Knickerbocker signaled that trust companies – intermediaries that accounted for nearly one-third of deposits in New York City – were at risk in ways distinct from other New York City intermediaries – that they appeared isolated from the New York Clearing House and its liquidity resources. And yet, the other New York City banks were subject to ramifications of the trust companies' problems. The perceived increase in the risk of the New York City financial market led interior banks to withdraw deposits from their correspondent New York City national banks in unusually large amounts (see Sprague (1910: 264) and Figure 6.1).

The increase in perceived risk across assets would be reflected in sharp declines in stock market values, increases in interest rates and related declines in long-term bond values, and, as already noted, a sharp increase in holding cash relative to risk-bearing liabilities (intermediated deposits).

The proximate cause of the 1907 banking crisis

Table 6.1 provides a summary time line for the events of the Panic of 1907. Trouble at the Heinze-Morse-Thomas banks was not a key factor in the panic, although the financial disarray of a failed corner attempt and related bank runs provided an essential catalyst for several subsequent events. Of the banks associated with these individuals, several were members of the New York Clearing House (Mercantile National, National Bank of North America, Mechanics and Traders, Fourteenth Street Bank, and New Amsterdam National). The Heinze-Morse-Thomas banks experienced bank runs, but there were no notable or widespread disruptions to banking activities in New York City during the days immediately following the corner failure. The lack of widespread panic-related activity was not surprising because of the relationship of these banks to the New York Clearing House. The aggregate of the Heinze-Morse-Thomas banking interests totaled $71 million in deposits, of which $56 million were deposits in the five clearing house member banks, and the New York Clearing House had existing policies aimed to rectify situations that threatened local banking conditions.

To prevent the bank runs from spreading, the New York Clearing House provided loans to those member institutions but also, as a condition of the aid, forced Heinze and Morse to resign from their banking interests and replaced the management of those banks. The New York Clearing House settled the financial situation by cooperation among its member institutions and shrewd decision making by its executive committee. Those decisions required accurate and timely information about the financial condition of its struggling member institutions, and clearing house representatives made detailed examinations at those institutions prior to the executive decisions to aid the member banks.

Until the completion of the examinations, there was still uncertainty about the outcome for the Mercantile National. The New York Clearing House initially made equivocal public statements regarding Mercantile National. For example, a clearing house representative expressed publicly that the clearing house would not pay off the depositors of the Mercantile National Bank, and that the aid that was offered by the New York Clearing House was temporary. The equivocation, noted in Bruner and Carr (2007: 61), is rarely acknowledged in academic treatments of the panic because on the following day, October 21, 1907, the New York Clearing House made a public statement announcing that the member banks had been examined in detail and that the New York Clearing House Association deemed them to be solvent.

Trusts and the Panic

The run on Knickerbocker Trust had reportedly begun as early as Friday, October 18, and the National Bank of Commerce had been extending credit to Knickerbocker Trust to cover those withdrawals. Wicker (2000: 90) describes how the vice president of the National Bank of Commerce along with the third vice president of Knickerbocker Trust asked the

New York Clearing House for a loan to Knickerbocker. The loan request was denied and justified effectively because the New York Clearing House was preserving its resources for its members.[2]

The run on Knickerbocker Trust took a spectacular turn for the worse when on October 21, 1907, the National Bank of Commerce announced that it would no longer be the clearing agent for the Knickerbocker Trust. The debit balance of the National Bank of Commerce at the New York Clearing House on October 22, 1907, was $7 million, and was largely assumed to reflect its dealings for Knickerbocker (*New York Tribune*, October 23, 1907: 1) because, as clearing agent, National Bank of Commerce held large correspondent balances for Knickerbocker. Legal considerations arising from the clearing agent relationship had financial ramifications for the National Bank of Commerce that provided a compelling incentive to limit its exposure to Knickerbocker's possible suspension. As the clearing agent for Knickerbocker, the National Bank of Commerce would have no priority as a claimant to Knickerbocker Trust assets if the trust suspended, and its assets went into receivership.[3] As Knickerbocker's clearing agent, the National Bank of Commerce would have to wait in line for its payment as an ordinary depositor. Analogously, Mercantile National Bank was clearing for Hamilton Bank, which was on the verge of failure. In that case, the New York Clearing House ordered the Mercantile National Bank to stop clearing for Hamilton Bank, a bank related to E.R. Thomas, to avoid potential losses from the possible suspension of Hamilton Bank. The Hamilton Bank failed on October 24, 1907.

On October 22, 1907, the Knickerbocker Trust Company was forced to suspend, and after that point, many other New York City trust companies were struck with widespread withdrawal of deposits. The runs at the Trust Company of America and the Lincoln Trust have gained the highest profile, however data on trust company balance sheets in 1907 show that the contraction in deposits was widespread across institutions.

Widespread depositor withdrawals from the Knickerbocker Trust forced its closure, yet there is no unambiguous evidence to conclude that it was either insolvent or that it was involved in the Heinze-Morse-Thomas scheme. Reasonable explanations for the run emphasize that the President of Knickerbocker Trust, Charles T. Barney, was associated with Charles Morse, a member of the Heinze group. Barney was on the Board of Directors of the National Bank of North America and the Mercantile National Bank (see Bruner and Carr 2007). His direct involvement in the Heinze-Morse stock corner activities has not been proven. The *New York Sun* (October 23, 1907: 2) reported that Knickerbocker Trust had extensive investments in real estate, although no further evidence uncovered so far can verify that claim.

Depositor withdrawals from Mercantile National Bank were unlike withdrawals from the Knickerbocker Trust Company because these intermediaries had clearly different relationships to the New York Clearing House. The New York Clearing House was effectively the lender of last resort in the New York City financial market. The Mercantile National Bank was a member of the New York Clearing House, and the Knickerbocker Trust Company was not a member. At the beginning of the crisis, the membership issue was front and center.

Newspaper reports were specific about how the New York Clearing House was aiding its members, and claimed that aid to members was for the sake of the general financial market. Clearing house representatives stated that the solution to the trust company runs would require the cooperation of trust companies to come up with their own solution to their problems.

Tallman and Moen (1990), Bruner and Carr (2007), Strouse (1999) and Wicker (2000) discuss the actions of J.P. Morgan and the New York Clearing House on October 24, 1907, to keep the stock market open and call loan funding available. Indirect evidence and secondary reports suggest that the national banks increased their loans on the call loan market to take over trust company loans and prevent the widespread liquidation of call loans. The national banks, however, were constrained by a reserve requirement on deposits that was higher than the reserve requirement for trusts. In addition, the large, correspondent banks in the New York Clearing House were also facing large-scale liquidation demands from their interior correspondents. However, the formation of "money pools" to address specific incidents like the shortage of credit for call loans on the stock market was inefficient and clumsy. Wicker (2000) argues that issuing clearing house loan certificates during a crisis was standard practice and would have provided the liquidity necessary for such instances. Sprague (1910: 257) argues that the delay in the issuance of clearing house loan certificates was the most serious error by the New York Clearing House during the Panic of 1907.

The large, New York City national banks were likely most sensitive to the widespread liquidation of call loans by trust companies. These banks held the largest proportion of correspondent bank balances, and invested those funds in the short-term call loan market on the New York Stock Exchange.

Figure 6.3 displays the daily (maximum) call loan interest rate for October 1, 1907, through February 19, 1908. The first sharp increase in this rate follows the failure of Knickerbocker Trust Company on October 22, 1907. The prevailing call rate for the next week hovered around 50 percent, although the effective rate likely would have been higher, because often there were no trades taking place even at these high interest rates.

On October 26, 1907, the New York Clearing House membership agreed to restrict the convertibility of deposits into cash and to permit the issuance of clearing house loan certificates to improve the liquidity of the New York financial market.

Clearing house loan certificates were an expedient method to economize on legal tender and specie as a mechanism for payment finality. It was a liability that had limited transferability – that is, it was transferrable to other clearing house members only. The economics of clearing house loan certificates is somewhat complex; the certificates were requested by banks, issued by the New York Clearing House, and effectively guaranteed by the entire membership of the clearing house association. Further, acceptance of clearing house loan certificates as final payment was a requirement of all members of the clearing house. Interest on the clearing house loan certificate was paid to holders of the clearing house loan certificate. In this case, the clearing house played the role of intermediary – the collateral was held by the clearing house and the clearing house administered the payment of interest. Borrowers could request additional issues of clearing house loan certificates and the New York Clearing House could require additional collateral or the replacement of collateral. Repayment was typically rapid because of the high interest rate (six percent) associated with their issue.

Clearing house loan certificate issues allowed the New York Clearing House banks to deliver cash to their interior depositors as well as continue to issue loans during the panic despite being short of cash reserves. In this instance, the main borrowers were: 1) Heinze banks and other banks subject to runs, and 2) large, correspondent banks. Tallman and Moen (2012) show that banker balances and clearing house loan certificate requests were highly correlated. Figure 6.4 displays the level of banker balances and the level of clearing house loan certificates among New York Clearing House banks. The larger a bank's role in the correspondent banking system, the larger the likely request for clearing house loan certificates from the New York Clearing House, and both of these characteristics were correlated with bank size.

The actions of national banks in the New York Clearing House have spurred investigation. Work by Donaldson (1993) examines the strategic incentives of New York Clearing House

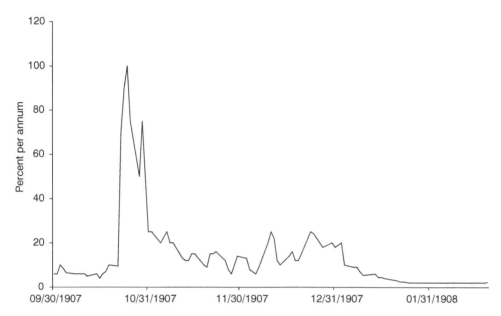

Figure 6.3 Daily maximum call loan interest rate

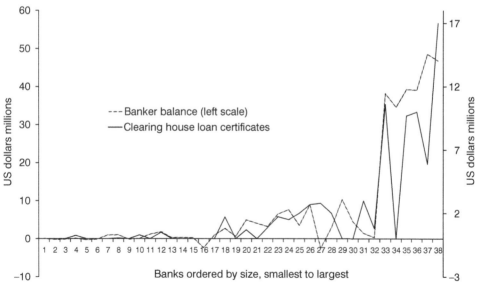

Figure 6.4 Bankers' balances versus clearing house loan certificates: New York Clearing House member banks

member banks to exploit their power over the stock of high-powered money during the panic. The transactions taken during the panic resulted in a reallocation of credit and deposits away from trust companies and toward national banks, clearly altering the trend within the financial industry, which had previously encouraged the growth of less heavily regulated intermediaries like trusts.

Trusts, the call loan market, and clearing house certificates

The run on trust companies in New York City provided a catalyst for transmitting the panic throughout the financial system. The interconnections between trust companies and banks – through banker balances, the call loan market, and through the railroad bond market – made the panic at trusts a financial crisis that still threatened commercial banks and the payments system. Even though trust companies were not part of the New York Clearing House, there was no "firewall" that allowed national banks to ignore the problems at trust companies. This characteristic of the Panic of 1907 highlighted the structural deficiencies of the "dual banking system" in the United States and the inability to insulate the payment system from capital and financial market shocks.

Table 6.2 displays the deposits of New York City trust companies, state banks and national banks on four separate call dates. The level of national bank deposits was clearly larger than deposit balances at trust companies alone, but was about the same as the combined deposit accounts of state banks and trusts. The level of deposits at New York City trust companies contracted by over 36 percent from August 22, 1907 to December 19, 1907, and totaled a contraction of over $200 million in deposits. In contrast, the deposits of New York City national banks rose by nearly $70 million, an increase of over six percent according to the call report data for December 3, 1907. State bank deposits also contracted by over ten percent, but that accounted for a decline of less than $40 million in deposits. The data highlight the substantial contraction in deposits that took place among trust companies during the Panic of 1907. Evidence from the final call date, November 27, 1908, shows that national bank deposits grew rapidly relative to their level in August 1907 (nearly 50 percent), whereas the deposits of trust companies were only five percent above the level in August 1907. The trust companies never fully recovered from the contraction in deposits arising from the panic (see Moen and Tallman 1992). Hansen (2011) shows further that "uptown" trust companies – those that competed with national banks for retail depositors – lost a relatively larger share of the deposit market to national banks.

New York City trust companies sparked the Panic of 1907 as runs on their deposits forced liquidation of assets and depletion of cash (and cash-like) reserves. In that first line of cash reserves, trusts held about $100 million in deposits in approved reserve depositories, mainly New York City national banks. From August 22 to December 19, 1907, trust companies

Table 6.2 Deposits in New York City intermediaries

Call Report Date	National	State	Trusts	Sum of State and Trusts	Aggregate Deposits
Thursday, August 22, 1907	1051.74	371.99	692.74	1064.74	2116.47
Tuesday, December 3, 1907	1120.62				
	6.55★				
Thursday, December 19, 1907		333.46	437.73	771.19	1891.81
		–10.36★	–36.81★	–27.57★	–10.61★
Friday, November 27, 1908	1546.37	437.25	724.03	1161.28	2707.65
	47.03★	17.54★	4.52★	9.07★	27.93★

★ denotes percentage change from August 22, 1907 level

Source: Annual Reports of the Comptroller of the Currency, Reports of the Superintendent of Banks of New York States, and Hagen (1932)

reduced their deposits at banks by over $30 million (Hagen 1932). In addition, trusts reportedly took actions in key markets that triggered financial distress in the call money market and in the stock and bond markets. Cleveland and Huertas (1985) suggest that trusts began calling-in large numbers of loans on October 24, 1907. Further, it is notable that New York Clearing House banks engaged in restrictions of the convertibility of deposits into cash, and yet trust companies did not restrict their payment to depositors throughout the panic. That said, repayments to depositors were through certified checks expressly "payable through the clearing house" (Sprague 1910: 258).

The liquidation of assets at trust companies during the Panic of 1907 took various forms. Deposit accounts at national banks were the first cash line after vault cash, and the sale of high-quality railroad bonds (which legally could be counted as reserves for trust companies in New York) likely took on an important role of raising cash. Evidence in Tallman and Moen (2011) and Rodgers and Wilson (2010) suggests that the liquidation of railroad bonds during the panic was unusual. Rodgers and Wilson (2010) argue that the unexplained gold inflows may have reflected an unusual increase in the purchases of U.S. financial assets (specifically, railroad bonds) by foreign investors engaged in arbitrage because the railroad bonds sold both on the New York and London exchanges. The panic apparently artificially lowered prices in New York.

How 1907 differed from 1873 and 1893

Although the panic withdrawals focused on trust companies, national banks in New York City still bore a significant burden of panic-related withdrawals by their correspondent banks. The New York Clearing House banks faced these demands as well in 1873 and 1893, but there were observable differences in the time-series behavior of the New York Clearing House aggregate bank balance sheets across these three panics. Figure 6.5 displays the loans, deposits and cash reserves of the New York Clearing House banks in 1873, 1893, and 1907. In the prior panics, loans, deposits and reserves fell during the related panic, whereas only in 1907 did the aggregate cash reserve balance among the New York Clearing House member banks fall while deposits remained fairly flat and loans increased.

In 1907, national banks in New York City were largely able to avoid widespread depositor withdrawals. Also, the New York Clearing House banks suspended convertibility of deposits into cash early in the crisis (the Knickerbocker Trust closed on October 22, 1907, and the New York Clearing House declared suspension of convertibility on October 26, 1907). Yet, it also indicates that there were transactions in which trust depositors moved to national banks, and trust loans were acquired by national banks. The analysis of national banking data alone will not indicate panic conditions in 1907 (see Smith 1984). Therefore it has been important to emphasize the inclusion of New York City trust company aggregates in any assessment of the financial ramifications of the 1907 banking crisis (see Moen and Tallman 1992).

The central banking movement

The Panic of 1907 struck mainly the trust companies and demonstrated that the New York Clearing House faced risks that arose from beyond their membership. Essentially, given the state of financial intermediation, the New York Clearing House banks could not control as well as in the previous panics the risks that they faced. Moen and Tallman (2007) argue that the growth of trusts and the risks indicated by the Panic of 1907 influenced the next generation of New York City bankers to support a central bank.

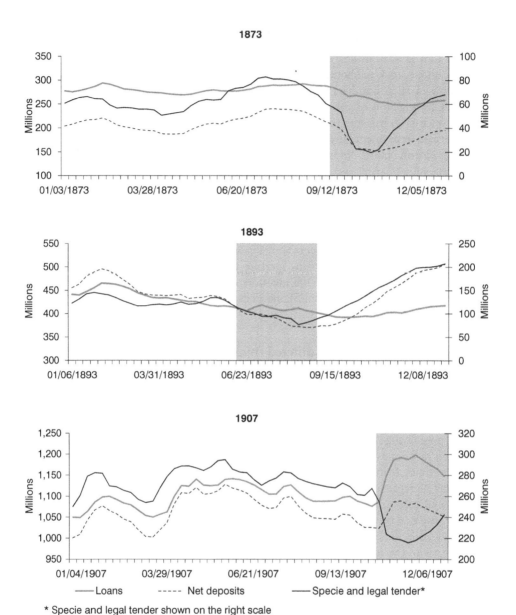

Figure 6.5 Loans, deposits, and cash reserves of New York Clearing House banks

Wicker (2005) credits Nelson Aldrich for the creation of a central bank in the United States, and suggests that the lack of financial crises in Europe influenced Aldrich to investigate a European model of a central bank as the basis for the central bank ideal for the United States. Broz (1997) suggests that New York bankers were interested in establishing a central banking institution in order to become competitive in the international markets. All the arguments listed above are feasible, and none of the arguments is exclusive of the others.

With the perspective of nearly 100 years of economic history, the Panic of 1907 provides no compelling evidence for the need to create a central bank in order to prevent financial panics. Friedman and Schwartz (1963) made what was a controversial suggestion that the Emergency Currency provisions of the Aldrich–Vreeland Act of 1908 (given the later amendment that such emergency currency would satisfy reserve requirements) was apparently successful in preventing a financial panic in 1914. Wicker (2000) proposes that the New York Clearing House and the large, correspondent national bank members had sufficient power to quell financial panics and that the observation of financial panics was an institutional failure. Further, given that runs on trust companies in New York City sparked the panic, requiring membership of trust companies in the New York Clearing House, may have been sufficient to remove trusts from among the potential sources of panics. Moen and Tallman (2000) suggest that trust company membership in the Chicago Clearing House kept those institutions relatively stable through the panic in contrast to New York City trust companies which were outside the New York Clearing House.

Measures of the associated real economic contraction

The real economic contraction associated with the financial panic in 1907 was among the deepest and sharpest contractions in the post-bellum U.S. experience. Figure 6.6 illustrates the annual percent change in the industrial production index compiled by Joseph Davis (2004) over the period 1863 to 1915. The contraction associated with the 1907 crisis is measured as a nearly 17 percent decline from 1907 to 1908. The two-year contraction in 1893 and 1894 of 9 percent and 7.5 percent, respectively, is roughly comparable as a panic-related output contraction, consistent with the widely held perception that the 1893 and 1907 financial crises were associated with the most severe real output contractions during the National Banking Era.

Balke and Gordon (1986) provide quarterly estimates of real GNP that extend back to 1875 covering a large subset of the National Banking Era, which allows a comparison of the time series profile of 1893 and 1907. Figure 6.7 compares the time series path of real GNP during the contraction relative to the relevant business cycle peak level of real GNP for

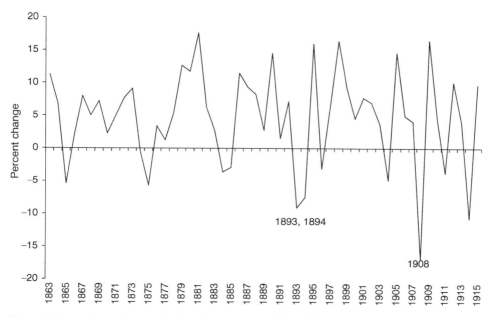

Figure 6.6 Annual growth rate of industrial production, 1863–1915

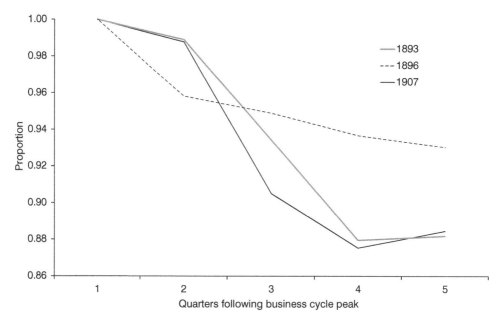

Figure 6.7 Real GNP during contractions taken relative to prior peak

three separate contractions during the period. In the figure, all the lines start at 1.0 and fall thereafter. For both 1893 and 1907, the measures contract by about 12 percent. The 1907 panic is associated with an economic downturn that is slightly steeper, but effectively both lines display a contraction of about the same magnitude. For comparison, the contraction of 1896 – associated with the fear that the U.S. would abandon the gold standard – displays a contraction of about seven percent, a substantial but more moderate contraction, and a contraction not associated with a banking crisis. These facts are consistent with observations made in Reinhart and Rogoff (2009) and empirical evidence produced by Bordo and Haubrich (2010) and Jalil (2012) that real economic contractions associated with banking and financial crises are more severe than otherwise.

Recent work by Jordà, Schularick, and Taylor (2011) indicates that 1907 was one of four pre-World War II "worldwide" financial crises, along with 1890, 1921, and 1930–31. Thus, the benefit of hindsight (along with more data and more powerful econometric tools) has increased the perceived severity of the financial and real economic contraction in 1907. Also, it is well-recognized that the panic arose from problems in the United States' financial system and economy (see Goodhart 1969 and Rich 1988).

Conclusion

The Panic of 1907 was an important financial and economic event in the evolution of the financial structure of the United States and as a signal of its growing worldwide economic influence. The economic contraction associated with the panic was severe and sharp, and comparable to the severe recession of 1893. The repercussions of the panic contributed momentum toward a successful political effort to establish a central banking institution (the Federal Reserve System) as well as attempts to reduce variation in the degrees of regulation across financial intermediaries.

Two distinct features of the 1907 crisis – its New York-centric character and the focus on an intermediary (the trust companies) that was not central to the payments system – have analogues in the recent 2007–2009 financial crisis. The investment banks, being a part of the so-called "shadow banking system," were effectively outside the regulatory oversight of the Federal Reserve System, and they did not have regular access to the Federal Reserve discount window. On a cursory level, the isolation of the investment banks from the lender of last resort appears comparable to the situation of trust companies in 1907. Future research and analysis can determine the relevance of the comparison for modern regulatory decisions. Regardless of the 100 years of separation, the shared characteristics in the two crises signify that historical episodes remain important sources for understanding modern financial crises.

Notes

1 Although the U.S. followed the gold standard since 1879, the commitment to gold was often in doubt until the Gold Standard Act of 1900.
2 Wicker (2000) considers the failure of Knickerbocker Trust a mistake that was the likely cause for the severity of the resulting panic. It is likely that, had the trust been a member of the New York Clearing House, the institution would have been assisted; that view is also expressed by Sprague (1910: 252). Alternatively, trust companies in New York City could have created an apparatus akin to the New York Clearing House, which could have provided support among trust companies subject to runs, but such arrangements typically take time.
3 Hansen (2011) provides a comprehensive discussion of the change in banking law that motivated National Bank of Commerce to relinquish its clearing agent responsibilities for Knickerbocker Trust.

References

Balke, N.S. and Gordon, R.J. (1986) 'Appendix B. Historical Data', in R.J. Gordon (ed.) *The American Business Cycle: Continuity and Change,* Chicago, IL: University of Chicago Press.
Bordo, M.D. and Haubrich, J.G. (2010) 'Credit crises, money and contractions: an historical view', *Journal of Monetary Economics,* 57(1): 1–18.
Broz, J.L. (1997) *The International Origins of the Federal Reserve System,* Ithaca, NY: Cornell University Press.
Bruner, R.F. and Carr, S.D. (2007) *The Panic of 1907: Lessons Learned from the Market's Perfect Storm,* New York: Wiley.
Cleveland, H.V.B. and Huertas, T.F. (1985) *Citibank: 1812–1970,* Cambridge, MA: Harvard University Press.
Davis, J.H. (2004) 'An annual index of U.S. industrial production, 1790–1915', *Quarterly Journal of Economics,* 119: 1177–215.
Donaldson, R.G. (1993) 'Financing banking crises: lessons from the panic of 1907', *Journal of Monetary Economics,* 31: 69–95.
Friedman, M. and Schwartz, A.J. (1963) *A Monetary History of the United States, 1867–1960,* Princeton, NJ: Princeton University Press.
Goodhart, C.A.E. (1969) *The New York Money Market and the Finance of Trade, 1900–1913,* Cambridge, MA: Harvard University Press.
Hagen, E.E. (1932) 'The panic of 1907', Masters of Arts Thesis, University of Wisconsin-Madison.
Hansen, B.A. (2011) 'Sometimes bad things happen to good trust companies: a re-examination of the trust company panic of 1907', Mary Washington University Working Paper.
Jalil, A. (2012) 'A new history of banking panics in the United States, 1825–1929: construction and implications', Unpublished manuscript, Reed College.
Jordà, Ò., Schularick, M. and Taylor, A.M. (2011) 'Financial crises, credit booms, and external imbalances: 140 years of lessons', NBER Working Paper No. 16567.
Kemmerer, E.W. (1910) *Seasonal Variations in the Relative Demand for Money and Capital in the United States; A Statistical Study,* Washington, DC: Government Printing Office.

Laughlin, J.L. (1912) *Banking Reform,* Chicago, IL: National Citizens League for the Promotion of a Sound Banking System.

Miron, J.A. (1986) 'Financial panics, the seasonality of the nominal interest rate, and the founding of the Fed', *American Economic Review,* 76(1): 125–140.

Moen, J.R. and Tallman, E.W. (1992) 'The bank panic of 1907: the role of trust companies', *Journal of Economic History,* 52: 611–30.

Moen, J.R. and Tallman, E.W. (2000) 'Clearinghouse membership and deposit contraction during the panic of 1907', *Journal of Economic History,* 60: 145–63.

Moen, J.R. and Tallman, E.W. (2007) 'Why didn't the United States establish a central bank until after the panic of 1907?' Unpublished manuscript.

Odell, K.A. and Weidenmier, M.D. (2004) 'Real shock, monetary aftershock: the 1906 San Francisco earthquake and the panic of 1907', *Journal of Economic History,* 64: 1002–27.

Reinhart, C.M. and Rogoff, K.S. (2009) *This Time is Different: Eight Centuries of Financial Folly,* Princeton, NJ: Princeton University Press.

Rich, G. (1988) *The Cross of Gold: Money and the Canadian Business Cycle, 1867–1913,* Ottawa: Carleton University Press.

Rodgers, M.T. and Wilson, B.K. (2010) 'Systemic risk, missing gold flows and the panic of 1907', Unpublished manuscript, Pace University.

Smith, B.D. (1984) 'Private information, deposit interest rates, and the "stability" of the banking system', *Journal of Monetary Economics,* 14: 293–317.

Sprague, O.M.W. (1910) *History of Crises under the National Banking System,* Washington, DC: Government Printing Office.

Strouse, J. (1999) *Morgan: American Financier,* New York: Random House.

Tallman, E.W. and Moen, J.R. (1990) 'Lessons from the panic of 1907', *Federal Reserve Bank of Atlanta Economic Review,* (May/June): 1–13.

Tallman, E.W. and Moen, J.R. (2011) 'The transmission of the financial crisis in 1907: an empirical investigation', presented at Past, Present and Policy 4th International Conference: The Sub-prime Crisis and How it Changed the Past, Graduate Institute, Geneva, 3–4 February 2011.

Tallman, E.W. and Moen, J.R. (2012) 'Liquidity creation without a central bank: clearing house loan certificates in the banking panic of 1907', *Journal of Financial Stability,* 8: 277–91.

Wicker, E.R. (2000) *Banking Panics of the Gilded Age,* New York: Cambridge University Press.

Wicker, E.R. (2005) *The Great Debate on Banking Reform: Nelson Aldrich and Origins of the Fed,* Columbus, OH: Ohio State University Press.

7

THE FOUNDING OF THE FEDERAL RESERVE SYSTEM

Mark Toma

Designing a monetary system

Mentally transport yourself to 1913. You have been charged with designing a new monetary system. Before jumping into the details of the task, you and your co-founders must answer the basic question that every institutional architect must answer: Do you create a top-down or a bottom-up system? More concretely, do you create a system whose policy is determined at the discretion of decision-makers at the top of a hierarchy, ideally motivated to do what is best for the economy? Or do you do you establish certain rules of the game where decisions are made bottom-up by individuals pursuing their self-interest? For the discretionary solution, the challenge is to design the system so that good leaders end up at the top. For the self-regulating solution, the challenge is to design rules that confront self-interested individuals with incentives that induce them to take actions that promote the common good.

Once this issue has been settled, you can turn to the design details. Now you and your co-founders must confront a problem that every *monetary* architect must confront: How do you avoid two bad outcomes – too much or too little money? First, consider the over-issue problem. If the money supplier issues more than the public demands, then the result is inflation. The money holder finds, through no fault of her own, that the purchasing power of her money balances dwindles over time. The classic solution, benefiting both sides, is for the issuer to commit to redeeming notes into a good, like gold, whose real value cannot be manipulated by the issuer and to make redemption easy. Then, money will be at least as good as gold, implying that the purchasing power of money cannot fall below the purchasing power of gold.

A second problem arises in the form of potential under-issue: The money issuer may fail to accommodate demand, triggering a scramble for liquidity that may result in some or all of the following: (1) a rise in the purchasing power of money relative to gold, (2) a rise in the rate of exchange between currency and its money substitute, demand deposits, (3) a rise in short-term interest rates. These price adjustments signal that currency has become scarcer – needlessly so if, under alternative institutional arrangements, the currency supplier would have been incentivized to accommodate.

Was the design problem confronted by the founders of the Federal Reserve one of over-issue, under-issue or both? To answer, we must briefly explore the nature of the monetary system that existed before the Fed's founding. That system, the National Banking System, was established by the Lincoln administration to solve its own design problem – how to help the North win the Civil War. Solving the war financing problem, however, did have a downside, producing a version of the under-issue problem or what came to be known as the problem of an inelastic currency. The creation of the Fed, some fifty years later, was meant to address this downside, a point driven home by the opening line of the Federal Reserve Act: "An Act to provide for the establishment of Federal reserve banks, *to furnish an elastic currency*...." (italics added). Before recounting the story of how the founders of the Fed crafted a new system to furnish an elastic currency, the next section outlines the nature of the elasticity problem under the National Banking System.

The National Banking System

Over-issue

Legislation giving rise to the National Banking System created two national currencies, U.S. notes and national bank notes. The U.S. notes (greenbacks) were issued by the Treasury and the national bank notes were issued by a new type of bank – nationally chartered banks – authorized to acquire the notes from the Treasury only after purchasing two-percent U.S. government bonds as collateral backing. After 1879, the U.S. notes were backed by a gold reserve of 100 percent housed at the Treasury, essentially making these notes commodity money. The national bank notes could be redeemed into lawful money (gold or U.S. notes) either at the national bank of issue or through redemption centers established by the Treasury. Each bank was required to contribute lawful money, into a redemption fund at the Treasury, equal to five percent of its outstanding notes. In the event that a national bank went bankrupt, the Treasury was obligated to immediately redeem its notes. For redemption purposes, the Treasury could use the redemption fund and the government bond collateral and was given first lien on all the assets of the bank and upon the personal liability of the stockholders (Friedman and Schwartz 1963: 21). After that, the Treasury would have to rely on the federal government's tax and borrowing capabilities.

Two considerations come into play in assessing whether these features of the National Banking System protected the currency holder from the over-issue problem. First, was redemption certain? Second, was redemption low cost?

For holders of U.S. notes, certainty of redemption was guaranteed by the 100 percent gold backing. For holders of national bank notes, certainty of redemption was a question of the magnitude of the federal government's taxing powers relative to its spending obligations, since the U.S. government stood as the ultimate backer. If the present value of current and expected future *maximum* taxes was less than the present value of current and expected future spending, then the federal government had no excess tax powers that could be used – by selling bonds – to redeem notes into gold. Note holders would have good reason to doubt the federal government's ability to raise funds on short notice to redeem notes.

How would a late-nineteenth- or early-twentieth-century note holder view the net tax powers of the federal government? Spending obligations were modest, but taxing powers also were modest since the federal government relied on taxes with narrow bases, mainly excise taxes and tariffs. Still, national notes were substantially backed – by reserves at the Treasury, by the government bond collateral, by the assets of the bank and by the personal liability of bank stockholders. A reasonable conjecture, therefore, is that holders of national bank notes, while not perceiving redemption to be certain, would have perceived it as likely.

Was redemption also low cost? Here, too, the answer is a qualified *yes*. An individual wanting lawful money for a national bank note issued by a distant bank could, of course, travel to the bank for redemption. More conveniently, she could take the note to her bank, exchange it for one of her bank's notes, which she could then redeem for lawful money. If desired, her bank could send those notes to a Treasury redemption center and receive lawful money from the redemption fund. Significantly, the costs of note redemption, e.g., the sorting of notes and the transportation costs, were not incurred by the sending bank; instead, they were assessed against the issuing bank (Champ, Freeman and Weber 1999: 568). So except for possible delays in receiving credit for notes sent to the Treasury, redemption costs were low.

The bottom line is that, while not sure-fire, the National Banking System did represent a credible solution to the over-issue problem. The cost of initiating redemption was relatively low. Once triggered, the likelihood that the notes would in fact be redeemed was relatively high.

Under-issue

Under-issue – the failure to promptly accommodate currency demand – would prove a bigger concern under the National Banking System. Chronic scarcity of money – say, a constant supply in the face of rising demand – was not the issue. The outcome in this case would be a persistent, equilibrating fall in the price level, with note-holders expecting and receiving a rising purchasing power. Rather, the problem was that supply did not promptly increase in response to temporary increases in demand.

The source of the problem was that neither of the two parties directly involved in currency supply – the national banks that issued the notes to the public and the Treasury that printed and delivered the notes to the national banks – had strong incentives to accommodate demand. The incentive problem faced by national banks stemmed from the requirement that they first acquire a specific bond – two-percent U.S. government bonds – before acquiring new notes. The requirement "funneled the banks' buying power into a single bond market and raised prices to prohibitive levels" (Horwitz 1990: 640), a problem made more severe by the fact that, after around 1880, the government used persistent budget surpluses to retire debt, thus reducing supply. Any unexpected relaxation of the collateral requirement or any easing of supply conditions in the market for two-percent government bonds might impose potentially significant capital losses on banks. Additionally, by making the entire banking system more fragile, the collateral requirement reduced depositor and note-holder confidence, increasing the likelihood that a relatively modest economic downturn would trigger numerous requests for note redemption, thus raising the overall costs of running the banking system. All told, the collateral requirement implied that accommodating the public's demand for currency was not always a profitable activity for national banks.

The incentive problem faced by the Treasury arguably was even more severe. Unlike private banks, the Treasury was a non-profit bureau that financed itself from a government budget. While the out-of-pocket expense of printing and delivering the notes was covered by the national bank requesting the notes, the Treasury still faced ancillary costs stemming primarily from the mandate that it verify and approve the government bond collateral backing new notes. Verification and approval costs would be particularly high during periods when the Treasury was called upon to respond quickly to numerous requests, requiring banks "to wait thirty days or more after depositing bonds before actually getting hold of new notes" (Horwitz 1990: 641). The problem of under-issue, in the form of upward inelasticity of note issue, was real.

Monetary reforms: discretion or self-regulation?

Currency inelasticity posed a particularly severe problem during an *active* season – the fall harvest season in the agriculturally-based economy of the nineteenth century – when the public sought to withdraw currency. As has been documented by numerous sources (e.g., Sprague 1910), a series of bank crises – accompanied by currency premiums and short-term interest rate spikes – did occur during the late 1800s and early 1900s. Both contemporary and modern economists generally agree that these crises were a major motivation for monetary reform. But what would be the nature of this solution? Would the National Banking System be replaced by a top-down system, headed by decision-makers exercising discretion, or by a bottom-up, self-regulating system?

One way of viewing the controversy is whether the Fed was to function as a modern central bank or as little more than a national clearinghouse, operating on automatic pilot. The policy debate was sparked by the central-bank-type open market operations in the early 1900s undertaken by Treasury Secretary Leslie Shaw during fall seasons of financial strain (see Timberlake 1993: 248–50). The Democratic Party tended to endorse Shaw's operations and wanted to institutionalize them in the form of a central bank with the tax powers of the federal government underwriting any losses incurred. The Republican Party favored a more decentralized, federalist structure that would automatically produce currency elasticity. The key innovative feature was a collection of competing government clearinghouses which would face a bottom-line and function alongside the already existing private clearinghouse system (Gorton 1985).

We all know the winning side, right? The Democratic Party swept the mid-term elections in 1910 and their candidate Woodrow Wilson won the Presidency in 1912. Then, on behalf of the Wilson administration, Senator Carter Class helped defeat a Republican bill, earlier offered by Senator Nelson Aldrich, and won passage of a Democratic bill, establishing a modern central bank in the form of the Federal Reserve System. Indeed, that passage of the Federal Reserve Act represented victory for Democrats and for discretion seems ingrained into the modern mindset.

The case for this modern consensus weakens considerably, however, with a more careful examination of the Fed's historical roots. For one thing, Elmus Wicker (2005) persuasively argues that Glass's plan adhered closely in its details to the one previously offered by Aldrich. Even more to the point, Richard Timberlake concludes that in creating the Fed, the founders rejected the discretionary central bank model, intending instead to create a system that would be largely self-regulating.

> Creation of the Federal Reserve banks was in part a reaction to the Treasury policies that Shaw had developed. Equally important was the anticipation that the new system would promote form-seasonal elasticity in the money supply … not through the discretion of a government official, but on the initiative of commercial bankers themselves through a supercommercial (Federal Reserve) bank. The emphasis shifted from discretionary policy by a government agency to automatic and self-regulating policy in the market. Indeed, the early Federal Reserve System, operating on a real-bills principle and on the doctrine of maintaining the discount rate above market rates of interest, was to be a self-regulating appendage to a more fundamental self-regulating system – the operational gold standard.
>
> (Timberlake 1993: 249–50)

Timberlake's characterization of the new system as a "self-regulating appendage to a more fundamental self-regulating system – the operational gold standard" is especially apt. The gold standard was the foundation of the system. But as emphasized in the introduction, an effective gold standard guarantees only that the price level will not rise above a certain ceiling level. To get an anchor – not just a ceiling – requires, in Timberlake's words, an appendage to the gold standard; an appendage that gives the Fed no choice but to passively supply the amount of money demanded at a price level over which it has no control.

To be sure, one need not be wedded to the particular appendage that Timberlake suggests – a real bills principle with penalty discount rates – to appreciate that some such device is needed to make the system truly self-regulating. Indeed, the next section argues that the decisive add-on to the gold standard was competition. The founders' intent was to replace an inflexible bureaucratic currency-issuing system – the National Banking System – with a more flexible, competitive currency-issuing system – the Federal Reserve System – where Reserve banks would act as clearinghouses in a market-like setting. If operated as planned, the new Fed would have little choice but to elastically supply currency at a price level that was determined in a market – the market for gold. The gold anchor would guard against Fed over-issue and competition against Fed under-issue of currency.

The Federal Reserve System

Over-issue

Perhaps the most significant features of the Federal Reserve Act were the creation of a new type of currency, the Federal Reserve note, to be supplied by a new type of financial institution, the Federal Reserve bank. In particular, the Act created twelve Reserve banks, each operating inside a distinct geographic boundary and each offering two monetary liabilities – deposits of member banks and Federal Reserve notes, with the notes of each Reserve bank bearing "upon their faces a distinctive letter and serial number" (Section 16). The Reserve banks were nominally owned by member banks, which were required to purchase stock in their district Reserve bank. Stock ownership, however, did not convey ordinary voting rights, nor could member banks sell their stock or buy stock held by others (Sections 2 and 5). In the absence of stockholder control, the power to make decisions on behalf of a Reserve bank was divided among the President of the Reserve bank (the Governor), the Board of Directors of the Reserve bank and the Federal Reserve Board, which was a central administrative body consisting of the U.S. Secretary of Treasury, the U.S. Comptroller and five members appointed by the President of the U.S.

In establishing a new currency, the founders of the Federal Reserve were aware that *certainty in redemption* was a key to overcoming the problem of over-issue. Section 16 of the Federal Reserve Act states that Federal Reserve notes "shall be redeemed in gold on demand at the Treasury Department of the United States … or in gold or lawful money at any Federal reserve bank." Section 16 also requires that each Reserve bank hold (1) gold in a redemption fund at the Treasury equal to five percent of its outstanding notes, (2) gold or lawful money equal to 40 percent of outstanding notes, as well as 35 percent of member bank deposits, with the 5 percent redemption fund at the Treasury counted as part of the 40 percent reserve against notes. Additionally, Reserve banks were required to supplement gold reserves with collateral in the form of bills and notes (commercial paper) accepted for discount. In the event a Reserve bank declared bankruptcy, the note-holder had first lien against all assets of the Reserve bank. If those proved insufficient, then, as a last resort, the tax powers of the federal government ("notes shall be obligations of the United States," Section 16) stood behind the Federal Reserve notes.

How do these features stack-up against corresponding features of the National Banking System? National bank notes were backed by (1) lawful money required to be held by a national bank in a redemption fund at the Treasury, (2) government bond collateral, (3) assets of a national bank and the personal liability of its stockholders and, as a last resort, (4) the tax powers of the federal government. Federal Reserve notes were backed by (1) gold or lawful money required to be held by a Reserve bank, including its redemption fund at the Treasury, (2) commercial paper collateral, (3) assets of a Reserve bank and, as a last resort, (4) the tax powers of the federal government.

While conditions (1) through (3) offer no clear-cut winner, the advantage seems to go to the Federal Reserve with respect to the ultimate backstop – federal tax powers, condition (4). The 16th Amendment to the U.S. Constitution, authorizing a federal income tax, was ratified in February 1913, just as congressional debate on the new monetary system was intensifying. At first the income tax was to apply only to the richest two percent of the population. But a forward-looking taxpayer would have solid grounds for forecasting that the tax base at some future date would be broadened. With enhanced powers to tax, government was in a position to make a commitment to the note-holding public that was more credible than at any time in the past: *If all else fails, the federal government stands ready to use its ability to borrow on the basis of future income tax collections to redeem your notes into gold.* On this basis, holders of Federal Reserve notes would have perceived the probability of redemption to be as high as or higher than the probability perceived by the pre-1913 holders of national bank notes.

Did the Federal Reserve System also do a better job of satisfying the second over-issue condition – that redemption cost is low? Here, the tables are turned. The individual holder of a national bank note simply visited the nearest national bank for redemption. Over-the-counter redemption for the holder of a Federal Reserve note required a visit to the Treasury, any Reserve bank, or any Reserve bank branch, none of which were necessarily nearby. Alternatively, the individual could send the Federal Reserve note to one of the above locations. Since express costs were assessed against the issuing Reserve bank, out-of-pocket costs would be low. Still, the note-holder would have to prepare the notes for mailing and wait for delivery of lawful money. Under the presumption that over-the-counter redemption at a nearby location is preferred to all other redemption options, note-holders would have perceived redemption to be less costly under the National Banking System.

One special provision of the Federal Reserve Act, however, may have allowed the general public to off-load the entire cost of redemption.

> Whenever Federal reserve notes issued through one Federal reserve bank shall be received by another Federal reserve bank they shall be promptly returned for credit or redemption to the Federal reserve bank through which they were originally issued. No Federal reserve bank shall pay out notes issued through another under penalty of a tax of ten per centum upon the face value of notes so paid out.
>
> (Section 16)

Here, a mechanism for routine *indirect* redemption is established. First, an individual visits her bank to deposit cash in her checking account. The bank may choose to hold the notes in anticipation of future withdrawals or send the notes to its Reserve bank in exchange for an increase in deposits. Assuming the Reserve bank was not the original issuer, Section 16 directs it to forward the notes to the issuing Reserve bank *for credit or redemption*. While not a foregone conclusion – individuals may seldom deposit cash, commercial banks may choose to hold deposited notes as vault cash, Reserve banks forwarding notes may ask for credit – the Federal Reserve Act provided for the possibility of routine indirect redemption.

Where do things stand with respect to the problem of over-issue under the Federal Reserve System? The note-holder knows that if certain steps are taken, redemption is all but inevitable due to the deep pockets of the federal government. Still, a question lingers – can redemption be triggered without substantial costs? For direct redemption, the answer is a qualified, *yes*. Note-holders are compensated for out-of-pocket costs of sending notes for redemption; the only costs incurred are in the form of inconvenience and waiting time. Moreover, note-holders may be able to avoid even these costs, if indirect redemption, as provided for in the Federal Reserve Act, is effective. Commenting on the clause in the Federal Reserve Act authorizing indirect redemption, H. Parker Willis and William H. Steiner – contemporary authorities on the operation of the early Fed – concluded "Redemption is thus fully provided for" (Willis and Steiner 1926: 136).[1]

Under-issue

The problem of under-issue in the form of upward-inelasticity of currency was the downfall of the National Banking System. Would inelasticity also prove the Achilles' heel of the Federal Reserve System? Viewed from one perspective, it would be a little shocking if the founders of the Fed dropped the ball on this issue. After all, the nation had just witnessed a long debate on how best to solve the elasticity problem. The big questions were (1) Was elasticity to be achieved by establishing a discretionary central bank or by setting up a self-regulating system, and (2) Was the chosen solution effective?

The debate at the turn of the century focused on the first question. Ultimately, Congress rejected both a monopoly central bank and a thorough-going decentralized system of legally unrestricted private banks. Instead of pure discretion or pure self-regulation, Congress created a system of twelve non-profit Reserve banks, each offering reserves to member banks in its district and each offering currency – unencumbered by a government bond collateral requirement – funneled through the banks to the general public. Did this hybrid system incentivize Reserve banks to accommodate the public's demand for currency? Were other government agencies involved, whose behavior might serve as bottlenecks to timely currency supply?

With respect to incentivized Reserve banks, two stumbling blocks stood in the way: Reserve banks as non-profit firms and as regional monopolists. Consider first the non-profit stumbling block. Reserve banks have an incentive to accommodate increased demands for currency only if so doing provides them with net benefits; more concretely, only if accommodation generates a flow of residual revenue that can be directly, or indirectly, consumed by the Reserve bank decision-makers. The Federal Reserve Act seemed to answer this question once and for all in a section titled, Division of Earnings:

> After all necessary expenses of a Reserve bank have been paid or provided for, the stockholders shall be entitled to receive an annual dividend of six per centum on the paid-in capital, which dividend shall be cumulative. After the foresaid dividend claims have been fully met, all the net earnings shall be paid to the United States as a franchise tax, except that one-half of such net earnings shall be paid into a surplus fund until it shall amount to forty per centum of the paid-in capital stock of such bank.
>
> (Section 7)

So the sequence of revenue disposition was (1) necessary expenses, (2) dividend payments to stockholders (member banks), (3) surplus fund, and, finally, (4) transfers to the United States (Treasury) in the form of a so-called franchise tax.

Where do Reserve bank decision-makers fit into the sequence? The apparent answer is that they do not. To be sure, the first draw on revenue goes to finance necessary expenses, with management compensation subsumed under necessary expenses. But once enough asset-backed currency has been issued to cover necessary expenses – along with dividend payments and the stipulated build-up of the surplus fund – the United States, not the Reserve banks, is in line to profit. Because there are no profits to be won, and *taken home*, the management team would not be advocates for accommodation – they would not care that the Treasury may receive a larger transfer payment. In a word, they would be simply *disinterested*.

Or would they? While the disinterested characterization may be consistent with a literal reading of the Federal Reserve Act – that Reserve banks transfer all revenues after paying necessary expenses, dividends and adding to the surplus fund – it is inconsistent with the economic literature on non-profit firms. The problem here is the word, *necessary*, preceding the word, *expenses*. A world of scarcity is a world of tradeoffs where, strictly speaking, nothing is an absolute necessity. In practice, decision-makers at each Reserve bank may see the clause, "necessary expenses," but they will behave as if it reads simply, "expenses." Or, in the language of the economist, decision-makers will engage in expense preference behavior, spending net revenues on goods that can be consumed in-house. Non-profit Reserve banks will have an incentive to supply currency to the public and reserves to banks so as to maximize this discretionary spending, with transfers of revenue to the government equaling zero in equilibrium.

Formally, replacing disinterested Reserve banks with discretionary spending maximizing Reserve banks solves the elasticity problem. Confronted by an economy-wide increase in currency demand, each Reserve bank finds that it can increase excess earnings, and hence discretionary spending, by accommodating demand in its region. Note, however, that the incentives are not as strong as with full-fledged, for-profit, competitive Reserve banks. For one thing, non-profit managers must consume net earnings as in-kind perks of office. Second, by carving the United States into 12 regions, the Federal Reserve Act seemed to give each Reserve bank monopoly power. Under competition, if an individual firm is not alert to an economy-wide increase in demand, a competing firm stands ready to fill the void. But in a regional monopoly system, with impregnable boundaries, no Reserve bank stands in waiting; demand in that region would go unsatisfied. Accordingly, a system of regional non-profit monopolies only *weakly* incentivizes accommodation.

However, a more careful reading of the Federal Reserve Act suggests that the characterization of Reserve banks as regional monopolists is misleading. To be sure, the Act did not allow a member bank in one region to borrow reserves from a Reserve bank in another region – *direct* competition through the discount window was illegal. But a true regional monopoly requires that all interconnections between regions be severed. If a member bank in one region is able to form a correspondent relationship with a member bank in another region – a bank is able to borrow from a bank in another region – then, via this bank-to-bank link, a Reserve bank in one region would be able to lend to banks in other regions.

Prior to the Fed, large national banks in urban centers frequently did form correspondent relationships with smaller banks inside and outside their region. In drafting the Federal Reserve Act, the founders made an explicit decision to retain the essential features of the correspondent system. Inter-regional borrowing and lending among banks could, and did, take place (Toma 1997: 29–30). In this sense, the Federal Reserve Act provided an avenue through which Reserve banks could *indirectly* compete in supplying reserve balances to out-of-district member banks as well as currency to the out-of-district general public.

Before concluding that the Federal Reserve System represented an effective solution to the currency elasticity problem, there is one more base to cover. Were there outside parties that may serve as a bottleneck to accommodation? We know from our discussion of the National Banking System that the Treasury was one such party with little incentive to insure the timely delivery of notes to national banks. The founders of the Federal Reserve System did not make the same mistake – note delivery would be brought within the Federal Reserve System proper. In particular, a Board-appointed Federal Reserve agent would be assigned to each Reserve bank and charged with the responsibilities of validating commercial paper for collateral-backing and of transporting the notes from the Treasury to the Reserve bank. Significantly, the Act stipulated that the agent's salary would be paid by his Federal Reserve bank, thus aligning the agent's interest with the Reserve bank's interest in the speedy delivery of Federal Reserve notes. The Federal Reserve agent, as an incentivized link between the Treasury and Reserve banks, represented a key ingredient in a decentralized, self-regulating Federal Reserve System.

The Federal Reserve Board represented perhaps an even more potent threat to currency elasticity. The Board enjoyed significant supervisory powers, the most important of which were to set discount rates and to define which bills would be eligible for rediscount (Federal Reserve Act, Sections 13 and 14). So empowered, the Board had the ability to shut down the flow of new currency through the discount window.

The Federal Reserve Act contained a loophole, however, which would allow Reserve banks to sidestep this potential bottleneck. The Act authorized the individual Reserve banks "To buy and sell, at home or abroad, bonds and notes of the United States" (Section 14). The authorization did contain the qualifier, "such purchases to be made in accordance with rules and regulations prescribed by the Federal Reserve Board" (Section 14). But, the limited nature of the Board's powers over open market operations, in contrast to their powers over discount loans, was recognized from the outset. Jane D'Arista in a passage introducing her much-neglected study prepared for a House Committee on Banking and Currency observes that

> a power struggle began almost immediately after the Reserve banks opened for business in November 1914, when the Federal Reserve Board pressured the Reserve banks for lower and more uniform discount rates and the Reserve bank governors resisted. The board won this round but lost the struggle. The Reserve banks won the struggle for power by dominating the system's open market operations.
>
> (D'Arista 1994: 4)

Open market operations provided a potential mechanism by which Reserve banks could end-run any impediments to currency elasticity arising from the Board's regulation of the discount window.

The founders' vision

The design flaw of the National Banking System was that it had no built-in mechanism that guaranteed upward elasticity of currency. The flaw stemmed from two attributes of the system: (1) the government bond collateral requirement and (2) bottlenecks in the process of delivering currency to the issuing banks. The challenge facing the founders of the Federal Reserve System was to remedy these defects – to create a system that would incentivize all parties involved in the supply of currency. The founders met this challenge by creating a decentralized self-regulating system, or, in Richard Timberlake's characterization, they created a "self-regulating appendage to a more fundamental self-regulating system – the operational gold standard." The operational gold standard was a hold-over from the National Banking System that guarded against over-issue. The really novel feature of the new system was the self-regulating appendage – a competitive network of non-profit Reserve banks, each facing a bottom-line, but without the government bond collateral requirement. At least on paper, the Reserve banks would face market pressures to accommodate surges in the public's demand for currency. They would be incentivized, in other words, to solve the fundamental defect of the National Banking System.

Did the founders' vision prove out in practice? A strong case can be made that it did, at least for the early years of the Federal Reserve. Indeed, the chapter title, "High Tide of the Federal Reserve System, 1921–1929," from Milton Friedman's and Anna Schwartz's *The Monetary History of the United States* (1963), bears testimony to the veracity of the founders' vision. During those early years, seasonal fluctuations in Federal Reserve credit tended to smooth seasonal variations in interest rates. A switch in decision-making power from autonomous Reserve banks to the Federal Reserve Board occurred, however, over the course of the 1920s – particularly the closing years of the decade – and the seasonal movement and general availability of Fed credit declined in the Depression years (Miron 1986: 136–37, Holland and Toma 1991: 669–71). A lingering question, in the spirit of Friedman and Schwartz's research agenda, is whether this reversal in policy can be attributed to the centralization of decision-making authority, a centralization that was not likely foreseen by the founders of the Federal Reserve.

Note

1 For a contrary view, see Selgin and White 1994.

References

Champ B., Freeman S. and Weber, W.E. (1999) 'Redemption costs and interest rates under the U.S. national banking system', *Journal of Money, Credit and Banking*, 31: 568–89.

D'Arista, J.W. (1994) *The Evolution of US Finance, Volume I*, London: M.E. Sharpe.

Friedman, M. and Schwartz, A.J. (1963) *A Monetary History of the United States, 1867–1960*, Princeton, NJ: Princeton University Press.

Gorton, G. (1985) 'Clearinghouses and the origin of central banking in the United States', *Journal of Economic History*, 45: 277–83.

Holland, S.A. and Toma, M. (1991) 'The role of the Federal Reserve as "lender of last resort" and the seasonal fluctuation of interest rates', *Journal of Money, Credit and Banking*, 23: 659–76.

Horwitz, S. (1990) 'Competitive currencies, legal restrictions, and the origins of the Fed: some evidence from the panic of 1907', *Southern Economic Journal*, 56: 639–49.

Miron, J.A. (1986) 'Financial panics, the seasonality of the nominal interest rate, and the founding of the Fed', *American Economic Review*, 76: 125–40.

Sprague, O.M.W. (1910) *History of Crises under the National Banking System*, Washington, DC: U.S. Government Printing Office.

Timberlake, R.H. (1993) *Monetary Policy in the United States*, Chicago, IL: University of Chicago Press.

Toma, M. (1997) *Competition and Monopoly in the Federal Reserve System 1914–1951*, Cambridge: Cambridge University Press.

Wicker, E. (2005) *The Great Debate on Banking Reform: Nelson Aldrich and the Origins of the Fed*, Columbus, OH: Ohio University Press.

Willis, H.P. and Steiner, W.H. (1926) *Federal Reserve Banking Practice*, New York: D. Appleton and Company.

8

WORLD WAR I

Jari Eloranta

But the study of history teaches us that all those States which in the decisive hour have been guided by purely commercial considerations have miserably come to grief. The sympathies of civilized nations are today, as in the battles of antiquity, still with the sturdy and the bold fighting armies; they are with the brave combatants who, in the words which Lessing puts in the mouth of Tellheim, are soldiers for their country, and fight out of the love which they bear to the cause.

(Crown Prince Wilhelm (son of the Kaiser) in 1913)[1]

Introduction

In August 1914 crowds rejoiced in the streets of many European cities due to the outbreak of the war.[2] Despite the vision of some, like Norman Angell in his 1909 bestseller *The Great Illusion* (Angell 1972), the increased economic interdependence of the great powers did not make a major international conflict impossible, or even force it to a swift conclusion. It seems that militarism, as displayed for example by the heir to the crown of the German empire in 1913, prevailed over other considerations. The end result was World War I, a pivotal event in human history, for a variety of reasons. First of all, it resulted in human suffering unprecedented in prior centuries or millennia. Millions of people died and were left maimed by this industrialized version of total war. The concept and practice of total war had, of course, been around for a long time, although World War I brought it to a new level by combining industrialized, globalized empires with new types of weapons capable of mass killing. The combatants had to harness the entire society and economic resources to fight this war, as well as attempt to disrupt their enemies' trade and ability to mobilize. Moreover, colonies and neutral countries were also affected by this conflict. Second, it brought the first era of globalization to an end and initiated an era of instability and protectionism that lasted until mid-century. Conversely, it also was the beginning of the end for European empires and triggered a wave of democratization, at least in the long run. In the short run, however, the new borders and nations created in the aftermath of the war were unstable, just like the economic climate of the interwar period, and encouraged the rise of populist groups and radical elements in European societies.

Finally, World War I was a deathblow to the European alliance system that had prevented great power conflicts, and it initiated a new phase in the march toward modernity with its benefits and vices. Warfare had graduated to a brutal affair in the miserable Western European trenches and the burnt villages of Eastern Europe. Great power politics were freed from the bonds of gentlemanly rules – a process that had already started by the 1790s and the French Revolution – and the practice of twentieth century warfare now resembled an industrialized mission. Restraints had been removed, and even genocide was now tried to advance nationalistic goals.[3] The war also upended the world economic system, with the European economic superpowers like Great Britain, France, and Germany deep in debt, and the United States now the new economic hegemon. However, the U.S. was not willing to play the role of the world's banker as Britain had, to coordinate the gold standard and facilitate the international trading system. Nor did it want to act as the arbiter of the post-war political settlements, at least after Woodrow Wilson's vision and membership in the League of Nations were rebuked soundly in the post-war presidential elections. The world after World War I was very different from the one that preceded it: alliances, international trade, European hegemony and colonialism, belief in short offensive wars, civilians as forbidden targets, and the gold standard were all casualties of the war, along with millions of human beings. This chapter will first examine the main causes of the war, especially the arms race that preceded the war. Then it will provide a macro-view of the costs, impacts, and outcomes of the war. It concludes with a discussion of the short- and long-term effects of the 1914–1918 world conflict.

The road to war

There were a plethora of causes for World War I. The list of explanations include (among other factors) alliances, nationalism, European imperialism, the (naval) arms race (Kennedy 1976, Modelski and Thompson 1988, Steiner 1977), shifting power balances (Geller and Singer 1998, Kennedy 1984, North et al. 1963a, North et al. 1963b), changes in strategic positions (Levy 1990–91, Mombauer 2001, Williamson 1988), diplomatic failures, Germany's perceived aggression,[4] mobilization plans (Keegan 1999, Taylor 1969, revised in Trachtenberg 1990–91), imperialism overreach, agricultural dependencies, economic interdependencies (Ferguson 1999, 2001, Kennedy 1989, Offer 1989), specific domestic causes (Ferguson 1994), a cult of the offensive among the officer corps in the various countries (Offer 1995, Strachan 2011, Van Evera 1984), international arms dealers (Tooley 2005), escalation of ethnic and regional conflicts (see, for example, Ferguson 2006), and, finally, the assassination of Archduke Ferdinand. It is very difficult to assign a greater explanatory value to some of these causes over others (Gillette 2006); however, it can be argued that the most important factors were changes in the power balance between nations and the resultant out-of-control arms race, which increased the risk of a multi-state conflict (Eloranta 2007). Accordingly, this chapter focuses on empires, the arms race, and the failure of globalization in order to understand how the war came about.

In the nineteenth century the process of globalization and empires were linked. By 1913, Europeans were the greatest imperialists in the history of the world, with 30 percent of the world's population living in European colonies outside Europe (Eloranta and Harrison 2010). Moreover, according to some estimates, Europeans or the former colonies of Europe in the Americas controlled 84 percent of the earth's land surface in 1914 either directly or indirectly. As described by Samuel Huntington, "by 1910 the world was more one politically and economically than at any other time in human history." Europeans were naturally dominant economically as well, and comprised the majority of the world's military spending (Eloranta 2007, Huntington 1996).

The pursuit of colonies by the existing great powers (like Britain and France) and new powers (like the new nations of Germany and Italy) contributed to frequent crises in the global political equilibrium among the powers and was one of the causal factors in the onset of both the world wars. Colonial conquests had become a zero-sum game – almost all possible areas suitable for conquest and/or raw materials extraction had been exhausted by the early twentieth century, thereby increasing the tensions between the main international players. It was no longer possible to divert attention from domestic problems, such as unequal distribution of income and unemployment, by engaging in further colonial adventures.

Following critics of empire like Lenin (1963) and Hobson (1965 (reprint)), it has been fashionable to link world trade and world empires with the causes of the two world wars. The truth is more complex, however. Neither globalization nor imperialism was the only cause of war in 1914. The nineteenth-century wave of globalization was a revolutionary process, almost by any historical standard. The industrializing parts of the world, as well as the colonies they were attached to, experienced tremendous growth in trade, especially in primary products, something that was unheard of during previous periods of trade expansion (O'Rourke and Williamson 2002). Globalization also increased the interdependency of all the trading nations, thereby increasing the opportunity costs of the war. Specifically, increased openness had made the European states more vulnerable to the loss of imported food and materials. By raising wages, economic growth had made the maintenance of standing armies more expensive. Businessmen across Europe were not pushing for war and therefore its outbreak came as a shock (Eloranta and Harrison 2010, Ferguson 1999). Yet other factors, beyond imperialism, were stronger in pushing the great powers toward an intensifying arms race. One of the most important was the industrialization of warfare, which increased the destructive efficiency of military equipment and gave industrialized states a bigger bang for their bucks (Ferguson 2001, McNeill 1982). Finally, the very fact of increased vulnerability to economic disruption probably heightened the propensity of the likely participants to gamble on a rapid offensive, once war became probable (Rowe 2005).

John Keegan (1999) describes a Europe thrust into war by communication failures and irreversible war plans that were designed for the "age-old quest for security in military superiority." To be sure, World War I was no accident, nor was it "caused" by the assassination of the heir to the Austro-Hungarian throne. However, Archduke Ferdinand's assassination did launch into motion a series of diplomatic offensives, acting like trigger mechanisms for a larger contraption. As Keegan argues, the mobilization plans and military resources of the great powers differed greatly, which necessitated the playing out of a complex game. For example, Germany had precise timetables in place to carry out the Schlieffen Plan – the quick defeat of France to avoid a long two-front war – whereas most of the participants knew that Russia would take a long time to mobilize its forces. Therefore it was logical for both the Russians (to get anywhere in case a war started) and the Germans (to make sure they would get a head start on their war plan) to start early; something that triggered similar responses among the other great powers. Alliances were simply the shell that housed the realities of the mobilization plans, and would prove relatively unimportant in their decision-making on military spending levels prior to the war.

Historians have tended to hold Germany particularly accountable for the pre-1914 arms race and the subsequent diplomatic breakdown (e.g., Berghahn 1973). Niall Ferguson (1999, 2001) has noted that, having started the arms race, Germany was unable to compete against its rivals, and was led therefore to gamble on a preemptive strike in 1914. Thus, the prewar

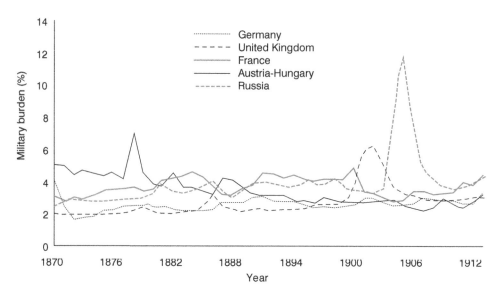

Figure 8.1 Military burdens of Great Britain, France, Germany, Austria-Hungary, and Russia, 1870–1913

Source: Eloranta (2007)

arms race, stimulated by the competition for colonies, was one of the main causes of the war, whereas the industrialization of armaments production contributed mainly to the length and destructiveness of the war. This arms race was under control, relatively speaking, until the early twentieth century, when several events disrupted the precarious equilibrium that existed between the great powers.

On the whole, both the United Kingdom and Germany spent less on their armed forces than most great powers. In the French case, the defense share (military spending as a percentage of central or federal government expenditures) mean remained quite similar during the nineteenth and early twentieth centuries, at little over 30 percent, whereas on average its military burden (military spending as a percentage of GDP) increased from 3.2 percent in 1815–1869 to 4.2 percent in 1870–1913, a higher share than most of its competitors. The British defense share mean declined about 2 percent to 36.7 percent from 1870–1913 compared to the early nineteenth century. However, the rapid growth of the British economy made it possible that the military burden actually declined a little to 2.6 percent, which is similar to what Germany was spending in the same period (as seen in Figure 8.1). For most countries the period leading to World War I meant higher military burdens than that, such as Japan's 6.1 percent. The United States, the new global economic (but not political) leader, however, spent only 0.7 percent of its GDP on average for military purposes, a trend that continued throughout the interwar period as well. Furthermore, the aggregate, systemic (based on a 16-country total), real military spending in this period increased consistently.

Several shocks upset this balance in the beginning of the twentieth century. First, the Russo-Japanese war (1904–1905) exposed weaknesses in Russian military power, led many nations to underestimate its military and economic potential, and forced great powers to at least briefly consider Japan as a major player (Eloranta 2007). Second, the arrival of a new type of battleship, the dreadnought, typified the intensification of the industrialized arms race, and forced the great powers to compete even harder for new weapons and potential strategic advantage over their rivals. Third, many colonies were also getting restless, as symbolized

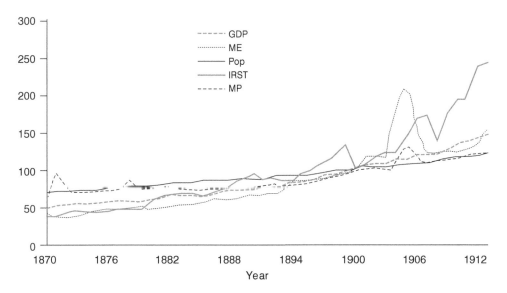

Figure 8.2 Indices of real GDP, real military spending (ME), total population (POP), iron and steel production (IRST), and military personnel (MP) as sixteen country totals, 1870–1913

Sources: Based on the sources listed in Eloranta (2007). GDP and military expenditure adjustments to real terms are also explained in the same article. The sixteen nations are: Austria-Hungary, Belgium, Denmark, France, Germany, Italy, Japan, the Netherlands, Norway, Portugal, Russia, Spain, Sweden, Switzerland, UK, and USA

for example by the Boer War in South Africa and the Boxer Rebellion in China. Fourth, the Balkans and the complicated conflicts that arose from the multitude of nationalistic, religious, ethnic, and political groupings – as well as the decline of one empire (the Ottomans), the fracturing of another (Austria-Hungary), the aspirations of a divided empire (the Russians), and the dreams of yet another (Italy) – ultimately spiraled out of control and provided the spark for the war. As seen in Figure 8.2, the potential combatants had an expanded resource base with which to fight the war, including larger and more industrialized economies with the ability to produce more weapons than ever before, and they were also arming themselves at an accelerating pace. These structural forces were unleashed when the heir to the Austro-Hungarian throne was assassinated in Sarajevo by a Serbian nationalist, Gavrilo Princip on June 28, 1914. The swift diplomatic responses by the Austro-Hungarian Empire and the machinations of the other nations quickly put Europe on the path of war, which officially began on July 28, 1914, with the Austro-Hungarian invasion of Serbia and the subsequent German offensives in the West (Stevenson 2011).

Macro-economic view: costs, impacts, and outcomes

The war divided most of the world, well beyond the European continent, into three camps: the Central Powers, who consisted of Germany, Austria-Hungary, Italy (only until 1915), the Ottoman Empire, and Bulgaria (1915 onward), as well as many of their colonies; the Allied Powers, comprising Russia, France, the UK, most of the Balkan states, Japan, Italy (from 1915 onward), Portugal (1915 onward), Romania (1915 onward), the United States (1917 onward), several Latin American nations (such as Brazil from 1917 onward), and many of their colonies; and neutral nations like Sweden and Switzerland. All three groups became entangled in the war to some extent, even the neutral states, because of the battle for naval superiority by the combatants and the extant business opportunities that arose due to the almost unlimited thirst for resources. In the West, the war became a stalemate as early as September 1914, after Germany's initial attack through Belgium was halted before reaching Paris by French and British troops. After that, both sides settled into almost four years of trench warfare, with intermittent attacks and insignificant gains. The loss of life, however, was not insignificant. Both sides engaged in futile offensive campaigns to gain even a little ground, with mass casualties. For example, in the Battle of the Somme in 1916 the British forces lost almost 58,000 men during the first hour of the campaign, and close to half a million in total during the offensive (Keegan 1999). Germans had similar losses in their campaigns. The introduction of new weaponry – such as more potent artillery, the machine gun, barbed wire and land mines, and chemical weapons – contributed to the mounting death tolls. Germany was not able to make a sustained effort to gain ground towards Paris until Spring 1918, when the so-called Ludendorff Offensive began. At this juncture they were able to concentrate all of their resources to the fight in the West, and made some significant headway initially. Ultimately the effort stalled, partially due to American reinforcements, and Germany's downhill slide toward ultimate defeat had begun.

In the East, things were different. Germany's plan was to leave the fighting there to the Austrians; however, after the disastrous initial battles they had with the Russians, Germans had to send troops eastward to prevent collapse. In fact, Germany achieved great success in the East, driving through Poland in 1915 and conquering Bucharest in 1916, all of which put great pressure on Russia. Dissatisfaction grew with the leadership of Czar Nicholas II, which ultimately led to his abdication in March 1917. The Bolshevik Revolution in October 1917 brought Lenin into power (although not conclusively until after the Civil War in 1922) who was willing to conclude a peace treaty with Germany in March 1918 in Brest-Litovsk. This treaty took Russia out of the war and ceded massive amounts of territory to Germany, thereby enabling them to concentrate their resources to the West, with aforementioned results (Keegan 1999).

The war was also fought in southern Europe, in the Middle East, and in the various European colonies. That meant that millions of people were directly or indirectly impacted by the war in places like Brazil, Liberia, Somalia, India, New Zealand, Australia, and so forth. Often the colonial military forces provided crucial military assistance and/or battlefield support in the European trenches. For example, close to 800,000 Indian fighters fought in World War I, with over 100,000 casualties in total. There also was a naval component to the war, something that was of great importance to the colonies as well as the European war economies. While big battleships that had been such a crucial part of the naval arms race prior to the war proved to be difficult to utilize in actual battles, both sides tried to impose blockades on one another to disrupt the enemy's war effort. The Germans tried to utilize their submarine fleet to sever Allied shipping lanes, and they escalated the use of U-boats almost every year of the war. From 1917 onwards they declared unrestricted submarine warfare the norm, in essence announcing that everything was fair game in their total war effort. Although they were unable to sink enough Allied ships to disrupt their supply lines, such efforts provoked the U.S. to enter the war eventually, and Britain still reigned supreme at sea (Davis and Engerman 2006).

Ultimately, World War I became a war that was decided by economic resources. As Niall Ferguson (1999) has pointed out, Germany did not mismanage its resources and thus lose the war. Quite the contrary: the Allies had massive advantages in terms of total GDP, population, military personnel, armaments production, and food supply throughout the conflict; a situation that became even more pronounced when the U.S. finally entered the war on their side. In November 1914, the Allies had 793 million people under their control compared to 151 million for the Central Powers. By the end of the war, the Allies controlled 1,272 million in terms of population (or 70 percent of world total), whereas the Central Powers' total was still under 200 million. Or, in terms of GDP, the Allies possessed a combined GDP of $1,761 billion (1990 Geary–Khamis dollars) at the end of the war, which was far superior to the less than $400 billion the Central Powers had in 1915. The Allies had a massive advantage in population, territory, and GDP throughout the war; this advantage became even more disproportionate as the war went on (Broadberry and Harrison 2005).

Allied great powers were ultimately able to mobilize their resources more effectively during the war. Even though the Central Powers initially did quite well with the limited resources they had, the Allies were able to mobilize their far superior resources better both at the home front and to the front lines. Their more democratic institutions supported the demands of the total war effort better than their authoritarian counterparts. Therefore, the richer countries mobilized more men and materiel for the war, and their war industries proved quite capable of adapting to fulfill the needs of the war machine (Broadberry and Harrison 2005). Moreover, having a large peasant population turned out to be a hindrance for the production of food under wartime constraints. In poorer countries, and even in affluent Germany, mobilization efforts siphoned off resources from agriculture and the farmers preferred to hoard food rather than sell it for low prices. As Avner Offer (1989) has argued, food (or the lack of it) played a crucial part in Germany's collapse. As seen in Table 8.1, Germany's problem was not so much that it was unable to mobilize resources for the war,

Table 8.1 Economic capabilities and military mobilization of the Great Powers, in 1914 and 1918

Year and Variable	Germany	UK	France	Austria-Hungary	Russia	USA
GDP per capita						
1914	3,059	4,927	3,236	2,876	1,488*	4,799
1918	2,983	5,459	2,396	2,555	–	5,659
Military Burden						
1914	14.90	14.15	10.36	30.2	–	0.90
1918	38.80	27.00	59.39	17.2*	–	8.05
Defense Share						
1914	54.86	64.62	60.10	–	–	47.97
1918	51.61	54.89	77.65	–	–	48.50
Military Personnel (% of Population)						
1914	1.30	1.16	1.99	1.60	0.78	0.17
1918	13.70	9.10	13.59	1.54	6.12*	2.81

★ in the absences of data, prior year's figure used to illustrate level of mobilization

Sources: See Eloranta (2007) and Eloranta and Harrison (2010) for details. GDP is expressed in 1990 Geary-Khamis U.S. dollars

but the fact that its main ally, Austria-Hungary, was a poor nation with limited resources and was plagued by the inability to mobilize effectively. The collective mobilization of resources by the Allies was too big an obstacle for Germany to overcome.

What about the total cost of the conflict? It has been estimated that about nine million combatants and twelve million civilians died during the so-called Great War, with substantial property damage especially in France, Belgium, and Poland. According to Rondo Cameron and Larry Neal (2003), the direct financial losses arising from the Great War were $180–230 billion (1914 U.S. dollars), whereas the indirect losses of property and capital rose to over $150 billion. According to the most recent estimates, the total economic losses arising from the war could be as high as $525 billion (1914 U.S. dollars, Broadberry and Harrison 2005). The total of battle and non-battle deaths varied between the combatants. Countries that lost the most lives were those most directly involved in the fighting. For example, smaller nations like Serbia-Montenegro and Romania lost 5.7 and 3.3 percent of their overall population in the conflict. Turkey, France, and Germany also lost more than 3 percent of their population. The most battle deaths in absolute numbers were incurred by Russia, 1.8 million in total. Allied losses were more comprehensive than those by the Central Powers, 5.4 million compared to 4 million (Broadberry and Harrison 2005). An enormous amount of human capital was lost and an entire generation was scarred by the physical and psychological toll of the war.

The individual participants of World War I devised different solutions to pay for the enormous burden of war. Germany and France were less willing to tax their populations to pay for the war effort. Britain in turn funded the conflict by using a variety of different taxes, in addition to other means (namely, borrowing). The war was a huge shock to the Western economies in particular, since it shattered the international trading system and the gold standard. Inflation was also a big problem, and most of the participants imposed price and wage controls, as well as rationing systems (Broadberry and Harrison 2005, Webber and Wildavsky 1986). In order to maximize war production, once it became apparent that the war would last much longer than the generals had initially assumed, most nations brought businessmen into government service, usually to oversee supply chains and mobilization plans. The kind of corporatism that saw its inception in the 1920s with Mussolini's Italy was introduced already during the war in a more limited form, and big business gained a foothold in government acquisitions for some time to come. In a way, this was the beginning of the so-called Military-Industrial Complex in its modern form (Eloranta 2009, Koistinen 1980, McNeill 1982).

Aftermath of the war and conclusions

The Central Powers lost the war due to inferior resources and their inability to mobilize at a rate that would have overcome this gap. The aftermath was messy for all the participants for a variety of reasons. First of all, the Allies were set on punishing Germany for the war, and implemented harsh conditions and reparations on Germany in the Treaty of Versailles in 1919. Britain and France were also keen on having Germany pay them first, and only then would they pay back their loans to the only economic superpower left standing, the United States. This led to a series of negotiations and ultimately failure to pay back many of those loans once the Great Depression hit. Furthermore, Weimar Germany was almost predestined to an existence of uncertainty and political turmoil. Second, the demobilization after the war was difficult to implement, since the combatants really did not have a precedent for such a large-scale operation. Many women felt slighted for having to leave their jobs in the factories to make room for the returning soldiers. Third, economic uncertainty was an inevitable outcome of the war, which the depression in 1920–21 drove home. Fourth, the apocalyptic legacy of the war was further reinforced by the devastating epidemic known as the Spanish influenza, which by some estimates killed more than 50 million people worldwide.

Among the losers of the war, in addition to the Central Powers, were globalization and international economic cooperation. Devastation also visited the countless families who lost members as a result of the war. Many economies now had to maneuver in an atmosphere of uncertainty and loss of human capital. The European alliance system, which was supposed to stop this kind of insanity, also crumbled. Certain ethnic communities that were wiped out by genocidal actions of nations and the rules of war of yesteryear, which protected civilians from harm and constrained warfare from encompassing societies as a whole, were scattered to the winds of history.

Were there any winners in this war? It is difficult to claim, for example, that Britain or France really "won" the war in the traditional sense. They incurred almost incomprehensible losses, and in the interest of quenching their sense of revenge they set into motion the machinery that would lead to World War II. Some of the new states that gained independence might be considered winners of the war, like Finland and Poland. But challenges remained for them as well, such as how to set up their governments and how to defend their borders against much stronger neighbors. Many of these new democracies were also very unstable, and would devolve into authoritarian and/or military dictatorships in the 1930s, especially in Eastern Europe. European colonialism now faced an uphill climb due to the economic costs of the war and contributions of the colonial troops, who expected reciprocity. Yet, instead of really attempting to assign "winners," we should look at World War I as the beginning of an era of total war and instability.

Notes

1 Available from http://www.firstworldwar.com/source/crownprincewilhelm1913.htm. Accessed June 12, 2011.
2 Although, as Niall Ferguson (1999, Chapter 7) has pointed out, there was no uniform enthusiasm for war among those crowds. Some were quite apprehensive about the future.
3 An example of this was the Turks killing over a million Armenians, as well as other nationalities before, during, and after the war (Rummel 1998).
4 One of the points of contention is the famous Fischer debate, which concentrated on whether Germany had deliberately caused the war and had far-reaching war plans. See, for expample, Fischer (1967), Langdon (1986), Ferguson (1994), as well as the discussion of the rationality of German military actions as a response to their inability to compete in terms of military spending in Ferguson (1999), and Germany's perception of others' weaknesses in Sagan (1986). See Kaiser (1983) for further discussion.

References

Angell, N. (1972) *The Great Illusion: A Study of the Relation of Military Power in Nations to Their Economic and Social Advantage*, New York: Garland Publishing, Inc.

Berghahn, V.R. (1973) *Germany and the Approach of War in 1914*, New York: St. Martin's Press.

Broadberry, S. and Harrison, M. (eds.) (2005) *The Economics of World War I*, Cambridge: Cambridge University Press.

Cameron, R. and Neal, L. (2003) *A Concise Economic History of the World: From Paleolithic Times to the Present*, 4th edn., Oxford: Oxford University Press.

Davis, L.E. and Engerman, S.L. (2006) *Naval Blockades in Peace and War: An Economic History since 1750*, Cambridge: Cambridge University Press.

Eloranta, J. (2007) 'From the great illusion to the Great War: military spending behaviour of the Great Powers, 1870–1913', *European Review of Economic History*, 11: 255–83.

Eloranta, J. (2009) 'Rent seeking and collusion in the military allocation decisions of Finland, Sweden, and Great Britain, 1920–38', *Economic History Review*, 62: 23–44.

Eloranta, J. and Harrison, M. (2010) 'War and disintegration, 1914–1950' in S. Broadberry and K.H. O'Rourke (eds.) *The Cambridge Economic History of Modern Europe, Volume 2: 1870 to the Present,* Cambridge: Cambridge University Press.

Ferguson, N. (1994) 'Public finance and national security: the domestic origins of the First World War revisited', *Past and Present*, 142: 141–68.

Ferguson, N. (1999) *The Pity of War: Explaining World War I*, New York: Basic Books.

Ferguson, N. (2001) *The Cash Nexus: Money and Power in the Modern World, 1700–2000*, New York: Basic Books.

Ferguson, N. (2006) *The War of the World: Twentieth-Century Conflict and the Descent of the West*, London: Allen Lane.

Fischer, F. (1967) *Germany's Aims in the First World War*, New York: W.W. Norton & Company Inc.

Geller, D.S. and Singer, J.D. (1998) *Nations at War: A Scientific Study of International Conflict.* Cambridge: Cambridge University Press.

Gillette, A. (2006) 'Why did they fight the Great War? A multi-level class analysis of the causes of the First World War', *The History Teacher,* 40: 45–58.

Hobson, J.A. (1965 reprint) *Imperialism*, Ann Arbor, MI: University of Michigan Press.

Huntington, S.P. (1996) *The Clash of Civilizations and the Remaking of World Order*, New York: Simon & Schuster.

Kaiser, D.E. (1983) 'Germany and the origins of the First World War', *Journal of Modern History,* 55: 442–74.

Keegan, J. (1999) *The First World War*, London: Hutchinson.

Kennedy, P. (1976) *The Rise and Fall of British Naval Mastery*, London: A. Lane.

Kennedy, P. (1989) *The Rise and Fall of the Great Powers: Economic Change and Military Conflict from 1500 to 2000*, London: Fontana.

Kennedy, P.M. (1984) 'The First World War and the international power system', *International Security,* 9: 7–40.

Koistinen, P.A.C. (1980) *The Military-Industrial Complex: A Historical Perspective,* New York: Praeger Publishers.

Langdon, J.W. (1986) 'Emerging from Fischer's shadow: recent examinations of the crisis of July 1914', *The History Teacher,* 20: 63–86.

Lenin, V.I. (1963) 'Imperialism, the highest stage of capitalism', in *Selected Works.* Moscow: Progress.

Levy, J.S. (1990–91) 'Preferences, constraints, and choices in July 1914', *International Security*, 15: 151–86.

McNeill, W.H. (1982) *The Pursuit of Power: Technology, Armed Force, and Society since A.D. 1000*, Chicago, IL: University of Chicago Press.

Modelski, G. and Thompson, W.R. (1988) *Seapower in Global Politics, 1494–1993*, Basingstoke: Macmillan Press.

Mombauer, A. (2001) *Helmuth von Moltke and the Origins of the First World War*, Cambridge: Cambridge University Press.

North, R.C., Holsti, O.R., Zaninovich, M.G. and Zinnes, D.A. (1963a) *Content Analysis: A Handbook with Applications for the Study of International Crisis*, Evanston, IL: Northwestern University Press.

North, R.C., Brody, R.A. and Holsti, O.R. (1963b) *Some Empirical Data on The Conflict Spiral,*. Stanford, CA: Stanford University.

Offer, A. (1989) *The First World War: An Agrarian Interpretation*, Oxford: Clarendon Press.

Offer, A. (1995) 'Going to war in 1914: a matter of honor?', *Politics & Society*, 23: 213–41.

O'Rourke, K.H. and Williamson, J.G. (2002) 'When did globalization begin?', *European Review of Economic History*, 6: 23–50.

Rowe, D. (2005) 'The tragedy of liberalism: how globalization caused the First World War', *Security Studies,* 14: 407–47.

Rummel, R.J. (1998) *Statistics of Democide: Genocide and Mass Murder since 1900*, Piscataway, NJ: Transaction Publishers.

Sagan, S.D. (1986) '1914 revisited: allies, offense, and instability', *International Security*, 11: 151–75.

Steiner, Z.S. (1977) *Britain and the Origins of the First World War*, London: Macmillan Press.

Stevenson, D. (2011) 'From Balkan conflict to global conflict: the spread of the First World War, 1914–1918', *Foreign Policy Analysis*, 7: 169–82.

Strachan, H. (2011) 'Clausewitz and the First World War', *Journal of Military History,* 75: 367–91.
Taylor, A.J.P. (1969) *War by Time-Table: How the First World War Began,* London: Macdonald & Co.
Tooley, T.H. (2005) 'Merchants of death revisited: armaments, bankers, and the First World War', *Journal of Libertarian Studies,* 19: 37–78.
Trachtenberg, M. (1990–91) 'The meaning of mobilization in 1914', *International Security,* 15: 120–50.
Van Evera, S. (1984) 'The cult of the offensive and the origins of the First World War', *International Security,* 9: 58–107.
Webber, C. and Wildavsky, A. (1986) *A History of Taxation and Expenditure in the Western World,* New York: Simon and Schuster.
Williamson, S.R. (1988) 'The origins of World War I', *Journal of Interdisciplinary History,* 18: 795–818.

9

THE CLASSICAL
GOLD STANDARD

Kris James Mitchener

Introduction

The classical gold standard was the first truly international monetary system based on fixed exchange rates. It emerged during the second half of the nineteenth century, lasted into the second decade of the twentieth century, and underpinned the growth in trade and overseas investment prior to World War I. At its peak, more than 35 countries and colonies used gold to back domestic currency issues, accounting for roughly 70 percent of the world's trade and 67 percent of its GDP (Chernyshoff, Jacks, and Taylor 2009). Under this regime, countries individually adhered to rules requiring them to fix the prices of their domestic currencies in terms of a specified amount of gold. Long-run adherents followed policy prescriptions (mainly, limitations on the issuance of domestic currency) that made the defense of these fixed exchange rates feasible. This chapter examines how the gold standard operated, why countries moved from silver and bimetallic standards to gold, what the costs and benefits of being on gold were, and how economies performed while part of this fixed-exchange regime.[1]

The gold standard's origin partly dates to a historical accident, in 1717, when master of the mint, Sir Isaac Newton, mistakenly set the price of silver in terms of its gold coins too high relative to the market-determined global price of silver. This mispricing drove all the silver coins from circulation and led to England having a currency backed only by gold. England later made gold legal tender in 1821.[2] Portugal was the next European country to adopt gold as its unit of account, in 1854, and most other larger economies from that continent joined gold in the 1870s (including Germany, Sweden, Denmark, Norway, the Netherlands, Belgium, France, and Switzerland).[3] Many later developing economies, including the United States, the periphery of Europe, and most of Latin America and Asia joined in the three subsequent decades. Some countries, such as Japan and Germany, were assisted in their ability to join gold by winning wars and acquiring specie through war indemnities imposed on the vanquished. China was a notable exception: it stayed on silver throughout the period prior to World War I (Friedman 1990, Mitchener and Voth 2010). Spain was another country that did not adopt gold, preferring a de facto fiat standard and floating exchange rate after 1883 so it had the option to monetize its fiscal deficits (Sabate, Gadea, and Escario 2006).

1914 marked the unofficial end of the classical gold standard period since countries found it increasingly difficult to maintain the free movement of gold once the hostilities of World War I commenced.

Operation of the gold standard

The classical gold standard had three key features that ensured its operation (Bloomfield 1981). First, the central bank or monetary authority set the mint parity – an officially determined price of gold in terms of domestic currency.[4] Second, countries permitted gold to be freely exported and imported, and the monetary authority stood ready to convert the home currency to gold upon demand.[5] Third, the monetary authority established a rule linking the money supply to its stock of gold. Some countries like Japan, Britain, Finland, Norway, and England adopted "fiduciary systems" whereby statutes allowed the monetary authorities to issue a fixed amount of paper currency unbacked by gold (but usually collateralized by government bonds). Additional paper money issuance had to be backed by gold reserves. Other countries like Belgium, the Netherlands, and Switzerland legalized so-called "proportional systems." In these countries, monetary laws decreed that the amount of gold (and, starting in the nineteenth century, also foreign exchange reserves) could not fall below some proportion of circulating paper currency (usually 35 to 40 percent) (Eichengreen 1996). By the first decade of the twentieth century, countries had increased the proportion of foreign exchange reserves used for backing their domestic note issues (i.e., currencies of countries that were themselves on gold) from 10 percent to 20 percent to satisfy these statutory rules.[6]

Fixed exchange rates between countries thus emerged as a result of each country fixing the price of its currency relative to the numéraire (gold).[7] Monetary authorities had to adhere to their monetary rules so that exchange rates would stay close to mint parity and not deviate beyond the so-called gold points.[8] If the spot rate deviated too much from the gold points, it could induce market participants to ship gold from one country to the other in order to capture arbitrage profits. This no-arbitrage condition in the market for precious metals tended to reinforce prevailing exchange rates as did credible commitments to the maintenance of fixed exchange rates (Eichengreen 1996).[9] Officer (1996) provides evidence that persistent violations in gold points between England and the U.S. did not exist and suggests that the gold standard was not inefficient in this manner. In contrast to previous studies which viewed the gold points as having been more or less stable over time, more recent research utilizing higher frequency data on the sterling–dollar rate suggests a process of increasing market integration over the course of the gold standard (Canjels, Prakash-Canjels, and Taylor 2004)

Regime stability and adjustment under the gold standard

One of the apparent features of the classical gold standard is its durability – lasting for more than 40 years – at least for the core countries. Theoretical work suggests that the gold standard was a smooth operating system that delivered price and exchange-rate stability – automatically eliminating balance-of-payment problems through adjustments in money, prices, and trade. As theorized by David Hume (1752), a fall in exports due to an external shock (e.g., a bad harvest) would be automatically corrected if a country were on the gold standard. All else equal, the trade balance would turn negative, resulting in an outflow of gold from the country. Because the monetary authority followed a rule that linked the supply of money to gold, the money supply would fall in response to the trade deficit. Following the quantity theory of money, prices would in turn fall, making exports relatively cheaper and imports more expensive. This automatic adjustment process (operating through the goods market) eventually balanced trade and eliminated the (initial) current account deficit.[10] Some have argued that limited use of sterilization policies (e.g., adjustments in the discount rate aimed at offsetting or moderating the effects of gold flows) during this period appear to have facilitated the automatic working of the specie-flow mechanism (Catão and Solomou 2005, Eichengreen and Flandreau 1997, Bordo and Schwartz 1984).

Hume's simple price–specie–flow mechanism provides an elegant explanation as to why convertibility crises may have been less frequent during the gold standard period.[11] It nonetheless makes strong assumptions that subsequently have been challenged by models emphasizing other adjustment mechanisms, including spending, capital flows, and the operation of the law of one price (Whale 1937, Ford 1962, Scammell 1965, McCloskey and Zecher 1976).[12] Moreover, in practice, countries deviated from Hume's price–specie–flow model. Monetary authorities often manipulated the financial (capital) account by changing discount rates (the rate of interest at which it was willing to discount money market paper) and/or intervening in gold markets. Following the situation of the earlier example, a country could reduce balance-of-payments pressure due to a trade deficit by raising its discount rate and attracting short-term capital flows from abroad. As the discount rate of a country rose, other domestic interest rates followed suit. Foreign investors in turn responded by purchasing short-term, interest-bearing assets in the country that raised its discount rate. Active and unfettered capital markets thus enabled capital to flow inward and offset the initial current account deficit.

Monetary authorities had other options besides the discount rate to correct current imbalances and minimize exchange rate instability. They could manipulate their backing ratios (since many held excess gold reserves) or they could use gold devices (including paying more than the statutory amount for gold bars, varying the purchase price of foreign coins, and extending interest free loans to gold importers) to intervene in the gold market and change the incentives for gold to flow in or out of the country. In short, adjustments due to payments imbalances were largely corrected through capital flows and transfers of currency balances in New York, London, Paris, and Berlin.

Monetary authorities playing by "the rules of the game" (a term coined by John Maynard Keynes well after the end of the classical gold standard) changed discount rates or engaged in open market operations to resolve balance-of-payments problems, but central banks possessed latitude in timing these actions as well as whether to even use them (perhaps placing some weight on domestic policy outcomes rather than external balance). Despite the belief that central banks needed to act in concert to avoid weakening their pegs, Bloomfield (1959) failed to find a tight relationship between short-run changes in gold reserves and discount rates. Subsequent research has shown frequent and sizeable violations to the "rules of the game" by core countries of the gold standard system.[13] Such violations are consistent with the notion that central banks in core countries may have been able to sterilize gold flows and pursue a degree of monetary independence for short periods so long as they stayed within the limits of the gold points (Eichengreen 1992, 1996, Bordo and Kydland 1995, Bordo and Schwartz 1996, Bordo and MacDonald 2005). Following these empirical observations and the theoretical work of Krugman (1991) and Svennson (1994), scholars began to describe the gold standard's operation as an early type of a target zone – a fixed exchange rate system with bands that are determined by the gold points. Bordo and MacDonald (2005) show that, within the gold points, monetary authorities had scope to violate the "rules of the game" temporarily and conduct independent monetary policy, in part because financial markets believed that government commitments to fixed exchange were credible, and would do whatever it would take to maintain gold convertibility at existing parities.

Recent research has suggested that other mechanisms may have provided some additional stability for the core countries during this period. Supply shocks occurred with frequencies similar to later periods, but Bayoumi and Eichengreen (1996) and Bordo (1993) suggest that the aggregate supply curves were steeper due to lower nominal rigidities.[14] As a result, adjustments in output and employment were quicker. Hatton and Williamson (1994, 1998) and Esteves and Khoudour-Casteras (2009) stress international mobility of labor during this era, which promoted labor market adjustment through in and out migration. Catão and Solomou (2005) emphasize that fluctuations in real exchange rates that arose from significant changes in the gold value of currencies on the periphery (due to imperfect gold pegs or alternative monetary standards) served as an additional adjustment mechanism.

Eichengreen (1996) argues that two factors, system credibility and cooperation, account for the stability of the gold standard system. First, isolation of central banks from political pressure (especially to respond to internal balance) enabled them to operate in a way that enhanced the credibility of the system. They could maintain a laser-like focus on the value of their currencies and on preventing gold outflows that might undermine reserve backing requirements. Since other policy goals were secondary to defending parities and departures were seen by the public as something that could only be contemplated in emergencies (i.e., wars), this policy regime stabilized financial markets in core countries and made monetary management easier (Eichengreen and Flandreau 1997). That is, the credibility of the regime assured investors such that if a currency started losing value, markets anticipated the central bank would defend the parity, and in anticipation of this, would buy currency and hence bid the price of the currency back toward parity. The belief by markets that the pegs were credible (at least in the core) often rendered official interventions redundant or unnecessary. Second, central banks cooperated in ways that limited a divergence in policy objectives. Central bank coordination in short-term interest rates ensured that gold flowed in stabilizing directions – at least in the core countries of Western Europe. And, this was made possible by the first condition, i.e., monetary authorities could do this, in part, because they were able to subvert internal balance (unemployment and output) to external balance.

Emergence and diffusion of the gold standard

Discussions for a global monetary standard began in earnest with an International Monetary Conference in 1867, although, as described above, adoption of the gold standard was only gradual.[15] Some countries, like France, actively resisted the move to gold and fought the influx of silver from neighboring countries (Germany) that had already moved to gold (Flandreau 1996). Economists and historians have speculated why countries clung to bimetallism, i.e. currency systems using both gold and silver in a fixed ratio. Flandreau (1996) argues bimetallism could have persisted and that there was nothing inevitable about the shift to gold. Some have suggested that technological hurdles in minting coins that were both small enough for daily use and sufficiently standardized to prevent counterfeiting stood in the way of adopting only gold (Redish 1990). But once steam presses were invented and counterfeiting became less of a problem, adoption of gold did not follow immediately. Silver discoveries in the early 1870s that affected the price of gold in terms of silver, an adequate supply of global gold, Germany's demonetization of silver, or the interests of the "creditor class" have also been suggested as reasons for the switch from bimetallism and silver standards to gold, but scholars have argued that none of these explanations has proved definitive

(Flandreau 1996). Morys (2007) argues that the early pan-European movement toward gold between the 1850s and early 1870s might have been motivated by having sufficient quantities of gold (a problem solved by gold discoveries in California and Australia in the 1850s), the relative convenience of gold coins versus silver, and concerns about the continued operation of a bimetallic standard.

Flandreau (1996) and Eichengreen (1996) posited that economies may have benefited from being on gold if their major trading partners were also on gold since being on the same monetary standard lowered the transactions costs of trade. If countries moved from paper currency to gold, then conducting trade under the auspices of fixed exchange rates would reduce exchange-rate risk and hence lower transaction costs. In addition, if trade bills were financed in currencies denominated in gold (as they were in the London money market) or purchases of goods were directly invoiced in currencies denominated in gold (e.g., pound sterling), then transaction costs might fall further with the global adoption of a single monetary standard. And, as more countries adopted gold, the reduction in transactions costs would be larger due to strategic complementarities. Hence, switching costs fell. These network effects thus may help explain the diffusion of the gold standard. Working in conjunction with the network effect, countries may have "scrambled for gold" if they anticipated that other countries would abandon silver or bimetallic standards. They would choose to adopt gold sooner rather than later so that they would not sell silver at depreciated prices (Gallarotti 1995).

Meissner (2005) tested whether network externalities were a factor tipping countries toward joining the gold standard. Such a test perhaps makes most sense after 1873, when Germany and France had joined the gold standard. That said, using duration analysis, he found that countries which traded more with countries already on gold switched to gold sooner. A one-standard-deviation increase in trade with gold standard countries decreased the time to adoption by roughly four years.[16] The results also appear to indicate that countries on silver standards (e.g., Holland) had a higher propensity to switch as more countries moved to gold and a smaller proportion of its trade was with other silver standard countries. Even Asian countries, which had an informal silver bloc, began to move to gold as more of their trade moved west to Britain, France, Germany, and the United States and less was with traditional (silver) trading partners like China (Mitchener and Voth 2010). This suggests that network externalities were part of the story for explaining the timing of when countries moved to gold; however, other factors, including the quality of fiscal institutions, the development of the banking sector, and economic development appear to have also influenced the timing of adoption.

Although many countries joined gold, for some it was hard to remain on the standard. The core countries of Western Europe, Japan, and the British Colonies were able to maintain formal links to gold through the outbreak of World War I, but the peg proved less durable in other parts of the globe, including Latin America and southern Europe (Bordo and Kydland 1995, Mitchener and Weidenmier 2009, Morys 2009).

Benefits of gold standard adoption

In addition to deciding when to join gold, a related literature has emerged that explores why countries adopted gold. While there is certainly potential for overlap between these two questions, the latter literature focuses on the costs and benefits of adoption rather than explaining the timing or sequence of countries adopting. In particular, this literature examines the decisions of policymakers.

Borrowing costs

The seminal paper by Bordo and Kydland (1995) established the notion that joining the gold standard affects policymaking. The authors suggest that being on the gold standard tied the hands of the monetary and fiscal authorities of a country by committing them to a rule, and this rule served as a credible commitment mechanism that solved the classic time-inconsistency problem (Kydland and Prescott 1977). Government policy is said to be time inconsistent when a policy plan that is determined to be optimal and to hold indefinitely into the future is subsequently revised. Suppose that a government sells debt to finance a war. From an *ex ante* perspective, it is optimal for the government to service its debt obligations. However, once the bonds have been sold, it is optimal for the government to default unless there is a commitment mechanism that ties the hands of monetary authorities. In the absence of a commitment mechanism, it is time inconsistent for the government to repay its debt obligations. Private agents will anticipate the government's incentive to default and they will not buy bonds, forcing the government to rely on taxes or money creation. Overall, the existence of an enforcement mechanism, such as a credible threat to deny the government access to borrowing in the future, means that a socially optimal, but time inconsistent policy of borrowing can be supported as an equilibrium outcome. Bordo and Kydland (1995) suggested that, as a credible commitment mechanism, adherence to the gold standard prevented the inflation and stagflation that later plagued economies in the 1970s. They also argued that it enabled monetary and fiscal authorities to employ seigniorage and obtain favorable rates of borrowing.

Bordo and Kydland (1995) also discuss how the gold standard operated as a contingent rule with an escape clause. Countries could suspend specie convertibility in the event of a war or a fiscal emergency; however, it was well understood that a country would return as soon as possible to specie convertibility at the pre-war parity. Generally, resumption occurred after a "reasonable" delay period during which a country would impose deflationary policies to retire fiat currency printed to finance emergency expenditure. The United States and France, for example, fought wars in the 1860s and 1870s and issued large amounts of irredeemable paper currency and debt. Following the end of these wars, both countries imposed deflationary policies to restore convertibility following the cessation of hostilities, and both had returned to a specie standard by 1880. (See Chapter 3 by Burdekin and Siklos in this volume for further discussion of the deflation of this period.)

To explore the empirical implications of viewing the gold standard as a contingent rule, Bordo and Rockoff (1996) and Obstfeld and Taylor (2003) examine the performance of sovereign bonds for countries that adopted gold and those that did not. In particular, these papers examine country risk (also called "political risk" or "default risk"), defined as the differential between gold or sterling-denominated bonds in the home country and the risk-free rate of borrowing (in this period, the British consol). The hypothesis being tested is that the monetary and fiscal probity associated with adopting gold ought to have been rewarded by markets in the form of lower borrowing costs. They find that the gold standard lowered sovereign or country risk by approximately 30–40 basis points.

A more recent series of papers suggests that borrowing costs were not significantly lower when countries adopted gold. Flandreau and Zumer (2004) find that the gold standard had no effect on sovereign yields once a broader set of economic and political variables controls are considered. They suggest that the size of public debts and other fiscal measures were particularly important in determining rates of sovereign borrowing. Ferguson and Schularick (2006) also find that the gold standard effect disappears once the sample of sovereign borrowers is expanded to include the universe of debtors on the London market.

In particular, they highlight the role of being part of an empire in reducing sovereign spreads. Using a sample of 55,000 sovereign bond returns, Alquist and Chabot (2010) find no association between gold standard adherence and lower borrowing rates. They focus on "excess returns," and show that, after conditioning on UK risk factors, countries off gold did not have excess returns relative to those on gold. Their results appear to be robust to allowing for sensitivities of portfolios to UK risk factors to vary according to whether a country was on the gold standard, to including proxies that capture the effect of fiscal, monetary, and trade shocks on the commitment to gold, and to controlling for the effect of membership in the British Empire.

Perhaps a more straightforward implication of the contingent rule literature is whether adopting the gold standard was perceived as credible. To examine whether investors considered the gold standard credible, one can look at whether the risk of exiting the gold standard was priced into the bonds of countries that had joined. The premium that investors demand for the risk of abandoning a fixed exchange rate and depreciating the currency is known as "currency risk," and a straightforward way of measuring this, using long-term sovereign bonds, is to calculate the yield spread between a country's paper bonds and gold bonds. The former are payable in domestic currency while the latter are payable in gold (or pound sterling). Using data on weekly sovereign bond prices of paper currency and pound sterling (or gold) denominated debt, Mitchener and Weidenmier (2009) identify the currency-risk component of sovereign yield spreads for nine of the largest emerging market borrowers for the period 1870–1913. Five years after a country joined the gold standard, paper currency bonds traded at significantly higher interest rates (more than 400 basis points on average) than a country's foreign currency debt denominated in pound sterling, suggesting investors did not perceive this hard peg as credible for emerging market borrowers. Investors also expected exchange rates to fall by roughly 20 percent even after emerging market borrowers had joined the gold standard. They find additional evidence that emerging market *short-term* interest rates also reflect market beliefs that exchange-rate pegs would not persist.

Trade

If lower borrowing costs did not materialize for many gold standard countries, were there other potential gains to adoption? One may have been that as more countries linked to gold, exchange-rate volatility declined, lowering the costs of trade in both goods and financial assets. In turn, real trade volumes between adopters of the fixed exchange rate regime ought to rise. Thus, research has focused on examining whether transacting in a single currency reduced trade costs either by lowering exchange-rate volatility or by reducing other transactions costs that arise from operating in multiple currencies.[17] Recent evidence suggests that trade costs were indeed lower during the classical gold standard period (Jacks 2006, Jacks, Meissner, and Novy 2011). And, as more countries adopted gold, such benefits could increase through network externalities.

Using quinquennial panel data for the period 1870–1910, Lopéz-Córdova and Meissner (2003) estimate a gravity model of bilateral trade flows to test for the effects of currency unions and gold-standard membership. After controlling for other influences such as distance, language, and a common border, they find a large, positive effect for historical currency unions as well as a large effect from gold-standard membership. Estevadeordal, Frantz, and Taylor (2003) and Flandreau and Maurel (2005) report similar results of increases in trade due to the gold standard of between 50 and 100 percent. Using a larger and more comprehensive database of bilateral trade flows from 1870–1913, Mitchener and Weidenmier (2008) find that gold increased bilateral trade by around 20 to 30 percent. The measured effects are significantly smaller than those reported in earlier studies, in part, because the latter paper includes substantially more trade pairs that are non-European. As a result, the effects on bilateral trade of being part of a formal political empire dwarf those of being part of the gold standard. Indeed, while currencies like the pound sterling were "as good as gold," it may have been the case that sterling was in many ways better than gold. British exporters and importers preferred to draw and be drawn on in pounds sterling. Investor and trader preference for carrying out transactions in sterling or sterling-denominated bills of exchange meant that it was advantageous for dominions and colonies to also carry out their transactions in sterling.

Although these studies correlate economic outcomes with the adoption of a hard peg, they provide less insight into why countries would willingly choose to tie the hands of their monetary authorities and join the gold standard. To get at this issue, one can examine the contemporaneous policy debates and identify factors that concerned leaders around the time of adoption. Then, one can test whether *ex ante* beliefs about the gold standard's effects matched *ex post* outcomes. Mitchener, Shizume, and Weidenmier (2010) take this approach in their study of Japan's decision to join gold in 1897. Evidence from the legislative debates of the 1890s suggests that policymakers believed gold standard adoption could impact borrowing costs, debt issuance, domestic investment, and trade. Their research finds no discernable trend in bond prices that would indicate that investors anticipated lower rates of borrowing, nor do they observe a boom in domestic investment in the wake of adopting the gold standard. Japanese policymakers of the nineteenth century also suggested that going onto gold would affect trade, but they were decidedly mixed as to whether it would increase it or reduce it. For example, opponents of adopting gold (like the business community that exported their wares) argued that Japan was receiving large benefits from being on a silver standard whereas proponents (like the ruling party) had suggested that Japan would benefit from lower transactions costs and reduced exchange-rate volatility. Both turned out to be correct. Estimates from a gravity model of Japanese exports suggest that Japan received a large boost in trade when Japan and its partners were on the silver standard. However, gold standard adoption also significantly boosted exports and trade. It appears to have done so in two ways. First, Japan adopted the currency system through which most of the world's trade was being conducted by the end of the nineteenth century. By joining the gold standard, it lowered transactions costs and exchange rate volatility vis-à-vis other gold standard countries. The fact that Japan abandoned its regional and historically relevant, silver-standard trading partners for the gold standard, enabled it to plug into the monetary system through which most of the world's trade was being conducted by the end of the nineteenth century. By 1897, approximately 60 percent of Japanese exports and total trade were with countries that were on the gold standard (or countries taking measures to join the gold club within a couple of years). Second, Japan's fortuitous timing of gold standard adoption proved beneficial for some of its exports. In particular, Japanese exports to silver standard countries received an additional boost in competitiveness because Japan adopted the gold standard right as silver began to appreciate against gold.

There are perhaps even more prominent political debates over the gold standard, which also suggest an important role for trade in terms of the decision of whether to adopt this monometallic standard. For example, in the United States, currency choice dominated political discussions in the last quarter of the nineteenth century. The "Greenback" movement sought to maintain the floating currency that had come about during the Civil War and later, and after silver was demonetized in 1873, joined forces with "silverites" (who wanted free coinage of silver) to prevent formal adoption of a gold standard. These monetary debates culminated in the 1896 presidential election, when William Jennings Bryan famously argued, "you shall not crucify mankind upon a cross of gold." Historians have traditionally emphasized that agrarian interests were opposed to a gold standard because of heavy debt burden, worsened by a gradual fall in prices between 1873 and 1896; they therefore favored silver or a floating currency in order to alleviate their debt burdens. Frieden (1997) argues that being on silver rather than gold would have also raised the prices of exports, including wheat, cotton, and minerals – all products for which tariffs or other forms of trade protection were less feasible alternatives – and therefore helped producers of such goods. On the other hand, manufacturers concentrated in the northeastern part of the country had no reason to support gold since they could achieve higher relative prices through trade protection. Evidence from congressional votes on monetary legislation suggests that concerns of exporters (farmers and miners) were more important in driving opposition to gold during this period than constituents' levels of debt (as measured by real estate debt). Nevertheless, the real burden of debt contracts would have been reduced through devaluation and exit from gold, helping to explain why opposition to gold proved broad based.

Capital market integration

If exchange-rate stability delivered decreased uncertainty, it may have also promoted financial market integration. As a result, it could have in turn pushed out the supply of capital available for overseas investment. Interest rate convergence took place as the gold standard spread around the world, indicating greater capital market integration. In some though not all regression specifications, Faria, Mauro, Minnoni, and Zaklan (2006) find evidence that the gold standard seems to have increased the supply of financing during the gold standard period, although their study points toward colonial relationships as being quantitatively more important. Esteves (2011) also finds that British and German capital outflows are positively associated with recipient countries being on the gold standard. Indeed, the flow of capital and levels of integration reached prior to 1914 were only obtained again after 1970, but it appears the causal link to gold is far from certain (Flandreau and Zumer 2004).

Macroeconomic performance under the gold standard

Prices, output, and policy constraints

Scholars have long associated the gold standard, not only with exchange rate stability, but also with price stability (Bordo 1981). Since money stocks were ultimately limited by the stock of gold, it was believed that changes in prices would be relatively small and that this system of fixed exchange rates would stabilize prices. However, Cooper (1982) argues that price stability did not occur in either the short run or long run. For example, his data on the United States show that short-run variations in wholesale prices were higher during the pre-World War I gold standard period than from 1949 to 1979: the standard deviation of annual movements in prices was 5.4 percent in the earlier period and only 4.8 percent in the latter period.

There were long secular swings in prices over the period of the gold standard, with deflation from the early 1870s up until 1896, and then inflation thereafter. Based on data from the core countries of the United Kingdom, Germany, France, and the United States, prices declined by between 40 and 50 percent until the gold discoveries of the late 1890s, and then rose by roughly equivalent amounts thereafter (Cooper 1982). The parabolic shape of price movements over the gold standard period thus produces the illusion of long-run stability, but offered little protection to financial contracts other than those with very long durations.

To understand why the standard view differs substantially from the observed outcomes, it is important to understand that prices will be stable only if the relative price between gold and other goods does not change (Barro 1979); however, if gold supplies vary substantially or the public's demand for gold is not perfectly elastic, then even the built-in nominal anchor will not guarantee price stability (Cooper 1982). Indeed, gold discoveries in the 1850s and 1890s were major shocks that changed global gold supplies. Rockoff (1984) and others have argued that nineteenth-century gold supplies were largely dominated by these discoveries and by a few technological improvements which appear to be exogenous to price movements. Eichengreen and McLean (1994) further show that gold production only responded to the implied changes in prices around these episodes with relatively long lags, and that regional production in major gold producers like Australia and the United States seems not to have always lined up with price movements. This suggests that actual linkages between gold and prices were weaker than theorized. In fact, under the gold standard, price stability and other domestic objectives were relinquished to the maintenance of exchange-rate stability.

Examining the time series behavior of macroeconomic variables provides some insight into whether the gold standard performed well relative to later periods. While there is some evidence that the pre-World War I gold standard delivered better output performance for countries like the UK and U.S. in comparison to the three decades after its collapse (Bordo 1981), broader samples of countries and comparisons to other time periods reveal somewhat different results. Comparing the performance of seven countries for the classical gold standard period and the period after 1973 (when no nominal anchor existed), Bordo (1993) finds no notable differences in output and inflation volatility. Recent research also suggests that the classical gold standard did not worsen exchange rate volatility and even buffered countries from terms-of-trade shocks (Chernyshoff, Jacks, and Taylor 2009), perhaps because wages and prices were more flexible than thereafter (Hanes and James 2003). Even if the gold standard delivered better output performance for some countries, it is quite clear it hinged on subverting internal objectives to external objectives. Moreover, any comparisons over time and across countries ultimately depend on whether it is possible to classify countries according to exchange rate regimes in meaningful ways. Rose (2011) suggests there is considerable difficulty in doing so for all but those countries with fixed exchange rates and capital mobility.

The policy trilemma and the periphery

Another way to view the constraints of the gold standard is in terms of the so-called open economy macroeconomics policy trilemma. In a world of fixed exchange rates and perfectly mobile capital, central banks or monetary authorities have very little room to employ monetary policy for domestic purposes or for internal balance. Changes in interest rates lead to inflows and outflows of currency and place pressure on the exchange rate to change. As a result, when countries adopted gold, policymakers lost a tool – the ability to fight a recession or to rein in a boom by changing the money supply or interest rates.[18] During the classical gold standard period, central banks thus subverted internal balance (objectives centered on full employment and output) to external balance (exchange-rate stability), in part because the costs of doing so were lower than later when the gold standard returned in the 1920s (Eichengreen 1996).

However, consider an economy on the periphery that is perhaps less diversified in its production and more reliant on commodities for exports. It would likely be subject to greater variance in output due to terms of trade shocks. For such a country, even if adopting the gold standard lowered borrowing costs or trade costs, choosing to adopt gold would be costlier than a more diversified economy as it would require larger adjustments in prices and output to maintain the peg. If this characterization describes countries on the periphery, they may have been bound to play by the "rules of the game" more so than others in order to convince markets of their commitments; this would mean raising interest rates when faced with gold drains and possessing little latitude to pursue domestic policy by postponing or delaying changes in discount rates.

Recent evidence indicates that gold shocks were sizable on the periphery, suggesting that adjustment would have to be larger and consequently more difficult to tolerate politically (Morys 2008).[19] A shaky or young new democracy (perhaps, for example, one in Latin America in the nineteenth century) may have thus found it less desirable to maintain a peg in light of the potential political costs to having lower domestic output or higher unemployment. The trilemma thus helps us understand why pegs were in fact harder to maintain on the periphery and why, outside the core countries, banking crises and convertibility crises were common events during the classical gold standard era. Countries in southern Europe and Latin America (e.g., Argentina, Portugal, Brazil, Italy, and Chile) were often forced to suspend gold, and widespread financial crises in the 1870s and 1890s took place.

As noted above, investors did not perceive many of the pegs on the periphery as credible: they believed that at some future date these countries would deviate from their policy rules and depreciate. And, if markets did not find the pegs credible, then capital could flow in de-stabilizing directions. Such was often the case at the periphery, where instability was commonplace, and cooperation and coordination from core central banks was largely missing. Perhaps central banks at the core were simply less willing to lend a hand to those economies facing such shocks or they were better suited for sharing the same currency (Eichengreen 1995, 1996, Aceña and Reis 2000). While there is little evidence that the gold standard itself was causally linked to a lower incidence of financial crises (Catão 2006, Adalet and Eichengreen 2005), some have suggested that remittances coming from millions of European workers who had moved to the Americas may have offset some of the instability resulting from weaker commitments to hard pegs (Esteves and Khoudour-Casteras 2009).

Acknowledgment

The author thanks Rui Pedro Esteves, David Jacks, Matthias Morys, Kirsten Wandschneider, and Marc Weidenmier for helpful comments and suggestions.

Notes

1 For review essays and comprehensive volumes on the classical gold standard complementary to the treatment here, see, for example, Bordo and Schwartz (1984), Eichengreen and Flandreau (1997), Meissner (2003), and Officer (2008).
2 Nogues-Marco (2011) develops a model and then describes how England's de facto monometallic standard emerged as a result of it choosing a legal bimetallic ratio that was "too high" relative to the market. Since the bullion market was integrated and Amsterdam's legal rate was much closer to the market's rate, silver was driven out of circulation in England while Holland was able to maintain bimetallism.
3 Some British colonies, such as those making up modern-day Canada and Australia, adopted gold in the 1850s.

4   Bank notes were convertible into gold and central banks evolved as issuers of these notes.
5   Some monetary authorities charged a fee, known as brassage, to coin bullion.
6   The practice of augmenting gold reserves with foreign exchange reserves became much more important during the interwar era when the gold standard was resurrected in the 1920s.
7   For example, during the classical gold era, Britain exchanged £3 17s 10½d per ounce of gold while the U.S. exchanged $20.67 per ounce of gold. Dividing the U.S. price of gold by the British price yields the par exchange rate of $4.867 per pound.
8   Small deviations existed due to insurance, shipping costs, and brassage.
9   Transactions between countries were often conducted using bills of exchange since these had lower transactions costs than payments settled in specie. When exchange rates deviated excessively from mint parity, beyond what were known as the "gold points," then transactions would switch to gold coin rather than bills of exchange (Morys 2008).
10 Hume's model was based on a gold coin standard, but in the late-nineteenth century, as described above, bank notes (backed by gold) primarily circulated. Monetary authorities could, in turn, either allow gold flows to have their full effect on the balance of payments or offset its effect through sterilization (Morys 2008).
11 It can also be used to demonstrate how commodity money standards can potentially promote price stability.
12 Adjustment through the capital or financial account was also inherently faster than through the changes in goods prices emphasized in Hume's model.
13 See Whale (1937), Pippenger (1984), Dutton (1984), Giovannini (1986), Davutyan and Parke (1995), Jeanne (1995), Morys (2007).
14 Chernyshoff, Jacks, and Taylor (2009) also indirectly document that nominal rigidities increased after World War I.
15 Attendees envisioned an international monetary system organized around either gold or silver. In addition to being easily recognizable and divisible, both gold and silver were suitable choices for money because, in the short run, it was difficult for governments to manipulate the stock of money: the supply is limited and new production is expensive. Moreover, both were commodity moneys, which tended to promote price stability in the long run (Bordo 1981, Friedman 1953). By the end of the conference, most delegates supported moving to gold (Russell 1898).
16 Of course, if one's principal trading partners were on silver, then there may have been network externalities to staying on silver.
17 During this period, there were few explicit financial instruments for hedging exchange-rate risk.
18 As discussed above, to the extent to which monetary authorities deviated from their parity but stayed within the gold points, core economies had some limited room to pursue independent monetary policy. This ability, however, hinged on credibility – something that was missing in the periphery.
19 Violations of gold points were more frequent on the periphery. It has been suggested that discount rate changes reflected changes in domestic cover ratios rather than keeping the exchange rate within the gold points, and those countries that could maintain convertibility, focused monetary policy on maintaining adequate reserves (Morys 2010).

References

Aceña, P.M. and Reis, J. (2000) *Monetary Standards in the Periphery: Paper, Silver, and Gold 1854–1933*, London: Macmillan Press, St. Martin's Press.

Adalet, M., and Eichengreen, B. (2005) 'Current account reversals: always a problem?', NBER Working Paper No. 11634.

Alquist, R. and Chabot, B. (2010) 'Did adhering to the gold standard reduce the cost of capital?', Federal Reserve Bank of Chicago, Working Paper No. 2010–13.

Barro, R. (1979) 'Money and the price level under the gold standard', *Economic Journal*, 89: 13–33.

Bloomfield, A. (1959) *Monetary Policy under the International Gold Standard, 1880–1914*, New York: Federal Reserve Bank of New York.

Bloomfield, A (1981) 'Gold standard', in D. Greenwald (ed.) *McGraw-Hill Encyclopedia of Economics*, New York: McGraw-Hill.

Bordo, M.D. (1981) 'The classical gold standard: some lessons for today', *Federal Reserve Bank of St. Louis Review*, 63: 2–17.

Bordo, M.D. (1993) 'The gold standard, Bretton Woods and other monetary regimes: a historical appraisal', Federal Reserve Bank of St. Louis *Review,* 75: 123–91.

Bordo, M.D. and Kydland, F.E. (1995) 'The gold standard as a rule: an essay in exploration', *Explorations in Economic History,* 32: 423–64.

Bordo, M.D. and MacDonald, R. (2005) 'Interest rate interactions in the classical gold standard, 1880–1914: was there any monetary independence?', *Journal of Monetary Economics,* 52: 307–27.

Bordo, M.D. and Rockoff, H. (1996) 'The gold standard as a "good housekeeping seal of approval"', *Journal of Economic History,* 56: 389–428.

Bordo, M.D. and Schwartz, A.J. (eds.) (1984) *A Retrospective on the Classical Gold Standard, 1821–1931,* Chicago, IL: University of Chicago Press.

Bordo, M.D. and Schwartz, A.J. (1996) 'The specie standard as a contingent rule: some evidence for core and peripheral countries, 1880–90', Departmental Working Papers 199411, Department of Economics, Rutgers University.

Canjels, E., Prakash-Canjels, G. and Taylor, A.M. (2004) 'Measuring market integration: foreign exchange arbitrage and the gold standard, 1879–1913', *Review of Economics and Statistics,* 86: 868–82.

Catão, L.A.V. (2006) 'sudden stops and currency drops: a historical look', IMF Working Paper No. 06–133.

Catão, L.A.V. and Solomou, S.L. (2005) 'Effective exchange rates and the classical gold standard adjustment', *American Economic Review,* 95: 1259–75.

Chernyshoff, N, Jacks, D.S. and Taylor, A.M. (2009) 'Stuck on gold: Real exchange rate volatility and the rise and fall of the gold standard, 1875–1939', *Journal of International Economics,* 77(2): 195–205.

Cooper, R. (1982) 'The gold standard: historical facts and future prospects', *Brookings Papers on Economic Activity,* 1982: 1–56.

Davutyan, N. and Parke, W. (1995) 'The operations of the Bank of England, 1890–1908: a dynamic probit approach,' *Journal of Money, Credit and Banking,* 27: 1099–112.

Dutton, J. (1984) 'The Bank of England and the rules of the game under the international gold standard: new evidence', in M.D. Bordo and A.J. Schwartz (eds.) *A Retrospective on the Classical Gold Standard, 1821–1931,* Chicago. IL: Chicago University Press.

Eichengreen, B. (1992) *Golden Fetters: The Gold Standard and the Great Depression, 1919–1939.* Oxford University Press.

Eichengreen, B. (1995) 'Central bank cooperation and exchange rate commitments: the classical and interwar gold standards compared', *Financial History Review,* 2: 99–117.

Eichengreen, B. (1996) *Globalizing Capital: A History of the International Monetary System,* Princeton, NJ: Princeton University Press.

Eichengreen, B. and Flandreau, M. (eds.) (1997) *The Gold Standard in Theory and History,* 2nd edn., London and New York: Routledge.

Eichengreen, B. and McLean, I.W. (1994) 'The supply of gold under the pre-1914 gold standard', *Economic History Review,* 47: 288–309.

Estevadeordal, A., Frantz, B. and Taylor, A.M. (2003) 'The rise and fall of world trade, 1870–1939', *The Quarterly Journal of Economics,* 118(2): 359–407.

Esteves, R.P. (2011) 'Between imperialism and capitalism: European capital exports before 1914', Working Paper, Oxford University, Department of Economics.

Esteves, R. and Khoudour-Casteras, D. (2009) 'A fantastic rain of gold: European migrants' remittances and balance of payments adjustment during the gold standard', *Journal of Economic History,* 69: 951–85.

Faria, A., Mauro, P., Minnoni, M. and Zaklan, A. (2006) 'The external financing of emerging market countries: evidence from two waves of financial globalization', IMF Working Paper WP/06/205.

Flandreau, M. (1996) 'The French crime of 1873: an essay on the emergence of the international gold standard, 1870–1880', *Journal of Economic History,* 56: 862–97.

Flandreau, M. and Maurel, M. (2005) 'Monetary union, trade integration, and business cycles in 19th century Europe', *Open Economies Review,* 16(2): 135–52.

Flandreau, M and Zumer, F. (2004) *The Making of Global Finance, 1880–1913,* Paris: OECD.

Ford, A.G. (1962) *The Gold Standard, 1880–1914: Britain and Argentina.* Oxford: Clarendon Press.

Frieden, J.A. (1997) 'Monetary populism in nineteenth-century America: an open economy interpretation', *Journal of Economic History,* 57: 367–95.

Friedman, M. (1953) 'Commodity-reserve currency', *Essays in Positive Economics,* Chicago, IL: University of Chicago Press

Friedman, M. (1990) 'Bimetallism revisited', *Journal of Economic Perspectives,* 4: 85–104.

Gallarotti, G.M. (1995) *The Anatomy of an International Monetary Regime: The Classical Gold Standard 1880–1914,* Oxford: Oxford University Press.

Giovannini, A. (1986) '"Rules of the game" during the international gold standard: England and Germany', *Journal of International Money and Finance,* 5: 467–83.

Hanes, C. and James, J.A. (2003) 'Wage adjustment under low inflation: evidence from U.S. history', *American Economic Review,* 93: 1414–24

Hatton, T.J. and Williamson, J.G (1994) 'What drove the mass migrations from Europe in the late nineteenth century?' *Population and Development Review,* 20: 1–27.

Hatton, T.J. and Williamson, J.G (1998) *The Age of Mass Migration: An Economic Analysis,* New York: Oxford University Press (1998).

Hume, D. (1752) *Of the Balance of Trade, Political Discourses,* Edinburgh, as reprinted in D. Hume (1955) *Writings on Economics,* ed. E. Rotwein. Madison, WI: University of Wisconsin Press.

Jacks, D.S. (2006) 'What drove 19th century commodity market integration?', *Explorations in Economic History,* 43: 383–412.

Jacks, D.S., Meissner, C.M. and Novy, D. (2011) 'Trade booms, trade busts, and trade costs', *Journal of International Economics,* 83: 185–201.

Jeanne, O. (1995) 'Monetary policy in England, 1893–1914: a structural VAR analysis', *Explorations in Economic History,* 32: 302–26.

Kydland, F.E. and Prescott, E.C. (1977) 'Rules rather than discretion: the inconsistency of optimal plans', *The Journal of Political Economy,* 85(3): 473–92.

Krugman, P. (1991) 'Target zone and exchange rate dynamics', *Quarterly Journal of Economics,* 106: 669–82.

López-Córdova, J.E. and Meissner, C.M. (2003) 'Exchange rate regimes and international trade: evidence from the classical gold standard era', *American Economic Review,* 93: 344–53.

McCloskey, D. and Zecher, R. (1976) 'How the gold standard worked, 1880–1913', in J.A. Frenkel and H.G. Johnson (eds.) *The Monetary Approach to the Balance of Payments.* London: George Allen and Unwin.

Meissner, C.M. (2003) 'The gold standard', in J. Mokyr (ed.) *Oxford Encyclopedia of Economic History,* Oxford: Oxford University Press.

Meissner, C.M. (2005) 'A new world order: explaining the international diffusion of the gold standard, 1870–1913', *Journal of International Economics,* 66: 385–406.

Mitchener, K.J. and Voth, H.J. (2010) 'Trading silver for gold: nineteenth-century Asian exports and the political economy of currency unions', in R.J. Barro and J.-W. Lee (eds.) *Costs and Benefits of Economic Integration in Asia,* Oxford: Oxford University Press.

Mitchener, K.J. and Weidenmier, M. (2008) 'Trade and empire', *Economic Journal,* 118: 1805–34.

Mitchener, K.J. and Weidenmier, M.D. (2009) 'Are hard pegs ever credible in emerging markets? Evidence from the classical gold standard', NBER Working Paper 15401.

Mitchener, K.J., Shizume, M. and Weidenmier, M.D. (2010) 'Why did countries adopt the gold standard? Lessons from Japan', *Journal of Economic History,* 70: 27–56.

Morys, M. (2007) 'The emergence of the classical gold standard', Working Paper, Oxford University.

Morys, M. (2008) 'Adjustment under the classical gold standard (1870s–1914): how costly did the external constraint come to the European periphery?', OeNB Workshop Paper 13.

Morys, M. (2009) 'South-Eastern European monetary history in a comparative perspective, 1870–1914', Bank of Greece Working Paper No. 94/2009.

Morys, M. (2010) 'Policy under the classical gold standard', CHERRY Working Paper 2010/01, Center for Historical Economics, University of York.

Nogues-Marco, P. (2011) 'Competing bimetallic ratios: Amsterdam, London, and bullion arbitrage in the 18th Century', Working Papers in Economic History, University Carlos III de Madrid, WP 11–03.

Obstfeld, M. and Taylor, A.M. (2003) 'Sovereign risk, credibility and the gold standard: 1870–1913 versus 1925–31', *Economic Journal,* 113: 241–75.

Officer, L.H. (1986) 'The efficiency of the dollar-sterling gold standard, 1890–1908', *Journal of Political Economy,* 94: 1038–73.

Officer, L.H. (1996) *Between the Dollar-Sterling Gold Points: Exchange Rates, Parity, and Market Behavior,* Cambridge: Cambridge University Press.

Officer, L.H. (2008) 'Gold standard', in R. Whaples (ed.) *EH.Net Encyclopedia.*

Pippenger, J. (1984) 'Bank of England operations, 1893–1913', in M.D. Bordo and A.J. Schwartz (eds.) *A Retrospective on the Classical Gold Standard, 1821–1931,* Chicago, IL: Chicago University Press.

Redish, A. (1990) 'The evolution of the gold standard in England', *Journal of Economic History,* 50: 789–806.

Rockoff, H. (1984) 'Some evidence on the real price of gold, its costs of production, and commodity prices', in M.D. Bordo and A.J. Schwartz (eds.) *A Retrospective on the Classical Gold Standard, 1821–1931,* Chicago, IL: University of Chicago Press.

Rose, A. (2011) 'Exchange rate regimes in the modern era: fixed, floating, and flaky', *Journal of Economic Literature,* 49: 652–72.

Russell, H. (1898) *International Monetary Conferences*, New York: Harper and Brothers.

Sabate, M., Gadea, M.D. and Escario, R. (2006) 'Does fiscal policy influence monetary policy? The case of Spain, 1874–1935', *Explorations in Economic History,* 43: 309–31.

Scammell, W.M. (1965) 'The working of the gold standard', *Bulletin of Economic Research*, 17(1): 32–45.

Svennson, L. (1994) 'The term structure of interest rates in a target zone', *Journal of Monetary Economics,* 28: 87–116.

Whale, P.B. (1937) 'The working of the pre-war gold standard', *Economica,* 4: 18–32.

PART II

The interwar era and World War II

10

THE 1920S

Martha L. Olney

The Roaring Twenties: for many, the visual images come from *The Great Gatsby* – a time of economic prosperity, extravagance, faster cars, shorter skirts, and jazz. Women could vote. Teenagers stayed in school. African-Americans migrated north. Electricity changed everything.

But against this apparent backdrop of economic prosperity and welcome social change were more ominous changes. The distributions of income and wealth became less equal. Farmers burdened by excessive debt lost their farms. Banks failed. Consumers financed their new cars and electrical appliances by taking on unprecedented levels of debt. Racial strife increased. Anti-immigrant fervor swept the nation. And of course, the 1920s served as prelude to the Great Depression which began as the decade concluded. It was, in short, a contradictory time.

A statistical look at the 1920s

The 1920s began with a sharp but short recession attributable to inventory adjustments in reaction to anticipated price swings (Romer 1993: Table 2). Two very mild contractions occurred in the middle of the decade: May 1923 to July 1924, and October 1926 to November 1927.[1] Neither was large enough to bring the annual real GDP growth rate (column (1) of Table 10.1) below zero. Generally, therefore, we think of the 1920s as a period of economic growth.

Unemployment in the 1920s (column (2) of Table 10.1) was quite low, rarely more than five percent after the economy recovered from the 1920–21 recession. The inflation rate (column (3) of Table 10.1), measured here as the annual rate of change of consumer prices, was also very moderate after 1922, never more than 3 percent and sometimes negative.

Figure 10.1 places the economic growth of the 1920s in a bit of historical context. The shaded section of Figure 10.1 is the 1920s. The economy grew more rapidly from 1923 to 1929 than it had in the years preceding World War I.

The unemployment rate in the 1920s, shown in Figure 10.2, is generally below the average rate for the decade preceding the United States' entry into World War I. Inflation for the same period is shown in Figure 10.3. The disruptions associated with World War I were followed by moderate inflation rates in the 1920s.

Table 10.1 Macroeconomic indicators, 1920–1929 (in percent)

Year	Real GDP Growth Rate (1)	Unemployment Rate (2)	Inflation Rate (3)
1920	−0.9	5.2	15.9
1921	−2.3	11.3	−10.8
1922	5.6	8.6	−6.5
1923	13.2	4.3	2.0
1924	3.1	5.3	0.0
1925	2.3	4.7	2.9
1926	6.5	2.9	0.5
1927	1.0	3.9	−1.4
1928	1.1	4.7	−1.4
1929	6.1	2.9	0.0

Sources: Column (1): Carter et al. 2006: Series Ca191. Percent change computed by author. Column (2): Carter et al. 2006: Series Ba 475. Column (3): Carter et al. 2006: Series Cc2. Percent change computed by author

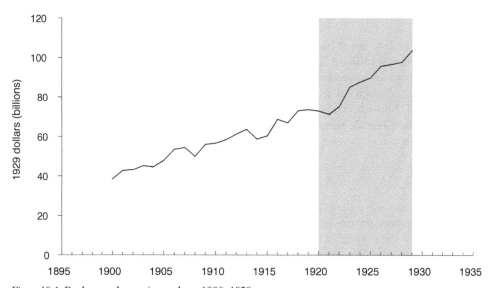

Figure 10.1 Real gross domestic product, 1900–1929

Source: Carter et al. 2006: Series Ca191

The population of the United States – 106 million in 1920 and 123 million in 1930 – grew about 1.5 percent annually during the 1920s. Ninety percent of the population was white. Immigration flows into the United States had been strong since the 1880s. In 1920 just over 13 percent of the U.S. population had been born abroad. The 1920 census marked the first time that more than half the U.S. population lived in urban areas (incorporated areas having 2,500 or more inhabitants): 51.3 percent of the population lived in urban areas in 1920 and 56.3 percent did so in 1930 (Carter et al. 2006: Series Aa23–Aa33). The farm

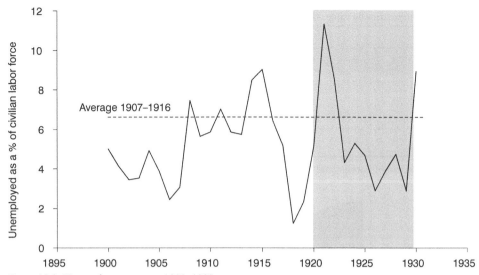

Figure 10.2 Unemployment rate, 1900–1930

Source: Carter et al. 2006: Series Ba475

Figure 10.3 Consumer price inflation rate, 1900–1930

Source: Carter et al. 2006: Series Cc2

population declined in absolute and relative numbers over the decade, dropping from 32.0 million people (30 percent of the total population) in 1920 to 30.5 million (under 25 percent) by 1930 (Carter et al. 2006: Series Da1–Da2).

The shift from a rural to urban population mirrored the shift in what the U.S. economy was producing. Table 10.2 shows the top 5 manufacturing industries by value added for 1914 and 1929. During the 1920s, the machinery and iron and steel industries became much more prominent in American manufacturing, reflecting increased industrialization.

Table 10.2 Top industries by value added in manufacturing (rank order)

1914	1929
Textiles	Machinery (excluding transportation)
Food products	Textiles
Chemicals	Food products
Machinery (excluding transportation)	Iron & steel
Forest products	Printing & publishing

Source: U.S. Bureau of Foreign and Domestic Commerce 1931: Table 813

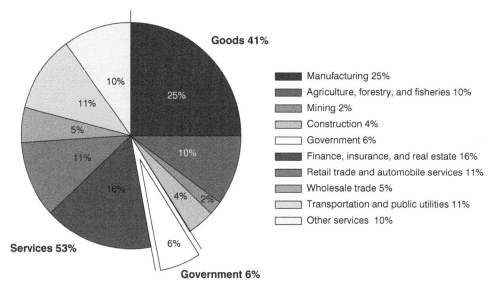

Goods 41%

■	Manufacturing 25%
▨	Agriculture, forestry, and fisheries 10%
▨	Mining 2%
▨	Construction 4%
▢	Government 6%
■	Finance, insurance, and real estate 16%
▨	Retail trade and automobile services 11%
▨	Wholesale trade 5%
▢	Transportation and public utilities 11%
▢	Other services 10%

Services 53%

Government 6%

Figure 10.4 National income by industry group, 1929

Source: Carter et al. 2006: Series Ca35–52

At the end of the 1920s, manufacturing was the largest single sector of the economy (see Figure 10.4). The goods-producing sectors – manufacturing, agriculture, mining, construction – together accounted for 41 percent of national income. The service-producing sectors – finance, trade, transportation, and other services – were 53 percent and the government sector was just 6 percent of national income.

Average income per worker, measured as nominal GDP per labor force member, was just under $2,000 through most of the 1920s (Carter et al. 2006: Series Ca10 and Ba470). This average masks stark inequality. Average annual earnings for waged manufacturing workers were $1,200 to $1,400 (U.S. Bureau of Foreign and Domestic Commerce 1931: Table 365). A farmer in the 1920s had an average annual income between $800 and $900 (Carter et al. 2006: Series Da4 and Da1295). A salaried worker in manufacturing earned about $2,200 per year (Douglas 1930: 361). A loaf of bread cost 10 cents, a new Ford Model T cost under $300, a two-bedroom house typically cost around $3,000 (The People History n.d.).

Inequality of income was at its twentieth century peak in the 1920s. The Gini coefficient for income was 0.49 in 1929 (Carter et al. 2006: Series Be23); a value of 0 indicates perfect equality and a value of 1 indicates perfect inequality. The share of income going to the top 10 percent of households increased sharply during the 1920s, rising from 38 percent in 1920 to over 46 percent in 1928 (Piketty and Saez 2003: Table II).

The social and political context

The United States entered World War I in 1917. Federal government spending surged from $0.7 billion in 1916 to $18.5 billion in 1919 (Carter et al. 2006: Series Ea585). Some of the increased spending was paid for with increased tax revenue, but the bulk of it was borrowed: outstanding federal government debt increased from $1 billion at the end of 1916 to over $25 billion at the end of 1919 (Carter et al. 2006: Series Ea650). The federal government sold over $21 billion of war bonds to families, banks, and financial institutions (Kimble 2006: 16)

The November 1918 end of World War I in Europe ushered in an era in America characterized by Warren Harding's 1920 Presidential campaign slogan: "Return to Normalcy." Americans seemed to long for what they perceived as the simpler prewar days. They expressed this longing in perhaps ironic ways: isolationism, anti-immigrant fervor, and racism.

One expression of isolationism was the U.S. Senate's refusal to join the League of Nations despite then-President Woodrow Wilson's urging. Blaming southern and eastern Europeans for America's political and economic woes, the period of isolationism was further manifested in the passage of two acts severely limiting immigration into the United States.

The Immigration Restriction Act of 1921 (also known as the Emergency Quota Act of 1921) established numerical quotas by country of origin: in any year, immigrants from any country could be no more than three percent of the population from that country who were resident in the United States at the time of the 1910 Census. The number of immigrants into the United States from Europe declined by half between 1921 and 1922 (Carter et al. 2006: Series Ad91).

A second restrictive act tightened immigration further. The Immigration Act of 1924 shifted the census benchmark to 1890 before the waves of migration from eastern and southern Europe, and limited the annual number of immigrants from any country to just two percent of the 1890 U.S. population from that country. The effect was dramatic. Immigration from Europe averaged over 800,000 persons annually between 1901 and 1914, but just over 150,000 per year between 1925 and 1930. From eastern Europe alone, the number of immigrants fell from an annual average of nearly 195,000 between 1901 and 1914 to just over 5,000 in the second half of the 1920s (Carter et al. 2006: Series Ad91, Ad114 and Ad115).

Race relations worsened in the 1920s. The Ku Klux Klan (KKK), a white supremacist organization that had its early origins in the years immediately following the Civil War, experienced a resurgence beginning in 1915. Its membership soared in the 1920s, peaking in 1924. Lynchings and other violent events occurred primarily but not exclusively in the South, against blacks, Jews, and immigrants (Newton 2007: 13–17).

Perhaps in reaction, a wave of south-to-north black migration occurred between 1910 and 1930. Although smaller than the post-World War II wave, the internal migration of black Americans to northern and midwestern states was unprecedented. In the 1920s, 750,000 blacks – about 8 percent of the southern black population – migrated from the South, splitting themselves about evenly between northern and midwestern states (Carter et al. 2006: Series Ac362–Ac413).

There is much more to the social and political history of the 1920s – prohibition, a rise of religious fundamentalism, the Jazz Age, and women's suffrage, to name a few. Here we have touched on just those aspects that are particularly relevant to our discussion of the economic history of the 1920s.

The macroeconomy: the demand side of the economy

Total spending in the macroeconomy is the sum of consumers' purchases, businesses' purchases of machinery and equipment plus construction spending, government agencies' purchases of goods and services, and net exports. In the 1920s, consumer spending was about 75 percent of total expenditure. Investment spending was about 15 percent, government purchases about 8 percent, and net exports were about 1 percent of total spending (Swanson and Williamson 1972: Table 1). We consider each of these sectors in turn.

Consumer spending

The 1920s witnessed what has come to be known as "The Consumer Durables Revolution" (Olney 1991). Consumer durables – cars, appliances, furniture, and other long-lasting items – were increasingly purchased by American families. The decade gave birth to the trend of American consumerism, a societal focus on the acquisition of material items and imbuing those items with the ability to determine the "goodness" of life.

The new items that families purchased had wide-ranging impacts on their lives. Automobiles were owned by just 26 percent of American families in 1920 but ownership surged to over 60 percent by 1930 (Lebergott 1993: 130). Automobiles allowed families to live further away from work, changing residential housing patterns. Car camping became a popular form of recreation in the 1920s (Costa 1999).

Proliferation of electricity was swift. In 1920, 35 percent of families had electric lighting, 8 percent owned a washing machine, and 9 percent owned a vacuum cleaner. Just a decade later – and before the New Deal electrification programs – 68 percent had electric lighting, 24 percent owned a washer, and 30 percent owned an electric vacuum cleaner (Lebergott 1993: 113).

Ironically, the time-saving nature of electrical appliances did not reduce the time that women spent working in the home. New theories of disease, of the science of sanitation, and of home economics were shared through popular literature and advertising. Together with a decline in the use of domestic servants, these new theories combined to create "more work for mother" in the homes of the 1920s (Cowan 1983; Mokyr 2000).

Why were families spending more on durable goods in the 1920s? Certainly increased income spurred families to spend more, as did decreases in the relative price of consumer durables. But the shift in demand was even greater due to the development of modern advertising and increased availability of consumer credit.

Advertising surged in the 1920s. During World War I, government-funded advertising campaigns had successfully encouraged purchase of war bonds (Kimble 2006: 15). Emboldened by this success, manufacturers turned increasingly to advertising. Money spent on advertising increased fourfold between 1915 and the 1920s (Olney 1991: 138). The number of magazine pages devoted to advertising and the size of the typical advertisement both increased (Olney 1991: Figures 5.1 and 5.3). Advertising copy began to focus on the consumers rather than on the products themselves, creating advertisements that emphasized "atmosphere" rather than the "reasons-why" someone should purchase a good (Marchand 1986: 206–34; Lears 1983: 157–59).

Increased credit availability also contributed to the boom in durable goods purchases. Consumer non-mortgage debt-to-income ratios more than doubled between 1920 and 1929 (Olney 1991: Table 4.1). Installment credit became in the 1920s the standard way to purchase consumer durable goods. An installment buyer provided a down payment and signed an agreement to make regular, monthly payments in exchange for immediate possession of the good. Down payments were substantial – as much as 30 percent for autos – and contract terms were relatively short, usually 12 to 24 months.

Three parties were involved in the installment sale: the buyer, the seller, and the sales finance company. The installment sale benefited all three parties. For the buyer, the entire purchase price need not be saved before the good was brought home. For the seller, the installment contract was immediately sold to a sales finance company, providing the seller with cash flow that enabled replenishment of inventory. For the sales finance company, installment sales contracts could be bundled and securitized allowing the sales finance company to obtain outside financing that funded yet more installment sales (Olney 1989).

The effective interest rate paid by many consumers on installment contracts was far in excess of any usury limit. But usury laws did not apply: the contract was not a loan per se but was a purchase-over-time. Consumers were largely unaware of the effective interest rate. Not only was the stated interest rate applied to the initial rather than the outstanding balance, but as much if not more of the financing costs were disguised as miscellaneous fees.

In contrast with informal credit from a merchant, an installment contract is secured by physical collateral: the good being purchased. Contracts allowed for repossession of the good if the contract was breached. So despite tense race relations in the 1920s, black Americans were able to obtain installment credit commensurate with their wealth and income (Olney 1998).

Retailing more generally was transformed in the 1920s. Chain stores such as the A&P increasingly eased out independent stores; indeed the "chain store problem" was a focus in 1929 as pundits worried – unnecessarily as it turned out – that chain stores would spell the death of the independent merchant (Lebhar 1932: xiii). The A&P had 4,224 stores and $195 million in sales in 1919. It reached its peak number of stores in 1930: 15,737 stores and $1,066 million in sales (Lebhar 1963: Table 7).

With the decline of independent grocers came as well a decline in personal relationships between grocer and customer. Those personal relationships had been key to an informal credit system that allowed many families to pay for their groceries some time after purchase. The new chain stores had lower prices than many independents but they were called "cash-and-carry" for a reason: their cash-only policies and lack of delivery distinguished them from the neighborhood grocer (Lebhar 1963: 31).

Chain stores were not limited to groceries. The major department, drug, and five-and-dime chain stores also witnessed spectacular growth in the 1920s. J.C. Penney had 197 stores and $29 million in sales in 1919, and 1,395 stores and $210 million in sales in 1929. Walgreen's had 23 stores and $2 million in sales in 1920, and 397 stores and $47 million in sales in 1929. Woolworth's grew from 1,081 stores and $119 million in sales in 1919 to 1,825 stores and $303 million in sales in 1929 (Lebhar 1963: Tables 5, 6, and 8).

Investment spending

Construction of structures and businesses purchases of machinery and equipment constitute what economists call "investment spending." Construction spending in the 1920s was about two-thirds of total investment. Purchases of machinery and equipment constituted the other third (Kuznets 1961: Table R-4).

Housing construction boomed in the first half of the 1920s. Housing starts peaked at 937,000 per year in 1925, having risen nearly fourfold since 1920 (Carter et al. 2006: Series Dc510). Why the boom? Fueled by earlier waves of immigration, household formation rates increased in the 1920s, increasing demand for houses. Speculation was common. Financing was relatively easy (Wheelock 2008: 135; White 2009). Banks typically wrote three-year mortgages with a balloon: the borrower's monthly payments would cover interest only, or interest plus a small amount of principal, and then the bulk of the principal – the balloon payment – would be due at the end of three years. When the balloon came due, banks refinanced the remaining loan principal. Savings and loans wrote longer-term mortgages, at an average of 11 years in the 1920s (Carter et al. 2006: Series Dc1198-Dc1200).

The boom ended after 1925. Housing starts fell by nearly 50 percent by 1929 to 509,000. Restrictive immigration rules enacted in 1921 and 1924 lowered the demand for houses. And a slowing of the rate of price increase made it more difficult for homeowners to refinance balloon payments, increasing defaults. Even before the Great Depression's start, the rate of foreclosure on houses doubled between 1926 and 1929 (Carter et al. 2006: Series Dc1257).

Capacity utilization fell at the end of the 1920s from its peak of over 90 percent in 1923 to 1926 to about 83 percent in 1929 (Baran and Sweezy 1966: 237). As factories were using less of their capacity, they added to their stock of equipment more slowly. Investment in equipment, which increased about 12 percent annually from 1922 to 1926, rose by only 4.5 percent per year to the end of the decade (Kuznets 1961: Table R-5).

Government

The federal government of the 1920s had few economic responsibilities. Social safety net programs were the province of state and local governments, not the federal government. The federal government provided $10 million in direct welfare aid in 1927 and another $1 million in transfers to state and local governments. By contrast $40 million in direct aid was provided by state governments in 1927 and $111 million was provided by local government agencies (Carter et al. 2006: Series Ea182, Ea224, Ea408, and Ea542).

The federal government took in more revenue than it spent throughout the 1920s and retired one-third of the bonds it had issued to finance World War I. The federal income tax had been established by the Sixteenth Amendment to the Constitution in 1913. In the late 1920s, corporate income taxes accounted for over 30 percent and individual income taxes accounted for nearly 25 percent of federal government revenue (Carter et al. 2006: Series Ea586-Ea588, Ea595, Ea596).

Individual income tax rates were reduced a number of times over the decade. Those earning below the median income level typically paid no income taxes. Taxpayers with taxable income of $20,000 – about ten times the median income – saw their average tax rate fall from 10 to 3 percent between 1920 and 1925. Those earning more than $1,000,000 annually paid an average tax rate of 66 percent in 1920 and only 24 percent just five years later (Carter et al. 2006: Series Ea761, Ea768, and Ea772).

Net exports

America's primary trading partners in the 1920s were the Americas and Europe. With World War I, U.S. exports and imports had both surged, rising in nominal terms from 15 to 20 percent annually between 1913 and 1920. Imports from Europe were down, but imports from the Americas and Asia rose. The U.S. trade surplus spiked as well (Carter et al. 2006: Series Ee 416–Ee417). The wartime surge in trade followed a dramatic drop in tariff rates in 1913 when Congress cut tariffs and introduced the federal income tax.

Once the war ended, exports declined. Agriculture was particularly hard hit. In response, Congress implemented the Emergency Tariff Act of 1921 and the Fordney–McCumber

Tariff Act of 1922. Average tariff rates increased between 1920 and 1922 from 16 percent to 38 percent of dutiable imports (Carter et al. 2006: Series Ee430). Nevertheless American exports did not return to their World War I heights at any point in the 1920s.

Tariff rates were a primary tool for manipulating trade because exchange rates were fixed by the international gold standard. For instance, an ounce of gold was worth $20.67 in the United States and £3 17s 10½d in England, making the exchange rate $4.867 per pound. When there was a trade imbalance, it was settled through international exchange of gold. Short of a devaluation of the gold value of its currency, a country could not depreciate its currency to increase its exports.

The supply side of the economy

Any economy is characterized not just by the demand factors discussed above, but also by what is termed the "supply side" of the economy. Here we look at the structure of the economy and at institutions that contribute to – or detract from – economic activity.

Agriculture

The agricultural sector, long a strength of the United States economy, suffered in the 1920s. During and immediately after World War I, farmers took on unprecedented levels of debt. Prices of agricultural goods had risen sharply during the war, making the acquisition of debt appear affordable.

Agriculture's woes became apparent as postwar crop prices fell. A bushel of corn sold for $1.51 in 1919, but averaged 77¢ between 1920 and 1929. A pound of cotton sold for 35.3¢ in 1919 but only 19.5¢ on average in the 1920s. A bushel of wheat which sold for $2.16 in 1919 brought in only $1.18 on average in the 1920s (Carter et al. 2006: Series Da697, Da757, and Da719).

Many farmers found themselves unable to pay their debts and banks increasingly foreclosed on their property. Farm foreclosure rates, which averaged 3.2 per 1,000 farms in the decades before World War I, averaged 17 per 1,000 from 1926 to 1929 (Alston 1983: 888). Foreclosure rates were highest in states with high levels of farm mortgage debt, relatively low farm earnings, and "*ex post* excessive expansion during the World War I agricultural boom" (Alston 1983: 903).

Financial institutions

Bank failures are usually associated with the 1930s. But throughout the 1920s, banks failed. From a high of over 30,000 banks in 1921, the number of banks declined to 25,000 by 1929 (and fell much further, to just over 14,000 by 1933). Nationally-chartered banks shied away from real estate loans at this time, leaving that market to state-chartered banks. And it was primarily state-chartered banks that failed. Bank failures were more frequent in rural areas where hard-hit farmers were unable to repay debt, and in insured banks which took on greater risk than did uninsured banks (Wheelock 1992, Hooks and Robinson 2002).

Particularly in the 1920s, commercial banks, trust companies, and investment companies each reached into the others' spheres. Legislative and economic changes were responsible. With the Federal Reserve Act of 1913, national commercial banks were allowed to move into trust operations. And then in the 1920s, traditional loan business stagnated in commercial banks, encouraging a move into more lucrative activities. Success in marketing war bonds for the U.S. government laid the groundwork for commercial banks' movement into marketing securities (White 1984, Mahoney 2001). National banks that engaged in the securities business increased from 72 in 1922 to 235 in 1929 (Peach 1941: 83). The number of investment banks increased from 485 in 1920 to 690 in 1928 (Mahoney 2001: 10).

The Federal Reserve

The Federal Reserve Act of 1913 had created the nation's central bank. The Federal Reserve System of the 1920s – the Fed – was a collection of twelve regional Federal Reserve Banks from San Francisco to Boston and a weak Federal Reserve Board in Washington, DC. The Fed's central policy-making body, the Federal Open Market Committee (FOMC), did not exist until the 1930s. As a result there was not a uniform monetary policy; each bank was responsible for its own policy (Wheelock 1991: 72–74, Richardson and Troost 2009). To the extent there was any system-wide leadership, that role in the 1920s fell to the Federal Reserve Bank of New York, led by Benjamin Strong until his death in 1928.

Monetary policy in the 1920s was centered on two features: the real bills doctrine and the gold standard. The real bills doctrine stipulated that banks could present for re-discount at the Fed only "real bills" – "notes, drafts, and bills of exchange arising out of actual commercial transactions" (Friedman and Schwartz 1963: 191). The doctrine was designed to limit speculative expansion of the money supply by linking increases in the monetary base to "real" activity as opposed to financial or speculative activity.

Under the gold standard, money was backed by gold: you could trade money – paper currency or bank deposits – for gold at a government-set price. The convertibility of money into gold put a limit on the money supply. When a country's gold stock declined, its money supply would also need to decline. When the gold stock rose, the money supply would also rise.

The interest rate charged by the Federal Reserve banks – the "discount rate" – could be manipulated to alter gold flows between other countries and the United States. An increase of the discount rate decreased gold outflows and spurred gold inflows. A decrease of the discount rate had the opposite effect: gold outflows increased and gold inflows decreased.

The gold standard was one reason the Fed postponed raising interest rates in the 1920s. The Fed recognized the stock market bubble but international concerns guided its interest rate policy. Low interest rates in the mid-1920s encouraged gold outflows and American investment abroad, part of America's assistance to the devastated post-war European economy. The Fed began tightening early in 1927 but reversed course in July 1927 and lowered interest rates to support the British pound sterling, an act later criticized as fueling the already raging stock market boom. Subsequently, Benjamin Strong argued for moving away from international cooperation which supported the gold standard, allowing the United States to base its interest rate policy on domestic concerns. The Fed then implemented a series of discount rate increases in 1928 and 1929 in an attempt to cool stock market speculation, doing so in the face of a weak economy (Eichengreen 1992: 13–14, 212–21, Wheelock 1991: 76–9).

By the time the Fed began raising interest rates, the bull market was well underway. Stock prices had risen 150 percent between 1921 and 1928 (Carter et al. 2006: Series Cj804). The number of shares traded on the New York Stock Exchange soared from 173 million in 1921 to 920 million in 1928, an increase of over 400 percent (Carter et al. 2006: Series Cj857).

Estimates of the extent of stock ownership in the 1920s vary from a range of 3 percent before World War I to 25 percent in 1929 (Ott 2009: 45) to point estimates such as 8 percent of the American population (Green 1971: 198). That small share of the public enjoyed tremendous gains. The market's meteoric rise had pushed stock prices in the Dow Jones Industrial Average up over 500 percent in eight years, from a low of 62.57 in mid-August 1921 to a high of 381.17 in early September 1929.

Business and labor

A wave of mergers – the "greatest revival of merger activity since the turn of the [twentieth] century" (Nelson 1959: 122) – occurred in the 1920s, aided in part by lax enforcement of antitrust laws (Borg et al. 1989: 130). Horizontal integration dominated as mergers were seen especially in primary metals, petroleum products, food products, chemicals, and transportation equipment (Eis 1969). From 1905 to 1919, there had been an average of just over 100 mergers and acquisitions annually, reflecting capital of $270 million. But from 1925 to 1929, mergers averaged nearly one per day with total capital of over $1,200 million annually (Carter et al. 2006: Series Ch416–Ch417). The mergers were not particularly profitable; shareholders typically suffered losses in the years immediately following a merger (Borg et al. 1989: 130).

Alongside the soaring demand for ownership shares was a desire to separate ownership from management. As a result, more and more businesses embraced the corporate form of governance (Wells 2010). The number of incorporations per year nearly doubled between the pre-war decade and the late 1920s (Carter et al. 2006: Series Ch293-Ch318).

Countering a potential backlash against big business may have been one reason for the 1920s surge in "welfare capitalism": provision of a variety of social services by an employer to its workers (Brandes 1976, Brody 1980: 49). Company picnics, organized sporting events, lunch rooms, encouragement to purchase property, health care … the list of services that employers provided in the 1920s went on and on. Providing services to employees was not simply a matter of doing the right thing: employers argued that protecting the wellbeing of their employees increased labor productivity (Fones-Wolf 1986: 234, Brody 1980: 57).

Welfare capitalism was also a means of lowering the incentive to unionize, substituting employer-provided benefits for those provided by the union (Brody 1980: 23, 57–59, Edwards 1979: 91–97). Combined with employer hostility toward unions and the postwar Red Scare, the 1920s witnessed a sharp decline in labor's membership and strength. Labor union membership doubled in the late 1910s, peaking in 1920 at about 5 million members. But by the mid-1920s, membership had declined to about 3.5 million (Carter et al. 2006: Series Ba4783, 4785, 4790). Work stoppages were common, averaging over 3,500 annually between 1916 and 1920 but only 600 per year by 1928 (Carter et al. 2006: Series Ba4954).

Education

The "high school movement" took place in the 1920s. No longer was an eighth-grade education the norm. Increasingly, the end degree for American youth was a high school diploma. In 1910, just 9 percent of 18-year-olds graduated from high school. By 1930, 30 percent did so. The rise of high schools was not uniform across the United States. High school graduation rates were highest in the Pacific and prairie states, and lowest in the industrial north and the South (Goldin and Katz 2008: 194–207).

Teenagers were more likely to stay in school if work opportunities were limited. In states with a strong manufacturing base, "good" jobs were available to men without a high school diploma, and high school graduation rates were lower. Graduation rates were also lower in states with weak support for public colleges and universities, lower income and wealth, a more diverse population, and a lower share of the population over 65 (Goldin and Katz 2008: 217).

Productivity

All of these forces combined in the 1920s to generate tremendous gains in productivity. Total factor productivity (TFP) grew faster in the 1920s than in any time period after World War II "driven by floor space savings and improved materials flow associated with newly laid out factories" (Field 2006: 227). Why was the factory layout new? Electricity. The move to electrical power allowed factories to move to a more efficient single-story layout. Moreover, electricity was so cheap by comparison with previous sources of power that manufacturers changed to labor-saving and capital-using production techniques, further increasing productivity (Woolf 1984: 185). The gains in productivity allowed for increased wages: the roar of the 1920s.

Conclusion

Few decades have attracted as much attention as the 1920s. It is a decade of conflicting messages. For economists: a booming economy obscured the seeds of the Great Depression that were sown in this decade. For social historians: consumerism, materialism, modernism … amid isolationism, racism, and xenophobia. For those who lived through it: the decade was a time of rapid social and economic change.

Note

1 Business cycle dates are determined by the Business Cycle Dating Committee of the National Bureau of Economic Research. See "U.S. Business Cycle Expansions and Contractions" (http://www.nber.org/cycles/cyclesmain.html, accessed November 1, 2011).

References

Alston, L.J. (1983) 'Farm foreclosures in the United States during the interwar period', *Journal of Economic History,* 43: 885–903.

Baran, P.A. and Sweezy, P.M. (1966) *Monopoly Capital: An Essay on the American Economic and Social Order,* New York: Modern Reader Paperbacks.

Borg, J.R., Borg, M.O. and Leeth, J.D. (1989) 'The success of mergers in the 1920s: a stock market appraisal of the second merger wave', *International Journal of Industrial Organization,* 7: 117–31.

Brandes, S.D. (1976) *American Welfare Capitalism, 1880–1940,* Chicago, IL: University of Chicago Press.

Brody, D. (1980) 'The rise and decline of welfare capitalism', in D. Brody (ed.) *Workers in Industrial America: Essays on the Twentieth Century Struggle,* New York: Oxford University Press.

Carter, S.B., Gartner, S.S., Haines, M.R., Olmstead, A.L., Sutch, R. and Wright G. (2006) *Historical Statistics of the United States, Earliest Times to the Present: Millennial Edition.* New York: Cambridge University Press.

Costa, D.L. (1999) 'American living standards: evidence from recreational expenditures', NBER Working Paper No. 7148.

Cowan, R.S. (1983) *More Work for Mother: The Ironies of Household Technology from the Open Hearth to the Microwave,* New York: Basic Books.

Douglas, P.H. (1930) *Real Wages in the United States, 1890–1926,* Boston, MA: Houghton Mifflin.

Edwards, R.C. (1979) *Contested Terrain: The Transformation of the Workplace in the Twentieth Century,* New York: Basic Books.

Eichengreen, B. (1992) *Golden Fetters: The Gold Standard and the Great Depression, 1919–1939,* New York: Oxford University Press.

Eis, C. (1969) 'The 1919–1930 merger movement in American industry', *Journal of Law and Economics,* 12: 267–96.

Field, A.J. (2006) 'Technological change and U.S. productivity growth in the interwar years', *Journal of Economic History,* 66: 203–36.

Fones-Wolf, E. (1986) 'Industrial recreation, the Second World War, and the revival of welfare capitalism, 1934–1960', *Business History Review,* 60: 232–57.

Friedman, M. and Schwartz, A.J. (1963) *A Monetary History of the United States 1867–1960,* Princeton, NJ: Princeton University Press.

Goldin, C. and Katz, L.F. (2008) *The Race Between Education and Technology,* Cambridge, MA: Harvard University Press.

Green, G.D. (1971) 'The economic impact of the stock market boom and crash of 1929', in Federal Reserve Bank of Boston, *Consumer Spending and Monetary Policy: The Linkages,* Monetary Conference: 189–220.

Hooks, L.M. and Robinson, K.J. (2002) 'Deposit insurance and moral hazard: evidence from Texas banking in the 1920s', *Journal of Economic History,* 62: 833–53.

Kimble, J.J. (2006) *Mobilizing the Home Front War Bonds and Domestic Propaganda,* College Station, TX: Texas A&M University Press.

Kuznets, S. (1961) *Capital in the American Economy,* Princeton, NJ: Princeton University Press.

Lears, T.J. (1983) 'The rise of American advertising', *Wilson Quarterly,* 7: 156–67.

Lebergott, S. (1993) *Pursuing Happiness: American Consumers in the Twentieth Century,* Princeton, NJ: Princeton University Press.

Lebhar, G.M. (1932) *The Chain Store: Boon or Bane?,* New York: Harper & Brothers.

Lebhar, G.M. (1963) *Chain Stores in America: 1859–1962,* New York: Chain Store Publishing Corporation.

Mahoney, P.G. (2001) 'The political economy of the Securities Act of 1933', *Journal of Legal Studies,* 30: 1–31.

Marchand, R. (1986) *Advertising the American Dream: Making Way for Modernity, 1920–1940,* Berkeley, CA: University of California Press.

Mokyr, J. (2000) 'Why "more work for mother?" knowledge and household behavior, 1870–1945', *Journal of Economic History,* 60: 1–41.

National Bureau of Economic Research (n.d) 'US Business Cycle Expansions and Contractions', http://www.nber.org/cycles/cyclesmain.html, (accessed Nov 1, 2011)

Nelson, R.L. (1959) *Merger Movements in American Industry, 1895–1956,* Princeton, NJ: Princeton University Press.

Newton, M. (2007) *The Ku Klux Klan: History, Organization, Language, Influence and Activities of America's Most Notorious Secret Society,* Jefferson, NC: McFarland.

Olney, M.L. (1989) 'Credit as a production-smoothing device: the case of automobiles, 1913–1938', *Journal of Economic History,* 49: 377–91.

Olney, M.L. (1991) *Buy Now, Pay Later: Advertising, Credit, and Consumer Durables in the 1920s,* Chapel Hill, NC: University of North Carolina Press.

Olney, M.L. (1998) 'When your word is not enough: race, collateral, and household credit', *Journal of Economic History,* 58: 408–31.

Ott, J.C. (2009) '"The free and open people's market": political ideology and retail brokerage at the New York Stock Exchange, 1913–1933', *Journal of American History,* 96: 44–71.

Peach, W.N. (1941) *Security Affiliates of National Banks,* Baltimore, MD: Johns Hopkins University Press.

Piketty, T. and Saez, E. (2003) 'Income inequality in the United States, 1913–1998', *Quarterly Journal of Economics,* 118: 1–39.

Richardson, G. and Troost, W. (2009) 'Monetary intervention mitigated banking panics during the Great Depression: quasi-experimental evidence from the Federal Reserve district border in Mississippi, 1929 to 1933', *Journal of Political Economy,* 117: 1031–73.

Romer, C.D. (1993) 'The nation in depression', *Journal of Economic Perspectives,* 7: 19–39.

Swanson J.A. and Williamson, S.H. (1972) 'Estimates of national product and income for the United States economy, 1919–1941', *Explorations in Economic History,* 10: 53–73.

The People History (n.d.) '1920's History', http://www.thepeoplehistory.com/1920s.html (accessed Feb. 20, 2012).

U.S. Bureau of Foreign and Domestic Commerce (1931) *Statistical Abstract of the United States*, Washington, DC: Government Printing Office.

Wells, H. (2010) 'The birth of corporate governance', *Seattle University Law Review*, 33: 1247–92.

Wheelock, D.C. (1991) *The Strategy and Consistency of Federal Reserve Monetary Policy, 1924–1933*, Cambridge: Cambridge University Press.

Wheelock, D.C. (1992) 'Regulation and bank failures: new evidence from the agricultural collapse of the 1920s', *Journal of Economic History*, 52: 806–25.

Wheelock, D.C. (2008) 'The federal response to home mortgage distress: lessons from the Great Depression', *Federal Reserve Bank of St. Louis Review*, 90: 133–48.

White, E.N. (1984) 'Banking innovation in the 1920s: the growth of national banks' financial services', *Business and Economic History*, 12: 92–104.

White, E.N. (2009) 'Lessons from the great American real estate boom and bust of the 1920s,' NBER Working Paper No. 15573.

Woolf, A.G. (1984) 'Electricity, productivity, and labor-saving: American manufacturing, 1900–1929', *Explorations in Economic History*, 21:176–91.

11

THE 1929 STOCK MARKET CRASH

Harold Bierman, Jr.

John K. Galbraith's *The Great Crash, 1929* (1961) is the most popular and widely read book about 1929 and the 1929 stock market crash. Although Galbraith's narrative makes extremely interesting reading, unfortunately it's not always fair and omits reasonable alternative interpretations of events. This chapter aims to provide a more accurate description of what went on, leading to a better understanding of the sequence of events in 1929 and in subsequent years.

Were the common stocks listed and traded on the New York Stock Exchange too high in September–October 1929? This crucial question cannot be answered with complete certainty, but a careful review of the financial evidence suggests that stocks were *not* overvalued at the time. There was a historical fall in stock prices in October 1929 (almost as bad as in 2008–2009), but large, rapid declines in the stock market are not uncommon. The causes (triggers) of each stock market crash are likely to be different and the consequences are likely to be a surprise to economic decision makers. It is very unlikely that federal government oversight can prevent future crashes, just as it failed to prevent the 1929 and the 2008 crashes.

This chapter will briefly review the stock market and economic conditions before October 1929, and then try to define the triggers of the 1929 crash and identify the most plausible subsequent factors that led to the Great Depression of the 1930s.

The economy in the 1920s and 1929

From 1925 to September 1929 the common stocks in the Dow Jones Industrials Average increased in value by 120 percent, which represents a compound annual growth rate of 21.8 percent. While this is a large rate of appreciation, it is not necessarily proof of an orgy of speculation.

The decade of the 1920s was an extremely prosperous one for the United States and the stock market with its rising prices reflecting this prosperity as well as the expectation that the prosperity would continue. But in 1929, the president, Congress, and the Federal Reserve Board worried about the speculation taking place in New York.

The fact that the stock market lost over 70 percent of its value from 1929 to 1932 indicates that the market, at least using one important criterion (actual performance of the market), was overvalued in 1929. Galbraith (1961: 16) implies that there was a speculative orgy and that the crash was predictable: "Early in 1928, the nature of the boom changed. The mass escape into make-believe, so much a part of the true speculative orgy, started in earnest." With the advantage of over thirty years of hindsight, Galbraith (1961: 29) had no difficulty identifying the end of the boom in 1929: "On the first of January of 1929, as a matter of probability, it was most likely that the boom would end before the year was out."

Compare this position with the fact that Irving Fisher, one of the leading economists in the United States at the time, was heavily invested in stocks and was bullish before and after the October sell offs; he lost his entire wealth (including his house) before stocks started to recover. In England, John Maynard Keynes, considered by many to be the world's leading economist during the first half of the twentieth century, and an acknowledged master of practical finance, also lost heavily. Nobel-laureate economist Paul Samuelson (1979: 9) quotes P. Sergeant Florence (another leading economist): "Keynes may have made his own fortune and that of King's College, but the investment trust of Keynes and Dennis Robertson managed to lose my fortune in 1929."

Galbraith's ability to "forecast" the market turn is not shared by all. Samuelson (1979: 9) admits that: "playing as I often do the experiment of studying price profiles with their dates concealed, I discovered that I would have been caught by the 1929 debacle." For many, "the collapse from 1929 to 1933 was neither foreseeable nor inevitable."

The stock price increases leading to October 1929 were not driven solely by fools or speculators. There were also intelligent, knowledgeable investors who were buying or holding stocks in September and October 1929. Also, leading economists, both then and now, could neither anticipate nor explain the October 1929 decline of the market. The evidence suggests that stocks were not obviously overpriced.

The nation's gross domestic product rose 3.4 percent per year from 1923 to 1929, allowing per capita income to rise from $8623 to $9678 (in 2011 dollars, *Historical Statistics:* series Ca9 and Ca11). Technological improvement appears to be the root cause behind this period of real growth and prosperity. Total factor productivity (output per unit of input) for the entire economy grew by 2.02 percent per year from 1919 to 1929 – the second highest rate during the entire twentieth century (Field 2011). The 1920s benefited from "transformative organizational and technological progress involving both new products (especially the automobile and electrical appliances) and a revolution in factory organization and design in which traditional methods of distributing power internally via metal shafts and leather belts were replaced with electrical wires and small electric motors." This electrification and reconfiguration had its roots decades earlier "but blossomed only in the 1920s." Total factor productivity growth in manufacturing reached 5.12 percent per year between 1919 and 1929, a rate which dwarfs all other decades. And these productivity growth rates were widespread – equaling 4.89 percent in non-durable goods and 5.06 percent in durables, whose transportation equipment sector reached 8.07 percent per year (Field 2011: 1, 3, 43, and 52–53). This productivity growth mitigated inflation. For the period of 1923–1929 wholesale prices went down 0.9 percent per year, reflecting moderate stable growth in the money supply during a period of healthy real growth.

Contemporaries recognized these economic strengths. For example, Irving Fisher's *Stock Market Crash and After* (1930) offers much data demonstrating that there was real growth in the manufacturing sector. The evidence presented goes a long way to explain Fisher's optimism regarding the level of stock prices. Fisher and others saw that manufacturing efficiency was rapidly increasing (output per worker) as was manufacturing output and the use of electricity.

Financial fundamentals and stock values

The financial fundamentals of the markets were also strong. During 1928, the price–earnings ratio for 45 industrial stocks increased from approximately 12 to approximately 14, before reaching 15 in 1929. While not low, these price earnings (P/E) ratios were by no means out of line historically. Values in this range would be considered reasonable by most market analysts. Burton G. Malkiel (1996: 389) shows that the future ten-year rates of return are higher when stocks are purchased at lower initial price-to-earnings ratios.

The rise in stock prices was not uniform across all industries. The stocks that went up the most were in industries where the economic fundamentals indicated there was cause for large amounts of optimism. They included airplanes, agricultural implements, chemicals, department stores, steel, utilities, telephone and telegraph, electrical equipment, oil, paper, and radio. These were reasonable choices for expectations of growth.

To put the P/E ratios of 10 to 15 in perspective, note that government bonds in 1929 yielded 3.4 percent. Industrial bonds of investment grade were yielding 5.1 percent.

If we assume corporations had zero growth and zero earnings retention, then a P/E of ten would imply a return on investment of 10 percent easily beating 3.4 percent. A P/E of 15 would imply a return on investment of 6.7 percent and again 3.4 percent is a poor second. Add growth possibilities and common stock dominated the government bond and industrial bond alternatives in 1929.

The Federal Reserve Bulletin in 1930 reported production in 1920 at an index of 87 (1923–1925 average equaled 100). The index went down to 67 in 1921, then climbed steadily (except for 1924) until it reached 118 in 1929. This is an annual growth rate in production of 3.1 percent. During the period commodity prices actually decreased. The production record for the ten-year period was exceptionally good.

During 1929, each of the first six months showed production increases in the United States. In June, the index was 125; in July, it went down to 119; in August, it was back up to 121; and in September, it increased to 123. Even in October the production index was 120. Looking at this widely publicized measure of industrial production, the stock market had little cause for fear. There was no identifiable seasonal trend cited by contemporaries.

Factory payrolls in September were at an index of 111 (an all-time high). The 1923–1925 average equaled 100. In October, the index dropped to 110, which beat all previous months and years except for September 1929. The factory employment measures were consistent with the payroll index.

Using the same 1923–1925 base years, the September unadjusted measure of freight car loadings was at 121 – also an all-time record. In October, the loadings dropped to 118, which was a performance second only to September's record measure.

Farm product prices throughout the year were equal to or higher than 101, and for the year were 105 (1923–1925 were the base years). In 1928 they had been 106, but only 99 in 1927 and 100 in 1926. In addition, the prices of nonfarm products had also gone down in 1929 compared to 1928.

In the first nine months of 1929, 1,436 firms announced increased dividends. In 1928, the number was only 955 and in 1927 it was 755. In September 1929, dividend increases were announced by 193 firms compared with 135 the year before. The financial news from corporations was very positive in September and October 1929.

But if the above numbers for dividends merely reflected the distribution of a larger percentage of earnings, there would be cause for concern. For September 1929, the percentage of earnings being paid out decreased to 64 percent. Not only dividends but also corporate earnings were increasing significantly in 1929.

The dividend yields were low compared to the call loan costs of 6 percent to 10 percent. But on the same date industrial bonds had yields to maturity ranging from 5 percent to 7 percent (there were "junk bonds" in 1929, but they went by a different name: "speculative"). If one wanted equity dividend yields that were higher than those of the common stock, one could buy industrial preferred stock yielding between 5.6 percent and 8 percent.

The May 1929 issue of *The National City Bank of New York Newsletter* indicated the earnings statements for the first quarter of surveyed firms showed a 31 percent increase compared to the first quarter of 1928. The August issue showed that for 650 firms the increase for the first six months of 1929 compared to 1928 was 24.4 percent. In September, the results were expanded to 916 firms with a 27.4 percent increase. The earnings for the third quarter for 638 firms were calculated to be 14.1 percent larger than for 1928. This is evidence that the general level of business activity and reported profits were excellent at the end of September 1929 and the middle of October 1929.

Barrie Wigmore (1985) researched the 1929 financial data for 135 firms. The market price as a percentage of year-end book value was 420 percent using the high prices and 181 percent using the low prices. However, the return on equity for the firms (using the year-end book value) was a high 16.5 percent. The dividend yield was 2.96 percent using the high prices and 5.90 percent using the low prices.

Article after article from January to October in business magazines carried news of outstanding economic performance. E.K. Burger and A.M. Leinbach, two staff writers for *The Magazine of Wall Street*, wrote in June 1929: "Business so far this year has astonished even the perennial optimists."

There was little hint of a severe weakness in the real economy in the months prior to October 1929. There is a great deal of evidence that in 1929 stock prices were not out of line with the real economics of the firms that had issued the stock. Leading economists were betting that common stock in the fall of 1929 was a good buy. Conventional financial reports of corporations gave cause for optimism relative to the 1929 earnings of corporations. Price–earnings ratios, dividend amounts and changes in dividends, and earnings and changes in earnings all gave cause for stock price optimism in September 1929.

Recent econometric work complements these more traditional approaches. McGrattan and Prescott (2004) use growth theory to estimate the fundamental value of corporate equity and compare it to actual stock valuations and find that using a conservative estimate of the fundamental value of U.S. corporations in 1929, a price multiple of 21 times earnings is justified. The observed maximum P/E in 1929 was 19 or less depending on which measure is used. "In other words," they conclude, "with regard to the value of the 1929 stock market, Irving Fisher was right" (2004: 1003). Likewise, Siegel (2003) uses an operational definition of a bubble as any time the realized asset return over a given future period is more than two standard deviations from its expected return. Using this framework, he shows that the crash of 1929 and 1987 prove not to be bubbles, but instead the low point in stock prices in 1932 is a "negative bubble."

Alternative views

The economics literature has not reached a consensus regarding whether or not there was a bubble in stock prices in 1929. The papers by Hamilton (1986), Flood and Hodrick (1990), Rappoport and White (1993) and the interview with, at that time, Fed Governor Ben Bernanke in Rolnick (2004) indicate just how difficult it is to econometrically identify asset bubbles, even after the fact. Although this chapter argues against the existence of a bubble, there are some scholars who reject the position that common stocks listed on the New York

Stock Exchange in the summer of 1929 were reasonably priced, conjecturing that there was a price bubble in the summer of 1929.

Kindleberger (1978) argues the stock market had detached from fundamentals by way of a credit-driven bubble fueled by the proliferation of brokers' loans. Credit creation fed the mania of speculation that ended in the Crash. White (1990), while acknowledging the econometric difficulty of identifying bubbles, goes on to make a qualitative case for the existence of a bubble in stock prices. Following Blanchard and Watson (1982), White (1990) suggests a bubble emerged because fundamentals had become difficult to assess due to major changes in industry. In addition, the entry of new and unsophisticated investors in the 1920s made speculation all the more likely. Rappoport and White (1993) identify a bubble in 1929 stock prices and associate it with information derived from rising premia on brokers' loans and rising margin requirements, both of which are indicative of rising fear of financial panic. But they qualify their conclusion by stating that standard statistical tests confirm that stock prices and dividends are cointegrated, which Campbell and Shiller (1987) indicate would not be the case if there was an asset price bubble. DeLong and Shleifer (1991) use closed-end mutual funds as the basis of their conclusion that there was a speculative bubble in stock prices. They observe the large difference between prices and net asset values of closed-end mutual funds to estimate that the stocks making up the S&P composite were priced at least 30 percent above fundamentals in late summer, 1929.[1]

What triggered the 1929 crash?

The stock market crash is conventionally said to have occurred on Thursday October 24 and Tuesday, October 29, 1929. These two dates have been dubbed Black Thursday and Black Tuesday, respectively. On September 3, 1929, the Dow Jones Industrial Average reached an all-time high of 381.2. At the end of the market day on Thursday October 24, the market was at 299.5 – a 21 percent decline from the market high. By November 13, 1929, the market had fallen to 230 – a drop of 40 percent from the market's high.

Investment trust formation and investing had driven up public utility stocks in 1928 and 1929. The trusts were, to a large extent, bought on margin by individuals. The sell off of utility stocks from October 16 to October 23 weakened prices and prompted "margin selling." Then on October 24, Black Thursday, the selling panic happened.

In the year 1929, public utility stock prices were generally in excess of twice their book values. (Book value is defined in this case as the value of the stock equity as computed and reported by the firms' accountants and auditors.) This relationship could be sustained only if the regulatory authorities were to decide to allow the utilities to earn more than the market's required return or there were larger than expected (by the regulators) earnings.

On August 2, 1929, *The New York Times* reported that the directors of the Edison Electric Illuminating Company of Boston had called a meeting of stockholders to obtain authorization for a stock split. The stock had risen in 1929 to a high of $440. Its book value was $164 (the ratio of price to book value was 2.6).

On Saturday October 12 the *Times* reported that on Friday the Massachusetts Department of Public Utilities had rejected the stock split. The heading said: "Bars Stock Split by Boston Edison. Criticizes Dividend Policy. Holds Rates Should Not Be Raised Until Company Can Reduce Charge for Electricity." Boston Edison lost 15 points for the day. The stock closed at $360 on Friday.

The Massachusetts Department of Public Utilities (*New York Times*, October 12: 27) rejected the stock split because it did not want to imply to investors that this was the "forerunner of substantial increases in dividends." Commissioners stated that the expectation of increased dividends was not justified. They offered "scathing criticisms of the company" and concluded "the public will take over such utilities as try to gobble up all profits available" (*New York Times*, October 12: 42). Boston Edison dropped 61 points at its low on Monday (October 14) but closed at 328, a loss of 32 points. On October 16, the *Times* reported that the governor of Massachusetts was launching a full investigation of Boston Edison including "dividends, depreciation, and surplus" (*New York Times*, October 12: 42).

Any acceptable financial model would argue that the primary effect of a two-for-one stock split would be to reduce the stock price by approximately 50 percent, leaving the total value of the stock essentially unchanged; thus the event would not be economically significant, and the stock split should have been easy to grant. But the Massachusetts Commission made it clear it had additional messages to communicate.

Massachusetts was not alone in challenging the profit levels of utilities. The Federal Trade Commission, New York City, and New York State were all questioning the status of public utility regulation. On October 17, *The New York Times* reported that the Committee on Public Service Securities of the Investment Banking Association warned against "speculative and uninformed buying." The committee published a report in which it "asks care in buying shares in utilities." As of September 1, 1929, all common stock listed on the NYSE had a value of $82.1 billion. The utilities industry at $14.8 billion of value thus represented 18 percent of the value of the outstanding shares.

In 1929, there were five important multipliers that meant that any change in a public utility's underlying value would result in a larger value change in the market and in the value of the investor's portfolio:

1 The ratio of share price to book value of an individual utility.
2 The ratio of market value of investment trust holding to market value of individual utilities (or holding companies) making up the trust.
3 The percentage of debt to assets of the utility.
4 The percentage of debt to assets of the holding company.
5 The percentage of debt to assets of the trust.

In addition, the many investors used margin debt to buy the stocks of the individual utility, the holding company, or the investment trust. Moreover, preferred stock was also used to increase the leverage used by various utility firms. The upshot is that utility investments were very heavily leveraged.

In the fall of 1929, many utility stocks that were somewhat high based on conventional calculations such as the ratios of price to book value came down. When regulators began to signal that these high market valuations warranted a reduction of prices, it triggered a drop in utility valuations which then snowballed into a broader stock market decline as leveraged buyers were forced to sell their stocks. The unusually high level of leverage triggered a substantial drop in the market, which reduced wealth levels and helped eliminate overall optimism among investors

The stock market crash and the Great Depression

Some observers, such as Galbraith, connect speculation in the late 1920s and the stock market crash (1961: 2) directly to the Depression of the 1930s: "The stock market crash and the speculation which made it inevitable had an important effect on the performance, or rather the malperformance, of the economy in the ensuing months and years." Friedman and Schwartz (1965) on the other hand, acknowledge that the stock market crash contributed to the problems in the economy but they give it only a secondary role. Thus, they state:

> Partly, no doubt, the stock market crash was a symptom of the underlying forces making for a severe contraction in economic activity. But partly also, its occurrence must have helped to deepen the contraction. It changed the atmosphere within which businessmen and others were making their plans, and spread uncertainty where dazzling hopes of a new era had prevailed.
>
> (Friedman and Schwartz 1965: 10)

They note that a fear of excessive speculation arising from easy money made the economic recovery more difficult (see their footnote p. 79), but they conclude that monetary forces, problems in the banking system and missteps of the Federal Reserve are the primary causes of the Great Depression – not the stock market crash.

Parker's chapter in this *Handbook* surveys the scholarly literature on the causes of the Great Depression, which gives pride of place to Friedman and Schwartz's argument and little support to the popular, Galbraithian notion that the stock market crash was an important factor.

Following the lead of Friedman and Schwartz and the other authors, it is concluded that the stock market crash of 1929 did not cause the Depression, but it made possible the Federal Reserve's decision to limit the money supply, which made economic recovery during the following years much more difficult and far less likely.

Conclusions

The *fear* of speculation in 1929 helped push the stock market to the brink of collapse. It is entirely possible that President Hoover's aggressive campaign against speculation, helped by the unrealistically priced public utilities hit by the Massachusetts Public Utility Commission and the vulnerable margin investors, brought about the October events, the selling panic, and its well-known consequences.

New York state Governor Franklin D. Roosevelt had already made several negative comments about the excessive incomes of New York state utilities, so the Massachusetts decision was looked at as an indication of events to come in New York state. The stock market realized that stock market prices that were almost three times book value could not be justified by a rate commission intent on allowing a fair return. The decline in public utility common stock prices led the decline across the market leading to the famed 1929 stock market crash.

History shows that the stock market has offered high returns compared to bonds as demonstrated in Siegel (1992). But a study of 1929 shows that there can be sudden drastic decreases in stock values. These decreases are very difficult to predict since they can occur despite healthy business activity. No one should invest in stocks unless they can withstand a 30 percent to 70 percent loss in value, a loss that can persist for a number of years.

For further comparisons of different stock market crashes throughout history, see for example, Romer (1990) for an analysis of 1929 versus 1987 and Bierman (2010) for an analysis of 1929 versus 2008.

Note

1 This type of calculation can be misleading, however. Consider that Berkshire Hathaway's common stock consistently sells at higher prices than the value of the component stocks held in its portfolio. Also, today most closed-end funds sell at a premium to their portfolio of investments (one reason being the tax status of unrealized gains).

References

Bierman, H., Jr. (2010) *Beating the Bear: Lessons from the 1929 Crash Applied to Today's World*, Santa Barbara, CA: Praeger.

Blanchard, O.J. and Watson, M.W. (1982) 'Bubbles, rational expectations and financial markets', in P. Wachtel (ed.) *Crises in the Economic and Financial Structure*, Lexington, MA: D.C. Heath and Co.

Burger, E.K. and Leinbach, A.M. (1929) 'Business', *The Magazine of Wall Street*, June 15, 289.

Campbell, J.Y. and Shiller, R.J. (1987) 'Cointegration and tests of present value models', *Journal of Political Economy*, 95: 1062–88.

Carter, S. et al. (2006) *Historical Statistics of the United States: Millennial Edition*, New York: Cambridge University Press.

DeLong, J.B. and Shleifer, A. (1991) 'The stock market bubble of 1929: evidence from closed-end mutual funds', *Journal of Economic History*, 51: 675–700.

Federal Reserve Bulletin (1930).

Field, A. (2011) *A Great Leap Forward: 1930s Depression and U.S. Economic Growth*, New Haven, CT: Yale University Press.

Fisher, I. (1930) *The Stock Market Crash and After*, New York: Macmillan.

Flood, R.P. and Hodrick, R.J. (1990) 'On testing for speculative bubbles', *Journal of Economic Perspectives*, 4: 85–101.

Friedman, M. and Schwartz, A.J. (1965) *The Great Contraction 1929–1933*, Princeton, NJ: Princeton University Press.

Galbraith, J.K. (1961) *The Great Crash*, Boston, MA: Houghton Mifflin.

Hamilton, J. (1986) 'On testing for self-fulfilling speculative price bubbles', *International Economic Review*, 27: 545–52.

Kindleberger, C.P. (1978) *Manias, Panics, and Crashes*, New York: Basic Books.

Malkiel, B.G. (1996) *A Random Walk Down Wall Street*, sixth edition, New York: Norton.

McGrattan, E.R. and Prescott, E. (2004) 'The 1929 stock market: Irving Fisher was right', *International Economic Review*, 45: 991–1009.

National City Bank of New York Newsletter, May 1929.

New York Times, various issues, October 1929.

Rappoport, P. and White, E.N. (1993) 'Was there a bubble in the 1929 stock market?', *Journal of Economic History*, 53: 549–74.

Rolnick, A. (2004) 'Interview with Ben S. Bernanke', *The Region*, Federal Reserve of Minneapolis, June.

Romer, C. (1990) 'The Great Crash and the onset of the Great Depression', *Quarterly Journal of Economics*, 105: 597–624.

Samuelson, P.A. (1979), 'Myths and realities about the Crash and Depression', *Journal of Portfolio Management*, 6: 7–10.

Siegel, J.J. (1992) 'The equity premium: stock and bond returns since 1802', *Financial Analysts Journal*, 48: 28–46.

Siegel, J.J. (2003) 'What is an asset price bubble? An operational definition', *European Financial Management*, 9: 11–24.

White, E.N. (1990) 'The stock market boom and crash of 1929 revisited', *Journal of Economic Perspectives*, 4: 67–83.

Wigmore, B.A. (1985) *The Crash and Its Aftermath*, Westport, CT: Greenwood Press.

12

BRITAIN'S WITHDRAWAL FROM THE GOLD STANDARD

The end of an epoch

Michael Kitson

It is safe to predict that Monday, September 21, 1931, will become an historic date; the suspension of the gold standard in Great Britain on that day, after the six years of painful effort which followed this country's return to gold in 1925, marks the definite end of an epoch in the world's financial and economic development.

(*Economist* 1931: 547)

Introduction

Britain's withdrawal from the interwar gold exchange standard (henceforth "the gold standard", not to be confused with "the classical gold standard" of an earlier period – on which, see Chapter 9) in September 1931 was the end of an epoch and the start of a new one. The gold standard was a fixed exchange rate regime which provided the framework for the global monetary system during much of the interwar period. When Britain withdrew, the whole system was undermined and began to fall apart. By the mid-1930s the system had been replaced by a world order where countries adopted independent and uncoordinated policies. But this lack of coordination and collaboration was preferable to the previous system, as the gold standard was a flawed construction which led to slow growth of the world economy and provided little flexibility for individual nations to deal with economic problems and international economic disturbances. This rigidity became particularly manifest in the Great Depression during the late 1920s and early 1930s where the gold standard led to countries adopting deflationary policies when they should have being doing the opposite. Following the end of the First World War, Britain decided to join the United States, Germany and other nations and returned to the gold standard in May 1925. This decision was a mistake which led to slow growth of the British economy in the 1920s and deepened the extent of the Great Depression. When Britain left the gold standard in September 1931 it provided the flexibility needed to introduce policies that increased aggregate demand which promoted recovery and stimulated growth for much of the rest of the decade.

This chapter traces the rise and fall of the gold standard in Britain. It considers the economic case for the gold standard and why this case was flawed. Furthermore, it considers how the gold standard harmed the British economy and how Britain's withdrawal from the system promoted recovery.

The economics of the gold standard

To examine the impact of both the return to, and the departure from, the gold standard it is important to evaluate how it was *supposed* to work. In particular, it depended on an implicit model of the economy where the flows of gold would ensure smooth adjustment of individual economies to changing economic conditions including the eradication of balance of payments surpluses and deficits. But in practice there were two main problems – one which was fundamental, the other which was operational. First, economies did not operate in the smooth frictionless way assumed by many proponents of the gold standard – and as assumed in many economic models. Second, intervention by governments and monetary authorities tended to disrupt and distort the, albeit imperfect, adjustment mechanisms that the gold standard did retain.

So how should the system have worked? First, assume that markets (for products, labor and so on) are working efficiently – markets respond quickly and effortlessly to shifts in supply and demand, and firms and workers are price-takers (as in competitive markets) and are not price makers (as in uncompetitive or imperfect markets). Thus, the economy will fully employ all available resources. Second, assume that an increase in the money supply leads to an increased demand for all goods – not just demand for financial assets – and excess money is definitely spent, not just hoarded (under the bed or somewhere else). These two assumptions are Say's Law and the quantity theory of money – two of the pillars of monetarism in its various guises. Next introduce a gold standard where each nation's currency is in the form of gold or in the form of a currency fully convertible into gold at a fixed price (thus creating a fixed exchange rate system). This should introduce a mechanism to ensure price stability and the automatic adjustment of trade deficits and surpluses – a mechanism first developed by David Hume and known as the price–specie–flow mechanism. According to Hume (1898: 333):

> Suppose four-fifths of all the money in Great Britain to be annihilated in one night, … what would be the consequence? Must not the price of all labour and commodities sink in proportion, … What nation could then dispute with us in any foreign market … In how little time … must this bring back the money which we had lost, and raise us to the level of all the neighboring nations? Where, after we have arrived, we immediately lose the advantage of the cheapness of labour and commodities; and the farther [sic] flowing in of money is stopped by our fulness and repletion.

The role of gold was to change (or "annihilate" in Hume's language) the money supply in response to global shifts in supply and demand. Take the case of country where there is excess supply of its goods and services, that is, it is running a trade deficit – buying more goods and services than it is selling to the rest of the world. This will lead to a loss of gold reserves and a contraction of its money supply. This in turn will lead to a fall in its price level compared to the rest of the world, which will improve its competitiveness and eradicate its trade deficit. Now, take the case of country where there is excess demand for its goods and services, that is, it is running a trade surplus – selling more goods and services than it buys from the rest of the world. This surplus will lead to an accumulation of gold reserves and an increase of its money supply. This in turn will lead to an increase in its price level compared to the rest of the world, which will lead to a reduction in competitiveness which will eradicate its trade surplus.

The economics of the gold standard were, therefore, dependent on highly restrictive assumptions about the way markets behave and also on the understanding that countries would freely permit their money supplies to be altered by the uninterrupted functioning of the price–specie–flow mechanism. If these assumptions were not correct, then the gold standard would not provide the means for economies to adjust to economic change. Instead, it would lock countries in to a fixed exchange rate system with little flexibility to accommodate the needs of individual economies.

The return to gold

The restoration of the gold standard progressed throughout the 1920s as all the major countries returned to the system. Britain returned to gold in 1925 and, as illustrated in Figure 12.1, by 1927 the vast majority of trading nations had joined the system which was, in effect, a global fixed exchange rate system (Kitson and Michie 1993). In Britain the conventional wisdom after the First World War was that a return to gold would provide stability and prosperity. The Cunliffe Committee, which was established to make recommendations for the development of the economy, reported in 1918 that "it is imperative that after the war, the conditions necessary for the maintenance of an effective gold standard should be restored without delay" (Cunliffe 1918). The commitment of the government to return to gold, combined with relatively high interest rates to facilitate the return, caused the sterling exchange rate to appreciate. In April 1925, the Chancellor of the Exchequer, Winston Churchill, restored sterling to the gold standard at its pre-war exchange rate of $4.86. According to Churchill (1925: cc. 52–8):

> A return to an effective gold standard has long been the settled and declared policy of this country. Every Expert Conference since the War – Brussels, Genoa – every expert Committee in this country, has urged the principle of a return to the gold standard. No responsible authority has advocated any other policy. No British Government – and every party has held office – no political party, no previous holder of the Office of Chancellor of the Exchequer has challenged, or so far as I am aware is now challenging, the principle of a reversion to the gold standard in international affairs at the earliest possible moment. It has always been taken as a matter of course that we should return to it, and the only questions open have been the difficult and the very delicate questions of how and when.

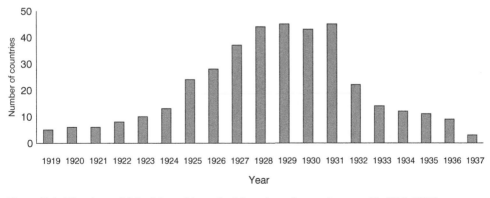

Figure 12.1 The rise and fall of the gold standard (number of countries on gold, 1919–1937)
Sources: Eichengreen (1992) and Kitson and Michie (1993)

Churchill was, of course, exaggerating. There were alternatives but, in political discourse, the various options for economic policy are very rarely clearly debated. This is a problem today, just as much as it was in the interwar period. But in the 1920s the conventional wisdom was that a return to gold would be good for the economy, although there were dissenters (on which, see Hume 1963; and Irwin 2011, on Cassel). The most prominent dissenter was John Maynard Keynes who wrote a stringent critique of the decision to return to gold (Keynes 1925). Keynes mainly focused on the decision to return at the pre-war parity, which he thought would lead to a loss of competitiveness for domestic businesses, rather than the fundamental flaws of the exchange rate system itself. Keynes (1925: 10) was scathing about Churchill, writing:

> Why did he do such a silly thing? Partly, perhaps, because he has no instinctive judgment to prevent him from making mistakes; partly because, lacking this instinctive judgment, he was deafened by the clamorous voices of conventional finance; and, most of all, because he was gravely misled by his experts.

But those experts were not to have their wisdom contaminated by Keynes. Keynes was a member of the Cunliffe Committee but his dissension led to Cunliffe calling for his resignation and arguing that: "Mr. Keynes, in commercial circles," … is … "not considered to have any knowledge or experience in practical exchange or business problems" (quoted in Moggridge 1995: 273).

Structurally flawed: "golden fetters" in the UK

Much of the discussion of the effectiveness of the gold standard has focused on whether it was allowed to operate according to the "rules of the game." It has been contended that problems were caused by governments or monetary authorities intervening to prevent the flows of gold adding to, or reducing, their money supply (Kitson 2003). A more fundamental problem was that markets rarely if ever worked according to the model that underpinned the gold standard. From the onset the fault lines of the gold standard were apparent. It was a fixed exchange rate system which contained countries with different economic structures and with different economic problems. In a floating exchange rate system, individual countries have some power to alter their exchange rate and monetary policy in response to national-specific factors or changing economic conditions. Within a fixed exchange rate system these powers are largely lost – a problem that has become recently apparent with the turmoil in the euro area and in particular the modern "Greek Tragedy." The effectiveness of the gold standard depended on the circulation of gold having the equilibrating properties discussed above. But it did not have these properties – even if countries did not meddle with gold flows. Instead the system was highly destabilizing, creating a deflationary bias in the global monetary system which hampered world economic growth and led to rising unemployment. It was to become one of the main causes of the Great Depression and the extent to which it spread internationally.

The countries that entered the gold standard had contrasting abilities to deal with its strictures and constraints (see Kitson and Michie 1993). The resilient countries were those that could maintain both a strong trade performance with high economic growth. Such countries did not have the problem of dealing with a balance of payments deficit by deflationary means. Two of the most resilient countries in the 1920s were the United States and France. The United States had emerged as the strongest industrial nation at the end of the nineteenth century based on its abundant raw materials, sustained investment and the development of new industries and new forms of industrial organization. France had recovered successfully from the First World War and had entered the gold standard at an undervalue exchange rate which provided a stimulus to export-led growth.

But not all countries were as resilient as the United States and France; in particular, Germany and Britain had fragile economies at that time. Both had emerged from the aftermath of the First World War with economic problems. Britain had been in relative decline since the 1870s and had become structurally dependent on traditional industries which were declining in importance in global markets. The German economy had been wrecked by the War and was further handicapped by the conditions of the peace settlement at Paris in 1919 (on which, see Keynes 1919). The problem for the fragile economies, such as Britain and Germany, was that they found it difficult to maintain a balance of payments equilibrium and a high level of domestic economic activity at the same time.

The problem for the reconstructed gold standard was that it did not comprise of similar economies with markets that were operating in the smooth frictionless manner of textbook economics. Instead, very dissimilar economies with different structures and different problems were combined together in an exchange rate system which provided little room to maneuver. All economies suffer from shifts in supply and demand and shocks of varying degrees of magnitude and severity. The response to such changes can broadly take two forms: a market response or a policy response. A market response depends on the quick, effective and painless adjustment of relative prices in response to shocks and shifts in supply and demand. In reality, most markets rarely operate like this – they are mainly slow-moving institutions and prices tend to be "sticky." Some can move quickly – such as financial markets – but this just makes adjustment more difficult for the slower moving product and labor markets. Take a collapse in global demand. In response, nominal exchange rates may move very quickly – but exporters will take time to reduce production, change prices and reallocate physical capital. And workers who lose their jobs may take considerable time to find new employment – and many may never succeed or may fail to regain employment as productive as that prevailing before the collapse.

The limitations and inadequacies of the market response often mean that the alternative of changing economic policy results in better economic outcomes. But entering a fixed exchange rate system – such as the gold standard – means that many of the policy adjustment mechanisms cannot be used. First, and most obviously, adjustment of the nominal exchange rate is not possible. The market response would be that this could be offset by adjustment of the real exchange rate – that is, the price level adjusts to maintain "equilibrium" of the exchange rate. But this process is often slow and uncertain. For the UK, most studies showed that the decision to return to the gold standard at the prewar parity led to a significant overvaluation of the real exchange rate in the period 1925–31 (Redmond 1980 and 1984). Overall, Keynes's (1925) contemporary estimate that sterling was overvalued by 10 percent proved to be a good approximation of many more recent estimates (Kitson and Michie 1993). It should also be emphasized that the real exchange rate was also significantly overvalued in the early 1920s (Kitson 2003 and Solomou 1996). The announcement of the intention of the return to gold led to rapid appreciation of the nominal exchange rate – but domestic prices relative to the rest of the world only adjusted slowly – leading a rise in the real exchange rate. According to Keynes (1925: 209–10): "the improvement in the exchange prior to the restoration of gold was due to a speculative anticipation of this event and to a movement of capital, and not to an intrinsic improvement in sterling itself."

The second policy mechanism that is inoperable in a fixed exchange rate system is the use of interest rates to achieve domestic economic objectives – such as economic growth, full employment, and low and stable inflation. Once a currency is locked into a fixed exchange rate system, interest rates have to be deployed to maintain the exchange rate parity. For the UK, this was a particular problem as sterling entered the gold standard, at an overvalued rate (as discussed above) which required relatively high interest rates to maintain demand for the currency. From 1923 there was a trend rise in the Bank of England's discount rate as the authorities had to tighten monetary policy to facilitate the return to gold at the pre-war parity (Kitson and Michie 1993). This contributed to the slow growth of the UK economy and persistently high unemployment during the 1920s (Kitson and Solomou 1990).

The third policy mechanism is the use of fiscal policy as a demand management tool. In a fixed exchange rate regime, the orthodox Mundell–Fleming model of open economy macroeconomics suggests that governments should use fiscal policy to manage the domestic economy (Mundell 1963 and Fleming 1962). For instance with slow growth, governments should engage in fiscal expansion which will increase output; this will put upward pressure on interest rates and the exchange rate. But as the latter is fixed, the monetary authorities will have to engage in monetary expansion to relieve the pressure, which in turn will boost aggregate demand. However, despite slow growth in the 1920s, fiscal policy was not used as a demand management tool. A more powerful orthodoxy was then dominant: the "Treasury view." The Treasury view asserted that fiscal policy has no impact on the level of economic activity and unemployment as any increase in government spending would "crowd out" an equal amount of private sector economic activity. As Winston Churchill, the Chancellor of the Exchequer, explained in 1929:

> The orthodox Treasury view ... is that when the Government borrow[s] in the money market it becomes a new competitor with industry and engrosses to itself resources which would otherwise have been employed by private enterprise, and in the process raises the rent of money to all who have need of it.
>
> (Churchill 1929, cc. 53)

The Treasury View was comprehensively debunked by Keynes (1936), and the use of fiscal policy in demand management became a cornerstone of economic policy in the "Golden Age of Capitalism" in the 1950s and 1960s.

Britain was suffering from slow growth and structural problems when it joined the gold standard. And the gold standard made these conditions worse. An overvalued exchange rate led to loss of competitiveness. The exchange rate straightjacket meant that there were few if any policy options to ameliorate the problem. When the Great Depression hit, the problems deteriorated further and were to ultimately result in the UK withdrawing from gold – which was the catalyst for the collapse of the entire system.

Gold and the Great Depression

The structural flaws of the gold standard were starkly exposed by the Great Depression. The causes of the Great Depression are subject to much debate, but the depth, length and spread of the Depression can largely be explained by the operation of the gold standard (Eichengreen 1992, Temin 1989). The gold standard operated as an effective mechanism for transmitting depression around the globe. As the Depression took hold in the U.S., loans to other countries (capital exports) were called in. This increased gold flows to the U.S., but drained gold reserves from other countries. For the countries losing gold to maintain convertibility of their exchange rate within the gold standard, they had to increase demand for their currency by raising interest rates. Thus as the world economy was moving into depression, the gold standard forced many countries to tighten monetary policy at the very time that policy should have been loosened.

In Britain the economy went into depression in 1929, although some indicators suggest that it was already in recession by 1928 (Solomou and Weale 1993). The first phase of the Depression was primarily caused by a collapse in exports as world trade went into severe decline (Corner 1956). The second phase was primarily caused by the policy response – which was in turn caused by the twin constraints of the gold standard and the Treasury View. The gold standard constraint led to a tightening of monetary policy, particularly in 1931 when the government raised interest rates in the forlorn attempt to maintain the value of sterling. This particularly harmed interest-sensitive sectors such as construction. As the British economy slowed, unemployment rose – and this led to pressure on the Government's finances as tax revenue fell and expenditure on unemployment benefits increased. The impact of such "fiscal stabilizers" is usually to dampen the impact of recessionary forces. But in Britain, policy was constrained by the Treasury View. For instance the May Report of July 1931 urged public sector wage cuts and large cuts in public spending, particularly in benefit payments to the unemployed. The gold standard and the Treasury View constraints reinforced each other as balancing the budget was considered as necessary for confidence in sterling. But the tightening of fiscal policy during a depression counteracted the impact of fiscal stabilizers – which in turn depressed economic activity even further.

The conduct of economic policy in Britain was closely bound up with shifts in the political landscape. In May 1929, the Labour Party formed a government with support from the Liberal Party. The government was committed to the Treasury View – but this commitment was to be tested by the Great Depression. The impact of the Depression was uneven with the industrial cities and regions – primarily in the north of Britain – suffering the most in terms of unemployment and poverty. These were the areas from which the Labour Party primarily garnered its support. Thus, the burden of fiscal austerity – involving public sector wage cuts and large cuts in benefit payments – would largely fall on the working class who were, in the main, supporters of the Labour Party. The dispute over public spending cuts divided the Labour Party and the Government – which was most evident after the publication in July 1931 of the May Report. There was economic and political turmoil, and in response the Prime Minister (Ramsey MacDonald) formed a "National Government" with the Conservative and the Liberal parties in August 1931. This led to MacDonald and his supporters being expelled from the Labour Party, and a General Election was called in October 1931 which subsequently resulted in a large majority for the Conservative Party. Thus, the National Government became Conservative-dominated, although MacDonald continued as Prime Minister until 1935.

The newly elected Government brought in emergency measures in an attempt to balance the budget and restore confidence in sterling. The budget of 10 September 1931 implemented cuts in public spending and wages of public sector workers. But this did not restore confidence either at home or abroad: while some of the British Navy mutinied, international investors took flight. Despite all the attempts to prop it up, on 21 September 1931 the Government was finally forced to abandon the gold standard, and immediately the sterling exchange rate fell by 25 percent.

The impact of the suspension of gold on the British economy:
"Nobody told us we could do that"

When Britain left the gold standard one prominent Labour politician pithily observed: "Nobody told us we could do that" (quoted in Moggridge 1969: 9). This is an example of a recurring refrain in British political discourse that there are few if any options in the conduct of economic policy. In the 1980s, Prime Minister Thatcher proclaimed that "there is no alternative"; more recently, the Chancellor of the Exchequer, George Osborne stated that there can be no plan B for economic policy. But there are always alternatives or different plans that can be implemented. And when Britain withdrew from the gold standard, this ushered in a new policy regime.

There were two primary benefits of the suspension of the gold standard. First, devaluation replaced persistent deflation, the fall in both the nominal and real exchange rate increased the competitiveness of domestic products including exports and import substitutes. According to Broadberry (1986), the devaluation led to an £80 million improvement in the balance of trade which, assuming a multiplier of 1.75, would have increased GDP by approximately 3 percent (Solomou 1996). It should be noted, however, that the competitive impact of devaluation was subsequently eroded as other countries followed Britain and also withdrew from the gold standard (on the global impact of the collapse of the gold standard, see Eichengreen and Sachs 1985, 1986). Second, the suspension of gold allowed the implementation of expansionary monetary policy as interest rates were no longer used to protect the exchange rate parity. The ending of the deflationary cycle brought about by the loss of gold reserves and the introduction of "cheap money" after 1932 have been identified as important stimuli for economic growth – in particular encouraging growth in the housing sector (Richardson 1967).

The withdrawal from the gold standard was quickly followed by another emergency measure, the introduction of widespread protectionism in November 1931 (measures which were formalized in 1932). The orthodox case, often based on the notion of comparative advantage and the case for free trade, is that protectionism either harmed growth (Capie 1983) or had little impact (Richardson 1967). But there is an alternative argument that under the special conditions of the early 1930s – depressed demand and wide-scale unemployment – protectionism helped to stimulate the economy (Kitson and Solomou 1990). This more optimistic assessment of protectionism suggests that it raised demand for British goods as imports were replaced by domestic products. The usual argument that tariffs are harmful did not apply in 1930s Britain. First, it did not lead to a misallocation of resources and inefficiency as Britain imposed tariffs on manufactured imports which competed with domestic products, and it did not impose tariffs on complementary imports such as raw materials and other inputs. Furthermore, the increased demand for their products allowed firms to exploit increasing returns. Second, the potential for "beggar thy neighbor" responses by other countries was negligible. Britain was the last major country to move away from free trade – most of its major competitors had developed their economies behind tariff walls limiting their potential to introduce additional protectionist policies which would harm British exports. During the 1930s, Britain's share of world exports was stable whereas it had been declining in the 1920s (Kitson and Solomou 1990). Thus, the optimistic assessment of protectionism suggest that it did not lead to a misallocation of resources but a mobilization of resources – it led to increased employment and output.

Although the new policy regime introduced at the end of 1931 was not based on strategic long-term planning, it did turn out to provide a coherent impetus for recovery and growth. The suspension of the gold standard led directly to a devalued exchange rate, cheap money and indirectly to the protectionism of British manufacturing. These policies together led to increased aggregate demand which led to a rapid rise of GDP from 1932. As Keynes argued:

> It is a wonderful thing for our business men and our manufacturers and our unemployed to taste hope again. But they must not allow anyone to put them back in the gold cage, where they have been pining out their hearts all these years.
>
> (News broadcast quoted in Backhouse and Bateman 2006: 11)

According to a narrow definition, the policy-induced recovery was not Keynesian as it did not involve expansionary fiscal policy. But a wider notion of Keynesianism stresses the importance of aggregate demand – and growth in the 1930s was very much demand induced – and central to this was the withdrawal from gold.

The impact of Britain's suspension of gold on the world economy

Britain's withdrawal from the gold standard triggered the global collapse of the exchange rate system. Other countries followed Britain and left the gold standard, including most of the dominions and empire, the Scandinavian countries and Canada and Japan; and the U.S. devalued in March 1933. As shown in Figure 12.1, by 1934 there were only 12 countries left on gold compared to 45 countries in 1931. Those remaining on gold included France, Belgium and the Netherlands; these countries only left the system later in the decade.

Overall, various studies have shown that those countries that withdrew from the gold standard – in particular those that left early – had superior economic performance compared to those that remained committed to gold (Eichengreen 1992, Eichengreen and Sachs 1985, Kitson and Michie 1994). Although there were variations in economic performance between individual countries, the comparative evidence suggests that countries that withdrew from gold had more flexibility to adjust their exchange rates and had the ability to use monetary and fiscal policies to help stimulate their domestic economies. Conversely, the countries that were committed to gold were hindered by both the constraints of the gold standard and by increasing overvaluation of their exchange rates as competitor countries left the exchange rate system and devalued.

The 1930s was a period of turbulence in the international economy. The withdrawal of sterling from the gold standard led to countries pursuing independent policies to achieve domestic economic goals. In many cases, such policies had competitive "beggar thy neighbor" impacts which would have been reduced by a coordinated international response to the Great Depression. But such a coordinated response was not feasible due to a lack of international leadership and a failure to appreciate the insights of Keynesian economics. Such a response had to wait until the Bretton Woods agreement in 1944 which provided the intellectual and institutional frameworks which would underpin the "golden age of capitalism" in the 1950s and 1960s.

The 1930s was a decade where high unemployment persisted; countries competed rather than collaborated, and political and social unrest led to the rise of fascism in many countries. But the roots of these problems can be traced to the operation of gold standard which was highly deflationary for many individual countries and the world economy as a whole.

Conclusions

The conventional wisdom in Britain in the early 1920s was that returning to the gold standard at the prewar parity would provide prosperity. This was a mistake. Instead it had a deflationary impact on the economy leading to slow growth. Furthermore, the constraints of being in the system initially led to Britain adopting contractionary policies during the Great Depression, at the very time when expansionary policies were needed. Under pressure from global financial markets, Britain could not maintain its exchange rate parity and was forced to withdrawal from the gold standard in 1931. Although unwanted by many at the time, this withdrawal provided the impetus for recovery from depression and sustained economic growth. It led to a more competitive exchange rate, expansionary monetary policy and helped usher in the protection of domestic manufacturing. The withdrawal of sterling from the gold standard was also the catalyst for the global collapse of the system. As the *Economist* pointed out at the time, this was the end of an epoch. And thankfully so. The gold standard epoch had hampered the growth of the world economy and amplified the Great Depression. The world economy was better off without it.

References

Backhouse, R.E. and Bateman, B.W. (2006) 'A cunning purchase: the life and work of Maynard Keynes', in R. Backhouse and B. Bateman (eds.) *The Cambridge Companion to Keynes*, Cambridge: Cambridge University Press.

Broadberry, S. (1986) *The British Economy between the Wars: A Macroeconomic Survey,* Oxford: Basil Blackwell.

Capie, F. (1983) *Depression and Protectionism: Britain between the Wars,* London: George Allen & Unwin.

Churchill, W. (1925) House of Commons, Financial Statement: Return to the Gold Standard, HC Deb 28, Hansard, April 1925, vol. 183 cc. 52–8.

Churchill, W. (1929) House of Commons, 227 HC Deb, Hansard, 1928–29, c. 53.

Corner, D.C. (1956) 'British exports and the British trade cycle', *Manchester School*, 24: 124–60.

Cunliffe Committee (1918) *Report of the Committee on Finance and Industry,* London: HM Stationery Office.

Economist (1931) 'The end of an epoch', 26 September 1931: 547.

Eichengreen, B. (1992) *Golden Fetters: The Gold Standard and the Great Depression, 1919–1939,* New York: Oxford University Press.

Eichengreen, B. and Sachs, J. (1985) 'Exchange rates and economic recovery in the 1930s', *Journal of Economic History*, 45: 925–46.

Eichengreen, B. and Sachs, J. (1986) 'Competitive devaluation and the Great Depression: a theoretical reassessment', *Economics Letters*, 22: 67–71.

Fleming, J.M. (1962) 'Domestic financial policies under fixed and floating exchange rates', IMF Staff Papers 9: 369–79. Reprinted in R.N. Cooper (ed.) (1969) *International Finance,* New York: Penguin Books.

Hume, D. (1898) *Essays, Moral, Political and Literary,* T.H. Green and T.H. Grose (eds.), Vol.1. London: Longmans.

Hume, L.J. (1963) 'The gold standard and deflation: issues and attitudes in the nineteen-twenties', *Economica*, 30: 225–42.

Irwin D. (2011) 'Anticipating the Great Depression? Gustav Cassel's analysis of the interwar gold standard', NBER Working Paper.

Keynes, J.M. (1919) *The Economic Consequences of the Peace,* London: Macmillan.

Keynes, J.M. (1925) 'The economic consequences of Mr. Churchill', reprinted in *Essays in Persuasion* (1972), London: Macmillan.

Keynes, J.M. (1936) *The General Theory of Employment, Interest and Money,* London: Macmillan.

Kitson, M. (2003) 'Slump and recovery: the UK experience' in T. Balderston (ed.) *World Economy and National Economies in the Interwar Slump,* Basingstoke: Palgrave.

Kitson, M. and Michie, J. (1993) *Coordinated Deflation: The Tale of Two Recessions,* London: Full Employment Forum.

Kitson, M. and Michie, J. (1994) 'Depression and recovery: lessons from the interwar period', in J. Michie and J.G. Smith (eds.) *Unemployment in Europe,* London: Academic Press.

Kitson, M. and Solomou, S. (1990) *Protectionism and Economic Revival: The British Interwar Economy,* Cambridge: Cambridge University Press.

Moggridge, D. (1969) *The Return to Gold, 1925: The Norman Conquest of $4.86,* Cambridge: Cambridge University Press.

Moggridge, D. (1995) *Maynard Keynes: An Economist's Biography,* London: Routledge.

Mundell, R.A. (1963) 'Capital mobility and stabilization policy under fixed and flexible exchange rates', *Canadian Journal of Economic and Political Science,* 29: 475–85, reprinted in Mundell, R.A. (1968) *International Economics,* New York: Macmillan.

Redmond, J. (1980) 'An indicator of the effective exchange rate of the pound in the nineteen-thirties', *Economic History Review,* 33: 83–91.

Redmond, J. (1984) 'The sterling overvaluation in 1925: a multilateral approach', *Economic History Review,* 37: 520–32.

Richardson, H.W. (1967) *Economic Recovery in Britain, 1932–39,* London: Weidenfeld & Nicholson.

Solomou, S. (1996) *Themes in Macroeconomic History: The UK Economy, 1919–1939,* Cambridge: Cambridge University Press.

Solomou, S. and Weale, M. (1993) 'Balanced estimates of national accounts where measurement errors are autocorrelated: the UK, 1920–38', *Journal of the Royal Statistical Society,* 156: 89–105.

Temin, P. (1989) *Lessons from the Great Depression,* Cambridge, MA: MIT Press.

13

THE GREAT DEPRESSION

Randall E. Parker

Introduction

The interwar era from 1919–1939 was a twenty year peace that separated the hostilities of the First and Second World Wars (discussed in Eloranta's and Higgs's chapters, respectively). The period was marked by the prosperity of the 1920s (discussed in Olney's chapter) together with the long recovery period from 1933–1939 (discussed in Fishback's and Ohanian's chapters). In between the roaring twenties and the post-1933 recovery, the world economy collapsed. Figure 13.1 shows the time path of U.S. industrial production from 1919:1–1939:12.

Peaking in July of 1929, industrial output fell almost continuously with but a few upward "breathers" (March–May 1931 and August–October 1932) on its downward plunge, hitting bottom in March 1933. Assessing the damage over those 45 months shows that industrial production fell 52 percent. Given that the United States produced one half of world industrial output in 1929, this decrease in U.S. production represented a one-quarter decline in world industrial output. Unemployment statistics tell a similar story, rising from 3 percent in August 1929 to 25 percent in March 1933.

This chapter focuses on the protracted fall and trough of the Great Depression. While the economic trauma the world witnessed in 2008, and continues to endure in 2012, is similar in many ways to the Great Depression, contemporary events do not begin to match the magnitude of the economic devastation that was evident worldwide in 1933. What were the forces that produced the most severe of all business cycle downturns and why was the Great Depression as deep and widespread as it turned out to be? As we will see, the depth and ubiquity of the Depression cannot be separated, primarily, from two schools of thought: one school that stresses the importance of the intransigent adherence to the interwar gold exchange standard and its fatally flawed structure and another school that focuses on the policy mistakes of the Federal Reserve and its faulty structure.[1]

The aftermath of World War I

In 1919, the United States and all of Europe took a look around and found their world in a smoldering heap of death and destruction. The previous four years had revealed warfare as it had never before been witnessed. Military engagements, such as the Battle of the Somme

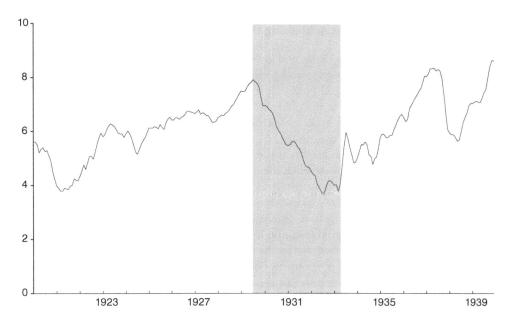

Figure 13.1 Industrial production 1919:1–1939:12

Source: Industrial production data are from the FRED economic data source of the Federal Reserve of St. Louis, 2007 = 100.

from July 1, 1916–November 18, 1916 which caused over one million casualties, were of an entirely new and unknown magnitude that shocked the human senses. The world powers longed to remake the world into something better than what had been endured for those dreadful four years from July 1914–November 1918.[2] So, naturally enough, they looked at a happier time in world history and reached back for what they had known prior to the war. They wanted to recreate what they had before 1914 when everyone agreed it was a better world. One of the key ingredients that fostered economic stability and made the pre-1914 period worthy of emulation was the gold standard. When viewed through the lens of history, the gold standard and prosperity appeared to be a package deal and were considered synonymous. The gold standard fixed exchange rates, and linked markets and the transfer of resources and value internationally. Certainly the empirical record from the late nineteenth and early twentieth centuries gave contemporary observers great faith and belief that the mingling of the gold standard and stable macroeconomic performance was not just a relation that emerged from historical coincidence but rather emanated from meaningful economic causality. Indeed, adherence to and maintenance of the gold standard was considered to be an unmistakable sign and coveted affirmation of a country's passage into economic adulthood and financial rectitude (Bordo and Rockoff 1996).

However, it was the reintroduction of the gold standard into a post-World War I world that had very much changed that set the stage for the Great Depression. The world of 1925 had little resemblance to the world of 1913. The world powers may have longed to recreate what they had before the war, the *status quo ante*. But the morphing of labor markets, unions, wage rigidity, the evolution of the social contract in many European countries and flaws in the structure of the gold standard insured that the efforts toward that recreation would fail. The functioning of the interwar gold standard would be entirely different…and the results devastating.

Re-establishing the gold standard

As discussed in the chapter by Olney and also by Field (2011), the decade from 1920–1929 was a period of economic progress and technological innovation. But it was also a time of financial turmoil as the world powers, particularly the U.S., Great Britain, France and Germany struggled to return to the gold standard.[3] Traditionally, countries suspended the gold standard when hostilities broke out. During the time of war, inflation in the general price level accompanied the expansion of government debt and the gearing up of the economy for wartime production. When the war was over, a country that was previously on the gold standard would re-establish the gold standard at the parity that existed before the war commenced. This was done by Great Britain after the Napoleonic Wars and by the United States after the Civil War, and each required deflation in the general level of prices to reset the dollar or pound sterling to its antebellum fixed price. (See the chapter by Burdekin and Siklos for a discussion of gold resumption and the deflation of the 1870s.) To not do so at the antebellum price was considered by the public to be a betrayal by the government and a confiscation of the wealth of government bond holders since re-establishment at a higher price would imply the erosion of purchasing power of the underlying value of bond holders' assets. Indeed, the dollar price of an ounce of gold had been established at $20.67 beginning in 1837 and it was to that price it was going to return after World War I.[4] While there was some argument regarding when and how the British would return to the gold standard, re-establishment at the price of £1 = $4.86 was not seriously questioned by either Prime Minister Baldwin or Montagu Norman, Governor of the Bank of England.[5] They ultimately brought the Chancellor of the Exchequer, Winston Churchill, over to their way of thinking, against the pleadings of John Maynard Keynes.[6]

The post-war deflation experience was different across countries. The Federal Reserve, in exercising its newly created independent monetary powers (in the sense of not having to accommodate wartime finance concerns), was able to engineer a sharp and short deflation which produced only a mild economic downturn that was quickly reversed. The United States went back on the gold standard in April of 1919, well before any of the countries in Europe. Although initially the recession of 1920–21 that followed the sharp deflation was thought to be a major economic disruption, subsequent scholarship has revealed its mild characteristics for the real economy (Romer 1988). The Federal Reserve faced its first independent test of its monetary powers and was perceived to have passed it convincingly (Friedman and Schwartz 1963, Eichengreen 1992). But the lessons that the Federal Reserve took away from this episode would prove to be very costly later in the decade.

The British did not fare as well as the U.S. in deflating and re-establishing the gold standard. With the re-establishment of the gold standard at prewar parity being the only option under serious consideration, deflation and falling wages were the avenues of adjustment, not devaluation. In maintaining the gold standard, internal balance of the domestic economy is subordinated to external balance and the preservation of the exchange rate and gold price of the domestic currency. Falling prices and wages (and higher interest rates) are the equilibrating mechanism. Indeed this is one of the main factors that led to the demise of the gold standard in the UK in September 1931 as Britain could no longer sustain the loss of gold reserves nor tolerate the deflation that was the necessary and only response to defend and preserve the exchange value of the pound (discussed in Kitson's chapter). After World War I, falling prices were needed to re-establish the exchange rate at £1 = $4.86. Since labor was the largest part of production costs, falling prices meant falling wages. However, the Britain known before World War I was not the Britain after World War I. Wage flexibility had been reduced as the early 1920s saw the emergence of union power, proposals for minimum wages and calls for the provision of state-provided family allowances or "living wages".[7] For the workers who fought and suffered during World War I, this adjustment of falling wages had gone too far. They bore the burden of the fight and now wanted to be treated as equals in the social contract, not simply to be dictated to by the government and firm owners. Although the UK went back on the gold standard in May of 1925, workers were not ready to just give in and capitulate. A general strike occurred from May 4, 1926 until May 13, 1926 that essentially shut the UK economy down. It ended when unions were told they could be held liable for losses during the strike and have their assets seized by the ownership of the firms they worked for. The labor movement lost this fight, but the future had been foretold.

Countries had to live with the exchange rate they chose when they went back on the gold standard. And for Britain, it is thought that the exchange rate they returned to was overvalued by about 10 percent. The combination of an overvalued pound with persistent deflation and labor unrest would make Britain's adherence to the gold standard untenable when the heat of the Great Depression was applied.

Given France's dreadful experience of 300 percent inflation during World War I (Beaudry and Portier 2002: 74) and the continued inflationary aftermath from 1921–1926 (see Eichengreen 1986), France was in no mood or position to deflate back to their pre-war parity of 25 francs per pound sterling in re-establishing the gold standard. When Raymond Poncaré was restored to power in 1926 he put in place a stabilization program that ended the deficits the French government had been running, stopped excessive money growth and successfully reduced expectations of inflation. The steady devaluation of the franc during the 1920s was also halted during this stabilization and the franc was back on the gold standard officially in June 1928 at one-fifth its 1913 exchange rate.[8] It is thought that the franc, based on purchasing power, was re-established at an exchange rate that was undervalued by 25 percent.[9] As indicated above, the parity at which a country returned to the gold standard was chosen unilaterally. Once chosen however, that was the rate that must be defended and would persist. The French were going to rejoin the international financial community at a severely undervalued currency, and French inflation would have been the necessary response to the forthcoming gold inflows the French were to experience. Inflation would have been the avenue to a sustainable equilibrium given this misalignment of exchange rates. But inflation was a non-starter for the French. This is one of the many flaws in the international gold exchange standard, and the stage for the Great Depression was now set.

The Midas touch

The interwar gold exchange standard that the world had wedded itself to was now in place and ready to operate. As long as the rules of the game were observed there was every reason to hope for a happy outcome for the international financial community's contribution to the recreation of the better world that had been known prior to 1914. That is, as long as the law of one price held, as long as countries that gained gold would inflate and countries that lost gold would deflate to observe the proper functioning of the price–specie–flow mechanism, as long as economic adjustments would be borne by prices and not quantities, as long as countries would trade internal imbalance (unemployment, falling wages, lost output) for external balance, and as long as countries would accept deflation in whatever dose was necessary to defend the gold price and exchange value of the national currency and never breathe a word or have a thought about devaluation, the gold standard would be operational. Any chink in the armor of the above list and the sanctity of the gold standard would begin to wobble. Check enough of the above items off the "ready-to-perform" list and the sanctity of the gold standard would crumble.

And that is what happened. The gold standard failed, as it was structured in 1928, because it was afflicted with six dysfunctional flaws.[10] First, and most damning, the gold standard was (and still is if it were to be adopted again) an engine for deflation anytime there was an increase in the relative price of gold. Given that the price of gold is fixed in dollar terms, *anything* that increases the relative price of gold compared to any other commodity must by necessity reduce the price of the other goods in terms of dollars, that is, impose deflation. Second, there was an asymmetry between gold-gaining countries and gold-losing countries. Countries that lost gold reserves *had* to deflate and reduce their money supplies while countries that gained gold *were not compelled* to inflate and increase their money supplies. If a country (or countries) that was attracting gold also decided to go down a contractionary economic path, it would continue to drain gold from other countries, export deflation and force further declines in the supplies of money in other countries. The Genoa Conference of 1922 that established guidelines for the return to gold did not contain any enforcement provision to compel countries to follow the rules of the gold standard (Irwin 2012). This would prove to be a pivotal cause of the spread of the Depression internationally. Third, countries that did not have reserve currencies could hold their minimum reserve balances in the form of gold and convertible foreign currencies, which is known as reserve pyramiding. As long as no threat of devaluation existed the system was stable. But any risk of devaluation sent countries fleeing from holding reserve currencies into gold, rather like the contractionary effects of the public switching from bank deposits to cash holdings. The result was a further contraction of the world money supply and further deflation. Moreover, France had little use for foreign exchange holdings and converted virtually all of their reserves into gold. Fourth, some central banks were restricted in their powers and indeed the Bank of France was prohibited from conducting open market operations (Eichengreen 1986). Thus, as France was amassing gold reserves, it was prevented from adhering to the rules of the gold standard and continued its export of deflation that consumed the world's economy. Fifth, when the gold standard was in jeopardy, the policy options available to improve the situation in fact exacerbated the conditions of the economy. Gold reserve losses promoted deflation and deflation was the only choice to preserve the exchange rate. If market participants questioned a country's commitment to gold, the relative price of gold would rise, more deflation would follow and interest rates would need to rise to stop gold outflow. This cycle of gold loss, deflation, higher interest rates, and unemployment ultimately is what led to Britain leaving the gold standard September 21, 1931. They no longer were able to, nor desired to, resist devaluing the pound. Finally, the sixth and last dysfunctional flaw has been discussed above. The misalignment of exchange rates provided a failure scenario for the world economy with the UK being overvalued by 10 percent and France undervalued by 25 percent, when all countries were officially back on the gold standard and the fact that these exchange rates were the ones that had to be lived with come what may.

The U.S. and France

In 1926 France held 7 percent of the world's gold reserves. By 1932 it held 27 percent of the world's gold reserves. "By 1932, France held nearly as much gold as the United States, though its economy was only about a fourth the size of the United States. Together, the United States and France held more than sixty percent of the world's gold stock in 1932"

(Irwin 2012). And that is the biggest piece of the puzzle needed to construct the narrative of the relation between the gold standard and the Great Depression.

In January 1928, a law was suspended that prohibited the export of capital from France so that securities of all national origin could come and go without restriction for the first time since 1918 (Hamilton 1987: 146). Once the process of officially stabilizing the franc was started in August 1926, at an undervalued exchange, money and gold came pouring into France from all corners of the globe. French gold holdings increased 76 percent between December 1926 and December 1928 of which gold flows from the United States alone represented the equivalent of 4 percent of the total stock of high-powered money in the U.S. during 1928 (Hamilton 1987: 147). In addition, Federal Reserve Bank of New York Governor Benjamin Strong had convinced Fed officials in 1927 of the need to assist the Bank of England in attempting to revive the British economy, especially after the traumatic general strike the year before. Knowing that unilateral action under the gold standard was futile, Montagu Norman asked for help and Strong complied. Monetary policy eased in the U.S. in 1927. By January 1928 , many in the Federal Reserve were convinced that speculative credit was driving the stock market surge and that this was Strong's fault[11] (see Meltzer's interview in Parker 2007). The monetary stimulus of 1927 was a mistake that needed to be unwound. In the real bills doctrine mind set of the time, credit creation was only to be countenanced in support of production. Self-liquidating loans made to support production and output were fine. Money creation for speculative purposes was anathema and supported the monetization of non-productive credit which would ultimately be inflationary. Further, in the belief system of the time, deflation was the inevitable result of inflation and inflation the result of speculative excess. Together with the loss of gold to France and the desire to address the rise in the stock market, the Federal Reserve became highly contractionary in January 1928 (Hamilton 1987).[12] The Fed had deflated quickly and with little consequence to the real economy in 1920–21 and it proceeded to repeat that episode. However, the Fed in 1928 did not appreciate the extent to which the successes of 1920–21 were a product of the unique circumstances that prevailed at that time. Europe was devastated after the war and export demand was strong for the U.S. Other countries were not on the gold standard yet in 1920–21 so that U.S. deflation was not matched by European deflation. Yet the Fed thought it could deflate again in 1928–29 with little consequence to the business cycle. However, the gold standard was now operational and was an engine for the international transmission of deflation (Eichengreen 1992, Parker 2007).

Depression

So in 1928–29 both the U.S. and France decided to take the path to falling prices, and the deflationary vortex that consumed most of the rest of the world had begun (Hamilton 1987, Bernanke and James 1991).[13] The structural dysfunctions of the gold standard and the gold standard's *mentalité* took it from there.[14] As gold flowed in, gold-gaining countries like France sterilized these inflows and compelled their trading partners to deflate and raise interest rates to stop the gold outflow. Preservation of the gold standard required deflation and it would be adhered to since the gold standard was the ideology and belief system that drove the actions of policy makers of that day. Consideration of actions outside the framework of the gold standard was unthinkable. Maintaining the orthodoxy of the gold standard would eventually restore order, if only there was the political will to persevere. This was the thinking of Benjamin Strong, U.S. president Herbert Hoover, Governor of the Federal Reserve System Eugene Meyer, Treasury Secretary Ogden Mills, Montagu Norman and Émile Moreau,

Governor of the Bank of France, to name some of the most important policy makers. And they stuck to it until they could not maintain it any longer (Britain) or there was a regime change (U.S.) and the unthinkable became thinkable. Or in the words of Eichengreen and Temin (2003: 212) only "until after an unprecedented crisis had rendered the respectable unrespectable and vice versa." Britain left gold on September 21, 1931 after a summer of bad financial news in Europe and a series of speculative attacks on the pound. They could no longer stomach interest rate increases and further deflation with a 20 percent unemployment rate. Moreover, their gold reserves had been drained to the point that they no longer found participation in the gold standard viable. After Britain departed, the U.S. continued to defend gold and this delivered "the knockout punch to the U.S. economy" (Hamilton 1988: 72). Uncertainty regarding the maintenance of the gold standard led to an increase in the relative price of gold and gold outflow. The gold standard prescription for this situation was higher interest rates and more deflation … and an intensified tumble to the bottom that finally came in March 1933. Leaving the gold standard was an executive decision and Hoover was going to stick with gold to the bitter end. And he did. It was only when Franklin Roosevelt took office in March 1933 that the gold standard was suspended and the allure of the Midas touch finally rejected. It was only after 25 percent unemployment, a massive wave of bank failures, a run on the dollar and the Federal Reserve of New York being reduced to a gold cover ratio of 24 percent that the gold standard and its orthodoxy were jettisoned.[15] Once this was done, recovery began almost immediately. In fact one of the strongest macroeconomic relations that economic research has identified is the empirical link between when a country left the gold standard and when recovery commenced. Brown (1940), Choudhri and Kochin (1980), Eichengreen and Sachs (1985), and Campa (1990) all overwhelmingly confirm that leaving the gold standard was a precondition for recovery. Regime change, as discussed by Temin (1989), finally freed the U.S. from the grip of the vertiginous downward deflation and depression cycle of August 1929–March 1933.

The monetary hypothesis

The hypothesis that the Great Depression was caused by a massive decline in the money supply is neatly summarized by the title of the seventh chapter, "The Great Contraction, 1929–1933," in the monumental work of Friedman and Schwartz (1963). A look at Figure 13.2 quickly reveals what Friedman and Schwartz had in mind. Note the dramatic fall in M2 from a high in August 1929 of $46.28 billion to a low of $29.75 billion in April 1933, a decline of 36 percent.

Great Contractions in the supply of money cause Great Depressions. Figure 13.2 also contains the answer to whom Friedman and Schwartz attribute the responsibility for this unfortunate economic record. By definition, the supply of money is the product of the monetary base multiplied by the money multiplier. Figure 13.2 shows that with a falling M2 and a constant monetary base, a crashing money multiplier is the culprit behind the falling money supply. The proper response from the monetary authorities should have been to accelerate the growth rate of the monetary base to counteract the falling multiplier and prevent the money supply from falling. Figure 13.2 demonstrates the monetary base had little to no movement during the protracted downward phase of the Depression. Its time path is virtually horizontal when the Depression was at its worst. The monetary base is certainly the one monetary variable that the Federal Reserve most closely controls and yet it did nothing to combat the epic fall in the money supply.[16] Looking at the equation of exchange where the money supply multiplied by the velocity of money equals nominal GDP, $M \times V = NGDP$,

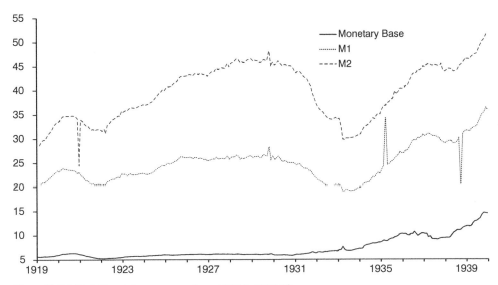

Figure 13.2 M1, M2 and the monetary base 1919:1–1939:12

Sources: M1 and M2 are from Friedman and Schwartz (1963) in billions of dollars. The monetary base is from the FRED economic data source of the Federal Reserve of St. Louis

with both the velocity of money and the money supply falling sharply, unless prices were perfectly flexible in the downward direction the inevitable result was depression. Yet, the Federal Reserve sat back and watched while the economy burned. In the monetary view, the culpability for the meltdown of the financial system, deflation, high real interest rates, and Depression can be laid squarely at the feet of the Federal Reserve and their series of policy errors.[17] In the words of Friedman and Schwartz (1963: 693):

> At all times throughout the 1929–33 contraction, alternative policies were available to the System by which it could have kept the stock of money from falling, and indeed could have increased it at almost any desired rate. Those policies did not involve radical innovations. They involved measures of a kind the System had taken in earlier years, of a kind explicitly contemplated by the founders of the System to meet precisely the kind of banking crisis that developed in late 1930 and persisted thereafter. They involved measures that were actually proposed and very likely would have been adopted under a slightly different bureaucratic structure or distribution of power, or even if the men in power had had somewhat different personalities. Until late 1931 – and we believe not even then – the alternative policies involved no conflict with the maintenance of the gold standard. Until September 1931, the problem that recurrently troubled the System was how to keep gold inflows under control, not the reverse.

So, inept monetary policy caused the Depression and it need not have turned out as it did. Different policies or different people would have produced different history.

The real question then becomes *why* did the people who ran the Federal Reserve act, or not act, as they did? It is not enough to just say it was a mistake and move on. The task of economic research and the key to a greater understanding of economic history is to discern what compelled the policy makers during the Depression to make the decisions they did in fact make. On these matters pertaining to the Federal Reserve, the chapter by James Butkiewicz provides an excellent discussion that will not be repeated here. For the purposes of this chapter, suffice it to say that during the 1929–33 period the leaders of the Federal Reserve had a list of beliefs, and might we say with the clarity of history, shortcomings, that molded the way they saw the world. This is not unique to those individuals as everyone else throughout history views events through their own experiences and their own theories of how the world works. However, taken together, at one time or another across a wide group of important people, these nine items were the largest part of the concatenation of forces that gave the world the Great Depression. Meltzer, in his interview in Parker (2007), spells out the items on this list:

1 The inability to distinguish between nominal and real interest rates.
2 The use of interest rates as an indicator of monetary tightness or ease.
3 Reliance and belief in the real bills doctrine which rendered monetary policy endogenous and completely passive with respect to the business cycle.
4 The use of borrowing volume as a measure of monetary tightness or ease. The thinking was if no one borrows then money must be plentiful.
5 The failure to act as lender of last resort.[18]
6 The belief that speculative excesses would be inflationary and must be purged.
7 Ignoring the rules of the gold standard.
8 Flawed institutional structure in both the Federal Reserve and the Bank of France.
9 As discussed at length above, the strict adherence to the gold standard orthodoxy as being the key to long-run prosperity.

Any one of these would probably not have generated the severity of the downturn that was experienced. The combination of all of them gave us the history contained in Figures 13.1 and 13.2.[19] But it need not have been as it turned out. Meltzer (2003) argues that if countries simply would have followed the rules of the gold standard, the Depression would not have happened. Moreover, McCallum (1990), Fackler and Parker (1994) and Bordo, Choudhri and Schwartz (1995) all demonstrate that if the Federal Reserve would have kept the money supply growing along its 1920s trend, the Great Depression would have been averted.

Current (and perhaps perpetual) debate and further readings

Perhaps the greatest remaining debate regarding the economics of the Great Depression concerns the extent to which the Federal Reserve was free to follow an independent monetary policy as long as it was functioning within a gold standard regime. Friedman and Schwartz (1963), Bordo, Choudhri and Schwartz (2002) and Hsieh and Romer (2006) conclude the Federal Reserve could have and should have done much more to avert the Depression and it was within its powers to have done so. Temin (1989), Eichengreen (1992) and Eichengreen and Temin (2000) argue that as long as the United States and other countries were locked into obedience to the gold standard, they were forced to choose deflation over devaluation. Monetary policies were crucially important, but they "were made in a particular institutional setting and global context."[20] And that of course was the gold standard and the constraints it placed upon policy makers. As long as the gold standard orthodoxy was followed, deflation and depression would result. Only a change of regime would break the cycle.

That is where the literature stands, as of 2012, and where it will probably remain. Perhaps the most measured reading of the debate is the work of Bernanke and Mihov (2000: 111) who conclude "the causes of world monetary contraction might be that damage resulted from 'self-inflicted wounds' prior to the financial crises of 1931, and 'forces beyond our control' between 1931 and 1933." Or said differently, there was room for monetary authorities to independently offset monetary contraction prior to the summer of 1931. But after the realities of massive bank failure in Europe and the U.S., and the British exit from the gold standard in September 1931, the gold standard and a country's commitment to its preservation called the tune until remaining on the gold standard was no longer viable and regime change came about.

The reader is referred to Parker (2011) for a comprehensive three-volume reference on the major pieces of research that have done the most to advance our understanding of the Great Depression. In particular, the seminal works of Bernanke (1983), Choudhri and Kochin (1980) and Eichengreen and Sachs (1985) deserve special mention. While Bernanke (1983) built upon the work of Friedman and Schwartz (1963), it furthered the ideas of Fisher (1933) and analyzed the role of information loss due to bank failures to help explain the protracted non-neutrality of money during the Depression. But more than this, the work of Bernanke energized a moribund literature and spurred a twenty-five-year burst of research on the interwar era that continues today. Further, the literature on the gold standard and the Great Depression had been virtually silent since Brown's classic work of 1940. Choudhri and Kochin (1980) brought the importance of the gold standard back to the discussion, and Eichengreen and Sachs (1985) laid the groundwork for the flurry of research on the gold standard in the late 1980s and beyond that has done so much to sharpen what we know about the interwar era. [21]

Conclusion

In a must-read new book titled *Why Nations Fail*, Daron Acemoglu and James Robinson make the convincing case that it is manmade economic and political institutions, how they are structured and the responsibility and accountability they provide to the people they serve that determine wealth and poverty, famine and plenty among nations. Leaving out the richness of the case made by Acemoglu and Robinson (2012) and putting it simply, nations fail because of flawed institutions.

This can also be the lesson to take away from the Great Depression. World economies fail because of flawed institutions and faulty international arrangements. At the top of this list for the interwar period of the flawed and faulty should be any institution that would permit the money supply to fall by 35 percent. The story told by Friedman and Schwartz (1963) of the lack of meaningful institutional decision-making structure at the Federal Reserve and the absence of corrective monetary policy action when it was at their disposal to implement makes the mantra "there will be no more 1930s" something the current leaders of the Federal Reserve are correctly chanting.

Also at the top of this list for the interwar period of the flawed and faulty should be the interwar gold standard. Men and nations executed some very severe policies to slavishly maintain this international financial system, until they could no longer take the pain. For some the pain lasted shorter periods of time (Japan, Sweden, UK, Canada, Norway, Australia and New Zealand, all left the gold standard by December 1931). For others it was much longer (the U.S. left in 1933 and France, Poland, Italy, and the Netherlands not until 1936). But in the end, relief only came once the gold standard was put back in the history books. The gold standard and the Great Depression are forever linked by the historical experience and empirical evidence of the interwar era.

Let us hope it is in the history books that the gold standard remains. Since the financial crisis of 2008, the voices advocating for a return to the gold standard have gotten louder and louder.[22] These quixotic longings are dangerous and must be resisted with all possible intellectual vigor. To praise the gold standard, long for its reemergence and advocate for its return ignores history. Yet, the gold standard is like a phoenix that rises from the ashes when the economy seems to be burning. Let us hope that the interwar gold exchange standard will be viewed as the pernicious anachronism that it is, and returned to the ash heap of history every time it rises.

Notes

1 There are some additional emerging avenues of research such as Ohanian (2009) and McGrattan (2010) that take a fresh look at wage policy and fiscal policy during the Depression, respectively. However, the "monetary hypothesis" and the "gold standard hypothesis" are the two major competing interpretations of the causes of the Great Depression.
2 For additional detail and insight see Temin (1989) and Eichengreen and Temin (2000).
3 See Ferguson and Temin (2003) and Ritschl (2003) for further discussion of the German experience during this period.
4 This was certainly the opinion of both Montagu Norman and Benjamin Strong. See Temin (1989: 14) for an expression of these sentiments in a memorandum written by Strong and sent to Norman on January 11, 1925.
5 Officially, doing the math, an ounce of gold was worth $20.67 in the United States and £3 17s 10½d in Great Britain. Therefore, the exchange rate works out to be $4.86 per pound. Note also that the value of money on the gold standard is backed up by some physical commodity, namely, gold. Thus the gold standard is referred to as a "commodity standard", as opposed to today's fiat standard, and also has the appellation of being a "hard money" monetary system.
6 See Keynes (1925) for reaction to the re-establishment of the pre-war parity. Also see Irwin (2011) for a discussion of the prescience of Gustav Cassel in predicting the demise of the gold standard as early as 1920.
7 See Eichengreen and Temin (2000: 191–92) for greater detail.
8 In January 1913 the French franc exchanged for 19.35 cents. In June 1928 the French franc traded for 3.93 cents. Remembering that the £1 = $4.86, the French franc went for 25 francs = £1 in 1913 to 125 francs = £1 in 1928.
9 See Hamilton (1987: 146).
10 Not to mention dysfunctional flaw seven where the world's money supply is held hostage in the long run to the discoveries of new gold deposits that can be mined and added to gold reserves. See Friedman and Schwartz (1963) for a discussion of the importance to the world economy of gold strikes in South Africa and Canada in the 1890s.
11 Adolf Miller, a founding Governor of the Federal Reserve System, certainly said so in testimony for the Banking Act of 1935.
12 Note, it really is irrelevant whether or not there was a speculative bubble in stocks at the time or if they were fairly priced. The Federal Reserve's perception was that there was a bubble and that is what it acted on.
13 Not all countries got caught up in the worldwide deflation. Spain was never on the gold standard at this time and missed the Great Depression completely. The Chinese were on a silver standard and missed the Depression too, although they had much else to be concerned with as Imperial Japan invaded Chinese Manchuria two days before Britain left the gold standard.
14 See Temin (1989). The French word *mentalité* translated into English, according to the Merriam-Webster online dictionary, means a set of thought processes, values and beliefs shared by members of a community. This definition could not be more fitting.
15 The statutory minimum cover ratio was 40 percent so there were not sufficient gold reserves to cover the currency that had been issued by the Federal Reserve of New York. See Meltzer (2003) and Wigmore (1987) for more extensive discussion of March 1933. Looking at the data for bank failures, it seems clear that the worst waves of bank failures centered around the episodes where the commitment to gold was most in question, the Summer of 1931 and March 1933.

16 See McMillin's chapter on recent monetary policy for insightful observations regarding the Federal Reserve's actions during the crisis of 2008 and how completely different they were compared to 1929–33.

17 See Hsieh and Romer (2006) for a more recent affirmation of these conclusions.

18 See Richardson and Troost (2009) for an important discussion and unique empirical approach showing how greater lending by the Fed would have moderated the financial crises and severity of the Depression. Also see Bordo and Wheelock (2011) for reasons why the Federal Reserve failed to live up to its role as lender of last resort during the Depression.

19 Certainly economic research and history will come up with a similar list for the financial crisis of 2008. Perhaps Gorton's chapter can be viewed as a starting point in this endeavor.

20 The quote is from Eichengreen in Parker (2007: 154).

21 Credit also goes to Kindleberger (1973) and Temin (1976) for introducing international considerations into the inquiry of the causes of the Great Depression, It should be noted that Abramovitz (1977) was the first to look at the international angle in the modern literature on the Great Depression. Unfortunately this paper was never published and copies of it are scattered to the winds of history.

22 Statements such as: "We need a currency that is as good as gold." "The gold standard was never really properly executed during the Depression so that evidence is irrelevant to today." "The gold standard worked fine during the Depression. It was the people that corrupted it." "The Federal Reserve cannot be trusted so we need an ironclad rule that would eliminate the Fed." The public policy pronouncements of Congressman Ron Paul are the most cited comments that contain these sentiments. He is not the only one who feels this way.

References

Abramovitz, M. (1977) 'Determinants of nominal-income and money-stock growth and the level of the balance of payments: two-country models under a specie standard', unpublished, Stanford University.

Acemoglu, D. and Robinson, J. (2012) *Why Nations Fail: The Origins of Power, Prosperity, and Poverty*, New York: Crown Business.

Beaudry, P. and Portier, F. (2002) 'The French Depression in the 1930s', *Review of Economic Dynamics*, 5: 73–99.

Bernanke, B. (1983) 'Nonmonetary effects of the financial crisis in the propagation of the Great Depression', *American Economic Review*, 73: 257–76.

Bernanke, B. and James, H. (1991) 'The gold standard, deflation, and financial crisis in the Great Depression: an international comparison', in R.G. Hubbard (ed.) *Financial Markets and Financial Crises*, Chicago: University of Chicago Press.

Bernanke, B. and Mihov, I. (2000) 'Deflation and monetary contraction in the Great Depression: an analysis by simple ratios', in B. Bernanke (ed.) *Essays on the Great Depression*, Princeton, NJ: Princeton University Press.

Bordo, M. and Rockoff, H. (1996) 'The gold standard as a "Good Housekeeping Seal of Approval"', *Journal of Economic History*, 56: 389–428.

Bordo, M. and Wheelock, D. (2011) 'The promise and performance of the Federal Reserve as lender of last resort 1914–1933', NBER working paper 16763.

Bordo, M., Choudhri, E. and Schwartz, A. (1995) 'Could stable money have averted the Great Contraction?' *Economic Inquiry*, 33: 484–505.

Bordo, M., Choudhri, E. and Schwartz, A. (2002) 'Was expansionary monetary policy feasible during the great contraction? An examination of the gold standard constraint', *Explorations in Economic History*, 39: 1–28.

Brown, W.A. (1940) *The International Gold Standard Reinterpreted, 1914–1934*, New York: National Bureau of Economic Research.

Campa, J. (1990) 'Exchange rates and economic recovery in the 1930s: an extension to Latin America', *Journal of Economic History*, 50: 677–82.

Choudhri, E.U. and Kochin, L.A. (1980) 'The exchange rate and the international transmission of business cycle disturbances', *Journal of Money, Credit and Banking*, 12: 565–74.

Eichengreen, B. (1986) 'The Bank of France and the sterilization of gold, 1926–1932', *Explorations in Economic History*, 23: 56–84.

Eichengreen, B. (1992) *Golden Fetters: The Gold Standard and the Great Depression, 1919–1939*, New York: Oxford University Press.

Eichengreen, B. and Sachs, J. (1985) 'Exchange rates and economic recovery in the 1930s', *Journal of Economic History*, 45: 925–46.

Eichengreen, B. and Temin, P. (2000) 'The gold standard and the Great Depression', *Contemporary European History*, 9: 183–207.

Eichengreen, B. and Temin, P. (2003) 'Afterword: Counterfactual histories of the Great Depression', in T. Balderston (ed.) *The World Economy and National Economies in the Interwar Slump*, New York: Palgrave Macmillan.

Fackler, J. and Parker, R. (1994) 'Accounting for the Great Depression: a historical decomposition', *Journal of Macroeconomics*, 16: 193–220.

Federal Reserve of St. Louis (n.d.) Federal Reserve Economic Data (FRED) http://research.stlouisfed.org/fred2/.

Ferguson, T. and Temin, P. (2003) 'Made in Germany: the German currency crisis of July 1931', *Research in Economic History*, 21: 1–53.

Field, A. (2011) *A Great Leap Forward: 1930s Depression and U.S. Economic Growth*, New Haven, CT: Yale University Press.

Fisher, I. (1933) 'The debt-deflation theory of great depressions', *Econometrica*, 1: 337–57.

Friedman, M. and Schwartz, A. (1963) *A Monetary History of the United States, 1867–1960*, Princeton, NJ: Princeton University Press.

Hamilton, J. (1987) 'Monetary factors in the Great Depression', *Journal of Monetary Economics*, 19: 145–69.

Hamilton, J. (1988) 'Role of the international gold standard in propagating the Great Depression', *Contemporary Policy Issues*, 6: 67–89.

Hsieh, C.-T. and Romer, C. (2006) 'Was the Federal Reserve constrained by the gold standard during the Great Depression? Evidence from the 1932 open market purchase program', *Journal of Economic History*, 66: 140–76.

Irwin, D. (2011) 'Anticipating the Great Depression? Gustav Cassel's analysis of the interwar gold standard', NBER working paper 17597.

Irwin, D. (2012) 'The French gold sink and the great deflation', Cato Papers on Public Policy, 2: forthcoming.

Keynes, J.M. (1925) *The Economic Consequences of Mr. Churchill*, London: Hogarth Press.

Kindleberger, C. (1973) *The World in Depression, 1929–1939*, Berkeley CA: University of California Press.

McCallum, B. (1990) 'Could a monetary base rule have prevented the Great Depression?' *Journal of Monetary Economics*, 26: 3–26.

McGrattan, E. (2010) 'Capital taxation during the Great Depression', Federal Reserve of Minneapolis working paper 670.

Meltzer, A.H. (2003) *A History of the Federal Reserve, Volume I*, Chicago, IL: University of Chicago Press.

Ohanian, L. (2009) 'What – or who – started the Great Depression?', *Journal of Economic Theory*, 144: 2310–35.

Parker, R. (2007) *The Economics of the Great Depression: A Twenty-First Century Look Back at the Economics of the Interwar Era*, Northampton, MA: Edward Elgar.

Parker, R. (2011) *The Seminal Works of the Great Depression, Volumes I–III*, Northampton, MA: Edward Elgar.

Richardson, G. and Troost, W. (2009) 'Monetary intervention mitigated banking panics during the Great Depression: quasi-experimental evidence from a Federal Reserve district border, 1929–1933', *Journal of Political Economy*, 117: 1031–73.

Ritschl, A. (2003) '"Dancing on a volcano": the economic recovery and collapse of Weimar Germany, 1924–33', in T. Balderston (ed.) *The World Economy and National Economies in the Interwar Slump*, New York: Palgrave Macmillan.

Romer, C. (1988) 'World War I and the postwar depression: a reappraisal based on alternative estimates of GNP', *Journal of Monetary Economics*, 22: 91–115.

Temin, P. (1976) 'Lessons for the present from the Great Depression', *American Economic Review*, 66: 40–45.

Temin, P. (1989) *Lessons from the Great Depression*, Cambridge, MA: MIT Press.

Wigmore, B. (1987) 'Was the bank holiday of 1933 caused by a run on the dollar?' *Journal of Economic History*, 47: 739–55.

14

THE MICROECONOMICS OF THE NEW DEAL DURING THE GREAT DEPRESSION

Price V. Fishback

Franklin Roosevelt's New Deal was the largest peace-time expansion in the federal government's role in the economy in American history. It was initiated after four years of economic devastation. By the beginning of 1933 unemployment rates had risen to nearly 25 percent of the labor force and annual real GDP had fallen to 30 percent of the 1929 level. Within the next six years, government spending as a share of GDP rose by nearly 5 percent.

So many people faced so many different types of troubles that Roosevelt and the newly elected Democratic Congress enacted policy changes in dozens of areas. If there was a unifying theme among the policies, it might have been to raise prices and wages in the face of the deflation that the economy had experienced. Yet, this theme covered only a few of the policies. A better description of the thinking was: "See a problem, develop a policy to try and fix it." People have lost their jobs: provide cash, food, and clothing to families and/or work relief jobs with subsistence earnings, build public works while paying full wages and seek to stimulate the economy while improving social overhead capital. Homeowners are losing their homes in foreclosure: purchase the troubled mortgages and refinance them. People don't trust the financial sector: regulate stocks, banks, savings and loans, and other financial institutions in new ways and create agencies to provide insurance against losses of deposits or on housing loans. Businesses and workers are facing problems across industries: allow employers, workers, and consumers in each industry to meet and set prices, wages, and quality of goods. Farm incomes have dropped: pay farmers to take land out of production and provide them with a variety of loans to help hold prices up and give them low-interest loans. Wages are too low: give unions the right to collective bargaining and establish minimum wages. The problems and responses ranged across nearly every aspect and sector of the economy.

Most New Deal policies were designed to achieve specific goals that were microeconomic in nature. For the past two decades scholars have been using modern quantitative methods to examine the impact of the various New Deal policies in local areas and for specific sectors of the economy. Because there were so many policy changes, the quantitative research has only begun to dig below the surface. This chapter summarizes the research findings related to the distribution of New Deal funds across areas and then describes the results of studies examining the impact of the following New Deal programs: relief and public works spending, farm programs, housing loans, and the National Recovery Administration.

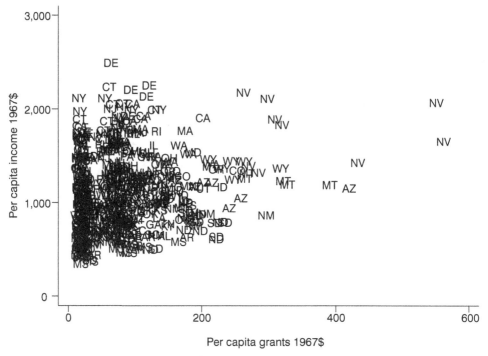

Figure 14.1 Per capita personal income and per capita federal grants in the state in 1967 dollars, 1930–40

Source: Fishback and Kachanovskaya (2011)

The distribution of New Deal funds across the country

The geographic distribution of New Deal funds has received the most attention in microeconomic studies of the New Deal. Leonard Arrington (1970) pointed out that per capita spending on New Deal programs varied dramatically across the states, as seen in Figure 14.1. Since then a cottage industry has produced a large number of publications seeking to explain the reasons why. The debate has centered on the extent to which the Roosevelt Administration followed their announcements that they had sought to promote "Relief, Recovery, and Reform," (the three Rs) or instead followed the more cynical aim of using government programs to build patronage and to "buy" voters to ensure the continuation of the Democrats' control of the presidency and the Congress.[1]

Nearly four decades of study shows that both sets of factors were important, although different study specifications give different weights to each factor. Most studies find evidence that the funds were distributed to some degree in the ways suggested by the rhetoric of the Roosevelt Administration. There are some signs that *total* spending was higher in areas with more economic problems. When the focus shifts to relief programs that explicitly focused on the poor, the signs of higher spending in areas with higher unemployment, more of an output drop, and lower long-term incomes are much stronger. Analysis by program suggests that many of the housing programs, like the Home Owners' Loan Corporation (HOLC) and the Federal Housing Administration (FHA) benefited higher income people, while many of the farm programs benefited large farmers.

Every study shows that politics mattered, particularly swing voting and higher voter turnout. Areas that had long supported Democrats fared well in some programs but not in others. Key Congressional leaders and members of key Congressional committees apparently were successful at "bringing home the bacon" to their constituents. Meanwhile, more federal relief spending was distributed in the months just prior to key national elections than in other years and at other times within the election years. The attitudes of state and local leaders and their administrative skills also determined the distribution. Some federal programs involved matching grants, while others required local governments to come up with projects to be funded.

In the final analysis further attempts to assign more exact weights to the three Rs and presidential politicking may be fruitless. Our measures of each are inexact at best, and we really have no metric for what was the "right" amount. Typically the most we can say is that a specific factor had an impact with only a rough idea of the weight. Further, good politics requires more than just strategic manipulation. Failure to deliver on at least some of the promises in the rhetoric would likely cause losses in the next election. Sorting out the differences is made more difficult by the great deal of overlap between the states that had high values for swing voting and presidential politicking and the states where economic problems were greatest (Fleck 2008).

The local impact of New Deal programs

Over the past two decades there has been increasing interest in measuring the impact of the New Deal at the local level. The wide range in per capita incomes and New Deal spending across the country illustrated in Figure 14.1 is similar to the range for a variety of New Deal programs and socio-economic outcomes. Scholars have therefore developed cross-sectional data and panel data sets for cities, counties, and states, as well as pseudo panels for individual census data from the Integrated Public Use Micro Series (IPUMS) to analyze the effects of the New Deal. All of the studies use multivariate analysis to control for correlates. The ones with panel data also use year fixed effects to control for factors that influenced all areas in each time period but varied over time, and area fixed effects for time-invariant features in the areas that varied from place to place. In situations where there are fears of endogeneity bias, a number of studies have explored the use of instrumental variables.

The impact of all federal grants on state economic activity

Macroeconomists have not spent much time focusing on the effects of fiscal stimulus in the Great Depression at the national level because it is generally agreed that the Roosevelt Administration did not try to run a Keynesian policy. The federal deficit remained small relative to the size of the problem in large part because tax revenues rose at roughly the same rate as federal distributions (Brown 1956, Peppers 1973, Fishback 2010). There are opportunities to examine the impact of differences in fiscal stimulus at the state level because Figure 14.1 shows that there was enormous variation in the per capita federal grants awarded and the per capita incomes in each state over the course of the 1930s. The figure also shows that there does not appear to be a strong positive relationship between per capita federal grants and per capita incomes in the raw data. The negative endogeneity bias from the Roosevelt Administration's attempts to offset downturns with more grant spending may well have worked against the expected positive benefits from the spending.

Regional models across the spectrum predict a positive relationship between per capita income and injections of spending in the form of multipliers. The area multipliers for injections of federal spending in regional models are driven by a variety of factors. A multiplier of one occurs when the spending feeds directly into state income such that a dollar per capita of federal spending raises income per capita by a dollar. The multiplier can grow larger than one if the grant spending not only employs workers in projects that would not have been built otherwise but also makes the private sector more productive or leads to spending that rolls over through the economy. Crowding out of private activity, like building an electric plant that would have been built by a private company, can lead to multipliers much less than one.

Since each local area was part of a larger economy, the impact of spending on income in the area receiving the funds was weakened to the extent that the grant money went to purchasing goods and services from other areas. Work relief grants suffered least from these leakages because over 80 percent of the money was spent on relief wages. The effects of federal injections were weakened further when local consumers purchased goods and services from other areas and when federal tax rates bit into the amount they had available to spend. Fishback, Horrace, and Kantor (2004, appendix) estimated in a simple regional federal model that if 80 percent of the grant was spent on wages, 80 percent of consumption was within the state, there was a 30 percent boost in productivity as a result of the grant, and the federal tax rate was about 7 percent, the multiplier of an additional dollar of per capita federal spending could exceed 2. However, if buyers imported 50 percent of their purchases, there was no productivity boost and no crowding out, and the other assumptions remained the same, the multiplier would be only 0.85. If there was crowding out of private activity or employment, the coefficient would be smaller still. It is true that each area can benefit from federal injections in other areas that purchase goods and services from them, but they get those benefits whether the federal government spends in that area or not. Thus, these multipliers give a sense of the benefit to local areas for lobbying for federal injections.

Fishback and Kachanovskaya (2011) develop a state panel data set with information on each year from 1930 to 1940 for various measures of economic activity and a variety of measures of federal government spending. In the process they control for changes in weather and year and state fixed effects, and they explore the use of state-specific time trends and a variety of instrumental variables. Their estimates suggest that the personal income multiplier from overall federal grant spending (and other broader measures) was roughly one. There was a stronger relative effect on retail spending and on purchases of automobiles. However, they do not find that the federal grants led to increases in private employment.

Relief and public works programs

The New Deal greatly expanded the value of grants and loans distributed by the federal government for the building of roads, dams, flood control, irrigation projects, federal buildings, and other national government public works. The projects simultaneously built new social overhead capital and also provided employment at full market wages for a significant number of skilled and unskilled workers through the normal contracting procedures. These projects accounted for about 20 percent of the total grants during the New Deal period listed in Table 14.1.

The lion's share of New Deal spending (roughly 62 percent) went to the federal government's new role as an emergency provider of relief for the unemployed and the poor through programs like the Federal Emergency Relief Administration (FERA), the Works Progress Administration (WPA) and the Social Security Public Assistance (SSPA) programs. The WPA and FERA programs were relief programs designed to replace incomes up to a very basic standard of living that was roughly 65 to 75 percent of the budget that social workers considered to be a maintenance budget for a manual worker (Stecker 1937: 5). Thus, for work relief jobs they limited working hours and paid hourly wages that were about half of the wages paid on public works projects. The Social Security Act of 1935 provided for federal matching grants to the states to provide aid to dependent children, the blind, and the poor elderly to help aid the poor once the states structured their existing programs or added new programs to meet the federal requirements.

The public works and relief spending tended to have stronger effects on state per capita personal incomes than overall spending. In Fishback and Kachanovskaya (2011), the point estimates for the multipliers are between 0.9 and 1.8, although the hypothesis of a multiplier of 1 cannot be rejected. In studies of counties during the 1930s, Fishback, Horrace, and Kantor (2005, 2006) find that an additional dollar of public works and relief spending over the course of the 1930s raised retail sales per capita in 1939 by 40 to 50 cents, while also stimulating in-migration into the county despite efforts by state and local officials to restrict access to relief to migrants.

The Tennessee Valley Authority, a government-sponsored corporation, developed a series of dams for flood control and electricity along the Tennessee River, which runs through Tennessee, Alabama, and slivers of Mississippi and Kentucky. Aside from the stimulus of the building projects, the TVA had the potential to lead to major long-run improvements in standards of living in the areas where it operated. Although many people have presumed that the TVA charged lower electric rates than the other utilities in the South, comparisons of the monthly bills for the vast majority of electricity consumers show no difference in the amounts paid per month. Comparisons of counties with and without access to TVA electricity show very little difference in the electrification of farms or in the growth of retail sales (Kitchens 2011a). The TVA dams did much to improve flood control in the southeast along multiple rivers but they had the unfortunate side effect of increasing problems with malaria because they created long coastlines with standing water in the areas that were flooded, which supported more mosquitoes. The TVA tried to change water levels, spread oil on the water, and use other methods to prevent mosquito hatches, but the efforts could not fully counteract the increase in mosquito activity (Kitchens 2011b).

Relief spending had a variety of salutary effects on a number of dimensions in American cities. By building public health facilities and providing funds and in-kind benefits to the poor and unemployed, families were better able to stave off disease. Using a panel of 114 cities from 1929 to 1940, Fishback, Haines, and Kantor (2007) find that about $2 million (in 2000$) in additional relief spending was associated with the reduction of one infant death, half a homicide, one suicide, 2.4 deaths from infectious disease, and one death from diarrhea in large urban areas between 1929 and 1940. The relief spending also gave young people enough income to return to normal fertility patterns.

Relief spending also struck at the roots of crime. Work relief had particularly strong effects because it replaced lost income and also occupied a significant amount of the recipient's time. In a city panel study of the 1930s, Johnson, Kantor, and Fishback (2010) find that a 10 percent increase in spending on work relief was associated with a 1.5 percent reduction in property crime. The relief spending was not as successful as private employment in reducing property crime; they also find that a 10 percent rise in employment in a city was associated with a 10 percent fall in property crime rates in the 1930s.

The one disappointing feature of the public works and work relief programs was that they did not appear to provide enough stimulus to generate a rise in private employment. A rise in public works spending that employed workers at full wages was likely to raise the number of government workers, but it would only increase private employment if there

Table 14.1 Total and per capita federal spending by program in millions of contemporary dollars for the period July 1, 1932 through June 30, 1939

	Acronym	Amounts from July 1, 1932 to June 30, 1939 (Millions $)	Per Capita	Category	First Fiscal Year with Significant Spending
Total Taxes Collected From States		26,061	213.11		
Nonrepayable Grants					
Works Progress Administration	WPA	6,844	55.97	Work Relief	1936
Veterans' Administration	VA	3,955	32.34	Relief	Pre 1933
Federal Emergency Relief Administration	FERA	3,059	25.02	Relief and Work Relief	1934
Agricultural Adjustment Administration	AAA	2,863	23.41	Agriculture	1934
Civilian Conservation Corps	CCC	2,130	17.42	Work Relief	1934
Public Roads Administration	PRA	1,613	13.19	Public Works	Pre 1933
Rivers and Harbors and Flood Control	RHFC	1,316	10.76	Public Works	Pre 1933
Public Works Administration – Nonfederal Projects	PWANF	1,032	8.44	Public Works	1934
Civil Works Administration	CWA	807	6.60	Relief/Public Works	1934
Social Security Act	SSA	759	6.21	Relief	1936
Public Works Administration – Federal Projects	PWAF	632	5.16	Public Works	1934
Balance from Relief Acts	BRA	376	3.08	Relief	1936
Public Buildings Administration	PBA	324	2.65	Public Works	Pre 1933
Bureau of Reclamation	BR	290	2.37	Public Works	1934
Farm Security Administration	FSA	273	2.24	Agriculture	1936
National Guard	NG	219	1.79	Military	Pre 1933
Public Works Administration – Housing Projects	PWAH	129	1.05	Public Works	1935
Nonrepayable Grants Total		27,180	222.26		
Repayable Loans					
Reconstruction Finance Corporation	RFC	4,782	39.11	All	1932
Farm Credit Administration	FCA	3,957	32.35	Agriculture	Pre 1933
Home Owners' Loan Corporation	HOLC	3,158	25.83	Home Finance	1934
Commodity Credit Corporation	CCC	1,186	9.70	Agriculture	1934
Public Works Administration	PWA	508	4.15	Public Works	1934

	Acronym	Amounts from July 1, 1932 to June 30, 1939 (Millions $)	Per Capita	Category	First Fiscal Year with Significant Spending
Farm Security Administration	FSA	337	2.76	Agriculture	1934
Home Owners' Loan Corporation and Treasury Investments in Bldg. and Savings and Loans Associations	HOLCT	266	2.17	Home Finance	1934
Federal Reserve Banks	FRB	125	1.02	Finance	1935
Rural Electrification Administration	REA	123	1.01	Agriculture	1936
Total Repayable		14,549	118.97		
Value of Loans Insured by Federal Housing Administration					
Title I – Refurbishing and Maintenance Loans		834	6.82	Home Finance	1936
Title II – Home Mortgages.		1,855	15.17	Home Finance	1936
Total Housing Loans Insured		2,689	21.99		

Source: Fishback and Kachanovskaya (2011). Categories included in grant totals but not listed include the Soil Conservation Service with $0.82 per capita, Agricultural Extension Work with $0.77, Vocational Education at $0.74, U.S. Employment Service at $0.65, Indian Service within the Civilian Conservation Corps at $0.42; Agricultural Experiment Stations at $0.29, Forest Service Roads at $0.28, Colleges of Agriculture and Mechanical Arts at $0.19, Forest Funds at $0.14, Mineral Lease Payments at $0.09, Land Utilization Programs at $0.09, Soldiers' and Sailors' Homes at $0.03, Special Funds at $0.02, Office of Education at $0.02, State Marine Schools at $0.01, Books for the Blind and Federal Water Project Payments. Categories included in Loan Totals but not listed include U.S. Housing Authority with $0.45 per capita, Farm Tenant Purchases with $0.27, and the Disaster Loan Corporation with $0.14.

were spillover increases in labor demand in the private sector. This effect was weakened and private employment could even fall if the presence of public works or work relief jobs created disincentives for workers to accept private employment, which in turn would drive up the wage for employers trying to attract workers. Both the positive and negative effects of work relief were weaker because it paid lower hourly earnings. During the 1930s some employers complained that work relief was creating disincentives for workers to accept private employment. In fact, a sizeable number of potential workers stayed on WPA projects for several years because they feared that the private jobs might last only a short period of time and they would have trouble returning to work relief (Margo 1993, Howard 1943).

A series of panel studies of local labor markets in the 1930s generally find no positive relationship between relief spending and private employment.[2] In the early years of the decade when unemployment was at its peak above 20 percent, Benjamin and Matthews (1992) find that the addition of one work relief job reduced private employment by about one-third of a job, while Neumann, Fishback, and Kantor (2010) find a slight positive effect of relief spending on private employment. After 1935, when unemployment rates fell below

20 percent, both studies find that an additional work relief job was associated with a reduction of up to nine-tenths of a private job. Fishback and Kachanovskaya's (2011) panel study of state multipliers finds small negative and statistically insignificant effects of overall spending and public works and relief spending on private employment.

One of the primary forms of direct relief was the development of old-age assistance, designed to allow the poor elderly to have enough income to remain in their homes. Over half the states had created some form of old age assistance by the time the Social Security Act of 1935 created matching grants to induce all states to improve or establish new programs. Higher benefits under the federal matching grant version of old-age assistance established under the Social Security framework after 1935 allowed more elderly men to retire from their jobs and more widowed women to live on their own (Costa 1999, Friedberg 1999, and Parsons 1991). Although death rates for the elderly fell after the introduction of Old Age Assistance (OAA) in each state, they also fell for other age groups at those same times. Thus, it does not appear that OAA was a causal factor lowering the elderly death rate in the 1930s. However, once penicillin and other drugs were created in the 1940s, increases in OAA benefits did appear to lower mortality rates (Stoian and Fishback 2010, Balan-Cohen 2008).

Farm programs

The shakeout after the rapid expansion in farm production during World War I had led to problems in the farm sector throughout the 1920s. The situation grew worse after 1929. The Roosevelt Administration sought to raise farm incomes by raising prices and to aid farmers through an expansion of their loan programs. The centerpiece of the New Deal program was the rental and benefit program administered by the Agricultural Adjustment Administration (AAA). The AAA, both before and after the initial version was declared unconstitutional, paid farmers to take land out of production in an attempt to limit output and raise prices. Meanwhile, the Farm Credit Administration (FCA) took over and expanded earlier mortgage programs, raising the federal government's share of mortgages from about 14 percent to roughly half of all farm mortgages. The FCA also offered crop and production loans and emergency loans. The Commodity Credit Corporation (CCC) made loans that were designed to put a floor on the prices received by farmers for their crops. The AAA and most loan programs ended up providing most of the aid to larger farmers. Meanwhile, the FERA provided relief aid to low-income farmers in programs later transferred to the Farm Security Administration, and the Resettlement Administration moved some farmers to better land. Loans and grants from other programs were provided to aid small family farms (Halcrow 1953, Alston and Ferrie 1999).

The original AAA program was meant to pay all types of farm operators, including cash and share tenants, who rented land by making cash and crop share payments to the farm owner. The situation for share croppers, who had labor contracts that paid them a share of the crop, was more tenuous, although the AAA administrators claimed that no one should be displaced by the payments and in fact claimed that there had been no displacement by 1935. Yet, many narratives suggest that in actual operation a number of share tenants and sharecroppers did not receive benefits from the AAA. The payments to take land out of production of the AAA crops also likely reduced the demand for labor because the land was either fallowed or shifted to less labor-intensive non-AAA crops. Thus, AAA recipients received a net benefit of the difference between the AAA payment and what they would have earned from the output had the land been used in that crop plus whatever benefits were gained from the alternative use of the land. Meanwhile, cuts in the demand for labor potentially led to lower earnings and fewer opportunities for farm laborers and sharecroppers and even tenants (Alston and Ferrie 1999, Biles 1994, Depew, Fishback, and Rhode 2012, Whatley 1983).

The findings from a variety of studies are consistent with a situation where the gains to AAA benefit recipients were offset by losses to farm workers, croppers and possibly tenants. Fishback, Horrace, and Kantor (2005, 2006) find that counties with more AAA spending per capita experienced slightly lower growth rates in retail sales and experienced more out-migration in the 1930s. In the state panel study by Fishback and Kachanovskaya (2011), increases in AAA spending had negative but statistically insignificant effects on per capita state incomes. Depew, Fishback, and Rhode (2012) find that increases in AAA cotton payments in 1933 and 1934 in the cotton counties were associated with declines in the number of managing share tenants and declines in the number of sharecroppers. The declines in the number of black and white croppers were similar in size, but the declines in the number of black managing share tenants were substantially larger than the declines in the number of white managing share tenants. Studies of the diffusion of tractors suggest that the AAA payments and farm loans stimulated the use of tractors, which in turn might have contributed to more replacement of labor in the South (Clarke 1994, Sorensen, Fishback, Kantor, and Rhode 2011, Whatley 1983).

The AAA programs' spillover effects on the health of the farm population in the South varied. Fishback, Haines, and Kantor (2001) find that areas with higher AAA spending were associated with higher infant mortality for both black and white families, with more damage for blacks than whites. On the other hand, the AAA's stimulus of out-migration of low income croppers and workers from poor areas where malaria was more of a problem appears to have had the side benefit of reducing malaria death rates (Barreca, Fishback, and Kantor 2011).

Over the long term the AAA had the positive effect of preventing later recurrences of the Dust Bowl of the 1930s. Farmers originally settled the Dust Bowl areas under the Homestead Act's restrictions on farm size. They had little incentive to spend the time building berms and using other methods to prevent soil erosion on these small farms because most of the benefits accrued to neighboring farms. When high winds combined with drought in the 1930s, the loose soils created enormous dust clouds in Kansas, Colorado, Oklahoma, and Texas. The AAA, particularly the reformed version after 1935, encouraged the development of large farms and required farmers receiving benefits to use techniques that cut soil erosion. When the same mix of strong winds and terrible droughts hit the region again in the 1970s, no Dust Bowl developed (Hansen and Libecap 2004).

Refinancing nonfarm mortgages through the HOLC

Housing markets began falling apart in the late 1920s after a strong building boom. In the late 1920s most nonfarm homeowners were limited to borrowing only 40 to 60 percent of the value of their homes and they were generally good credit risks at the time they borrowed. The high unemployment of the Depression forced many into deep trouble. To combat the growing potential for foreclosures, the Roosevelt Administration established the Home Owners' Loan Corporation (HOLC). The corporation purchased roughly 10 percent of all U.S. nonfarm mortgages from lenders for a cost equal to about 5.7 percent of GDP and then turned around and refinanced the mortgages on generous terms. The typical borrower refinanced by the HOLC was in deep enough trouble that he had typically stopped making mortgage and tax payments 2.5 years before the HOLC purchased the loan.

The HOLC focused its publicity and reports on the relief provided to home owners, but it provided as much or more relief to the lenders. The HOLC served as a "bad bank" by purchasing toxic assets from the lenders with HOLC bonds guaranteed by the federal government. To get lenders to participate, the HOLC gave them a good deal. In nearly half of the cases the lender received bond values that covered not only the principal owed on the loan but also all of the interest payments missed and any taxes on the home the lender had paid. In the rest of the cases the bond values fully covered the principal and taxes and most of the interest payments missed (Rose 2011).

The borrowers also received a good deal. Roughly half of the borrowers received small reductions in the interest they owed, but virtually no one received a reduction in the principal owed. The HOLC interest rate was 5 percent at a time when interest rates ranged from 6 to 8 percent across the country for high quality mortgages. The true subsidy was probably higher because the HOLC later foreclosed on 20 percent of the loans refinanced at a typical 30 percent loss. The HOLC also adopted a 15-year amortized loan that spread payments evenly across the life of the loan. These replaced loans that either required a large balloon payment of principal after five years or involved membership contracts with a building and loan association that contained a risk of increases in payments if other borrowers failed to make their membership payments.

How much did the program cost the taxpayer? An audit by the U.S. Comptroller General shows that the lending program lost roughly $53 million, or 2 percent of the roughly $3 billion total value of loans, after all costs of capital were considered in the government accounting process. This cost to the taxpayer understates the true subsidy to housing markets that arose from federal guarantees of the HOLC bonds that financed the program. Had the HOLC run such a risky program without the federal guarantee, the interest rate on HOLC bonds would likely have been at least one percent higher. Each one percent rise in the interest rate on the bonds would have raised the subsidy by roughly $300 million, or 10 percent of the value of the loans refinanced (Fishback, Rose, and Snowden 2012).

Was the cost worth it? Two independent studies of county housing markets across the country find strong effects of HOLC loans in smaller counties. An increase in HOLC lending from zero to the average amount in these places staved off roughly 20 percent of the potential drop in housing prices from 1930 to 1940, and as much as 67 percent of the potential drop from 1934 to 1940. The change also contributed to raising the number of home owners by about 10 to 15 percent in these communities. Neither study finds much effect in larger cities, however, possibly because larger cities had better established networks of lenders who were more effective at protecting the group against failures. Nor did the studies find an increase in housing construction associated with the replacement of the toxic assets on the lenders' books.[3]

The National Recovery Administration

As the price level fell 30 percent between 1929 and 1933, many industry leaders complained of "cutthroat" competition that drove prices down and forced many firms to close. The Roosevelt Administration responded by establishing the National Recovery Administration (NRA), which was meant to foster the development of "fair codes of competition" in each industry. Industrialists, workers, and consumers in each industry met to establish rules for minimum prices, quality standards, trade practices, wages, hours limits, and working conditions. Once the code was approved by the NRA, it legally bound all firms in the industry, even those not involved in writing the code. While waiting for the codes to be written, a large number of firms signed President's Reemployment Agreements (PRAs) in the summer of 1933 that required them to raise wages without cutting the number of their employees. In many of the sectors the codes were largely written by the leaders of trade associations with some influence by consumers, because relatively few industries had a strong union presence. Many small firms complained that the codes favored the large firms that were so prominent in writing them (Bellush 1975).

Economists bluntly describe the NRA codes as cartel arrangements with the federal government as enforcer because the industries were given anti-trust exemptions. Even with government's backing, industries with more diverse firms and products had trouble coming to agreement on the codes and then trying to enforce them (Alexander 1997, Klein and Taylor 2008). The successful cartels typically had more complex codes that established restrictions on capacity, production quotas, and provided for data collection for monitoring. The extent to which cartels raised prices and lowered output depended heavily on these rules (Klein and Taylor 2008, Taylor 2007, 2010). Most were relieved when the NRA was struck down as unconstitutional and did not press for an alternative policy (Alexander and Libecap 2000).

Cole and Ohanian (2004) develop a dynamic structural model of the economy to examine the impact of the NRA policies and later attempts to maintain wages by establishing a minimum wage and recognizing unions' rights to collective bargaining. They find that the policies played a major role in preventing the type of quick recovery in employment and output that typically follows sharp recessions. On the other hand, Eggertsson (2008) develops a similar model that examines the simultaneous effects of the NRA, the move off of the gold standard, and increases in deficit financing. Eggertsson argues that all three measures led to a sharp change in people's expectations of future price declines. In his counterfactual, output would have dropped further after 1933, and the NRA was one of the policies that contributed to an increase in output and a reduction of unemployment.

Taylor (2011) does not find nearly so dramatic effects when he examines the impact of the PRA and NRA on panels of monthly data from 1927 through 1937 for up to 66 industries. After controlling for industry fixed effects, a time trend, and macro policy, he shows that the number of workers employed and hourly wage rates were higher under the PRA and the NRA than in other periods, but these benefits were offset by reductions in average weekly hours that led to lower total hours worked and lower weekly earnings. Similarly, the introduction of the minimum wage under the Fair Labor Standard Acts did not have strong effects, in part because the minimum was below wages in most parts of the country. Where it was binding in the South, many firms exploited loopholes to get around it (Seltzer 1997).

Conclusion

The economic and quantitative analysis of the microeconomics of the New Deal is still in its infancy. A large number of policies have still not been studied carefully, and there are many other questions that still can be answered about the policies that have received emphasis here. Thus far, the quantitative analyses appear to suggest that the most successful programs for socio-economic welfare of the population were the public works and relief programs and the HOLC. The public works and relief programs appear to have raised incomes and consumption, although not with multipliers of 2 or 3 that are often used in consulting reports for stadiums and other infrastructure. They also helped reduce mortality on a variety of dimensions and contributed to lower crime rates. Outside of larger cities, the HOLC loan purchase and refinance program helped counteract the drops in housing prices and home ownership that people feared would continue throughout the 1930s, although the purchase of toxic assets from lenders does not seem to have stimulated building activity. The farm program helped large farm owners and those who were paid AAA benefits, but may have redistributed incomes in ways that harmed farm workers and farm laborers.

Notes

1 The discussion in this section is an overview of findings from Anderson and Tollison (1991), Arrington (1970), Couch and Shughart (1998), Fishback, Kantor, and Wallis (2003), Fleck (1999a, 1999c, 2001a, 2001b; 2008), Neumann, Fishback, and Kantor (2010), Stromberg (2004), Wallis (1984, 1985, 1987, 1991, 1998, 2001), and Wright (1974).

2 The emphasis here is on the panel studies. Wallis and Benjamin (1981) find no positive effects in a cross-sectional analysis, and Fleck (1999b) finds that a marginal relief job increased measured unemployment (which included relief workers) likely by attracting discouraged workers back into the labor force.

3 See Fishback et al. 2011, Courtemanche and Snowden 2011. For studies of other programs, see Kollmann and Fishback 2011).

References

Alexander, B. (1997) 'Failed cooperation in heterogeneous industries under the National Recovery Administration', *Journal of Economic History*, 57: 322–44.

Alexander, B. and Libecap, G. (2000) 'The effect of cost heterogeneity in the success and failure of the New Deal's agricultural and industrial programs', *Explorations in Economic History*, 37: 370–400.

Alston, L.J. and Ferrie, J. (1999) *Southern Paternalism and the American Welfare State*, New York: Cambridge University Press.

Anderson, G.M. and Tollison, R.D. (1991) 'Congressional influence and patterns of New Deal spending, 1933–1939', *Journal of Law and Economics*, 34: 161–75.

Arrington, L.J. (1970) 'Western agriculture and the New Deal', *Agricultural History*, 49: 337–16.

Balan-Cohen, A. (2008) 'The effect on elderly mortality: evidence from the old age assistance programs in the United States', Unpublished working paper, Tufts University.

Barreca, A., Fishback, P. and Kantor, S. (2011) 'Agricultural policy, migration, and malaria in the U.S. in the 1930s', National Bureau of Economic Research Working Paper No. 17526.

Bellush, B. (1975) *The Failure of the NRA*, New York: Norton.

Benjamin, D. and Mathews, K.G.P. (1992) *U.S. and U.K. Unemployment between the Wars: A Doleful Story*, Institute for Economic Affairs, London.

Biles, R. (1994) *The South and the New Deal*, Lexington, KY: University of Kentucky Press.

Brown, E.C. 1956, 'Fiscal policy in the 'thirties: a reappraisal', *American Economic Review*, 46: 857–79.

Clarke, S. (1994) *Regulation and the Revolution in United States Farm Productivity*, New York: Cambridge University Press.

Cole, H. and Ohanian, L. (2004) 'New Deal policies and the persistence of the Great Depression: a general equilibrium analysis', *Journal of Political Economy*, 112: 779–816.

Costa, D.L. (1999) 'A house of her own: old age assistance and the living arrangements of older nonmarried women', *Journal of Public Economics*, 72: 39–59.

Couch, J. and Shughart II, W. (1998) *The Political Economy of the New Deal*, New York: Edward Elgar.

Courtemanche, C. and Snowden, K. (2011) 'Repairing a mortgage crisis: HOLC lending and its impact on local housing markets', *Journal of Economic History*, 71: 307–37.

Depew, B., Fishback, P. and Rhode, P. (2012) 'New Deal or no deal in the cotton south: the effect of the AAA on the labor structure in agriculture', Working Paper, University of Arizona.

Eggertsson, G. (2008) 'Great expectations and the end of the Depression', *American Economic Review*, 98: 1476–1516.

Fishback, P. (2010) 'Monetary and fiscal policy during the Great Depression', *Oxford Review of Economic Policy*, 26: 385–413.

Fishback, P. and Kachanovskaya, V. (2011) 'In search of the multiplier for federal spending in the states during the Great Depression', National Bureau of Economic Research Working Paper No. 16561.

Fishback, P., Flores-Lagunes, A., Horrace, W., Kantor, S. and Treber, J. (2011) 'The influence of the home owners' loan corporation on housing markets during the 1930s', *Review of Financial Studies*, 24: 1782–1813.

Fishback, P.V., Haines, M.R. and Kantor, S. (2001) 'The impact of the New Deal on black and white infant mortality in the south', *Explorations in Economic History*, 38: 93–122.

Fishback, P.V., Haines. M.R. and Kantor, S. (2007) 'Births, deaths, and New Deal relief during the Great Depression', *Review of Economics and Statistics*, 89: 1–14.

Fishback, P., Horrace, W. and Kantor, S. (2004) 'Did New Deal grant programs stimulate local economies? A study of federal grants and retail sales during the Great Depression,' National Bureau of Economic Research Working Paper W8108.

Fishback, P., Horrace, W. and Kantor, S. (2005) 'Did New Deal grant programs stimulate local economies? A study of federal grants and retail sales during the Great Depression', *Journal of Economic History*, 65: 36–71.

Fishback, P., Horrace, W. and Kantor, S. (2006) 'The impact of New Deal Expenditures on mobility during the Great Depression', *Explorations in Economic History*, 43: 179–222.

Fishback, P., Kantor, S. and Wallis, J. (2003) 'Can the New Deal's three R's be rehabilitated? A program-by-program, county-by-county analysis', *Explorations in Economic History*, 40: 278–307.

Fishback, P., Rose, J. and Snowden, K. (2012) 'HOLC: fending off foreclosures in the Great Depression', Unpublished Book Manuscript.

Fleck, R. (1999a) 'Electoral incentives, public policy, and the New deal realignment', *Southern Economic Journal*, 63: 377–404.

Fleck, R. (1999b) 'The marginal effect of New Deal relief work on county-level unemployment statistics', *Journal of Economic History*, 59: 659–87.

Fleck, R. (1999c) 'The value of the vote: a model and test of the effects of turnout on distributive policy,' *Economic Inquiry*, 37: 609–23.

Fleck, R. (2001a) 'Inter-party competition, intra-party competition, and distributive policy: a model and test using New Deal data', *Public Choice*, 108: 77–100.

Fleck, R. (2001b) 'Population, land, economic conditions, and the allocation of New Deal spending', *Explorations in Economic History*, 38: 296–304.

Fleck, R. (2008) 'Voter influence and big policy change: the positive political economy of the New Deal', *Journal of Political Economy*, 116: 1–37.

Friedberg, L. (1999) 'The effect of old age assistance on retirement', *Journal of Public Economics*, 71: 213–32.

Halcrow, H.G. (1953) *Agricultural Policy of the United States*, New York: Prentice-Hall.

Hansen, Z. and Libecap, G. (2004) 'Small farms, externalities, and the Dust Bowl of the 1930s', *Journal of Political Economy*, 112: 665–94.

Howard, D.S. (1943) *The WPA and Federal Relief Policy*, New York: Russell Sage Foundation.

Johnson, R., Fishback, P., and Kantor, S. (2010) 'Striking at the roots of crime: the impact of social welfare spending on crime during the Great Depression', *Journal of Law and Economics*, 53: 715–40.

Kitchens, C. (2011a) 'A dam problem: TVA's fight against malaria 1926–1951', Working Paper, University of Arizona.

Kitchens, C. (2011b) 'The role of publicly provided electricity in economic development: the experience of the Tennessee Valley Authority, 1929–1955', Working Paper, University of Arizona.

Klein, P. and Taylor, J. (2008) 'Anatomy of a cartel: the National Industrial Recovery Act of 1933 and the compliance crisis of 1934', *Research in Economic History*, 26: 235–71.

Kollmann, T. and Fishback, P. (2011) 'The New Deal, race, and home ownership in the 1920s and 1930s', *American Economic Review Papers and Proceedings*, 101: 366–70.

Margo, R. (1993) 'Employment and unemployment in the 1930s', *Journal of Economic Perspectives*, 7: 41–59.

Neumann, T., Fishback, P. and Kantor, S. (2010) 'The dynamics of relief spending and the private urban labor market during the New Deal', *Journal of Economic History*, 70: 195–220.

Parsons, D.O. (1991) 'Male retirement behavior in the United States, 1930–1950', *Journal of Economic History*, 51: 657–74.

Peppers, L. (1973) 'Full employment surplus analysis and structural change: the 1930s', *Explorations in Economic History*, 10: 197–210.

Rose, J. (2011) 'The incredible HOLC: mortgage relief during the Great Depression', *Journal of Money, Credit, and Banking*, 43: 1073–1107.

Seltzer, A.J. (1997) 'The effects of the Fair Labor Standards Act of 1938 on the southern seamless hosiery and lumber industries', *Journal of Economic History*, 57: 396–415.

Sorensen, T., Fishback, P., Kantor, S. and Rhode, P. (2011) 'The New Deal and the diffusion of tractors in the 1930s', Working paper, University of Arizona.

Stecker, M.L. (1937) *Intercity Differences in Cost of Living in March 1935, 59 Cities*, Works Progress Administration Research Monograph XII, Washington, DC: U.S. Government Printing Office.

Stoian, A. and Fishback, P. (2010) 'Welfare spending and mortality rates for the elderly before the Social Security era', *Explorations in Economic History*, 47: 1–27.

Stromberg, D. (2004). 'Radio's impact on public spending', *Quarterly Journal of Economics*, 119: 189–221.

Taylor, J. (2007) 'Cartel codes attributes and cartel performance: an industry-level analysis of the National Industrial Recovery Act', *Journal of Law and Economics*, 50: 597–624.

Taylor, J. (2010) 'The welfare impact of collusion under various industry characteristics: a panel examination of efficient cartel theory', *B.E. Journal of Economic Analysis & Policy*, 10(1): Article 97.

Taylor, J. (2011) 'Work-sharing during the Great Depression: did the "President's Reemployment Agreement" promote reemployment?', *Economica*, 78: 133–58.

Wallis, J.J. (1984) 'The birth of the old federalism: financing the New Deal, 1932–1940', *Journal of Economic History*, 44: 139–59.

Wallis, J.J. (1985) 'Why 1933? The origins and timing of national government growth, 1933–1940', *Research in Economic History*, 4: 1–51.

Wallis, J.J. (1987) 'Employment, politics, and economic recovery during the Great Depression', *Review of Economics and Statistics*, 69: 516–20.

Wallis, J.J. (1991) 'The political economy of New Deal fiscal federalism', *Economic Inquiry*, 39: 510–24.

Wallis, J.J. (1998) 'The political economy of New Deal spending revisited, again: with and without Nevada', *Explorations in Economic History*, 35: 140–70.

Wallis, J.J. (2001) 'The political economy of New Deal Spending, yet again: a reply to Fleck', *Explorations in Economic History*, 38: 305–14.

Wallis, J.J. and Benjamin, D.K. (1981) 'Public relief and private employment in the Great Depression', *Journal of Economic History*, 41: 97–102.

Whatley, W.C. (1983) 'Labor for the picking: the New Deal in the south', *Journal of Economic History*, 43: 905–29.

Wright, G. (1974) 'The political economy of New Deal spending: an econometric analysis', *Review of Economics and Statistics*, 56: 30–38.

15

THE MACROECONOMIC IMPACT OF THE NEW DEAL

Lee E. Ohanian

Introduction

The New Deal was a collection of policies adopted in response to the Great Depression that were designed to alleviate economic hardship and promote economic recovery. This chapter analyzes the contribution of New Deal recovery policies to macroeconomic activity. The focus is on the centerpiece of President Roosevelt's New Deal, which were the policies that were aimed at fostering industrial recovery and expanding private sector employment. This includes the National Industrial Recovery Act (NIRA) and the National Labor Relations Act (NLRA), which are among the most significant government interventions in the private economy. The chapter evaluates the impact of these policies on aggregate output, labor, consumption and investment. The evidence indicates that these policies significantly retarded economic recovery by suppressing competition in some product and labor markets which in turn raised relative prices and real wages, thereby depressing employment and output. This suggests that New Deal industrial and labor policies not only failed to promote recovery, but instead delayed recovery by several years.

The failure of the U.S. economy to recover from the Depression

Table 15.1 shows detrended per-adult real output and its components from 1929–1939, with data normalized so that trend values for each variable are equal to 100.

In what follows, 1929–33 is referred to as the downturn phase of the Depression, and 1933–39 as the recovery phase. The data are detrended by removing a 1.9 percent annual growth rate from the data, as in Cole and Ohanian (1999, 2007). Detrending time series data is standard in business cycle analysis (e.g. see Cooley 1995), but often is not used in analyses of the Depression (see for example Temin 1976, Romer 1990, or Bernanke 1995). The decade long duration of the Depression means that detrending is quantitatively important and Table 15.1 highlights the extent to which the recovery was indeed slow when compared to trend growth.

Table 15.1 shows that the economy had recovered little relative to trend six years after the 1933 trough. Per capita GNP was 26 percent below trend in 1939, compared to its trough value of 38 percent below trend in 1933. In terms of final expenditures, there was virtually

Table 15.1 Consumption, investment, and other components of GNP, 1929–39 (1929 = 100)

		Consumption				Foreign Trade	
Year	Real GNP	Durables	Non Durables	Investment Nonresidential	Government Purchases	Exports	Imports
1929	100.0	100.0	100.0	100.0	100.0	100.0	100.0
1930	87.4	76.2	90.9	79.2	105.1	85.3	84.9
1931	78.1	63.4	85.4	49.4	105.4	70.6	72.4
1932	65.2	46.7	76.0	27.9	97.3	54.5	58.1
1933	61.9	44.4	72.2	24.6	91.7	52.8	60.8
1934	64.6	49.0	72.1	28.4	101.1	52.8	58.3
1935	68.1	58.9	73.1	34.4	100.1	53.8	69.3
1936	74.9	70.8	77.0	45.9	113.9	55.1	71.9
1937	76.0	72.2	77.2	53.6	106.3	64.3	78.3
1938	70.6	56.3	74.3	37.8	112.0	62.8	58.3
1939	73.5	64.3	75.0	40.5	112.9	61.7	61.6

Source: Cole and Ohanian (2007)

Note: Data from the U.S. Department of Commerce, Bureau of Economic Analysis. All data are divided by the working-age population (16 years and older). Data are also detrended by dividing each variable by its long-run trend growth rate (1.9 percent)

no recovery in consumption of nondurables and services, which was little changed between 1933 and 1939. And while investment rose from its remarkably low trough value of 1933 of 75 percent below trend, it still was 60 percent below trend in 1939.

Regarding the supply side of the economy, most of the increase in output that occurred between 1933 and 1939 was the result of higher productivity, rather than higher labor input. Specifically, output per capita (y/n) is the product of output per hour (y/h) and hours per person (h/n):

$$\frac{y}{n} = \frac{y}{h}\frac{h}{n}$$

Tables 15.2 and 15.3 show labor input and productivity during the 1930s. Table 15.2 shows three different measures of aggregate labor input and two measures of sectoral labor, all of which are divided by the adult population.

All of the aggregate measures of labor input declined substantially during the downturn and remained well below normal afterwards with only modest recovery. In 1939, total employment per person was 12.5 percent below its 1929 level, total hours worked, which is conceptually the best measure of labor input, was about 21 percent below its 1929 level, and private hours worked was about 25 percent below its 1929 level. Note that agricultural labor input changed very little during the downturn, as it was not until later that farm hours declined.

Table 15.3 shows aggregate labor productivity (output per hour worked) and total factor productivity (TFP). Both productivity measures declined considerably in the downturn, but recovered very quickly afterwards.

Table 15.2 Five measures of labor input, divided by working-age population, 1930–39 (1929 = 100)

Year	Aggregate measures			Sectoral measures	
	Total employment	Total hours	Private hours	Farm hours	Manufacturing hours
1930	93.8	92.0	91.5	99.0	83.5
1931	86.7	83.6	82.8	101.6	67.2
1932	78.9	73.5	72.4	98.6	53.0
1933	78.6	72.7	70.8	98.8	56.1
1934	83.7	71.8	68.7	89.1	58.4
1935	85.4	74.8	71.4	93.1	64.8
1936	89.8	80.7	75.8	90.9	74.2
1937	90.8	83.1	79.5	98.8	79.3
1938	86.1	76.4	71.7	92.4	62.3
1939	87.5	78.8	74.4	93.2	71.2

Source: Cole and Ohanian (2007)

Note: Data from Kendrick, John W. 1961. *Productivity trends in the United States*. Princeton, NJ: Princeton University Press (for NBER)

Table 15.3 Three measures of productivity, 1930–39 (1929 = 100)

Year	GNP/hour	TFP	
		Private domestic	Private nonfarm
1930	95.3	94.8	94.8
1931	95.2	93.4	92.0
1932	89.4	87.6	85.8
1933	84.8	85.7	82.7
1934	90.3	93.1	92.7
1935	94.8	96.3	95.3
1936	93.7	99.5	99.5
1937	95.1	100.1	99.3
1938	94.6	99.9	98.1
1939	95.2	102.6	100.1

Source: Cole and Ohanian (2007)

Note: Data from Kendrick, John W. 1961. Productivity trends in the United States. Princeton, NJ: Princeton University Press (for NBER)

These data indicate that the recovery from the Depression was weak, despite the fact that productivity, which is considered by most economists to be the central factor driving long-run economic growth, recovered very quickly. The analysis next considers how fast the economy would normally have recovered, given observed productivity growth beginning in 1933.

Estimates of output use the standard optimal growth model as discussed in Cole and Ohanian (1999, 2004, 2007), in which consumers allocate time between market and non-market uses, allocate income between consumption and investment, and in which there are both long-run deterministic productivity growth and stochastic transitory productivity shocks. Standard parameter values (taken from Cole and Ohanian 2007) enable calculation of the path of normal output, labor input, consumption, and investment given the sequence of observed productivity and given the actual level of the capital stock in 1933. Figure 15.1 shows predicted output for 1929–1939 and compares it to actual output for these years.

Standard neoclassical growth theory predicts a recovery that was much faster than what actually occurred. In particular, the low capital stock, reflecting very low investment during the downturn, coupled with rapid productivity growth, would normally have led to much higher labor input and a much faster recovery than observed. Moreover, the prediction of a fast recovery is consistent with actual recoveries from severe recessions in the U.S. For example, Table 15.4 shows that the recovery from the 1981–82 recession, which was the most severe recession in the half century following the Great Depression, was very rapid, with employment and output very close to trend levels about a year after the recession trough.

Why didn't the economy recover?

This section uses a diagnostic framework developed by Cole and Ohanian (2002), Chari, Kehoe, and McGrattan (2007), and Mulligan (2002) to identify possible reasons for why

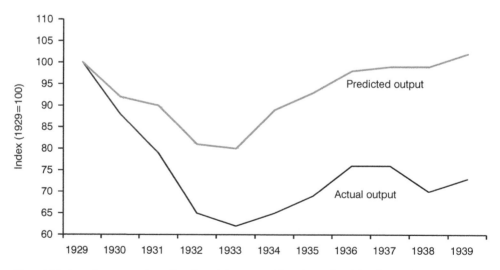

Figure 15.1 Actual output and predicted model output with only productivity change: 1929–1939

Source: Cole and Ohanian (2007)

Note: The series on actual output is divided by the working-age population (16 years and older) and is also detrended by dividing by its long-run trend growth rate (1.9 percent)

Table 15.4 Detrended levels of output and its components in 1981-III to 1982-IV recession. Measured quarterly from trough, peak=100

Quarters From Trough	Output	Consumption	Investment	Government Purchases	Employment	Compensation to Employees
0	93.5	98.8	74.4	99.8	95.1	100.6
1	94.0	99.0	76.5	99.8	95.0	101.3
2	95.4	100.2	83.2	99.9	95.7	100.6
3	96.5	101.2	88.1	100.8	96.6	100.0
4	97.7	102.0	96.7	98.3	98.0	99.4
5	98.7	102.0	105.8	98.4	99.1	99.2
6	99.7	102.6	108.6	99.8	100.1	98.8

Source: Output and components, Bureau of Economic Analysis. Employment, Bureau of Labor Statistics

labor didn't recover, despite rapid productivity growth. This procedure uses time series data together with the equations characterizing the solution to the growth model described above to assess whether these equations are approximately satisfied or whether they are distorted. Note that any difference in output, labor, consumption, or investment from trend is necessarily associated with a deviation in at least one first order condition in the growth model.

The only equation that is substantially distorted is the household first order condition that equates the marginal rate of substitution between consumption and leisure to the real wage rate. The analysis uses real per-adult consumption of nondurables and services relative to trend, hours worked per adult, and the manufacturing wage from Beney (1936) deflated by the GNP deflator, and measured relative to trend.

There is a historically large distortion in this equation, reflecting the fact that both consumption and hours worked were well below normal levels, and that the real wage was well above normal, which means that the opportunity cost of working was much less than the benefit of working. Between 1934 and 1939, this distortion is about 50 percent above its level in 1933. In comparison, Ohanian and Raffo (2012) document that this distortion at the trough of postwar U.S. recessions was only 4.5 percent above its level at the previous business cycle peak.

This diagnostic statistic raises the central question about the failure of labor to recover: why didn't the real wage fall to increase labor and output? The high level of unemployment should have resulted in enormous competitive pressure to reduce wages and expand employment. The fact that wages were well above trend and in fact continued to rise during the New Deal suggests that labor market policies prevented the real wage from falling and clearing the labor market.

New Deal labor and industrial policies

This diagnostic evidence is consistent with a number of New Deal recovery policies that were aimed at suppressing competition and raising wages and relative prices in a number of sectors. This included the National Industrial Recovery Act (NIRA), which was the centerpiece of Roosevelt's recovery programs. The NIRA was purposely designed to limit competition and raise prices and wages in most of the non-farm private economy.[1] The NIRA accomplished this by permitting industry to cartelize provided that industry immediately raised wages and agreed to collective bargaining with workers.

The Act covered over 500 industries, representing about 80 percent of non-farm private employment. Each industry formed a "code of fair competition" that was approved by the National Recovery Administration and that became the operating rules for each industry. The code was enforced by a code authority, which typically was comprised of members from the industry.

The NIRA codes included several textbook characteristics of cartels: minimum prices within industry, restrictions on expanding capacity and production limits, resale price maintenance, basing point pricing, in which pricing consists of a base price plus transportation costs, which thereby facilitates collusion, and open price systems, which required that any firm planning to reduce price must preannounce the price cut to the code authority, who in turn would notify all other firms. Following this notification, the announcing firm was required to wait a specific period before changing its price. The purpose of this waiting period was for the code authority and other industry members to persuade the announcing firm to cancel its price cut.

In some industries, the code authority determined minimum price directly, either as the authority's assessment of a fair market price or as its assessment of the minimum cost of production. In other codes, such as the iron and steel industry and the pulp and paper industry, the authority indirectly set the minimum price by rejecting any price that was so low it would promote "unfair" competition. Codes of fair competition also included explicit provisions for profits. Some minimum prices explicitly included depreciation, rent, royalties, directors' fees, research and development expenses, amortization, patents, maintenance and repairs, and bad debts and profit margins as a percentage of cost.

The NIRA ended in May 1935, when the Supreme Court ruled in *Schecter Poultry Corp. vs. United States* that the NIRA was an unconstitutional delegation of legislative power. Roosevelt strongly opposed the court's decision: "The fundamental purposes and principles of the NIRA are sound. To abandon them is unthinkable. It would spell the return to industrial and labor chaos" (quoted in Hawley 1966: 124). But policymakers found ways to continue anticompetitive policies during the New Deal through new labor legislation and by ignoring the antitrust rules. In fact, anticompetitive policies, particularly labor policies, became even more pronounced after the *Schecter* decision, and as will be shown below, real wages and relative prices were even higher after the NIRA. This contradicts the widely-accepted view that distortions to competition ended after the *Schecter* decision.

The main New Deal labor policy after the NIRA was the NLRA, also known as the Wagner Act, which was passed on July 27, 1935. This gave considerably more bargaining power to workers to raise wages than under the NIRA. The NLRA gave workers the right to organize and bargain collectively. It prohibited management from refusing to engage in collective bargaining with government-recognized unions, discriminating among employees for union affiliation, or forcing employees to join a company union. The act also established the National Labor Relations Board (NLRB) to enforce wage agreements and the rules of the NLRA.

Union membership and strikes rose rapidly under the NLRA. Union membership rose from about 13 percent of employment in 1935 to about 29 percent of employment in 1939, and strike activity similarly increased from 14 million strike days in 1936 to about 28 million in 1937. Moreover, strikes were much more effective in raising worker bargaining power during the New Deal than during other times because the NLRA was initially interpreted as to permit workers to take unprecedented actions against firms that destroyed profits.

The most important of these was the "sit-down strike," in which strikers forcibly occupied factories to halt production. The sit-down strike was the key factor in unionizing the auto and steel industries (see Kennedy 1999: 310–17). Sit-down strikes in GM auto body plants in late 1936 and early 1937 brought GM production to a virtual halt. There was no federal intervention to aid GM, despite support of GM's position by Vice President John Nance Garner. Consequently, GM was forced to recognize the United Auto Workers to end the strike. Shortly after the GM sit-down strikes, U.S. Steel recognized the Steel Worker's Organizing Committee to avoid a sit-down strike. This period, in which workers were implicitly permitted to forcibly occupy factories, stands in sharp contrast with pre-New Deal government policy on strikes. Bernstein (1963) documents that police action was frequently used to break strikes before the New Deal, and firms were often allowed to use violence against workers during strikes and even during union organizing drives.

Regarding the continuation of cartelization, there is considerable evidence that the government largely ignored antitrust prosecution after the NIRA. Hawley (1966) notes that the government tacitly permitted collusion, particularly in industries that paid high wages. He cites a number of Federal Trade Commission (FTC) studies documenting price fixing and production limits in a number of industries following the *Schecter* decision. Post-NIRA collusion was facilitated by trade practices formed under the NIRA, including basing point pricing. Cole and Ohanian (2004) document that Interior Secretary Harold Ickes complained to Roosevelt that he received identical bids from steel firms on 257 different occasions (Hawley 1966) between June 1935 and May 1936. The bids were not only identical but 50 percent higher than foreign steel prices (Ickes 1953–54).

This price difference was sufficiently large that Ickes was allowed to order the steel from German suppliers. Roosevelt canceled the German contract, however, after pressure from both the steel trade association and the steel labor union. And despite wide scale collusion, the Attorney General announced that steel producers would not be prosecuted. Hawley documents that the steel case was just one example of the failure of the government to enforce the antitrust laws. The number of antitrust cases initiated fell from an average of 12.5 new cases per year during the 1920s, which was in itself a period of limited enforcement, to an average of 6.5 cases per year between 1935 and 1938. Moreover, several of these new cases were initiated in order to prosecute racketeering, rather than pure restraint of trade.

It is striking that policies that so grossly suppressed competition would be adopted. Economists today broadly agree that reducing competition reduces employment and output, and that maximizing competition leads to superior economic outcomes. But Roosevelt and his advisors believed that competition was damaging and that the Depression was the result of "excessive competition" that reduced prices and wages, which they believed reduced employment and output. Moreover, note that this 1930s view regarding the impact of changes in nominal prices and wages on employment and output tends to mistake general price movements for relative price movements. Roosevelt expressed his views about competition as follows:

> A mere builder of more industrial plants, a creator of more railroad systems, an organizer of more corporations, is as likely to be a danger as a help. Our task is not necessarily producing more goods. It is the soberer, less dramatic business of administering resources and plants already in hand.
>
> (Quoted in Kennedy 1999: 373)

Many of Roosevelt's advisors worked as economic planners during World War I, and argued that wartime economic planning would bring recovery. Hugh Johnson, who was one of Roosevelt's main economic advisors and the main administrator of the NIRA, argued that the economy grew during World War I because the government ignored antitrust laws. Johnson (1935) argued that competition wasted resources, and that wartime planning facilitated cooperation between firms, which in turn, according to Johnson, raised wages and output. World War I economic planning, with its focus on firm cooperation taking the place of competition between firms, was the foundation for New Deal policies.

And it was not just FDR and his advisors who believed that suppressing competition to raise prices and wages would increase employment and output. Ohanian (2009) describes how Herbert Hoover had very similar views. As Commerce Secretary under Harding and Coolidge, Hoover significantly fostered cartelization by helping industries develop trade associations which were designed to help firms share information on costs and prices and to coordinate on product quality and standardization. In November 1929, President Hoover promised industry that he would protect them from unionization and permit collusion as long as firms increased nominal wages, or at least maintained prevailing nominal wage levels. Industry complied, but maintaining nominal wages led to large increases in real wages as deflation accelerated.

The largest manufacturing firms did not cut nominal wages until Fall 1931, after it became clear that Hoover was unwilling to support policies that would provide guaranteed minimum profit levels. Ohanian (2009) develops a model of Hoover's policy and finds that Hoover's nominal wage setting in conjunction with deflation accounts for about 60 percent of the decline of output and labor input in the early stages of the Great Depression.

The impact of New Deal policies on wages and prices

Cole and Ohanian (2004) present evidence that New Deal labor and industrial policies had a significant impact on relative prices and real wages. Tables 15.5 and 15.6 compare wage and price statistics between industries cartelized by New Deal policies and non-cartelized industries. Table 15.5 shows annual industry-level data for wages in three sectors covered by New Deal policies – manufacturing, bituminous coal, and petroleum products – and two sectors not covered – anthracite coal and all farm products.

The farm sector was not covered by these industrial and labor policies, while anthracite coal was a de facto uncovered sector. It was to have been under the umbrella of the NIRA, but the industry and its coal miners failed to reach an agreement.

Real wages in the three covered sectors rose after the NIRA was adopted and remained high through the rest of the decade. Manufacturing, bituminous coal, and petroleum wages were between 24 and 33 percent above trend in 1939. In contrast, the farm wage was 31 percent below trend, and anthracite coal was 6 percent below trend. It is striking that the bituminous coal miners – who successfully negotiated under the NIRA – increased their wages significantly, while anthracite coal miners – who did not successfully negotiate under the NIRA – were unable to raise their wages.

Monthly Conference Board data in Table 15.6 (Beney 1936, Hanes 1996) report real wages in 11 manufacturing industries for which there are also price data. It shows significant increases in all 11 industries, occurring after the NIRA was passed.

Real wages are indexed to 100 in February 1933 (a few months prior to the passage of the NIRA) to focus on the effect of the adoption of the policies on real wages. All of these wages were significantly higher at the end of 1933, six months after the act was passed. The smallest increase was 7 percent (farm implements), and the largest increase was 46 percent (boots and shoes). These wages remained high through the end of the NIRA (May 1935) and also after

Table 15.5 Indexed real wages relative to trend

Sector	1930	1931	1932	1933	1934	1935	1936	1937	1938	1939
Manufacturing	101.7	106.3	105.1	102.9	110.8	112.0	111.6	118.9	122.9	123.6
Bituminous coal	101.2	104.8	91.4	90.4	110.1	119.1	125.3	127.8	130.9	132.7
Anthracite coal	–	–	100.0	100.0	92.7	90.3	89.9	89.1	94.1	94.4
Petroleum	–	–	100.0	103.6	108.9	113.6	115.4	124.8	129.1	128.8
Farm	94.6	78.8	63.0	60.9	60.8	64.1	67.7	72.9	68.5	68.6

Source: Cole and Ohanian (2004)

Note: Wages are deflated by the GNP deflator and a 1.4 percent trend, which is the growth rate of manufacturing compensation in the postward period. They are indexed to be 100 in 1929, except for the wages in anthracite coal and petroleum, which are indexed to 1932=100 because of data availability

Table 15.6 Montly wages relative to GNP deflator (February 1933=100)

	April 1933	December 1933	June 1934	May 1935	December 1935	June 1936
Leather tanning	96.6	124	122.2	121.9	123	124.9
Boots and shoes	104.7	145.9	138.1	139	139.7	137
Cotton	96.7	142	133.2	135.2	133.4	134.3
Iron/steel	100.2	123.1	122.7	124.6	125	127
Foundries and machine shops	99.4	112.6	111.9	113.4	113.6	115.9
Autos	98.9	115.5	121.3	121	123.1	125.8
Chemicals	102.8	117.6	118.2	121.5	123.1	124.1
Pulp/paper	100.7	117.5	111.4	115.3	116.4	117.9
Rubber manufacturing	100.7	121.3	125.9	134.1	137	128.6
Furniture	102.3	118.9	125.9	129.2	129	130.3
Farm implements	96.5	107.1	105.6	115.3	116.9	113.7

Source: Cole and Ohanian (2004)

the Act was ruled unconstitutional. The average real wage increase across these 11 categories in June 1936 relative to February 1933 was 25.4 percent.

These wage premia in the cartelized sectors are considerably higher than most estimates of union wage premia, which some authors have used to gauge labor market distortions. There are two key reasons why estimates of union/nonunion wage premia are not the right statistics for evaluating New Deal wage increases. One is that the NIRA raised wages of both union and nonunion workers. Very few workers were in unions in 1933, and the NIRA took this into account by forcing firms to raise wages of all workers to get cartelization benefits. Another reason why union wage premia are poor estimates of the impact of New Deal wage increases is that most estimates of union wage premia come from post–World War II data. These data are not good estimates because postwar union bargaining power was lower than worker bargaining power during the New Deal.

By fostering cartels and collusion, New Deal policies also increased relative prices in several industries for which data are available from the Bureau of Labor Statistics. Where possible, industries in which both wage and price data are available are matched. Table 15.7 shows relative price data from several industries covered before the NIRA was passed and continuing through the 1930s after the *Schecter* decision.

Prices for nearly all industries that were effectively covered by these policies rose shortly after the NIRA was passed, and remained high throughout the decade. As in the case of real wages, the contrast between the two coal industries is revealing. Note that the relative price of bituminous coal (covered by the NIRA) rose after the NIRA was passed and remained high through 1939. In contrast, the relative price of anthracite coal (not covered by the NIRA) was unchanged after the NIRA passed and then declined moderately over the rest of the decade.

These wage and price data provide substantial evidence that New Deal policies significantly raised relative prices and real wages in the industries covered by these policies, while prices and wages did not rise in industries that either were not covered by these policies or, as in the case of anthracite coal, in which the industry was unable to negotiate and collude. There is additional evidence, including studies by the National Recovery Review Board (NRRB), which was an independent agency charged with assessing whether the NIRA was creating monopoly. The NRRB produced three studies that assessed industries covering about 50 percent of NIRA employment, and concluded that there was substantial evidence of monopoly in most industries. The FTC studied a number of manufacturing industries following the *Schecter* decision and concluded that there was very little competition in many concentrated industries after the NIRA.

The impact of New Deal policies on economic activity

Standard theory indicates that New Deal cartelization policies distorted resource allocation and reduced employment and output. Cole and Ohanian (2004) quantify the effect of the New Deal on the slow recovery by developing a general equilibrium model tailored to capture key aspects of these policies. The model's foundation is a multisector neoclassical growth model that allows for the fact that not all of the economy was impacted by these policies. In the model, sectoral intermediate outputs, which are produced using capital and labor, are combined to produce a single final output good which is divided between consumption and investment. The model includes a dynamic bargaining model between labor and capital that is similar to the actual bargaining process that occurred during the 1930s. The model is an insider–outsider model, as in Blanchard and Summers (1986) and Lindbeck and Snower (1988), in which the workers in the industries covered by cartel policies receive higher wages than those in industries that are not covered. But in contrast to other insider–outsider models, the number of workers within the cartelized industries is endogenously determined by the current group of insiders. Thus, the model can quantitatively address the impact of these policies on employment within an optimizing framework.

The model develops a representative family construct, in which family members work in different industries. Even though the cartel and noncartel sectors pay different wages, household members pool incomes so that each member has the same consumption level. There are four possible time allocations for household members: (1) work in a high-wage cartel industry, if already employed in that industry, (2) work in a competitive sector, (3) search for a high-wage cartel job, and (4) nonmarket time allocation.

In the model of New Deal policies, workers and firms within an industry bargain each period over the wage and the number of workers that will be hired. The bargaining is conducted

Table 15.7 Wholesale prices relative to the personal consumption services deflator (February 1933=100)

Industry	April 1933	December 1933	June 1934	May 1935	December 1935	June 1936	June 1937	June 1938	June 1939
Leather/hides	102.1	131.2	126.1	127.5	137.8	126.7	128.5	143	121.1
Textiles	131.8	149.2	143.8	133.1	140.4	131.9	142.3	116.9	120.1
Furniture	99.4	110.3	108.1	105.3	105.3	103.9	112.2	106.2	103
All home furnishings	98.9	112	111.6	109.5	109.5	107.9	115.3	110.1	108.2
Anthracite coal	91.8	91.9	85.3	80.8	91.8	84.1	78.2	76.8	77.8
Bituminous coal	98.4	114.1	117.8	117	119.3	117.8	115.6	112.2	110.1
Petroleum products	94.8	150.4	145.2	145.2	142.6	162.4	167	150	139.9
Chemicals	100.6	100.3	97.9	108.8	108.8	107.8	104.6	99.7	97.4
Drugs/pharmaceuticals	99.6	107.7	131.3	133	133	138.6	144.8	127.4	129.1
Iron/steel	97.9	108.2	97	114.6	108.7	108.2	120.2	119.3	112.6
Nonferrous metals	106.5	144.2	145.9	147.1	147.1	146.8	185.3	133	144.2
Structural steels	100	106.2	113.8	110.6	110.6	109.7	131	126.4	120
All metal products	99.4	107.9	111.5	109.9	110.1	107.9	115.4	113.5	110.1
Autos	99.4	100	102.9	102	102	–	–	96.5	93.5
Pulp/paper	98.1	114.4	114	108.5	108.5	107.1	122.8	108.4	101.3
Auto tires	87.8	101.4	103	103.7	103.7	102.3	123.3	123.2	129.8
Rubber	121.3	295.1	446.9	400.8	400.8	413	626.2	394.1	515.5
Farm equipment	100	102.4	107.9	110.6	118.8	109.8	105.5	105.7	102.7
All building materials	100.6	122.6	123.8	119.3	119.3	119.1	129.3	117.5	117.2
Average	103.2	117.1	120	122.6	123.7	116.8	124.6	117.9	113.8

Source: Cole and Ohanian (2004)

Note: The average does not include rubber

within a dynamic game in which workers make a take-it-or-leave-it offer. If the firms accept, then the government permits the industry to collude and act as a monopolist. If the firms do not accept the workers' offer, then with probability ω they collude and pay the wage that prevails in the non-cartel sector, and with probability $(1 - \omega)$ the government discovers that a wage agreement was not reached, and forces the industry to operate competitively. This latter feature captures the fact that New Deal cartelization was sanctioned only if industry reached an agreement with their workers.

Thus, workers must make an offer that industry weakly prefers to rejecting. Worker bargaining power in the model thus depends on the value of ω. Specifically, firms will accept an offer only if profits by accepting the offer (Π^A) are higher than expected profits $E(\Pi^R)$ from rejecting. Formally, this is given by:

$$\Pi^A \geq E\left(\Pi^R\right) = (1 - \omega)\Pi^R$$

This expression shows that worker bargaining power is high for ω close to one, as in this case workers capture most of the monopoly rents from cartelization. Alternatively, if ω is zero then industry captures most of the monopoly rents, as in this case industry can collude without paying premium wages. The model reduces to a multi-sector growth model with monopoly in one sector in this latter case.

The key parameters in this model are the fraction of industries that are effectively cartelized and the bargaining parameter ω. Cole and Ohanian assume that about one-third of the economy is cartelized, which represents the share of the economy at that time devoted to manufacturing, petroleum, and mining. They choose a value of about 0.85 for ω so that the cartel wage in the steady state of the model equals the observed real manufacturing wage in 1939 of about 17 percent above trend.

Cartel policies impact employment and output substantially. Cole and Ohanian (2004) find that steady-state output, consumption, and hours are all about 16 percent below trend. This accounts for about two-thirds of the extent that these actual variables remained below trend. Investment represents a larger deviation between the model and data, as actual investment remained about 50 percent below trend, compared to model investment, which is about 16 percent below trend. Table 15.8 shows the model simulations for the impact of the New Deal on the economy.

The end of New Deal industrial and labor policies

By the late 1930s, Roosevelt acknowledged the impact of cartelization on the economy in a speech: "the American economy has become a concealed cartel system. The disappearance of price competition is one of the primary causes of present difficulties" (quoted in Hawley 1966: 412).

New Deal labor and industrial policies began to change around this time, and continued to evolve in the 1940s and World War II. Trust-buster Thurman Arnold was appointed as Assistant Attorney General and ran the antitrust division at the Department of Justice. Arnold doubled the antitrust workforce in the Department of Justice and initiated a number of antitrust cases.

Labor policies changed considerably beginning in the late 1930s. The Supreme Court ruled against sit-down strikes in 1939. Labor policy continued to change during World War II, when the National War Labor Board (NWLB) refused to approve a large wage increase for Bethlehem Steel's workers. From that point on, the NWLB's "Little Steel" decision severely impacted bargaining power, as only cost-of-living wage increases were approved. Union strikes in

Table 15.8 Predicted path of US economy in cartel model (1933=1)

	Output	Consumption	Investment	Employment
1934	0.77	0.85	0.40	0.82
1935	0.81	0.85	0.62	0.84
1936	0.86	0.85	0.87	0.89
1937	0.87	0.86	0.90	0.90
1938	0.86	0.86	0.86	0.89
1939	0.87	0.86	0.88	0.89

Source: Cole and Ohanian (2004)

response to the Little Steel decision pushed public opinion against unions, and the Taft–Hartley Act, which revised the National Labor Relations Act by reducing worker bargaining power, was passed in 1947. Postwar wage premia never again approached the levels of the late 1930s.

Conclusion

The economy remained far below trend throughout the New Deal, in part reflecting New Deal industrial and labor policies that substantially distorted the normal competitive forces of supply and demand. These policies depressed employment and output by raising prices and wages well above normal, competitive levels in many sectors.

Research by Cole and Ohanian (2004) suggests that the economy would have recovered much more quickly in the absence of these policies. Moreover, this new research provides a very different interpretation of the Depression compared with that of Keynes (1936), who argued that low investment, reflecting pessimistic investor expectations, prevented employment from recovering, and that significant government intervention was required for the economy to recover. In contrast, the view presented here indicates that investment was low because of significant government interventions that depressed employment.

It is important to note that this chapter does not analyze the negative impact of other government interventions on the economy, and in particular, the impact of interventions on investment, including increased uncertainty regarding property rights (see Higgs 1997), or the large increase in capital taxation that occurred under the New Deal (see McGrattan 2012). Future research should focus on integrating these various factors into a single model framework to study how these three factors – cartelization, uncertainty, and higher taxes – interacted with each other to prolong the Depression.

Note

1 Exempt industries included steam railroads, nonprofits, domestic services, and professional services.

References

Beney, M.A. (1936) *Wages, Hours, and Employment in the United States, 1914–1936,* New York: National Industrial Conference Board.

Bernanke, B.S. (1995) 'The macroeconomics of the Great Depression: a comparative approach', *Journal of Money, Credit and Banking,* 27: 1–28.

Bernstein, I. (1960) *The Lean Years: A History of the American Worker, 1920–1933*, New York: Houghton Mifflin.

Blanchard, O.J., and Summers, L.H. (1986) 'Hysteresis and the European unemployment problem', NBER Chapters, in *NBER Macroeconomics Annual 1986*, vol 1. Cambridge, MA: National Bureau of Economic Research.

Chari, V.V., Kehoe, P.J. and McGrattan, E.R. (2007) 'Business cycle accounting', *Econometrica*, 75: 781–836.

Cole, H.L. and Ohanian, L.E. (1999) 'The Great Depression in the United States from a neoclassical perspective', *Quarterly Review Federal Reserve Bank of Minneapolis*: 2–24.

Cole, H.L. and Ohanian, L.E. (2002) 'The U.S. and U.K. Great Depressions through the lens of neoclassical growth theory', *American Economic Review*, 92: 28–32.

Cole, H.L. and Ohanian, L.E. (2004) 'New Deal policies and the persistence of the Great Depression: a general equilibrium analysis', *Journal of Political Economy*, 112: 779–816.

Cole, H.L. and Ohanian, L.E. (2007) 'A second look at the U.S. Great Depression from a neoclassical perspective' (revised and updated), in T. Kehoe and E. Prescott, (eds.) *Great Depressions of the Twentieth Century*, Minneapolis, MN: Federal Reserve Bank of Minneapolis.

Cooley, T.F. (ed.) (1995) *Frontiers of Business Cycle Research*, Princeton, NJ: Princeton University Press.

Hanes, C. (1996) 'Changes in the cyclical behavior of real wage rates, 1870–1990', *Journal of Economic History*, 56: 837–61.

Hawley, E.W. (1966) *The New Deal and the Problem of Monopoly: A Study in Economic Ambivalence*, Princeton, NJ: Princeton University Press.

Higgs, R. (1997) 'Regime uncertainty', *Independent Review*, 1: 561–90.

Ickes, H.L. (1953–54) *The Secret Diary of Harold Ickes*, New York: Simon and Schuster.

Johnson, H.S. (1935) *The Blue Eagle, from Egg to Earth*, Garden City, New York: Doubleday, Doran.

Kennedy, D.M. (1999) *Freedom from Fear: The American People in Depression and War, 1929–1945*, New York: Oxford University Press.

Keynes, J.M. (1936) *The General Theory of Employment, Interest and Money*, London: Macmillan.

Lindbeck, A. and Snower, D.J. (1988) *The Insider–Outsider Theory of Employment and Unemployment*, Cambridge, MA: MIT Press.

McGrattan, E.R. (2012) 'Capital taxation and the U.S. Great Depression', *Quarterly Journal of Economics*, 127: 1515–50.

Mulligan, C.B. (2002) 'A century of labor–leisure distortions', NBER Working Papers 8774, Cambridge, MA: National Bureau of Economic Research.

Ohanian, L.E. (2009) 'What – or who – started the Great Depression?', *Journal of Economic Theory*, 144: 2310–35.

Ohanian, L.E. and Raffo, A. (2012) 'Hours worked over the business cycle: evidence from OECD countries, 1960–2010', *Journal of Monetary Economics*, 59(1): 40–56.

Romer, C.D. (1990) 'The Great Crash and the onset of the Great Depression', *Quarterly Journal of Economics*, 105: 597–624.

Temin, P. (1976) *Did Monetary Forces Cause the Great Depression?*, New York: W.W Norton.

16

MONETARY POLICY DURING THE GREAT DEPRESSION

James L. Butkiewicz

The Federal Reserve System was created to end the banking panics that plagued the United States economy from the end of the Civil War through the early twentieth century. Yet the greatest series of banking panics in American history occurred in the early 1930s, on the Federal Reserve's watch. And the Federal Reserve's failure to stop the banking crises as it allowed the money supply to fall is widely believed by economists to be one key reason why a business recession turned into the Great Depression.

The Federal Reserve's policies at this time have been extensively studied by economists. While there is general agreement that monetary policy failed, numerous explanations have been offered as to the reason for this failure.

Monetary policy during the Great Depression is best understood as occurring in four phases. The first phase is the Great Contraction (Friedman and Schwartz 1963: Chapter 7). Monetary policy before and during the contraction was determined by Federal Reserve decisions and inactions. The lessons learned from this experience have informed subsequent policy decisions to the present day.

The second phase of the Depression is a recovery from 1933 through 1937. Monetary policy during this period was dominated by President Franklin Roosevelt's decision to devalue the dollar in terms of gold and the Treasury's monetization of the resulting gold inflow. In response to the failure of policy during the contraction, numerous pieces of legislation were enacted during this recovery period significantly increasing and altering the Federal Reserve's powers.

In 1937 before reaching full employment, the economy fell into another recession, the third phase of the Depression. While other factors may have contributed to the economic reversal, another Federal Reserve policy decision, a series of increases in required reserves, and the Treasury's sterilization (neutralizing) of gold inflows are blamed, at least in part, for the 1937–1938 recession. The final phase began with a partial reversal of the increase in required reserves and renewed monetization of gold inflows. These policies resumed the recovery that continued to the U.S. entry into World War II. War-related government spending and monetary ease during the war more than completed the recovery.

Understanding Depression-era monetary policy requires understanding the structure, tools and traditions of the Federal Reserve System at that time. The system then differed significantly from the system we know today.

The Depression-era Federal Reserve System

The Federal Reserve Act was passed in 1913 and the system began operations in November 1914. The Federal Reserve System (the Fed) was comprised of twelve district banks and a governing board in Washington, D.C. All nationally chartered banks were required to become members of the Fed. State chartered banks could join, but most did not. Member banks were required to hold reserves at Federal Reserve banks against customer deposits. Reserve requirements were fixed by law and the Fed used its policy tools to alter the supply of available reserves.

Initially, the Fed's primary policy tool was its discount rate, the interest rate charged to banks borrowing from the Fed. Discount lending provided reserves (new money) to banks. When banks held more reserves than required, they would use the excess to make additional loans. When extending a new loan, a bank credited the borrower with additional deposited funds, increasing the bank's required reserves.

The Federal Reserve banks affected banks' willingness to lend by altering their individual discount rates relative to the rates banks charged on loans. Increasing the discount rate was a contractionary (tight) policy discouraging bank lending and decreasing economic activity. Lowering the discount rate was an expansionary (easy) monetary policy intended to encourage bank lending and economic expansion. Since banks created deposits when extending credit, changes in bank lending changed the money supply as well.

The Fed also engaged in open-market operations, initially for income, but subsequently as its primary policy tool to alter the supply of bank reserves. The Fed bought bills: trade and bankers' acceptances which were short-term securities financing economic activity. The Fed set its bill-buying rate and purchased all bills offered at face value less the discount of the Fed's bill-buying rate. When the Fed set its discount and bill-buying rates, it had no control over the exact amount banks borrowed or the quantity of bills offered.

The Fed also purchased U.S. government securities. When purchasing government securities, the Fed could exercise precise control over the dollar value of purchases and sales. In the early 1920s the Fed began utilizing open-market operations in government securities as its primary policy tool. Purchases of securities expanded the supply of bank reserves and currency in the hands of the non-bank public: an expansionary monetary policy. Sales had the opposite, contractionary, effect.[1]

The Federal Reserve Act established two criteria to guide monetary policy. The first was based on the "real bills" doctrine. This doctrine maintained that if lending were limited to financing productive economic activity, the supply of credit would passively adjust to meet the needs of the economy and never result in inflation. Consistent with this theory, the Federal Reserve Act specified that acceptable collateral for discount lending was limited to short-term commercial and agricultural loans. Loans on this basis were believed to finance productive economic activity, and would automatically expand and contract with changes in economic activity, including seasonal demands emanating primarily from the agricultural sector. Loans based on other collateral, especially securities and real estate, were considered to be speculative and inflationary. Lending for speculative purposes would result in an inflation inevitably followed by deflation. Now discredited, the "real bills" doctrine was one of the two principles of policy for the early Fed.[2]

The other principle of policy was based on the gold standard. The value of the dollar was defined as $20.67 per ounce of gold. The gold content of the dollar also defined the dollar exchange rate with other currencies having a defined gold content. Central banks in gold standard countries, including the Fed, were required to hold gold reserves to back their currency notes and bank deposits with the central banks. The policy principle was to vary the discount rate in response to gold flows. According to the "rules of the game," a central bank should lower its interest rate in response to gold inflows and raise the rate in response to outflows. Interest rate adjustments were expected to affect economic activity to maintain or restore balance of payments equilibrium and limit the creation of money to avoid inflation.

The Fed was also created to be a lender of last resort, lending to banks in times of crisis. This function would prevent banking panics. However, the Act provided no guidelines for dealing with panics (Bordo and Wheelock 2011).

The Federal Reserve Act never specified how the Fed would resolve potential conflicts between its various objectives. A speculative attack on the dollar exchange rate could also lead to a banking crisis and economic contraction. Defending the exchange rate required a higher discount rate. Assisting banks required lending freely, possibly raising fear of inflation that induced further speculation. Combating a recession required a lower interest rate. There was no clear ranking of priorities for this or similar conflicting situations.

Responsibility for the conduct of monetary policy in the early Fed was also poorly defined. The Secretary of Treasury was the *ex officio* Chairman of the Federal Reserve Board. The Comptroller of the Currency, a Treasury official responsible for the national banking system, was also a member of the Board. There were initially five, and later six, appointed Board members. The Treasury dominated the Fed during its first years of operation. An easy monetary policy maintained low interest rates, enabling the Treasury to borrow cheaply to finance the government's war-related spending.

After World War I the Fed gained a degree of independence and authority for policy passed to the governors of the district banks.[3] They would recommend changes in interest rates and open-market holdings of securities. The Board could approve or disapprove recommended changes. The Board at times attempted to initiate policy, and while it had the legal authority to do so under certain conditions, these attempts were resented by the governors and often resulted in contentious disputes.

Benjamin Strong of the New York Federal Reserve Bank was first among the twelve governors. Through his abilities and force of character he directed monetary policy during the 1920s. Strong believed that the district banks should determine policy. He worked to unify the district banks and opposed yielding power to political appointees, that is, the Board. He both created opposition to the Board and utilized existing opposition to the Board to weaken the Board's operational authority (Chandler 1958). The Board also suffered from a very poor reputation; its members generally lacked the respect of the bank governors (Chandler 1958: 256–7, Hyman 1976: 113).

Following Strong's untimely death in 1928, a power struggle between the Board and the Fed banks ensued. The Board attempted to increase its operational control by creating a new committee to determine open-market policy. This change, expanding the committee from five to all twelve district bank governors, weakened, rather than strengthened the Board's influence. When a new Board Governor, Eugene Meyer, attempted to pursue expansionary policies during the contraction, the history of conflict between the Board and banks proved to be a significant obstacle.

The great contraction

The monetary and economic contractions from 1929 through 1933 were the worst in American history. Annual economic measures indicate that real gross domestic product (GDP) fell by 27 percent, and unemployment increased from 3 percent to 25 percent.

Monthly data from July 1929 through March 1933, the business cycle turning points, indicate that the broad measure of money, M2, fell by 35 percent, consumer prices fell 27 percent, and industrial production fell 52 percent.[4]

By 1924 Ben Strong had established three objectives for monetary policy: a high and stable level of business activity and stable prices, avoiding the use of credit for stock speculation, and assisting monetary reconstruction, that is, the restoration of the gold standard in Europe (Chandler 1958: 199). In an effort to curb stock speculation, all twelve Federal Reserve banks increased their discount rates in early 1928. In most cases the increase was from 3.5 percent to 5 percent.[5] In addition the bill buying rate was increased and open-market sales were made, making policy contractionary (Hamilton 1987).

In 1928–29 policy goals conflicted. Stopping stock speculation required an increased discount rate, but this policy was contractionary and initiated a recession in August 1929. International stability required U.S. lending abroad, but the tight U.S. policy forced other nations to tighten their policies, and many other nations' recessions began before the U.S. recession (Eichengreen 1992: 222).

In spite of the Fed's attempt to end speculation in stocks, the market continued to rise throughout 1928 and much of 1929. The Dow Jones Industrial Average peaked on September 3, 1929 and then declined, at first in an orderly fashion. But order turned to panic selling on October 28 and 29, the latter the infamous "Black Tuesday." The New York Fed made sizable open-market purchases to keep markets liquid and functional. However, the Board felt their approval should have been obtained before the purchases were made. The Board warned that any further purchases should not be made without their approval.

From the beginning of 1928 through September 1929, monetary conditions were tight. The monetary base, the sum of bank reserves and currency in the hands of the public, fell slightly, and the two measures of money, M1 (currency plus checking deposits) and M2 (M1 plus saving and time deposits) were flat.[6] Short- and long-term interest rates both increased throughout the year. The increase in short-term rates was greater, such that short rates on high-quality assets rose above the rate on the best-quality corporate bonds. An inverted yield curve, when short rates rise above long rates, indicates monetary tightness.[7]

After a one-month surge due to the New York Fed's open-market purchases in October 1929, all three monetary aggregates fell, and the rate of decline of the base increased. After the crash, Federal Reserve Banks began reducing their discount rates. Still the amount of borrowing from the Fed decreased, reducing Federal Reserve credit and the monetary base.[8] In the first months of the contraction, the decrease in the money supplies was due to the decreased base.

In October 1930 the first of a series of bank panics broke out (Friedman and Schwartz 1963: 308–13; Wicker 1996: Chapter 2). The banking difficulties changed the nature of the monetary contraction. The nonbank public immediately increased their holdings of currency relative to bank deposits, and within a few months banks increased their holdings of excess reserves.[9] Normally, bank reserves are expanded into a multiple amount of deposits through what is known as the money multiplier process. However, there is no multiplier effect for currency or excess reserves, so increases in these items subtract from bank reserves and reduce the money multiplier and money supplies (Friedman and Schwartz 1963: Appendix B). Although gold inflows increased the base, both money measures contracted due to the decreased multiplier. As the bank panics affected mostly nonmember banks, the Fed felt no obligation to act as the lender of last resort, and Federal Reserve credit decreased. Banking failures continued into 1931 and the public and banks responded by further increasing currency and excess reserves, continuing the decreases in the money multipliers and money supplies.

Banking difficulties spread across Europe in the spring and summer of 1931, forcing countries to abandon the gold standard or impose restrictions stopping the loss of gold. In September gold losses forced Great Britain to leave the gold standard and float the pound exchange rate.[10] Fear that the United States would follow caused a gold drain and a new, more severe banking panic, resulting in drains of both gold and currency.

The Fed reacted by applying conventional gold standard rules, increasing the discount and bill buying rates. As banks sought to replenish reserves lost to gold and currency drains, discounts and bills bought both increased, increasing the base. However, the currency drain, reducing the multiplier, more than offset the increase in the base, and the money supply measures both continued to decrease.

In September 1930 President Hoover appointed Eugene Meyer as Governor of the Federal Reserve Board. Meyer had written to Hoover prior to his appointment that he felt open-market purchases by the Fed might help reverse the recession. However, upon assuming his position he hesitated because he felt a "dangerously" high level of foreign deposits in the U.S. posed a threat to the gold standard, so he urged the Fed banks to lower their discount rates to reduce foreign balances. Then in the spring and summer of 1931 he advocated a policy of open-market purchases to combat the recession. Most of the Fed bank officials opposed Meyer. The tradition of hostility between the Board and banks prevented an expansionary policy. In the crisis following Britain's departure from gold in 1931, it was Meyer who urged increasing discount rates, as his first priority was always to maintain the gold standard (Butkiewicz 2008).

In 1932 Meyer obtained new legislation creating the Reconstruction Finance Corporation (RFC) and the Glass–Steagall Act of 1932 allowing the Fed to use government securities as collateral for Federal Reserve notes (currency). The RFC lent money to banks, particularly nonmember banks that could not borrow from the Fed. Meyer's goal was to restore confidence in banks and reduce hoarding, the public's increased holding of currency due to fear of bank failures (Butkiewicz 2008).

At this time the Fed was required to hold collateral for its outstanding notes (currency) of 40 percent gold and 60 percent eligible paper (loans eligible to serve as collateral for discount lending by the Fed) or gold (Federal Reserve Board 1932: 143–44). As bank discounts with the Fed had fallen to very low levels by July 1931, the Fed had to substitute gold as collateral due to a lack of eligible paper. Open-market purchases would have increased bank reserves and notes outstanding, requiring additional gold to meet reserve and collateral requirements. Fed officials opposed to open-market purchases argued that the Fed lacked sufficient gold to make purchases, the "free gold" argument. The Glass–Steagall Act of 1932 authorized the substitution of government securities for eligible paper, overcoming the "free gold" objection.

Between February and August 1932, the Fed purchased over $1.1 billion of government securities, the largest program of purchases in Federal Reserve history to that time. However, the program lowered interest rates causing gold outflows, and the RFC failed to reduce hoarding as public currency holdings grew from fear of bank failures, since there was no federal deposit insurance. The program increased bank reserves by a meager $166 million. In spite of signs of an incipient turn in the economy, the program of purchases was judged a failure because banks did not lend, and many Fed bank officials, worried about their dwindling gold reserves, voted to end the purchases (Butkiewicz 2008).

When the purchases ended, Fed policy stagnated. A return gold flow increased the base, but continued hoarding of currency and bank accumulation of excess reserves decreased the money supplies. The economic decline continued.

Banking failures beginning in late 1932 (Friedman and Schwartz 1963) and the declaration of a bank holiday in the state on Michigan on February 14, 1933 (Butkiewicz 1999, Wicker 1996) ignited another financial crisis. Many states soon declared bank holidays and on inauguration day, March 4, 1933, the governors of New York, Illinois and several other states declared bank holidays. Even the Federal Reserve and financial markets closed. President Roosevelt's first act was to declare a national banking holiday beginning Monday, March 6 and lasting until the next week when government-authorized banks were allowed to reopen. The holiday ended the panic.

During this final panic there was an increased internal drain of currency, some in the form of gold coin and gold certificates (currency), and an external drain of gold. President-elect Roosevelt refused to reveal his position on the gold standard, and fear of devaluation of the dollar in terms of gold, that proved to be correct, caused these gold drains. On March 3 the Board was forced to suspend the Fed's gold reserve requirement for thirty days, as the New York bank's gold reserves fell to 24 percent, below the minimum required (Meltzer 2003: 386–87, Wigmore 1987).

During the final crisis the Fed took no action other than to increase the New York and Chicago discount rates and the bill buying rates in the first days of March to stem the gold drain. No open-market purchases were made to reduce the pressure on banks from the internal and external drains.

The reasons for the Fed's decisions and inactions during the Great Contraction have been extensively debated. Friedman and Schwartz (1963) blame the lack of leadership and disharmony within the system following Ben Strong's death, as well as an incorrect policy principle, the "real bills" doctrine. Trescott (1982) agrees with Friedman and Schwartz that Fed policy changed during the contraction. His econometric estimates indicate that if the same policies had been followed in 1930–33 as had been followed in 1924–29, the Fed's security holding would have been 50 percent higher, increasing the base by $1.1 billion.

Brunner and Meltzer (1964, 1968) and Meltzer (2003) argue that Fed policy did not change between the 1920s and the contraction. The failure of policy was due to the Fed's attachment to the "real bills" doctrine. By the "real bills" doctrine, a low level of member bank borrowing and low nominal interest rates were indicators of monetary ease. The low rates during the 1929–33 contraction indicated to the Fed that policy was "easy." Open-market purchases when interest rates and discount lending were low would result in an expansion of speculative lending and inflation, followed by deflation and depression, so there was nothing more the Fed could do.

Wicker (1965, 1966) also argues that Fed policy was consistent, but focused primarily on international concerns, the gold standard, rather than domestic issues as Friedman and Schwartz argue. He concludes that Fed officials were confused by the behavior of excess reserves and did not understand how open-market operations could be used for economic stabilization.

Wicker and Meltzer both dispute the Friedman–Schwartz claim that had Strong lived, policy would have followed a different path. Meltzer and Wicker both argue that Strong's commitment to the gold standard would have resulted in policies similar to those actually followed.

Wheelock (1991) also disputes the idea that Strong's death changed policy. Based on his statistical analysis of Fed policies during this period, he concludes that the Fed focused on member banks' reserves throughout the 1920s and contraction. A low level of discount borrowings indicated policy "ease." The decentralized system and focus on the gold standard also contributed to policy ineffectiveness.

Kindleberger (1973) blames the collapse of commodity prices and international lending for the Depression. British leadership had waned and the U.S. was not ready to fill the void. The failure of an international lender of last resort to emerge to replace Britain was the reason for the economic collapse.

Eichengreen (1992) and Temin (1989) argue that the gold standard constrained the Fed's policy, and that devaluing the dollar or floating the exchange rate were not considered viable options. Butkiewicz (2008), examining the role of Governor Meyer, finds that his attempts to expand were constrained by discord within the system and Meyer's own inflexible commitment to the gold standard.

Friedman (Moreau 1991: xii–xiii) states that French absorption of the world's gold reserves deserves more blame than given in his previous work (Friedman and Schwartz 1963). Irwin (2010: 23) argues that French accumulation of gold and lack of U.S. lending caused the global depression. Mouré (1991: 201) argues that French officials urged the U.S to increase its discount rate in 1931, a decision that worsened the Depression. Butkiewicz (2008) also finds evidence of French urgings for tighter U.S. monetary policy.

Regardless of these disparate explanations of the failure of policy, there is general agreement that the Fed's monetary policy failings were a major cause of the contraction. While other factors, including fiscal policy changes in taxes and transfers, and tariffs were contributory, the impact of the monetary collapse on output and prices is clearly evident in the data. Figure 16.1 depicts monthly indices of M2 and industrial production during the years 1919–1941.[11] The correspondence between the trends in money and production is evident. Figure 16.2 depicts the index values for consumer prices and M2. While the primary impact of monetary changes during this period is on output, the corresponding fluctuations in money and prices are evident in the figure.

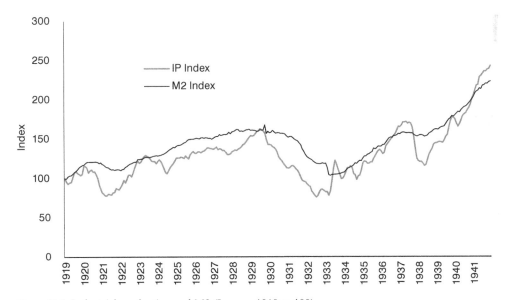

Figure 16.1 Industrial production and M2 (January 1919 = 100)

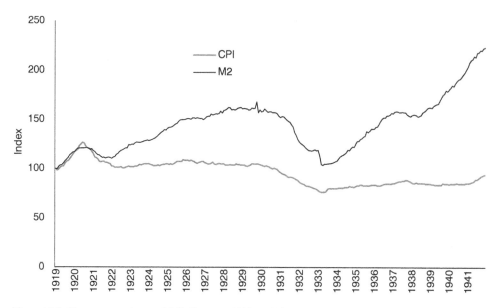

Figure 16.2 Consumer prices and M2 (January 1919 = 100)

The golden recovery

President-elect Roosevelt had been evasive when asked whether he would maintain the gold standard. His declaration of the bank holiday also prohibited anyone from making payments in gold, temporarily suspending the gold standard (Friedman and Schwartz 1963: 462–65). In April an executive order required banks to surrender all monetary gold to the Federal Reserve banks and individuals were to surrender all gold in excess of $100. Also in April the dollar exchange rate was floated in an effort to increase prices. In October the President directed the RFC to buy gold to increase the price, and in December an order required the delivery of all remaining monetary gold to the Treasury. All surrendered gold was redeemed at the official price of $20.67, even though the market price had increased during this time. On January 30, 1934 the Gold Reserve Act was passed outlawing private ownership of gold, requiring the Fed to surrender all monetary gold to the Treasury, and authorizing the President to set a new official price, which he set at $35 per ounce. The Treasury now controlled all operations in gold, and gold payments were made only to foreign governments.

A major obstacle to devaluation had been the "gold clause," dating from the Civil War period. To protect lenders against devaluation, many debt securities, including government bonds and private contracts stipulated that payment was required in gold or its dollar equivalent. Thus, a devaluation of the dollar from $20 to $30 per ounce would have increased the nominal value of debts carrying a gold clause by 50 percent. A joint resolution of Congress in June 1933 abrogated the gold clause, removing this obstacle, and in January 1935 the Supreme Court upheld the Congressional resolution.

Immediately following the official devaluation of the dollar, gold inflows into the U.S. surged, increasing the monetary gold stock by $7.9 billion between January 1934 and May 1937. Correspondingly, the broad money supply increased by 52 percent from March 1933 through May 1937, the business cycle trough and peak. Industrial production more than doubled, increasing by 121 percent, while consumer prices increased by 14 percent. Annual real GDP increased by 44 percent while unemployment fell to 14 percent.

President Roosevelt appointed Marriner Eccles as Governor of the Federal Reserve Board in 1934, promising Eccles that the Board's powers would be strengthened (Barber 1996: 86). Various legislation, including the Banking Act of 1933 (a.k.a. the Glass–Steagall Act), the Securities Exchange Act of 1934, and the Banking Act of 1935 altered and expanded the powers of the Federal Reserve System. Control of open-market operations was vested in the new Federal Open Market Committee, controlled by the renamed Board of Governors.[12] Discount loans could be made based on any acceptable security, ending the tie to the "real bills" doctrine. The Fed was given the authority to change member bank reserve requirements. To control stock market speculation, the Fed was authorized to set margin requirements, the amount of down payment required when borrowing to purchase stock. Speculation could now be controlled without changing monetary policy. Payment of interest on checking deposits was prohibited, and interest rates paid on savings and time deposits were regulated by the newly created Federal Deposit Insurance Corporation (FDIC).

In spite of its vastly expanded powers, the Fed contributed nothing to the recovery. Increased discount lending and bills bought during the March 1933 crisis increased Federal Reserve credit by $1 billion, but it then fell by over $700 million in April. Between then and May 1937, Federal Reserve credit increased by a mere $62 million. Monetary policy was determined by the Treasury's gold policy.

The recession of 1937–1938

From 1934 through 1941 the Fed's discount rate was high relative to market rates of interest (Friedman and Schwartz 1963: 514). The high discount rate encouraged member banks to accumulate excess reserves to meet liquidity needs as an alternative to borrowing from the Fed. The Fed, still focused on member bank borrowing even though discount lending had fallen to negligible levels, viewed the accumulated excess reserves as negative borrowing that could fund an inflationary credit expansion. As the excess reserves served no useful purpose, Fed officials believed they could be eliminated without any monetary effect (Meltzer 2003: 490–500).

The accumulation of excess reserves explains the Fed's inaction during 1933–1937. Open-market purchases would add to idle excess reserves, increasing the potential for inflation. Being an independent institution, the Fed generated its own income from its discount lending and open-market portfolio to pay for its expenses. While open-market sales would reduce excess reserves, the level of excess reserves in January 1936 was greater than the Fed's portfolio of government securities, so sales would reduce the Fed's income to almost zero, as discounts and bill holdings at that time together totaled a mere $11 million, yielding very little interest income at the prevailing low rates of interest.

The Fed decided to exercise its new power and doubled reserve requirements in three steps from August 16, 1936 to May 1, 1937 to reduce excess reserves.[13] The Fed's belief that this would have no monetary effect proved incorrect. Banks now held the additional required reserves, and while excess reserves initially fell, banks sought to replenish their excess reserves such that by July of 1938, excess reserves equaled the January 1936 total, and soon exceeded the previous high level.

As Federal Reserve credit was roughly constant between 1933 and 1937, the growth in the base and excess reserves was fueled by gold inflows responding to the higher price for gold and also European fear of Nazi Germany. At the end of 1936, President Roosevelt ordered the Treasury to sterilize the gold inflows. The Treasury issued new gold certificates to the Fed for the gold it obtained,[14] but then sold bonds, increasing its cash holdings by draining cash from the economy. From December 1936 through July 1937, gold certificates and Treasury cash increased by equal amounts (Meltzer 2003: 504–07).

Together these two actions reversed the preceding monetary expansion. The increased reserve requirements and continued accumulation of excess reserves increased the ratio of bank reserves to deposits, decreasing the money multiplier. The Treasury sterilization program slowed the growth of the base. As a result, from May 1937 through June 1938, M2 fell 2.4 percent. Friedman and Schwartz note that this is the third largest decline in their historical record (1963: 545).

The tightening of monetary policy had the predictable economic impact, likely augmented by fiscal tightening from the initiation of payroll taxes in 1937 (no benefits were paid until 1940), the enactment of an undistributed profits tax in 1936, and the end of bonus payments to World War I veterans in 1936. From 1936 to 1937, unemployment increased from 14 percent to 19 percent. Real GDP fell 3.4 percent. During the recession from May 1937 through June 1938, industrial production fell 32 percent, and consumer prices fell 2 percent.

The recovery is completed

The recession prompted a reversal of monetary policy. Pressured by President Roosevelt (Bordo and James 2010: 131) the Fed reversed the third of the three increases in reserve requirements in April 1938. Other than this change in required reserves, the Fed continued to remain inactive, with very little variation in Federal Reserve credit.

Monetary policy was still determined by the Treasury. The Treasury reversed its sterilization of gold and allowed the continued gold inflow due to capital flight from Europe to increase the monetary base. From the cycle trough in June 1938 to December 1941, monetary gold increased by almost $10 billion and the base increased by over $9 billion.

The expansion of the base and increased multiplier expanded the money supply by 45 percent from June 1938 through December 1941, the eve of the U.S. entry into World War II. Over the same period, industrial production increased 108 percent and consumer prices rose 10 percent. Annual real GDP grew by 38 percent and the annual unemployment rate fell to 9.9 percent.

Romer (1992) estimates that by 1941, the monetary expansion had returned real GDP to its pre-Depression trend, so the Depression ended before the U.S. entered the war. She allows that the war contributed to the recovery in the sense that the outbreak of war in Europe in 1939 was at least part of the reason for the capital flight from Europe and resulting gold inflows into the U.S.

Conclusion

Monetary policy during the Great Depression is largely a study of failure. The Fed increased interest rates in 1928 attempting to end stock speculation. Stock prices continued to rise through September 1929, but the tightening of policy resulted in a recession beginning in August 1929. Then, the Fed failed to act as the lender of last resort it was created to be when the banking panics broke out.

The Fed did not allow the gold inflows during 1929–1931 to increase the money supply, but failed to sterilize the outflows after Britain left gold in September 1931. Its only response to this crisis was the conventional gold standard response of raising its discount and bill-buying rates, worsening the contraction.

When an expansionary program of purchases of government securities was initiated in 1932, disagreements within the System and concern about gold losses caused the program to be terminated, even though some Fed officials wanted to continue the purchases. The Fed's only response to the final crisis in 1933 was to raise its discount rate in a futile effort to stop gold outflows.

The Fed's incorrect understanding of banks' accumulation of excess reserves led to another policy error, the doubling of required reserves in 1936–1937, resulting in a recession before the recovery from the Depression was complete. Due to its concerns about the inflationary potential of excess reserves, the Fed also opposed the expansion of the base from gold inflows (Meltzer 2003: 530). Fortunately, except for its sterilization of inflows in 1937, the Treasury allowed the gold flows to expand the money supply and stimulate the recovery.

The many studies of this era offer varied reasons for the policy failures: a lack of leadership, an incorrect theory of policy, the constraint of the gold standard, and a lack of understanding of how Fed actions affected the money supply and the economy. Hopefully, the lessons learned from this era can be applied to better direct future policy in the pursuit of price stability and maximum sustainable economic growth.

Notes

1 Fed officials at the time understood that open-market operations caused member banks to change borrowings in a way that partially or totally offset open-market actions: the "scissors effect."

2 Many within the Fed soon realized that there was no connection between the collateral for a loan and the use of funds obtained through the loan.

3 The heads of the twelve district banks held the title of governor. One of the appointed members of the Board was designated governor and a second vice governor. The Board governor was its chief operating office. The titles were changed by the Banking Act of 1935; heads of the twelve district banks were designated as presidents, and the Board became the Board of Governors, with a chairman and vice chairman.

4 The M2 data are from Friedman and Schwartz (1963). Data for GDP, consumer prices and industrial production are from the Federal Reserve Bank of St. Louis data base, Fred, at http://research. stlouisfed.org/fred2/. Unemployment data are from U.S. Bureau of Economic Analysis (1973), BLS series B2.

5 Interest rate data are from Board of Governors of the Federal Reserve System (1943: Section 12).

6 Data for the monetary base and M1 are also from Friedman and Schwartz (1963).

7 Banks engage in asset transformation (liquidity creation), borrowing short-term funds and lending for longer terms, profiting on the spread between short- and long-term rates. An inverted yield curve confounds the asset transformation process, reducing banks' profitability.

8 Federal Reserve credit is the amount of money the Fed supplies toward the monetary base. Federal Reserve credit consists of discount lending, bills bought, open-market purchases of government securities and minor items. Data for Federal Reserve credit are from Board of Governors of the Federal Reserve System (1943: 369–72). The monetary base is the sum of Federal Reserve credit, Treasury currency and monetary gold, less Treasury cash and deposits with the Fed, and other minor accounts.

9 Currency ratios are computed using currency and deposit data from Friedman and Schwartz (1963). Excess reserve data are from the Board of Governors of the Federal Reserve System (1943: 369–72).

10 Britain's gold losses stemmed from its balance of payments deficit. Eliminating this deficit to stop gold losses required price deflation (and further decreases in output) in Britain, increasing the price of gold relative to goods and services. The alternative was to devalue or float the exchange rate, either of which increased the price of gold (and foreign currencies) relative to prices in Britain.

11 Because the values of the two series are so different, an index depicts the percentage change from the initial January 1919 value.

12 The Treasury Secretary and Comptroller of the Currency were removed from the Board, and the number of appointed members was increased to seven.

13 Data for reserve requirements are available in Board of Governors of the Federal Reserve System (1943: 400).

14 These gold certificates could be held only by Federal Reserve banks. Private citizens had been ordered to surrender all monetary gold, including gold certificates, to the Treasury by January 1934 (Friedman and Schwartz 1963: 470).

References

Barber, W.J. (1996) *Designs within Disorder: Franklin D. Roosevelt, the Economists, and the Shaping of American Economic Policy, 1933–1945,* Cambridge: Cambridge University Press.

Board of Governors of the Federal Reserve System (1943) *Banking and Monetary Statistics, 1914–1941,* Washington, DC: Board of Governors of the Federal Reserve System.

Bordo, M. and James, H. (2010) 'The Great Depression analogy', *Financial History Review,* 17: 127–40.

Bordo, M. and Wheelock, D.C. (2011) 'The promise and performance of the Federal Reserve as lender of last resort 1914–1933', Norges Bank Working Paper 2011/01.

Brunner, K. and Meltzer, A.H. (1964) 'The Federal Reserve's attachment to the free reserve concept', Staff Analysis, Subcommittee on Domestic Finance, Committee on Banking and Currency. U.S. House of Representatives, 88th Congress, 2nd Session. Washington, DC: U.S. Government Printing Office.

Brunner, K. and Meltzer, A.H. (1968) 'What did we learn from the monetary experience of the United States in the Great Depression?', *Canadian Journal of Economics,* 1: 334–48.

Bureau of Economic Analysis (1973) *Long Term Economic Growth, 1860–1970,* Washington, DC: U.S. Government Printing Office.

Butkiewicz, J.L. (1999) 'The Reconstruction Finance Corporation, the gold standard, and the banking panic of 1933', *Southern Economic Journal,* 66: 271–93.

Butkiewicz, J.L. (2008) 'Governor Eugene Meyer and the Great Contraction', *Research in Economic History,* 26: 273–307.

Chandler, L.V. (1958) *Benjamin Strong, Central Banker,* Washington, DC: Brookings Institution.

Eichengreen, B. (1992) *Golden Fetters: The Gold Standard and the Great Depression, 1919–1939,* New York: Oxford University Press.

Federal Reserve Bank of St. Louis. (n.d.) Fred database. http://research.stlouisfed.org/fred2/.

Federal Reserve Board (1932) *Federal Reserve Bulletin,* March. Washington, DC: U.S. Goverment Printing Office.

Friedman, M. and Schwartz, A.J. (1963) *A Monetary History of the United States. 1867–1960,* Princeton, NJ: Princeton University Press.

Hamilton, J.D. (1987) 'Monetary factors in the Great Depression', *Journal of Monetary Economics,* 19: 145–69.

Hyman, S. (1976) *Marriner S. Eccles,* Stanford CA: Stanford University Graduate School of Business.

Irwin, D.A. (2010) 'Did France cause the Great Depression?' unpublished manuscript, Dartmouth College.

Kindleberger, C.P. (1973) *The World in Depression, 1929–1939,* Berkeley, CA: University of California Press.

Meltzer, A.H. (2003) *A History of the Federal Reserve. Volume I: 1913–1951,* Chicago, IL: University of Chicago Press.

Moreau, E. (1991) *The Golden Franc: Memories of the Governor of the Bank of France: The Stabilization of the Franc (1926–1928).* Translated by S.D. Stoller and T.C. Roberts. Boulder, CO: Westview Press.

Mouré, K. (1991) *Managing the Franc Poincaré: Economic Understanding and Political Constraint in French Monetary Policy, 1928–1936,* Cambridge: Cambridge University Press.

Romer, C.D. (1992) 'What ended the Great Depression?' *Journal of Economic History,* 52: 757–84.

Temin, P. (1989) *Lessons from the Great Depression,* Cambridge, MA: MIT Press.

Trescott, P.B. (1982) 'Federal Reserve policy in the Great Contraction: a counterfactual assessment', *Explorations in Economic History,* 19: 211–20.

Wheelock, D.C. (1991) *The Strategy and Consistency of Federal Reserve Monetary Policy, 1924–1933,* Cambridge: Cambridge University Press.

Wicker, E.R. (1965) 'Federal Reserve monetary policy, 1922–1933: a reinterpretation', *Journal of Political Economy,* 63: 325–43.

Wicker, E.R. (1966) *Federal Reserve Monetary Policy 1917–1933,* New York: Random House.

Wicker, E.R. (1996) *The Banking Panics of the Great Depression,* Cambridge: Cambridge University Press.

Wigmore, B.A. (1987) 'Was the bank holiday of 1933 caused by a run on the dollar?', *Journal of Economic History,* 47: 739–55.

17

WORLD WAR II

Robert Higgs

For many European and Asian countries, World War II was unquestionably the most important event of the twentieth century, both in general and in its economic aspects. For the United States, it was also very important, although many economists and economic historians view the Great Depression as an event of equal or greater economic importance. The war engaged most of the world's countries and all of its great powers. It lasted four to six years, depending on the country, and arguably several years longer for Japan and China, whose engagement some historians date from Japan's initiation of war against China in 1937 or its invasion of Manchuria in 1931. The war ended in May 1945 in Europe, in August 1945 in Asia.

More than 100 million military personnel were mobilized in the course of the war. A greater number was employed in producing munitions, other supplies, and services in support of the armed forces. The war had pervasive effects on virtually every aspect of economic life in the great powers. In Europe and Asia, it caused vast devastation. Altogether, probably more than 60 million persons lost their lives as a result of the war, and enormous quantities of capital houses and apartment buildings, factories, mills, port facilities, railroads, and other forms of fixed capital were destroyed or heavily damaged. Millions of people were left homeless or forced to move to distant places. In the midst of this disarray and destruction, governments strove to increase military outputs and to convert civilian production facilities and labor forces to military production. Thus, apart from any change in overall production, each of the major belligerents drastically altered the productive structure of its economy to serve the ends of war (Harrison 1998).

As usual, war entailed the exertion of greater government powers and a corresponding diminution of economic liberties. Each of the great powers developed or greatly expanded its military–industrial complex. Production of civilian goods and services was forcibly squeezed, in some places to very low levels, in order to serve military ends. Populations were subjected to regimentation of all sorts, from conscription of labor to rationing of consumer goods to physical allocation of raw and intermediate materials for industrial use. The market-price system was set aside more or less completely in favor of central planning, wage and price controls, and physical resource allocation for war-related purposes. Production of guns trumped production of butter, even in the United States, which escaped the devastation of its cities and the tremendous loss of life that other great powers, especially the USSR, China, and Germany, suffered.

Strange to say, many historians and economists have viewed the war as a positive economic event for the United States. It is generally interpreted as having "got the economy out of the Great Depression," restored "full employment," and created the conditions for the sustained prosperity that Americans enjoyed in the postwar era. This interpretation, however, rests on a faulty theoretical and empirical foundation, and during the past 20 years it has come under increasing professional challenge (see, for example, the studies collected in Higgs 2006; also Field 2008). Thus, even for the United States, the war is coming to be seen as, if not the unmitigated disaster experienced by the other major belligerents, nevertheless an extremely costly and unsettling event, rather than the "Good War" or a "carnival of consumption," as many historians have represented it.

In view of the vast scope of the economic events associated with World War II, and given the limitations of a short chapter, the remainder of this discussion deals exclusively with the United States. For a wider view, encompassing the war economies of other countries, consult Harrison (1998) and the articles on particular countries in Dear and Foot (1995), which are useful points of departure.

Before Pearl Harbor

Soon after World War I, a revulsion against the war and its then seemingly pointless sacrifices set in, and during the 1920s and 1930s, Americans for the most part supported measures to preserve U.S. neutrality and to keep the armed forces on a near-starvation diet. In the Senate, the Nye Committee hearings of 1934–36 cast an accusing light on the "merchants of death," the financiers and industrialists whom in those days many people blamed for the disappointing U.S. engagement in the Great War. To preclude foreign entanglements that might drag the country into a future war, Congress passed strict neutrality laws in 1935, 1936, and 1937, and a less strict law in 1939. Therefore, despite some interwar planning by the War Department, the Navy Department, and a handful of big businessmen, the nation possessed scant preparation for engagement in a great war when the conflagration broke out in Europe in 1939. The U.S. Army, with only 190,000 officers and men (U.S. Bureau of the Census 1975: 1141), was the world's sixteenth largest. Nor did the United States possess anything that deserved to be called a substantial munitions industry.

Whereas Woodrow Wilson in 1914 had urged his fellow citizens to remain neutral in thought as well as deed, Franklin D. Roosevelt in 1939 declared: "This nation will remain a neutral nation, [but] I cannot ask that every American remain neutral in thought as well" (Kennedy 1999: 427). Roosevelt himself had no intention of remaining neutral in either thought or deed, however, and he worked deviously but relentlessly for more than two years to push the United States ever closer to outright belligerency, finally gaining his objective when U.S. economic sanctions against, and an unacceptable ultimatum to, the Japanese provoked them to make a desperate gamble by attacking U.S. forces in Hawaii and the Philippines (Kennedy 1999: 426–515, Garrett 2003).

Meanwhile, the government had begun to mobilize and organize resources for war much more seriously after France and the Low Countries fell to Hitler's forces in the spring of 1940. A series of makeshift planning agencies guided these preparations: the National Defense Advisory Commission, the Office of Production Management, the Office of Price Administration and Civilian Supply, and the Supply Priorities and Allocations Board, all of which drew their authority from presidential directives and operated under FDR's tight control within the Executive Office of the President. Only after the attack on Pearl Harbor did Congress enact war-powers laws that created a firm statutory foundation for the War Production Board (WPB) and the other agencies that would direct the wartime command economy during the next four years.

Of all the measures taken during the 18-month "defense period" that preceded the formal U.S. declaration of war, none loomed larger than the re-establishment of military conscription. A proposal to reinstitute the draft ignited a fierce national debate in 1940. Ultimately, however, the nation's first peacetime national conscription law was enacted on September 16, 1940. Still, the draft remained a contentious measure, and when the law came up for extension in the summer of 1941, with a provision to retain the existing draftees in service beyond the 12 months originally stipulated, the House passed it by the narrowest possible margin, 203 to 202.

After Pearl Harbor

After the United States formally entered the war, the draft laws received periodic amendment. The ages of men subject to induction were extended at both ends to cover the span 18 to 45 inclusive, and the period of service became the duration of the war plus six months. Deferments remained controversial, especially the general exemption of agricultural workers. Many men joined the Navy or the Army Air Forces to escape the draft and the consequent likelihood of assignment to the dreaded infantry. As during World War I, local civilian boards rather than the military itself administered the draft system, which contributed greatly to its acceptance by the draftees and their families. Secretary of War Henry L. Stimson praised the system as "a triumph of decentralization" (Stimson and Bundy 1947: 162).

Of the 16 million who served in the armed forces at some time during the war, more than 10 million, or some 63 percent, were drafted outright (Chambers 1987: 254–55; Higgs 1987: 200–02). The buildup of this enormous conscription-fed armed force has a crucial bearing on the claims made during and since the war that U.S. participation in World War II "got the economy out of the Great Depression." The explanation that has usually accompanied this claim is that "wartime prosperity" resulted from massive government spending financed for the most part by borrowing and the Fed's creation of money. Although the government's fiscal policies during the war certainly had great importance in many respects, the core of the claim about elimination of the Depression relates to the reduction of unemployment, not to the increase of national output (which consisted entirely of military outputs, not of civilian goods and services (Higgs 1992: 44–49)). The truth, however, is simple: overwhelmingly, the reduction of unemployment occurred because of the buildup of the armed forces.

As Table 17.1 shows, the uniformed, active-duty ranks of the armed forces increased by 11.6 million persons between mid-1940 and mid-1945. That increase alone was more than sufficient to account for the simultaneous reduction of unemployment by 7.9 million persons. However, during those five years, the armed forces also increased their civilian employment by 2.3 million persons, and "private" employment in military-supply industries increased by 10.7 million (the increase had been even greater during the peak war-production years 1943 and 1944). While this gigantic diversion of labor to military purposes was proceeding, however, total *nonwar-related* employment actually fell by 7 million persons (again, the drop had been even greater in 1943 and 1944).

No one needs a macroeconomic model to understand these events – not Keynesianism, not monetarism, not any modern refinements of those theories. The government forced millions of men into the armed forces, paid millions of others to equip those men with guns and

Table 17.1 Employment, unemployment, and labor force, 1940–48 (millions of persons at mid-year)

Year	Uniformed military on active duty	Civilian military employees	Military supply industry employees	Total employed non-war-related	Unemployed	Total labor force
1940	0.5	0.3	0.3	46.1	8.8	55.9
1941	1.8	0.6	2.5	45.2	6.8	56.9
1942	3.9	1.3	10.0	39.6	4.1	58.9
1943	9.0	2.2	13.4	36.0	1.9	62.5
1944	11.5	2.2	12.6	38.1	0.9	65.3
1945	12.1	2.6	11.0	39.1	0.9	65.7
1946	3.0	1.4	1.2	55.9	1.7	63.1
1947	1.6	0.9	0.8	55.4	2.3	61.0
1948	1.4	0.9	1.0	56.4	2.4	62.1

Source: U.S. Department of Defense, Office of the Assistant Secretary of Defense (Controller) (1987: 126)

ammunition, and hence unemployment disappeared. None of this, however, had anything to do with the creation of genuine prosperity, and in no way does it support the oft-repeated claims that the war brought about a "carnival of consumption" (Blum 1976: 90) and that "economically speaking, Americans had never had it so good" (Melman 1985: 15). It would have been miraculous indeed if the U.S. economy had managed to improve the well-being of consumers (either currently or, via investment, subsequently) while reducing nonwar-related employment by more than 10 million persons, or some 15 percent (22 percent between 1940 and 1943), and no such miracle occurred. The workweek increased, to be sure, yet total civilian hours worked (including hours worked in private military-supply industries) increased by less than 21 percent between 1940 and the wartime peak in 1943 (Higgs 2009: 3).

The government did spend gargantuan amounts of money to prosecute the war; never before or since did the government's fiscal activities so dominate the nominal economy. As Table 17.2 shows, federal outlays increased from $9.5 billion in fiscal year 1940 to $92.7 billion in fiscal year 1945, at which time these outlays amounted to almost 44 percent of officially measured GNP (U.S. Bureau of the Census 1975: 224).

To get the wherewithal to pay for this huge gush of spending, the government proceeded to impose new taxes, to increase the rates of existing taxes, and to lower the thresholds above which people became liable for the payment of taxes. Annual excise-tax revenue more than trebled between 1940 and 1945. Employment-tax revenue more than doubled. The major sources of increased revenue, however, were individual and corporate income taxes. The latter zoomed from $1.0 billion in 1940 to $16.4 billion in 1945 (the greater part representing an "excess profits" tax), while individual income taxes jumped from $1.1 billion to more than $18.4 billion (U.S. Bureau of the Census 1975: 1105). Before the war, fewer than 15 million individuals filed an income-tax return; in 1945, approximately 50 million did so. And not only did most income earners have to pay, they also had to pay at much higher rates: the bottom bracket rose from 4.4 percent on income in excess of $4,000 in 1940 to 23 percent on income in excess of $2,000 in 1945. The top rate reached a virtually confiscatory rate of 94 percent on income in excess of $200,000 (U.S. Bureau of the Census 1975: 1095, 1110). In

Table 17.2 Federal receipts, outlays, and surplus (fiscal years), federal debt and money stock (mid-year), and GDP Deflator, 1940–48 (billions of current dollars, except deflator)

Year	Federal receipts	Federal outlays	Surplus or deficit (-)	Federal debt	Money stock	GDP deflator (1996=100)
1940	6.548	9.468	–2.920	50.7	54.3	10.3
1941	8.712	13.653	–4.941	57.5	61.3	11.0
1942	14.634	35.137	–20.503	79.2	69.0	–
1943	24.001	78.555	–54.554	142.6	90.4	–
1944	43.747	91.304	–47.557	204.1	104.6	–
1945	45.159	92.712	–47.553	260.1	124.7	–
1946	39.296	55.232	–15.936	271.0	139.3	–
1947	38.514	34.496	4.018	257.1	146.0	–
1948	41.560	29.764	11.796	252.0	146.9	17.3

Sources: Cols. 1–3, U.S. Office of Management and Budget (2002: 21); col. 4, U.S. Bureau of the Census (1975: 1105); col. 5, Friedman and Schwartz (1963: 716-18); col. 6, Johnson and Williamson (2002)

one mighty push, the government had completed the transformation of the income tax from a "class tax" to a "mass tax," which it would remain afterward. Moreover, payroll withholding of income taxes, which the government imposed midway through the war, also remained an essential component of the great federal revenue-reaping machine.

Notwithstanding the vast increase in taxation, the government's revenues amounted to less than half of its outlays (see Table 17.2), and it had to obtain the rest by borrowing. Therefore, the national debt swelled from $51 billion in mid-1940 to $271 billion in mid-1946. The Fed bought some $20 billion of government bonds itself, thereby acting as a de facto printing press for the Treasury, and it aided the government's bond sales indirectly by adopting policies that dramatically expanded the volume of commercial-bank reserves and thereby contributed to the rapid increase of money and credit, which pumped up the demand for government bonds. As Table 17.2 shows, the money stock increased by 171 percent between mid-1940 and mid-1948 (the latter being the first year almost completely free of the effects of wartime price controls), while the GDP deflator rose 68 percent.

Table 17.2 lists no figures for the GDP deflator from 1942 through 1947. Such figures have been computed and too many economists and historians have taken them seriously. In truth, however, the operation of a massive military-procurement system combined with a shrunken civilian economy subject to comprehensive price controls renders all such price-index calculations so problematic that for most purposes it is best not to use them at all (Higgs 1992: 49–52). The government began to dictate selected prices in 1941 and expanded and tightened the controls considerably in 1942 after enactment of the Emergency Price Control Act in January and the Economic Stabilization Act in October. Not until late 1946 did the government abandon the price controls, and not until 1948 had the economy shaken off the direct effects of those controls nearly completely.

A massive bureaucracy, the Office of Price Administration (OPA), administered the maze of controls and, because the price controls gave rise to pervasive shortages, the related rationing of a number of important consumer goods, including gasoline, tires, canned foods, meats, fats, sugar, clothing, and shoes. Although many people evaded the price controls and rationing restrictions and a black market flourished for many items, the OPA controls of basic consumer markets proved a major nuisance to civilians from 1942 through 1946 (Rockoff 1984: 85–176).

Consumers might well have counted it a blessing that the rationed goods were available at all, because many other goods were not. Early in 1942 the War Production Board forced the cessation of civilian automobile production, compelling this great industry to turn its factories and managerial talents to the production of war goods such as army tanks and bomber planes. Many other consumer durable goods, including most household appliances, were either unavailable or available only in tightly limited quantities during the war. New construction of private residential housing came to a virtual halt as the government diverted construction materials to the building of military bases and other war-related facilities ,and to the construction of housing for munitions workers in places where existing living accommodations could not shelter the influx of Rosies seeking to rivet.

Closure of the civilian automobile industry was only one of thousands of measures taken by the WPB, the central agency of the government's wartime command economy (for many details, see U.S. Civilian Production Administration 1947). In 1940 and 1941, the WPB's predecessor agencies had begun to issue priority ratings similar to those the War Industries Board used during World War I to give precedence to orders placed by critical munitions producers. Although the WPB inherited this system, expanded and refined it, and to some extent continued to use it throughout the war, the system proved highly unsatisfactory in practice. Excessive issuance of high priority ratings gave rise to "priorities inflation" and thus rendered the system incapable of serving its intended purpose. In 1943 the WPB implemented a Controlled Materials Plan for allocating three critical metals – steel, copper, and aluminum – to the major procurement agencies (Army, Navy, Army Air Forces, Maritime Commission, and Lend-Lease), which in turn allocated their quotas down the chain of their contractors and subcontractors. The idea was that the tail composed of these three materials would wag the dog of the entire war-production program. Although the authorities claimed success for this plan, they continued to supplement it with an array of other controls besides priorities, including spot allocations and production scheduling. Like any system of central planning, the entire apparatus was pervaded by conflicts, inconsistencies, and mistakes. The authors of one of the most careful studies of the system make liberal use of terms such as "administrative chaos," "administrative anarchy," "chasm between plan and operation," and "trial-and-error fumbling" (Novick, Anshen, and Truppner 1949: 110, 140, 219, 291, 394, 395, 400, 403), and they conclude that the successes of the wartime planned economy were "less a testimony to the effectiveness with which we mobilized our resources than they are to the tremendous economic wealth which this nation possessed" (Novick, Anshen, and Truppner 1949: 9).

Amid the sound and fury of the wartime command economy, no area proved more troublesome than labor. Owing to the massive withdrawal of prime workers from the civilian labor force by the draft and voluntary enlistments, labor grew ever scarcer, and the civilian labor force consisted increasingly of youths, elderly people, and inexperienced women who were drawn to seek employment, especially in the relatively high-paying munitions industries such as aircraft manufacturing and shipbuilding. The War Manpower Commission attempted to steer labor to the occupations and locations where it would make the greatest contribution to the war-production program, but labor proved difficult to steer. Toward the end of the war the president proposed that a national-service law be enacted that in effect would make all workers subject to an industrial draft, but powerful opponents of this idea, including the labor unions and the major business associations, blocked its congressional approval.

Labor unions continued to flex their muscles during the war. They strove constantly to push wages and other compensation above the limits the government had set in an effort to restrain the wage–price spiral that its inflationary monetary policy was causing. In general, the government enforced a "maintenance of membership" rule, which helped the unions to add some four million new members to their ranks – an increase of approximately 40 percent during the war years. Some powerful unions, most prominently the railroad operating brotherhoods and the United Mine Workers (UMW), took advantage of their choke-hold on the production of critical war services and materials to demand large wage increases, striking when their demands were not met. Twice in 1943 the government seized the bituminous coal mines and threatened to draft the striking miners, but the miners eventually achieved their objectives for the most part. Altogether, the government took over more than 40 production facilities – sometimes entire industries – during the war, and half that many during the immediate postwar years, to settle union-management disputes and thus to avoid protracted work stoppages (for detailed information about wartime seizures, see Justice Frankfurter's concurring opinion in *Youngstown Sheet & Tube Co. et. al. v. Sawyer*, 343 U.S. 679 at 621–27).

Not content with the regimentation of workers and capitalists in the private sector, the government undertook to build enormous industrial facilities on its own account, thus embracing war socialism in its pure form. Of the $25.8 billion invested in new manufacturing plants and equipment between mid-1940 and mid-1945, $17.2 billion, or precisely two-thirds, was federally financed, much of it directly by the armed forces, and the rest for the most part by the Defense Plant Corporation, a wartime subsidiary of the Reconstruction Finance Corporation (Higgs 1993: 180, citing WPB data). RFC head Jesse Jones observed:

> At the close of World War II, Defense Plant Corporation's investment alone embraced 96 per cent of the nation's synthetic rubber capacity, 90 per cent in magnesium metal, 71 per cent in the manufacture of aircraft and their engines, 58 per cent in aluminum metal, and nearly 50 per cent of the facilities for fabricating aluminum.
>
> (Jones 1951: 316)

The Navy and the Maritime Commission plowed some $2.2 billion into the construction of shipyards and plants for the production of ship components (Lane 1951: 397). Much of the government's wartime capital formation had little or no value for civilian production, and the government received only pennies on the dollar for the plants and equipment it sold to private purchasers after the war (Higgs 2004).

Legacies

The fiscal effects of World War II loomed large. In fiscal year 1940, when the Depression still lingered and the government was spending heavily for a number of relief programs, federal outlays amounted to $9.5 billion; but in fiscal year 1948, after the wartime command system had come and gone and the economy was once again enjoying genuine prosperity, outlays amounted to $29.8 billion, or 214 percent more (see Table 17.2), even though a 68 percent increase would have been sufficient to compensate for the fallen purchasing power of the dollar. Relative to GNP, federal outlays amounted to 10 percent in fiscal year 1940 and 12.2 percent in fiscal year 1948 (computed from data from Table 17.2 and U.S. Bureau of the Census 1975: 224). Federal receipts had grown much more, however: by 535 percent between fiscal years 1940 and 1948. (In the former year the budget had a large deficit, in the latter year a much larger surplus – see Table 17.2.)

The huge increase in federal revenues testified to the power of the wartime tax system, which the government retained when the war ended. Although some taxes were terminated, and some reductions were made in tax rates, many of the wartime changes remained, including the capture of the masses in the income-tax net and the payroll withholding of taxes to prevent employees from avoiding payment. In 1940 the lowest individual tax rate was 4.4 percent on income in excess of $4,000; in 1948 it was 16.6 percent on income in excess of $2,000 (equivalent to little more than half that amount in 1940 dollars). In 1948, 11.5 million of the persons who paid individual federal income tax, or some 55 percent, had the tax withheld by employers (U.S. Bureau of the Census 1975: 1091, 1095). With this war-spawned tax system, the federal government possessed the fiscal engine it would use to propel the postwar warfare-welfare state.

Despite the huge increase in taxation during the war, the government had borrowed more than half of the funds it expended; hence, the national debt had ballooned from $51 billion in mid-1940 to $271 billion in mid-1946. Although a small amount was repaid in the late 1940s, the huge war-spawned debt was destined to remain forever, becoming even greater almost every year (notwithstanding that until the 1980s, the debt declined relative to GDP).

The misleadingly named Lend-Lease program, whereby the government had transferred some $50 billion worth of goods and services to allied nations during the war, clearly prefigured the adoption of the postwar Marshall Plan, whereby some $12.5 billion was transferred to European governments during 1948–51 to aid their countries' recovery from the war's devastation. (See Crafts' chapter in this volume.) The way was then clear for the U.S. government to undertake a wider-ranging, permanent foreign-aid program, which has continued to the present.

The postwar foreign-aid program was but one aspect of the nation's new commitment to "internationalism." As the war ended, the United States and the USSR transformed their wartime alliance seamlessly into outright enmity and 45 years of Cold War, a conflict with far-reaching political, social, cultural, and economic consequences (Higgs 1994, Leebaert 2002), including the devastating "limited" wars in Korea and Vietnam. World War II had shattered the nation's traditional commitment to avoiding military entanglements outside the Western Hemisphere. Pursuit of global hegemony, by military and other means, became the de facto U.S. policy after 1945.

On the receiving end of much of the Cold War spending was the conglomeration of military contracting companies, universities, consultants, labor unions, and other recipients who formed one vertex of what became known as the military–industrial–congressional complex. The contractual arrangements that tied the parties of this arrangement together had been forged into their modern forms first during the "defense period" prior to World War II (Higgs 1993), and the dimensions of the system had swelled during the war. When the government's spending for military purposes plunged after 1945, the system endured a few lean years, but the outbreak of fighting in Korea in 1950 served as a catalyst for a big rebound, and the major participants have continued to prosper ever since, despite the alternating ups and downs of the defense budget (Higgs 2001, Higgs 2006: 124–208). The modern military–industrial–congressional complex constitutes perhaps the most consequential of the many institutional legacies of World War II.

Perhaps even more auspicious, however, was the war's ideological legacy. On the one hand, the war shattered the remaining remnants of serious opposition to government intervention among business people. The war, observed Calvin Hoover, "conditioned them to accept a degree of governmental intervention and control after the war which they had deeply resented prior to it" (Hoover 1959: 212). Hence, even during the pro-business Eisenhower administration, no attempt was made to get rid of the pervasive interventionist programs that the government had created during Franklin D. Roosevelt's presidency. Moreover, the general public's prevailing interpretation of the wartime experience gave unprecedented ideological support to a big federal government actively engaged in a wide range of domestic and international tasks (Higgs 1997: 318). Passage of the Employment Act of 1946 formally committed the federal government to ongoing responsibility for the economy's successful operation.

References

Blum, J.M. (1976) *V Was for Victory: Politics and American Culture during World War II*. New York: Harcourt Brace Jovanovich.

Chambers, J.W. III. (1987) *To Raise an Army: The Draft Comes to Modern America*, New York: Free Press.

Dear, I.C.B., and Foot, M.R.D. (eds.) (1995) *The Oxford Companion to World War II*, Oxford: Oxford University Press.

Field, A.J. (2008) 'The impact of the Second World War on U.S. productivity growth', *Economic History Review*, 61: 672–94.

Garrett, G. (2003) *Defend America First: The Antiwar Editorials of the Saturday Evening Post, 1939–1942*, Caldwell, ID: Caxton Press.

Harrison, M. (ed.) (1998) *The Economics of World War II*, Cambridge: Cambridge University Press.

Higgs, R. (1987) *Crisis and Leviathan: Critical Episodes in the Growth of American Government*, New York: Oxford University Press.

Higgs, R. (1992) 'Wartime prosperity? A reassessment of the U.S. economy in the 1940s', *Journal of Economic History*, 52: 41–60.

Higgs, R. (1993) 'Private profit, public risk: institutional antecedents of the modern military procurement system in the Rearmament Program of 1940–1941', in G.T. Mills and H. Rockoff (eds) *The Sinews of War: Essays on the Economic History of World War II*, Ames, IA: Iowa State University Press.

Higgs, R. (1994) 'The Cold War economy: opportunity costs, ideology, and the politics of crisis', *Explorations in Economic History*, 31: 283312.

Higgs, R. (1997) 'War and leviathan in twentieth-century America: conscription as the keystone', in J.V. Denson (ed) *The Costs of War: America's Pyrrhic Victories*, New Brunswick, NJ: Transaction Publishers.

Higgs, R. (2001) 'The Cold War is over, but U.S. preparation for it continues', *Independent Review*, 6: 287–305.

Higgs, R. (2004) 'Wartime socialization of investment: a reassessment of U.S. capital formation in the 1940s', *Journal of Economic History*, 64: 500–20.

Higgs, R. (2006) *Depression, War, and Cold War: Studies in Political Economy*, New York: Oxford University Press.

Higgs, R. (2009) 'A revealing window on the U.S. economy in depression and war: hours worked, 1929–1950', *Libertarian Papers*, 1, no. 4. Available at http://www.libertarianpapers.org/articles/2009/lp-1-4.doc.

Hoover, C.B. (1959) *The Economy, Liberty, and the State*, New York: Twentieth Century Fund.

Jones, J.H. (1951) *Fifty Billion Dollars: My Thirteen Years with the RFC (1932–1945)*, New York: Macmillan.

Kennedy, D.M. (1999) *Freedom from Fear: The American People in Depression and War, 1929–1945*, New York: Oxford University Press.

Lane, F.C. (1951) *Ships for Victory: A History of Shipbuilding under the U.S. Maritime Commission in World War II*, Baltimore, MD: Johns Hopkins Press.

Leebaert, D. (2002) *The Fifty-Year Wound: The True Price of America's Cold War Victory*, Boston, MA: Little, Brown.

Melman, S. (1985) *The Permanent War Economy: American Capitalism in Decline*, rev. edn., New York: Simon and Schuster.

Novick, D., Anshen, M. and Truppner, W.C. (1949) *Wartime Production Controls*, New York: Columbia University Press.

Rockoff, H. (1984) *Drastic Measures: A History of Wage and Price Controls in the United States,* Cambridge: Cambridge University Press.

Stimson, H.L. and Bundy, M. (1947) *On Active Service in Peace and War,* London: Hutchinson.

U.S. Bureau of the Census (1975) *Historical Statistics of the United States, Colonial Times to 1975,* Washington, DC: U.S. Government Printing Office.

U.S. Civilian Production Administration (1947) *Industrial Mobilization for War: History of the War Production Board and Predecessor Agencies, 1940–1945,* Washington, DC: U.S. Government Printing Office.

U.S. Department of Defense, Office of the Assistant Secretary of Defense (Controller) (1987) *National Defense Budget Estimates for FY1988/1989,* Washington, DC: U.S. Department of Defense.

U.S. Office of Management and Budget (2002) *Budget of the United States Government, Fiscal Year 2003: Historical Tables,* Washington, DC: U.S. Office of Management and Budget.

PART III

Post-World War II era

18

THE MARSHALL PLAN

Nicholas Crafts

Introduction

The Marshall Plan was a major program of aid which transferred $12.5 billion from the United States to Western Europe during the years 1948 to 1951. The phrase "Marshall Plan" has an iconic status, as is reflected in repeated calls over time for a new Marshall Plan for Eastern Europe (in the 1990s), for Africa (in the 2000s), and now for the Middle East. This suggests both that it qualifies for inclusion in this *Handbook* and also that it is important to be clear what it comprised, to evaluate its achievements, and to explain its successes and failures.

From the perspective of European economic history, the Marshall Plan has attracted a great deal of attention because it represents the prologue to an extraordinarily rapid phase of economic growth, the so-called "Golden Age" of the 1950s and 1960s, which came so soon after the traumatic shock of World War II and its aftermath. This raises the issue of whether it made a crucial difference to the reconstruction and subsequent growth performance of Western Europe. Since this turns mainly on an analysis of the medium-term indirect effects that the Marshall Plan may have had on institutions and economic policy choices rather than the immediate short-run impact of aid on investment or imports, the answer to this question involves difficult counterfactuals and is unavoidably somewhat controversial.

From the perspective of today's economic policymakers, the Marshall Plan can be studied with a view to deeper understanding of the question of the effectiveness of aid in stimulating economic growth, an issue which has produced an enormous literature over the last 15 years or so. It can also be viewed as a structural-adjustment program with similarities to the interventions made by the World Bank from the 1980s onwards, and its content has distinct similarities to the policies embodied in the Washington Consensus. This directs attention to lessons that might be drawn from the experience of the Marshall Plan for structural-adjustment lending.

The historiography of the Marshall Plan was initially dominated by accounts of a massive success story, for example, Mayne (1970). A well-known revisionist account was presented by Milward (1984) which argued both that the direct effects of inflows of aid on economic growth were small and also that the United States was not really able to reconstruct Europe according to its own blueprint. The reaction to this view can be found most notably in the work of Eichengreen and his several collaborators (Eichengreen and Uzan 1992, Casella and Eichengreen 1993, DeLong and Eichengreen 1993) which stressed the role of the Marshall Plan in promoting financial stabilization, market liberalization and the social contract on which the "economic miracle" was based.

The context

A good starting point is to consider two questions which are central to establishing the context of the Marshall Plan, namely, "why did the United States decide to implement it?" and "how promising were the opportunities for economic growth in Europe at the end of the 1940s?"

The idea of the Marshall Plan, later formally designated as the European Recovery Program (ERP), was first put forward by Secretary of State George C. Marshall in a commencement speech at Harvard University on June 5, 1947.[1] In the speech, Marshall noted that Europe's immediate needs for imported commodities, especially food, were much greater than its current ability to pay and that without substantial help Europe faced economic, social and political deterioration of a very grave character. The purpose of aid would be to permit the emergence of political and social conditions in which free institutions could exist and to provide a cure rather than a palliative.

The circumstances to which Marshall was alluding were, first, that Europe had a large current account balance of payments deficit running at about $9 billion per year in 1946–47 matched by an American surplus of a similar amount, and second, that with the perception of a looming communist threat in Europe the Marshall Plan would be the Truman administration's response. The current account problem could not be dealt with by borrowing from private capital markets at a time when international capital mobility was heavily restricted and currencies were inconvertible.

The United States had already given substantial amounts of aid; between July 1945 and the end of 1947 flows amounted to $13 billion and the GARIOA program was underway.[2] In the absence of the Cold War, the support of Congress for such a further big aid program would have been inconceivable (Cronin 2001). The communist coup in Czechoslovakia in February 1948 ensured that the European Recovery Act would be passed with a large majority but it should also be recognized that the provision of aid through in-kind transfers had business support from exporters and agricultural interests, and that labor unions were placated by provisions that the supply of goods to Europe would be carried on American ships loaded by American dockworkers (Gardner 2001).[3]

The rhetoric that the Marshall Plan was vital for saving Europe prevailed. The explicit objectives of the ERP can be summarized as increasing European production, expanding European countries' foreign trade both within Europe and with the rest of the world, achieving financial stabilization, and developing economic cooperation notably through what in 1950 eventually became the European Payments Union (EPU) (Wexler 1983). An important subtext, notwithstanding French resistance, was the rehabilitation of the German economy as an integral part of West-European trade able to supply capital goods to its trading partners.

Although times were hard in the years immediately after World War II, the medium-term prospects for European economic growth were quite bright provided that countries did not pursue damaging economic policies as, in different ways, many Latin American economies and the Soviet bloc would do. In fact, the scene was set for rapid catch-up growth to reduce the large American productivity lead which had built up over the first half of the twentieth century both through reducing inefficiencies in the allocation of resources and the management of firms, and through successful technology transfer. Abramovitz and David (1996) note that catch-up growth would be sustained by enhanced "technological congruence" and "social capability." In other words, American technology was now more cost effective in European conditions than it had been in earlier decades, and incentive structures in European countries were more conducive to effective assimilation of that technology. Technology transfer surged on the back of European investments in human capital, foreign direct investment (especially by American multinationals), a greater role for codified as opposed to tacit knowledge, and economic integration leading to larger markets (Nelson and Wright 1992).

In any event, Western Europe was very different from the typical country or region for which so-called Marshall Plans have been proposed in the last 20 years. It had a capitalist tradition and a long history of reasonably successful market economies. We do not have quality of governance measures for the 1940s but it is clear that European countries in that period would score much better for the indicators now compiled by the World Bank like "rule of law," "control of corruption," "regulatory quality" or "government effectiveness" than the average third-world country today. This augured well for growth and, at the same time, increased the probability that Marshall Aid could make a positive difference.

The details of the Marshall Plan

The basic mechanisms by which the Marshall Plan was implemented were as follows. First, European economies were allocated aid according to their dollar balance of payments deficits. American goods were shipped to meet the requests of individual countries. Second, each recipient country deposited the equivalent amount to pay for these imports in a so-called Counterpart Fund. The balances in these funds could be reclaimed for approved uses; approval was determined by the Marshall Plan authorities in the guise of the European Cooperation Agency (ECA) which had a resident mission in each country. Third, a productivity assistance program which aimed at reducing the productivity gap between Europe and the United States was established. This financed study tours by Europeans and provided follow-up technical services; it lasted in total for 10 years during which $300 million was spent (Silberman et al. 1996). Fourth, each recipient country signed a bilateral treaty with the United States which committed them *inter alia* to follow policies of financial stability and trade liberalization, including most-favored-nation treatment for West Germany. Fifth, the Organization for European Economic Cooperation (OEEC) which was established in April 1948 provided "conditional aid" of about $1.5 billion to back an intra-Western European multilateral payments agreement. In 1950 Marshall Aid recipients became members of the European Payments Union (EPU).

The EPU was a mechanism that addressed the problem of the absence of multilateral trade settlements in a world of inconvertible currencies and dollar shortage. In such circumstances, the volume of trade between each pair of countries is constrained to the lower of the amount of imports and exports because a surplus with one country cannot be used to offset a deficit with another. The EPU provided a multilateral clearing system supplemented by a credit line for countries temporarily in overall deficit. This was facilitated by the United States through conditional Marshall Aid acting as the main "structural creditor" to address the difficulty that would otherwise have arisen from the prospect that some countries were likely to be persistent debtors.[4]

Table 18.1 sets out the amounts received by the major recipients of Marshall Aid. Although the amount of aid provided by the United States was generous and amounted to an average of

Table 18.1 The distribution of U.S. Aid, 1948–1951 ($ million and % of GDP)

	$ million	*% of GDP*
United Kingdom	2826.0	1.8
France	2444.8	2.2
Italy	1315.7	2.3
West Germany	1297.3	1.5
Netherlands	877.2	4.0
Austria	560.8	5.7
Belgium & Luxembourg	546.6	2.2
European Payments Union	350.0	N/A
Denmark	257.4	2.2
Norway	236.7	2.5
Sweden	118.5	0.4

Note: Other countries not listed here received funds

Sources: Bossuat (2008) and Eichengreen and Uzan (1992)

Table 18.2 Composition of aid, 1948–1951 (%)

	UK	*France*	*West Germany*	*Italy*	*Others*	*Total*
Food, feed, fertilizer	30	10	43	17	30	26
Petroleum, coal	12	23	4	14	10	13
Raw cotton	9	14	19	25	5	11
Other raw materials	25	13	15	6	13	15
Machinery, vehicles	6	17	3	15	14	12
Tobacco	8	1	5	0	3	4
Other commodities	0	1	1	0	1	1
Ocean freight	3	12	8	9	4	6
EPU	1	0	0	0	11	4
Miscellaneous	4	8	3	13	9	8

Notes: "Miscellaneous" includes shipments made but not yet documented, and technical services.

Source: United States, *Statistical Abstract* (1952)

a little over 1 percent of GDP, the annual inflow to the recipients was modest in terms of their GDP at around 2 percent on average, although there was considerable variation. Table 18.2 describes the composition of aid shipments. Food was the largest category, especially at the outset, with capital goods accounting for only a small share. Table 18.3 reports on the use of counterpart funds in the largest economies which varied substantially. France, Italy and West Germany used most of their funds to boost production, although the composition of expenditure was quite different, By contrast, the United Kingdom used 97 percent of its funds to reduce the national debt (recorded as contributing to financial stability).

Table 18.3 Approvals for withdrawal of counterpart funds, 1948–1952 ($ million)

	France	West Germany	Italy	United Kingdom	Total
Power	738.4	182.6	1.0	0.0	1025.5
Transport & Communication	294.2	86.8	348.9	0.0	957.5
Agriculture	234.1	70.7	204.8	0.2	817.6
Manufacturing	249.2	218.7	22.6	0.0	681.7
Mining	340.6	91.8	0.0	0.0	481.8
Other Production	69.1	103.1	246.5	2.0	502.2
Total Production	1925.6	753.7	823.8	2.2	4466.3
Financial Stability	171.4	0.0	0.0	1706.7	2583.3
Housing & Public Buildings	314.4	97.7	172.7	0.0	767.5
Other	291.4	157.7	45.9	53.9	834.2
Total	2702.8	1009.1	1042.4	1762.8	8651.3

Note: Total includes other countries not separately listed

Source: Mayer (1969)

Direct effects on growth

Growth accounting provides a useful starting point for thinking about the direct effects of the Marshall Plan on growth. The basic formula is

$$\Delta Y / Y = \alpha \Delta K / K + \beta \Delta L / L + \Delta A / A$$

where Y is output, K is capital, L is labor, A is total factor productivity (TFP) while α and β are the output elasticities of capital and labor, respectively. TFP growth will reflect improvements in the efficiency with which inputs are used and improvements in technology. This approach directs attention to effects that the Marshall Plan had by financing more investment and so raising $\Delta K/K$, and also on TFP growth through the productivity assistance program.

Conventional growth accounting would suggest that the impact of the Marshall Plan via investment must have been quite modest. The rate of growth of the capital stock = $(I/Y)/(K/Y) = (I/K)$ where I is investment. If all Marshall Plan inflows went to raise I/Y, the share of investment in GDP, on average across recipient countries this would have gone up by about 2 percentage points, and with K/Y, the capital to output ratio, at about 2 this would imply that $\Delta K/K$ rose by about 1 percentage point. In growth accounting it would be conventional to assume that $\alpha = 0.35$ so the maximum effect on annual GDP growth would be about 0.35 percentage points. In fact, a relatively small share of the aid either in terms of ERP shipments or counterpart funds was spent on capital goods so the minimum effect might be much lower. In practice, the use of aid for other purposes to some extent released funds for investment so the actual effect lay somewhere between these bounds. Reasoning of this kind underlay the conclusion in Milward (1984: 107–08) that this kind of growth effect was small.

This analysis can be made more sophisticated by thinking in terms of a three-gap model (Bacha 1990). This takes into account that growth is a function of investment but also that investment may require not only savings but also imported inputs and complementary

Table 18.4 The Marshall Plan: effect of an aid inflow of 2% of GDP (percentage points)

	Impact of	Growth effect
Investment/GDP	+ 0.72	+ 0.3
Current Account	−0.25	0
Government Spending	0	0

Note: Zero indicates an insignificant coefficient

Source: Derived from Eichengreen and Uzan (1992)

provision of infrastructure. Thus, aid can have positive growth effects through relaxing savings, foreign-exchange or fiscal constraints. Eichengreen and Uzan (1992) developed an analysis of this type which at the same time provided an econometric estimate of the actual effect of Marshall Aid on investment; their results are summarized in Table 18.4. They confirm the basic conclusion that the direct effects of Marshall Aid on growth were modest. There is no effect through alleviating a fiscal constraint and while $1 allows a 12 cent increase in the balance of payments deficit this had no significant effect on growth performance. $1 of aid was found to raise investment by 0.36 cents (well below the maximum postulated above) but this is found to have a relatively large output elasticity compared with conventional assumptions. The bottom line is that the direct effect of an average inflow of 2 percent of GDP would have raised the growth rate by 0.3 percentage points during the years 1948–51.

The unimportance of the foreign exchange constraint suggests that resource bottlenecks were less important than is sometimes believed. DeLong and Eichengreen (1993) buttressed this conclusion by considering coal where Europe imported about 7 percent of its consumption from the United States. Using an input–output analysis, they obtained an upper-bound estimate that elimination of these coal imports would have reduced GDP by no more than 3 percent. Bottlenecks perhaps deserve more investigation and it has been suggested that they may have been particularly important in Germany where Borchardt and Buchheim (1991) argue that the Marshall Plan was important in delivering raw materials to the cotton industry and that counterpart funds mattered considerably for investment in the electricity industry.

It has been claimed that the productivity assistance program had big effects through increasing TFP. Silberman et al. (1996) asserted that productivity increases of 25 to 50 percent were common in firms following a study tour just through raising awareness of what was possible.[5] However, the evidence for big productivity effects is not convincing. These authors note that there was no proper evaluation using control groups at the time (1996: 449). A cross-section regression study which took account of whether or not there had been a report by the Anglo-American Productivity Council found no effect on a British industrial sector's productivity growth in the early postwar period (Broadberry and Crafts 1996). This may be explained by the general belief that American methods were inappropriate in British conditions, the bargaining power of workers who opposed change and the weakness of competition which permitted the survival of inefficient firms. The productivity assistance program had no leverage to remove these obstacles.

Indirect effects on growth

The Marshall Plan not only provided flows of aid, it changed the environment in which economic policy was conducted. The indirect effects on long-term growth which resulted were probably much more important than the short-run growth accounting impacts discussed above but they are harder to quantify. The channels through which these effects may have been transmitted include facilitating macroeconomic stabilization in the early postwar years, conditionality which *inter alia* promoted European economic integration, and providing an impetus towards postwar settlements which underpinned a cooperative equilibrium between firms and their workers in which high investment was the *quid pro quo* for wage moderation. The literature stresses effects working through investment but there may have been positive implications for TFP growth as well.

Stabilization which ended the threat of postwar inflation required that government budget deficits be reduced and liquidity creation stemmed. The potential contribution of Marshall Plan aid was to reduce the sacrifices required to achieve this and thus to make easier a political compromise that would suffice to end a "war of attrition." It has been argued 2 to 2.5 percent of GDP might go a long way in this context and that in some countries, notably France and Italy, the Marshall Plan was a key ingredient facilitating early stabilization (Casella and Eichengreen 1993). This claim has some theoretical plausibility but is not easy to confirm.[6]

Conditionality was embedded in the Marshall Plan in several ways. First, the bilateral treaty that each country had to sign was an agreement that embodied sound macroeconomic policies and a commitment to trade liberalization. Second, the requirement for American permission for the use of counterpart funds gave the ERP authorities both some control over the use of resources and ostensibly bargaining power with regard to domestic policy decisions. Third, Marshall aid gave the Americans leverage to encourage recipients to join the European Payments Union which also entailed reducing barriers to trade and adopting most-favored-nation treatment of imports from other members. This had the implication that West Germany would be reintegrated into European trade and able to resume its role as major exporter of capital goods.

The use of conditionality by the United States was clearly subject to important limitations. In particular, the strong American preference for moderate governments in France and Italy meant that counterpart funds had to be released to them and could not be used to influence domestic economic policies (Esposito 1995). Similarly, the United Kingdom's importance as an ally gave it substantial bargaining power over the implementation of the ERP – for example, there was no serious attempt to dissuade the British government from its extensive nationalization program (Burnham 1990). Moreover, the design for European trading arrangements was negotiated, notably with regard to British and French concerns, rather than imposed and the EPU did not match the original American plans for a free-trade customs union and early current-account convertibility (Milward 1984).

Nevertheless, the EPU represented an important success as a mechanism for restoring West Germany to its central role in the European economy (Berger and Ritschl 1995) and for promoting trade growth. The EPU was a second-best way of reviving European trade and multilateral settlements compared with full current-account convertibility, but it speeded up the process by solving a coordination problem. It lasted until 1958 by which time intra-European trade was 2.3 times that of 1950 and a gravity-model analysis confirms that the EPU had a large positive effect on trade levels (Eichengreen 1993). This can be seen as a stepping stone to further trade liberalization through increases in the political clout of exporting firms relative to import-competing firms (Baldwin 2006). The long-term effect of economic integration raised European income levels substantially, by nearly 20 percent by the mid-1970s according to estimates by Badinger (2005). This was perhaps the most important way in which the long-term effect of the Marshall Plan was to raise TFP.[7]

This account may seem to suggest a route by which the Marshall Plan had a major effect on postwar European economic growth. The obvious and very important qualification is, of course, that there were other routes to achieving trade-led growth. They may have taken a bit longer but by the early 1950s, at least for countries other than Germany, they were becoming increasingly feasible as reconstruction continued, exchange rates were adjusted, and the dollar shortage evaporated. Exclusion from the Marshall Plan and the EPU postponed but did not preclude trade liberalization, as the case of Spain shows.[8] The difficult issue which remains is what the net benefit of the Marshall Plan was relative to a counterfactual of a feasible alternative liberalization strategy.

DeLong and Eichengreen maintained that there was a further long-term effect of the Marshall Plan on long-run growth, namely, that it facilitated the negotiation of a "social contract" that delivered a high investment rate. They suggested that this was "vital but … difficult to quantify" (1993: 192). The idea is that the social contract which involves wage restraint by workers in return for high investment by firms was underpinned by governments through their fiscal and welfare policies and through restrictions on capital mobility and the extent of foreign competition. Marshall aid and the EPU were conducive to setting up these arrangements.

There is evidence that coordinated wage bargaining conducted by industry-level peak organizations, which were conducive to the patience which is required to support such a cooperative equilibrium, was good for investment and growth during the Golden Age and that the effects were quite large (Gilmore 2009). It should be recognized, however, that participation in the Marshall Plan was neither necessary nor sufficient for this outcome. Thus, Sweden had institutions of this kind (the so-called "Swedish Model") but the Marshall Plan played no part in their development, while wage moderation in Italy was underpinned by Lewis-type "unlimited" supply of labor rather than corporatism (Crouch 1993). Moreover, game-theoretic analysis shows that social contracts of this kind are very fragile and were vulnerable to many possible shocks, notwithstanding Marshall aid (Cameron and Wallace 2002).[9]

All this confirms that it is hard to say what difference the Marshall Plan made although it surely was helpful. In any event, insofar as it was favorable to the adoption of policies conducive to faster economic growth it should be remembered that Europe was fertile ground with high-quality human capital and institutions together with a history of successful market economies.

Lessons for today

In recent years there has been a massive literature on the effectiveness of aid in stimulating economic growth. It is now clear that, on average, aid has not resulted in increased growth in developing countries as the meta-analysis by Doucouliagos and Paldam (2011) confirms. There remains some controversy about whether aid has favorable effects in countries which have good governance and good policy environments, as was once firmly believed by World Bank economists following in the footsteps of Burnside and Dollar (2000). This claim does not appear very robust (Easterly 2003) and the very careful analysis by Rajan and Subramanian (2008) was unable to reject the null hypothesis that aid has no effect on growth in any circumstances.

All agree that the Marshall Plan was good for growth, even though as we have seen there is great scope still to differ on the magnitude of the effect. So, why was the Marshall Plan different? The answer partly does seem to be that there was a favorable institutional and policy environment with reasonably competent governments that could implement reforms and use the funds effectively. In these conditions, it is argued, the Marshall Plan had positive effects which might not be replicated elsewhere (Eichengreen and Uzan 1992). This suggests that the Burnside–Dollar argument may have more going for it than recent econometric analysis has been able to show. The possibilities seem to be either that there are measurement difficulties in identifying the conditions in which aid can work and/or that the Western European economies in the late 1940s had better institutions and policies than are typically found in developing-country samples.

The Marshall Plan can be thought of a "structural adjustment program" (SAP) as that is to say policy-based lending with conditionality, similar in essence to the concessionary lending of the World Bank after 1980; indeed, DeLong and Eichengreen (1993) called it "History's Most Successful Adjustment Program." Since there has been considerable skepticism about SAP lending and the use of conditionality, again the question arises what made the Marshall Plan different. The main point is similar, namely, that the evidence is that success or failure of World Bank programs resulted primarily from domestic political economy considerations. On average, success is most likely with recently elected democratic governments. The implication of the Marshall Plan period, as with the World Bank experience, is that "The key to successful adjustment lending is to find good candidates to support" (Dollar and Svensson 2000: 896). Put another way, the Marshall Plan might have been able to "tip the balance" where countries were, in any case, basically well disposed to the reforms that it advocated (Eichengreen 2001).

Looking at the Marshall Plan as a structural adjustment program also reveals that it had a common core with the Washington Consensus as originally formulated by Williamson (1990).[10] This comprises support for policies that are conducive to macroeconomic stabilization, are outwardly orientated, and strengthen the operations of the market economy. It includes trade but not capital-account liberalization as in the so-called "Bretton Woods Compromise" (Rodrik 2002). Since the Washington Consensus as set out by Williamson can be seen as advocating that developing countries should reform their policy mix to make it more similar to OECD orthodoxy, this is not so surprising. The greater success of the Marshall Plan than the Washington Consensus quite possibly reflects the institutional environment of Latin America compared with Western Europe rather than the basic mindset of the designers.[11]

All this tends to suggest that those who have called for a new "Marshall Plan for Africa" either do not mean it literally or have a serious misconception as to what it entailed. It seems unlikely that the average supporter of this kind of proposal really has in mind a structural adjustment program based on Washington-Consensus principles. On the other hand, they probably do believe that the aid inflows were much greater than the historical average of 2 to 2.5 percent of GDP and they probably do not realize that the success of the Marshall Plan in stimulating growth is quite unusual compared with the general record of aid effectiveness. In important respects, Africa in the 2000s is very different from Western Europe in the 1940s and it is perfectly reasonable to be skeptical that a "Marshall Plan for Africa" would deliver anything remotely similar to the results claimed by DeLong and Eichengreen (1993) for the real Marshall Plan.

Notes

1 Marshall was awarded the Nobel Peace Prize in 1953 for his role as architect of and advocate for the Marshall Plan.
2 GARIOA is an acronym for Government Relief in Occupied Areas, which financed imports of food, petroleum and fertilizers. Germany received aid under this program from July 1946 to March 1950, and during the period of overlap with the Marshall Plan received more from GARIOA.

3 Congressional support would presumably not have been forthcoming if the Soviet Union had accepted the American offer that it could participate together with its Eastern-European satellites. For a game-theoretic analysis which claims that this was an offer whose refusal was rationally anticipated, see Gardner (2001).

4 For a fuller account of the intricate details of the operation of the European Payments Union, see Eichengreen (1993).

5 It should be noted that James Silberman, the lead author of this paper, was not an impartial observer; he conceived and launched the productivity assistance program of the Marshall Plan in his capacity as Chief of Productivity and Technology Development at the Bureau of Labor Statistics.

6 The idea has been formalized in terms of a model proposed by Alesina and Drazen (1991) in which inflation results from a distributional conflict over who will bear the costs of stabilization. Delay in making concessions is rational as long as the costs of stabilization are borne unevenly and there is uncertainty about the staying power of rivals. Aid reduces the fiscal burden on the group that concedes first (the Left in late-1940s France and Italy) and thus induces earlier concessions; for a formal analysis and qualifications to this result see Casella and Eichengreen (1996).

7 Higher TFP could come through improvements in allocative and productive efficiency and through the expediting of technology transfer. Studies which find a strong positive impact of trade on income levels, for example, Frankel and Romer (1999) incorporate these effects.

8 Spain undertook a unilateral reform program in 1959 with help from the IMF which greatly reduced barriers to trade and exchange-rate distortions. This also had a significant positive effect on growth of income per person, raising it by almost 1 percentage point per year through the mid-1970s (Prados de la Escosura et al. 2011).

9 The key to sustaining the equilibrium is that both sides have low discount rates. This can be expected to be less likely if capital becomes more mobile, exchange rates are no longer fixed, technological progress slows down or inflation becomes more volatile. This suggests that the economic environment of the 1950s, rather than the Marshall Plan, played a relatively large role in underpinning "social contracts"; for further analysis, see Cameron and Wallace (2002).

10 This is on the basis of taking the Washington Consensus in terms of its economic dimensions rather than its alleged ideological connotations of neo-liberalism or market fundamentalism.

11 If it is accepted that the original Washington-Consensus reforms in Latin America had modest success in raising growth (Birdsall et al. 2010) and the more grandiose claims for the Marshall Plan are discounted, then the results are perhaps not as different as commonly assumed.

References

Abramovitz, M. and David, P.A. (1996) 'Convergence and delayed catch-up: productivity leadership and the waning of American exceptionalism', in R. Landau, T. Taylor and G. Wright (eds.) *The Mosaic of Economic Growth*, Stanford, CA: Stanford University Press.

Alesina, A. and Drazen, A. (1991) 'Why are stabilizations delayed?', *American Economic Review*, 81: 1170–88.

Bacha, E.L. (1990) 'A three-gap model of foreign transfers and the GDP growth rate in developing countries', *Journal of Development Economics*, 32: 279–96.

Badinger, H. (2005) 'Growth effects of economic integration: evidence from the EU member states', *Review of World Economics*, 141: 50–78.

Baldwin, R. (2006) 'Multilateralising regionalism: spaghetti bowls as building blocks on the path to global free trade', *The World Economy*, 29: 1451–1518.

Berger, H. and Ritschl, A. (1995) 'Germany and the political economy of the Marshall Plan, 1947–52: a re-revisionist view', in B. Eichengreen (ed.) *Europe's Postwar Recovery*, Cambridge: Cambridge University Press.

Birdsall, N., de la Torre, A. and Caicedo, F.V. (2010) 'The Washington consensus: assessing a damaged brand', World Bank Policy Research Working Paper No. 5316.

Borchardt, K. and Buchheim, C. (1991) 'The Marshall Plan and key economic sectors: a microeconomic perspective', in C.S. Maier and G. Bischof (eds.) *The Marshall Plan and Germany*, Oxford: Berg.

Bossuat, G. (2008) 'The Marshall Plan: history and legacy', in E. Sorel and P.C. Padoan (eds.) *The Marshall Plan: Lessons Learnt for the 21st Century*, Paris: OECD.

Broadberry, S.N. and Crafts, N.F.R. (1996) 'British economic policy and industrial performance in the early post-war period', *Business History*, 38: 65–91.

Burnham, P. (1990) *The Political Economy of Postwar Reconstruction*, Basingstoke: Macmillan.

Burnside, C. and Dollar, D. (2000) 'Aid, policies and growth', *American Economic Review*, 90: 847–68.

Cameron, G. and Wallace, C. (2002) 'Macroeconomic performance in the Bretton Woods era and after', *Oxford Review of Economic Policy*, 18: 479–94.

Casella, A. and Eichengreen, B. (1993) 'Halting inflation in Italy and France after the Second World War', in M.D. Bordo and F. Capie (eds.) *Monetary Regimes in Transition*, Cambridge: Cambridge University Press.

Casella, A. and Eichengreen, B. (1996) 'Can foreign aid accelerate stabilization?', *Economic Journal*, 106: 605–19.

Cronin, J.E. (2001) 'The Marshall Plan and Cold War political discourse', in M. Schain (ed.) *The Marshall Plan: Fifty Years Later*, Basingstoke: Palgrave.

Crouch, C. (1993) *Industrial Relations and European State Traditions*, Oxford: Clarendon Press.

DeLong, J.B. and Eichengreen, B. (1993) 'The Marshall Plan: history's most successful adjustment program', in R. Dornbusch, W. Nolling and R. Layard (eds.) *Postwar Economic Reconstruction and Lessons for the East Today*, Cambridge, MA.: MIT Press.

Dollar, D. and Svensson, J. (2000) 'What explains the success or failure of structural adjustment programmes?', *Economic Journal*, 110: 894–917.

Doucouliagos, H. and Paldam, M. (2011) 'The ineffectiveness of development aid on growth: an update', *European Journal of Political Economy*, 27: 399–404.

Easterly, W. (2003) 'Can foreign aid buy growth?', *Journal of Economic Perspectives*, 17: 23–48.

Eichengreen, B. (1993) *Reconstructing Europe's Trade and Payments*, Manchester: Manchester University Press.

Eichengreen, B. (2001) 'The market and the Marshall Plan', in M. Schain (ed.) *The Marshall Plan: Fifty Years After*, Basingstoke: Palgrave.

Eichengreen, B. and Uzan, M. (1992) 'The Marshall Plan: economic effects and implications for Eastern Europe and the former USSR', *Economic Policy*, 14: 13–75.

Esposito, C. (1995) 'Influencing aid recipients: Marshall Plan lessons for contemporary aid donors', in B. Eichengreen (ed.) *Europe's Postwar Recovery*, Cambridge: Cambridge University Press.

Frankel, J.A. and Romer, D. (1999) 'Does trade cause growth?', *American Economic Review*, 89: 379–99.

Gardner, R. (2001) 'The Marshall Plan fifty years later: three what-ifs and a when', in M. Schain (ed.) *The Marshall Plan: Fifty Years After*, Basingstoke: Palgrave.

Gilmore, O. (2009) 'Corporatism and growth since 1945: testing the Eichengreen Hypothesis', unpublished MSc dissertation, University of Warwick.

Mayer, H.C. (1969) *German Recovery and the Marshall Plan, 1948–1952*, Bonn: Atlantic Forum.

Mayne, R.J. (1970) *The Recovery of Europe: from Devastation to Unity*, London: Weidenfeld and Nicolson.

Milward, A.S. (1984) *The Reconstruction of Western Europe, 1945–1951*, London: Methuen.

Nelson, R.R. and Wright, G. (1992) 'The rise and fall of American technological leadership: the Postwar Era in historical perspective', *Journal of Economic Literature*, 30: 1931–64.

Prados de la Escosura, L., Rosés, J.R. and Sanz Villarroya, I. (2011) 'Economic reforms and growth in Franco's Spain', *Revista de Historia Economica*, 30: 45–89.

Rajan, R.G. and Subramanian, A. (2008) 'Aid and growth: what does the cross-country evidence really show?', *Review of Economics and Statistics*, 90: 643–65.

Rodrik, D. (2002) 'Feasible globalizations', NBER Working Paper No. 9129, Camdridge, MA: NBER.

Silberman, J., Weiss, C. and Dutz, M. (1996) 'Marshall Plan productivity assistance: a unique program of mass technology transfer and a precedent for the former Soviet Union', *Technology in Society*, 18: 443–60.

Wexler, I. (1983) *The Marshall Plan Revisited: the European Recovery Program in Economic Perspective*, Westport, CT.: Greenwood Press.

Williamson, J. (1990) 'What Washington means by policy reform', in J. Williamson (ed.) *Latin American Adjustment: How Much Has Happened?* Washington, DC: Institute for International Economics.

19

THE RIOTS OF THE 1960S

William J. Collins[1]

This chapter describes the wave of urban riots that occurred in predominantly African-American neighborhoods during the 1960s. These events marked the twentieth century's high point of racial tension and civil disorder in the United States. An enduring irony of the 1960s is that the riots broke out just as the political system, in response to a nonviolent campaign for change, finally renewed the civil rights that had been promised 100 years earlier. The riots came soon after Congress passed the Civil Rights Act of 1964, which targeted discrimination in labor markets, and the Voting Rights Act of 1965, which sought to reverse the disenfranchisement of African Americans in the South. Congress passed the Fair Housing Act of 1968, the period's third major piece of civil rights legislation, soon after the massive outbreak of riots in the wake of Martin Luther King's murder.

The riots of the 1960s were neither the first nor last examples of destructive civil disorders in American history. However, they were different in ways that make the period stand out from others. Prior to the 1940s, most race-related riots were instigated by whites who attacked blacks, as in the infamous 1919 riot in Chicago and the 1921 riots in Tulsa. In 1943, there were riots bearing a closer resemblance to those that occurred in the 1960s, including clashes between black civilians and police, looting of retail establishments, and arson. But in comparison with the 1943 riots, those of the 1960s were unprecedented in scale and scope. Hundreds of riots broke out all over the United States in the space of a few years. To the extent that the outbreaks had particular targets, Sugrue (2008: 326) points out that most violence was directed toward the police and local shops in black neighborhoods. White residential neighborhoods were rarely affected directly. Most riots were not severe in terms of loss of life or property damage, but several were extremely serious by historical standards.

After the 1960s, there were more large-scale, destructive riots, such as outbreaks in Miami in 1980, Los Angeles in 1992, and Cincinnati in 2001. In the last 40 years, however, the United States has not experienced anything comparable to the wave of riots that occurred in the 1960s. So, these events and the indelible images conveyed in the media—cities in flame, open violence between civilians and police, rampant looting, tanks in the streets, Mayor Daley's "shoot to kill" order and so on—continue to cast a large shadow in discussions of "what happened" in American cities in the 1960s.

In August 1965, the eruption of a riot in Watts, a predominantly black section of Los Angeles, ushered in this unusually violent period in American urban history. The precipitating event was the arrest of a young man for allegedly driving while intoxicated, which drew a crowd and then escalated out of control. During the ensuing riot, 34 people were killed, more than 1,000 people were injured, and 3,000 instances of arson were recorded. Elsewhere, there had been much smaller riots prior to Watts, including events in Philadelphia and New York City in 1964. These early, relatively small events were indicators of simmering tensions in black neighborhoods and might also have signaled the ascendance of a new "model" of collective action in which violent confrontation and destructive behavior eclipsed the non-violent methods of protest espoused in the early Civil Rights Movement. In any case, it is clear that sheer scale of the Watts riot marked a turning point in American history.

Table 19.1 reports information on the frequency and severity of riots, organized by year of occurrence. Table 19.2 enumerates the location and timing of the largest riots. Following a definition established early in the sociological literature's efforts to test hypotheses about the riots' causes and to better understand the spatial distribution of riots (Spilerman 1970, 1971), the data discussed here refer to events that were spontaneous, included at least 30 participants, some of whom were black, and resulted in property damage, looting, or other "aggressive behavior." Disturbances that were directly associated with organized protests or that occurred in school settings are not included. The dataset underlying Table 19.1 was compiled by Gregg Carter (1986), who extended and improved Seymour Spilerman's original data. The basic sources of information on riots in this period are the Congressional Quarterly Service's Report (1967), the Kerner Commission Report (discussed below), reports in the *New York Times*, and the "Riot Data Review" compiled by the Lemberg Center for the Study of Violence at Brandeis University. In sum, Carter's dataset covers the years 1964 to 1971 and includes the dates and locations of more than 700 civil disturbances, as well as the associated number of deaths, injuries, arrests, and occurrences of arson. Estimates of property damage tend to vary widely, and to my knowledge such estimates are not available on a consistent, nationwide basis. Collins and Margo (2007) define a simple index of riot severity that combines the various elements reported in Carter's dataset.[2] This measure of riot severity (S) is "absolute" in the sense that it is not scaled by population. Measurement error in the underlying components of riot activity (e.g., injuries) implies that a precise ordering of riots in terms of severity is unattainable. Moreover, reasonable people could disagree about whether some components (e.g., deaths) deserve more weight than others in forming such an index, and therefore a unique ordering is not possible even in theory. Nonetheless, the components are fairly highly correlated, and the simple index does summarize the available information and roughly characterizes the relative magnitude of the events.

Riots occurred throughout the eight-year period covered in Table 19.1, but the bulk of riot activity was concentrated in just two years, 1967 and 1968, which account for 3.3 out of 5.0 total index points and 65 percent of all deaths. The "severity" was heavily concentrated in a relatively small number of events and cities, not spread evenly over them. For example, no deaths occurred in 91 percent of the 752 riots underlying Table 19.1, and 90 percent of the riots have severity index values of less than 0.01. By far, the deadliest riots were in Detroit in July 1967 (43 deaths), Los Angeles in August 1965 (34 deaths), and Newark in July 1967 (24 deaths). Using the index as a broader severity measure, the riot in Washington, DC, following Martin Luther King's assassination (S = 0.34) joins Los Angeles in 1965 (0.48), Detroit in 1967 (0.44), and Newark in 1967 (0.23) as the most severe events on record.

Table 19.1 Frequency and severity of riots, 1964–1971

	1964	1965	1966	1967	1968	1969	1970	1971	Total
Number of Riots	11	11	53	158	289	124	68	38	752
Days of Rioting	34	20	109	408	739	284	126	82	1,802
Number of Deaths	2	35	11	83	66	13	13	5	228
Number Injured	996	1,132	525	2,801	5,302	861	710	414	12,741
Number Arrested	2,917	4,219	5,107	17,011	31,680	4,730	2,027	1,408	69,099
Occurrences of Arson	238	3,006	812	4,627	6,041	369	283	459	15,835
Index Value	0.163	0.504	0.275	1.349	1.956	0.374	0.230	0.149	5.000

Notes: See text for definition of a riot and description of the index. Note that counts of injuries and arson may be subject to error. Systematic, nationwide data on property damage do not exist to my knowledge.

Source: The data were compiled and described in Carter (1986)

Table 19.2 Dates and locations of ten severe riots, 1964–1971

	Date	Deaths	Index
Los Angeles	August 1965	34	0.48
Detroit	July 1967	43	0.44
Washington, DC	April 1968	11	0.34
Newark	July 1967	24	0.23
Baltimore	April 1968	6	0.19
Chicago	April 1968	9	0.14
Cleveland	July 1966	4	0.11
Mobile	April 1968	0	0.09
Milwaukee	July 1967	4	0.07
Pittsburgh	April 1968	1	0.06

Notes: See text for definition of a riot and description of the index. Notable riots that are not on the list include: Cleveland, Ohio, July 1968, 10 deaths; Kansas City, Missouri, April 1968, 6 deaths; and Augusta, Georgia, May 1970, 6 deaths. These riots had relatively small numbers of arrests, injuries, arsons, and/or days of rioting and therefore smaller index values than those listed above.

Source: The data were compiled and described in Carter (1986)

The causes and diffusion of the riots

The study of the 1960s riots' causes and diffusion draws on and contributes to a broader body of scholarship on civil disorders and collective violence. Theories of civil disorders attempt to understand why a collection of individuals, who are often similar in some dimensions (e.g., race and neighborhood) but heterogeneous in other dimensions (e.g., education, employment status, place of birth), would come together spontaneously and wreak havoc in places where only a few days before, nothing seemed particularly out of the ordinary. The key elements of a formal model might entail underlying grievances that are unaddressed by existing political channels, differences across persons and changes over time in the expected gains and losses (broadly defined) from rioting, and a spark that sets in motion the dynamics of a riot—something that suddenly raises the perceived gains, lowers the perceived costs, or both, for a critical mass of potential participants at a point in time and space. Potential "gains" in this setting are not necessarily pecuniary, though some certainly valued the opportunity to loot goods from stores. They might include satisfaction from the confrontation with police and the destruction of shops, or expectations of policy changes in response to the riot. Potential "losses" might include the risk of injury, death, or arrest. For reference, DiPasquale and Glaeser (1998) set out a tractable model along these lines, drawing inspiration from Tullock (1971), Kuran (1989), and Grossman (1991).

Three kinds of questions have been featured prominently in studies of the 1960s riots. First, did differences in cities' characteristics or differences in the economic circumstances of African Americans in cities translate into differences in the likelihood or severity of riots? Because scholars have ample evidence on the location and severity of riots as well as detailed economic and demographic information about cities from the decennial census, this question lends itself to fairly straightforward statistical analysis. Second, given the timing and location of any particular riot, is there evidence that the violence was "contagious" to other cities, and if so how were the riots transmitted from place to place? This is a more difficult question to answer because it requires careful attention to the exact timing and sequencing of events and to the nature of networks of information and influence, some of which are not easily observed. A third kind of question is more "time series" than spatial in nature: Why did the wave of riots crest in the late 1960s and then diminish sharply? In approaching this question, it is difficult to discern among competing hypotheses or measure the relative contributions of various factors through statistical analysis. Historical perspectives, such as Sugrue (2008), Thernstrom and Thernstrom (1997), and Fine (1989), provide context for the rise of black militancy and the frustration that boiled over into riots, especially among young men in northern cities in the 1960s.

The starting point for many discussions of the riots' causes and diffusion is the report of the National Advisory Commission on Civil Disorders, also known as the Kerner Commission Report (Kerner et al. 1968). The Commission was formed in the wake of the 1967 riots in Newark and Detroit and issued its report before the next wave of riots in 1968. The Commission debunked the conspiracy theory that the riots were organized events, and it ultimately blamed the riots on residential segregation, poverty, and frustration with the pace of social change, all of which the report described as functions of historical and contemporary discrimination. More specific grievances identified by the Commission included police practices, unemployment, and inadequate housing. The Commission recommended programs to alleviate conditions in ghettos, improve relations with local police forces, and speed the racial integration of workplaces, suburbs, and schools.

Since then, social scientists have sought to identify city-level factors associated with the incidence and severity of the riots, many of which were suggested as contributing factors by the Kerner Commission. The typical empirical approach to studying variation in riot occurrence and severity has entailed measuring correlations or estimating regression models that relate riots to observable city-level economic and demographic characteristics, mostly drawn from the decennial census volumes. A particularly striking finding is that after accounting for each city's black population size and region, relatively little variation in cross-city riot severity can be accounted for by pre-riot city-level measures of African-Americans' economic status, either in absolute terms or relative to whites. The size of the local black population is strongly associated with larger riots, which is consistent with a simple model in which a sufficient number of individuals are required to initiate and sustain a riot. Location in the South is associated with less riot activity, which is consistent with the expected costs of rioting being high there (or the expected benefits being low) relative to other regions. It is also consistent with an interpretation that emphasizes the relative stability of black communities in the South compared to those elsewhere. Beyond these two variables, Spilerman (1976: 789) concludes that "the severity of a disturbance, as well as its location, appears not to have been contingent upon Negro living conditions or their social or economic status in a community." The point is not that the 1960s riots were unrelated to blacks' economic or social status in the United States at the time, but rather that the *variation* in riot severity across places was highly unpredictable.

This interpretation is consistent with detailed chronologies that suggest that the period's truly severe riots were highly idiosyncratic events. In many cases, there were identifiable, idiosyncratic "sparks" that, through a series of unforeseen complications, turned a routine event into a minor altercation, and a minor altercation into a full-blown riot. In Detroit, a raid on a "blind pig" (an after-hours drinking establishment) escalated into the decade's deadliest riot. In Newark, rioting commenced after the arrest and rumored beating of a taxi driver. Another identifiable spark—the murder of Martin Luther King—initiated a large share of the riot activity that occurred in 1968.

As mentioned above, the idea that riots beget more riots through contagion is more difficult to evaluate than simple hypotheses about whether pre-existing city characteristics predict the likelihood or severity of a riot. Although early scholars did attempt to pin down the contagion phenomenon, the most sophisticated and thoughtful work in the area is fairly recent. In particular, Daniel Myers (2000, 2010) finds that severe riots in large cities inspired imitation, especially among smaller cities in the same media market, but that this contagion effect was rather short-lived (decaying within a week). These findings are important additions to our understanding of how civil unrest spreads geographically within short time spans, considerations that may be increasingly important as the speed and global reach of communication networks expand (e.g., relatively new social media have been widely employed in recent uprisings in the Middle East). In the context of the literature that seeks to understand the patterns across time and place of the 1960s riots, Myers's findings complement the longstanding empirical emphasis on pre-existing local characteristics, especially black population size and region. The findings also open the way for further consideration of how information networks functioned in this important period of social turmoil and change.

The effects of the riots

In comparison with studies of the riots' causes, scholarship on the riots' effects is less extensive. Nonetheless, the riots' effects are central to our interpretation of their historical significance. Did the riots affect the course of urban economies? Did they really matter for the cities and neighborhoods in which they occurred? Or were they merely destructive sideshows to a deeper story of urban economic change? The challenge for researchers is to estimate the counterfactual trend of places that were affected by the riots. That is, one must imagine what their post-1960 trends would have been *without* the riots.

Because the riots never destroyed a large portion of a city's capital stock, the direct economic effects through that channel were probably quite limited. Strong effects through other channels, however, are plausible. In particular, in models of spatial equilibrium, in which people and firms locate to maximize utility or profits (Roback 1982, Moretti 2011), an event that affects perceived local amenities, such as security or taxes, or affects local productivity can drain a place of population, property value, and income. Property value trends are particularly interesting in the context of urban riots because they reflect a broad range of forward-looking considerations that ultimately feed into demand for residence in a particular location.

Collins and Margo (2004, 2007) attempt to measure the "treatment effects" of riots in labor markets and housing markets. If, conditional on black population size and region, variation in riot severity across cities was essentially randomly distributed, then parsimonious ordinary-least-squares (OLS) regressions may provide useful estimates of the riots' effects on various economic outcomes. Given the existing body of research on cross-city variation in the severity of the riots, a simple OLS approach to measurement is defensible, but it is straightforward to check the OLS regression results' robustness to the inclusion of several additional control variables.

Table 19.3 shows simple comparisons of property value trends across three groups of cities with different levels of riot severity. The property value information pertains to owner-occupied residential housing and is from the decennial *Census of Housing*, which is the most consistent long-run, nationally representative source of information. Nominal property value appreciation was slower in high-riot-severity cities than elsewhere, especially for black-owned residential properties. This general finding is confirmed in regressions that adjust for observable differences across cities in pre-1960 property value trends, residential segregation, manufacturing employment, crime, and region. There is no evidence of a rebound in relative property values between 1970 and 1980. Overall, it appears that between 1960 and 1980 black-owned property declined in value by about 14 percent in high-severity cities compared to low-severity cities, after adjusting for observable city-level characteristics. Readers are referred to Collins and Margo (2007) for a more extensive discussion of the regression analysis, including instrumental variable estimates.

One interpretation of the relatively strong effect on black-owned property values is that these properties were likely to be closer to the riots than other properties in the city due to the high degree of residential segregation. If the effects of the riots were strongly concentrated in the neighborhoods close to riot activity, then the value of black-owned housing might have been differentially affected. Collins and Smith (2007) examine census-tract data, which describe economic and demographic characteristics of neighborhood-sized areas within cities. Within Cleveland, they find evidence that proximity to the riots is negatively correlated with post-riot property value and population growth. Importantly, proximity to the riot area is not negatively correlated with property value and population trends *before* the riots.

Collins and Margo (2004) find that the labor market outcomes of African Americans deteriorated in cities with severe riots relative to other places. Median family income and adult males' employment and income all show signs of relative decline in cities with severe riots,

Table 19.3 Comparisons of owner-occupied residential property value trends

	Low Severity Riot Cities	Medium Severity Riot Cities	High Severity Riot Cities	High–Low Difference
Mean Severity Index	0.003	0.021	0.195	0.192
Black households				
1960–1970: Mean change in log median value, 1960–70	0.384	0.318	0.270	–0.114
1960–1980: Mean change in log median value, 1960–80	1.327	1.166	1.021	–0.306
All households				
1960–1970: Mean change in log median value	0.303	0.264	0.251	–0.052
1960–80: Mean change in log median value	1.303	1.152	1.101	–0.202
Pre-trend, 1950–60: Mean change in log median value	0.344	0.346	0.314	–0.030

Notes and sources: *The Census of Housing* reports the median value of owner-occupied property for the 104 cities studied by Collins and Margo (2007), all of which had at least 100,000 residents in 1960. After splitting the sample into low, medium, and high severity categories, the table reports the within-severity-category mean change in log property values from 1960 to 1970 or 1960 to 1980, for black households or for all households in each city (unweighted). See Collins and Margo (2007) for regression analysis that adjusts for differences in city size, region, pre-trends, and other observable city characteristics.

controlling for other characteristics. For instance, OLS regressions reveal that average growth in median black family income between 1960 and 1980 was approximately 8 to 12 percent lower in cities with severe riots than elsewhere, conditional on basic city characteristics in 1960. This is consistent with the riots negatively affecting local labor demand, and again the effects persist into the 1970s with no signs of reversion.

The work described above has several limitations and leaves open important questions for future research. First, these studies primarily examine census data on places, and they are unable to track individuals or households over time. In essence, the studies compare changes over time across geographic areas, and the underlying populations of those areas could change. To the extent such changes are responses to the riots, it is appropriate to include them as part of the estimated "riot effect" *on places*, but this is conceptually distinct from measuring the effect on specific individuals or households that were directly involved in the riots, by choice or accident.

Second, because the empirical work is based on cross-place comparisons, general equilibrium effects of the riots could bias the results. For instance, if cities with low riot severity attracted economic activity from cities with high riot severity, then estimates that use low riot severity cities as a basis for comparison (i.e., as the basis for the "counterfactual" trend) will overstate the true effect of the riots on the high severity locations. On the other hand, if the wave of riots made people or businesses wary of locating in any central city, perhaps pushing economic activity to suburban locations, then comparisons across low and high severity central cities will understate the true effect of the riots. In this scenario, cross-city comparisons would highlight differences among cities but would not capture the common negative effect shared by all cities.

Third, it is unclear exactly how the riots led to worse labor market outcomes and lower property values. With the census data, Collins and Margo are able to link the riots to changes in average outcomes for cities, and to do so in a way that is plausibly causal. It is difficult, however, to get beyond that "reduced form" link to a deeper understanding of the process of urban decline with existing data.

Fourth, whereas the studies mentioned above focus on labor market and housing market outcomes, one might hypothesize that a wide range of other important responses occurred. Moreover, one could conjecture that these responses had implications for the likelihood of riots after 1970, or that these responses fed back into observed housing market and labor market variables within cities. For example, changes in police practices and hiring, changes in black political clout within cities, changes in the expected profitability of businesses located in central cities, and the post-riot demands for law and order are just a few possibilities that come to mind immediately. All may have some basis in anecdotal evidence, but they await more careful empirical investigation.[3]

Notes

1 This chapter draws on collaborative papers with Robert A. Margo and Fred H. Smith. Gregg Carter graciously provided his data on riots. The author is solely responsible for interpretations expressed in this article.
2 Each riot (indexed by j) is assigned a value $S_j = \sum \left(X_{ij} / X_{iT} \right)$, where X_{ij} is a component of severity (i indexes deaths, injuries, arrests, arson, and days of rioting) and X_{iT} is the sum of component X_{ij} across all riots. Thus, S_j is the proportion of all riot deaths that occurred during riot j, plus the proportion of all riot injuries that occurred during riot j, plus the proportion of all arrests, and so on. Summed over all riots, there are five total index points, reflecting the five components that enter the calculation. For each city, we add the index values for each riot that occurred in that city to form a cumulative riot severity measure.
3 See also Hahn (1970), Welch (1975), and Kelly and Snyder (1980) for early studies of changes in the wake of the riots.

References

Carter, G.L. (1986) 'The 1960s black riots revisited: city level explanations of their severity', *Sociological Inquiry*, 56: 210–28.
Collins, W.J. and Margo, R.A. (2004) 'The labor market effects of the 1960s riots', in W. Gale and J. Pack (eds.) *Brookings-Wharton Papers on Urban Affairs 2004*, Washington, DC: Brookings Institution.
Collins, W.J. and Margo, R.A. (2007) 'The economic aftermath of the 1960s riots in American cities: evidence from property values', *Journal of Economic History*, 67: 849–83.
Collins, W.J. and Smith, F.H. (2007) 'A neighborhood-level view of riots, property values, and population loss: Cleveland 1950–1980', *Explorations in Economic History*, 44: 365–86.
Congressional Quarterly Service (1967) *Urban Problems and Civil Disorder: Special Report No. 36*, Washington, DC: CQ Roll Call.
DiPasquale, D. and Glaeser, E.L. (1998) 'The Los Angeles riot and the economics of urban unrest', *Journal of Urban Economics*, 43: 52–78.
Fine, S. (1989) *Violence in the Model City: The Cavanagh Administration, Race Relations, and the Detroit Riot of 1967*, Ann Arbor, MI: University of Michigan Press.
Grossman, H. (1991) 'A general equilibrium model of insurrections', *American Economic Review*, 81: 912–22.

Hahn, H. (1970) 'Civic responses to riots: a reappraisal of Kerner Commission data', *Public Opinion Quarterly*, 34: 101–07.

Kelly, W.R. and Snyder, D. (1980) 'Racial violence and socioeconomic changes among blacks in the United States', *Social Forces*, 58: 739–60.

Kerner, O. et al. (1968) *Report of the National Advisory Commission on Civil Disorders*, New York: New York Times Company.

Kuran, T. (1989) 'Sparks and prairie fires: a theory of unanticipated political revolution', *Public Choice*, 61: 41–74.

Moretti, E. (2011) 'Local labor markets', in O. Ashenfelter and D. Card (eds.) *Handbook of Labor Economics, Volume 4B*, Amsterdam: North Holland.

Myers, D.J. (2000) 'The diffusion of collective violence: infectiousness, susceptibility, and mass media networks', *American Journal of Sociology*, 106: 173–208.

Myers, D.J. (2010) 'Violent protest and heterogeneous diffusion processes: the spread of U.S. racial rioting from 1964 to 1971', *Mobilization: An International Journal*, 15: 289–321.

Roback, J. (1982) 'Wage, rents, and the quality of life', *Journal of Political Economy*, 90: 1257–78.

Spilerman, S. (1970) 'The causes of racial disturbances: a comparison of alternative explanations', *American Sociological Review*, 35: 627–49.

Spilerman, S. (1971) 'The causes of racial disturbances: test of an explanation', *American Sociological Review*, 36: 427–42.

Spilerman, S. (1976) 'Structural characteristics of cities and the severity of racial disorders', *American Sociological Review*, 41: 771–93.

Sugrue, T. (2008) *Sweet Land of Liberty: The Forgotten Struggle for Civil Rights in the North*, New York: Random House.

Thernstrom, S. and Thernstrom, A. (1997) *America in Black and White: One Nation, Indivisible*, New York: Simon & Schuster.

Tullock, G.S. (1971) 'The paradox of revolution', *Public Choice*, 11: 89–99.

Welch, S. (1975) 'The impact of urban riots on urban expenditures', *American Journal of Political Science*, 19: 741–60.

20

THE GREAT INFLATION OF THE 1970S

Robert L. Hetzel[1]

The economics profession has developed very little consensus regarding the nature of macroeconomic phenomena. One reason for this lack of consensus is the difficulty of passing from correlations in the historical data to cause and effect relations. Economists cannot perform the controlled experiments that render causation unambiguous, such as those used in the physical sciences. In macroeconomics, this difficulty in inferring structural relationships from reduced-form relationships appears most prominently in controversy over interpretation of the unemployment–inflation correlations summarized in Phillips curves.

As a result, in the case of the Phillips curve, economists disagree over whether policymakers can manipulate inflation and output in a way that yields predictable outcomes. The decades of the 1960s and 1970s are especially interesting because of the ability to identify a change in monetary policy designed to manipulate unemployment in a way intended to yield acceptable behavior for inflation. As much as is possible in macroeconomics, this attempt constituted a "controlled experiment."

This policy of using monetary and fiscal policy to lower the unemployment rate accompanied rising inflation and recurrent recessions. Measured by year-over-year changes in the consumer price index (CPI), inflation rose irregularly starting from 1 percent in the early 1960s. It peaked at 5.7 percent in 1970, at 11.0 percent in 1974, and finally at 13.5 percent in 1980. Also, a succession of recessions occurred with business cycle peaks in December 1969, November 1973, January 1980, and July 1981.

The debate over the cause of this economic dysfunction took the name of Monetarist–Keynesian. Monetarists attributed the poor outcomes to the activist policy to lower unemployment known as fine-tuning. Keynesians pointed to adverse shocks like inflation shocks. This debate addressed the fundamental issues of macroeconomics: What is the nature of the shocks that impinge on the economy and how efficacious is the price system in attenuating those shocks?

The Keynesian consensus

At least until the end of the 1970s, Keynesians dominated the intellectual and policymaking environment. The post-World War II Keynesian consensus emerged out of the juxtaposition

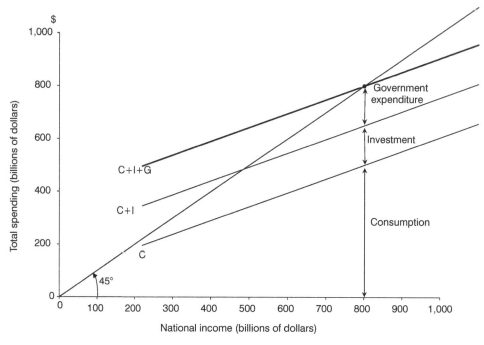

Figure 20.1 Effects of government expenditure on income determination

Source: The figure is from Samuelson (1967, 233)

of the high unemployment rates of the Great Depression with the low unemployment rates of World War II. Economists inferred from the Depression with its low level of interest rates that the price system does not work well to maintain full employment. They inferred from World War II with its high level of defense spending that government spending can maintain full employment.

For Keynesians, a corollary of the assumption that the price system is a weak reed for maintaining full employment was the impotence of monetary policy. This reasoning came from the correct proposition that the transmission of monetary policy works through asset prices and the associated interest rates on those assets plus two incorrect propositions. The first incorrect proposition was that a "low" real interest rate implies expansionary monetary policy and the second was that interest rates (nominal and real) were low in the Depression.[2]

According to the Keynesian view, the driving force of cyclical fluctuations is "animal spirits," that is, swings from optimism to pessimism about the future on the part of investors. These swings are unpredictable and untethered in that they occur independently of rules implemented by the central bank. Because they overwhelm the stabilizing properties of the real interest rate and monetary policy, shocks produce changes in output largely unmitigated by the working of the price system. As expressed in the Keynesian cross shown in Figure 20.1 (adapted from Samuelson 1967: 233), the economy adjusts to swings in investment through amplified swings in output (the multiplier).

Consider the horizontal axis as measuring income, the vertical axis as measuring spending, and the 45° line as measuring the necessary ex-post equality between income and spending. Aggregate demand, shown as the diagonal line intersecting the 45° line, includes the two components: consumption (C) and investment (I). At the income level of $800 billion,

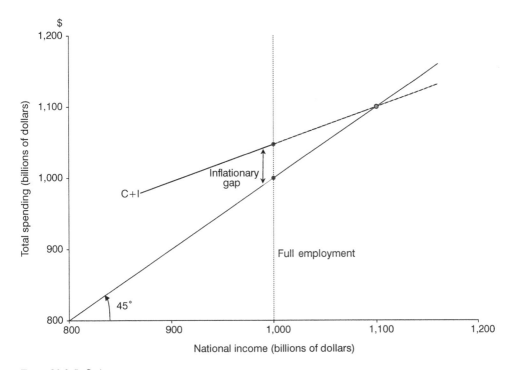

Figure 20.2 Inflationary gap

Source: The figure is from Samuelson (1967, 233)

aggregate demand (spending) falls short of the 45° line. That is, ex ante, spending (*C*+*I*) is less than income. The counterpart of this shortfall in spending is excessive saving.

In the absence of government expenditure, real output would decline to the point where the *C*+*I* line intersects the 45° line. Output must decline sufficiently for the saving of the public to decline to the exogenously-given level of investment. The greater the marginal propensity to consume out of income, that is, the steeper the *C*+*I* line, the more that output and income must fall to effect the required reduction in saving (the multiplier). Output must adjust to swings in investment with no assurance that it will end up at the full employment level. The mechanism for keeping aggregate demand at the full employment level is government expenditure, in particular, deficit spending.

Figure 20.2 (Samuelson 1967: 231) illustrates the Keynesian view of inflation as determined by real forces. At the full employment level of output of $1 trillion, ex ante, spending (aggregate demand) exceeds income. This "inflationary gap" produces inflation. Because changes in the price level serve no equilibrating function, inflation is not self-correcting.[3] Again, government expenditure is the equilibrating mechanism. Now, government needs to run a budget surplus to reduce aggregate demand. Government needs to save because the public saves too little.

Keynesians believed that the price system worked so poorly that for almost indefinite periods of time the unemployment rate could exceed the unemployment rate consistent with full employment. The output gap remained negative in that actual output minus full-employment (potential) output remained negative. Keynesians advocated deficit spending to raise aggregate demand to its full-employment level. To complete their policy program, Keynesians needed to know how much inflation would accompany the full employment of resources. To answer that question, they turned to an empirical relationship – the Phillips curve. Interpreted as a structural relationship, the Phillips curve implied a hard-wired relationship between inflation and unemployment. This relationship appeared to offer a prediction for the amount of inflation that would occur at different levels of an output gap or employment gap.

The monetarist challenge

In the most famous challenge to the propositions of Keynesianism, Milton Friedman (1968) criticized the idea of a stable relationship between a nominal variable (inflation) and a real variable (unemployment). He predicted the breakdown of the Phillips curve as offering a menu of choice between unemployment and inflation. Friedman (1968: 11) wrote:

> The temporary trade-off [between inflation and unemployment] comes not from inflation per se, but from unanticipated inflation. ... It [the central bank] cannot use its control over nominal quantities to peg a real quantity.

According to Friedman, in the absence of monetary disorder, the price system works well to determine distinct "natural" values of real variables like the unemployment rate. Moreover, "the monetary authority ... cannot know what the 'natural' rate is." As a result, the central bank must follow a rule that allows the price system to determine real variables. Friedman (1960) argued for a rule in the form of low, steady money growth by arguing that historically the country would have been better off both in recessions – with faster money growth instead of the contemporaneously prevailing low money growth – and in inflations – with slower money growth instead of the contemporaneously prevailing high money growth.

The efficient operation of the price system requires the central bank to follow a rule that makes the price level evolve in a predictable fashion. Given such a rule, because of their self-interest in setting an optimal relative price, firms collectively set dollar prices in a way that adjusts for predictable changes in the price level while individually setting market-clearing relative prices. As formalized by Lucas (1972), firms collectively adjust dollar prices in a way conditioned by the systematic part of monetary policy (rational expectations). With that adjustment for expected inflation, relative prices summarize aggregate dispersed information so that market-clearing prices allocate resources efficiently.

In contrast, the price system works only poorly when the central bank causes the price level to evolve unpredictably. Firms set dollar prices with the intention only of setting relative prices. Collectively, however, the dollar prices they set determine the price level. The price level adjusts to give the public the real money balances it desires to make transactions. When the central bank creates money in a way that causes the price level to evolve erratically, firms have no way of collectively coordinating changes in dollar prices in a way that both preserves market-clearing relative prices while at the same time discovering the price level that endows the nominal quantity of money with the real purchasing power desired by the public. There is no private market mechanism to coordinate this latter social good aspect of firm behavior in setting the price level.

The rational-expectations assumption about the efficient use of information by market participants (Lucas 1972) implies a "classical dichotomy." The central bank can follow a rule that allows for separation of the determination of nominal variables (the price level) and real variables (relative prices). Based on a common understanding of the central bank's inflation target, firms make relative-price maintaining changes in dollar prices while also making relative-price altering changes in dollar prices.

On the one hand, through the expectational environment it creates for firms that set prices for multiple periods, the central bank controls trend inflation (leaving inflation shocks to impart random changes to the price level). On the other hand, by following a rule that allows market forces to determine the real interest rate, the central bank delegates the control of real variables to the working of market forces.

Samuelson and Solow propose a "vast" experiment

In the 1950s, given the economic conservatism of the Eisenhower administration with its focus on balanced budgets and concern for the balance of payments and gold outflows, the Keynesian orthodoxy exercised negligible influence on policy. In the 1960 election pitting John F. Kennedy against Richard Nixon, the former's pledge to get the country moving brought macroeconomic policy into play. The contentious political issue was whether a national objective of full employment would cause inflation. That objective was widely taken to be the 4 percent unemployment rate that prevailed after World War II. In a paper that reads like a position paper for Kennedy as presidential candidate, Samuelson and Solow (1960 [1966]) asked what inflation rate would emerge if aggregate-demand management engineered full employment. To answer this question, they extended the empirical work by A.W. Phillips (1958).

Using annual data for the United Kingdom from 1861 through 1957, Phillips demonstrated an inverse relationship between the rate of change of nominal money wages and the unemployment rate. Samuelson and Solow recreated this "Phillips curve" using U.S. data. The "problem" was that for data from the 1950s this curve indicated that price stability would require a 6 percent unemployment rate. Nevertheless, Samuelson and Solow (1960 [1966]: 1351) chose 3 percent as their "nonperfectionist's goal" for unemployment (point B on their graph, which translates wage into price inflation, adapted here as Figure 20.3). The specific issue then became whether their Phillips curve drawn using U.S. data offered a good prediction of the inflation rate consistent with a 3 percent unemployment rate.

To understand the issue as formulated by Samuelson and Solow, one needs to know that they considered inflation to be a real phenomenon rather than a monetary phenomenon. As a real phenomenon, there is no single explanation for inflation. Most broadly, the Keynesian taxonomy of the causes of inflation contains two kingdoms. Aggregate-demand (demand-pull) inflation arises from a high level or aggregate demand ($C+I+G$) that stresses the rate of resource utilization. Cost-push inflation arises from increases in relative prices particular to individual markets that pass through to the price level.

To predict the inflation consistent with a policy of aggregate-demand management aimed at full employment, Samuelson and Solow (1960 [1966]: 1348) assumed that the empirical Phillips curve they had identified was:

> a reversible supply curve for labor along which an aggregate demand curve slides. … [M]ovements along the curve might be dubbed standard demand-pull, and shifts of the curve might represent the institutional changes on which cost-push theories rest.

According to their analysis, the answer to the question of what inflation rate would emerge with a 3 percent unemployment rate depended upon whether the U.S. Phillips curve had shifted upward because of cost-push inflation or did indeed reflect the level of demand-pull inflation at the stress on resources indicated by that unemployment rate. Because they did

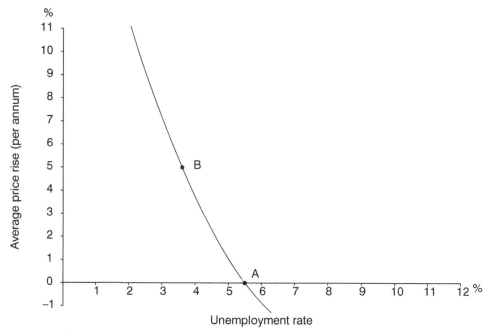

Figure 20.3 Phillips curve

Source: Figure is from Samuelson & Solow (1960 [1966], 1351)

not actually know the level of unemployment consistent with full employment, Samuelson and Solow (1960 [1966]: 1350) argued that only the "vast experiment" of targeting 3 percent unemployment could determine whether their empirically estimated Phillips curve had been pushed up by cost-push inflation. Nevertheless, they made clear their view of the enormous social costs of controlling inflation through targeting an unemployment rate of 6 percent in the face of cost-push inflation.

Specifically, Samuelson and Solow (1960 [1966]: 1352, 1353) argued that such a "low-pressure economy might build up within itself over the years larger and larger amounts of structural unemployment" and could lead to "class warfare and social conflict." They mentioned "direct wage and price controls" as a possible way "to lessen the degree of disharmony between full employment and price stability." Later, Samuelson expressed his view that if the inflation consistent with low unemployment were of the demand-pull variety, it was a reasonable price to pay. Samuelson (1963 [1966]: 1543) wrote that "The late Sumner Slichter said: 'If some price creep is the price we must pay for growth and prosperity, and perhaps it often is, then it is the lesser evil to pay this price.'"

Unlike Samuelson and Solow in their academic work, President Kennedy's Council of Economic Advisers entertained no uncertainty over the correct explanation for an empirical Phillips curve that had shifted upward from its pre-World World II level. The shift was due to cost-push inflation not demand-pull inflation. At the urging of his Council, in the 1962 *Economic Report of the President*, President Kennedy set 4 percent as a national goal for the unemployment rate and urged wage "guideposts" to control cost-push inflation (Hetzel 2008, Ch. 6). Two pictures from the 1960s *Economic Report of the President* capture the Keynesian spirit of the 1960s. Figure 20.4 from the 1962 *Report* shows the Council's estimate of the negative output gap that existed at levels of output associated with unemployment rates in

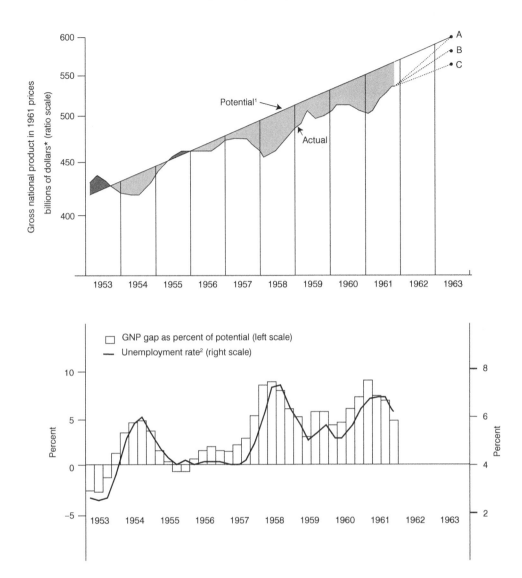

Figure 20.4 Gross national product, actual and potential, and unemployment rate

*Seasonally Adjusted Annual Rates
1 Trend line through middle of 1955
2 Unemployment as percent of civilian labor force, seasonally adjusted
Note: A, B, and C represent GNP in middle of 1963 assuming unemployment rate of 4%, 5%, and 6%, respectively.

Sources: Department of Commerce, Department of Labor, and Council of Economic Advisers

excess of 4 percent. As evident from the persistently negative output gap shown in the chart, the Council assumed that the price system failed to maintain aggregate demand at a level sufficient to maintain full employment.

Figure 20.5 from the 1969 *Report* plotted an empirical Phillips curve using paired observations of inflation and the unemployment rate for the years 1954 through 1968. The

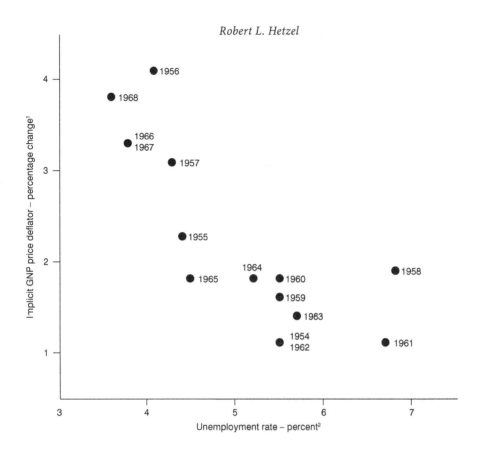

Figure 20.5 Price performance and unemployment

1 Change during year, calculated from end of year deflators (derived by averaging fourth quarter of a given year and first quarter of subsequent year)
2 Average for the year

inverse relationship appeared to exhibit a causal relationship running from the degree of real aggregate demand, which varies inversely with the unemployment rate, to the inflation rate. It appeared to measure demand-pull inflation. Figure 20.5, however, left unanswered the issue that arose within the Keynesian framework of whether the inflation that arose at a 4 percent unemployment rate represented cost-push or demand-pull inflation. That is, had cost-push inflation raised the entire level of the curve? What happened to make a reality the "vast experiment" of Samuelson and Solow necessary to answer this question?

In the last part of the 1960s, deep social fissures developed around the Vietnam War and militancy in the civil rights movement. Those divisions appeared in the negative reaction of the conservative white middle class to protests against the Vietnam War and to inner-city riots. A bipartisan political consensus developed over the desirability of low unemployment as a social balm. Keynesian economics promised to deliver that result at a predictable cost in terms of inflation.

Also, at the end of the 1960s, monetary policy replaced fiscal policy as the economic profession's preferred instrument of aggregate-demand management. That happened through a combination of economic results and political reality. In June 1968, Congress passed a 10 percent income tax surcharge to dampen aggregate demand. The federal budget deficit turned into a small surplus. However, continued high rates of money growth trumped the effect of the tax increase, and growth in aggregate nominal (dollar) demand continued at an inflationary pace. Moreover, in 1969, political wrangling over an extension of the income tax surcharge made clear that fiscal policy was an unwieldy instrument for aggregate demand management.

Arthur Burns, who became chairman of the Board of Governors and the FOMC (Federal Open Market Committee) in February 1970, was critical to making monetary policy an instrument of aggregate demand management. Burns was not a Keynesian. However, his views on monetary policy reflected those of the conservative business community, which was receptive to wage controls to restrain an inflation it attributed to wage-push inflation. Burns was willing to sign on to expansionary monetary policy provided that the Nixon administration gave him the wage controls he wanted to control inflation (Hetzel 1998, 2008). With the August 1971 Camp David announcement of wage and price controls, the Nixon administration brought Burns on board for an expansionary monetary policy. Monetary policy then became subject to the politics of persuading the Pay Board, with its representatives from labor, business, and the public, to adopt the low wage guidelines Burns wanted.

The country got the Samuelson and Solow "vast experiment": a policy of aggregate demand management to create a low unemployment rate and price controls to restrain cost-push inflation. Monetarists argued that the result was stagflation: high inflation with high unemployment. Figure 20.6, reproduced from Stockman (1996: 906) shows how over succeeding time periods (1960–1969, 1970–1973, 1974–1979, and 1980–1983) the Phillips curve shifted upward. Initially, however, both the economics profession and policy makers interpreted stagflation as evidence of cost-push inflation. Although later Lucas and Sargent (1981: 304) talked about "econometric failure of a grand scale," the professional consensus in favor of Keynesian economics did not change until the early 1980s.

A monetarist taxonomy of stop-go monetary policy

The period prior to 1981 is an extraordinary laboratory for the monetary economist because of the existence of a monetary aggregate (M1) that was both interest-insensitive and stably related to nominal expenditure (GDP). For that reason, the behavior of M1 offered a reliable measure of the expansionary or contractionary thrust of monetary policy. As argued by monetarists, the destabilizing features of monetary policy appeared in a long-term increase in money growth superimposed over monetary acceleration in economic recoveries and monetary decelerations in economic recessions. The latter characteristic of monetary policy earned the nickname of stop-go monetary policy.

The go phases of monetary policy represented an attempt by the Fed to eliminate a presumed negative output gap (unemployment in excess of 4 percent). In the go phases, the FOMC raised the funds rate only well after cyclical troughs and then only cautiously in its attempt to reduce the excess unemployment presumed by a negative output gap. The high rates of money growth in the go phases created inflation. In response to that inflation, in the stop phases, the FOMC raised the funds rate sufficiently to create a negative output gap. It then lowered the funds rate after the resulting cyclical peak but only cautiously out of a desire to reduce the inflationary expectations in the bond market (Hetzel 2008: Chs. 23–25, Hetzel 2012a: Ch. 8). This restrictive policy constituted the stop phase of the alternation between restrictive and expansionary monetary policy.

As shown in Figure 20.7, the failure of monetary policy was not the absence of a strong interest-rate response to realized inflation but rather the failure of the Fed to follow a rule that prevented the emergence of inflation. After the onset of high money growth, nominal

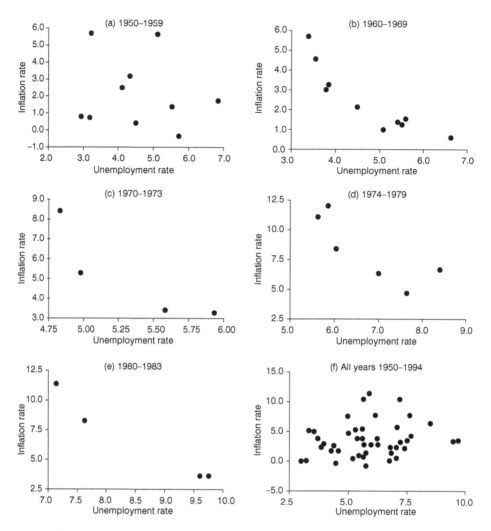

Figure 20.6 Inflation and unemployment in the United States

expenditure increased with a lag of six months followed by increased inflation after another year (Friedman 1989). Responding directly to negative output gaps and then directly to realized inflation destabilized the economy because of the long lags involved in the impact of monetary policy actions on the economy.

As summarized in his long-and-variable-lags argument, Friedman (1960) had already made this critique of activist policy. Friedman (1984: 27) wrote later:

> Each increase in monetary growth was followed by a rise in inflation, which led the authorities to reduce monetary growth sharply, which in turn produced economic recession. The political pressures created by rising unemployment led the Fed to reverse course at the first sign that inflation was tapering off. The Fed took its foot, as it were, off the brake and stepped on the gas. After an interval of about six months, the acceleration in monetary growth was followed by economic recovery, then a decline in unemployment, and, after another year or so, by accelerated inflation.

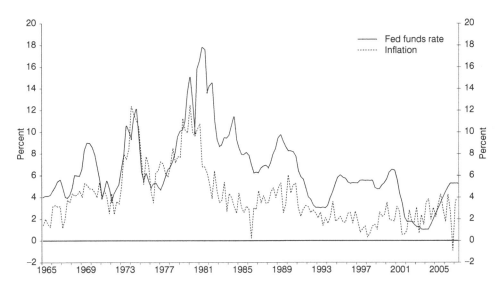

Figure 20.7 Fed funds rate and inflation

Notes: Quarterly observations of annualized percentage changes in the personal consumption expenditures deflator. Data from Bureau of Economic Analysis and Federal Reserve Board, via Haver Analytics

> This roller coaster was superimposed on a rising trend. Each peak in monetary growth was higher than the preceding peak. ... Each inflationary peak was higher than the preceding peak.

The assumption made sometimes that the FOMC did not respond strongly to inflation in the 1970s comes from a failure to distinguish between realized and ex-ante real interest rates. Using the Livingston survey of professional forecasters to measure inflationary expectations in financial markets, Figure 20.8 shows how realized inflation consistently exceeded expected inflation in the 1970s. Based on expected inflation, nominal rates of interest did translate into high real rates of interest in the stop phases.

Figures 20.9 and 20.10 show the cyclical inertia imparted by the Fed to real short-term interest rates. Figure 20.9 fits a trend line between cyclical peaks to real personal consumption expenditures (real PCE). Figure 20.10 shows how consumption falls below trend in recession (the dashed minus the solid line in Figure 20.9). Figure 20.10 also plots the short-term real interest rate calculated as the commercial paper rate minus inflation forecasts from the Board of Governors' staff document called the Greenbook. The two series (nominal interest rate and inflation forecasts) are matched by date and roughly by maturity.[4] As shown in Figure 20.10, when inflation rose, the Fed pushed up the short-term real interest rate. Despite a growing negative output gap, because of its concern about inflationary expectations, the FOMC maintained an elevated level of the real interest rate well into recessions (Hetzel 2012a: Ch. 8).

In the 1970 recession, the contrast between the decline in consumption below trend and high real interest rates is clear. In the 1974 recession, high real rates preceded the cyclical peak in October 1973 and then fell. However, real rates increased again in late summer and fall 1974 when FOMC chairman Burns, as part of bargaining with Congress, overrode FOMC procedures for setting the funds rate. Burns was reluctant to cut the funds rate without

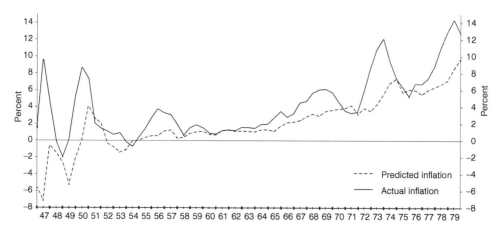

Figure 20.8 Livingston Survey: predicted and subsequently realized one-year inflation

Notes: Predicted inflation is the mean of predicted one-year-ahead CPI inflation from the Livingston Survey. The Philadelphia Fed maintains the survey currently (data from www.phil.frb.org/econ1). The survey comes out in June and December. The questionnaire is mailed early in May and November. Therefore, the one-year inflation forecast is for the 13 month period from May to June of the following year for the June release and for the 13 month priod from November to December of the following year for the December release. The June release inflation forecast is matched with an average of the realized annualized monthly CPI inflation rates starting in June of the same year and ending in June of the subsequent year. The December release inflation forecast is matched with an average of realized annualized monthly CPI inflation rates starting in December of the same year and ending in December of the subsequent year. The light tick mark is the June release forecast and the heavy tick mark is the December release forecast.

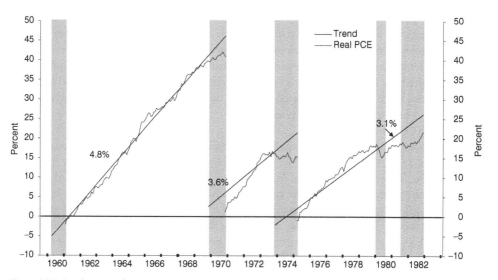

Figure 20.9 Real personal consumption expenditures and trend

Notes: Observations are the natural logarithm of monthly observations on real personal consumption expenditures (PCE) normalized using the value at the prior business cycle peak. Trend lines are fitted to these observations and the trend line is extended through the subsequent recession. Data from the Commerce Department via Haver Analytics. Shaded areas indicate NBER recessions. Heavy tick marks indicate December

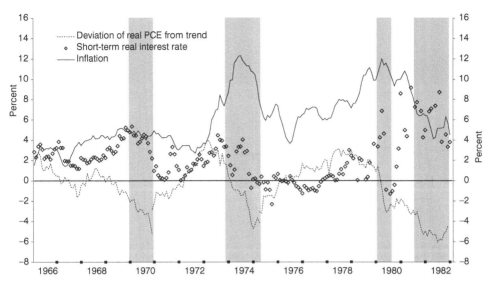

Figure 20.10 Deviation of real PCE from trend, short-term real interest rate, and inflation: 1966–1982

Notes: "Deviation of Real PCE from Trend" is the difference between the actual values and trend lines shown in Figure 20.9. Inflation is twelve-month perecentage changes in the personal consumption expenditures deflator. The "Short-term Real Interest Rate" is the commercial paper rate minus the corresponding inflation forecast made by the staff of the Board of Governors. It is the real interest rate series labelled "Overall Inflation Forecast" shown in Figure 11.2, Hetzel (2012a). Data from the Commerce Department via Haver Analytics. Shaded areas indicate NBER recessions. Heavy tick marks indicate December

congressional action to restrain spending (Hetzel 2008: Ch. 10). The Volcker disinflation era is confusing because of the brief stop-go cycle set off by the Carter credit controls announced in March 1980 and then withdrawn in July 1980. However, the overall pattern is clear over the period of disinflation from 1980 through 1982. Despite a clear decline in real economic activity, the Fed maintained a high level of short-term real interest rates.

The cyclical inertia introduced into the short-term interest rate by stop-go disrupted the working of the price system and produced the monetary accelerations and decelerations shown in Figure 20.11. As shown, the M1 steps fitted to M1 growth rates fell prior to recession. They then rose in recovery. Over the entire period, they also rose. The result was cyclical instability and rising trend inflation.

The change in the policymaking and intellectual consensus

Another "vast" experiment, this one unforeseen by Samuelson and Solow, occurred in the early 1980s. The Volcker–Greenspan FOMCs succeeded in controlling inflation without the need to engineer periodic bouts of high unemployment. By the early 1980s, countries became willing to turn the control of inflation over to their central banks while accepting the consequences for unemployment. The contrast between Depression-era high unemployment with World War II-era low unemployment had supported the Keynesian consensus. The contrast between the economic instability during the Great Inflation with the economic stability of the Great Moderation allowed formation of a new consensus.

During the Great Moderation, the rule-like monetary policy necessary to re-anchor inflationary expectations undertaken by the Volcker FOMC supplanted the earlier

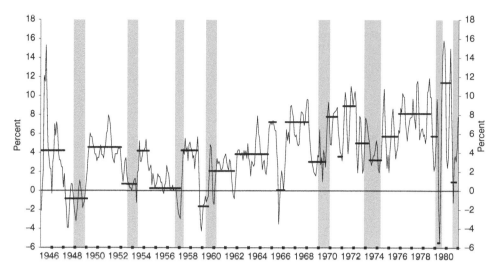

Figure 20.11 M1 step function and recessions: 1946–1981

Notes: Series are a three-month moving average of the annualized monthly money growth rates and a step function fitted to monthly annualized growth rates of money. Data on money (M1) from January 1946 to December 1958 from Friedman & Schwartz (1970). From January 1959 to December 1980 data from Board of Governors. January 1981 to December 1981 M1 is "shift-adjusted M1" (Bennett 1982). Shaded areas indicate NBER recessions. Heavy tick marks indicate December

discretionary policy of aggregate demand management. The former policy of "fine tuning" had attempted in an ongoing way to exploit the trade-off between unemployment and the inflation presumed caused by recurrent inflation shocks. By the early 1990s, the economics profession became receptive to the New Neoclassical Synthesis or New Keynesian model (Goodfriend and King 1997). The core of this model is a real business cycle model in which the price system works well to mitigate the effects of shocks on output and unemployment. The model also includes forward-looking agents with expectations disciplined by the systematic behavior of the central bank. With credible monetary policy, inflation shocks do not affect the long-run inflationary expectations of price-setting firms and thus do not propagate in the extrapolative way assumed in Keynesian Phillips curves.

Concluding comment

In the Volcker–Greenspan era, the Fed had to conduct policy in a rule-like spirit to re-anchor inflationary expectations unhinged in the stop-go period (Hetzel 2008, Goodfriend 2004, and Goodfriend and King 2005). However, the Fed never synthesized and communicated the change in its behavior. Instead, it continued to employ the language of discretion. With this language, the Fed explains each policy action as a unique event based on the contemporaneous state of the economy. The language precludes discussion of consistency in policy actions imposed to discipline market expectations. As a result, despite the dramatic experiment undertaken in the stop-go era, the actual change in monetary policy that occurred remained unarticulated.

Hetzel (2012b) argues that the language of discretion, which always allows for ex-post rationalization of Fed actions, does not allow the Fed to learn in any systematic way from historical experience. Hetzel (2012a) attributes the 2008–2009 recession to contractionary monetary policy in 2008. In a way comparable to the stop phases of stop-go monetary policy, the FOMC attempted to allow a negative output gap to develop by imparting inertia to declines in the funds rate while the economy weakened. The intention was to engineer a moderate amount of weakness in the economy to reduce inflation. However, as occurred in the stop-go era, this attempt at manipulating the trade-offs offered by a structural Phillips curve failed.

Notes

1 The ideas expressed here are those of the author, not the Federal Reserve Bank of Richmond.
2 Hetzel (2012a) argued that the regional Federal Reserve Banks kept the (nominal and real) marginal cost of funds to the banking system high. Expected deflation raised nominal rates significantly.
3 Samuelson and Solow (1960, 1339) wrote:

   [G]overnment plus investors plus consumers want, in real terms among them, more than 100 percent of the wartime or boomtime available producible output. So prices have to rise to cheat the slow-to-spend of their desired shares. But the price rise closes the inflationary gap only temporarily, as the higher price level breeds higher incomes all around and the real gap reopens itself continually. And so the inflation goes on...

4 For a description of the construction of the series, see Hetzel (2008, Ch. 4, Appendix: Series on the Real Interest Rate). Darin and Hetzel (1995) show that the Board staff inflation forecasts used to generate this series were representative of the forecasts made by other forecasters.

References

Darin, R. and Hetzel, R.L. (1995) 'An empirical measure of the real rate of interest', *Federal Reserve Bank of Richmond Economic Quarterly,* 81: 17–47.
Economic Report of the President, various issues,Washington D.C.: U.S. Govt. Printing Office.
Friedman, M. (1960) *A Program for Monetary Stability*, New York: Fordham University Press.
Friedman, M. (1968) 'The role of monetary policy', *American Economic Review*, 58: 1–17.
Friedman, M. (1984) 'Monetary policy for the 1980s', in J.H. Moore (ed.) *To Promote Prosperity: U.S. Domestic Policy in the Mid-1980s,* Stanford, CA: Hoover Institution Press.
Friedman, M. (1989) 'The quantity theory of money', in J. Eatwell, M. Milgate, and P. Newman (eds.) *The New Palgrave Money*, New York: W.W. Norton.
Friedman, M. and Schwartz, A.J. (1970) *Monetary Statistics of the United States*, New York: National Bureau of Economic Research.
Goodfriend, M. (2004) 'The monetary policy debate since October 1979: lessons for theory and practice', Paper for 'Reflections on Monetary Policy: 25 years after October 1979', Conference at Federal Reserve Bank of St. Louis, October 7–8.
Goodfriend, M. and King, R.G. (1997) 'The new neoclassical synthesis', in B.S. Bernanke and J. Rotemberg (eds.) *Macroeconomics Annual,* Cambridge, MA: NBER.
Goodfriend, M. and King, R.G (2005) 'The incredible Volcker disinflation', *Journal of Monetary Economics,* 52: 981–1015.
Hetzel, R.L. (1998) 'Arthur Burns and inflation', *Federal Reserve Bank of Richmond Economic Quarterly,* 84: 21–44.
Hetzel, R.L. (2008) *The Monetary Policy of the Federal Reserve: A History*, Cambridge: Cambridge University Press.
Hetzel, R.L. (2012a) *The Great Recession: Market Failure or Policy Failure?* Cambridge: Cambridge University Press.
Hetzel, R.L. (2012b) 'Central bank accountability and independence: are they inconsistent?' *Journal of Macroeconomics* 34: 616–25.
Lucas, R.E., Jr. (1972) 'Expectations and the neutrality of money', *Journal of Economic Theory*, 4: 103–24.
Lucas, R.E., Jr. and Sargent, T.J. (1981) 'After Keynesian macroeconomics', in R.E. Lucas, Jr. and T.J. Sargent (eds.) *Rational Expectations and Econometric Practice*, vol. 1, Minneapolis, MN: University of Minnesota Press.

Phillips, A.W. (1958) 'The relation between unemployment and the rate of change of money wage rates in the United Kingdom, 1861–1957', *Economica*, 25: 283–99.

Samuelson, P.A. (1963 [1966]) 'A brief survey of post-Keynesian developments', in J.E. Stiglitz (ed.) *The Collected Scientific Papers of Paul A. Samuelson*, vol. 2, no. 115, 1534–50. Cambridge, MA: The MIT Press.

Samuelson, P.A. (1967) *Economics: An Introductory Analysis*, New York: McGraw-Hill Book Company.

Samuelson, P. and Solow R. (1960 [1966]) 'Analytical aspects of anti-inflation policy', in J. Stiglitz (ed.) *The Collected Scientific Papers of Paul A. Samuelson*, vol. 2, no. 102, 1966: 1336–53, Cambridge, MA: The MIT Press.

Stockman, A.C. (1996) *Introduction to Economics*, Orlando, FL: Dryden Press.

21

HISTORICAL OIL SHOCKS

James D. Hamilton

1859–1899: Let there be light

Illuminants, lubricants, and solvents in the 1850s were obtained from a variety of sources, such as oil from lard or whales, alcohol from agricultural products, and turpentine from wood. Several commercial enterprises produced petroleum or gas from treatment of coal, asphalt, coal-tars, and even shale. But a new era began when Edwin Drake successfully produced commercially usable quantities of crude oil from a 69-foot well in Pennsylvania in 1859.

From the beginning, this was recognized as an extremely valuable commodity, as *Derrick's Hand-Book of Petroleum* (1898: 706) described:

> Petroleum was in fair demand at the time of Colonel Drake and his associates … for practical experiments had proved that it made a better illuminant than could be manufactured from cannel coal by the Gessner and Downer processes. All that could be obtained from the surface springs along Oil creek and the salt wells of the Allegheny valley found a ready market at prices ranging from 75 cents to $1.50 and even $2.00 per gallon.

With about 40 gallons in a barrel, the upper range quoted corresponds to $80 per barrel of crude oil, or $1,900/barrel in 2009 dollars. Given the expensive process of making oil from coal and the small volumes in which an individual household consumed the product, obtaining oil by drilling into the earth appeared to be a bargain:

> Drake's discovery broke the market. The fact that the precious oil could be obtained in apparently inexhaustible quantities by drilling wells in the rocky crust of the earth, was a great surprise. The first product of the Drake well was sold at 50 cents a gallon, and the price for oil is generally given at $20.00 a barrel from August, 1859 down to the close of the year.

As production from Pennsylvania wells increased, the price quickly fell, averaging $9.60/barrel during 1860, which would correspond to $228/barrel in 2009 dollars.

Not surprisingly, such prices stimulated a fury of drilling efforts throughout the region. Production quadrupled from a half million barrels in 1860 to over 2 million in 1861, and the price quickly dropped to $2 a barrel by the end of 1860 and 10 cents a barrel by the end of 1861. Many new would-be oil barons abandoned the industry just as quickly as they had entered.

1862–1864: The first oil shock

The onset of the U.S. Civil War brought about a surge in prices and commodity demands generally. The effects on the oil market were amplified by the cut-off of supplies of turpentine from the South and more importantly by the introduction of a tax on alcohol, which rose from 20¢/gallon in 1862 to $2/gallon by 1865 (Ripy 1999) – in contrast to the 10¢/gallon tax on petroleum-derived illuminants. Assuming a yield of about 20 gallons of illuminant per barrel of crude, each 10¢/gallon tax differential on illuminant amounted to a $2/barrel competitive advantage for oil. As a result, the tax essentially eliminated alcohol as a competitor to petroleum as a source for illuminants. Moreover, the price collapse of 1861 had led to the closure of many of the initial drilling operations, while water flooding and other problems forced out many others. The result was that oil production began to decline after 1862, even as new pressures on demand grew (see Figure 21.1).

Figure 21.2 plots the inflation-adjusted price of oil from 1860 to 2009.[1] The price is plotted on a logarithmic scale, so that a vertical move of 10 units corresponds approximately to a 10 percent price change.[2] As a result of these big increases in demand and drops in supply, the increase in the relative price of oil during the U.S. Civil War was as big as the rise during the 1970s.

1865–1899: Evolution of the industry

After the war, demand for all commodities fell significantly. At the same time, drilling in promising new areas of Pennsylvania had resulted in a renewed growth in production. The result was a second collapse in prices in 1866, though more modest than that observed in 1860–61. Two similar boom-bust cycles were repeated over the next decade, with relative stability at low prices becoming the norm after development of very large new fields in other parts of Pennsylvania. By 1890, oil production from Pennsylvania and New York was five times what it had been in 1870. Production in other states had grown to account for 38 percent of the U.S. total, and Russia was producing almost as much oil as the United States. These factors and the recession of 1890–91 had brought oil back down to 56¢/barrel by 1892.

However, that proved to be the end of the easy production from the original Pennsylvanian oilfields. Annual production from Pennsylvania fell by 14 million barrels between 1891 and 1894 (see Figure 21.1), and indeed even with the more technologically advanced secondary recovery techniques adopted in much later decades, never again reached the levels seen in 1891 (Caplinger 1997). Williamson and Daum (1959: 577) suggested that the decline in production from the Appalachian field (Pennsylvania, West Virginia, and parts of Ohio and New York) along with a loss of world access to Russian production due to a cholera epidemic in Baku in 1894 were responsible for the spike in oil prices in 1895.

Dvir and Rogoff (2010) emphasized the parallels between the behavior of oil prices in the nineteenth century and that subsequently observed in the last quarter of the twentieth century. There are some similarities, in terms of the interaction between the exhaustion in

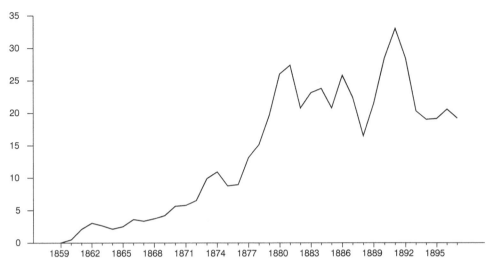

Figure 21.1 Estimated oil production from Pennsylvania and New York, in millions of barrels per year, 1859–1897

Source: *Derrick's Hand-Book* 1898: 804–05

Figure 21.2 One hundred times the natural logarithm of the real price of oil, 1860–2009, in 2009 U.S. dollars

Source: British Petroleum 2010; Jenkins 1985: Table 18; and Carter et al. 2006: Table E 135–166, consumer prices indexes (BLS), all items, 1800 to 1970, as detailed in footnote 1

production of key fields with strong demand, and in either century there were buyers who were willing to pay a very high price. But despite similarities, there are also some profound differences. First, oil was of much less economic importance in the nineteenth century. In 1900, the U.S. produced 63.6 million barrels of oil. At an average price of $1.19/barrel, that represents $75.7 million, which is only 0.4 percent of 1900 estimated GNP of $18,700 million. For comparison, in 2008, the U.S. consumed 7.1 billion barrels of oil at an average price of $97.26/barrel, for an economic value of $692 billion, or 4.8 percent of GDP.

1900–1945: Power and transportation

There is another key respect in which petroleum came to represent a fundamentally different economic product as the twentieth century unfolded. In the nineteenth century, the value of oil primarily derived from its usefulness for fabricating illuminants. As the twentieth century developed, electric lighting came to replace these, while petroleum gained increasing importance for commercial and industrial heat and power as well as transportation, first for railroads and later for motor vehicles. Figure 21.3 shows that U.S. motor vehicle registrations rose from 0.1 vehicle per 1,000 residents in 1900 to 87 by 1920 and 816 in 2008.

In addition to growing importance in terms of direct economic value, oil came to become an integral part of many other key economic sectors such as automobile manufacturing and sales, which as we shall see would turn out to be an important factor in business cycles after World War II.

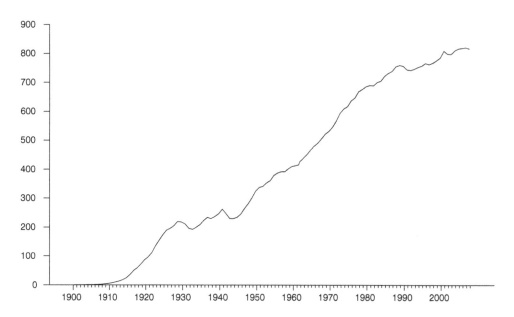

Figure 21.3 Total U.S. vehicle registrations per thousand U.S. residents, 1900–2008

Source: Carter et al. 2006: Table Aa6-8 and Table Df339-342, U.S. Department of Census, 2010 Statistical Abstract, and U.S. Department of Transportation, Federal Highway Administration, Highway Statistics, annual reports

The West Coast gasoline famine of 1920

Problems in the gasoline market on the U.S. west coast in 1920 might be viewed as the first oil-related shock of the transportation era. U.S. consumption of crude oil had increased 53 percent between 1915 and 1919 and increased an additional 27 percent in 1920 alone (Pogue 1921: 61). Olmstead and Rhode (1985: 1044–45) provided this description:

> In the spring and summer of 1920 a serious gasoline famine crippled the entire West Coast, shutting down businesses and threatening vital services. Motorists endured hour-long lines to receive 2-gallon rations, and, in many localities, fuel was unavailable for as long as a week at a time....
>
> [A]uthorities in Wenatchee, Washington, grounded almost 100 automobiles after spotting them late one Saturday night "on pleasure bent." Police ordered distributors not to serve these "joyriders" for the duration of the shortage.
>
> Seattle police began arresting drivers who left their parked vehicles idling. Everywhere individuals caught hoarding or using their privileged status to earn black market profits were cut off and even prosecuted. Many localities issued ration cards, and most major cities seriously considered it …
>
> On July 2 in Oakland, California, 150 cars queued at one station impeding traffic over a four-block area. On July 16, Standard's stations in Long Beach relaxed restrictions so that after 2:00 P.M., all cars (as opposed to only commercial vehicles) could buy up to 2 gallons. This caused such a jam that "it was necessary for the assistant special agent to spend two hours in keeping the traffic from blocking the streets" … Drivers in the Pacific Northwest endured 2-gallon rations for several months, and even with these limits stations often closed by 9:00 A.M. In San Francisco, gunplay erupted in a dispute over ration entitlements.

Petroleum was still much less important for the economy in 1920 than it was to become after World War II. Moreover, these problems seem to have been confined to the West Coast, a much less populated region than it was later to become. It is nevertheless perhaps worth noting that these shortages coincided with a U.S. business cycle contraction that the NBER dates as beginning January 1920 and ending July 1921, a correlation which as we will see would be repeated quite frequently later in the century.[3]

The Great Depression and state regulation

Huge gains in production from Texas, California, and Oklahoma quickly eliminated the regional shortages of 1920 and induced a downward trend in oil prices over the next decade, with oil prices falling 40 percent between 1920 and 1926. The decline in demand associated with advent of the Great Depression in 1929 magnified the price impact of phenomenal new discoveries such as the gigantic East Texas field which began production in 1930. By 1931, the price of oil had dropped an additional 66 percent from its value in 1926.

These competitive pressures facing the industry interacted with another challenge that had been present from the beginning – how to efficiently manage a given reservoir. The industry had initially been guided by the rule of capture, which resulted in a chaotic race among producers to extract the oil from wells on adjacent properties. For example, the gusher in Spindletop, Texas, in 1901 was soon being exploited by over a hundred different companies (Yergin 1991: 70) with more than three wells per acre (Williamson et al. 1963: 555). This kind of development presented a classic tragedy of the commons problem in which significantly less oil was eventually extracted than would have been possible with better management of the reservoir. The legitimate need for better-defined property rights interacted with the three other tides of the Great Depression – growing supplies, falling demand, and a shifting political consensus favoring more regulation of industry and restrictions on competition.

The result was that the United States emerged from the Great Depression with some profound changes in the degree of government supervision of the industry. At the state level, the key players were regulatory agencies such as the Texas Railroad Commission (TRC) and the Oklahoma Corporation Commission. The states' power was supplemented at the federal level by provisions of the National Industrial Recovery Act of 1933 and the Connally Hot Oil Act of 1935, which prohibited interstate shipments of oil produced in violation of the state regulatory limits.

Of the state agencies, the most important was Texas, which accounted for 40 percent of the crude petroleum produced in the United States between 1935 and 1960. The TRC's mandate was to "prevent waste," which from the beginning was a mixture of the legitimate engineering issue of efficient field management and the more controversial economic goal of restricting production in order to ensure that producers received a higher price. As the system evolved, the TRC would assign a "maximum efficient rate" at which oil could be extracted from a given well, and then specify an allowable monthly production flow for that well at some level at or below the maximum efficient rate.

In terms of the narrow objective of preserving the long-run producing potential of oil fields, these regulatory efforts would be judged to be a success. For example, Williamson et al. (1963: 554) noted that in fields in Texas and Oklahoma that were exploited before regulation, within four to six years the fields were producing less than one-tenth of what they had at their peak. By contrast, fields developed after regulations were in place were still producing at 50–60 percent of their peak levels 15 years later. Once production from the entire state of Texas peaked in 1972, the decline rate was fairly gradual (see Figure 21.4), in contrast to the abrupt drops that were associated with the frenetic development of the Pennsylvanian fields seen in Figure 21.1.

1946–1972: The early postwar era

The United States has always been the world's biggest consumer of oil, and remained the world's biggest producer of petroleum until 1974 when it was surpassed by the Soviet Union. In the initial postwar era, prices throughout the world were quoted relative to that for oil in the Gulf of Mexico (Adelman 1972 Chapter 5), making the Texas Railroad Commission a key player in the world oil market.

Although state regulation surely increased the quantity of oil that would ultimately be recovered from U.S. fields, it also had important consequences for the behavior of prices. The production allowables set by the Texas Railroad Commission came to be based on an assessment of current market demand rather than pure considerations of conservation. Each month, the TRC would forecast product demand at the current price and set allowable production levels consistent with this demand. The result was that discounts or premiums were rarely allowed to continue long enough to lead to a change in posted prices, and the nominal price of oil was usually constant from one month to the next. On the other hand, the commissions would often take advantage of external supply disruptions to produce occasional abrupt changes in oil prices in the early postwar era (see Figure 21.5). The nominal price of oil in the era of the Texas Railroad Commission thus turned out to be a fairly unique time series, changing only in response to specific identifiable events.[4]

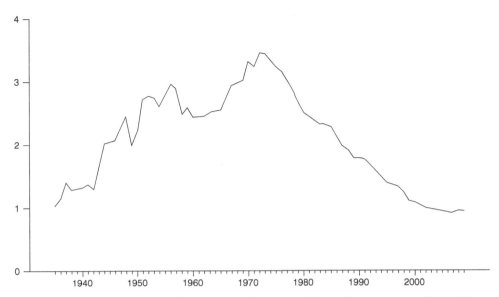

Figure 21.4 Annual oil production from the state of Texas in millions of barrels per day, 1935–2009

Source: Railroad Commission of Texas (http://www.rrc.state.tx.us/data/production/oilwellcounts.php)

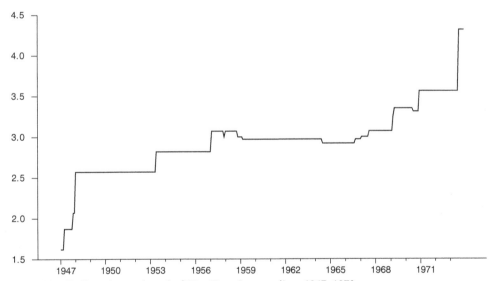

Figure 21.5 Dollar price per barrel of West Texas Intermediate, 1947–1973

Source: Average monthly spot oil price, from Federal Reserve Bank of St. Louis (http://research.stlouisfed.org/fred2/data/OILPRICE.txt)

1947–1948: Postwar dislocations

The end of World War II marked a sharp acceleration in the transition to the automotive era. U.S. demand for petroleum products increased 12 percent between 1945 and 1947 (Williamson et al. 1963: 805) and U.S. motor vehicle registrations increased by 22 percent (see Figure 21.3). The price of crude oil increased 80 percent over these two years, but this proved insufficient to prevent spot accounts of shortages. Standard Oil of Indiana and Phillips Petroleum Company announced plans in June of 1947 to ration gasoline allocations to dealers,[5] and in the fall there were reports of shortages in Michigan, Ohio, New Jersey, and Alabama.[6] Fuel oil shortages resulted in thousands without heat that winter.[7] An overall decline in residential construction spending began in 1948:Q3, with the first postwar U.S. recession dated as beginning in November of 1948.

1952–1953: Supply disruptions and the Korean conflict

The price of oil was frozen during the Korean War as a result of an order from the Office of Price Stabilization in effect from January 25, 1950 to February 13, 1953.[8] Prime Minister Mohammad Mossadegh nationalized Iran's oil industry in the summer of 1951, and a world boycott of Iran in response removed 19 million barrels of monthly Iranian production from world markets.[9] A separate strike by U.S. oil refinery workers on April 30, 1952 shut down a third of the nation's refineries.[10] In response, the United States and British governments each ordered a 30 percent cut in delivery of fuel for civilian flights, while Canada suspended all private flying.[11] Kansas City and Toledo instituted voluntary plans to ration gasoline for automobiles, while Chicago halted operations of 300 municipal buses.[12] When the price controls were lifted in June of 1953, the posted price of West Texas Intermediate increased 10 percent. The second postwar recession is dated as beginning the following month.

1956–1957: Suez Crisis

Egyptian President Nasser nationalized the Suez Canal in July of 1956. Hoping to regain control of the canal, Britain and France encouraged Israel to invade Egypt's Sinai territories on October 29, followed shortly after by their own military forces. During the conflict, 40 ships were sunk, blocking the canal through which 1.5 million barrels per day of oil were transported. Pumping stations for the Iraq Petroleum Company's pipeline, through which an additional half-million barrels per day moved through Syria to ports in the eastern Mediterranean, were also sabotaged.[13] Total oil production from the Middle East fell by 1.7 million barrels per day in November 1956. As seen in Figure 21.6, that represented 10.1 percent of total world output at the time, which is a bigger fraction of world production than would be removed in any of the subsequent oil shocks that would be experienced over the following decades.

These events had dramatic immediate economic consequences for Europe, which had been relying on the Middle East for two-thirds of its petroleum. Consider for example this account from the *New York Times*:[14]

> LONDON, December 1 – Europe's oil shortage resulting from the Suez Canal crisis was being felt more fully this week-end. … Dwindling gasoline supplies brought sharp cuts in motoring, reductions in work weeks and the threat of layoffs in automobile factories.
>
> There was no heat in some buildings; radiators were only tepid in others. Hotels closed off blocks of rooms to save fuel oil. … [T]he Netherlands, Switzerland, and Belgium have banned [Sunday driving]. Britain, Denmark, and France have imposed rationing.
>
> Nearly all British automobile manufacturers have reduced production and put their employees on a 4-day instead of a 5-day workweek. … Volvo, a leading Swedish car manufacturer, has cut production 30 percent.

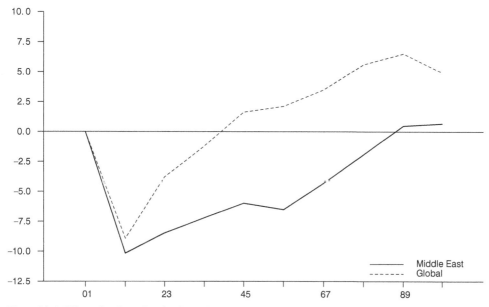

Figure 21.6 Oil production after the Suez Crisis

Notes: Dashed line: change in monthly global crude oil production from October 1956 as a percentage of October 1956 levels. Solid line: change in monthly Middle East oil production from October 1956 as a percentage of global levels in October 1956. Horizontal axis: number of months from October 1956

Source: *Oil and Gas Journal,* various issues from November 5, 1956 to July 3, 1957

> In both London and Paris, long lines have formed outside stations selling gasoline. ... Last Sunday, the Automobile Association reported that 70 percent of the service stations in Britain were closed.
>
> Dutch hotel-keepers estimated that the ban on Sunday driving had cost them up to 85 percent of the business they normally would have expected.

Within a few months, production from outside the Middle East was able to fill in much of the gap. For example, U.S. exports of crude oil and refined products increased a third of a million barrels per day in December.[15] By February, total world production of petroleum was back up to where it had been in October. Middle East production had returned to its pre-crisis levels by June of 1957 (see Figure 21.6).

Notwithstanding, overall real U.S. exports of goods and services started to fall after the first quarter of 1957 in what proved to be an 18 percent decline over the next year. This decline in exports was one of the factors contributing to the third postwar U.S. recession that began in August of that year.

1969–1970: Modest price increases

The oil price increases in 1969 and 1970 were in part a response to the broader inflationary pressures of the late 1960s (see Figure 21.7). However, the institutional peculiarities of the oil market caused these to be manifest in the form of the abrupt discrete adjustments observed in Figures 21.5 and 21.7 rather than a smooth continuous adaptation. The immediate precipitating

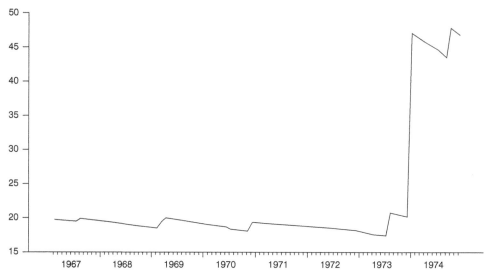

Figure 21.7 Price of oil in 2009 dollars, 1967–74

Notes: February 1967 to December 1974. Price of West Texas Intermediate deflated by CPI

events for the end-of-decade price increases included a strike by east coast fuel oil deliverers in December of 1968, which was associated with local accounts of consumer shortages,[16] and followed by a nationwide strike on January 4 of the Oil, Chemical, and Atomic Workers Union. After settlement of the latter strike, Texaco led the majors in announcing a 7 percent increase in the price of all grades of crude oil on February 24, 1969, citing higher labor costs as the justification.[17] The rupture of the Trans-Arabian pipeline in May 1970 in Syria may have helped precipitate a second 8 percent jump in the nominal price of oil later that year. The fifth postwar recession is dated as beginning in December of 1969, 10 months after the first price increase.

1973–1996: The age of OPEC

It is helpful to put subsequent events into the perspective of some critical broader trends. In the late 1960s, the Texas Railroad Commission was rapidly increasing the allowable production levels for oil wells in the state, and eliminated the "conservation" restrictions in 1972 (see Figure 21.8). The subsequent drop in production from Texas fields observed in Figure 21.4 was due not to state regulation but rather to declining flow rates for mature fields. Oil production for the United States as a whole also peaked in 1971, despite the production incentives subsequently to be provided by huge price increases after 1973 and the exploitation of the giant Alaskan oilfield in the 1980s (see Figure 21.9).

Although there proved to be abundant supplies available in the Middle East to replace declining U.S. production, the transition from a world petroleum market centered in the Gulf of Mexico to one centered in the Persian Gulf did not occur smoothly. In addition to the depletion of U.S. oil fields, Barsky and Kilian (2001) pointed to a number of other factors that would have warranted an increase in the relative price of oil in the early 1970s. Among these was the U.S. unilateral termination of the rights of foreign central banks to convert dollars to gold. The end of the Bretton Woods system caused a depreciation of the dollar and increase in the dollar price of most internationally traded commodities. In addition, the nominal yield on three-month Treasury bills was below the realized CPI inflation rate from

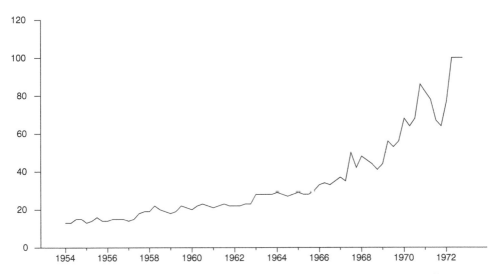

Figure 21.8 Texas Railroad Commission allowable production as a percent of maximum efficient rate, 1954–1972

Source: Railroad Commission of Texas, Annual Reports

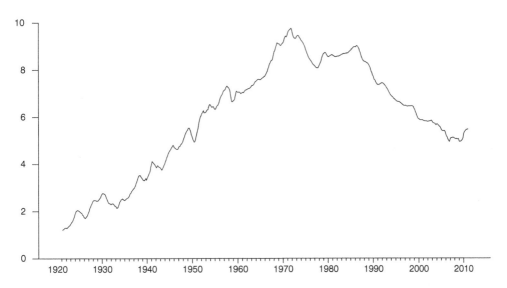

Figure 21.9 U.S. field production of crude oil, 1920–2010

Notes: December 1920 to September 2010. Average over preceding 12 months in millions of barrels per day

Source: Energy Information Administration (http://tonto.eia.doe.gov/dnav/pet/pet_crd_crpdn_adc_mbblpd_m.htm)

August 1972 to August 1974. These negative real interest rates may also have contributed to increases in relative commodity prices (Frankel 2008). Between August 1971 and August 1973, the producer price index for lumber increased 42 percent. The PPI for iron and steel was up 8 percent, while nonferrous metals increased 19 percent and foodstuffs and feedstuffs 96 percent. The 10 percent increase in the producer price index for crude petroleum between August 1971 and August 1973 was if anything more moderate than many other commodities. Given declining production rates from U.S. fields, further increases in the price of oil would have been expected.

Another factor making the transition to a higher oil import share more bumpy was the system of price controls implemented by President Nixon in conjunction with the abandonment of Bretton Woods in 1971. By the spring of 1973, many gasoline stations had trouble obtaining wholesale gasoline, and consumers began to be affected, as described for example in this report from the *New York Times*:[18]

> With more than 1,000 filling stations closed for lack of gasoline, according to a Government survey, and with thousands more rationing the amount a motorist may buy, the shortage is becoming a palpable fact of life for millions in this automobile-oriented country.

The sixth postwar recession began in November 1973, just after the dramatic geopolitical events that most remember from this period.

1973–1974: OPEC embargo

Syria and Egypt led an attack on Israel that began on October 6, 1973. On October 17, the Arab members of the Organization of Petroleum Exporting Countries (OPEC) announced an embargo on oil exports to selected countries viewed as supporting Israel, which was followed by significant cutbacks in OPEC's total oil production. Production from Arab members of OPEC in November was down 4.4 million barrels per day from what it had been in September, a shortfall corresponding to 7.5 percent of global output.[19] Increases in production from other countries such as Iran offset only a small part of this (see Figure 21.10). On January 1, 1974, the Persian Gulf countries doubled the price of oil.

Accounts of gasoline shortages returned, such as this report from the *New York Times*:[20]

> HARTFORD, Dec 27 – "Some of the customers get all hot and heavy," [Exxon service station attendant Grant] McMillan said. "They scream up and down … It's ridiculous."
>
> The scene is a familiar one in Connecticut as service station managers find themselves having to decide whether to ration their gasoline or sell it as fast as they can and cut the number of arguments…
>
> "People driving along, if they see anyone getting tanked up, they pull in and get in line," said Bruce Faucher, an attendant at [a Citgo] station. "If we don't limit them, we'd be out in a couple of hours and wouldn't have any for our regular customers."

Frech and Lee (1987) estimated that time spent waiting in queues to purchase gasoline added 12 percent to the cost of gasoline for urban residents in December 1973 and 50 percent in March 1974. They assessed the problem to be more severe in rural areas, with estimated costs of 24 percent and 84 percent, respectively.

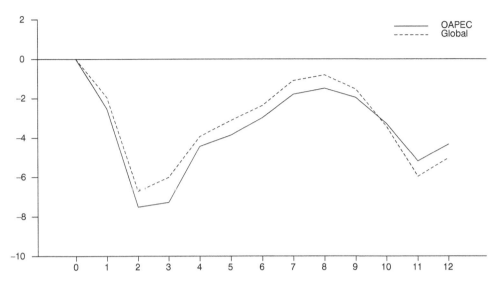

Figure 21.10 Oil production after the 1973 Arab–Israeli War

Notes: Dashed line: change in monthly global crude oil production from September 1973 as a percentage of September 1973 levels. Solid line: change in monthly oil production of Arab members of OPEC from September 1973 as a percentage of global levels in September 1973. Horizontal axis: number of months from September 1973

Source: Energy Information Administration, Monthly Energy Review, Tables 11.1a and 11.1b (http:// tonto.eia.doe.gov/merquery/mer_data.asp?table=T11.01a)

Barsky and Kilian (2001) have emphasized the importance of the economic motivations noted earlier rather than the Arab–Israeli War itself as explanations for the embargo. They noted that the Arab oil producers had discussed the possibility of an embargo prior to the war, and that the embargo was lifted without the achievement of its purported political objectives. While there is no doubt that economic considerations were very important, Hamilton (2003: 389) argued that geopolitical factors played a role as well:

> If economic factors were the cause, it is difficult to see why such factors would have caused Arab oil producers to reach a different decision from non-Arab oil producers. Second, the embargo appeared to be spearheaded not by the biggest oil producers, who would be expected to have the most important economic stake, but rather by the most militant Arab nations, some of whom had no oil to sell at all.

My conclusion is that, while it is extremely important to view the oil price increases of 1973–74 in a broader economic context, the specific timing, magnitude, and nature of the supply cutbacks were closely related to geopolitical events.

1978–1979: Iranian revolution

The 1973 Arab–Israeli War turned out to be only the beginning of a turbulent decade in the Middle East. Figure 21.11 plots the monthly oil production for five of the key members of OPEC since 1973. Iran (top panel) in defiance of the Arab states had increased its oil production during the 1973–74 embargo, but was experiencing large public protests in 1978.

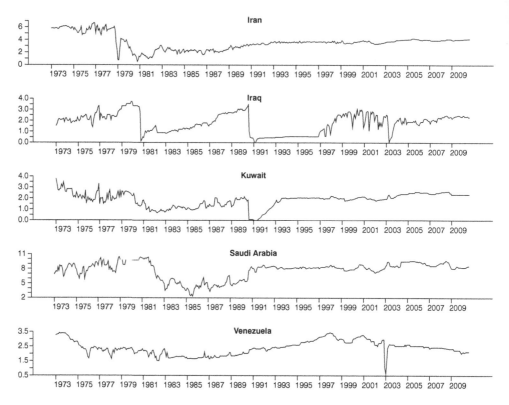

Figure 21.11 Monthly production rates (in millions of barrels per day) for five OPEC Members

Notes: 1973:M1–2010:M8

Source: Energy Information Administration, Monthly Energy Review, Table 11.1a (http://tonto.eia. doe.gov/merquery/mer_data.asp?table=T11.01a)

Strikes spread to the oil sector by the fall of 1978, bringing Iranian oil production down by 4.8 million barrels per day (or 7 percent of world production at the time) between October 1978 and January 1979. In January the Shah fled the country, and Sheikh Khomeini seized power in February. About a third of the lost Iranian production was made up by increases from Saudi Arabia and elsewhere (see Figure 21.12).

Gasoline queues were again a characteristic of this episode, as seen in this report from the *New York Times*:[21]

> LOS ANGELES, May 4 – "It's horrible; it's just like it was five years ago," Beverly Lyons, whose Buick was mired 32nd in a queue of more than 60 cars outside a Mobil station, said shortly after 8 o'clock this morning.
>
> I've been here an hour; my daughter expects her baby this weekend," she added. "I've got to get some gas!"
>
> Throughout much of California today, and especially so in the Los Angeles area, there were scenes reminiscent of the nation's 1974 gasoline crisis.
>
> Lines of autos, vans, pickup trucks and motor homes, some of the lines were a half mile or longer, backed up from service stations in a rush for gasoline that appeared to be the result of a moderately tight supply of fuel locally that has been aggravated by panic buying.

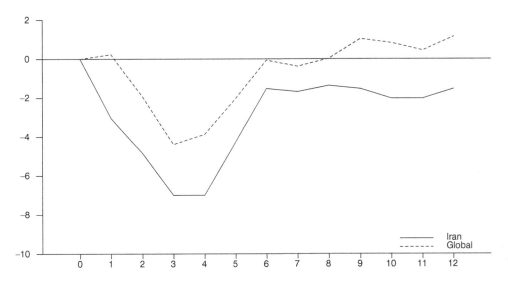

Figure 21.12 Oil production after the 1978 Iranian Revolution

Notes: Dashed line: change in monthly global crude oil production from October 1978 as a percentage of October 1978 levels. Solid line: change in monthly Iranian oil production from October 1978 as a percentage of global levels in October 1978. Horizontal axis: number of months from October 1978

Source: Energy Information Administration, Monthly Energy Review, Tables 11.1a and 11.1b (http://tonto.eia.doe.gov/merquery/mer_data.asp?table=T11.01a)

Frech and Lee (1987) estimated that time spent waiting in line added about a third to the money cost for Americans to buy gasoline in May of 1979. The seventh postwar recession is dated as beginning in January of 1980.

1980–1981: Iran–Iraq war

Iranian production had returned to about half of its pre-revolutionary levels later in 1979, but was knocked out again when Iraq (second panel of Figure 21.11) launched a war against the country in September of 1980. The combined loss of production from the two countries again amounted to about 6 percent of world production at the time, though within a few months, this shortfall had been made up elsewhere (see Figure 21.13).

Whether one perceives the Iranian Revolution and Iran–Iraq war as two separate shocks or a single prolonged episode can depend on the oil price measure. Some series, such as West Texas Intermediate (WTI) plotted in Figure 21.14, suggest one ongoing event, with the real price of oil doubling between 1978 and 1981. Other measures, such as the U.S. producer price index for crude petroleum or consumer price index for gasoline, exhibit two distinct spurts. Interpreting any price series is again confounded by the role of price controls on crude petroleum, which remained in effect in the United States until January 1981.

The National Bureau of Economic Research characterizes the economic difficulties at this time as being two separate economic recessions, with the seventh postwar recession ending in July 1980 but followed very quickly by the eighth postwar recession beginning July of 1981.

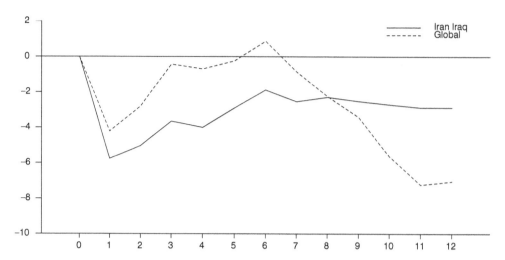

Figure 21.13 Oil production after the Iran–Iraq War

Notes: Dashed line: change in monthly global crude oil production from September 1980 as a percentage of September 1980 levels. Solid line: change in monthly oil production of Iran and Iraq from September 1980 as a percentage of global levels in September 1980. Horizontal axis: number of months from September 1980

Source: Energy Information Administration, Monthly Energy Review, Tables 11.1a and 11.1b (http://tonto.eia.doe.gov/merquery/mer_data.asp?table=T11.01a)

Figure 21.14 Price of oil in 2009 dollars

Notes: January 1973 to October 2010. Price of West Texas Intermediate deflated by CPI

1981–1986: The great price collapse

The war between Iran and Iraq would continue for years, with oil production from the two countries very slow to recover. However, the longer term demand response of consuming countries to the price hikes of the 1970s proved to be quite substantial, and world petroleum consumption declined significantly in the early 1980s. Saudi Arabia voluntarily shut down three-fourths of its production between 1981 and 1985, though this was not enough to prevent a 25 percent decline in the nominal price of oil and significantly bigger decline in the real price. The Saudis abandoned those efforts, beginning to ramp production back up in 1986, causing the price of oil to collapse from $27/barrel in 1985 to $12/barrel at the low point in 1986. Although a favorable development from the perspective of oil consumers, this represented an "oil shock" for the producers. Hamilton and Owyang (forthcoming) found that the U.S. oil-producing states experienced their own regional recession in the mid 1980s.

1990–1991: First Persian Gulf war

By 1990, Iraqi production had returned to its levels of the late 1970s, only to collapse again (and bring Kuwait's substantial production down with it) when the country invaded Kuwait in August 1990. The two countries accounted for nearly 9 percent of world production (see Figure 21.15), and there were concerns at the time that the conflict might spill over into Saudi Arabia. Though there were no gasoline queues in America this time around, the price of crude oil doubled within the space of a few months. The price spike proved to be of short duration, however, as the Saudis used the substantial excess capacity that they had been maintaining throughout the decade to restore world production by November to the levels seen prior to the conflict. The ninth postwar U.S. recession is dated as beginning in July of 1990.

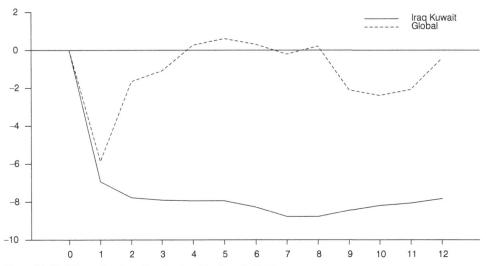

Figure 21.15 Oil production after the first Persian Gulf War

Notes: Dashed line: change in monthly global crude oil production from August 1990 as a percentage of August 1990 levels. Solid line: change in monthly oil production of Iraq and Kuwait from August 1990 as a percentage of global levels in August 1990. Horizontal axis: number of months from August 1990

Source: Energy Information Administration, Monthly Energy Review, Tables 11.1a and 11.1b (http://tonto.eia.doe.gov/merquery/mer_data.asp?table=T11.01a)

1997–2010: A new industrial age

The last generation has experienced a profound transformation for billions of the world's citizens as countries made the transition from agricultural to modern industrial economies. This has made a tremendous difference not only in their standards of living, but also for the world oil market. A subset of the newly industrialized economies used only 17 percent of world's petroleum in 1998 but accounts for 69 percent of the increase in global oil consumption since then.[22] Particularly noteworthy are the 1.3 billion residents of China. China's 6.3 percent compound annual growth rate for petroleum consumption since 1998, if it continues for the next decade, would put the country at current American levels of oil consumption by 2022 and double current U.S. levels by 2033. And such extrapolations do not seem out of the question. Already China is the world's biggest market for buying new cars. Even so, China only has one passenger vehicle per 30 residents, compared with one vehicle per 1.3 residents in the United States (Hamilton 2009a: 193). Whereas short-run movements in oil prices in the first half-century following World War II were dominated by developments in the Middle East, the challenges of meeting petroleum demand from the newly industrialized countries has been the most important theme of the last 15 years.

1997–1998: East Asian crisis

The phenomenal growth in many of these countries had begun long before 1997, as economists marveled at the miracle of the "Asian tigers." And although their contribution to world petroleum consumption at the time was modest, the Hotelling Principle suggests that a belief that their growth rate would continue could have been a factor boosting oil prices in the mid 1990s.[23] But in the summer of 1997, Thailand, South Korea, and other countries were subject to a flight from their currency and serious stresses on the financial system. Investors developed doubts about the Asian growth story, putting economic and financial strains on a number of other Asian countries. The dollar price of oil soon followed them down, falling below $12 a barrel by the end of 1998. In real terms, that was the lowest price since 1972, and a price that perhaps never will be seen again.

1999–2000: Resumed growth

The Asian crisis proved to be short-lived, as the region returned to growth and the new industrialization proved itself to be very real indeed. World petroleum consumption returned to strong growth in 1999, and by the end of the year, the oil price was back up to where it had been at the start of 1997. The price of West Texas Intermediate continued to climb an additional 38 percent between November 1999 and November 2000, after which it fell again in the face of a broader global economic downturn. The tenth postwar U.S. recession began in March of 2001.

2003: Venezuelan unrest and the second Persian Gulf war

A general strike eliminated 2.1 million barrels per day of oil production from Venezuela in December of 2002 and January of 2003. This was followed shortly after by the U.S. attack on Iraq, which removed an additional 2.2 million barrels per day over April to July. These would both be characterized as exogenous geopolitical events, and they show up dramatically

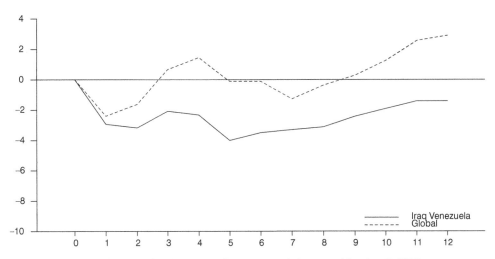

Figure 21.16 Oil production after the Venezuelan unrest and the second Persian Gulf War

Notes: Dashed line: change in monthly global crude oil production from November 2002 as a percentage of November 2002 levels. Solid line: change in monthly oil production of Venezuela and Iraq from November 2002 as a percentage of global levels in November 2002. Horizontal axis: number of months from November 2002

Source: Energy Information Administration, Monthly Energy Review, Tables 11.1a and 11.1b (http://tonto.eia.doe.gov/merquery/mer_data.asp?table=T11.01a)

in Figure 21.11. Kilian (2008) argued they should be included in the list of postwar oil shocks. However, the affected supply was a much smaller share of the global market than many of the other events discussed here, and the disruptions had little apparent effect on global oil supplies (see Figure 21.16). Indeed, when one takes a 12-month moving average of global petroleum production, one sees nothing but phenomenal growth throughout 2003 (Figure 21.17). While oil prices rose between November 2002 and February 2003, the spike proved to be modest and short lived (see Figure 21.14).

2007–2008: Growing demand and stagnant supply

Global economic growth in 2004 and 2005 was quite impressive, with the IMF estimating that real gross world product grew at an average annual rate of 4.7 percent.[24] World oil consumption grew 5 million barrels per day over this period, or 3 percent per year. These strong demand pressures were the key reason for the steady increase in the price of oil over this period, though there was initially enough excess capacity to keep production growing along with demand.

However, as seen in Figure 21.17, production did not continue to grow after 2005. Unlike many other historical oil shocks, there was no dramatic geopolitical event associated with this. Ongoing instability in places like Iraq and Nigeria was a contributing factor. Another is that several of the oil fields that had helped sustain earlier production gains reached maturity with relatively rapid decline rates. Production from the North Sea accounted for 8 percent of world production in 2001, but had fallen more than 2 million barrels per day from these levels by the end of 2007.[25] Mexico's Cantarell, which recently had been the world's second-largest producing field, saw its production decline 1 million barrels per day between 2005 and 2008. Indonesia, one of the original members of the Organization of

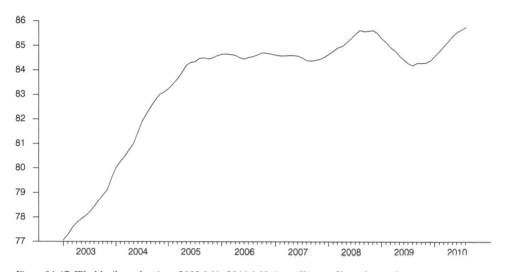

Figure 21.17 World oil production, 2003:M1–2010:M9, in millions of barrels per day

Notes: Includes lease condensate, natural gas plant liquids, other liquids, and refinery process gain

Source: Energy Information Administration, International Petroleum Monthly (http://www.eia.doe.gov/emeu/ipsr/t44.xls)

Petroleum Exporting Countries, saw its production peak in 1998 and is today an importer rather than an exporter of oil.

But the most important country in recent years has surely been Saudi Arabia. The kingdom accounted for 13 percent of global field production in 2005, and had played an active role as the world's residual supplier during the 1980s and 1990s, increasing production whenever needed. Many analysts had assumed that the Saudis would continue to play this role, increasing production to accommodate growing demand in the 2000s.[26] In the event, however, Saudi production was 850,000 barrels per day lower in 2007 than it had been in 2005.

Explanations for the Saudi decline vary. Their magnificent Ghawar field has been in production since 1951 and in recent years has perhaps accounted for 6 percent of world production all by itself. Simmons (2005) was persuaded that Ghawar may have peaked.

Gately (2001), on the other hand, argued that it would not be in the economic interest of OPEC to provide the increased production that many analysts had assumed. Although they reached their conclusions for different reasons, both Simmons and Gately were correct in their prediction that Saudi production would fail to increase as other analysts had assumed it would.

Notwithstanding, demand continued to grow, with world real GDP increasing an additional 5 percent per year in 2006 and 2007, a faster rate of economic growth than had accompanied the 5 million barrels per day increased oil consumption between 2003 and 2005. China alone increased its consumption by 840,000 barrels per day between 2005 and 2007. With no more oil being produced, that meant other countries had to decrease their consumption despite strongly growing incomes. The short-run price elasticity of oil demand has never been very high (Hamilton 2009a), and may have been even smaller over the last decade (Hughes, Knittel, and Sperling 2008), meaning that a very large price increase was necessary to contain demand. Hamilton (2009b: 231) provided illustrative assumptions under which a large shift of the demand curve in the face of a limited increase in supply would have warranted an increase in the price of oil from $55 a barrel in 2005 to $142 a barrel in 2008.[27]

Others have suggested that the return to negative ex post real interest rates in August 2007 and the large flows of investment dollars into commodity futures markets magnified these fundamentals and introduced a speculative bubble in the price of oil and other commodities. Weyant and Huntington (2010: 50) surveyed the literature on this possibility and concluded:

> In summary, there has been no significant statistical evidence for a speculative bubble in the recent oil price boom except for some weak evidence during the first half of 2008. In particular, the direct link between the oil price movements and commodity index funds have not been well developed in existing empirical studies.

For further discussion see Hamilton (2009b), Tang and Xiong (2010), Kilian and Murphy (2010), and Büyükşahin and Robe (2010). Whatever the cause, the oil price spike of 2007–2008 was by some measures the biggest in postwar experience, and the U.S. recession that began in December of 2007 was likewise the worst in postwar experience, though of course the financial crisis rather than any oil-related disruptions was the leading contributing factor in that downturn.[28]

Discussion

Table 21.1 summarizes key features of the postwar events discussed in the preceding sections. The first column indicates months in which there were contemporary accounts of consumer rationing of gasoline. Ramey and Vine (2010) have emphasized that nonprice rationing can significantly amplify the economic dislocations associated with oil shocks. There were at least some such accounts for six of the seven episodes prior to 1980, but none since then.

The third column indicates whether price controls on crude oil or gasoline were in place at the time. This is relevant for a number of reasons. First, price controls are of course a major explanation for why nonprice rationing such as reported in column 1 would be observed. And although there were no explicit price controls in effect in 1947, the threat that they might be imposed at any time was quite significant (Goodwin and Herren 1975), and this is presumably one reason why reports of rationing are also associated with this episode. No price controls were in effect in the United States in 1956, but they do appear to have been in use in Europe, where the rationing at the time was reported.

Second, price controls were sometimes an important factor contributing to the episode itself. Controls can inhibit markets from responding efficiently to the challenges and can be one cause of inadequate or misallocated supply. In addition, the lifting of price controls was often the explanation for the discrete jump eventually observed in prices, as was the case for example in June 1953 and February 1981. The gradual lifting of price ceilings was likewise a reason that events such as the exile of the Shah of Iran in January of 1979 showed up in oil prices only gradually over time.

Price controls also complicate what one means by the magnitude of the observed price change associated with a given episode. Particularly during the 1970s, there was a very involved set of regulations with elaborate rules for different categories of crude oil. Commonly used measures of oil prices look quite different from each other over this period. Hamilton (2011) found that the producer price index for crude petroleum has a better correlation over this period with the prices consumers actually paid for gasoline

Table 21.1 Summary of significant postwar events

Gasoline shortages	Price increase	Price controls	Key factors	Business cycle peak
Nov 47–Dec 47	Nov 47–Jan 48 (37%)	no (threatened)	strong demand, supply constraints	Nov 48
May 52	Jun 53 (10%)	yes	strike, controls lifted	Jul 53
Nov 56–Dec 56 (Europe)	Jan 57–Feb 57 (9%)	yes (Europe)	Suez Crisis	Aug 57
none	none	no	–	Apr 60
none	Feb 69 (7%) Nov 70 (8%)	no	strike, strong demand, supply constraints	Dec 69
Jun 73	Apr 73–Sep 73 (16%)	yes	strong demand, supply constraints, OAPEC embargo	Nov 73
Dec 73–Mar 74	Nov 73–Feb 74 (51%)			
May 79–Jul 79	May 79–Jan 80 (57%)	yes	Iranian revolution	Jan 80
none	Nov 80–Feb 81 (45%)	yes	Iran–Iraq War, controls lifted	Jul 81
none	Aug 90–Oct 90 (93%)	no	Gulf War I	Jul 90
none	Dec 99–Nov 00 (38%)	no	strong demand	Mar 01
none	Nov 02–Mar 03 (28%)	no	Venezuela unrest, Gulf War II	none
none	Feb 07–Jun 08 (145%)	no	strong demand, stagnant supply	Dec 07

than do other popular measures such as the price of West Texas Intermediate or the refiner acquisition cost. I have for this reason used the crude petroleum PPI over the period 1973–1981 as the basis for calculating the magnitude of the price change reported in the second column of Table 21.1. For all other dates the reported price change is based on the monthly WTI.

The fourth column of Table 21.1 summarizes key contributing factors in each episode. Many of these episodes were associated with dramatic geopolitical developments arising out of conflicts in the Middle East. Strong demand confronting a limited supply response also contributed to many of these episodes. The table collects the price increases of 1973–74 together, though in many respects the shortages in the spring of 1973 and the winter of 1973–74 were distinct events with distinct causes. The modest price spikes of 1969 and 1970 have likewise been grouped together for purposes of the summary.

The discrete character of oil price changes seen in Figure 21.5 for the era of the Texas Railroad Commission makes the choice of dates to include in the table rather straightforward prior to 1972. After 1972, oil prices changed continuously, and there is more subjective judgment involved in determining which events are significant enough to be included. For example, the price increase of 2000 could well be viewed as the continuation of a trend that started with the trough reached after the southeast Asian crisis of 1997. However, the price increases in 1998 and 1999 only restored the price level back to where it had been in January 1997. Based on the evidence reported in Hamilton (2003), the episode is dated in Table 21.1 as beginning with the new highs reached in December 1999.

An alternative approach to the narrative summary provided by Table 21.1 is to try to use statistical methods to determine what constitutes an oil shock (e.g., Hamilton 2003), or to disentangle broadly defined shocks to oil supply from changes in demand arising from growing global income, as in Kilian (2009) and Baumeister and Peersman (2009). Although it is very helpful to bring such methods to these questions, the identifying assumptions necessary to interpret such decompositions are controversial. Kilian (2009) and Baumeister and Peersman (2009) attributed a bigger role to demand disturbances in episodes such as the oil price increase of the late 1970s than the narrative approach adopted here has suggested, and also explored the possible contribution of speculative demand and inventory building to the price increases.

As noted in the previous sections, these historical episodes were often followed by economic recessions in the United States. The last column of Table 21.1 reports the starting date of U.S. recessions as determined by the National Bureau of Economic Research. All but one of the eleven postwar recessions were associated with an increase in the price of oil, the single exception being the recession of 1960. Likewise, all but one of the twelve oil price episodes listed in Table 21.1 were accompanied by U.S. recessions, the single exception being the 2003 oil price increase associated with the Venezuelan unrest and second Persian Gulf war.

The correlation between oil shocks and economic recessions appears to be too strong to be just a coincidence (Hamilton 1983a, 1985). And although demand pressure associated with the later stages of a business cycle expansion seems to have been a contributing factor in a number of these episodes, statistically one cannot predict the oil price changes prior to 1973 on the basis of prior developments in the U.S. economy (Hamilton 1983a). Moreover, supply disruptions arising from dramatic geopolitical events are prominent causes of a number of the most important episodes. Insofar as events such as the Suez Crisis and first Persian Gulf war were not caused by U.S. business cycle dynamics, a correlation between these events and subsequent economic downturns should be viewed as causal. This is not to claim that the oil price increases themselves were the sole cause of most postwar recessions. Instead the indicated conclusion is that oil shocks were a contributing factor in at least some postwar recessions.

That an oil price increase could exert some drag on the economy of an oil-importing country should not be controversial. On the supply side, energy is a factor of production, and an exogenous decrease in its supply would be expected to be associated with a decline in productivity. However, standard neoclassical reasoning suggests that the size of such an effect should be small. If the dollar value of the lost energy is less than the dollar value of the lost production, it would pay the firm to bid up the price of energy so as to maintain production. But the dollar value of the lost energy is relatively modest compared with the dollar value of production lost in a recession. For example, the global production shortfall associated with the OPEC embargo (the area above the dashed line in Figure 21.10) averaged 2.3 million barrels per day over the six months following September 1973. Even at a price of $12/barrel, this only represents a market value of $5.1 billion spread over the entire world economy. By contrast, U.S. real GDP declined at a 2.5 percent annual rate between 1974:Q1 and 1975:Q1, which would represent about $38 billion annually in 1974 dollars for the U.S. alone. The dollar value of output lost in the recession exceeded the dollar value of the lost energy by an order of magnitude.

Alternatively, oil shocks could affect the economy through the demand side. The short-run elasticity of oil demand is very low.[29] If consumers try to maintain their real purchases of energy in the face of rising prices, their saving or spending on other goods must fall commensurately. Although there are offsetting income gains for domestic oil producers, the marginal propensity to spend out of oil company windfall profits may be low, and by 1974, more than a third of U.S. oil was imported. Again, however, the direct effects one could assign to this mechanism are limited. For example, between September 1973 and July 1974, U.S. consumer purchases of energy goods and services increased by $14.4 billion at an annual rate,[30] yet the output decline was more than twice this amount.

Hamilton (1988) stressed the importance of the composition of consumer spending in addition to its overall level. For example, one of the key responses seen following an increase in oil prices is a decline in automobile spending, particularly the larger vehicles manufactured in the United States (Edelstein and Kilian 2009, Ramey and Vine 2010). Insofar as specialized labor and capital devoted to the manufacture and sales of those vehicles are difficult to shift into other uses, the result can be a drop in income that is greater than the lost purchasing power by the original consumers. Table 21.2 reproduces the calculations in Hamilton (2009b) on the behavior of real GDP in the five quarters following each of five historical oil shocks, and the specific contribution made to this total from motor vehicles and parts alone.[31] This did seem to make a material contribution in many cases. For example, in the five quarters following the oil price increases of 1979:Q2 and 1990:Q3, real GDP would have increased rather than fallen had there been no decline in autos. In addition, there appears to be an important response of consumer sentiment to rapid increases in energy prices (Edelstein and Kilian 2009). Combining these changes in spending with traditional Keynesian multiplier effects appears to be the most plausible explanation for why oil shocks have often been followed by economic downturns.

In addition to disruptions in supply arising from geopolitical events, another contributing factor for several of the historical episodes is the interaction of growing petroleum demand with production declines from the mature producing fields on which the world had come to depend. In the postwar experience, this appears to be part of the story behind the 1973–74 and 2007–08 oil price spikes, and, going back in time, in the 1862–64 and 1895 price run-ups as well. It is unclear as of this writing where the added global production will come from to replace traditional sources such as the North Sea, Mexico, and Saudi Arabia, if production from the latter has indeed peaked.

Table 21.2 Real GDP growth (annual rate) and contribution of autos to the overall GDP growth rate in five historical episodes

Period	GDP growth rate	Contribution of autos
1974:Q1–1975:Q1	–2.5%	–0.5%
1979:Q2–1980:Q2	–0.4%	–0.8%
1981:Q2–1982:Q2	–1.5%	–0.2%
1990:Q3–1991:Q3	–0.1%	–0.3%
2007:Q4–2008:Q4	–2.3%	–0.5%

Source: Hamilton (2009b)

But given the record of geopolitical instability in the Middle East, and the projected phenomenal surge in demand from the newly industrialized countries, it seems quite reasonable to expect that within the next decade we will have an additional row of data to add to Table 21.1 with which to inform our understanding of the economic consequences of oil shocks.

Acknowledgments

I am grateful to Lutz Kilian, Randall Parker and Robert Whaples for helpful suggestions.

Notes

1 The number plotted is the series for oil prices in 2009 dollars from British Petroleum, *Statistical Review of World Energy 2010,* which are also the numbers used by Dvir and Rogoff (2010). The source for the BP nominal price series appears to be the same as Jenkins (1985: Table 18), which were then evidently deflated using the consumer price index (BLS) for all items from *Historical Statistics of the United States,* Table E135-166. Since Jenkins' original series goes back to 1860, that value ($9.59/barrel, almost identical to that reported in *Derrick's Hand-Book* (1898: 711)) is also included in the figure provided here. As noted in the text, the early Pennsylvanian market started even higher than this and was somewhat chaotic.

2 If $100 \times \left[\ln(P_t) - \ln(P_s) \right] = 10$ then $P_t / P_s = e^{0.1} = 1.105,$ meaning that P_t is 10.5% higher than P_s.

3 Interestingly, McMillin and Parker (1994) also found evidence that over the period 1924:M2–1938:M6, oil price changes could help predict subsequent changes in industrial production, with the effects both economically and statistically significant.

4 This and the following discussion draws heavily from Hamilton (1983b, 1985).

5 *New York Times,* June 25, 1947, 1:6; June 27, 33:2.

6 *New York Times,* August 12, 1947, 46:1; August 22, 9:2; November 3, 25:7; November 19, 24:3.

7 *New York Times,* January 5, 1948, 11:2.

8 From the *New York Times,* May 8, 1951, 45:1: The Office of Price Stabilization "announced a regulation establishing ceiling prices for new oil, generally at prices posted on January 25, for any given pool. Prices for crude oil have been governed up to now by the general price 'freeze' which set the ceilings at the highest price attained between December 19, 1950 and January 25."

9 *International Petroleum Trade,* Bureau of Mines, U.S. Department of Interior, May 1952, p. 52.

10 *Wall Street Journal,* May 7, 1952, p. 2.

11 *Wall Street Journal,* May 5, 1952, 3:1; May 7, 2:2; May 12, 2:2.

12 *New York Times,* May 5, 1952, 1:6; May 9, 16:7.

13 *Oil and Gas Journal,* Nov 12, 1956, 122–5.

14 *New York Times,* Dec 2, 1956, 1:5.

15 *Minerals Yearbook,* 1957, p. 453.

16 *New York Times,* Dec 25, 1968, 1:3; Dec 27, 1:5.

17 *New York Times,* Feb 25, 1969, 53:3.

18 *New York Times,* Jun 8, 1973, 51:1.

19 Kilian (2008) suggested that this calculation overstates the effects of the embargo. He argued that production by Saudi Arabia and Kuwait was unusually high in September 1973 and that there would have been some decreases from those levels even in the absence of an embargo.

20 *New York Times,* Dec 18, 1973, 12.

21 *New York Times,* May 5, 1979, 11.

22 These calculations are based on Brazil, China, Hong Kong, India, Singapore, South Korea, Taiwan, and Thailand. Data source: EIA, total petroleum consumption (http://tonto.eia.doe.gov/cfapps/ipdbproject/iedindex3.cfm?tid=5&pid=5&aid=2&cid=regions&syid=1980&eyid=2009&unit=TBPD).

23 World oil consumption grew by more than 2 per cent per year between 1994 and 1997. Moreover, if oil producers correctly anticipated the growth in petroleum demand from the newly industrialized countries, it would have paid them to hold off some production in 1995 in anticipation of higher

prices to come. By this mechanism, the perceived future growth rate can affect the current price. See Hamilton (2009a: Section 3.3) for a discussion of the Hotelling Principle.

24 Details for the these calculations are provided in Hamilton (2009b: 229).
25 Energy Information Administration, *Monthly Energy Review*, Table 11.1b (http://tonto.eia.doe.gov/merquery/mer_data.asp?table=T11.01b).
26 See for example International Energy Agency, *World Economic Outlook*, 2007.
27 Other research supporting the conclusion that strong global economic growth was the cause of the 2007–08 oil price run-up include Kilian (2009) and Kilian and Hicks (2011).
28 Hamilton (2009b) nevertheless noted some avenues by which the oil shock contributed directly to the financial crisis itself.
29 See for example the literature surveys by Dahl and Sterner (1991), Dahl (1993), Espey (1998), Graham and Glaister (2004) and Brons, et al. (2008). Examples of studies finding higher elasticities include Baumeister and Peersman (2009) and Davis and Kilian (2011).
30 Bureau of Economic Analysis, Table 2.3.5.U.
31 Subsequent to April 2009, the GDP figures for 2007 and 2008 were substantially revised. This accounts for the difference between the numbers in the last row of Table 21.2 and those reported in Hamilton (2009b).

References

Adelman, M.A. (1972) *The World Petroleum Market*, Baltimore, MD: Johns Hopkins University Press.
Barsky, R.B. and Kilian, L. (2001) 'Do we really know that oil caused the Great Stagflation? A monetary alternative', in B.S. Bernanke and K. Rogoff (eds.) *NBER Macroeconomics Annual 2001*, Cambridge, MA: MIT Press.
Baumeister, C. and Peersman, G. (2009) 'Time-varying effects of oil supply shocks on the U.S. economy', working paper, Ghent University.
British Petroleum (2010) *Statistical Review of World Energy 2010*, London: British Petroleum Corporation, available at http://www.bp.com/liveassets/bp_internet/globalbp/globalbp_uk_english/reports_and_publications/statistical_energy_review_2008/STAGING/local_assets/2010_downloads/statistical_review_of_world_energy_full_report_2010.pdf
Brons, M., Nijkamp, P., Pels, E. and Rietveld, P. (2008) 'A meta-analysis of the price elasticity of gasoline demand: a SUR approach', *Energy Economics*, 30: 2105–22.
Büyükşahin, B. and Robe, M.A. (2010) 'Speculators, commodities, and cross-market linkages', working paper, American University.
Caplinger, M.W. (1997) 'Allegheny oil heritage project: a contextual overview of crude oil production in Pennsylvania', Historic American Engineering Record (HAER), No. PA-436, Prints and Photographs Division, Library of Congress, Washington, DC, available at http://www.as.wvu.edu/ihtia/ ANF%20Oil%20Context.pdf
Carter, S.B., Gartner, S.S., Haines, M.R., Olmstead, A.L., Sutch, R. and Wright, G. (eds.) (2006) *Historical Statistics of the United States Millennial Edition*, New York: Cambridge University Press.
Dahl, C.A. (1993) 'A survey of oil demand elasticities for developing countries', *OPEC Review*, 17: 399–419.
Dahl, C.A. and Sterner, T. (1991) 'Analysing gasoline demand elasticities: a survey', *Energy Economics*, 13: 203–10.
Davis, L.W. and Kilian, L. (2011) 'Estimating the effect of a gasoline tax on carbon emissions', *Journal of Applied Econometrics*, 16(7): 1187–1214.
Derrick's Hand-Book of Petroleum: A Complete Chronological and Statistical Review of Petroleum Developments from 1859 to 1898 (1898), Oil City, PA: Derrick Publishing Company.
Dvir, E. and Rogoff, K.S. (2010) 'The three epochs of oil', working paper, Boston College.
Edelstein, P. and Kilian, L. (2009) 'How sensitive are consumer expenditures to retail energy prices?' *Journal of Monetary Economics*, 56: 766–79.
Espey, M. (1998) 'Gasoline demand revisited: an international meta-analysis of elasticities', *Energy Economics*, 20: 273–95.
Frankel, J.A. (2008) 'The effect of monetary policy on real commodity prices', in J. Campbell (ed.) *Asset Prices and Monetary Policy*, Chicago, IL: University of Chicago Press.
Frech, H.E. III, and Lee, W.C. (1987) 'The welfare cost of rationing-by-queuing across markets: theory and estimates from the U.S. gasoline crises', *Quarterly Journal of Economics*, 102: 97–108.

Gately, D. (2001) 'How plausible is the consensus projection of oil below $25 and Persian Gulf oil capacity and output doubling by 2020?', *Energy Journal*, 22: 1–27.

Goodwin, C.D. and Herren, R.S. (1975) 'The Truman administration: problems and policies unfold', in C.D. Goodwin (ed.) *Exhortation and Controls: The Search for a Wage-Price Policy: 1945–1971*, Washington, DC: Brookings Institution.

Graham, D.J. and Glaister, S. (2004) 'Road traffic demand elasticity estimates: a review', *Transport Reviews*, 24: 261–74.

Hamilton, J.D. (1983a) 'Oil and the macroeconomy since World War II', *Journal of Political Economy*, 91: 228–48.

Hamilton, J.D. (1983b) 'The macroeconomic effects of petroleum supply disruptions', unpublished thesis, University of California, Berkeley.

Hamilton, J.D. (1985) 'Historical causes of postwar oil shocks and recessions', *Energy Journal*, 6: 97–116.

Hamilton, J.D. (1988) 'A neoclassical model of unemployment and the business cycle', *Journal of Political Economy*, 96: 593–617.

Hamilton, J.D. (2003) 'What is an oil shock?', *Journal of Econometrics*, 113: 363–98.

Hamilton, J.D. (2009a) 'Understanding crude oil prices', *Energy Journal*, 30: 179–206.

Hamilton, J.D. (2009b) 'Causes and consequences of the oil shock of 2007–2008', *Brookings Papers on Economic Activity*, Spring 2009: 215–61.

Hamilton, J.D. (2011) 'Nonlinearities and the macroeconomic effects of oil prices', *Macroeconomic Dynamics*, 15(S3): 364–78.

Hamilton, J.D. and Owyang, M.T. (forthcoming) 'The propagation of regional recessions', *Review of Economics and Statistics*.

Hughes, J.E., Knittel, C.R. and Sperling, D. (2008) 'Evidence of a shift in the short-run price elasticity of gasoline demand', *Energy Journal*, 29: 93–114.

Jenkins, G. (1985) *Oil Economists' Handbook*, London: British Petroleum Company.

Kilian, L. (2008) 'Exogenous oil supply shocks: how big are they and how much do they matter for the U.S. economy?' *Review of Economics and Statistics*, 90: 216–40.

Kilian, L. (2009) 'Not all oil price shocks are alike: disentangling demand and supply shocks in the crude oil market', *American Economic Review*, 99: 1053–69.

Kilian, L. and Hicks, B. (2011) 'Did unexpectedly strong economic growth cause the oil price shock of 2003–2008?', working paper, University of Michigan.

Kilian, L. and Murphy, D.P. (2010) 'The role of inventories and speculative trading in the global market for crude oil', working paper, University of Michigan.

McMillin, W.D. and Parker, R.E. (1994) 'An empirical analysis of oil price shocks in the interwar period', *Economic Inquiry*, 32: 486–97.

Olmstead, A. and Rhode, P. (1985) 'Rationing without government: the West Coast gas famine of 1920', *American Economic* Review, 75: 1044–55.

Pogue, J.E. (1921) *The Economics of Petroleum*, New York: John Wiley & Sons.

Ramey, V.A. and Vine, D.J. (2010) 'Oil, automobiles, and the U.S. economy: how much have things really changed?', in D. Acemoglu and M. Woodford (eds.), *NBER Macroeconomics Annual 2010*, 333–68. Cambridge, MA: National Bureau of Economic Research.

Ripy, T.B. (1999) *Federal Excise Taxes on Alcoholic Beverages: A Summary of Present Law and a Brief History*, Congressional Research Service Report RL30238, available at http://stuff.mit.edu/afs/sipb/contrib/wikileaks-crs/wikileaks-crs-reports/RL30238

Simmons, M.R. (2005) *Twilight in the Desert: The Coming Saudi Oil Shock and the World Economy*, Hoboken, NJ: John Wiley & Sons.

Tang, K. and Xiong, W. (2010) 'Index investment and financialization of commodities', working paper, Princeton University.

Weyant, J.P. and Huntington, H.G. (2010) 'Inventory of research and analysis on overall oil price determinants', working paper, Stanford University.

Williamson, H.F. and Daum, A.R. (1959) *The American Petroleum Industry: The Age of Illumination 1859–1899*, Evanston, IL: Northwestern University Press.

Williamson, H.F., Andreano, R.L., Daum, A.R. and Klose, G.C. (1963) *The American Petroleum Industry: The Age of Energy 1899–1959*, Evanston, IL: Northwestern University Press.

Yergin, D. (1991) *The Prize: The Epic Quest for Oil, Money, and Power*, New York: Simon and Schuster.

22

THE 1970S

The decade the Phillips Curve died

Arnold Kling

Introduction

The 1970s was a tumultuous decade for the American economy and for macroeconomic theory. The breakdown of one of the most important macroeconomic relationships, the unemployment-inflation trade-off known as the Phillips Curve, played a central role in the drama.

Some of the key developments in economic theory and in the economic environment unfolded as follows:

- In 1958, British economic historian A.W. Phillips (1958) published an article documenting an inverse relationship between nominal wage changes and the unemployment rate in England for nearly a century.
- In 1960, Paul Samuelson and Robert Solow (1960) dubbed this relationship the Phillips Curve and suggested that American policy makers could use it as a tool to help decide policies for aggregate demand management.[1]
- In 1967, Milton Friedman (1968) gave the Presidential Address to the American Economic Association, in which he challenged the interpretation of the Phillips Curve as a relationship in which causality runs from unemployment to inflation and that the trade-off between unemployment and inflation is stable. Instead, he propounded what became known as the "natural rate hypothesis."[2]
- In 1970 a collection of papers that explored the theory of the Phillips Curve, which became known as "the Phelps volume" (Phelps 1970), boosted the natural rate hypothesis.
- In August, 1971, President Nixon abruptly changed economic policy, including the imposition of a three-month freeze on wages and prices. This was followed by other forms of wage and price controls for the next two years.
- In October, 1973, a war in the Middle East resulted in an "oil boycott" by Arab producers unhappy with American policy. This began a period in which the Organization of Petroleum Exporting Countries (OPEC) was apparently able to achieve some success in acting as a cartel, restricting oil output and driving up prices. (See Chapter 21 by James Hamilton in this *Handbook*.)

- In 1976, Robert Lucas (1976) published "Econometric Policy Evaluation: A Critique." This paper called into question the stability of relationships, such as the Phillips Curve, if individuals have rational expectations.
- In 1978, the Federal Reserve Bank of Boston (1978) published a conference volume that was devoted to burying the Phillips Curve.

The rest of this chapter will proceed as follows. First, I will use a simple linear model of the inflation-unemployment trade-off to show how dramatically the 1970s diverged from previous macroeconomic performance. Next, I will look at the impact of the 1970s on macroeconomic theory and macroeconometric modeling. Next, I will discuss the macroeconomic thinking that emerged until the recent financial crisis and its aftermath. In a sense, macroeconomics from 1980 through 2008 can be viewed as a long post-mortem on the demise of the simple Phillips Curve in the 1970s. Instead, more complex theories of expectations and aggregate supply were adopted. Finally, I will look briefly at the implications of more recent events for the Phillips Curve.

A simple one-for-one trade-off

The Phillips Curve is supposed to be a curve. That is, at low levels of unemployment, an additional reduction in unemployment is presumed to bring about a larger increase in inflation than is the case at high levels of unemployment. However, the inflation–unemployment trade-off could have been reasonably approximated by a straight line during the 1950s and 1960s.

We can neatly divide the history from the 1950s through the present into thirteen-year periods, starting in 1956. The breakdown of the Phillips Curve took place during the second of those periods.

From 1956 through 1968, inflation averaged 2.19 percent and unemployment averaged 5.0 percent.[3] Because the sum of the two is 7.19 percent, a simple linear model of the trade-off is:

Inflation = 7.19 – unemployment

By construction, this linear trade-off means that every one percentage point increase in the unemployment rate lowers the inflation rate by one percentage point. This one-for-one trade-off is not necessarily the empirical estimate that most closely fits the data. However, it works quite well over the 1956–1968 period. Inflation had a mean of 2.19 percent with a standard deviation of 1.11 percent. The standard error of this simple linear model is 0.61 percent, which means that it has an R^2 of close to 70 percent.

Thus, as of 1969, an economist might reasonably have described inflation and unemployment in terms of a one-for-one trade-off, with an average "misery index" (the sum of inflation and unemployment) of 7.19 percent. What took place subsequently, however, was radically different. Table 22.1 presents the performance of this inflation-prediction equation over four thirteen-year periods.

Note that this table uses the simple one-for-one trade-off estimated for 1956–1968, not allowing for any subsequent shifts in average inflation and unemployment. This simple model fits well from 1956–1968 and again from 1995–2007. From 1982–1994, the trade-off exists, but at a higher average level of inflation and unemployment, so that the "misery index" averaged 10.65 percent, compared with 7.19 percent in 1956–1968. However, for the period from 1969–1981, the linear trade-off fails dramatically to predict the behavior of inflation. This is when the dramatic breakdown of the Phillips Curve took place.

Table 22.1 Inflation, unemployment, and a simple linear trade-off model

	1956–1968	1969–1981	1982–1994	1995–2007	1956–2007
Average Unemployment	5	6.19	6.99	5	5.8
Average inflation	2.19	7.81	3.66	2.67	4.09
Standard error	0.61	7.67	3.79	1.04	4.32
Largest underprediction	1.4	12.33	6.34	1.68	12.33
Largest overprediction	−0.84	none	none	−1.09	−1.09

Notes: An underprediction is when the inflation rate exceeds what would have been predicted, given the unemployment rate, by the simple linear trade-off. Within a thirteen-year period, the largest underprediction is the amount of the underprediction in the year where this value is the highest. Similarly for the largest overprediction, an overprediction is when the inflation rate falls below what would have been predicted, given the unemployment rate, by the linear trade-off

From 1973 to 1974, inflation climbed from 9 percent to 12 percent, while unemployment increased also, from 4.9 percent to 5.6 percent. This perverse behavior may have been the result of the breakdown of the wage–price control regime that was in place from 1971 through 1973. Otherwise, even in the 1970s. in years when inflation went up. unemployment went down, and vice-versa.

Late in the 1970s, the inflation rate shot up, going from 5.0 percent in 1976 to 6.7 percent, 9.0 percent, and 13.2 percent in 1977, 1978, and 1979, respectively. This painful acceleration took place in spite of the fact that the unemployment rate was 7.0 percent, 6.1 percent and 5.8 percent in 1977–79, respectively. The simple linear trade-off would have predicted inflation of 1.4 percent or less in those years. However, the worst year for the linear trade-off would have been 1980, when the unemployment rate of 7.2 percent implied almost zero inflation, while actual inflation was 12.35 percent.

The great debates

The Phillips Curve provoked vigorous debate among macroeconomists, both before and after the simplest empirical version broke down. This debate focused on considerations of both theory and econometric methods.

Keynesians interpreted the Phillips Curve as a model of inflation. The macroeconometric models treated inflation as resulting from the combination of a wage-setting equation and a price-markup equation. In the wage-setting equation, there is a Phillips Curve trade-off between the rate of increase in nominal wages and the unemployment rate. In the price-markup equation, prices are set as a markup over unit labor costs, which are affected primarily by wages.

The price-markup equation serves to align real wages with average productivity of labor. Thus, the real wage does not have a marked cyclical tendency according to the standard macroeconometric models of the late 1960s and early 1970s.

The wage-setting equation determines the change in nominal wages, and consequently the rate of inflation. The theory is that as unemployment gets lower, workers are in a stronger bargaining position, and they are able to extract larger wage increases.

Although low aggregate unemployment gives workers stronger bargaining power in an individual industry, in the economy as a whole this wage bargaining is a zero-sum game. The real wage is determined by the price mark-up, so that the only thing that wage negotiations achieve overall is a higher rate of inflation.

Given this view of the inflation process, Keynesian economists in the 1960s favored "incomes policies" to restrain inflation. Labor unions individually were attempting to increase their relative wages, but collectively the effect was to increase overall inflation. It seemed to make sense for government to discourage this unproductive competition for income shares.

Both the non-monetarist view of inflation and the implication that government should play a role in the process of setting wages were opposed by Milton Friedman. His Presidential Address to the American Economic Association in 1967 was a significant attack on the Keynesian theory of the Phillips Curve. Friedman proposed that we begin with a notion of a "natural rate of unemployment," which he defined as

> the level that would be ground out by the Walrasian system of general equilibrium equations, provided there is imbedded in them the actual structural characteristics of the labor and commodity markets, including market imperfections, stochastic variability in demands and supplies, the cost of gathering information about job vacancies and labor availabilities, the cost of mobility, and so on.
>
> (Friedman 1968: 8)

One property of the natural rate of unemployment is that the average real wage is at an equilibrium level. There should be no tendency for real wages to rise or to fall.

Friedman argued that if the monetary authority attempts to drive the unemployment rate below the natural rate, it must cause an increase in prices, with wages lagging behind. This will temporarily increase labor demand. However, workers will be unsatisfied with real wages *ex post*, and they will demand higher nominal wages going forward. If the monetary authority remains passive, then real wages and employment return to their natural levels. On the other hand, if the monetary authority persists in trying to drive down unemployment, it has to raise the inflation rate still further, until workers start to ask for even higher rates of wage increases. The more persistent the monetary authority, the higher will be the rate of inflation.

Friedman (1968: 11) concluded, "there is always a temporary trade-off between inflation and unemployment; there is no permanent trade-off."

Implicitly, this analysis reverses the causality from the Keynesian norm. Rather than think in terms of causality running from unemployment to inflation, we are to think of causality as running from *unanticipated* inflation to lower unemployment. The monetary authority can cause an increase in inflation. At first, this will be unanticipated, reducing real wage rates and increasing employment. However, once inflation becomes anticipated it will have no effect on real wage rates or employment.

The logic of Friedman's argument posed an immediate challenge to the conventional wisdom in macroeconomics. It stimulated more research and analysis of the microeconomic foundations of the trade-off between inflation and unemployment, with the Phelps volume a prominent early example. It also caused some macroeconometric modelers to adopt the concept of a natural rate of unemployment. Wage growth was measured relative to expected inflation (typically measured as an average of recent past inflation). If unemployment was low, wages would grow faster than expected inflation. If unemployment was high, wages would grow more slowly than expected inflation. The unemployment rate at which wages would grow at exactly the rate of expected inflation was called either the "natural rate" or, more literally, the "non-accelerating inflation rate of unemployment," or NAIRU.

While mainstream economists adopted the idea of the NAIRU, they did not adopt Friedman's policy prescriptions. Unlike Friedman, they took the view that they could recognize when unemployment was above the NAIRU, in which case they believed that policies to raise aggregate demand were warranted. In addition, mainstream economists continued to advocate incomes policies as a means of controlling inflation.

Incomes policies were given a thorough trial for two years, starting in August of 1971, when President Nixon announced a three-month freeze on wages and prices. Although there was some improvement in both inflation and unemployment in 1972, the overall verdict on these policies was negative. They distorted markets and were administratively unworkable.

On the theoretical front, Robert Lucas and others challenged the idea of even a temporary trade-off between inflation and unemployment. They argued against the simple model of inflation expectations as backward-looking. Instead, suppose that at the other extreme workers have "rational" expectations, in that they do their best to anticipate all factors that could affect inflation going forward, including future actions by the monetary authority.

If workers have "rational" expectations, then on average they should not be surprised by monetary expansion. This means that the unanticipated component of inflation should be small and not under the control of the monetary authority. Combining rational expectations of inflation with Friedman's view that only unanticipated inflation affects employment, the conclusion is that the unemployment cannot be affected by monetary policy.

The arguments of Lucas and others created a revival of classical economics, in which monetary policy affects inflation without affecting unemployment. Anticipated money growth produces only inflation, and under rational expectations all but the purely random fluctuations in money growth are anticipated.

Against this revived classical economics, Keynesians argued that episodes of high unemployment, such as the Great Depression, are difficult to explain within a classical paradigm. Surely, they argued, workers in the 1930s were not making persistent large errors about inflation that caused them to insist on overly high real wage rates.

Part of the rational expectations revolution was directed against the large macroeconometric models. The Lucas Critique suggested that the models would create the illusion that monetary policy could affect output, because the models were fit on the basis of backward-looking expectations. However, if activist monetary policy were to be tried and economic agents began to take anticipated policy into account, then the models would break down.

With respect to forecasting key economic variables, the macroeconometric models did suffer major breakdowns in the 1970s. Jeremy Siegel noted that

> Almost every one of the nearly two dozen of the nation's top economists invited to President Ford's anti-inflation conference in Washington in September 1974 was unaware that the U.S. economy was in the midst of its most severe postwar recession to date. McNees, studying the forecasts issued by five prominent forecasters in 1974, found that the median forecast overestimated gross national product (GNP) growth by 6 percentage points and underestimated inflation by 4 percentage points.
> (Siegel 2002: 212)[4]

The rational expectations hypothesis changed the lens through which macroeconomists looked at data. Rational expectations introduced some similarities between the theory of the behavior of macroeconomic variables and that of financial variables in an efficient market. In an efficient market, with all past information reflected in forecasts, prices of long-term financial instruments, most notably common stocks, should approximately follow a random walk. Similarly, under plausible assumptions about consumer preferences, economists argued that macroeconomic variables, such as consumer spending, should follow a random walk (Hall 1978).

In part because a random walk became an interesting "null hypothesis" for a number of macroeconomic variables, economists began to examine more closely the properties of time-series data. What they found was that many macroeconomic variables did not exhibit stationary behavior. They did not tend to revert to a long-run mean or even to a long-term trend. Instead, deviations in, say, the level of real GDP, tend to persist. Only if one takes the first difference of GDP, that is the change between the level one quarter and the level the next quarter, will the series be stationary.

This poses a problem for empirical macroeconomics that has never been completely solved. Studying data in levels, ignoring nonstationarity, introduces spurious correlations. On the other hand, studying data in differences, in order to work with stationary time series, tends to amplify the noise in the data relative to the signal, resulting in weak estimates for the effect of any one variable on the other.

For the Phillips Curve, this means that if one uses the change in the inflation rate as the dependent variable (which would correct the nonstationarity in the inflation time series), the measured effect of any other variable, such as the unemployment rate, will tend to be quite small. The effect of the unemployment rate on inflation is likely to be cumulative and diffuse over time. Differencing the inflation data tends to obscure any such diffuse cumulative effects.[5]

In short, by 1980, macroeconometric models in general, and the Phillips Curve in particular, had at least three strikes against them. First, their forecasting experience had been dismal in the 1970s. Second, they were vulnerable to the Lucas Critique, which suggested that the parameters in the models would not remain stable if individuals were forming forward-looking expectations in a rational way. Finally, the modelers were not able to treat nonstationary data in a satisfactory way, leading to concerns that the relationships represented by the model coefficients were spurious.

The long post-mortem

For most macroeconomists, the 1970s was a traumatic decade, and the profession spent the next quarter century attempting to explain and recover from this episode. Only a minority clung to a Phillips Curve with backward-looking expectations.

Those who would still defend the Phillips Curve faced the challenge of explaining the combination of high rates of inflation and unemployment in the 1970s. The stories that were most widely proposed to account for this period included oil price shocks, other supply factors, and chronic over-optimism on the part of the Federal Reserve.

In the 1970s, there were two spikes in the price of oil. The first began with the Arab oil embargo in October of 1973. The impact of this adverse supply shift may have been exacerbated by the regime of price controls, which resulted in gasoline lines and other symptoms of allocative inefficiency. Another spike took place after the Iranian revolution of 1979 and during the Iran–Iraq war that began in 1980. (Once again see Chapter 21 by James Hamilton in this *Handbook*.)

In textbook macroeconomics, an oil shock shifts the aggregate supply curve upward. In theory, this should cause a one-time increase in the price level and reduction in aggregate output. However, with wage–price feedback effects, one could argue that it would lead to an increase in the rate of inflation, not just a one-time jump in the price level.

In general, the 1970s was a period of a "productivity slowdown." The trend growth rate in labor productivity declined, in part because of the reduction in energy supplies but also perhaps because of other factors. For example, the entry of the Baby Boom generation into the labor force created a relative excess of inexperienced workers, which could cause productivity growth to decelerate.

Finally, and perhaps most important, the Federal Reserve probably took an overly optimistic view of the economy, particularly the NAIRU. If, based on experience in the 1960s, the Fed thought that the NAIRU was somewhere between 4 and 5 percent, while the actual NAIRU may have been somewhere around 6 percent, the Fed would have committed the exact mistake that Friedman had warned about in his 1967 address. That is, by aiming for an unemployment rate below the natural rate, the Fed produced ever-increasing inflation, while continually falling short of its (unrealistic) goal of lower unemployment.

In fact, Friedman's anti-Keynesian heterodox views of 1967 became the fallback position of those still committed to the Keynesian Phillips Curve view in the 1980s and 1990s. They incorporated the NAIRU into their thinking, and they took a pessimistic view that the NAIRU was close to 6 percent, until the late 1990s when it appeared that the economy could tolerate lower unemployment rates without causing inflation to accelerate.[6] Those who continued to work with macroeconometric models made sure that the models satisfied the theoretical expectation that in the long run money growth would drive inflation but be neutral with respect to employment. However, they continued to employ backward-looking models of expectation formation, so that their models still embodied a short-run trade-off between inflation and unemployment.

In general, however, this was not the path followed by academic macroeconomists. In the economics journals, the macroeconomics that emerged after the 1970s was very different from that which preceded it. Whereas pre-1970s macroeconomics might have been cavalier about microeconomic foundations, post-1970s macro was meticulous about microfoundations. Whereas pre-1970s macroeconometric models took the issue of expectations casually, using past behavior as an indicator of expectations for future behavior, post-1970s macroeconomic modeling tried to address the Lucas Critique and rational expectations. Whereas pre-1970s macroeconomics ignored the relationship between inflation and money growth, post-1970s macroeconomics treated inflation as determined by the rate of money growth, with possible allowances for wage or price stickiness that in turn can lead to fluctuations in output.

A useful snapshot of post-1970s macroeconomics was written by Olivier Blanchard (2008), shortly before the financial crisis worsened in 2008. Blanchard pointed out that post-1970s economics initially diverged, with the more radical of the classical revivalists proposing what became known as the Real Business Cycle model, in which economic fluctuations are determined by productivity shocks rather than by changes in aggregate demand. The other camp, labeled New Keynesian, developed microeconomic models that might explain wage and price stickiness.

In Blanchard's view, there was in the decade prior to the financial crisis of 2008 a softening of the disagreement between the two macroeconomic camps. According to Blanchard, all agreed that the evidence for the significance of demand shocks was too strong to be ignored. At the same time, all agreed that methodological critiques of the rational expectations advocates should be dealt with. The result was a convergence toward using rigorous neoclassical models to analyze the effects of Keynesian-type nominal rigidities. According to Blanchard (2008: 8), this emerging consensus includes, "A Phillips-curve like relation, in which inflation depends on both output and anticipations of future inflation."

I should emphasize that this is not a pre-1970s Phillips Curve. It includes explicitly forward-looking measures of inflation. It does not present the monetary authority with a menu of choices for unemployment and inflation. At best, the newer models can describe what sorts of policy rules serve to amplify or dampen fluctuations in the face of various sorts of external shocks.

One common finding is that targeting the rate of inflation can be a useful rule. Of course, if a model is driven by nominal rigidities, then giving participants a predictable path for the price level is likely to be the best policy rule. Thus, the policy implications derived from these models are pretty much "baked in" to the assumptions.

Recent developments

Has the Phillips Curve returned? We saw earlier that the simple, one-for-one linear trade-off estimated on the basis of 1956–1968 experience fits the 1995–2007 period remarkably well. For that span, we do not need to rely on models of expectations or even a NAIRU in order to explain movements in inflation.

From 2004 through 2007, inflation averaged 3.4 percent. With the onset of a new, deep recession, inflation fell to about 1.4 percent on average in 2008 and 2009. With the high rate of unemployment, the simple linear trade-off would have expected inflation to average about –0.4 percent in 2008 and 2009. The simple trade-off is correct in predicting lower inflation, but it over-estimates the extent of the decline.

Many economists expect inflation to remain low because of the weak economy, which suggests at least an implicit belief in the Phillips Curve. Financial markets appear to share this view, based on the inflation expectations that can be inferred from comparing yields on inflation-indexed Treasury bonds with comparable nominal bonds.

On the other hand, the consensus that Blanchard saw in 2008 appears to have evaporated. Bitter arguments have erupted between Keynesians and neoclassical economists in web postings and occasionally in newspaper opinion columns.[7]

The disputes over policy are also highly charged. Keynesian economists have tended to support fiscal stimulus and "quantitative easing" of monetary policy, while neoclassical economists have expressed vociferous opposition.

Thus, while the 1970s may be gone, they are not forgotten. The doubts about the stability of the Phillips Curve, and hence about the reliability of macroeconometric models and about the effectiveness of policies to increase aggregate demand, are still salient to many economists.

Notes

1 Humphrey (1985) points out that the fame that Samuelson and Solow gave to Phillips was perhaps undeserved. Humphrey lists many antecedent discussions of the inflation–unemployment trade-off, going back to David Hume.
2 Phillips himself may have been closer to the Friedman view than to the Samuelson–Solow view. See Leeson and Young (2008).
3 These figures are derived from data downloaded from the Bureau of Labor Statistics web site in November of 2010. Inflation is measured as the December–December percent change in the all-urban Consumer Price Index. Unemployment is measured as the annual average of the civilian unemployment rate.
4 Siegel cites McNees (1992).
5 There was much more work done in the 1970s and later on macroeconometric methodology. The interested reader should examine topics such as vector autoregression and cointegration.
6 For a defense of the Phillips Curve and of the view that the NAIRU was 6 percent, see Fuhrer (1995).
7 Some of the arcane academic dispute even found its way into a Congressional hearing. See Solow (2010).

References

Blanchard, O. (2008) 'The state of macro', MIT Working Paper 08–17.

Federal Reserve Bank of Boston (1978) *After the Phillips Curve: Persistence of High Inflation and High Unemployment*, Federal Reserve Bank of Boston Conference Series, 19. Boston, MA: Federal Reserve Bank of Boston.

Friedman, M. (1968) 'The role of monetary policy', *American Economic Review*, 58: 1–17.

Fuhrer, J.C. (1995) 'The Phillips Curve is alive and well', *New England Economic Review*, March–April: 41–56.

Hall, R.E. (1978) 'Stochastic implications of the life-cycle permanent-income hypothesis', *Journal of Political Economy*, 86: 971–87.

Humphrey, T.M. (1985) 'The early history of the Phillips Curve', *Federal Reserve Bank of Richmond Economic Review*, 71: 17–24.

Leeson, R. and Young, W. (2008) 'Mythical expectations', in R. Leeson (ed.) *The Anti-Keynesian Tradition*, New York: Palgrave MacMillan.

Lucas, R.E., Jr. (1976) 'Econometric policy evaluation: a critique', *Carnegie-Rochester Conference Series on Public Policy*, 1: 19–46.

McNees, S. (1992) 'How large are economic forecast errors?', *New England Economic Review*, July–August: 25–33.

Phelps, E. (1970) *Microeconomic Foundations of Employment and Inflation Theory*, New York: W.W. Norton.

Phillips, A.W. (1958) 'The relation between unemployment and the rate of change of money wage rates in the United Kingdom, 1861–1957', *Economica*, 25: 283–99.

Samuelson, P.A. and Solow, R.M. (1960) 'Analytical aspects of anti-inflation policy', *American Economic Review*, 50: 177–94.

Siegel, J. (2002) *Stocks for the Long Run,* 3rd edition, New York: McGraw-Hill.

Solow, R.M. (2010) Testimony before the House Committee on Science and Technology, July 20, 2010, available at http://democrats.science.house.gov/Media/file/Commdocs/hearings/2010/Oversight/20july/Solow_Testimony.pdf

23

THE RISE AND FALL OF THE BRETTON WOODS SYSTEM

Barry Eichengreen

Romanticizing the Bretton Woods System

The Bretton Woods international monetary system is all too easily romanticized. There is the high drama of an international conference in the leafy resort town of Bretton Woods, New Hampshire over three weeks in the summer of 1944. There is the compelling tale of two great minds, John Maynard Keynes and Harry Dexter White, crossing intellectual swords over the shape of the postwar monetary world. There is the romantic assertion that the establishment of the Bretton Woods System inaugurated an era of international monetary and financial stability the likes of which the world has never seen before or since, and in so doing gave birth to a golden quarter-century of economic growth.

The Bretton Woods System is also too easily confused. For some the term "Bretton Woods System" connotes the international monetary institution, the International Monetary Fund, created as a result of the Bretton Woods negotiations, and the regime of pegged but adjustable exchange rates that it helped to oversee from the late 1940s through the early 1970s. Others use the label to denote something more specific: a system in which countries kept their currencies stable and also maintained convertibility for international transactions on current account – something that was done by more than a small handful of countries only from the beginning of 1959. Still others mean something broader: a system or order involving not just stable exchange rates but also an open trading system and a social compact in which capital and labor agreed to suppress distributional conflicts in order to share the fruits of growth.

Finally, experience with the Bretton Woods System is too easily distorted. It is used with ulterior motives. Some point to Bretton Woods as "proof" that it is possible for central banks and governments to stabilize exchange rates for extended periods. Others point to Bretton Woods in order to "show" that the world would be better off with stricter limits on international capital flows. Still others point to experience under Bretton Woods, when European countries and Japan pegged their currencies to the dollar and enjoyed a long period of export-led growth, to "substantiate" their argument that China is justified in pursuing analogous policies today (Dooley, Folkerts-Landau and Garber 2003).

The only protection against this tendency to romanticize, confuse and distort the Bretton Woods System is the discipline of evidence. In other words, it is to consider the history.

The rise of the Bretton Woods System

The successful conclusion of the International Monetary and Financial Conference of the United and Associated Nations (the Bretton Woods Conference) and the ability of the 44 countries assembled there to reach an agreement on the shape of the postwar monetary order reflected years of careful planning and negotiation, first at the national level, then bilaterally between the United Kingdom and the United States, and finally at a preparatory conference in Atlantic City, New Jersey, while World War II was still underway. In formulating their plans, the British and American teams, led by Keynes and White, channeled the lessons drawn by their countries' respective policy elites from efforts to rebuild the international monetary and financial order after World War I and the disastrous consequences that flowed from the subsequent collapse of that laboriously reconstructed system. Although other countries had views and offered plans, with France still occupied, the Soviet Union preoccupied, and Germany and Japan still enemy powers, the negotiations were effectively an Anglo–American show.

The Americans attached priority to reconstructing an open trading system and believed that international monetary arrangements should be subordinated to this end. The U.S. displayed the self-serving confidence characteristic of the leading exporter in insisting that countries that trade with one another do not go to war. (British commentators like Norman Angell (1910) had made analogous arguments before World War I when Britain was the leading trading nation.) To promote trade and cement the peace, the Americans observed, exchange rates should be fixed. Countries should be required to remove controls, financial and nonfinancial, that might limit freedom of international transactions.

The British view was that it would be folly to repeat the post–World War I mistake of attempting to restore fixed exchange rates and unfettered capital flows. For Keynes and his colleagues, those arrangements had been associated with the descent into the Great Depression; their abandonment had been associated with recovery. More recently, Britain had suffered through nearly five years of total war, including not just extensive loss of life but aerial bombardment of its major cities, and incurred an immense burden of financial obligations to its allies. Informed by their country's wartime loss of shipping capacity and by the fact that it would need substantial amounts of imported capital equipment for postwar reconstruction, British planners anticipated that the balance of payments would be weak. It followed that they favored more scope for adjusting exchange rates, more restrictions on freedom of capital transactions, and more credits for deficit countries.

From this starting point flowed the compromise enshrined in the Articles of Agreement of the International Monetary Fund (IMF). Exchange rates would be pegged within plus/minus one percent margins to satisfy the Americans but adjustable to reassure the British that they would not be prevented by a weak balance of payments from pursuing full employment. To ensure that countries would not manipulate their currencies at their neighbors' expense, such exchange rate changes would be permitted only in the event that a country experienced a "fundamental [balance-of-payments] disequilibrium," a condition to be verified by the IMF. Current account restrictions would be lifted to encourage trade but controls on capital flows retained to provide insulation from destabilizing capital movements. Countries experiencing temporary balance-of-payments difficulties would be able to borrow from the Fund to ease the burden of adjustment, although the IMF quotas conceded by the Americans, who anticipated being lenders and not borrowers, were only a fraction of those proposed by the British.

It is revealing also to recall what the Articles of Agreement did not include. They did not include a concrete, binding schedule for completion of the transition to current account convertibility, although the Americans did seek to impose one on the British as a condition of the postwar Anglo–American loan. This meant that it would be some years – in practice close to 15 – before the Bretton Woods System was fully up and running. The Articles did not include effective sanctions to force chronic balance-of-payments-surplus countries to adjust – the Americans not wishing to expose themselves to the risk of being sanctioned – only a vaguely-worded scarce currency clause that was never invoked. This allowed one of the awkward asymmetries that had riddled the operation of the interwar gold standard to carry over to the postwar period. They did not include a precise definition of the condition of "fundamental disequilibrium" that was supposed to govern the adjustment of currencies. This allowed a country when contemplating whether to adjust its currency to do pretty much as it pleased. They did not provide for the creation of a new international reserve unit, which Keynes dubbed "bancor," to augment the supply of international reserves. While gold was still recognized and held as international reserves, its new supply was limited. This meant that the main way for countries to accumulate additional reserves was by running balance-of-payments surpluses vis-à-vis the United States, and acquiring dollars, which were "as good as gold," reflecting American economic and financial might and the U.S. commitment to pay out the yellow metal to foreign governments and central banks at a fixed price of $35 an ounce. This would turn out to be a very serious flaw in the structure of the system.

Between 1945 and 1958, the broad outlines of the Bretton Woods System took shape. Countries declared par values for their currencies against gold and the dollar. They began relaxing and removing exchange controls and import licensing requirements. European countries, having negotiated bilateral clearing arrangements as a way of restarting their trade, moved next to multilateralize them. The 1949 devaluations against the dollar, in which Britain led and some two dozen other countries followed, moved Europe another step toward competitive balance against the United States. This helped to relieve the so-called "dollar shortage," reduce the U.S. trade surplus, and permit further market opening in Europe. Participation in the Marshall Plan obliged the recipients to stabilize their currencies and liberalize their trade but also enabled them to augment their international reserves. The European Payments Union, established with seed money from the Marshall Plan, was an early reserve pooling arrangement and provided insurance for countries like West Germany experiencing temporary balance-of-payments difficulties in the course of opening up. The Organization of European Economic Cooperation, the club of Marshall Plan recipients (and forerunner of today's OECD), promulgated a Code of Liberalization to coordinate the movement to current account convertibility.

There were only a couple of additional parity changes in this period. In practice, the main way in which countries regulated the balance of payments from the late 1940s through the late 1950s was by varying the pace at which they relaxed and removed exchange controls. Adjustment was easier against the backdrop of relatively rapid growth made possible by reconstruction and catch-up following the war. It was easier as a result of the social compact sometimes known as the Bretton Woods order. This was also an era in which, it should be noted, the IMF played a limited role. The U.S. did not permit Marshall Plan recipients to borrow from the Fund, since such double dipping would have undercut the ability of America to influence their economic policies. The IMF was given little notice and not asked permission when the UK devalued in 1949. West Germany only joined the Fund in 1952. The first Standby Arrangement and with it development of the notion that conditions should be attached to IMF loan packages came also in 1952. The IMF provided assistance to the UK in 1956, averting another disorderly sterling devaluation, but only after Britain agreed to withdraw its troops from Suez and the U.S. permitted the Fund to go ahead. The IMF also provided France with Standby Arrangements in 1956 and 1958 as the country experienced serial balance-of-payments problems. The Fund was active also in Latin America, but its lending programs there were small.

The high Bretton Woods System

The 1960s were the heyday of Bretton Woods. Technically one should speak of the "long 1960s" from 1959 through 1971 as the heyday of Bretton Woods or the high Bretton Woods era. It was inaugurated by the European move to current account convertibility at the end of 1958. Japan then joined the club by instituting current account convertibility (essentially allowing its currency to be freely bought and sold for trade-related transactions) in 1964. From this point, adjustments in domestic policy and, failing that, IMF finance were needed to maintain and restore balance-of-payments equilibrium and keep exchange rates stable. Considerable importance was attached to the latter. Devaluation was seen as resulting in a loss of face, revaluation in a loss of competitiveness, and on both grounds created a reluctance to allow changes in par values. Among the industrial countries there were a limited number of devaluations, like Britain's in 1967, and revaluations, like Germany's and the Netherlands's in 1961 and 1969, but these were rare. With capital mobility continually on the rise, discussion of parity changes could excite anticipatory capital flows, making it safer to avoid even contemplation of such changes. Such exchange rate changes as occurred were often excessively delayed and, as a result, took the form of unsettlingly large devaluations and revaluations rather than a series of timely, small adjustments.

With limited demand for its services in the industrial world, the IMF became increasingly active in the developing world, negotiating nearly 200 Standby Arrangements with literally scores of countries. And with African independence, there were more developing countries to become active in. There were a substantial number of step devaluations of currencies by developing countries – by one count more than 40 in this period.

The United States was at the center of the high Bretton Woods System. By 1959, its currency had been pegged to gold at a fixed nominal price for fully a quarter of a century, something that no other country could claim. The liquidity of its financial markets was unrivalled, and those markets were open to foreign central banks and governments (or at least to the central banks and governments of the Free World). The U.S. was not just industrial producer and exporter *numero uno* but also the leading foreign investor (causing the Europeans to complain of the "invasion" of American companies and U.S. "expropriation" of European firms). It followed as night follows day that other countries pegged their currencies to the dollar and, when seeking to augment their reserves, accumulated U.S. Treasury securities.

But virtually from the start of the high Bretton Woods years – from 1959 – questions arose about the stability of the system. With growth in the catch-up economies of Europe and Japan outstripping that in the United States, doubts were expressed about U.S. competitiveness and complaints registered in Washington, D.C. about the inability of the U.S. to devalue – or, putting the point in more politically-correct terms, about the reluctance of the competitors to revalue. The U.S. current account surplus disappeared in 1959. The OEEC warned that Europe's chronic payments surpluses and the ongoing drain of gold from the United States threatened the stability of the system. The gross foreign liabilities of U.S. monetary authorities, deposit banks and the government first exceeded U.S. monetary gold reserves in 1960, creating the at least hypothetical possibility of a run on the country's monetary gold. Senator John F. Kennedy was compelled to issue a statement in the late stages of that year's presidential campaign that, in the event he was elected, he would not attempt to devalue the dollar or, in Rooseveltian fashion, tinker with the price of gold.

To be sure, other countries could and did take action to support the operation of the system. The lending capacity of the IMF was expanded in 1961. Another locus of cooperation was the Gold Pool, established to maintain the link between the official U.S. price of gold of $35 and the price at which gold traded on the London market (Eichengreen 2007). The motivation was fear that, were the market price to significantly exceed the official price, the incentive for arbitrage would become irresistible and a run on U.S. gold reserves would ensue. The European members of the pool (France, Germany, Italy, the UK, Belgium, the Netherlands and Switzerland) agreed to provide half of however much gold had to be supplied to the market in order to prevent the price from rising significantly above $35, thereby sharing this burden with the United States and limiting the danger that market pressures would exhaust U.S. gold reserves.

But while other countries had a collective interest in preserving the system, they also had an individual interest in maintaining their gold reserves. In the early years of the agreement, gold sales by the two main producers, South Africa and the Soviet Union, were enough to stabilize the market price. Starting in 1965, however, this was no longer true, forcing members of the pool to sell gold into the market. Several European governments quietly reconstituted their gold reserves by demanding that the U.S. redeem some of their U.S. Treasury securities for gold. In 1967, France made its dissatisfaction with the arrangement known by withdrawing from the pool. Soon thereafter, in March 1968, the London price of gold shot up – in effect, there was a run on the pool – and its operation was suspended. The private market price of gold was cut loose from the official price. This marked the advent of the "two tier gold market" in which official transactions in gold took place at one price, for the moment $35 an ounce, while private transactions took place at a higher price determined by the balance of supply and demand.

The fundamental factor driving these developments was, of course, the entirely natural tendency for other advanced countries to begin closing the gap in per capita incomes and productivity vis-à-vis the United States that had opened up in the course of three decades of depression and war. The result was a world economy whose growth outpaced that of the United States, the country that effectively monopolized the provision of international reserves. In particular, the world economy was growing faster than U.S. gold reserves which were not growing at all.

This flaw at the heart of the Bretton Woods System had been identified already by the Belgian economist Robert Triffin in 1947 (Triffin 1947). With the expansion of the volume of world trade and payments, countries naturally sought to augment the reserve stocks with which they smoothed their balance of payments and defended their exchange rates against speculation. But the more they accumulated U.S. dollars, the greater became the disproportion between U.S. monetary obligations to foreigners and U.S. gold reserves, and in turn the incentive to run on U.S. gold. In principle, the United States could take steps to strengthen its balance of payments and limit the pace at which foreigners accumulated claims on the country, be those steps devaluation of the dollar, foreign acquiescence permitting, or the adoption of restrictive monetary and fiscal policies. But then other countries would be denied additional reserves. The international economy would be starved of liquidity, and global trade and growth would suffer. Either way – whether or not the U.S. provided other countries with additional dollars – tensions would build up. Triffin wrote of this problem repeatedly over the course of two decades. In time it became known as the Triffin Dilemma.

If the flaw in the structure of the system was well known, then so was the solution. This was to create through the IMF a synthetic unit, along the lines of Keynes' bancor, to supplement and ultimately supplant the dollar as international reserves. With benefit of hindsight, it is remarkable that serious discussion of the possibility got underway only in 1964, fully 20 years after the Bretton Woods Conference and five years after the restoration of current account convertibility in Europe. Discussions were initiated by a committee of the Group of Ten, made up of representatives of the U.S., Canada, Japan and seven European countries. Although the clock was ticking on Bretton Woods, considerable time was needed to reach an agreement. U.S. officials were initially reluctant to support the creation of a synthetic reserve unit for fear that this would diminish the international role of the dollar. French officials were reluctant on the grounds that doing so might relieve the pressure on the United States to reduce its balance of payments deficit. German officials feared the inflationary consequences.

But as the Gold Pool teetered, negotiations acquired a sense of urgency. Discussions proceeded on two tracks: in yet another Group of Ten study group, and in the Executive Board of the IMF. The U.S. came around to the view that supplementing the dollar with another form of reserves was unavoidable. Germany accepted the role of obedient ally. France, finding itself without support from other European countries, withdrew its opposition.

In this way agreement was finally reached on authorizing the IMF to issue Special Drawing Rights (SDRs). SDRs were initially linked to gold at a value of one U.S. dollar. The new unit would be allocated to IMF members in proportion to their existing rights to borrow from the Fund. Governments would be obliged to accept these bookkeeping claims from other governments and in transactions with the IMF itself. Through the periodic issuance of SDRs, the IMF could now provide countries with the additional reserves needed to support their expanding trade and payments without adding to the dollar overhang. It was agreed to amend the IMF's Articles of Agreement to provide for issuance of the new unit in August 1967.

The fall of the Bretton Woods System

But the hour was already late. The amendment to the Articles still had to be ratified, a process that was only completed in May 1968. Next followed legislative ratification by a supermajority of IMF members. It was then necessary to activate the facility and actually create SDRs, overcoming the reservations of countries like Germany that still feared inflationary effects. A first allocation finally took place in January 1970. By this time the foreign liabilities of the Fed, U.S. banks and the U.S. government exceeded U.S. monetary gold reserves by a factor of four. It was unlikely that even massive issuance of SDRs, sufficient to prevent this ratio from rising further, would be enough to stabilize the system. It seemed only a matter of time before there was a run on U.S. gold reserves. And the fact that U.S. policy turned increasingly expansionary, shifting the U.S. merchandise trade balance first from surplus to balance in 1968–69 and then, after a brief recession-induced respite, back into deficit, only reinforced the pressure.

The slow-motion run on U.S. gold gained momentum in the first half of 1971. In early August, France leaked its intention of cashing in dollars for gold. Then on August 13, seeking to move before it was too late, Britain asked the United States to swap $750 million of dollars for gold. In response, President Richard Nixon shut the gold window, suspending the payment of gold to official foreign claimants (Gowa 1983). This was the first of a series of milestones leading to the eventual end of the Bretton Woods System.

The United States, as the nth country in a system with $n-1$ exchange rates, had been frustrated by its inability to devalue. With other countries declaring par values for their currencies in dollars, the U.S. could not alter its exchange rate without their cooperation. The crisis presented an opportunity to change this status quo. In conjunction with the decision to shut the gold window, Nixon imposed a temporary 10 percent import surcharge to be removed only upon the successful conclusion of currency realignment negotiations.

Those negotiations occupied the balance of 1971. The U.S. sought a sizeable devaluation; the American economy's recovery from the 1969–70 recession continued to disappoint, and there was an election looming in 1972; both considerations inclined it to favor a sharp change in the value of the dollar. But other governments feared that substantial revaluation of their currencies would mean a substantial loss of competitiveness. At a bilateral summit in the Azores, U.S. and French officials squared the circle, agreeing that the dollar should be devalued by precisely 7.9 percent. Then in a Bretton-Woods-style conference at the Smithsonian Institution in Washington, D.C. in December, the Group of Ten agreed by how much each individual currency would be revalued by the dollar to achieve this now officially-enshrined figure.

But the idea that countries had scientifically calibrated the precise amounts by which exchange rate parities had to be altered in order to restore balance and stability was, of course, an illusion. The Smithsonian Agreement, hailed by Nixon as "the most significant monetary achievement in the history of the world," did nothing to resolve the contradictions of the system. Bretton Woods as reconstructed at the Smithsonian staggered on through the spring of 1973, when another run on the dollar commenced. Capital flowed out of the United States and into its Group of Ten partners, subjecting them to increasingly intense inflationary pressures. Seeing no alternative, they cut loose from the dollar, allowing their currencies to float upward. This marked the definitive end of Bretton Woods.

Implications

What broader implications flow from this experience? A first implication is that Bretton Woods is properly seen not as a unique epoch in international monetary history but as one of a series of stages in the evolution of international monetary relations over the course of the twentieth century. Bretton Woods shared important elements in common with its predecessor – the dual roles of gold and the dollar in providing international liquidity, for example – and also with the system that succeeded it, in which the dollar played only a slightly diminished role. Bretton Woods' pegged-but-adjustable exchange rates were a stage in the transition from the pegged rates of the gold-exchange standard to the still more flexible rates of the regime that followed.

Second, international monetary relations in this period rested heavily on a special set of historical circumstances. They rested on the economic dominance of the United States in the aftermath of World War II, which allowed for the construction of a system that revolved around the dollar. They rested on the fact of the Cold War, which provided powerful incentives for the Group of Ten countries to cooperate in supporting and stabilizing the system. They rested on the potential for rapid catch-up growth across much of the industrialized world – rapid growth making it easier to reconcile the imperatives of internal and external balance. They rested on the legacy of the Great Depression, which bequeathed tight capital controls and rigorous financial regulation that suppressed the worst manifestations of financial instability.

But, third and finally, the Bretton Woods years are not accurately seen as an interlude of admirable stability. In fact, the Bretton Woods era was characterized by an ongoing sense of crisis. Long before the system was fully functional, keen observers worried about its demise. It operated in the manner intended by its architects for barely a decade, from 1959 through 1968 – or, depending on what one means by "in the manner," perhaps through 1971. That short period saw continuous reform negotiations that acquired increased urgency as the system displayed growing signs of instability. This continuing pressure for reform, reflecting dissatisfaction with the operation of the international monetary mechanism, was another thing that the Bretton Woods System had in common with the regime that succeeded it.

References

Angell, N. (1910) *The Great Illusion: A Study of the Relation of Military Power in Nations to Their Economic and Social Advantage,* London: W. Heinemann.

Dooley, M., Folkerts-Landau, D. and Garber, P. (2003) 'An essay on the revived Bretton Woods system', NBER Working Paper no. 9971. Cambridge, MA: NBER.

Eichengreen, B. (2007) *Global Imbalances and the Lessons of Bretton Woods,* Cambridge, MA: MIT Press.

Gowa, J. (1983) *Closing the Gold Window: Domestic Politics and the End of Bretton Woods,* Ithaca, NY: Cornell University Press.

Triffin, R. (1947) 'National central banking and the international economy', *Postwar Economic Studies,* 7: 46–81.

24

DISINFLATION, 1979–1982

Allan H. Meltzer[1]

Disinflation from 1979 to 1982 is a unique event in U.S. economic history. All previous disinflations – reductions in the inflation rate – followed wartime inflations. The disinflation that began in 1979 occurred almost a decade after the Vietnam War ended, and it was unrelated to the end of that war. Also, the disinflation came after several earlier attempts failed because the Federal Reserve, federal government and many in the public considered the cost of disinflation too high. By 1979, the public, and their representatives, were willing to accept temporarily higher unemployment to reduce inflation.

Start of the disinflation

Disinflation started in October 1979, a few months after President Carter appointed Paul Volcker Chairman of the Board of Governors of the Federal Reserve System. At the time, Volcker served as President of the Federal Reserve Bank of New York, but he had served earlier as Undersecretary for Monetary Affairs in the Nixon Treasury Department and, earlier, as a Treasury official in the Kennedy administration. He was critical of the Federal Reserve's policy and had dissented in the spring of 1979. The New York president is ex officio vice-chair of the Federal Open Market Committee (FOMC) that decides on monetary policy. Dissent by the vice-chair is rare, possibly unique on these occasions.

Paul Volcker dissented because he was opposed to the rising rate of inflation and the costs inflation imposed on the economy. In August 1979, when he assumed leadership of the Federal Reserve, the reported annualized inflation rate reached 11 percent, the highest peacetime rate to that time. His appointment not only put a committed anti-inflationist in charge of monetary policy but gave responsibility to a trained economist who accepted that inflation resulted from money growth that exceeded growth of real output. He described his view as "practical monetarism."

The appointment was a major change for President Carter. His administration had never shown much commitment to price stability or low inflation. Its prior anti-inflation efforts consisted mainly of rhetoric urging restraint by business and labor unions supported by guidelines for less inflationary private actions. These actions had little, if any, effect, but guidelines and administrative action were the main recommendations he received from his advisers.

When the president interviewed Paul Volcker, Volcker told him that he intended to act more determinedly against inflation than his predecessors had done. President Carter assured him that he wanted less inflation. Neither the president nor Volcker thought at the time that the Federal Reserve would raise the federal funds rate to 20 percent or that the unemployment rate would reach 10.8 percent.

President Carter's acceptance of disinflation led by the Federal Reserve probably had two principal origins. First, polling data at the time showed the public believed inflation was the principal domestic problem. That had not happened during the long rise in the inflation rate. President Carter planned to run for reelection, so the public's concern became his. Second, he lost confidence in the advice he received about inflation. He replaced Secretary of the Treasury Blumenthal, his chief economic spokesman, with Federal Reserve Chairman Miller. The exchange rate crisis in October 1978 may have convinced him that rising inflation and a depreciating exchange rate responded to excessive monetary growth. The first U.S. response to exchange rate depreciation of 14 percent against the German mark and 23 percent against the Japanese yen between May and October 1978 failed. In late October, the administration announced policy changes to strengthen the dollar. The new policy called for fiscal changes and voluntary wage-price guidelines.

The market's response came swiftly. Following the policy announcement, the dollar quickly fell 1.7 percent against the mark and the yen and about 4 percent in the week against an index of developed country exchange rates. The United States responded by raising the Federal Reserve discount rate by 1 percentage point and by offering bonds denominated in foreign currencies. The Federal Reserve also raised reserve requirements for large time deposits.

The market's reaction to these monetary changes reversed the decline in the dollar exchange rate. The dollar index rose 5.3 percent and continued to rise. Tighter monetary policy convinced market participants that the United States intended to strengthen the dollar. President Carter learned that monetary policy achieved what earlier actions did not.

The president's Domestic Policy Adviser, Stuart Eizenstat, described Volcker's appointment this way: "With inflation raging and the president's popularity plunging the president believed the economic situation was dire, and he wanted someone who would apply tough medicine" (Meltzer 2009: 1009).

First steps

Soon after taking office, the Volcker FOMC raised the discount rate. The market did not consider the action a harbinger of sustained anti-inflation policy. Volcker understood that more decisive, sustained action was required, but he was skeptical that the FOMC would vote to raise interest rates high enough, fast enough, to succeed. Further, he did not know how high to raise rates, so he decided to let the market decide. This meant controlling bank reserve growth and had the benefit that he could shift responsibility for higher interest rates to the market and away from the Federal Reserve.

On a trip to Belgrade for the International Monetary Fund meeting, he explained his plan to control reserves and reduce money growth to Treasury Secretary Miller and Council of Economic Advisors Chair Schultze. En route the plane stopped in Germany where Chancellor Schmidt strongly endorsed the plan. After an early return from Belgrade, Volcker called a special meeting of the FOMC for Saturday, October 6. Volcker proposed reserve targeting as a temporary change to show that the FOMC would make a determined effort to reduce inflation. He insisted on adopting a program at that meeting that would alter expectations. He did not insist on reserve targets.

The October 6 program had three parts. First, the FOMC adopted reserve targeting to reduce money growth (M1) to 5 percent in fourth quarter 1979. The actual vote was 8 to 3, but the 3 who initially opposed changed their votes so the vote could be recorded as unanimous. The committee voted to let the federal funds rise from the prevailing 11.5 percent to as high as 15.5 percent. Second, the Board approved a 12 percent discount rate for New York, a one percentage point increase. All other Reserve banks followed. Third, the Board raised marginal reserve requirements by 8 percentage points for banks with $100 million of managed liabilities. The Board avoided Congressional criticism by limiting the increase to large banks.

The Board hoped that these actions would generate a positive market response. That didn't happen. The market had difficulty in interpreting reserve targeting, so long-term interest rates rose. The Federal Reserve had announced its commitment to anti-inflation action several times before, but it had not followed through when unemployment rose. Markets were not convinced that this time would be different, that the Federal Reserve would maintain the program once recession started.

The commitment to reserve targeting was never absolute. Volcker did not propose to leave the federal funds rate unconstrained. At the October 6, 1979 meeting, he told the members that "in practice the kind of range we have is one-eighth of a point roughly" (Meltzer 2009: 1028, fn. 24). The range would increase. Volcker did not say what the limits would be. He left that to his judgment. In subsequent months, the rate reached 20 percent, a record. Volcker and most others did not anticipate that response. To his credit and the FOMC's determination, they did not prevent the rise.

Markets reacted negatively to the administration's budget proposals in January. Influential members of president's party in Congress criticized monetary policy because it raised interest rates and unemployment. Many had long favored controls that restricted credit. They urged President Carter to change course. The president brought together a group of advisers to discuss credit controls and reductions in government spending. Paul Volcker was a member of the group, despite the Federal Reserve's much discussed independence. The group agreed on some spending reductions and requested the Federal Reserve to impose credit controls. The president submitted some spending reductions to Congress and asked the Federal Reserve to impose controls on consumer and business credit. He left the decision about the types of controls to the Federal Reserve. Since Volcker was part of the advisory group, he supported the recommendation. Only Governor Henry Wallich voted against it.

The Board adopted very modest controls. It exempted credit cards and most consumer borrowing. The public wanted lower inflation, so they acted eagerly to reduce new credit extension. They cut up and mailed credit cards to the Federal Reserve and the Treasury, and they reduced spending and borrowing drastically. Policymakers were surprised, then alarmed, by the response. Controls began in March 1980. Real GDP fell by an annualized rate of almost 8 percentage points in the second quarter. Early in the summer, the Federal Reserve ended controls and began an expansive policy to limit or reverse the decline.

The policy reversal lowered interest rates and increased money growth. Markets reacted by increasing expected inflation. They believed the Federal Reserve had ended its anti-inflation policy to prevent the rise in the unemployment rate. They had seen this response several times; they expected it; and now it was confirmed.

Anti-inflation policy restored

In the fall of 1980, before the November election, the FOMC raised interest rates and renewed its decision to reduce inflation. This time would be different. Paul Volcker was determined to reduce inflation. Ronald Reagan ran for office on a program that promised lower inflation, lower tax rates, renewed economic growth, and increased defense spending. Despite warnings from his aides that high market interest rates would hurt his prospects, President Carter rejected calls for stimulus and did not criticize the Federal Reserve during the 1980 campaign.

Reagan won a decisive election victory including a Republican majority in the Senate. Soon after inauguration, he announced the Economic Recovery Plan. It called for tax rate reduction, spending reduction, and slower money growth.[2]

President Reagan stood firmly behind the anti-inflation policy. His administration was divided. Some "supply-siders" at the Treasury wanted increased money growth to assure that reduced tax rates increased spending for consumption and investment. "Monetarists" wanted slower money growth. The internal argument raged, but President Reagan did not participate. He told the Federal Reserve to continue its policy. For his part, Paul Volcker chose to ignore the divided advice from different parts of the new administration. He proceeded as he wished to proceed.

One impediment to improved monetary control came just at the time the Federal Reserve decided to focus on control of money. After lengthy negotiation, Congress repealed interest rate regulations. Time deposits at commercial banks and thrift associations had been subject to controls whenever market interest rates rose above posted ceiling rates. Removing controls with market interest rates at historic highs caused changes in the public's allocation of deposits that added variability to the portfolio response to high inflation. Money growth rates were very variable and difficult to interpret.

Three Federal Reserve decisions added to the problem of interpreting monetary changes. First, a great deal of attention focused on reported weekly growth rates that are subject to large random variation because of weather, changes in Treasury balances and many other sources including Federal Reserve actions. Second, the Federal Reserve did not have a useful model for member bank borrowing. The Board was reluctant to raise the discount rate it charged for bank borrowing as the federal funds rate rose. At times the banks could borrow at a rate 3 or 4 percentage points below the funds rate. This subsidy increased borrowed reserves and money growth, reducing control. Third, the Federal Reserve adopted lagged reserve accounting in the late 1960s. Required reserves depended on deposits two weeks earlier. If a bank's reserves were insufficient to meet requirements, the bank borrowed from its Reserve bank.

Despite many proposals from its staff and outsiders, the Board did not eliminate lagged reserve accounting until after its experiment with reserve control ended and it no longer mattered. The Board continued the, at times, large subsidy to borrowing. The result: reserve control was erratic. Also, some careful empirical studies suggest that the account manager retreated to interest rate control at times (Schreft 1980).

Volcker made an important change that was critical for success of his policy. He abandoned forecasts of inflation based on the Phillips curve. He insisted that by reducing inflation he would reduce the unemployment rates. The Phillips curve assumed there was a tradeoff; higher inflation reduced the unemployment rate. Volcker pointed out publicly and internally that in the 1970s inflation and unemployment increased together. His policy would lower both, he said.

Early in his chairmanship, he was asked on a popular television show, *Face the Nation*, what he would do when unemployment rose. He replied that the question assumed there was a tradeoff between inflation and unemployment. He believed, to the contrary, that he would lower both. He maintained this position throughout his chairmanship. His successor continued his policy, but the Phillips curve returned as a policy guide after Alan Greenspan retired in 2006.

By abandoning Phillips curve forecasts, Chairman Volcker could make a significant change in Federal Reserve policy. He directed efforts mainly toward reducing inflation. Once credit controls ended, the main policy objective shifted from preventing an increase in unemployment to achieving lower inflation. By insisting that the Federal Reserve controlled reserves, not interest rates, market rates could rise to reflect public concerns about inflation.

Leading Keynesian economists criticized the disinflation policy. James Tobin (1983: 297) said, "I would expect the process to be lengthy and costly, characterized by recession, stunted recoveries, and high and rising unemployment." He was right about cost and rising unemployment, but his estimate that disinflation would take ten years was much too pessimistic and greatly overestimated the cost. Only two years elapsed from the time the Federal Reserve renewed its disinflation policy in October 1980 to the end of the experiment in October 1982. And most of the disinflation ended a few months earlier, but the unemployment rate reached 10.8 percent at its peak in November 1982.

Public support for disinflation helped considerably to make high interest and rising unemployment politically acceptable. The public voted for Ronald Reagan, committed to reducing inflation, and leading members of Congress, including chairs of the House and Senate Banking Committees supported the policy. Criticism rose as the 1982 Congressional election approached. By that time, most of the work had been done. Many observers claim that the high rates paid on time and saving deposits and bank certificates of deposit contributed to some public willingness to support disinflation.

Sustaining anti-inflation policy

Federal Reserve commitment to reduce inflation had happened before. FOMC members spoke about the importance of controlling inflation several times. In previous episodes, their commitment vanished when unemployment rates rose. A comparable change occurred in 1980, when credit controls interrupted the anti-inflation policy.

Volcker made many speeches and testified in Congress to his continuing commitment. He was eager to assure his audience that he did not intend to change direction until inflation fell to low levels. An example from a 1980 press conference illustrates his effort.

> Question: How high an unemployment rate are you prepared to accept in order to break inflation?

> Answer: That kind of puts me in a position of I accept or unaccept or whatever. You know my basic philosophy is over time we have no choice but to deal with the inflationary situation because over time inflation and unemployment go together. … The growth situation and the unemployment situation will be better in an atmosphere of monetary stability than they have been in recent years.
> (Volcker papers, Federal Reserve Bank of New York, Box 97657, January 2, 1980, 6. Quoted in Meltzer 2009: 1034)

Volcker's statement, made repeatedly, changed Federal Reserve policy in two major ways. First, it looked ahead months or years to a time when the policy had its effect on the economy. One of the FOMC's frequent errors is that it responds to current events ignoring the future. Second, Volcker discarded the Phillips curve and greatly reduced Federal Reserve concern about the unemployment rate. Unemployment would fall when inflation fell.

The problem was that market participants and many of the public remained skeptical that the FOMC would maintain the anti-inflation policy. Past experience reinforced by the expansion following the credit control program strengthened these concerns. Despite a return to recession in 1980, interest rates remained high. The ten-year constant maturity Treasury bond reached 13.2 percent in February 1980. Forecasts of expected inflation one quarter ahead reached 9.98 percent in second quarter 1980. The GDP deflator reached a peak at 12.1 percent in fourth quarter 1980.

The Federal Reserve's initial failure to control money growth added to general skepticisms. In October 1979, at the start of the new policy, money growth reached a 14 percent annual rate, against a 4.5 percent rate target for fourth quarter 1979. This was an inauspicious start. The FOMC let the federal funds rate rise to 17 percent, the highest level reached to that time. This painful experience of surges in bank borrowing, money growth, and interest rates would be repeated many times.

The Federal Reserve traditionally gave most attention to current changes in the economy and the financial markets. Volcker recognized that the disinflation policy had to persist for an indefinite time. Presidents Willes (Minneapolis) and Roos (St. Louis) wanted to announce money targets for the next three years to condition market expectations and recognize that disinflation would take time. Governor Teeters led the opposition, pointing out that they did not have enough information to look three years ahead.

Financial deregulation added to the difficulty of interpreting monetary changes. The Fed staff responded by setting monetary targets for a quarter ahead that were consistent with annual growth rates announced in Congressional hearings. But the FOMC never announced the inflation goal it sought to achieve, and it did not discuss whether its objective was to slow or stop steady-state inflation or whether it included one-time price level changes as part of its objective. It did not discuss either objectives or how it defined inflation. In this, it continued to plod along the bumpy path set by current data. The members continued to argue over small differences. They did not respond to President Willes' comment that the best procedure would be to choose a non-inflationary rate of money growth and continue to produce it.

Control of short-term money growth raised concerns about the Fed's ability to reduce inflation. Volcker looked longer-term. His was an eclectic pragmatic position:

> When I look at all these risks, what impresses me is that the greatest risk in the world is not whether we miss our targets or not. I don't want to miss our targets, but we have to put that in perspective of what is going on in the rest of the world.
> (quoted in Meltzer 2009: 1057, at the May 20, 1980 FOMC meeting)

At the meeting Governor Wallich noted that many observers thought the desk had returned to an interest rate control policy. The desk staff agreed.

FOMC members did not have a common way of forecasting future inflation and unemployment. Some like Governor Teeters and the Board staff used a Phillips curve. Others believed the inflation rate depended on expectations and credibility. Volcker was the leader of this group. Once the market became convinced that the FOMC would sustain its policy, expected and actual inflation would fall, and unemployment rate would move toward full employment. No one expressed any belief about when that would happen. As usual, no one attempted to reconcile the different views. Volcker's view proved to be correct.

For 1980 as a whole, M1 growth (currency and demand deposits) was 7.1 percent against a target of 4.0 to 6.5 percent. At one campaign stop, President Carter responded to a question by saying he wished the Federal Reserve would give more attention to interest rates, but he added that the Federal Reserve was an independent agency. That is his only criticism of the policy after credit controls. And he rejected staff proposals for fiscal stimulus, especially an investment tax credit.

Although the FOMC in practice did not exercise tight monetary control, remained uncertain about interpretation of financial market changes, subsidized bank borrowing at times, and did nothing to improve monetary control, the major change remained a shift from adjusting policy to reduce unemployment to reducing the inflation rate. In response to a question about how weak the economy would be allowed to become, Volcker responded:

> We have been put in a position or have taken the position ... that we are going to do something about inflation maybe not regardless of the state of economic activity but certainly more than we did before ... It is a very important distinction.
>
> (Meltzer 2009: 1074)

Persistence succeeded. Early in May 1981, the Board approved an increase in the discount rate to 14 percent and a federal funds rate between 18 and 22 percent. By June, the funds rate was above 19 percent, the highest rate ever recorded. At the time, the unemployment rate was 7.5 percent and rising. The increased interest rate was a strong signal that Volcker's FOMC did not intend to respond to the unemployment rate until inflation fell. Market expectations changed. Within a year, inflation fell to about 4 percent. The evidence of policy persistence was rewarded. In April 1981 the twelve-month rate of CPI price rise fell below 10 percent for the first time in two years.

Fiscal stimulus took the form of reductions in marginal tax rates especially in 1982 and 1983. The rate reductions brought the conflict within the administration to the fore. Supply side proponents wanted faster money growth to increase the response following the tax cuts. Monetarists opposed. They wanted better inflation control. The conflict left Volcker and the FOMC free of administration pressure. They could do as they wished supported by President Reagan, who did not interfere. Volcker continued to claim that lower inflation would reduce unemployment.

The dollar was the world currency. The anti-inflation policy brought a major appreciation of the exchange rate. From its July 1980 trough to its February 1985 peak, the trade-weighted dollar index appreciated 87 percent. Since many loans are dominated in dollars and commodities are priced in dollars, costs of refunding and costs of production rose everywhere. The FOMC discussed intervention, especially coordinated intervention with the Germans, but Volcker was hesitant, and nothing happened.

International loans to developing countries became a major problem. Many developing countries borrowed in dollars to pay for increased oil prices and for other purposes as well. As the dollar appreciated, refunding costs rose. Starting with Mexico in 1982, countries defaulted on debt service, adding a major international dimension to the economy's problems.

A moving average of four-quarter changes in the rate of change of nominal hourly compensation reached a peak of 11 percent at the beginning of 1981. It then began a steady decline until it reached about 4 percent by early 1983. The compensation series is much less influenced by one-time changes in energy and food prices or other discrete events. The FOMC decisions to raise the funds rate in spring 1981 despite 7.5 percent unemployment reinforced the growing belief that the Federal Reserve would continue disinflating. The prompt response of wage growth to the renewed disinflation policy in autumn 1980 contradicted the many computer models showing very slow response to disinflation.

By early 1982, to the extent that the FOMC had a consensus on policy, it fractured. Monthly money growth rates fluctuated over a wide range. Frank Morris (Boston) wanted to continue disinflation but end monetary targets. Governor Nancy Teeters wanted to expand enough to reduce the unemployment rate. Pressure for policy change also came from Congress. These pressures increased as the mid-term election approached.

Paul Volcker acknowledged the control problems, but he remained committed to the policy and procedures. The data suggest that beginning in February 1982, the Federal Reserve used an interest rate target (Meltzer 2009: 1099–1100). Nevertheless, despite a 9 percent unemployment rate, in March 1982, the FOMC voted 9 to 2 to keep the federal funds rate between 12 and 16 percent.

Volcker actively defended the policy before many different groups. One of these was the homebuilders, one of the industries most adversely affected by high interest rates. Volcker told their convention that the Federal Reserve had to continue the policy until inflation fell to low levels. Relaxing restraint postponed disinflation. The Federal Reserve would have to start over. Skepticism about its commitment would have to be overcome again. Despite their financial losses, the builders applauded his forthright statement.

Ending "practical monetarism"

The retreat from "practical monetarism" differed from its start. In October 1979, the Federal Reserve wanted to publicize the major changes. From July to November 1982, it avoided explicit announcements. Volcker directed the decisions and actions, changing slowly in a series of stages after observing market and public responses.

Second, FOMC members wanted to reduce interest rates. Governor Teeters was the most strident, but she had support from Governors Gramley, Rice and Partee. Events appear to have been more important than the Governor's criticisms. At the July 1, 1982 Board meeting, the Board approved a $700 million loan to Mexico under the "swap" program. Both central banks concealed the loan by transferring the loan on the day before reserves were added and returning the money the next day. But there was no doubt in Volcker's mind that continued Mexican debt service was at risk. Loans to Mexico from nine major U.S. banks amounted to $60 billion, 45 percent of the banks' capital. And Mexico was not alone. Loans to all Latin American countries amounted to twice the lending banks' capital. Most of the countries seemed likely to follow Mexico into default.

Heightened domestic financial fragility added to the problems that policy had to confront. In May, a small securities firm, Drysdale, was unable to pay interest on the government securities it had sold short. Drysdale had about $20 million in capital but $6.5 billion in securities; it owed $160 million in interest payments to nearly 30 financial lenders. In late June an Oklahoma bank, Penn Square, became bankrupt. It had large loans to oil companies that became worthless when oil prices fell. Major banks had bought some of Penn Square's loans. Continental Illinois held $1 billion. It had financed its lending by borrowing in the short-term market. Foreign banks were among the lenders to Continental. The problem seemed likely to grow.

In July, Volcker began to shift back to targeting the federal funds rate. At its May meeting, the FOMC lowered the funds rate to a 10 to 15 percent range voting 11 to 1 for the lower rate.

Real long-term rates remained as high as 7.5 percent. Real GDP growth rose 1.2 percent in the second quarter but fell at a 3.2 percent rate in the third quarter. As election approached, Congress became more active. Legislation setting money targets or putting a ceiling on interest rates gained supporters but did not pass. White House Chief of Staff, James Baker, hinted that perhaps Federal Reserve independence should be curtailed.

At the FOMC meeting, talk was about bankruptcies, banking distress, and the difficulty of interpreting money growth rates. Pressed by economic events and political pressures, the FOMC moved to lower the funds rate. Volcker urged gradual steps fearing that a large change would arouse inflationary expectations and force reversal. On July 19, the Board approved a 0.5 percent reduction in the discount rate to 11.5 percent followed by further reductions that reached 10 percent on August 26. The funds rate followed. By late August nominal Treasury bond yields fell to 12.5 percent, the lowest rate since January 1981.

The disinflation was over, but the announced end did not come until October. Between July and October, the FOMC continued discussions of the desirability of policy changes. A principal argument against was that the move would be interpreted as a response to rising pressure from Congress ahead of the election. One example was a bill introduced by Senator Byrd (WV) requiring the Federal Reserve to lower interest rates and end reserve targeting. Many senators joined in the attack on independence.

Volcker steered between the two extremes. He gradually lowered the funds rate and, at a telephone conference on September 24, he proposed targeting member bank borrowing. This returned the FOMC to the indirect interest rate target it used in the 1920s, similar to the free reserve target of the 1950s.

The market was slow to recognize that policy changed in July. When money growth rose in early September without a response by the Fed, stock price indexes rose 4 percent in a week. The disinflation policy ended. But no announcement came from the Fed until October.

At the October 5 FOMC meeting, the few remaining vestiges of reserve targeting and monetary control ended. Volcker spoke first to state his concerns about foreign trade, financial fragility internationally and domestically, and dollar appreciation that exacerbated the Latin American debt problems.

In August he had asked the committee to give him authority to prevent an increase in market rates. They refused, so rates rose. At the October meeting, he again requested that authority. He would not accept a renewed restriction on his freedom to implement "an operational approach that modestly moves the funds rate down" (Meltzer 2009: 1119.)

M1 rose at a 20 percent annual rate in October. The Federal Reserve did not respond. When Volcker spoke to the Business Council, he insisted that policy had not changed. Special factors affecting monetary aggregates became the explanation. Volcker continued to claim that the rejection of money targets was a temporary change. The Federal Reserve did not announce a new operating tactic.

Conclusion

The 1979–82 disinflation differs from most Federal Reserve postwar actions in two principal ways. First, it gave principal emphasis to inflation control and much less attention to unemployment. Volcker believed and often said that inflation and the unemployment rate would fall together. He dismissed forecasts based on a Phillips curve tradeoff. Time proved him right. By the mid-1980s, the economy began the longest period on record with steady growth, small recessions, low inflation and low unemployment rates.

Second, the Volcker Fed focused on a goal – lower inflation – that could be reached only if policy continued to pursue that goal. The Federal Reserve before Volcker was overly responsive to near-term events over which it could have little influence. After 2004, the Fed returned to its former policy.

The end of reserve targeting and a return to rapid growth in 1983 did not end skepticism. Real interest rates on long-term Treasury bonds remained elevated until 1985. Markets seemed convinced that with growth, inflation would return. When that didn't happen, Federal Reserve credibility strengthened.

The recovery after 1982 began with historically high real interest rates. As on many other prior occasions, real base growth dominated real interest rates. Real base growth declined before every recession from 1920 to 1991. Real interest rates often do not rise in advance of recessions. And as in the recovery after 1982, the economy recovered and grew despite historically high real long-term interest rates. Economists and central bankers have been slow to read that message.

The 1979–82 policy succeeded because the Volcker Fed persisted. Many skeptics who doubted that the Fed would ignore the rise in unemployment changed their opinion when the FOMC raised interest rates in spring 1981 despite high unemployment. Many of the public supported the policy. They wanted an end to high inflation. Most members of Congress supported the effort. President Reagan actively encouraged Volcker.

Volcker's commitment was an essential reason for success in lowering inflation. Economists err, however, if they neglect public and political support. Congress and the administration can hinder or prevent the Federal Reserve from achieving its objectives. One lesson from the Volcker disinflation is that models of optimal policy err seriously if they neglect politics and political economy.

Notes

1 Volume 2, Book 2 of Meltzer (2009) is the basis of this chapter and has much supporting detail.
2 I wrote a draft of the section on monetary policy. The administration moderated my proposal at the Fed's request.

References

Meltzer, A.H. (2009) *A History of the Federal Reserve: Volume 2, Book 2*, Chicago, IL: University of Chicago Press.
Schreft, S.L. (1980) 'Credit controls: 1980', *Federal Reserve Bank of Richmond Economic Review*, 76: 25–51.
Tobin, J. (1983) 'Okun on macroeconomic policy: a final comment', in J. Tobin (ed.) *Macroeconomics, Prices and Quantities*, pp. 297–300, Washington, DC: Brookings.

25

THE RISE OF CHINA

Loren Brandt

Introduction

Since the onset of economic reform in the late 1970s, China has enjoyed rates of growth in real GDP in the vicinity of 8 percent per year, and the Chinese economy today is nearly 15 times larger than it was 35 years ago (NBS 2010). Of course, on a per capita basis, GDP in purchasing power parity (PPP) terms is still only one-fifth of that in the most advanced countries.[1] However, with a population of nearly 1.3 billion, the Chinese economy is on track in the next few years to surpass that of the U.S. as the world's largest. By fact of its size and high growth rate, China's economy is currently the source of around 20 percent of the annual growth in global GDP. Today, China figures prominently in nearly every pressing international issue from global recovery to global warming.

This is not the first time in history that the Chinese economy was quantitatively so important. Estimates of Dwight Perkins (1967) and Angus Madisson (2007) suggest that with a population in excess of 300 million at the end of the eighteenth century the Chinese economy was producing close to a quarter of the world's GDP.[2] Moreover, Kenneth Pomeranz (2000), Li Bozhong (2000) and others contend that in China's most advanced localities, including the Jiangnan region in the Lower Yangzi, and the Pearl River Delta, China achieved a level of development and standard of living that may have paralleled that in the more advanced parts of Europe.[3]

China's exact level of development at the end of the eighteenth century is a source of ongoing academic debate (Allen et. al. 2011). Probably much less in dispute is the economy's trajectory, and the fact that for much of the next 150–175 years or so, China became an economic laggard. As a result, the gap in most measurable indicators of the level of economic and social development between China and the rapidly industrializing countries in the West, and later, Japan and the Asian Tigers (Korea, Hong Kong, Taiwan and Singapore) only widened until the onset of economic reforms in the late 1970s began to reverse the trend.

The long fall before the rise

The nineteenth century was not kind to China and a combination of external shocks and internal disruption (the White Lotus Rebellion, 1796–1805 and the Taiping Rebellion, 1850–

1864) revealed critical weaknesses in its traditional institutions and political economy. In the historiography of China for the period, probably no event has taken on more import—symbolic or otherwise—than the Opium Wars.

Prior to the 1800s, China's trade with the rest of the world was a highly imbalanced affair, with Chinese exports of tea, silk and porcelains helping to finance imports of New World silver that supported the rising commercialization in the economy.[4] British merchants, frustrated by the difficulty of penetrating the Chinese market and the constraints of the "Canton" system[5], lobbied London for the better part of half of a century to obtain wider access from China for their goods and wares. Britain largely failed, but in the context of a triangular trade involving India, merchants found a market for opium in China.

The rise in opium imports the first third of the nineteenth century was accompanied by a shift in China's balance of payments and a reversal of longstanding silver inflows. Believing that these were "causally" linked[6] and concerned about their negative impact, China tried to put an end to the opium trade, with war (First Opium War, 1839–1842) soon breaking out. British military superiority quickly won the day, and with the signing of the Nanking Treaty of 1842, China entered into the first of a series of treaties commonly referred to as the "Unequal Treaties".[7] Under the Nanking Treaty, China was required to make reparation payments to the victors, to open up four ports to international trade, and ceded Hong Kong to Great Britain for 150 years. Terms of future treaties dictated the opening up of additional treaty ports, the loss of tariff autonomy, and the extension of rights of extra-territoriality in the treaty ports themselves.

Through the last half of the nineteenth century, trade grew, but overall, the impact of this "forced" opening on the Chinese economy was geographically confined and relatively small (Murphey 1977). By the end of the century, imports and exports combined still represented no more than a few percentage points of GDP, and the Chinese economy looked very much like it did a century earlier: predominantly rural and agricultural. China also went through a costly and disruptive civil war (Taiping Rebellion), revealing further weakness in the authority and span of control of the central government. In contrast to Meiji Japan, and slightly earlier, continental Europe, to which the Industrial Revolution successfully spread, Qing China was unable to leverage the benefits of openness and the economic advantages of backwardness, most notably, cheap labor and access to new technology and know-how, to put its economy on a new growth trajectory. The key obstacle here was a tightly linked and well-entrenched set of economic, social and political institutions (Brandt, Ma and Rawski 2011), which were very slow to adapt. In some cases, these interests blocked outright the transfer of new technology and know-how essential to modern economic growth (Brown 1979). More generally, government-led modernizing efforts were weak and ineffective (Perkins 1967).

Over time new pressures in China originating from within the treaty port sector as well as outside helped to erode some of these centuries-old institutions, and on the margin modernization efforts began to take hold. The end of prohibition on foreign factories in the treaty ports, for example, sparked a rise in foreign direct investment (FDI) centered on Shanghai and the lower Yangzi, and indirectly helped to foster the development of private business in China. The introduction of the steamship and the construction of a number of major railroad lines complemented a well-developed system of traditional transport, and reduced transportation costs. A modern banking system also emerged, and with it paper currency spread once again as the most important medium of exchange in the Chinese economy. Governmental reform proceeded, both during the final years of the Qing (1644–1911), and then through the Republican period (1911–1949), however not without frequent setbacks. All of the above changes were complemented by a slow makeover in the fabric of Chinese society, a product of new paths of upward economic and social mobility (Yuchtman 2010).

How far did this proceed? Estimates of John Chang (1969), Thomas Rawski (1989) and others suggest that through the first three decades of the twentieth century these forces propelled growth in China's modern sector (industry, finance, transportation, and so on) , and promoted structural change in the economy. Moreover, two important regions, namely, the lower Yangzi and the northeast, may have experienced the onset of modern economic growth, i.e. sustained increase in per capita incomes, as increases in the modern sector were either complemented by growth in agriculture and the traditional non-agricultural sectors, or at minimum offset any reduction in their size (Ma 2008, Mizoguchi and Umemura 1988).

Assessments at the aggregate level are much harder. At its peak, and after growing through the first three decades of the twentieth century at a rate of 8 percent per annum, the modern sector still never represented more than 15 percent of GDP (Liu and Yeh 1965). A majority of the population continued to live in the countryside and derived a livelihood from either agriculture – the source of two-thirds of GDP in the mid-1930s – or the traditional non-agricultural sector, which included handicraft industry, commerce and transport. Unfortunately, existing data only allow estimates of growth in the farm/traditional sector with relatively wide margins of error. More than likely, there was enormous heterogeneity in the impact of these developments on the rural economy, with some areas benefitting from growing demand and links with a small but dynamic urban economy, while others were largely cut-off, or possibly adversely affected.

China appears to have weathered the impact of the Great Depression better than most. But the cities and countryside were badly disrupted soon thereafter. From 1937 to 1945 China was engaged in a costly war against Japan, in which the CCP (Chinese Communist Party) and KMT (Kuomintang) joined together—at least in principle—to defeat the Japanese. Between 1945 and 1949, they would fight each other.

The socialist period: 1949–1978

With the defeat of the KMT in 1949 and their departure to Taiwan, the CCP inherited a badly devastated economy in the midst of hyperinflation. It also found itself facing an increasingly hostile international environment, and external threats. Ending the hyperinflation, completing land reform[8], and economic recovery occupied much of the new government's attention the next few years. Shortly thereafter, and borrowing from the Soviet Union, China established a set of institutions that would help define the economic system for the better part of the next three decades.[9] The essential features of the system included the nationalization of industry and state ownership, the elimination of markets in favor of an elaborate system of state planning, and the end of household farming and the re-organization of households in the countryside into rural collectives (Naughton 1995).[10]

The system was highly successful in mobilizing resources and directing them to priority areas, notably, heavy industry, but inefficiencies of the sort inherent in any system of planning, and weak material incentives in industry and agriculture worked against this, as did Maoist policies promoting local self-sufficiency. These problems were exacerbated during episodes such as the Great Leap Forward (1958–1960) and the Cultural Revolution (1965–1976) when politics and ideological considerations figured even more prominently in economic policymaking.[11] Indeed, political failure and costly economic policies largely explain the huge loss of life estimated to be in upwards of 30 million associated with the Great Leap Famine between 1959 and 1961 (Peng 1987, Dikötter 2010).

Estimates suggest that over this period Chinese real GDP grew 6 percent per annum and on a per capita basis at a rate of 4 percent[12], surpassing those in other large low-income countries such as India, Pakistan, Indonesia, Egypt and Brazil (Morawetz 1978). Industry's share of GDP also rose from only 10 percent in the early 1950s to nearly 45 percent by the late 1970s as new industrial and technological capabilities were developed (Perkins 1988). These numbers are misleading however. Under socialism growth occurred almost entirely along the extensive margin as a result of factor accumulation. Moreover, with total factor productivity (TFP) declining during much of the last half of the 1960s and up until the late 1970s, growth was sustained only by a rising share of GDP channeled into investment. As a result, output per person increased, but consumption did not.

On the positive side, investments by the state in health, education and welfare combined with highly egalitarian systems of distribution within both the urban and rural sectors to deliver major improvements in life expectancy, maternal and infant mortality, and literacy. Overall however, average consumption languished: Rationing was pervasive and the material standard of living on the eve of economic reform was likely comparable to the level of two decades earlier (Lardy 1983). In the countryside, where more than 80 percent of the population lived and worked, calorie availability may have actually been lower.

The weak link here was Chinese agriculture, which failed to generate a growing marketable surplus that could be used to support a larger population outside of agriculture. Indeed, the percentage of the population living in the cities in 1978—18 percent—was no higher than it was 15 years earlier (NBS 2010). Once again, the problems were system-related as any potential gains from increases in irrigated area, the use of new higher-yielding varieties and chemical fertilizers, and mechanization were more than offset by rising inefficiencies (Lardy 1983).

In the historiography of the People's Republic of China (PRC), the rural-basis of CCP support is often singled out in explaining their rise and defeat of the KMT. Paradoxically, through much of the first three decades of the PRC, agriculture was repeatedly under-valued, and this constituency largely ignored. Even using China's own "bare-minimum" poverty line for the period, the number of individuals living in poverty in the countryside was estimated to be upwards of 250 million (Vermeer 1982), or a third of the Chinese rural population at that time. If one was to use the World Bank's $US 1 a day as a benchmark, the number might actually be twice this. In addition, a huge gap also emerged in the incomes (and consumption) between those living in the countryside, and those fortunate enough to enjoy urban registration (Rawski 1982).

The reform era: 1978–present

The end of the Cultural Revolution and death of Mao late in 1976 helped set in motion a process of economic and political reforms that have not fully played out. The risks and enormity of the task facing China's political elite at this juncture in Chinese history cannot be underestimated, if for no reason other than there was little in the way of international experience to help guide them in this difficult transition. On top of this, there were powerful vested interests to contend with that were the major beneficiaries of the old system. The huge economic dislocation that accompanied a similar process in Eastern Europe a decade or so latter is a sobering reminder of the economic and political pitfalls that can easily accompany such a process (Svejnar 2002).

Three and half decades of reforms have helped transform China from a highly closed, planned economy into an open, dynamic market economy in which the state plays a smaller, albeit still important, role. Reform has also extended to China's highly authoritarian political system (Xu 2011). Although the CCP maintains its monopoly on political power, reform has helped to transform the Party from the "personality-ruled party" under Mao to a "system governed by rules, clear lines of authority and collective-making decisions" (Shirk 1993); opened up party membership to newly emerging groups, e.g. entrepreneurs; and tied political promotion at every level of the political hierarchy to economic growth. The highly decentralized nature of the Chinese economy inherited from the planning period played to reforms that "incentivized" cadre behavior in this way.

But at the outset, reform efforts were motivated by two more immediate concerns: food security, and a widening gap in productivity and living standards between China and its east Asian neighbors. Both threatened the legitimacy of the CCP. With agriculture continuing to falter, concerns of a return to famine-like conditions of the late 1950s were surfacing. Moreover, after nearly two decades of economic, political and social turmoil, the success of the Asian tigers, especially Taiwan, was an embarrassing reminder of earlier expectations and unfulfilled promises.

Rural reform, incremental opening of the economy to foreign trade and investment, enlivening state-owned enterprises (SOEs), and fiscal decentralization formed the core of the early reform initiatives. All were important but a case can be made that reform would not have proceeded very far without the early success in the countryside, which exceeded all expectations including those of China's paramount leader, Deng Xiaoping (Vogel 2011). Moreover, we see in the rural reforms key elements of China's success through the first phase of reform, namely, the ability to dismantle the old command economy without disrupting economic growth, and institutional innovation.

At the heart of the rural reform was the re-introduction of household farming through the Household Responsibility System (HRS). Under HRS, ownership rights to the land remained with the collective or village, and households were extended usufruct rights in return for meeting "fixed" rental-like obligations. Household incentives in farming were enhanced by price and marketing reforms. It is probably no irony that these reforms were first experimented with in the provinces of Sichuan and Anhui, two of the hardest hit provinces during the Great Leap Forward.[13] Reforms spread rapidly to other provinces, and, by 1983, 95 percent of all households were under HRS.

The rapid growth in farm output—grain production increased by a third between 1978 and 1984 with output of cash crops and farm sidelines growing even more rapidly—helped to solve the immediate "food" problem, and simultaneously freed up huge amounts of labor formerly trapped in collective agriculture (Lin 1992). New outlets emerged for this labor in the form of small family-run enterprises and collectively-owned and managed township and village enterprises (TVEs), the growth of which also benefitted from the rapid rise in incomes and liberalization of the non-farm sector in the countryside. Between 1978 and 1995, employment in rural enterprises grew by over 100 million, and in industry, their output increased to more than a third of the gross value of industrial output.[14] This dynamism was especially evident in the coastal provinces, and built on the growth of commune and brigade-run enterprises of the socialist period, as well the human and social capital from the pre-1949 era that survived.

Isolated from the West for the better part of three decades, the importation of new technology and know-how and links with international production networks were viewed as critical to the modernization efforts of Chinese industry. In 1979, China cautiously set up four Special Economic Zones in the southern coastal provinces of Guangdong and Fujian to encourage foreign direct investment (FDI) in labor-intensive export processing activity. The timing could not have been better, and coincided with rapidly rising labor costs facing entrepreneurs in Taiwan and Hong Kong who were involved in export activity. Local leaders outside these four zones were soon lobbying Beijing for similar powers and authority, and competition for FDI among regions intensified. Rapid growth of processing exports helped to relax a binding foreign exchange constraint, and China's early "embrace of globalism" (Branstetter and Lardy 2008) was extended to encouraging investment by multinational firms in strategic sectors. Entry was often limited to establishing joint ventures with state-owned firms, but in return for the transfer of managerial, organization and technical know-how, these firms were promised access to a potentially rapidly growing domestic market.

Outside of a relatively small collectively-owned sector, the urban economy and industry were initially dominated by state-owned enterprises. These same institutions were also important providers of housing and social services to individuals working in these firms. With no social safety net outside of these firms, reform options such as bankruptcy and layoffs were deemed politically infeasible at this time. As a result, through the first decade and a half of reform, efforts focused on improving productivity within SOEs, while facilitating the growth of the economy outside of the state and plan.

SOE managers were extended new autonomy from supervisory agencies, and incentives were enhanced through profit retention and individual bonuses. Competition also increased through new entry. With the implementation of the "dual-track system," firms were allowed to find new market outlets for their production after fulfilling plan obligations fixed at levels of the early 1980s. Retention of the planned component of output served two useful purposes: first, it helped to prevent the disruption to industry of the sort observed in Eastern Europe; and second, it minimized opposition to reform from those who would have lost the rents associated with control over planned allocation (Lau, Qian and Roland 2002). At the same time, production outside of the plan offered non-state firms access to key inputs. China soon grew "out of the plan" (Naughton 1995), and by the early 1990s, the planned component of industrial output was below 20 percent.

Last, these reforms were accompanied by a marked decentralization of China's fiscal system, and an end to an older system in which the center effectively controlled revenues and expenditures at all levels of government. Combined with the existing decentralization over economic management and an increasingly meritocratic personnel system for cadres tied to economic growth, these changes gave local governments the incentive, the resources, and the policy tools to promote local economic growth with an intensity and determination rarely visible in other economies.

The first 15 years of reform delivered impressive results that were widely enjoyed among nearly all segments of society. Poverty, which had been almost exclusively a rural problem dropped precipitously, and inequality fell early on with a narrowing in the urban–rural gap (Ravallion and Chen 2007). But problems loomed. Soft-budget constraints of firms in the state sector undermined incentives, and productivity growth in the state sector lagged significantly behind the more dynamic non-state sector which now extended to private enterprises. Only lending from the state-controlled banking system helped to sustain expansion and wage increases in the state sector on par with that outside, leaving non-performing loans to accumulate in the state-dominated banking system. In addition, decentralization in the fiscal system left the center without the fiscal resources needed to finance public investment and achieve distributive objectives. Central government revenue fell to only 3 percent of GDP (Wong and Bird 2008). After initially falling, inequality was also on the rise, with current estimates suggesting a Gini coefficient upwards of 0.50 in 2010.

These tensions between economic decentralization, fiscal constraints and redistributive objectives were manifest in inflationary cycles that peaked in 1985, 1989, and 1993 (Brandt and Zhu 2000).

In the mid-1990s policy makers tackled these issues head on through a series of ambitious reforms that recentralized the fiscal system; restructured the SOE sector; reorganized the financial sector and recapitalized the banks; and with the decision to enter World Trade Organization (WTO) in 2001, exposed the domestic economy to increasing competition and more deeply engaged the international economy. Unlike the earlier reform initiatives however, there were clearly losers here, as most small and medium sized SOEs were either privatized or shut down, and upwards of 50 million workers were furloughed from the state sector.

A number of alternative, and by no means mutually exclusive, explanations have been offered for this sharp break in policy and the ability of the CCP to carry through a set of reforms that would have seemed nearly impossible to carry out earlier. Was it the product of slowly emerging consensus that the desired long-run outcome of reform was a market economy in which the role of the state was to be radically redefined (Qian 2000)? Alternatively, did it reflect a reconfiguration of political power that accompanied the dying off of key party elders, including Deng Xiaoping, each of whom had their own power base, and in the past was able to block reforms detrimental to the supporters (Naughton 2008)? Or, was it an effort by the CCP to shed support to an increasingly costly constituency in order to sustain economic growth, while providing the Party with the financial and fiscal resources necessary to rebuild patronage and achieve its larger strategic objectives?

Since the mid-to-late 1990s, economic growth has averaged over 10 percent per annum, with China weathering the external shocks from the Asian financial crisis (1997–1998), and the most recent world financial crisis (2008–2010) fairly well. Central government fiscal revenue increased to nearly 11 percent of GDP. Inward foreign direct investment, much of which is focused on the domestic economy, increased to more than $US 100 billion in 2010, and is now accompanied by significant outward FDI, much of which is in natural resources. Estimates also identify a half or more of GDP growth as the product of productivity growth, coming from rising TFP within sectors, as well as the result of the reallocation of labor and capital to more highly valued sectors (Brandt and Zhu 2010). Upgrading and productivity growth in the manufacturing sector have been especially pronounced, however services, which were more insulated from WTO-related reforms, have lagged. These achievements have also been accompanied by relaxation on earlier restrictions on geographic mobility, setting in motion probably the largest migration in human history: The recent 2010 population census puts the number of migrants or "floating" population at 150 million (Chan, forthcoming).

Economic dynamism, however, has been accompanied by severe distortions that are easily overlooked when an economy grows as rapidly as China's, and can be linked to repression in the financial sector, an under-valued exchange rate, poorly defined property rights in land, as well as industrial policies often restricting market access and entry. Since the early 2000s, two clear symptoms of these distortions have been the falling (rising) share of consumption (investment) in GDP, and a significant and persistent current account surplus (Lardy 2012). In 2010, the share of GDP going to investment rose to over 50 percent, probably the highest in the world's history, and up from 35.3 percent in 2000, while China's foreign exchange reserves increased to more than $US 3.6 trillion.[15] The state has been essential to China's economic transformation and modernization, but other policies (and politics) are also effectively behind a massive redistribution of income between individuals, sectors and regions that is likely serving other political and strategic objectives, and contributing to China's high and rising level of inequality.

Within the current decade, the rate of growth of the Chinese economy will slow, albeit to levels that are still considerably higher than we observe in advanced countries. This decline will reflect the impact of a host of factors, including the narrowing in its technological gap with the West, falling rates of investment, a contraction in the absolute size of its labor force and more rapidly rising wages, as well as the rapid aging of the population. Japan, Korea and Taiwan also experienced reductions in their high rates of growth at a similar point in development, and so it is simply a matter of time. As growth rates fall however, the costs of these distortions will loom even larger, and China's success in moving up the ranks of the middle-income countries and in keeping a lid on social tensions will depend on its ability to deal with the difficult political economy issues that are the source of these distortions. Given China's new role as an engine of growth in the international economy, and its rapid expansion outwards, we can be certain that the consequences from any failure to deal with these issues will not only be felt in China, but will extend past China's borders as well.

Notes

1 Based on estimates from the World Bank's International Comparison Program database, www.databank.worldbank.org, accessed May 29, 2012.
2 Comparable estimates by the Conference Board for 2011 are 15.8 percent for China and 18.6 percent for the U.S., respectively. Estimates are taken from http://www.conference-board.org/data/globaloutlook.cfm, accessed February 17, 2012.
3 Similarities in the local economies extended from a high level of commercialization and market development, to rates of literacy, land productivity, and development of the non-agricultural sector, as well as household demographic behavior. Pomeranz (2000) also argues that China and Europe shared a common land constraint, which becomes the important point of departure for the two regions in his analysis.
4 Overall, these exports represented a relatively small percentage of the Chinese economy. On an annual basis, so were the silver imports, but on a cumulative basis they were huge and the major source of the increase in China's money supply during the seventeenth and eighteenth centuries.
5 The Canton (present day Guangzhou) system required that all trade between China and European countries go through that city, and further limited involvement on the Chinese side to a guild of merchants (the *cohong*) that had been extended monopoly rights over this trade by the Qing government.
6 Recent research by Lin (2006) and Irigoin (2009) offers alternative explanations for the reversal in silver flows including the rising gold price of silver, falling domestic demand for silver, and a breakdown of the Spanish peso standard.
7 The Unequal Treaties refer to a series of treaties including the Treaty of Nanjing (1842), the Treaties of Tianjin (1858 and 1861), and the Treaty of Shiminoseki (1895) that were imposed on China by foreign powers during the nineteenth and early twentieth century, and which represented a loss of national sovereignty.
8 Estimates of Charles Roll (1980) suggest that more than 40 percent of farm land was redistributed through land reform. Several million individuals were also likely executed as part of efforts to consolidate control over the countryside.
9 In the 1950s, China also benefitted from Soviet aid, but by the late 1950s the relationship had soured.
10 There were some differences however, and Chinese planning was never as extensive as the Soviet Union's, and remained much more decentralized (Wong 1985).
11 In both periods, for example, the right of households to farm small private plots was eliminated and the role of rural markets heavily curtailed.
12 Estimates of the rate of growth during this period are sensitive to the choice of base-year for deflators. On this point, see Perkins and Rawski (2008).

13 Institutional reforms similar to HRS were in fact implemented in these same two provinces in the early 1960s.
14 By the early 1990s, any remaining advantages enjoyed by the collectively owned TVEs over privately owned firms disappeared, and as a result, they were privatized en masse.
15 These distortions are also reflected in nagging differences in the returns to labor and capital across firms, sectors and region, and rising inequality.

References

Allen, R.C, Bassino, J-P, Ma, D., Moll-Murata, C. and van Zanden, J.L. (2011) 'Wages, prices, and living standards in China, Japan, and Europe, 1738–1925', *Economic History Review*, 64: 8–38.

Brandt, L., Ma, D., and Rawski, T.G. (2011) 'From divergence to convergence: reevaluating the economic history behind China's economic boom', Mimeo.

Brandt, L. and Zhu, X. (2000) 'Redistribution in a decentralizing economy: growth and inflation in China under reform', *Journal of Political Economy*, 108: 422–51.

Brandt, L. and Zhu, X. (2010) 'Accounting for growth in China', Working paper, University of Toronto.

Branstetter, L. and Lardy, N.R. (2008) 'China's embrace of globalization', in L. Brandt and T.G. Rawski (eds.) *China's Great Economic Transformation*, Cambridge and New York: Cambridge University Press.

Brown, S. R. (1979) 'The Ewo filature: a study in the transfer of technology to China in the 19th century', *Technology and Culture*, 20: 550–68.

Chan, K.W., (forthcoming) 'China's internal migration', in I. Ness and P. Bellwood (eds.) *The Encyclopedia of Global Migration*, Oxford: Blackwell Publishing.

Chang, J.K. (1969) *Industrial Development in Pre-Communist China: A Quantitative Analysis,* Chicago, Il: Aldine.

Dikötter, F. (2010) *Mao's Great Famine: The History of China's Most Devastating Catastrophe, 1958–1962,* New York: Walker & Co.

Irigoin, A. (2009) 'The end of the Silver Era: the consequences of the breakdown of the Spanish peso standard in China and the United States, 1780s-1850s', *Journal of World History*, 20: 215–20.

Lardy, N. (1983) *Agriculture in China's Modern Economic Development,* New York: Cambridge University Press.

Lardy, N. (2012) *Sustaining China's Economic Growth after the Global Financial Crisis,* Washington, DC: Peterson Institute for International Economics.

Lau, L., Qian, Y. and Roland, G. (2002) 'Reform without losers: an interpretation of China's dual-track approach to transition', *Journal of Political Economy*, 108: 120–43.

Li, B. (2000) *Jiangnan de zaoqi gongyehua: 1550–1850 nian. [Jiangnan's Early Industrialization, 1550–1850]*, Beijing: Shehui Kexue wenxian chubanshe.

Lin, J.Y. (1992) 'Rural reforms and agricultural growth in China', *American Economic Review*, 82: 34–51.

Lin, M. (2006) *China Upside Down: Currency, Society and Ideologies, 1808–1856,* Cambridge, MA: Harvard University Asia Center.

Liu, T. and Yeh. K.C. (1965) *The Economy of the Chinese Mainland: National Income and Economic Development, 1933–1959,* Princeton, NJ: Princeton University Press.

Ma, D. (2008) 'Economic growth in the lower Yangzi region of China in 1911–1937: a quantitative and historical analysis', *Journal of Economic History*, 68: 355–92.

Madisson, A. (2007) *Chinese Economic Performance in the Long Run,* second edn., revised and updated, Paris: Development Centre of the Organization for Economic Cooperation and Development.

Mizoguchi, T. and Umemura, M. (1988) *Kyū Nihon shokuminchi keizai tōkei: suikei to bunseki,* Tokyo: Toyo Keizai Shinposha.

Morawetz, D. (1978) *Twenty-five Years of Economic Development, 1950 to 1975,* Baltimore, MD: Johns Hopkins University Press.

Murphey, R. (1977) *The Outsiders: The Western Experience in India and China,* Ann Arbor, MI: University of Michigan Press.

NBS (National Bureau of Statistics) (2010) *Zhongguo Tongji Nianjian, 2010 [China Statistical Yearbook, 2010]*, Beijing: China Statistical Press.

Naughton, B. (1995) *Growing Out of the Plan: Chinese Economic Reform, 1978–1993,* Cambridge: Cambridge University Press.

Naughton, B. (2008) 'A political economy of China's economic transition', in L. Brandt and T.G. Rawski (eds.) *China's Great Economic Transformation*, Cambridge: Cambridge University Press.

Peng, X. (1987) 'Demographic consequences of the Great Leap Forward in China's provinces', *Population and Development Review*, 13: 639–70.

Perkins, D.H. (1967) 'Government as an obstacle to industrialization: the case of nineteenth century China', *Journal of Economic History*, 27: 478–92.

Perkins, D.H. (1988) 'Reforming China's economic system', *Journal of Economic Literature*, 26: 601–45.

Perkins, D.H. and Rawski, T.G. (2008) 'Forecasting China's economic growth to 2025', in L. Brandt and T.G. Rawski (eds.) *China's Great Economic Transformation*, Cambridge: Cambridge University Press.

Pomeranz, K. (2000) *The Great Divergence: China, Europe, and the Making of the Modern World Economy*, Princeton, NJ: Princeton University Press.

Qian, Y. (2000) 'The process of China's market transition (1978–1998): the evolutionary, historical, and comparative perspectives', *Journal of Institutional and Theoretical Economics*, 156: 151–71.

Ravallion, M. and Chen. S. (2007) 'China's (uneven) progress against poverty', *Journal of Development Economics*, 82: 1–42.

Rawski, T.G. (1982) 'The simple arithmetic of Chinese income,' *Keizai Kenkyu*, 33: 12–26.

Rawski, T.G. (1989) *Economic Growth in Prewar China*, Berkeley, CA: University of California Press.

Roll, C.R. (1980) *The Distribution of Rural Incomes in China: A Comparison of the 1930s and the 1950s*, New York: Garland.

Shirk, S. (1993) *The Political Logic of Economic Reform in China*, Berkeley, CA: University of California Press.

Svejnar, J. (2002) 'Transition economies: performance and challenges', *Journal of Economic Perspectives*, 16: 3–28.

Vermeer, E.B. (1982) 'Income differentials in rural China', *China Quarterly*, 89: 1–33.

Vogel, E. (2011) *Deng Xiaoping and Transformation of China*, Cambridge, MA: Harvard University Press.

Wong, C.(1985) 'Material allocation and decentralization: impact of the local sector on industrial reform', in E.J. Perry and C. Wong (eds.) *The Political Economy of Reform in Post-Mao China*, Cambridge, MA: Council on East Asian Studies/Harvard University.

Wong, C., and Bird, R.M. (2008) 'China's fiscal system: a work in progress', in L. Brandt and T.G. Rawski (eds.) *China's Great Economic Transformation*, Cambridge: Cambridge University Press.

Xu, C. (2011) 'The fundamental institutions of China's reform and development', *Journal of Economic Literature*, 49(4): 1076–151.

Yuchtman, N. (2010) 'Teaching to the tests: an economic analysis of educational institutions in late Imperial and Republican China', Mimeo.

26

THE RISE OF INDIA

Areendam Chanda

Introduction

While India started out the twentieth century as the "Jewel in the Crown," for most of the post-independence period, India's economy laid claim to a range of unenviable metaphors such as "Hindu rate of growth," the "license Raj," and the "lumbering elephant." It would not be unfair to judge the twentieth century as a lost economic century except the past 25 years have been an entirely different story from the economic history of India from 1900 to 1985.

The fact of the matter is that India was expected to "rise" after independence. It started off as the world's largest democracy, home to a multitude of ethnic and linguistic groups and was led by Nehru who was a proponent of a modern industrialized India. This vision extended to his willingness to involve international scholars in shaping India's development policy. Of course, policy making in an economy so large, complex and chaotic can be a challenge. Basu (1992) notes that India's annual population increase is equal to the size of Australia. Nevertheless, any great hopes for India quickly dissipated, as Nehru decided to adopt a socialist economic structure with an emphasis on economic independence and social justice. As the decades passed India began to fall behind many other developing countries. Figure 26.1 traces India's GDP per capita from 1950 to 2009 and Figure 26.2 traces India's relative GDP per capita to that of U.S. and the entire world for the period 1960–2009. As Figure 26.1 shows, India's GDP per capita increased from about US$700 in 1950 to US$1000 in 1980, i.e., a 42 percent increase over a 30-year period and an annual growth rate of 1.2 percent.[1] However, between 1980 and 2009, the next thirty year period, GDP per capita increased from US$1000 to US$3200, a 220 percent increase and an annual growth rate of 4.0 percent. Figure 26.2 demonstrates that India fell behind the world slightly in the 1960s and 1970s. This trend was partly reversed in the 1980s and a rapid convergence has been taking place since the mid-1990s.

While India's performance during most of the second half of the twentieth century was disappointing, it is important to note that unlike most other developing countries, India did not suffer from any major economic crises or extended political instability. Indeed, DeLong (2003), uses the phrase "average India." In the 1980s, however, India broke away from being average. To understand India's economic performance since the 1980s, one needs

303

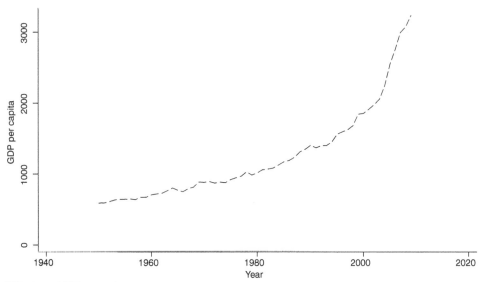

PPP adjusted GDP per capita from Penn World Tables v7.0 (Heston et al, 2011)

Figure 26.1 India's GDP per capita, 1950–2009

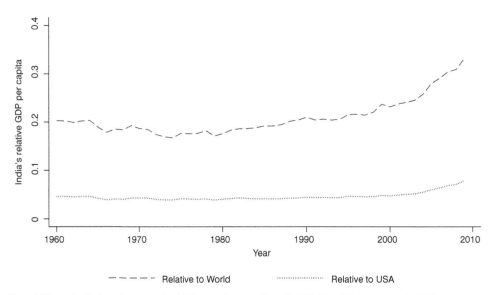

World GDP per Capita based on sample of 111 countries from Penn World Tables v7.0 (Heston et al, 2011)

Figure 26.2 India's relative GDP per capita, 1960–2009

to understand what was in place before independence. Therefore this chapter begins with some important aspects of colonization. Some of the institutional settings from colonized India, such as the land tenure system, continue to affect India's agricultural productivity even today. The chapter next discusses the post-independence period preceding the growth takeoff. "Average India" can be divided into two parts – the era of Nehru's leadership until his death in 1964 and the further relative decline of the economy until about 1980.[2] There is however considerable disagreement among scholars as to when exactly the rise began.

It is clear that some deregulation began in the late 1970s and early 1980s and growth was considerably higher in that decade. However, it was really in the mid-1980s when a major bout of deregulation took place leading to accelerated growth in the last few years of the decade. In terms of actual policy making though, it was only in 1990–91 with the balance of payments crisis that the government explicitly forsook the economic dirigisme of the past. The chapter concludes by highlighting some important aspects of the Indian economy that are still problematic and can potentially derail the growth train.

India before independence

India gained independence from the British on August 15, 1947. During the period of colonization, India fell squarely into what is now commonly labeled an "extractive colonization."[3] While European merchants started arriving in India at least as early as 1498, the British East India Company's ascent is usually traced to the Battle of Plassey in 1757. The British government took direct control over India only in 1857 after a failed revolt by a collection of Indian rulers. During the nineteenth century, India was part of a global system of trade and commerce. India's exports were primarily agricultural and it moved away from being a finished textiles producer to a supplier of raw materials for the British cotton mills. Hence, some scholars argue that India suffered from deindustrialization during the colonial period. Moreover, the country had to "pay" for the British government's expenses in India and this was alleged to have been a drain on India's resources.

For the purposes of this chapter there are two key aspects of colonization that deserve attention. First, Roy (2002) notes that in the second half of the nineteenth century net domestic product per capita grew at a rate between 0.5 and 1 percent annually. From 1914 to 1947, it actually *fell* at 0.5 percent per year. Moreover, independence itself did not alter the change of pace of India's industrialization. In particular, the share of national income in industry showed an anemic but slow increase over the entire twentieth century while the industrial share of the workforce remained around 10 percent for almost all of the twentieth century.

Second, since agricultural land was an important source of tax revenue, it was necessary for the British to have a well-defined tax system with property rights in place. Depending upon the region of the country, the British imposed a landlord-based system, a village-based system or a cultivator-based system of property rights and revenue sharing. In practice the contracts or "settlements" often went to the wrong person due to mistaken identity, political reasons or poor information. Moreover, the type of contract that was enforced in a particular region was also based on incorrect prior information. Out of these various contracts, the landlord-based system which involved a fixed nominal revenue into perpetuity, was the most exploitative. Despite the enactment of land reforms almost immediately after independence, it has been shown that the regions with the landlord-based system continued to suffer in terms of agricultural productivity and investments even 40 years later.[4]

The Nehru years (1947–1964)

The policymaking regime that dominated in India immediately after independence owes much of its vision to the country's first prime minister, Jawaharlal Nehru. Nehru enjoyed almost unparalleled popularity until his death in 1964. He was the prime minister during this entire period and was able to pursue economic policies that were in tune with his vision of a modern India.[5] Nehru's view was that political freedom from the West could not be attained without economic independence. As a result a large emphasis was placed on the concept of self-sufficiency. This did not necessarily entail the erection of barriers to international trade as much as ensuring that the country's consumption needs were largely met by domestic production. Inevitably this would mean centralized decision making and the introduction of restrictions on both the degree of private ownership of industrial activities and even the amount of private production that was to be allowed. Apart from the introduction of laws to achieve these goals, the government also embarked on five-year plans beginning in 1951. At the core of these plans was the focus on state ownership of infrastructure and capital goods industries. The idea was that if the country was to depend on imports for heavy machinery, railways, and automobiles then India would remain enslaved to foreign countries. As a result, during this period, restrictive industrial policies were introduced, particularly the Industrial Policy Resolution in 1956. This resolution divided industries in the manufacturing sector into three different categories. The first category of 17 major industries was reserved only for state monopolies. These included railways, iron and steel, shipbuilding, telecommunication equipment, mining, etc. By the beginning of the second five-year plan in 1956, the public sector accounted for 61 percent of all investment (Panagariya 2008).

In addition to the introduction of state ownership, the Industries (Development and Regulation) Act in 1951 led to the practice of licensing. It set down the guidelines that ensured planned investment and production were in line with national goals, small industries were encouraged, and it created rules allowing the government to take over private firms and introduce price controls among other things. Finally, the agricultural sector, despite accounting for an overwhelming share of the economy, received little attention. This reflected Nehru's preoccupation with industry. The major policy change worth noting was the introduction of land reforms that were implemented to undo the deleterious effects of the Zamindari system that had been institutionalized by the British as mentioned earlier. Nevertheless the success of these reforms varied across states.

It should be noted that growth during this period averaged 3.7 percent per year. Combined with annual population growth of 1.9 percent, this implies an annual growth rate of GDP per capita of 1.8 percent. This is certainly higher than the negative growth rates during much of the first half of the twentieth century. Nevertheless, it was hardly adequate for any sort of catch-up with rich countries and was well below the nation's potential.

Falling behind years (1965–81)

Following Nehru's death, Lal Bahadur Shastri became prime minister and brought a more agrarian-centered perspective into policy making. However, his tenure was cut short due to his death in 1966. Nehru's daughter, Indira Gandhi was appointed prime minister and she remained prime minister until 1984 except for a three-year period (1977–80). During the first ten years of this period, 1965–75, the growth rate of the Indian economy fell substantially compared to the earlier years so that the growth rate of GDP per capita was again near zero. During this period, India engaged in two wars with Pakistan (1965, 1971), experienced several droughts (1965–67, 1971–73) and was also hit by the worldwide oil price shock. Nevertheless, one of the signature developments during this period was the leftward evolution of policy making. An effort to consolidate her power within the Congress and growing divisions between India and the U.S. reinforced Gandhi's socialist agenda. The overall annual growth rate registered by the economy during the entire 16-year period was almost a full percent lower than the earlier period.

Agriculture in India was characterized by inefficient farm size, poor irrigation infrastructure, and a lack of access to credit and insurance markets. The neglect of the sector by the government during the earlier period implied that very few technological innovations had been adopted to increase productivity. When coupled with the droughts in the mid-1960s, along with expansionary fiscal policies and increased foreign borrowing, these led to the creation of a macroeconomic crisis and a contraction of the economy. Thereafter, an unprecedented level of interference in private economic activities began. These manifested themselves through new restrictions on the operation of large firms (via the Monopolies and Restrictive Trade Practices Act, 1969) and the introduction of another round of licensing policies. The backdrop was a feeling that earlier licensing rules were being misused by big business houses to concentrate economic power. To counter such allegations, the government restricted any new activity of large business houses to a very narrow set of industries. In addition to the usual licensing requirements, virtually any change in business plans including new undertakings, capacity expansion, and mergers required permission. The government would only allow investment activity if it did not lead to further concentration and did not harm small-scale firms or cottage industry. The government also introduced a more elaborate system of licensing activities. Virtually all these policies were set up to favor small firms such that it became almost impossible for large enterprises to manufacture labor-intensive products, thus precluding any efficiency gains from scale.

During this period virtually all incentives for foreign firms to invest in India were choked off due to the introduction of new regulations on the operation of foreign firms and foreign investment via the Foreign Exchange Regulation Act in 1973. The Act required almost all foreign firms to either dilute their foreign equity shares to 40 percent or else close their business. Finally, this was also the period that saw an acceleration of the nationalization of banks through an act in 1969 leading to 84 percent of bank branches belonging to government-owned banks. This was further expanded to cover six more of the largest private sector banks in 1980 (Panagariya 2008).

Like the earlier period, a notable exception during this time period was agriculture. However, in this case the development was positive. After the repeated droughts in the 1960s, the government introduced high-yielding varieties of wheat to north India with resounding success. By the end of the 1970s the country was self-sufficient in food grain production.

The 1980s: dilution of regulation

There has been an active debate regarding when India actually began to move to a pro-market regime. Most of this debate surrounds the choice of an initial year for "take-off." There is no doubt that the balance of payments crisis and the sharp abandonment of socialist policies makes 1991 a watershed year in Indian history. However, most of the disagreements arise because there are clear indications that Indira Gandhi had moved somewhat toward the center by the early 1980s. Moreover, her son, Rajiv Gandhi, who became prime minister after her assassination in 1984, pursued deregulation with a hitherto unseen enthusiasm. DeLong (2003) notes that in terms of GDP growth rates, the period 1980–90 was almost 6 percent compared to the growth rate of 3.7 percent for the preceding 30 years. Similarly Rodrik and Subramaniam (2008) observe that the growth rate in GDP per capita during the period 1980–2000 was 3.7 percent which was twice that of 1.7 percent in the preceding 30 years. Bosworth and Collins (2003) find that annual output per worker growth and productivity growth in the 1980s was 3.9 percent and 2.5 percent. The corresponding numbers for the 1990s were 3.3 percent and 1.3 percent. This indicates the decade leading up to major reforms saw higher productivity growth than the decade following their onset.

Panagariya (2008) is skeptical of most of the research suggesting that the 1980s was a takeoff decade. While he does not question the general move away from the interventionist policies, he notes that most of the high growth rates in the 1980s actually come from the last three years of the decade when the economy averaged 8 percent rates of growth while the first seven years saw the economy average less than 5 percent rates of growth. Thus, in his view, the Indian growth miracle really should be seen as beginning from 1987–88.

To understand the source of the shifts in the policy-making regime, we need to return to the 1970s. By the middle of the 1970s, two consecutive drought years combined with worldwide oil price shocks had led to runaway inflation – the consumer price index had risen by more than 20 percent. While the number is nowhere near as destabilizing as rates observed commonly in many developing countries, Indians have had a very low appetite for such inflation rates. The weakened economy along with a court judgment that Indira Gandhi had fraudulently won her parliament seat put her in a precarious position. In an attempt to consolidate power, she declared a state of emergency and suspended all democratic rights. The period of emergency lasted for a little less than two years (June 1975 to March 1977) when she called for fresh elections. However, she was defeated in those elections and remained out of power until 1980. Dissatisfaction with the performance of other political parties during the intervening years ensured that she came back to power in 1980 with a resounding majority. Unlike her earlier years, this time around there was a gradual reversal of many of the highly restrictive policies on licensing and investment. It became easier for firms to expand capacity, diversify their production, and invest in industries previously reserved for state monopolies such as telecommunications. In addition price controls on important items like cement and aluminum were removed.

A wave of deregulation followed the election of Rajiv Gandhi as prime minister in early 1985. As one of the youngest elected leaders of the executive branch ever in modern democracies, he was less influenced by the socialist ideas of earlier leaders including his own mother and grandfather. Moreover, the overwhelming majority with which he was elected ensured that he could implement policies that were more representative of a youthful India. The changes were apparent in his government's first budget which reduced marginal tax rates and tariffs, replaced import quotas with tariffs, expanded the open general license program for imports, and further relaxed restrictions on big businesses and licensing. Thus it was not surprising that growth accelerated at the end of the1980s. DeLong (2003) notes that GDP per worker in India by then was at least a third higher than what one would have predicted a decade earlier.

To conclude, the 1980s were a period that certainly reflected a movement away from the socialist path but there was little indication that the country was poised for the wholesale elimination of barriers to trade and investment. Nevertheless the reforms that took place were enough to bestow India with a growth rate higher than ever experienced since independence.

1991: the rise of India

Though growth in India accelerated during the 1980s, so did public expenditures. While in the early 1980s the fiscal deficit stood at around 8 percent of GDP, by 1990, the deficit had reached a value of 10.4 percent of GDP. These were also accompanied by increasing borrowing abroad and thus rising current account deficits. The stock of foreign exchange reserves began to fall precipitously and by 1990–91 the country had only enough left to service one month's worth of imports. This led to the balance of payments crisis in 1991 and intervention by the International Monetary Fund and the World Bank which initiated the process of reforms. It should also be noted that while the crisis was deepening, India was in the midst of parliamentary elections. Midway through the elections, Rajiv Gandhi was assassinated. The elections resulted in a victory for the Congress party with support from the left. Narsimha Rao became prime minister. Rao appointed Manmohan Singh, an Oxford-educated former professor of economics and a former governor of the Reserve Bank of India, as the Minister of Finance. The pro-reform agenda of both Rao and Singh helped shape the wide-ranging reforms that were enacted during the next few years. The reforms were more or less a complete about face. While the 1980s reflected a dilution of the licensing and regulatory regime, the reforms in the early 1990s reflected more or less a complete abandonment of that regime. The stifling industrial licensing regime was abolished and the public sector had its role reduced to only a few key industries. Foreign direct investment and capital flows into the stock markets and for mergers and acquisitions were now welcome. There was a wholesale reduction of tariffs and other barriers to international trade. In the financial sector the entry of both domestic and foreign players in the banking and capital markets was liberalized. This is also true for insurance which was earlier a government oligopoly.

For the past 20 years, India has been singularly a success story. In the 1990s the growth rate of GDP per capita averaged 4.0 percent (excluding 1991 – the crisis year). This was only marginally higher than the 1980s (3.5 percent). The first decade of the twenty-first century was quite another story with the growth rate of GDP per capita averaging 5.8 percent per annum. There seem to be two phases of growth performance. Up until 2004, the growth rate of GDP per capita averaged 3.7 percent. However since then the growth rate has further accelerated to 6.7 percent.

It is too early to tell whether the new higher growth rate will be sustained, but a promising sign is that this growth encompassed the years of a major recession in developed countries. A cause for optimism is the more or less emerging growth consensus or liberalization consensus. While initially it seemed that economic reform was taking place at gunpoint with the 1991 crisis, over time the reforms have become accepted more widely. During the entire period since the reforms began, the Indian government has been run by coalition parties. Both the centrist Congress party and the more right of center Bhartiya Janata Party have pushed reforms. At the state level, the aspirations of the people for change have led to either unprecedented re-election of pro-reform chief ministers (e.g. Nitish Kumar in Bihar in 2010) or to the stunning defeat of the Communist Party in West Bengal in 2011 after 34 years of unchallenged majority rule.

Poverty and inequality

Since independence, economic policy making in India has centered on self-sufficiency and a concern for equity. However, it is probable that this overriding concern for "growth with equity" came at a significant cost. Clearly the industrial licensing regimes aimed at restricting the size of big business houses and the simultaneous protections granted to small-scale industries reflect this bias. Unfortunately, for most of India's pre-reform period there was hardly any growth nor any reduction in poverty. The good news is that by all accounts, there has been a significant reduction in poverty since the beginning of the reforms. According to Himanshu (2007), the poverty ratio, defined as the proportion of people with per capita consumption below official poverty lines, in rural India had declined from 46.5 percent in

1983–84, to 37.2 percent in 1993–94 and further to 28.7 percent in 2004–05. For urban India, the numbers were 43.6 percent, 32.6 percent and 25.9 percent respectively.[6] As far as inequality is concerned, the Gini coefficients show slight increases in both rural and urban inequality but more so for the latter. In 2004–05 the Gini coefficient for rural India was at around 30.5 as opposed to 28.6 in 1993–94, but the former number is equal to values observed in the 1980s. The Gini for urban India had increased from 34.4 to 37.6 which is seen by many as a cause for concern.

Another area of concern is the differences in per capita income across states. It is now more or less accepted that per capita state domestic product has been diverging since the onset of reforms. For example, in 1960, the ratio of per capita income for Punjab (one of the richest large states) to Bihar (one of the poorest) was 1.6. By 1991, the ratio had risen to 3 and by 2009 it was slightly higher at 3.5. Kochar et al. (2006) have also documented that there has been divergence in income between states. They also note that with increasing decentralization, state-level policies and institutions have begun to matter more and this can explain some of the divergence. For example, both Bihar and Orissa, two of the poorest large states, have recorded double digit growth for the past five years.[7] With free flow of labor and easy flow of information, people are more likely to migrate to richer states and this can set in motion other channels of convergence.[8]

Structural transformation

Figure 26.3 tells the well-known but unusual story of Indian structural transformation. First, over almost six decades the share of agriculture (and allied activities) has declined, falling to 18 percent of GDP in 2008–09. Over the past two decades, the decline has been fairly rapid and in general this is in line with any modernizing economy. A rise in services offset most of the decline in agriculture's share. Only the first phase (1950–65) saw an appreciable rise in the manufacturing sector and only in the past five years has the manufacturing sector's share picked up. These trends are more or less typical of countries with the same per capita income as India (Kochar et al. 2006).

Table 26.1 lists the labor share of each of the major three sectors. Despite the decline in the output share of agriculture, the labor share reflects considerable inertia. This has translated into very poor labor productivity growth for agriculture, but considerably high productivity growth for the service and manufacturing sectors. Kochar et al. (2006) note some of the idiosyncrasies in Indian manufacturing: an unusual concentration of above medium-sized firms. Most of these large firms are capital intensive and reflect state monopolies. However, even though there is a concentration of large firms, across the spectrum, Indian manufacturing firms tend to be about only one-tenth the size of firms in the same industry in other countries. Finally, in addition to a capital-intensive bias, firms also exhibit a skill bias. The share of manufacturing in skill-intensive firms between 1980 and 1996 was identical to those of Malaysia and South Korea, which have considerably higher per capita incomes.[9] Another important issue that confronts this sector is the share of the unorganized or informal sector in manufacturing. Panagariya (2008: 284) drawing on the work of Saha et al. (2004) notes that within manufacturing, the informal sector accounted for 94 percent of the labor force in 1999–2000.[10]

The fact that Indian firms are so small compared to their international counterparts, the unusually high skill shares and the extraordinarily large size of the informal sector are probably due to the rigid labor laws that began to be introduced in India under the Industrial Disputes Act of 1947. While the Act stipulated the conditions under which firms

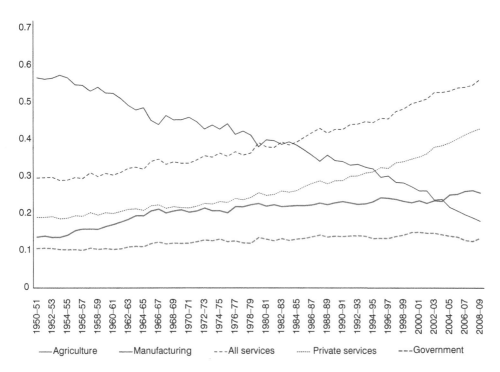

Figure 26.3 Sectoral shares in GDP, 1950–2009

Note: All Services is the sum of private services and government

Table 26.1 Sectoral composition of the labor force

Year	Agriculture	Manufacturing	All Services
1951	0.70	0.08	0.22
1961	0.72	0.11	0.17
1971	0.72	0.11	0.16
1981	0.66	0.13	0.21
1991	0.61	0.12	0.27
2009	0.52	0.14	0.34

Source: Data for all years except 2009 are taken from the ILO LABORSTA database. For 2009, the data comes from the CIA Factbook

have to negotiate labor agreements in the face of disputes, state governments have over time introduced several amendments. Nevertheless, at its core, it makes it virtually impossible for firms with 100 or more employees to lay off workers. Not surprisingly Besley and Burgess (2004) find that states which strengthened these laws in favor of workers experienced lower output growth, employment, investment and productivity in formal manufacturing and also increases in urban poverty. Another area that has evaded reform is bankruptcy laws. In a recent survey, the World Bank (2011) finds that on average it takes seven years for a company to close a business. Thus, while delicensing since the mid-1980s has made entry of firms easier, the lack of any reform on labor dispute laws and bankruptcy laws make exit more difficult. Not surprisingly, the manufacturing sector's share has hardly changed over the past 25 years.

As Table 26.1 suggests, agriculture's labor share has fallen much more slowly than its output share. The absence of adequate land reforms has played an important role in this trend. Land reforms, enacted in 1949, aimed to provide more secure tenancy rights, redistribute land ownership and reduce the size of landholdings to provide more ownership to the landless laborers, abolish intermediaries, and consolidate landholdings to increase efficiency. Like the case of labor market regulations, while the central government initiated land reforms, it was up to the states to actually implement them and there has been considerable heterogeneity in terms of actual implementation. Besley and Burgess (2000) show that land reforms have reduced poverty at the state level. However, Ghatak and Roy (2007) note reforms have had a *negative* effect on agricultural productivity. However, on further investigation they find that this is largely due to the effect of consolidation of land holdings. On the other hand, tenancy reforms have had insignificant effects. These results underscore the fact that land reforms in many cases have been *de jure* and actual implementation has been weak except in a few states such as West Bengal and Kerala.[11] Unfortunately, like labor reform, enacting sweeping changes in the agricultural sector remains a politically sensitive issue.

Education

Outside India, particularly in the West, the emergence of a successful Indian immigrant community along with the rise of the IT sector in the India often creates misperceptions regarding India's human capital stocks. In reality, India's literacy rate has historically been better than only the poorest sub-Saharan African countries. While the situation has improved considerably, with gross enrollment rates near 100 percent in primary education, secondary enrollment is still only 60 percent. Large firms in India tend to be skill-intensive. The rapidly growing service sectors in India (information and communication technologies, finance, business services, etc.) are all very skill-intensive sectors. Part of this lopsided development is due to the fact that the government of India has long ignored primary education while favoring higher education. For example, even in 2006, the expenditure per student relative to GDP per capita was 8.6 percent for primary education and 53.2 percent for higher education. Developed economies like Japan and Australia recorded values in the range of 15–20 percent for both categories for the same year.[12]

While the level of educational attainment has increased, the quality of public education remains dismal. One of the oft-repeated indicators in this area of research is the teacher absenteeism rate. Reporting results from an exhaustive survey by the Government of India, Chaudury et al. (2006) note that 25 percent of all public school teachers were absent on a typical day. Given this poor record, it is not surprising that Muralidharan and Kremer (2008) note that even in rural India, 28 percent of schools in 2003 were private and 40 percent of the private enrollment was in schools that opened within the preceding five years. Reacting to the concerns about the lack of proper provisioning of public schools, in 2004 the Indian government introduced a "cess" of 2 percent on all central taxes and duties to fund elementary education.[13] In 2007, an additional cess of 1 percent was imposed for higher education. It is too early to tell whether these will help raise education expenditures as a share of GDP to 6 percent – the government's avowed goal.

Institutions and economic growth

Acemoglu and Johnson (2005: 949) distinguish between two different types of institutions:

> "property rights institutions," which protect citizens against expropriation by the government and powerful elites, and "contracting institutions," which enable private contracts between citizens.

They capture property rights institutions by variables such as the risk of expropriation index which measure the risk of expropriation of private foreign investment, from 0 to 10, with a higher score meaning less risk averaged over 1985–1995. For contracting institutions they look at variables that try to measure the complexity and number of procedures involved in collecting debt, for example, bounced checks. They find a strong negative association between GDP per capita and risk of expropriation but little relation between GDP per capita and measures of contracting institutions. It is of interest to note that India is somewhat of an outlier in their study. Its institutional quality indicator is far superior relative to its GDP per capita when compared to the rest of the sample. Given that there is no strong overall relationship between procedural complexity and GDP per capita, it is difficult to make any strong conclusion, though here India is clearly a country with lower than average income and higher than average complexity.

The first finding, that the risk of expropriation in India is relatively low compared to its GDP per capita, is interesting and something that others have already dwelled on. Rodrik and Subramaniam (2008) also note that in 1980, India was already underachieving relative to its long-run institutional quality. They note that the reforms of the late 1980s and early 1990s, while unprecedented for India, were not too dissimilar in scale to those undertaken by Latin American and sub-Saharan African countries. Yet these countries have not shown anywhere near the growth rates for a sustained period like India has over the past 20-plus years.[14]

Conclusion

Since the beginning of the reforms in India, many have doubted their sustainability and their efficaciousness. This is not surprising given India's own chaotic style of democracy and the fact that many other developing countries have started off with similar reforms but have failed to maintain the pace. Over the past two decades, comparisons between India and China by "experts" shifted from why India could never replicate China's success to why reforms in India are more viable in the longer run. This suggests that India's two decades of sustained growth have been somewhat of a surprise. This chapter attempts to provide a broad perspective on India's performance. It is impossible to do full justice to the economic history and the complex issues that are present in India within one chapter. For example, there are many potential roadblocks that have not been mentioned – the complete lack of urban planning, center-state fiscal relations and the fiscal deficit in general, the poor provision of public services, the still dismal situation of electricity generation and distribution, and India's international trade and finance positions. While the media are at once both filled with hyperbole and skepticism about India's future economic growth, there is no doubt that the relentless unfurling of the process makes it an exciting time not just to stay updated but to also explore interesting research questions.

Notes

1 The values are taken from Heston et al. (2011) and are PPP adjusted using 2005 as the base year.
2 For much of this I follow Panagariya's (2008) categorization.
3 As opposed to a "settler" colony.
4 See Banerjee and Iyer (2005). Their work also provides an excellent exposition of the British land tax system.
5 As an aside, for those not familiar with Indian history, Mahatma Gandhi and Nehru had very different views on the future trajectory of the Indian economy. Gandhi viewed India's development in the villages while Nehru wanted India to become a self-sufficient industrialized nation.
6 There has been a vigorous debate on the measurement and trends in poverty. See Deaton and Kozel (2005) for more on this.
7 There is also now an active literature that involves the ranking of states in terms of business friendliness, etc., that further creates competitive pressure. For an exhaustive discussion on these kinds of rankings, see D'Souza (2011).
8 Chanda (2011) finds that Bihar's migration rate increased from 3 percent in 1999–2000 to 12 percent in 2007–08 – the highest value for any state. In addition Bihar has the second highest value for remittances relative to state domestic product at 5.5 percent. (Kerala has the highest share on account of its large emigrant population in the Middle East.)
9 Malaysia's per capita income in 2010 was estimated to be about US$14,000, South Korea's US$30,000 and India's US$3500 (Source: https://www.cia.gov/library/publications/the-world-factbook/).
10 The informal sector usually includes household production. The unorganized sector according to the definition of the Government of India includes enterprises that either a) employ less than 10 workers or b) 20 workers and less but use no electricity.
11 Both states have historically elected the Communist Party which has been more active in pursuing not just land redistribution but more importantly, improving tenancy rights.
12 All data in this paragraph come from the World Bank website data.worldbank.org/indicators.
13 A cess is an indirect tax imposed on services and is usually calculated as a tax on a tax.
14 Bockstette, Chanda and Putterman (2002) argue that countries like India which have long histories of formal institutions have better prospects of long-run growth.

References

Acemoglu, D. and Johnson, S. (2005) 'Unbundling institutions', *Journal of Political Economy*, 113: 949–95.

Banerjee, A. and Iyer, L. (2005) 'History, institutions, and economic performance: the legacy of colonial land tenure systems in India', *American Economic Review*, 95: 1190–1213.

Basu, K. (1992) 'Markets, laws and governments', in B. Jalan (ed.) *The Indian Economy: Problems and Prospects,* New Delhi: Penguin Books.

Besley, T. and Burgess, R. (2000) 'Land reform, poverty reduction, and growth: evidence from India', *Quarterly Journal of Economics*, 115: 389–430.

Besley, T. and Burgess, R. (2004) 'Can labor regulation hinder economic performance? Evidence from India', *Quarterly Journal of Economics*, 119: 91–134.

Bockstette, V., Chanda, A. and Putterman, L. (2002) 'States and markets: the advantages of an early start', *Journal of Economic Growth*, 7: 347–70.

Bosworth, B. and Collins, S. (2003) 'The empirics of growth: an update', *Brookings Papers on Economics Activity*, No. 2: 113–79.

Chanda, A. (2011) 'Growth theoretical appraisal of Bihar's economic performance', mimeo, International Growth Center, London School of Economics.

Chaudhury, N., Hammer, J., Kremer, M., Muralidharan, K. and Halsey Rogers, F. (2006) 'Missing in action: teacher and health worker absence in developing countries', *Journal of Economic Perspectives,* 20(1): 91–116.

Deaton, A. and Kozel, V. (2005) 'Data and dogma: the great India poverty debate', *World Bank Research Observer*, 20: 177–99.

DeLong, J.B. (2003) 'India since independence: an analytical growth narrative', in D. Rodrik (ed) *In Search of Prosperity,* Princeton, NJ: Princeton University Press.

D'Souza, E. (2011) 'What constrains business? The role of the "Single Window" in Gujarat, India', Working Paper, International Growth Center, London School of Economics.

Ghatak, M. and Roy, S. (2007) 'Land reform and agricultural productivity in India: a review of the evidence', *Oxford Review of Economic Policy*, 23: 251–69.

Heston, A., Summers, R. and Bettina, A. (2011) *Penn World Table Version 7.0*, Center for International Comparisons of Production, Income and Prices at the University of Pennsylvania. http://pwt.econ.upenn.edu/php_site/pwt_index.php

Himanshu, (2007) 'Recent trends in poverty and inequality: some preliminary results', *Economic and Political Weekly*, February 10: 497–508.

Kochhar, K., Kumar, U., Rajan, R., Subramanian, A. and Tokatlidis, I. (2006) 'India's pattern of development: what happened, what follows?' *Journal of Monetary Economics*, 53: 981–1019.

Muralidharan, K. and Kremer, M. (2008) 'Public and private schools in rural India', in P. Peterson and R. Chakrabarti (ed.) *School Choice International*, Cambridge, MA: MIT Press.

Panagariya, A. (2008) *India: The Emerging Giant*, New York: Oxford University Press.

Rodrik, D. and Subramaniam, A. (2008) 'From "Hindu Growth" to productivity surge: the mystery of Indian growth transition', in A. Subramaniam (ed.) *India's Turn*, New Delhi: Oxford University Press.

Roy, T. (2002) 'Economic history and modern India: redefining the link', *Journal of Economic Perspectives*, 16: 109–30.

Saha, V., Kar, A. and Baskaran, T. (2004) 'Contribution of informal sector and informal employment in Indian economy', paper presented at the Seventh Meeting of the Expert Group on Informal Sector Statistics (Delhi Group), New Delhi, February 2–4.

World Bank (2011) *Doing Business 2011: Making a Difference for Entrepreneurs*, Washington, DC: World Bank.

27

THE BUBBLE BURST
AND STAGNATION
OF JAPAN

Etsuro Shioji

This chapter reviews the collapse of asset price bubbles in Japan in the early 1990s and its long lasting consequences.[1] Particular attention is paid to the way these experiences have shaped debates among economists on the causes of the stagnation.

Prelude to the bubble

The Japanese economy, devastated by the destruction from World War II, came back strongly in the 1950s and the 1960s. Figure 27.1 presents the evolution of real GDP growth rates. Between 1956 and 1972, the average annual rate of growth was 9.3 percent.[2] This impressive growth ended in 1973 when the first oil crisis hit. In 1974, Japan recorded negative growth, as did most of the world economies. After this, it entered an era of "steady growth," with real GDP growth rates between 1975 and 1985 averaging 3.8 percent. Retrospectively, the oil crisis was merely a trigger. The growth deceleration mirrored a deeper structural change. Due to the rapid technological catch-up in the 1950s and 1960s, there was little room for Japanese firms to grow through further foreign technology adoption. They now needed to develop their own frontiers, which is an inherently more difficult task. This also meant a new, potentially decisive role for the financial market: finding borrowers with promising new projects and truly innovative ideas. The question was whether the market was really up to the job.

The banking system in Japan at that time was characterized by the so-called "convoy system." The notion was that all the banks, including the least competitive ones, were under the protection of the Ministry of Finance. At the same time, banks were subject to the Ministry's strict regulations. A bankruptcy of a commercial bank was considered unthinkable. Indeed, regulation was so prevalent that a bank could not even decide the interest rate it paid on time deposits.[3]

Another important characteristic of the banking system was its hierarchical nature. At the top there were thirteen major banks, known as "city banks." Many of them were at the core of the corporate conglomerates known as "financial *keirestu*,"[4] e.g., Sumitomo and Mitsubishi. To those thirteen, one can add three "long-term credit banks." They had originally been set up to exclusively supply long-term funds to corporations in the years following World War II. But, their roles were becoming increasingly indistinguishable from

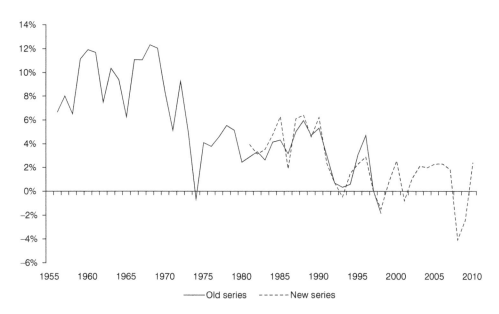

Figure 27.1 Real GDP growth rate of Japan

Source: ESRI (Economic and Social Research Institute, Cabinet Office)

Note: "Old series" is based on 1968SNA and uses calendar year 1990 as the fixed base year. "New Series" is based on 1993SNA and is a chained series, with calendar year 2000 as the reference year.

those of the "city banks." Then there were "regional banks (first-tier and secondary)" which were expected to serve local customers within a single prefecture. Below them were even smaller "credit associations" and "credit unions." The banking system was also supplemented by "non-banks," financial institutions financed by other companies to make loans, such as consumer credit companies and housing loan companies.

It should be noted that, in reality, the "tight" regulations of the system literally applied only to banks at the top. Going down the hierarchical structure, institutions were subject to less strict surveillance by the Ministry of Finance. The smaller ones, especially "non-banks," found loopholes to regulations during the bubble period. In addition, "agricultural cooperatives" effectively acted as banks in rural areas, and yet were not under the jurisdiction of the Ministry of Finance.

But the biggest giant in the financial system was the government-owned Post Office, which in 1984 collected 29 percent of overall deposits in Japan.[5] Postal savings deposits were a seriously competitive alternative to deposits offered by commercial banks since the former were perceived to be government-guaranteed assets; there was a nation-wide network of post offices deployed to collect them, and the rate of interest was comparable to those offered by banks. On the lending side, as major commercial banks were trying to move into new business territories such as housing loans and lending to smaller firms, the presence of the Housing Loan Corporation and the Small Business Finance Corporations, public institutions that provided low-cost loans to households and small businesses, made such moves difficult.

By the mid-1980s this system was seriously outdated. Up to that time, with governmental protection, banks could expect to reap more or less guaranteed profits by continuing business with their traditional borrowers. Consequently, there were few incentives for banks to spend resources to search for potentially promising new borrowers. In fact, it is believed that they had limited incentives to develop skills to conduct such screening. Instead, the practice of collateral-based lending was prevalent. On the other hand, deregulation was progressing at differing speeds across different sectors of the financial market. The most important development was growth of the corporate bond market. Once practically non-existent, it emerged as an important source of funds for the best performing firms in Japan.[6] As a result, "over-banking" had become a serious issue: banks were still absorbing much of the household sector's money in the form of deposits,[7] but they were losing high-quality borrowers.

One of the biggest issues in international economic relationships in the mid-1980s was U.S. current account deficits with Japan. As a response, the Plaza Accord was signed in September 1985 which resulted in a rapid appreciation of the Japanese yen. At the time, 1 U.S. dollar was equal to 236.9 yen. A year later, the yen had appreciated to 154.8 yen per dollar. There was an outcry, especially from major Japanese exporting sectors, for policy actions to counteract this effect. Japan's real GDP growth rate for 1986 was just 1.9 percent.[8]

The bubble

The Japanese bubble took off in 1987. Figure 27.2 presents the evolution of a representative stock price index in Japan, TOPIX. Between January 1987 and December 1989, it went up from 1649 to 2860. Figure 27.3 reports the price of commercial land for six major cities in Japan (a biannual statistic). Between the second half of 1986 and the first half of 1990, it had more than doubled, from 222 to 525. The growth rate of real GDP between 1987 and 1990 was 5.8 percent per annum.

Analysis suggests that two forces were behind the bubble. The first was a loose monetary policy. Figure 27.4 shows the evolution of the call rate, the key interbank lending rate for Japan. Toward the end of 1985, the Bank of Japan (BOJ) set it to be around 8 percent. It was down

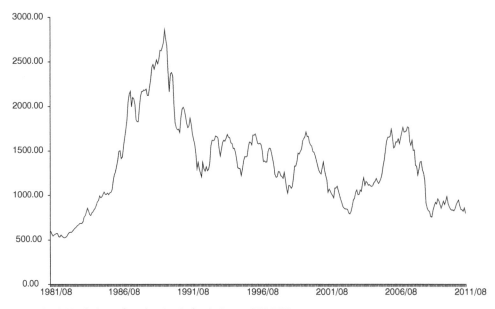

Figure 27.2 Evolution of stock price index in Japan (TOPIX)

Source: Tokyo Stock Exchange

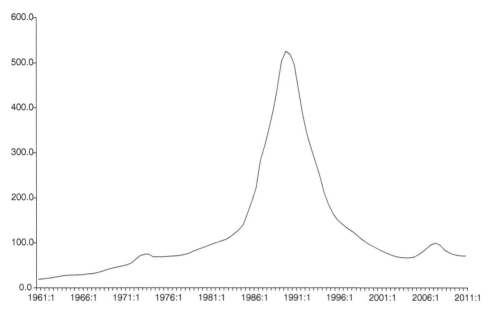

Figure 27.3 Evolution of land price index in Japan (six major cities, commercial use)

Source: Japan Real Estate Institute

Note: Biannual data

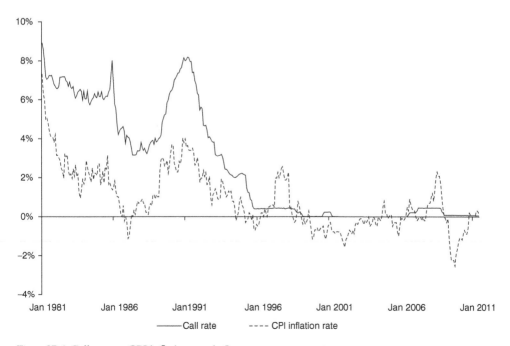

Figure 27.4 Call rate vs. CPI inflation rate in Japan

Source: Call rate = Bank of Japan, CPI = Statistics Bureau

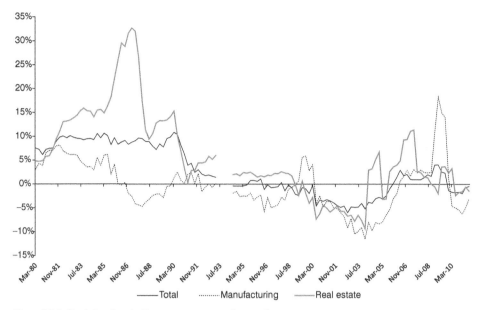

Figure 27.5 Bank lending in Japan, percentage change from a year ago

Source: Bank of Japan.

Note: Discontinuity is due to a change in definition

to about 3 percent by mid 1987. Even more noteworthy are expansions in credit. Figure 27.5 shows year-to-year growth rates in overall bank loans, loans to manufacturing, and loans to the real estate sector. In the first quarter of 1987, total loan growth was 8.8 percent, while real estate loans were growing at 32.7 percent. On the other hand, the number for manufacturing was negative at –2.5 percent: this indicates that banks were losing their traditional customers to the bond market. Why was this massive credit expansion left unchecked? First, as already noted, there was strong pressure from industries to counteract the depressing effects of the strong yen. Second, inflation was apparently under control. Figure 27.4 also shows the trend in the CPI inflation rate. Between 1987 and 1988, the average inflation rate was as low as 0.4 percent.

Even today, there is no consensus about why loose monetary policy was associated with the formation of a bubble, or why a monetary expansion sometimes leads not to a general price increase but rather to a boom concentrated in asset markets. Indeed, economics has difficulty identifying asset bubbles even after they happen, never mind in real time. But the Japanese experience, like that of the U.S. in the 2000s, suggests that finding answers to the questions above holds a key to understanding bubble phenomena.

The second cause of the Japanese bubble lay in the banking system. As previously noted, banks were losing easy profit opportunities, namely corporations with high creditworthiness, to other types of financial markets such as the corporate bond market. When faced with the massive supply of funds flowing on to their balance sheets, they turned to alternative profit opportunities, namely, the real estate sector. The practice of collateral-based lending created a positive feedback loop: rising land prices prompted a series of upward revaluations of land as collateral, and this in turn fueled a further real estate boom. Banks had little incentive to limit their risk-taking under the protection of the convoy system. This was a typical example of a moral hazard problem, that is, excessive risk-taking encouraged by guarantees of compensation for losses.

In standard macroeconomic theory, "rational bubbles" occur in the situation of over-accumulation of capital (called "dynamic inefficiency"), and the presence of a bubble enhances efficiency through crowding out capital investment (see, e.g., Blanchard and Fischer 1989: Chapter 5). But Japanese experiences point to the contrary. A large amount of money was spent on building new resort facilities and expensive golf courses, which turned out to be money losers. Investment in foreign assets such as the purchases of the Pebble Beach Golf Course in California and the Rockefeller Center in New York, to name just two, mostly turned sour.

The collapse

Asset prices began to decline in 1990. Once this started, it happened fast, especially in the stock market. By August 1992, TOPIX was down to 1208 (Figure 27.2) – a drop of 58 percent from the peak only 32 months earlier. The decline in the land price index was slower, but it still went down to 143 by the second half of 1996 – a drop of 73 percent over 6.5 years (Figure 27.3). Three policy changes are believed to have triggered the collapse. The first is the quantitative restriction on real estate loans implemented in March 1990 which required the growth rate in real estate lending to be less than or equal to that of overall lending. The second is the introduction of a land price tax which was legislated in 1990 and implemented in 1992. The third is a series of interest rate hikes by the BOJ: the call rate was around 4 percent in early 1989 but went up to 8 percent by the end of 1990 (Figure 27.4). Those anti-bubble measures probably came too late, but if stopping the bubble was the objective, they were all very effective, perhaps too much so.

The collapse did more than reverse what the bubble had accomplished. As the collateral values declined, bank lending shrank, which induced a further decline in asset values, i.e., a negative feedback loop emerged. The severity of this vicious circle was magnified by the bad loans problem which will be reviewed in the next section.

From creeping instability to financial crisis

At the time of the bubble collapse, it was largely considered a minor correction which would lead to a sound state of the economy. But behind the scene, a crisis was about to unfold, albeit gradually.

The stock market crash lowered profits in the corporate sector by making it difficult to raise funds. The crash in the land market lowered the values of collateral. Thus much of lending that existed at the end of the bubble era turned into non-performing loans.

Four reasons why the collapse did not result in an immediate financial crisis have been identified. First, in the first half of the 1990s, there was still a widespread expectation of an eventual turnaround of the economy. Second, the "convoy system" had created a perception that the government would not let banks fail. Third, under the mutual stock holding practice of the "financial *keiretsu*," banks held a major portion of stocks in the corporate sector. As they had acquired those shares long before the bubble period, even as of the early 1990s, they still had tremendous unrealized capital gains. Under Bank for International Settlements (BIS) regulations, which were introduced in Japan in 1993, banks were allowed to incorporate about half of those gains as a part of their tier two capital. This gave them a cushion to absorb their losses. Fourth, unclear accounting rules at the time made it possible for the banks to conceal much of their losses.

It should be noted, at the same time, that precisely for those four reasons, the banking sector postponed the inevitable fate of facing the problems with bad loans, that is, forcing unprofitable borrowers to restructure (or to simply liquidate) while taking losses themselves. This wait-and-see strategy made sense for the top managers who could expect to retire soon. But economically, Japan wasted a few precious years because of that. In the meantime, financial intermediation came to a stand still. Faced with an enormous risk of defaults on existing loans, banks cut new lending. At the same time they kept lending to their ailing old customers to keep them afloat, for fear that their own financial problems would be revealed. In retrospect, the economy was not going to get the kind of quick recovery that those bankers were hoping for as long as they were all in this waiting mode.

The first sign that the situation was unsustainable came from real estate financing. In 1996, the government proposed to inject public money into troubled housing loan corporations. This caused a public outrage, which forced the government to promise to use no further tax money to help the financial sector. Also, some smaller financial institutions, such as Kizu Credit Union, failed, causing mini bank runs.

The reaction of monetary policy makers to the collapse is also believed to have been slow. Figure 27.4 shows that the BOJ did not start lowering the interbank lending rate until 1991; it was subsequently lowered to around 0.5 percent by mid-1995. Fiscal policy shifted to stimulative mode in 1992 but, faced with a mounting debt, changed its focus to debt reduction in 1997; the consumption tax rate was raised from 3 percent to 5 percent in March of 1997.

Between 1997 and 1998, the Japanese economy had a major crisis. The crisis was triggered by the failure of a modest securities company called Sanyo Securities on November 5, 1997. On this day, it defaulted on its debt in the call market, the first default by a Japanese financial company in the post-World War II period. This created a panic and sent the call market into paralysis, making it difficult for already struggling financial institutions to survive. On November 15, Hokkaido Takushoku Bank failed. It was one of the "city banks" at the top of the old hierarchy, whose failure was considered unthinkable until then. On November 24, Yamaichi Securities, one of the four largest securities companies in Japan, failed. In 1998, the media frequently reported on the crises of Japan Long-Term Credit Bank and Nippon Credit Bank, two of the once-mighty "long-term credit banks."

The crisis gave rise to what was called the "Japan Premium." This is the premium that Japanese financial institutions had to pay to raise funds in overseas markets due to concerns over the stability of their financial system. Figure 27.6 shows its evolution. In both late 1997 and October 1998, it went up to almost 0.7 percent.

This crisis was a typical manifestation of "systemic risk": as financial institutions are interconnected through the web of lending and borrowing, a fear of default in one place could trigger a chain reaction of heightened counter-party risks. As a consequence, even healthy banks could greatly suffer through the possibility of liquidity shortage or potential threatened insolvency. This induces a massive financial disintermediation and sends the entire economy into a crisis. GDP growth rates in 1997, 1998, and 1999 were 0.0 percent, −1.5 percent, and 0.7 percent, respectively (Figure 27.1). An obvious remedy would be to draw a clearly defined line between healthier banks and troubled ones, and to protect the former from systemic risk by injecting public money if necessary, while encouraging the latter to clean up their problems, and, if they fail, taking them out of the system quickly. A big question is how to accomplish the latter job without causing a panic.

Why was Japan unable to avoid the crisis? One reason was that, seven years after the bubble collapse, the country was still so unprepared against such a risk. For example, there was no legal framework to deal with a failure of a systemically important bank; under the old system,

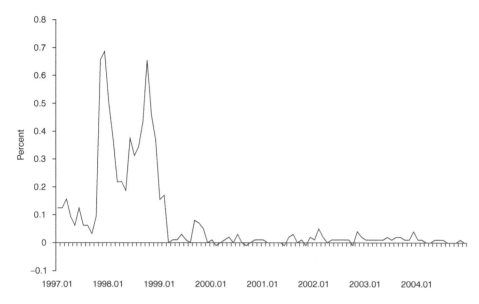

Figure 27.6 Japan premium (percent)

Source: Bank of Japan

Note: Defined as TIBOR – LIBOR (Tokyo Interbank Offered Rate – London Interbank Offered Rate)

it was just not supposed to happen. Only when it faced the crisis did the Japanese government come up with the following five policy changes: (1) In October 1998, the parliament legislated a framework to nationalize failing banks temporarily. Based on this, the two troubled "long-term credit banks" were nationalized. (2) The government started injecting public money into the financial system. Its first attempt in March 1998, which involved 1.8 trillion yen, was largely ineffective, as the money was divided exactly equally between major banks, without consideration of their financial health. The second wave, which started in 1999 for which the government had set aside 60 trillion yen, was more meaningful. It favored relatively healthy banks and shielded them from the crisis, while punishing those with deeper problems, giving them incentives to act swiftly to clean up their balance sheets.

Other notable developments included (3) introduction of "Prompt Corrective Action" which empowers the newly established Financial Services Agency to order restructuring to those banks that fail to meet the BIS capital standards, (4) a shift to stricter and more transparent guidelines for banks to report their non-performing loans, and (5) establishment of the Resolution and Collection Corporation that purchases bad loans from banks. With those five reforms in place, Japan was finally equipped with sufficient apparatus to deal with the financial crisis. The fear of an imminent fallout had subsided by the end of 1999.

It should be noted, however, that the instability due to the bad loans problem persisted until 2002. In fact, according to the Financial Services Agency, the ratio of non-performing loans to total credit for all the "city banks" was 5.1 percent in March 1999. It went up, not down, to 8.7 percent in March 2002. GDP growth was at 2.6 percent in 2000, but in 2001 and 2002, it was –0.8 percent and 1.1 percent. After all, capital injection per se does not make bad loans disappear. It requires banks that are determined to clean up their balance sheets. At this point, bank managers were still reluctant to reveal the true extent of their balance sheet problems and to post substantial realized losses.

Macroeconomic policy reactions to the crisis

The Bank of Japan reacted to the crisis by lowering the already low interest rate further. In 1998, it lowered the target rate to 0.25 percent. In February 1999, it effectively lowered the target rate to zero. This is called the Zero Interest Rate Policy (ZIRP). Interestingly, this was followed by another, lesser noticed new policy initiative. In April 1999, the BOJ announced that ZIRP would be continued "until deflationary concerns are dispelled." This was the BOJ's first attempt to influence the private sector through changing the private sector's expectations on the future course of policy actions. Such an effect is called the "Policy Duration Effect." This historical announcement, however, did not seem to have much impact, perhaps because the conditions for policy duration were not specified clearly enough.

After a brief departure from ZIRP (for which the BOJ was heavily criticized), in March 2001, the BOJ adopted the unprecedented "Quantitative Easing" (QE) policy. Under QE, the Bank of Japan targeted outstanding bank reserves. The target was achieved mainly through purchases of the Japanese government bonds. The target was set at 5 trillion yen initially, and then was raised on several occasions.

It is debatable whether QE had an impact on the economy much beyond that of ZIRP. Evidence suggests that it did have the effect of flattening the yield curve through the policy duration effect, and perhaps also through eliminating some risk premia along the way. But its macroeconomic impact is less clear. As most of the added monetary base stayed within the banking sector, no significant impact on M2 is apparent. Also, deflation persisted. On the other hand, there is little doubt that both ZIRP and QE acted as great stabilizers of the financial market. Under these policies, banks were given unlimited access to zero-cost funds. Concerns over possible liquidity shortages were gone.

The Japanese government, burdened by its heavy debt with a public debt-to-GDP ratio equal to 100.5 percent in 1997 according to the OECD (refer to Figure 27.7 which depicts the evolution of this ratio; the number includes debts of local governments), was about to embark on an ambitious fiscal consolidation program when the crisis hit. In 1998, the program was suspended and the policy stance turned expansionary. The general government deficit-to-GDP ratio was 4.0 percent in 1997, but went up to 11.2 percent and 7.4 percent, respectively, in 1998 and 1999 (OECD). It was perceived, however, that the stimulus did not work, and there was a growing concern over further accumulation of public debt. The public debt-to-GDP ratio increased to 143.7 percent in 2001 (Figure 27.7). Under the cabinet of Prime Minister Koizumi, which was formed in 2001, fiscal policy once again shifted to a contractionary mode.

What caused the "Lost Decade"?

The bubble and the following crash led to a stagnation which lasted over ten years, called the "Lost Decade" of the Japanese economy. Between 1991 and 2002, the average annual growth rate of real GDP was just 0.9 percent. There has been a heated debate on its main cause and appropriate policy responses.

The initial reaction from researchers was to treat these events as another typical downturn caused by aggregate demand deficiency (just a very large one). Based on this view, the proposed solution was to stimulate aggregate demand through expansionary monetary and/ or fiscal policies. But what could have caused such a decline in demand? There are four popular candidates:

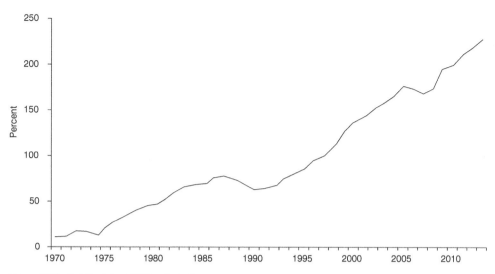

Figure 27.7 Public debt–GDP ratio in Japan

Source: OECD *Economic Outlook* No. 90 (2011) database

Note: General government gross financial liabilities (i.e., includes debts of both central and local governments), historical estimates and future forecasts

1 *Credit crunch*: As explained above, the bad loans problem led to cuts in new lending or what is known as the "reluctance to lend" problem. It is widely believed that many banks were even refraining from loans to small but sound borrowers in an effort to maintain their relationships with large but troubled ones. This depressed investment. In a collection of micro data studies, Kazuo Ogawa shows that investment, particularly that of medium-sized and small firms, in Japan is sensitive to financial frictions (refer to, for example, Ogawa 2003). Also, Motonishi and Yoshikawa (1999), using time series data, show that the lending attitude of banks significantly affects investment by medium-sized and small firms.

2 *Inadequate monetary policy*: Many regard monetary policy during this period as a sequence of "too little, too late" actions. They point to persistent deflation (Figure 27.4) as a sign of failed monetary policy. But what could be achieved by monetary policy once the economy hits the zero bound? Some argue that the BOJ simply should have printed more money, either through expanding QE much further, or by purchasing a wider range of private assets or through foreign exchange market interventions. Others point to inappropriate management of expectations of the private sector. In today's macroeconomic theory, monetary policy works not only through manipulating today's interest rate, but also through changing the private sector's perception for the future course of policy. They argue that, through introduction of "inflation targeting," the BOJ could have utilized the expectation channel far more effectively (Ito 2001).[9]

3 *Inadequate fiscal policy*: Others point to insufficient fiscal stimulus. The expansionary policy in the late 1990s failed to lift the economy out of a recession not because of its ineffectiveness but because it was not large enough. A challenge for this view would be how to convincingly argue that the large budget deficits and enormous growth in the public debt should not have been such a major concern.

4 *Uncertainty and precautionary saving*: Horioka (2006) argues that households during this period were facing considerable uncertainty concerning future disposable income and job availability. For example, there was uncertainty regarding who would eventually pay for the large budget deficits. Such uncertainty might have induced precautionary saving, as for example in a Ricardian forward-looking household, and thus reduced consumption demand.

Hayashi and Prescott (2002) offer a different view. They find that the growth rate of total factor productivity (TFP) had declined considerably in this period. They calibrate a real business cycle model for the Japanese economy (which, by construction, has no place for demand deficiency) and demonstrate that the deceleration in TFP can account for much of the slowdown. Thus, demand deficiency does not seem to be a major factor in explaining the lost decade.

An important contribution of Hayashi and Prescott was that it ignited a heated debate within the profession. One notable development was progress in productivity measurement. Various improved estimates of TFP were proposed, incorporating such elements as variable capacity utilization. One of these studies, Kawamoto (2005), finds no evidence of TFP growth deceleration for the 1990s, contrary to the finding of Hayashi and Prescott. Perhaps the most comprehensive estimate at present is available in the Japan Industrial Productivity (JIP) Database: it indicates that the average TFP growth rates for the periods 1980–1990 and 1990–2000 were 2 percent and 0 percent per annum, respectively, indicating a sizable decline.[10]

The question remains why a mere financial market problem could lead to a productivity slowdown in the real sector. Studies along this line focus on the misallocation of resources. As was argued, banks reduced lending to new and potentially productive borrowers, while continuing to lend to unprofitable customers (so-called "Evergreening"). Caballero, Hoshi and Kashyap (2008) argue that the latter practice produced a group of "zombie firms" that congested the market and lowered profitability of healthier firms. Fukao and Kwon (2006) and Nishimura, Nakajima and Kiyota (2005) compare TFP levels of incumbent firms and exiting firms using micro data, and find that more productive firms were being forced out of the market. Another likely cause of resource allocation failure was the rigid labor market practice in Japan: under the once-lauded long-term employment system in Japan, firms are reluctant to cut down the size of their core workforce. A by-product of this convention is that the labor market for mid-career workers is very thin and inactive. As a consequence, there was little mobility of workers across different industrial sectors. This is believed to have slowed down a necessary structural adjustment of the Japanese economy.

The debate continues even today. A weakness with the demand deficiency view is that, in typical Keynesian macroeconomics, excess supply arises due to nominal price stickiness, and is supposed to be a temporary phenomenon. It may not provide an adequate explanation for a decade long stagnation. On the other hand, the productivity view may have a hard time explaining the coexistence of weak output and falling prices. In traditional macroeconomics, a productivity slowdown leads to a fall in aggregate supply, which results in inflation, not deflation. Of course, in modern dynamic theories, productivity plays a more complex role: if a current productivity slowdown induces households to revise their estimates of permanent income downward, or if it lowers firms' expected future marginal product of capital, it could reduce demand as well as supply (Miyao 2006). Whether it could reduce demand *more than* supply, for a sustained period of time, needs further investigation.

The preceding discussion of deflation presumes that it was a consequence of a *temporary* negative GDP gap. Alternatively, it might reflect a downward shift in the *trend* inflation rate.

Given that deflation has outlived the lost decade by far (at the time of this writing, there is no sign of an end to it), seeking such a separate explanation might be a promising direction for future research.

End of the Lost Decade?

In 2002, the Japanese government, led by economic minister Heizo Takenaka, implemented a set of new policies that is commonly known as the "Takenaka Plan." This required commercial banks to adopt tougher accounting standards and to reduce the amount of bad loans by half: a non-compliant bank would have faced a threat of nationalization. In March of 2002, the total amount of non-performing loans among major banks was at its peak at 27.6 trillion yen. In March 2005, it was down to 13.6 trillion yen, roughly achieving the goal of the plan (Hoshi and Kashyap 2011).

Between 2003 and 2007, Japan enjoyed a sustained but modest recovery, with an average real GDP growth rate of 2.1 percent (Figure 27.1). The CPI inflation rate approached zero (Figure 27.4). Economists are again divided on the interpretation. Some see this as a sign that the resolution of the bad loans problem finally freed the country from the structural problems. Others, based on the demand-side view, argue that this recovery was a consequence of stronger exports, which were in turn due to strong world-wide economic growth.

During the world financial crisis of 2008–2009, the performance of the Japanese economy was the worst among industrialized economies: GDP growth rates for 2008 and 2009 were –4.1 percent and –2.4 percent, respectively. Deflation deepened again. This caused a fear that perhaps Japan's "lost decade" was not over after all, and that it was in the midst of a "lost two decades." Many of those who take this long-term pessimistic view point to Japan's rapidly aging society and the near certainty of a declining population (see Figure 27.8).[11] The ever higher public debt–to-GDP ratio also poses a threat to the hope for sustained economic growth (refer, again, to Figure 27.7). After a weak sign of recovery in 2010, in March 2011, Japan was hit by the devastating Great East Japan Earthquake and the nuclear plant accident

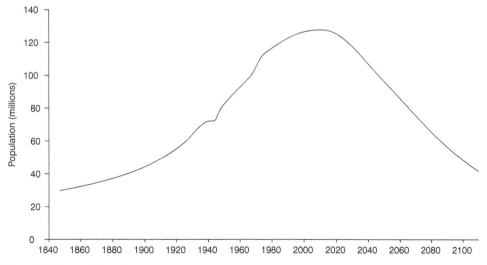

Figure 27.8 Population of Japan

Source: Statistics Bureau (historical estimates, up to 2009) and National Institute of Population and Social Security Research (forecasts, from 2010).

in Fukushima. At the time of this writing (June 2012), the pessimistic view seems to be gaining popularity within Japan. The author's opinion is that very long-term issues such as demography can be discussed separately from the problems of the lost decade, which had roots in the financial market, regardless of which of the opposing views one takes.

Notes

1 Komine (2011a, 2011b) provides a comprehensive and valuable record of the history of the Japanese economy between the 1970s and 2006.
2 Refer to the note to Figure 27.1 for details on the underlying statistics. Throughout this chapter, real GDP numbers are for Japanese fiscal years, which start in April and end in March.
3 Although the Ministry of Finance never stated this "protection" explicitly, everybody implicitly understood that it was the policy of the ministry. The banks, in exchange, were highly regulated and often accepted ex-Ministry of Finance officials as their company executives. Once the government started to lift those regulations, the implicit guarantees provided fertile ground for moral hazard on the part of the banks.
4 According to Ito (1991: 178), financial *keiretsu* is "a financial grouping that effects horizontal integration – a set of firms in different industries – through cross holding of stocks and lending from a main bank." The word "*keiretsu*" literally means "company chains."
5 Based on data from the Statistics Bureau of Japan.
6 According to Komine (2011a), at the beginning of the 1980s, major firms in Japan raised 8.5 percent of their funds by corporate bonds. By 1989, the share had gone up to 17.4 percent.
7 Deposits (banks and the postal savings combined) constituted 56.7 percent of household assets in 1984, according to the Statistics Bureau of Japan.
8 From here onwards, real GDP refers to numbers from the chained indices with the calendar year 2000 as the reference year.
9 The "Policy Duration Effect" reviewed in the previous section also works through expectations. The difference is that this channel works through changing expectations of the financial sector, which shifts the yield curve. It is not necessarily clear how the effect is transmitted to the non-financial sector. Inflation targeting, on the other hand, is supposed to work mainly through expectations of the non-financial corporate sector and households, and thus can be expected to have a more direct impact on the macroeconomy (if successful).
10 Source: http://www.rieti.go.jp/jp/database/JIP2011/index.html. The numbers are for the market sector.
11 Although the total population in Japan did not start to decline until 2008, it is noteworthy that the working age population (those aged between 15 and 64) already started to decrease in 2000. This decline is expected to accelerate in the near future.

References

Blanchard, O. and Fischer, S. (1989) *Lectures on Macroeconomics*, Cambridge, MA: MIT Press.
Caballero, R.J., Hoshi, T. and Kashyap, A.K. (2008) 'Zombie lending and depressed restructuring in Japan', *American Economic Review*, 98: 1943–77.
Fukao, K. and Kwon, H.U. (2006) 'Why did Japan's TFP growth slowdown in the lost decade? An empirical analysis based on firm-level data of manufacturing firms', *Japanese Economic Review*, 57: 195–228.
Hayashi, F. and Prescott, E. (2002) 'The 1990s in Japan: a lost decade', *Review of Economic Dynamics*, 5: 235–61.
Horioka, C.Y. (2006) 'The causes of Japan's "lost decade": the role of household consumption', *Japan and the World Economy*, 18: 378–400.
Hoshi, T. and Kashyap, A.K. (2011) 'Why did Japan stop growing?', report submitted to the National Institute of Research Advancement.
Ito, T. (1991) *The Japanese Economy*, Cambridge, MA: MIT Press.
Ito, T. (2001) *Inflation Targeting* (in Japanese), Tokyo: Nihon Keizai Shinbunsha.

Kawamoto, T. (2005) 'What do the purified Solow residuals tell us about Japan's lost decade?', *Monetary and Economic Studies,* 23: 113–48.

Komine, T. (ed.) (2011a) *Records of the Japanese Economy 1* (in Japanese), Tokyo: Economic and Social Research Institute.

Komine, T. (ed.) (2011b) *Records of the Japanese Economy 2* (in Japanese), Tokyo: Economic and Social Research Institute.

Miyao, R. (2006) 'Causes of fluctuations of the Japanese economy: roles of productivity shocks' (in Japanese), Bank of Japan Working Paper 06-J-1.

Motonishi, T. and Yoshikawa, H. (1999) 'Causes of the long stagnation of Japan during the 1990s: financial or real?', *Journal of the Japanese and International Economies,* 13: 181–200.

Nishimura, K.G., Nakajima, T. and Kiyota, K. (2005) 'Does the natural selection mechanism still work in severe recessions?: Examination of the Japanese economy in the 1990s', *Journal of Economic Behavior and Organization,* 58: 53–78.

Ogawa, K. (2003) 'Financial distress and corporate investment: the Japanese case in the 90s', Institute of Social and Economic Research Working Paper No. 584.

28

THE DEMISE OF THE
SOVIET UNION

Richard E. Ericson

Introduction

For most of the twentieth century, the Soviet Union stood like a colossus over Eurasia, a political, military, and economic challenge to the West and its way of life. As discussed by Hayek (1994), the Soviet Union represented a way of organizing economic life and development that was diametrically opposed to the natural market ordering that had supported, indeed driven, Western economic development and prosperity into the early twentieth century. With its authoritarian, indeed (at least initially) totalitarian, political system and centrally planned "command" economic system, it appeared to turn a backward, illiterate, overwhelmingly rural/agricultural society into an industrialized, urbanized, scientifically advanced, military superpower in record time. From an agrarian backwater, the Soviet Union became a viable alternative model of the potential future of the social, political, and economic organization of humanity.

Apparent Soviet rates of growth were historically unprecedented, providing the world's first economic development miracle, and threatening to overtake, "bury" in Khrushchev's words, the most advanced economies. And in doing so, it provided, in the middle of the twentieth century, a model of rapid modernization and economic development, one seen as worthy of emulation by developing economies around the world.[1] It also had an impact on the development of economic policy in Western Europe, where Socialist governments introduced massive industrial nationalization and national economic planning in their democratic polities. Even in the United States, the "rationality" of the Soviet planned approach to managing economic growth, macroeconomic stability, and equity in distribution, was accepted in major textbooks and by numerous economists who called for national planning as an inevitable historical development, a part of convergence of systems to a common, rational, socially controlled form of economic organization.[2]

Yet, in the early 1990s, the Soviet Union, and its touted economic system, vanished in one of the more spectacular economic collapses in recorded history. The system, presented as a model for the future, collapsed into economic chaos, and the superpower disintegrated into fifteen largely underdeveloped countries. What happened? How should we understand this history changing event?

This chapter explores the sources and course of this remarkable event. As with all historical change, the factors behind it are both structural and conjunctural. The former relate to the nature of the system, its inherent characteristics, strengths and vulnerabilities. They created capabilities and vulnerabilities, the foundation upon which performance was based. The latter refer to the specific circumstances, decisions, and actions, in the environment created by the structural factors, that triggered the event and determined the precise timing of its occurrence. Thus it begins by discussing the nature of the command economy, and how it helps "explain" both the phenomenal successes and the growing economic failures of the Soviet economic system. That nature made the system highly stable, resistant to change, with every prospect of long-run survival, despite increasing performance problems. Yet those problems, in the face of the growing success of market capitalist systems, led the Soviet leadership to undertake measures, reforms, that proved disastrous to the viability of the system – the conjunctural factors. Spurred by diminishing success relative to the developed capitalist world, the Soviet leadership, under Communist Party General Secretary, and then President of the USSR, Mikhail S. Gorbachev, forced systemic changes that essentially destroyed the command economy. In the face of losing economic competition with the West, the Soviet economic system committed suicide.

The command economy: experiment of the century

Nature and defining characteristics

A command economy is one in which the coordination of economic activity, essential to the viability and functioning of a complex social economy, is undertaken through administrative means – commands, directives, targets and regulations – rather than by a market mechanism. Economic agents in a command economy, in particular production organizations, operate primarily by virtue of specific directives from higher authority in an administrative/political hierarchy, that is, under the "command principle."

(Ericson 2008: 1)

The Soviet "command" system, the economic engine behind Soviet power and military prowess, reflected a conscious effort to take total control over human activity and destiny. It was developed to implement the utopian dream of a "knowing" elite, the Communist Party: the creation of a fully rational society, one in which no aspect of human activity was to be left to chance, outside of social control. It reflected the socialist culmination of the enlightenment ideal of a rationally managed economy, one consistent with the scientific laws of history. And as such, it brooked no opposition to, no deviation from, the ultimate social goal as interpreted by that elite.

In pursuit of this objective, the command economy strove for total control over all economic activity. The inherent impossibility of such control forced the leadership and its implementing agencies to relinquish operational (direct) control over non-priority areas, and focus on those critical to determining the direction, structure and outcomes of material production, the physical basis of the new society. Although implementation details, even in priority areas, had to be left in the hands of poorly informed, self-interested subordinates, this aspiration led to unprecedented control over economic behavior, and ongoing efforts to reinforce and expand that control, efforts in large part defining the Soviet command economy.

This imperative of control, by a small "leading" group ultimately responsible for its fate, required the centralization of all important decisions, and hence required structures making central planning, *ex ante* coordination, and *ex post* management of economic activity both feasible and effective. This posed an increasingly overwhelming task as the economy developed and grew in size and complexity. To manage the vast amounts of information required both for planning and for the provision of operational instructions/commands to implementing agents, a complete, elaborated hierarchy, in which both information and instructions might be, respectively, aggregated to the top and disaggregated to the bottom, was found necessary. Economic activity was determined in and controlled by nested hierarchical structures, each facing a relatively simple subproblem of planning and implementation, working with economic aggregates at all but the lowest level.[3]

This simplification of the economic planning and management problems allowed effective focus on priorities and the achievement of sufficiently important goals. In doing so, however, it rendered decisions crude, consistent only (at best) with respect to planning aggregates; and systematically isolated decision makers, at all but the highest levels, from the consequences of their decisions, a source of fundamental irresponsibility in operational decision making.[4] Further, priorities were achieved at the expense of non-priority sectors and activities, which were still subject to mandatory targets and arbitrary interventions from above, but had to fend for themselves without taking resources from priority uses or disrupting more important (from the perspective of the highest authorities) activities. Hence, resulting plans, necessarily developed in haste on the basis of delayed and partial information, were always incomplete, and suffered numerous inconsistencies which, however, could not be allowed to disrupt the achievement of priorities.

The consequence of this imperative was the destruction of markets and market institutions, the foundation of any economic autonomy, and their replacement with a set of institutions antithetical to proper market functioning. Thus institutions were required for enforcing subordinate obedience both to plans and operational interventions from above, and restricting subordinate autonomy. In particular, strict control over the physical allocation of all material and human resources had to be maintained, and subordinate capabilities for unauthorized "initiative" had to be severely limited. This included rationing material inputs and access to labor and capital, and severely limiting access to, and the effective power of, "money" – the generalized command over goods and services that is the foundation of any effective economic agent autonomy in a complex social economy.

From the physical rationing of key materials and products, and the tight regulation of the incentives and parameters guiding allocation at levels of detail beyond central purview, to the severe restrictions on the flexibility/capabilities of subordinates to respond to problems, the institutions of the command economy strove to block all unauthorized initiative and force strict compliance with planned/commanded (both explicitly and implicitly) activities.[5] Thus information from planners was rationed on a need-to-know basis, liquidity was provided only when and as needed, and Soviet "money" was restricted to a mere unit of measurement and account, where possible.[6] Indeed, monetary funds were neither necessary nor sufficient for any transactions within the state sectors, and balances were subject to arbitrary confiscation or enhancement as deemed fitting by the higher economic organs. Monetary functions were also limited, but not void, outside sectors amenable to central planning and control, as indicated below (Garvy 1977, Ericson 1991, 2008). Further, all incentives were tied to service to the (party and) state as interpreted by superiors in the hierarchy, with individual wellbeing dependent on such service. And arbitrary discretion (*ex post*) was necessarily left in the hands of, in particular political (Party), superiors to alter commands in order to fix problems, to get things done.

Of course, large areas of economic activity proved too complex, or insufficiently important, to be centrally planned and directly managed. Thus households and many agricultural organizations remained outside the formal state sector, necessarily operating in a (partially) monetized environment, and hence had to be dealt with through "quasi-markets" for labor, consumers' goods, and some agricultural produce. Here money was necessarily more active than in the state-managed sectors, opening opportunities for decentralized initiative and so posing a continual threat to effective state control.[7] Hence its availability and use had to be subject to as strict monitoring and control as possible, a primary task of the Soviet dual monetary system. Yet, despite extraordinary controls built into this system (Garvy 1977) the inevitable errors in planning and surprises in implementation led to growing "liquidity" outside of centralized controls, undermining "plan discipline" and the ability to effectively manage economic activity. And this increasingly fed the growth of a second economy outside of, if largely parasitic on, the state "planned" command economy.[8]

This created a system *fundamentally different from* that of modern market economies, as can be seen in a summary of its essential characteristics (Ericson 1991).

1   A hierarchical structure of authority in which all choices must be made, and conflicts resolved, in principle, at a level superior to all sides of the issue, with sole vertical accountability for actions and outcomes.
2   Rigid, highly centralized planning of production and distribution.
3   A commitment to maximal resource utilization, implying "tautness" and pressure in planning.
4   Formal rationing, i.e. administrative allocation in physical or quasi-physical terms, of producers' goods and services.
5   Exhaustive price control, yielding multiple and contradictory systems of centrally fixed, economically inflexible, prices.
6   The lack of any liquidity or flexible response capability (e.g. reserves, excess capacity) in the system, and in particular the lack of any true money.
7   The lack of any legal alternatives to given economic relationships, and the inability of any subordinate to legally alter any of these relationships.
8   Absolute and arbitrary control by superiors of the norms, indices, and parameters of plan assignments, performance evaluation, and rewards.
9   Incentives geared to meeting the plans and desires of evaluating superiors, and not to the economic consequences of decisions taken at levels below the very top.

Characteristics (1) to (4) provided the framework for effective central control; characteristics (5) to (7) limited or eliminated subordinate autonomy; characteristics (8) and (9) gave the center the ability to steer subordinate behavior. Together these characteristics imply a summary derivative characteristic:

10 The *systematic separation* (due to the hierarchical structure) of the *loci of (four) prerequisites* for proper, efficient action in any situation: correct location, correct information, authority to act, and command over the physical means of action. In particular, the dispersion of usable information and its separation from the loci of decision making authority was critical to the nature and functioning of the system.

These characteristics determined a coherent, stable configuration of mutually supporting institutions, one that systematically rejected (rendered dysfunctional) partial reforms affecting one or more of them, as long as most remained intact.[9]

Strengths and weaknesses

This was a system well suited, indeed built, for "mass mobilization." It embedded the advantages of centralization (Grossman 1963) and was ideally suited to exploit advantages of backwardness (Gerschenkron 1962). These characteristics implied an *effectiveness* in achieving sufficiently important, large-scale and quantifiable goals and priorities, those so important that cost could be no barrier. Thus the new Soviet industrial structure, mass collectivization and urbanization, wartime mobilization, and recovery from the devastation of war and occupation were all achieved in record time (Nove 1992). Yet despite this "effectiveness," it was inherently economically inefficient.

These characteristics imply an unavoidable, deep economic inefficiency in all that was accomplished. Fine economic cost–benefit trade-offs, indeed all but the crudest aggregate trade-offs, were beyond the capability of the system. Such trade-offs require detailed and precise information of particular and changing circumstances, and of fine valuations of all relevant materials and activities, and hence require *decentralized* authority and decision making.[10] Further, they invariably, in some circumstances, indicate that some central objectives should not be pursued; cost–benefit analysis implies constraints on behavior – explicitly rejected in the Soviet approach to planning. Therefore, economic efficiency and cost had to remain distant secondary considerations, as the central authorities had neither the capability, nor truly the desire, to let them disrupt central planning and control over economic activity.

As the economy grew and became more complex, social and economic goals became less tangible, less amenable to command implementation; there were no more complete development examples to emulate. Objectives became less clear, more multifaceted, and priorities proliferated, as the development focus switched from building physical structures to intangibles such as a high rate of technological progress, progressive structural change, satisfying consumer preferences, etc. Thus the command mechanism gradually lost its ability to cope with the changing economy, displaying a growing impotence, obvious to the Party leadership by the early 1980s. Yet for decades, the mutually reinforcing characteristics of the command system persevered, despite repeated attempts to improve performance through reforms. The system remained stable, functioned coherently, until Gorbachev's *perestroika* attacked, simultaneously, a critical mass of its characteristics.

Implications for performance

Both the strengths and the weaknesses were clearly reflected in Soviet economic performance. They generated substantial achievement, particularly when it was clear in the underdeveloped economy of the 1920s through the 1950s what needed to be done. But they also generated substantial waste along the way. Structures and technologies from the advanced economies were readily adopted by forcibly mobilizing and focusing resources, both material and human, without regard to cost, to attain state priorities in record time, as all other demands on resources could be ignored or minimized. Thus the mobilization of labor (full employment) and of capital (massive investment) and the reallocation of land usage were effectively and quickly implemented. And vast military power was generated, challenging the United States, despite an economic base only 22 percent to 33 percent as large.[11] Although a rather egalitarian income distribution, with unshakable job security, was guaranteed, household incomes were kept low, if slowly and systematically increasing. Consumer choice was quite limited; consumption was not a state priority, and was sacrificed to support industrial and military development.

These characteristics also generated the negative characteristics that have come to be associated with the Soviet economy. Extraordinary waste and obvious economic inefficiencies accompanied virtually every achievement. Except for the highest priority, closely monitored projects, implementation was shoddy, with measurable quantity of output substituting for quality. The assortment of products and technologies used was extremely limited to avoid overwhelming detail in planning, sharply limiting technological quality of products. Indeed, quality and qualitative objectives proved too abstract, too ephemeral, to be commanded. Known technologies could be readily implemented and replicated, but innovation proved impossible to plan and command. Only in the military/space sector, by dint of extraordinary concentration of resources and effort, was innovation and frontier technological progress maintained.[12]

These problems were particularly prevalent and acute in the non-priority sectors: consumers' goods and services, housing, basic materials processing, and in all aspects of agricultural production, processing, and distribution. This was reflected in the low, if slowly growing, standard of living, and an increasing resort to "second economy" activities/outlets for both income and consumers' goods and services, as the "first economy" faltered in providing results outside of priority areas.[13] As the Soviet economy grew in size and complexity, there was an unavoidable, inexorable deterioration of performance, even in priority areas, with measured growth devolving to stagnation by the early 1980s. That deterioration was slowed by the growing second economy, which compensated for inefficiencies in even the priority sectors, and the 1970s rise in price of the Soviet primary export, oil, allowing import of both technology and consumers' goods.

The system managers saw these problems coming even in the 1950s – for example, Malenkov's (1954) abortive consumerism; Khrushchev's (1957–63) *SovNarKhoz* reforms; Kosygin's (1965–67) and Brezhnev's (1967–79) repeated reforms (Nove 1992). Their response, prior to Gorbachev, was however, timid, attempting to protect the *status quo* while tinkering with the structure and functioning of the economic mechanism, without changing or even challenging its basic (command-administrative) nature. And they (tacitly) allowed unofficial mechanisms (the second economy) to deal with the growing complexity, the coordination and consumption failures, of the command economy. This preserved the stability, continuity, and decline of the economic system, and the power and perquisites of its leadership.

The collapse of an economic system

Performance to 1982

The initial performance of the Soviet economic system, in terms of apparent growth of output, urbanization, education, living standards, and military power was quite impressive, even if less than Soviet claims. Abram Bergson's (1978) careful reconstructions from dubious Soviet statistics showed a doubling in national income under the first two five-year plans (1928–37) and a further near doubling by 1950, following recovery from the devastation of World War II.[14] This development occurred by virtue of a massive sustained commitment of resources, both material and human, to the industrialization and urbanization of the inherited agrarian economy. Agriculture was squeezed by collectivization, all personal consumption drastically constrained, and education and health services focused on mass training and preparation of the peasantry for industrial employment and urban life (Nove 1992). Market behavior was criminalized, removing market constraints on planners'

Table 28.1 Soviet performance: annual rates of growth (%)

Index	1928–40	1940–50	1950–60	1960–70	1970–75	1975–80	1980–85
GNP	5.8	2.2	5.7	5.2	3.7	2.6	2.0
Factor productivity	1.7	1.6	1.4	0.9	1.5	–0.8	–1.2
Labor productivity	1.8	1.4	4.0	3.0	2.2	1.4	1.3
Capital productivity	–2.9	3.4	–3.5	2.6	–3.9	–3.9	–4.0
GNP/capita	3.6	2.9	3.9	3.9	2.7	1.8	1.1

Source: Ofer 1987: 1778

choices, and industrial and urban development forced. This was naturally accompanied by microeconomic distortions, evident waste and inefficiencies, but the economy was rich in natural resources, largely self-sufficient before the war, and able to impose desired outcomes regardless of human and material costs.

Following the death of Stalin (March 1953) the use of violence and terror to achieve development objectives diminished. The new leadership, no longer willing to live in terror, backed away from the extreme suppression of personal consumption, the extreme exploitation of the agricultural peasantry, and the hyper-centralized organization of economic activity. This change was also triggered by an evident decline in macroeconomic performance together with serious deprivation of much of the population – they had sacrificed all to win the war, and deserved a better life! Khrushchev, criticizing the "excesses" of Stalin, initiated a cultural thaw and a decentralization of the management and control of the Soviet economy to regional authorities – the *SovNarKhoz* system.[15] These changes produced a revival of strong economic growth in the 1950s, the basis of Khrushchev's claim to Nixon that "we will bury you" by surpassing the U.S. economy in the 1980s. But this opening to decentralized initiative proved inconsistent with the core institutions of the command economy. In the absence of proper market interface, it also introduced serious economic/regional coordination problems, and an evident substantial loss of control by the central authorities over economic priorities and the course of development. This was reflected, by the end of the decade, in again diminishing growth, coupled with increasingly obvious evidence of economic waste, failed plans, a stagnating standard of living, and a growing technological lag behind the West.

Thus the radical 1957 reform was progressively "re-reformed" through 1963 to impose greater central coordination and control, and then reversed in the major Brezhnev–Kosygin economic reforms of 1965–67, following their 1964 coup which retired Khrushchev. Those reforms re-imposed the classic Soviet command economy (characterized above) with greater, but still severely limited, enterprise autonomy, restructured the (imposed) price system, and created a new centralized organ (GOSSNAB) to plan and manage materials and equipment rationing. And again there was an initial burst in economic growth, maintaining the hope of economically overtaking the West, and the U.S. in particular.

Failure of "partial reform"

By the early 1970s, however, it became clear that Soviet economic growth was declining, and economic waste/inefficiency growing, despite the hopes put into reforms to improve the functioning of the socialist economy.[16] Thus the Soviet leadership authorized a continuing series of further "reforms," each addressing a perceived inadequacy in the functioning of the economy. Although the reforms were wide-ranging, addressing administrative reorganization, planning processes and parameters, the functioning of the material supply/rationing system, incentives both within firms and above the firm level, and decentralization in implementation, they remained partial, often introduced piecemeal as experiments. And none of them challenged the nature, the essence, of the command economy – the dedication to overriding central control with its necessary consequences. Instead they tinkered with economic policies and procedures, replacing or re-reforming earlier reforms, each change anticipating noticeable improvement, and each resulting in disappointment. Reforms consistent with the nature of the command system, those enhancing hierarchical monitoring and control or benefits to higher authorities, remained in place, elaborating the structures of command, but still failing to noticeably improve performance (Kontorovich 1988, 2008).

Those reforms that challenged the command principle, that moved toward true subordinate autonomy and allowing real market interaction, threatened the viability of the command mechanism, and were systematically re-reformed to impotence, or outright reversed. Indeed, for the survival of the system, they had to be, as they resulted in breakdown of planned coordination (in the absence of markets) and the disruption and/or loss of control over economic processes, the disruption of higher objectives and priorities. This aptly named "treadmill" of reforms (Schroeder 1979) did nothing to reverse the dismal performance trends, with output growth falling to near zero and productivity growth turning negative by 1982. This resilience in the face of repeated reforms reflected the inherent unreformability of the command system, both a strength and a structural flaw that lay behind its eventual collapse.

The perceived need for "deeper" reform

By the early 1980s, it was clear to all that the response of the system to its growing economic problems was inadequate.[17] The economy and society were stagnating. Partial reforms were not working, and the top leadership of the party was incapacitated by age and unwilling to decide on any change. Both the Soviet economy and Soviet society had sunk into a deep stagnation, and were perceived by all to be falling ever further behind the developed West. There was an evident feeling of a need to shake things up, to overcome inertia and get people motivated and working again, in part by removing petty plan restrictions on, and allowing greater initiative by, subordinates and individuals.

In both the Party and educated society, massive, subsurface, discussions were taking place, questioning the way the economy functioned. Special secret studies were commissioned by the Party. One particularly influential such study was in a Novosibirsk Report by sociologist Tatiana Zaslavskaia.[18] It contained a sociological critique of the deadening impact of the command system and argued for a humane socialism, with room for individual initiative and reward. It was not opposed to socialism or central planning *per se*, but did oppose its Soviet implementation.

This debate remained muffled until Brezhnev's death (November 1982) brought it into the open. Brezhnev's successor, KGB head Yuri Andropov, pushed to implement some suggestions, launching yet another reform – the Large-Scale Experiment (Six Ministries) – that again granted managers in these ministries greater enterprise autonomy in investment decisions and in providing incentives to workers and managers, albeit within plan control figures, and greater responsibility for results of their economic activities. This was coupled with a strong discipline campaign, severely punishing absenteeism and failure to carry out directives. Both sets of measures provided an apparent boost to performance that quickly faded, and then vanished with Andropov's death (February 1984) and the appointment of Brezhnev's older colleague Konstantin Chernenko. That deadened debate and muzzled changes until he too died on March 10, 1985. He was succeeded by the next generation: a young man with a "nice smile, hiding teeth of steel"[19] was selected by system's "Board of Directors" [Politburo] – Mikhail Sergeyevich Gorbachev.

Gorbachev and perestroika

Gorbachev strove to save Soviet socialism by radically reforming the command economy. He sought to allow decentralized initiative, with associated personal risks and rewards, in order to provide incentives without sacrificing overall central control or socialist ideals. The economy was to be steered by general central directives and development policies, but no longer directly centrally administered, in pursuit of an equitable collective future that preserved the gains of socialism.[20] Thus he pursued a vision inherently incompatible with the nature of the command economy. He ultimately sought to introduce tame, manageable "socialist markets" to allow efficient implementation of the social and economic goals indicated by the party, creating a socialist market economy rather similar to that imagined of the NEP (New Economic Policy) period from 1921–29. It however took some time for him to fully formulate this vision.

Thus he began where his mentor and predecessor, Yuri Andropov, had left off, with the vigorous implementation of what were believed to be the "best" of the reforms of the prior two decades, with a new, strong emphasis on providing incentives to mobilize the effort, creativity and initiative of individuals. This reform program was accompanied by a drive to accelerate growth in economic output and productivity, both of which appeared to be turning negative by 1985. It was encapsulated in the Twelfth Five-Year (1986–1990) Plan's massive investment push that was focused on the machine building and engineering sectors.[21]

This ambitious program, launched under the slogan *Uskorenie* (Acceleration), directed a massive increase in investment, a revival and extension of Andropov's "Large-Scale Experiment," more tinkering with plan indicators and performance reward parameters, a partial decentralization of investment and price setting, and further administrative streamlining and rationalization, reallocating planning and control tasks and simplifying administrative controls. More radically, Gorbachev forced through a liberalization of foreign trade, allowing for the first time since the mid-1920s direct contact between some Soviet ministries and firms and the foreign firms with which they hoped to deal.

But the heart of the program, building on the discussion of the early 1980s, was the focus on the human factor. New rights and opportunities were offered to individuals, to economic decision makers, in the hope that they would find better ways to implement what were thought to be generally shared social goals. And new incentives, both positive and negative, were provided. The old Soviet "social contract" of security and stability of well-being in return for obedience, effort, and abdicating control over one's life, was to be replaced by a new one granting greater rights and responsibilities, and the opportunity to do better than others through one's own efforts, but without guarantees and at the risk of suffering economic failure. Thus unemployment and unexpected adverse price changes became possibilities, and private economic activity, at least at the level of individuals and families, a path to potential enrichment. To further enhance individual incentives, a wide-ranging "discipline campaign" was also launched to enforce plan, production and labor discipline and counteract "free riding" on socialist benefits. It included a crackdown on corruption, particularly in the

Table 28.2 Economic performance during *perestroika*: annual rates of growth (%)

Index	1981–85	1985	1986	1987	1988	1989	1990	1991
GNP	1.9	0.8	4.1	1.3	2.1	1.5	–3.5	–17.0
Industry	2.0	2.0	2.4	3.0	2.7	–0.6	–2.8	–7.8
Agriculture	1.2	–3.9	11.2	–3.8	–0.4	6.1	–3.6	–7.0
Investment	3.3	2.1	5.3	1.7	4.5	0.6	–6.0	–25.0
Consumption per capita	0.8	0.2	–2.1	0.3	2.9	2.5	1.4	–14.8

Source: CIA, *Handbook of Economic Statistics, CPAS 91–10001*, September 1991: 62–69. 1991 figures from OECD (1995)

national republics, substantial turnover in higher administrative ranks (a generational transfer of power), a crackdown on absenteeism, and an attack on unearned incomes (during the summer of 1986) – i.e. those beyond what the (generally local) authorities thought desirable.

This was complemented and reinforced by perhaps the most radical policy of all: *glasnost*. This was a policy of openness, reversing the traditional Russian/Soviet approach of hierarchically structuring and limiting information to only those with a need to know, limiting criticism to only those authorized to exercise it. It was aimed at mobilizing and harnessing the input and enthusiasm of society to the great task of modernizing the Soviet Union and its economy. But it opened the floodgates to historical revelation and revision, criticism of not only shortcomings in operation but of the very essence of the Socialist command economy and its leadership, past and present, and of the sacred institutions and myths of the Soviet system. And it provided information useful for "unauthorized" initiatives, for deviation from "socially desirable" activities.

The initial impact once again appeared quite positive as firms absorbed the increase in investment resources, the discipline campaign raised labor inputs, and the weather cooperated in producing a bumper crop. But all these factors rapidly faded. The price of oil, the primary source of hard currency earnings, collapsed; investment plans proved overambitious, unsupported by resources; the discipline campaign soon became disruptive of regular economic activity; and economic agents figured out how to exploit new powers and opportunities in their own interest rather than that of fulfillment of the plan. Production disruptions, shortages, and waste of materials became increasingly prevalent, and hoped-for increases in efficiency and quality of product failed to appear. Gorbachev's response to this increasingly dysfunctional impact of his reforms was to deepen and radicalize, rather than repeal them, breaking with the conservative response of his predecessors when their reforms had faltered.

Gorbachev deeply believed, as the memoir literature shows,[22] that the Soviet socialist system was reformable, if only the spirit were willing, and vested interests overcome. But that, he soon came to believe, would require more than marginal improvements (*sovershenstvovanniia*) in the economic mechanism of the Soviet economy, more than the prior tinkering with the economic system. A more radical institutional reform, preserving and strengthening Soviet socialism, was needed. At the January 1987 Plenum of the CPSU; he declared the intent to undertake such a comprehensive reform of the economic system itself; and at the June 1987 Plenum; basic documents outlining a fundamental reform and the skeleton of a new socialist market economy were approved and ordered to be implemented in the coming year.[23] This was to prove a critical conjuctural factor in the system's collapse.

This was a truly radical reform, attacking the foundations, the very logic, of the command economy. The cornerstone of the reform was the Law on State Enterprise that codified the central actor in the new decentralized, socialist market economy, the autonomous state enterprise. It was to be self-financing, negotiating many of its own contractual prices and trading with other such enterprises and foreign firms. It was also to be self-managing, operating under a self-developed plan, drawn up to be consistent, it was hoped, with social plans and state directives, and guided by state orders and stable planning and financial norms. Thus firms were free to dispose of all output above (diminishing) state orders, although most prices remained fixed, and to finance their own investment and development. Central planning was to become longer run and financial outcome oriented, rather than physical output oriented, setting basic directions and guidelines, only commanding the allocation of a few hundred structure-forming commodities, and allowing firms to fill in the details to determine, on their own, how to achieve good financial results.

Once again, unintended consequences dominated the outcomes. One major consequence was that enterprise labor collectives found themselves empowered to take what they wanted from the enterprise's earnings, leading to rapid expansion of currency in circulation and growing inflationary pressure, albeit repressed by price controls.[24] Controlled prices, together with enterprise freedom to select outputs and partners, and the planned lack of competition (sellers' market) led to increasing disruption of production and growing shortages. Facing mandatory targets for only part of their output, firms reduced production of non-mandated items, and shifted their product mix toward higher-priced products and those easiest to produce given existing capacities and reserves. This disrupted supply to other enterprises, undercutting their ability to meet state orders, contributing to a broadening output contraction through 1989, 1990 and 1991.[25]

At the same time, the intermediating administrative and political organs, which had made central control effective, had their rights and powers undercut, rendering them impotent in the face of growing economic chaos. Macroeconomic imbalances, including the first recognized Soviet budget deficits, grew together with the monetary overhang, generating unprecedented repressed inflation and shortages in consumers' and investment "markets." Again, however, there was an initial spurt of economic activity as firms rushed to exploit new opportunities, launch investments, and cut old commitments. But by the end of 1988 it became clear that this spurt in activity was unsustainable as output stagnated, and microeconomic chaos and distributional inequity grew, far exceeding the worst expectations of the central authorities. To the highest leadership, innocent of economic understanding, this looked like sabotage by bureaucrats and old hierarchical structures.

So Gorbachev "doubled down" on radical reform, launching a third phase to undercut these vested, anti-reform interests. The essence of this stage was the attempt to outflank those structures by introducing some real competition into the system without, however, giving up control over its overall development or socialist nature. Thus the door was further opened to foreign capital through liberalized joint-venture laws, currency liberalization and auctions to determine a "market" exchange rate in the hope of attracting foreign technology and know-how, backed by hard currency, to the modernization effort. This liberalization was also intended to provide effective competition for large-scale Soviet state industry. On the consumer side of the economy, a liberal Law on Cooperation was promulgated in 1988, greatly enhancing the rights and opportunities for small producers' cooperatives and greatly expanding the role of active money in the economy. Opportunities for individual labor activity, allowed since 1986, were also expanded, again enhancing the power and reach of entrepreneurial initiative and active money. These were intended to produce consumers' goods and services, and producers' services, thereby providing competition to state enterprises and absorbing labor released by state firms as they became more efficient.

Finally, some competition was introduced in the political sphere through a policy of *democratization,* aimed at undercutting entrenched political interests by increasing citizen participation in decision processes, and by mobilizing representative bodies (soviets) through contested elections of their members. These bodies were given enhanced administrative power, and legislative authority in the social and economic spheres was decentralized to these regional and local organs. This created new centers of political power – republic, regional, and local soviets – with a popular base of support outside the direct control of the party and state apparatus. And it provided a basis for effective action based on the critiques raised by the increasingly venomous un- and anti-Soviet discourse inadvertently fostered by the policy of *glasnost.*

Chaos and collapse

The primary consequence of these policies was an aggravation and deepening of the evident economic crisis. Measured productivity continued to plummet, production slowed with increasing disruptions, shortages multiplied, stores became virtually emptied of consumers' goods, and prices began an inexorable rise despite continuing controls. Overall, the reforms appeared ineffective, or dysfunctional. Foreign companies displayed much hesitation about entering the Soviet market, although increasing imports, financed by foreign borrowing, did ameliorate shortages. The introduction of domestic competition through private cooperative enterprise did have a noticeable impact, but one that rapidly got out of hand, generating massive *unintended* negative consequences. Incomes visibly differentiated creating obvious inequality; speculative and arbitrage activities flourished, often carried out by fly-by-night (pseudo-) cooperatives. Corruption became obvious, and crime against private and personal property, including fraud and extortion, flourished, with criminal gangs, second economy entrepreneurs and petty officials actively involved. Thus a firm base for the growth and legitimation of criminal organizations was laid; they were just engaging in private, cooperative business.[26]

The leadership increasingly expressed an evident dismay at these reform outcomes, as well as a deep lack of understanding of why they were having such a negative impact. Further, democratization backfired from the perspective of supporting reform. Newly empowered legislatures and their leaders were clearly interested in political power, autonomy from the center, the revival of local (ethnic/national) culture and dignity, and the control over local natural and capital resources. This led in 1989–90 to a war of laws as many regions tried to invalidate Soviet laws and impose their own laws, norms, and economic controls, particularly over valuable resources (oil, minerals and metal ores, timber, etc.). The elections that were to rally support for reform instead gave voice to dissatisfaction with reform consequences, with blame for economic stagnation and decay, and the chaos of recent years, being increasingly placed on *perestroika.* Finally, this limited democratization revealed the totality of the collapse of the authority of the Party – the only universal glue holding the command economy together.

The Soviet leadership in 1991 faced a deepening crisis, clearly reflected in disastrous economic statistics. Growing economic chaos and signs of obvious social, economic and political disintegration led to a new phase, one of retreat, with partial reversal of some reforms (e.g. worker election of managers), growing confusion, and accelerating disintegration, rather than the vigorous reassertion of central authority and wholesale reversal of reform as had occurred with earlier reforms. This failure to act decisively reflected a loss of both control

Table 28.3 Economic performance, 1991

Indicator	% change	Indicator	% change
Gross national product (GNP)	−17.0		
Net material product (NMP)	−15.0	Consumer prices	+196.0
Industrial output	−7.8	Producer prices	+240.0
Agricultural output	−7.0	Cash emission	+480.0
National income (used)	−16.0	Credit emission	+210.0
Consumption	−13.0	Budget deficit	over +500.0
Investment	−25.0		

Source: *Ekonomika i zhizn'*, #6, 1992

instruments and confidence of the will to act on the part of the ruling elite, aggravated by a genuine lack of understanding of what was going wrong. It also reflected growing corruption, from the temptations of private enrichment of that elite, generating divisions that further obstructed coherent action.

The system drifted through 1990 and 1991 as a great socialist transition debate unfolded, reopening the whole issue of social control of the economy. The debate subjected the centralized, political determination of economic objectives to withering attack. Even the "reformist" conception of a Socialist Market Economy, and indeed the very desirability of socialism itself, came under direct assault. And this naturally generated a reaction, a reassertion of Soviet, even Stalinist, orthodoxy by some debate participants, setting the background for major policy struggles over the needed direction of reforms.[27] Indeed, under the Pavlov government (January–August, 1991) "anti-crisis stabilization" replaced "reform" as the official policy objective, while various plans for continuing/deepening the reform were proposed and debated, without a choice being made. Among these, the most radical was the Shatalin–Yavlinsky 500-Day Plan for radical marketization with total abandonment of the command economy. The other reform plans (Abalkin, Ryzhkov, Aganbegian) all relied on various degrees of state-led development of a socialist market economy – a compromise between radical marketization and Soviet plan orthodoxy, while some political voices called for a return to discipline and rigorous central planning.[28]

Alongside these debates, the national republics sought exit from the chaos through "economic autonomy," which Gorbachev, if not most of the central party leadership, appeared willing to grant. In short order, demand grew for political autonomy and then national independence, particularly in the Baltic and Caucasian republics. Gorbachev hoped to end this flight of the republics through signing a new constitutional agreement preserving the Soviet Union, if in a far more decentralized form. A referendum to that end was held in June 1991 in which a majority of the population voted in favor of its preservation. However, government opponents of the reforms, and of the obvious weakening of the Soviet Union they engendered, acted on the eve of the signing of the new Union agreement, removing Gorbachev from power by sealing him in a Crimean state dacha, and taking formal power into the hands of their State Committee on the Emergency Situation (GKChP) August 19, 1991. This was a last gasp effort of the Soviet government to reimpose order and discipline, and save the Union.

The new regime lasted only three days, while its leaders sank into drunkenness and indecision, before succumbing under popular pressure and the spirited resistance of the recently elected President of the Russian Federated Soviet Socialist Republic, Boris N. Yeltsin. Gorbachev was returned to the Soviet Presidency, but not to power, as Yeltsin and other regional and republic leaders effectively controlled the course of events. Most republics, with Russia in the lead, moved to seize effective sovereignty in the face of an accelerating economic collapse. Within three months, the leaders of the three core Slavic republics of the Soviet Union met in Belovezhsk, outside Minsk, and agreed to dissolve the Soviet Union and create a loose confederation of sovereign states, the CIS (Commonwealth of Independent States). The failure of the August coup, Yeltsin's initiative, and the Belovezhsky agreements (CIS) effectively ended the Soviet Union and the command economy on December 25, 1991.

Why *perestroika* destroyed the Soviet system

The logic of perestroika's *failure*

Perestroika grew naturally out of decades of piecemeal, if at times wide-ranging, "reforms" aimed at improving/"perfecting" (*sovershenstvovanie*) the socialist (command-administrative[29]) system of the Soviet economy. These reforms were driven by slowly growing, but persistent, microeconomic dysfunction (evident waste, mal-coordination, etc.) and inexorably, if slowly, deteriorating economic growth. As seen above, these partial reforms had no lasting positive impact on economic performance, leaving the economy sinking toward stagnation. That stagnation, achieved as the post-war generation of Soviet leaders began dying off, set the stage for a more radical approach; partial reform/improvement of the system had not worked. Yet the system appeared completely stable, able to move forward and maintain a slow but steady rise standard of living for the indefinite future.[30]

Gorbachev and his advisors assumed that this was a result of insufficient boldness of reform, of insufficient trust in the socialist aspirations and instincts of Soviet citizens.[31] Assuming that Soviet society fully accepted this socialist vision, they sought to liberate it from petty constraints and to allow individual initiative to be mobilized in pursuit of that vision. *Perestroika* thus went beyond the prior reform paradigm; it grew, albeit unintentionally, into a fundamental attack on the logic of the system, challenging its essential defining characteristics. Knowing that the prior partial reforms had failed to improve the functioning of the system, Gorbachev and his advisors ploughed ahead with ever more radical reform, determined to impose significant change despite the escalating signals of problems from below. The authoritarian system allowed them to do so, ignoring feedback until it was too late.

Thus increasingly radical measures, challenging the foundations of the command economy, were launched one after another, if rarely brought to fulfillment. These measures disrupted the coherence of that system, yet themselves failed to comprise a coherent package of alternative economic mechanisms. Indeed, progressive Soviet economists, with their profound ignorance of economics, played a destructive role as they recommended mixing policies and institutions from progressive world experience without comprehending the institutional embeddedness of such policies in those other economies. Important decisions, by the structure of the system, could be, and were, taken without feedback from below, where "simulation" of performance and pleading of "special circumstances" clouded real performance data about the impact of the policies launched. In this distorted informational environment, the leadership lost trust in reports from below which, coupled with driving impatience, led them to rapidly revise/"improve" policies, undercutting them before they had a chance to do what they had been designed to do. And, in the name of reform, the leadership systematically abandoned the key levers of economic control of the command economy. Hierarchical structures of state planning and implementation, the rationing of resources, strict control over prices and financial transfers, and operational intervention of party organs in economic allocation and operations were abandoned, as were the key priorities at which the command economy excelled: industrial investment, producers' goods production, the military, etc. And this disorganization of the mechanisms of command implementation led to a loss of coordination in the implementation of reforms across both sectors and institutional arrangements. When the consequent economic incoherence brought further disruption and deterioration in performance, increasingly radical *political* reforms were introduced to uproot or push aside the opposition believed to lie at the root of failure of these reform attempts. These reforms, in turn, further undercut the legitimacy and ability to control that politically-inspired and politically-driven economic system.

Increasingly *perestroika* freed Soviet institutions and agents from the behavioral constraints and coordinating controls of the command economy. In effect, it granted them *de facto* license to exploit resources – political, institutional, economic and material – at their disposal in their personal interests, without the institutional constraints of either the command economy or a law-based market system and its financial infrastructure. The leadership naively assumed that reform-stimulated individual initiative would be exercised only in the interests of state and society. Individuals and firms were to exercise initiative only to make current structures, organizations, and interactions work better, and to refrain from lucrative opportunities that were disruptive of received interactions, to limit the "excessive" acquisition of personal wealth. The pursuit of any interests beyond what the leadership wanted was considered sabotage. "State" values and valuations were to be accepted by economic agents, who should only marginally adjust them in the pursuit of efficiency and effectiveness of state operations.

There was absolutely no comprehension of the extreme distortions, the explosive tensions, built into the existing singular structure of industrial and "commercial" interactions, and the bizarre relative prices that had evolved over seventy years of rigid and economically uninformed controls. Thus the natural incentives of implementing agents were destructive of the structure of the inherited system. And that was aggravated by continuing Soviet institutions that blocked market feedback mechanisms that might have channeled agent behavior in more desirable directions: the dual monetary system, rendering budget constraints vacuous; insufficiently flexible prices, with critical input prices still fixed; planned absence of alternative suppliers and users for virtually all products; total absence of market intermediaries, etc. Finally, the uncomprehending haste of the political leadership, brooking no opposition and piling uncoordinated reform upon ill thought-out reform, launched a downward spiral of economic performance as institutional and economic collapse accelerated. Only the political collapse was faster. The Soviet Union, largely for political reasons, disintegrated in the last few months of 1991, leaving all policy in a state of collapse, and fifteen new state economies in free fall.

Suicide of a system

Gorbachev's policies drove a process that led to the unraveling of the command economy, as its essential pillars were systematically, if uncomprehendingly, attacked. The social and political policy of *glasnost*, aimed at developing an informed, active Soviet citizenry, undercut legitimacy of the system and hence the willingness to both command and to obey. Political and economic "*democratization*" undercut the ability of critical political organs to direct and manage economic activity, empowered workers' collectives to manage production and incomes without responsibility for the outcomes, while *"sovietization"* created indecisive, economically incompetent, collective bodies at the regional and local levels. Finally, *ekonomicheskaia perestroika* (economic restructuring and decentralization) without real markets, prices, money, or a hard "bottom line," disorganized economic activity and its coordination, leading to a growing breakdown of economic intermediation and activity, while self-interested behavior, unanchored in market discipline or institutions, was systematically dysfunctional, disruptive of productive economic activity. The resulting systemic breakdown in 1990–91 reflected the fundamental nature of the command economy, and the truly radical scope and depth, relative to the system, of the changes introduced by Gorbachev. Indeed, they attempted a truly radical reform of an inherently unreformable system.

The system, the command economy, was unreformable as a logically consistent, self-contained entity (Ericson 1991, Kornai 1992) comprising a tight set of necessary, mutually supporting characteristics. Each component was a natural, and indeed essential, part of the overall system, organically linked to every other essential component. While the shape and form, the superficial features, of each component could vary tremendously, the essence of each was inextricably bound to the logic of command, the logic of centralized direction, control, and coordination of economic activity. Thus, reforms/changes *consistent with the logic* of the system were successfully adopted, without altering its nature or the quality of its performance. These included such things as administrative restructuring, planning refinements, incentive scheme refinements, and priority changes. Where the reforms were restorative, involved recentralization or administrative rearrangement within the hierarchical structures of command, they entered the system, elaborating its hierarchical structures to accommodate increasing size and complexity. Such reforms became a refinement or improvement of the economic mechanism of developed socialism.

However, where the reforms were contrary to command – decentralizing, or extended subordinate discretion and autonomy, reforms that attacked or sought to fundamentally change one or more essential characteristics of the system – they soon ran foul of the existing structures, introducing dysfunction: deviation from plans and priorities, mal-coordination, diversion of resources, private enrichment, unjustified differentials in performance, etc. Such reforms were *inconsistent* with the rest of the system and hence with the proper functioning of the command economy, leading to increasing disruption and breakdown. This created a clearly untenable situation, to which the authorities, in particular those mid-level economic officials responsible for maintaining balance and smooth functioning of the production process economy-wide, had in the past regularly responded by reversing or "re-reforming" the reform in question. Reforms such as introducing real decentralized trade, monetizing interaction (real money), introducing real financial incentives, allowing local control over investment or product line/assortment, etc., all attacked the foundations of the system and hence had to be eliminated, however real the problem they had been introduced to address. Thus bureaucratic resistance, sabotage of the reforms, was a rational response of those whose duty it was to implement economic plans and outcomes.[32] This is the logic of the Treadmill of Reforms – fiddling with the system without affecting its *essential nature,* without challenging its underlying logic: reforms with no essential impact survived, while those that made things worse were reversed/re-reformed, and often retried later as they attacked real problems. Thus the command economy was, in a fundamental sense, unreformable. That, however, was not understood by Gorbachev and his closest economic and political advisors.

Instead, they took a different lesson to heart, as seen in the evolution of *perestroika*. Assuming the system's reformability, and the ultimate viability, indeed superiority, of planned socialist organization of the economy, they pushed for ever greater radicalization as reform stalled. In doing so, they failed to appreciate the consequences of economic and social liberalization within command institutional structures, the impact of the incentives and opportunities created. The organizational structures of the command economy remained in place, blocking the development of new market structures, of market feedback and prices, that might have channeled decentralized activity into socially useful directions. In particular, the continuing dual monetary system allowed the hemorrhaging of both cash and credits into the hands of uncontrolled economic actors, who effectively faced no financial constraints, no "bottom line." So disproportions in activities, waste of social resources, and diversion for private usage faced no natural barriers; the market price mechanism was effectively disabled.

When liberalizations yielded negative social and economic consequences, Gorbachev and his advisors assumed that must be the result of political opposition, of sabotage by those whose power was threatened by the liberalizations. Thus political liberalization, undercutting the supposed resistance, was launched on top of social and economic liberalization. The social and economic forces liberated from direct party and administrative controls, from prior constraint on words and actions, were now free to exploit resources and arbitrage opportunities created by the shortcomings and then collapse of plans in their own personal interests. And those tasked in the command economy with maintaining social coordination and focus were now deprived of the power of immediate intervention, of effective instruments of control. In particular, the Communist Party of the Soviet Union, the lynch-pin of the system of command and control, was forcibly – by direct order of the General Secretary, the ultimate executive authority in the party – removed from economic responsibility, and was forced to compete for political authority with national social and political forces.

And that proved to be fatal to the command economy.

Concluding comments

On Christmas day, 1991, Mikhail S. Gorbachev was escorted from his Kremlin office, and the flag of the Soviet Union came down, replaced by the Russian Federation tricolor. This marked the formal end of the greatest social experiment of the twentieth century, of an epic effort to remake society and economy, indeed mankind, into a rationally planned, socially directed and controlled egalitarian world inexorably marching toward a utopian future. While that experiment had long been faltering, the Soviet leadership, and the world, accepted it as an ongoing "work in progress," a viable alternative to market capitalism that indeed was pulling, by its example, both developing and developed market economies toward an inevitable, more collectivist, planned future. Hence Gorbachev could not conceive that his reforms, his efforts to render the command economy more flexible, innovative and humane, would destroy that economic system. And neither could most outside specialists/ Sovietologists and observers.

Yet the implementation of those reforms, the increasingly radical *glasnost, perestroika* and *demokratizatsiya*, systematically undercut the foundations of the Soviet system, its authoritative party, command economy and authoritarian society. The reforms disorganized, then destroyed, existing political, economic and social institutions, leaving society and the economy in chaos by late 1991, with the leadership deadlocked in debate and gripped by misunderstandings of what was happening. The August 19, 1991 coup against Gorbachev by the leaders of the political, military and security services marked the last gasp of the dying system, an attempt to stop a process of disintegration already gone too far. Yeltsin's visible resistance and cooptation of key military units blocked the coup, freed Gorbachev from house arrest, and completely marginalized him, as Yeltsin, recently democratically elected President of the newly proclaimed autonomous Russian Federation, seized the mantle of leadership and proclaimed Russia's turn from socialism toward a normal European society and market economy. Meeting with the leaders of the other two large slavic Soviet socialist republics – Ukraine and Belarus – in Belovezhsk outside Minsk, Yeltsin joined them in dissolving the USSR and forming a new, post-Soviet Commonwealth of Independent States which was in short order joined by most of the other former Soviet republics, all of which had declared national independence from the Soviet Union.

Each of the fifteen new former Soviet states inherited a piece of the crumbling command economy, and each had its economic capabilities and activities further disrupted by the breaking of (planned) "chains" of supply and demand, as new national borders arose between suppliers and users and economic agents pursued new opportunities at the cost of old relations. Further, each was faced with the unprecedented task of building a market economy, with its myriad formal and informal institutions and culture of interaction, on the ruins of a system that had systematically attacked, and largely destroyed, all aspects of modern markets. Thus each was plunged into a deep "transitional" recession/depression without the economic institutions to deal with it. The great experiment, brought to an end by the demise of the Soviet Union, ended as tragedy for the peoples on which it had been carried out. It also posed on-going challenges for economists to understand how to resolve the problem of building successful market economies, not just in a development context, but in the face of surviving economic structures, institutions and understandings that are hostile to, and destructive of true market development. But that is a story for the twenty-first century.

Notes

1 The post-war development literature to the mid 1960s is full of praise for Soviet economic "achievements" and the Soviet model of economic development. See Wilber (1969), Spulber (1964), and Dodge and Wilber (1970).

2 Samuelson's textbook, *Economics*, in its fourth through seventh editions pointed to the advantages of Soviet economic planning. John Kenneth Galbraith's (1967) influential monograph was a leading voice in advocating this development.

3 A vast literature arose on decentralized, information/communication efficient procedures for planning that maintained central control over the economy. See Heal (1986) for a survey.

4 This is most vividly illustrated in the discussions of plan allocations, their implementation, and incentives for plan performance in Nove (1986).

5 Informal "institutions" and patterns of behavior of those forced to live within these institutions, of course, softened the impact of the command logic and structures, allowing corruption and a "second economy" to aid in managing the impossible central planning and coordination tasks required to truly implement a command economy.

6 As experience had shown that, outside of emergency war-time rationing, the direct planning of consumption allocations was an impossible task, money was given a limited "active" role in the *ex post* implementation of planned allocations of consumers' goods and services.

7 Ericson (2006) develops the threat of "active" money to the proper functioning of the command economy.

8 The "second economy" involved privately motivated and/or illegal economic activity that fed off the irrationalities of the "first" (centrally planned and administered) economy. It fed off arbitrage opportunities, production and trade opportunities created by inconsistencies/gaps in the plan, and by the inability of money and prices to play an active role in allocating resources. It thrived on theft, bribery, and the entrepreneurial seizing of opportunities created by the economic irrationalities of the planned system. It increasingly over time reallocated resources, goods and services, and created (largely hidden) pools of wealth, undermining both the functioning and the legitimacy of the "planned" economic system. See the discussions in Grossman (1977) and Alexeev (2008).

9 For a detailed discussion of how reforms inconsistent with these characteristics were undermined and reversed, see Kontorovich (1988) on the Kosygin reforms and his broader analysis in Kontorovich (2008).

10 The logic behind this is clearly laid out in Grossman (1963).

11 See Rowen and Wolf (1990).

12 See Amman, Cooper and Davies (1977).

13 The classic summary description is in Grossman (1977).

14 Bergson calculated growth in 1937 constant prices. Soviet calculations using 1926–27 constant prices showed 3.86 and 7.68 fold growth to 1937 and 1950 respectively, exploiting the Laspeyres index distortion (Gerschenkron Effect). See Ofer (1987).

15 Nove (1992). For a recent study see Kibita (2011).

16 This was particularly clear in the increasingly wasteful use of capital, evidenced (Table 28.1) by its negative productivity growth since the mid 1960s, dragging total factor productivity growth below zero from the mid 1970s.

17 Visitors to the Soviet Union at the time all noted a deep cynicism and resignation about future stagnation, in particular among the *intelligentsia*. See, for example, Smith (1984).

18 This was smuggled out of the Soviet Union and presented to the West by Phil Hanson (1984).

19 In the words of Andrei Gromyko, Soviet foreign minister and senior Politburo member, when nominating Gorbachev to be selected General Secretary of the CPSU.

20 Gorbachev (1987), especially section 3 of Chapter 2.

21 These sectors were to be the engine of acceleration by dramatically increasing the quality and technological level of equipment and machinery produced for use in these and in the other sectors of the economy, thereby drastically raising productivity and growth rates throughout the economy. For a thorough analysis, see the papers in Joint Economic Committee, U.S. Congress, 1987, *Gorbachev's Economic Plans*, Part I, The Agenda of Economic Change, pp. 1–121, especially Stanley H. Cohen, "Soviet Intensive Economic Development Strategy in Perspective," pp. 10–21.

22 See Ellman and Kontorovich (1998) for thorough discussion.

23 The *Osnovnye napravleniia* [Basic provisions] and the Law on State Enterprise were approved at the Plenum. Ten basic implementing decrees were promulgated July 17, 1987, codifying Gorbachev's vision of a Socialist Market Economy. See Ericson (1989).

24 The non-market monetary system (Garvy 1977) lacked the ability to control high-powered money, while automatically financing any planned expenditures.

25 See the discussion in Krueger (1993).

26 See Volkov (2002).

27 From the beginning, Politburo member Egor Ligachev led opposition to *perestroika* in the party, while the most vocal public statement of Stalinist nostalgia came at the beginning of this debate from a chemistry teacher Nina Andreeva in the newspaper, *Sovetskaia Rossiia*, March 13, 1988.

28 See Åslund (1991) for the details of the Soviet economic debates of the period.

29 A descriptive term introduced by Gorbachev at the January (1987) Plenum of the CPSU.

30 See the compendium of scholarly papers by leading Western experts in Joint Economic Committee (1982) and the Bergson and Levine (1983) conference volume with papers by leading Sovietologists arguing the stability and likely longevity of the Soviet economic system, despite its myriad problems.

31 See his address to the world on Soviet new thinking, Gorbachev (1987).

32 See Kontorovich (1988: 313–14) and Litwack (1991: 264).

References

Alexeev, M. (2008) 'Second economy', *New Palgrave Dictionary of Economics*, second edition, New York: Palgrave.

Amman, R., Cooper J.M. and Davies, R.W. (1977) (eds.) *The Technological Level of Soviet Industry*, New Haven, CT: Yale University Press.

Åslund, A. (1991) *Gorbachev's Struggle for Economic Reform*, second edition, Ithaca, NY: Cornell University Press.

Bergson, A. (1978) *The Real National Income of Soviet Russia since 1928*, Cambridge, MA: Harvard University Press.

Bergson, A. and Levine, H.S. (1983) (eds.) *The Soviet Economy: Toward the Year 2000*, London: Allen & Unwin.

Dodge, N. and Wilber, C.K. (1970) 'The relevance of Soviet industrial experience for less developed economies', *Soviet Studies*, 21: 330–49.

Ellman, M. and Kontorovich, V. (1998) *The Destruction of the Soviet Economic System: An Insiders' History*, Armonk, NY: M.E. Sharpe.

Ericson, R.E. (1989) 'Soviet economic reforms: the motivation and content of *Perestroika*', *Journal of International Affairs*, 42: 317–31.

Ericson, R.E. (1991) 'The traditional Soviet-type economic system', *Journal of Economic Perspectives*, 5: 11–28.

Ericson, R.E. (2006) 'Command vs. shadow: the conflicted soul of the Soviet economy', *Comparative Economics Systems*, 48: 1–17.

Ericson, R.E. (2008) 'Command economy', *New Palgrave Dictionary of Economics*, second edition, III: 1–53, New York: Palgrave.

Galbraith, J.K. (1967) *The New Industrial State,* New York: Houghton-Mifflin.

Garvy, G. (1977) *Money, Financial Flows, and Credit in the Soviet Union*, Cambridge, MA: Ballinger.

Gerschenkron, A. (1962) *Economic Backwardness in Historical Perspective*, Cambridge, MA: Harvard University Press.

Gorbachev, M.S. (1987) *Perestroika*, New York: Harper & Row.

Grossman, G. (1963) 'Notes for a theory of the command economy', *Soviet Studies,* 15: 101–23.

Grossman, G. (1977) 'The second economy of the USSR', *Problems of Communism*, 26: 25–40.

Hanson, P. (1984) 'Novosibirsk report', *Survey*, Spring.

Hayek, F.A. (1944) *The Road to Serfdom.* Chicago, IL: The University of Chicago Press.

Heal, G. (1986) "Planning', Chapter 29 in K.J. Arrow and M.D. Intrilligator (eds.) *Handbook of Mathematical Economic,* volume III: 1483–1511, Amsterdam: North-Holland.

Joint Economic Committee Congress of the United States (1982) *Soviet Economy in the 1980s: Problems and Prospects*, Washington, DC: U.S. Government Printing Office.

Joint Economic Committee Congress of the United States (1987) *Gorbachev's Economic Plans*, Washington, DC: U.S. Government Printing Office.

Kibita, N. (2011) *Soviet Economic Management under Khushchev: The Sovnarkhoz Reform,* London: Routledge.

Kontorovich, V. (1988) 'Lessons of the 1965 Soviet economic reform', *Soviet Studies*, 40: 308–16.

Kontorovich, V. (2008) 'Soviet economic reform', *New Palgrave Dictionary of Economics*, second edition, New York: Palgrave.

Kornai, J. (1992) *The Socialist System,* Princeton, NJ: Princeton University Press.

Krueger, G. (1993) 'Priorities in central planning', *Journal of Comparative Economics*, 17: 646–62.

Litwack, J.M. (1991) 'Discretionary behaviour and Soviet economic reform', *Soviet Studies*, 43: 255–80.

Nove, A. (1986) *The Soviet Economic System,* London: George Allen & Unwin.

Nove, A. (1992) *An Economic History of the USSR*, third edition, Baltimore, MD: Penguin.

OECD (1995) *OECD Economic Surveys: Russian Federation,* Paris: OECD Publications.

Ofer, G. (1987) 'Soviet economic growth: 1928–1985: a survey article', *Journal of Economic Literature*, 25: 1767–1833.

Rowen, H.S. and Wolf, C. (eds.) (1990) *The Impoverished Superpower,* San Francisco, CA: ICS Press.

Schroeder, G. (1979) 'The Soviet economy on a treadmill of reforms', in Joint Economic Committee Congress of the United States, *Soviet Economy in a Time of Change,* Washington, DC: U.S. Government Printing Office.

Smith, H. (1984) *The Russians,* New York: Crown, 1983.

Spulber, N. (1964) *Soviet Strategy for Economic Growth,* Bloomington, IN: Indiana University Press.

Volkov, V. (2002) *Violent Entrepreneurs*, Ithaca, NY: Cornell University Press.

Wilber, C.K. (1969) *The Soviet Model and Underdeveloped Countries*, Chapel Hill, NC: UNC Press.

29

DEVELOPMENT OF TRADE INSTITUTIONS AND ADVENT OF GLOBALIZATION SINCE THE END OF WORLD WAR II

Teresa Gramm

Introduction

In the aftermath of World War II and the protectionism of the Depression era, as the decade of the 1950s approached, international trade as a share of world output had fallen to levels not seen since the beginning of the twentieth century. In contrast, the rise of world trade in the second half of the twentieth century, with all the associated gains from trade for all trading partners, was one of the economic miracles of the postwar era.

As much as economists bemoan the protectionism that exists today, the dramatic fall in world-wide tariff rates and the emergence of multilateral trade negotiations and institutions such as the General Agreement on Tariffs and Trade (GATT)/World Trade Organization (WTO) aimed at freeing trade can be seen as a real success of economic reasoning over political expediency. But despite the correlation between falling tariff rates and growing trade, there is the perhaps not-so-obvious question of causality: what explains the growth in world trade?

Trade expansion

The Great Depression, protectionism and World War II together reduced trade considerably. The Smoot–Hawley Tariff of 1930 increased the already high average U.S. tariff rates by about 17 percent from 40.1 percent to 47.1 percent. However, the fact that most duties were specific (as opposed to ad valorem) combined with the massive deflation of the period and served to magnify its effect, so that effective average tariffs increased by a total of 50 percent from 40.1 percent to 60 percent. Due to the increased effective protectionism and the contacting economy, import volumes fell dramatically in the United States. Half of the 40 percent decline in the volume of imports can be attributed to the combined effects of Smoot–Hawley and deflation, while 7 percent was due to Smoot–Hawley alone (Irwin 1998: 333).

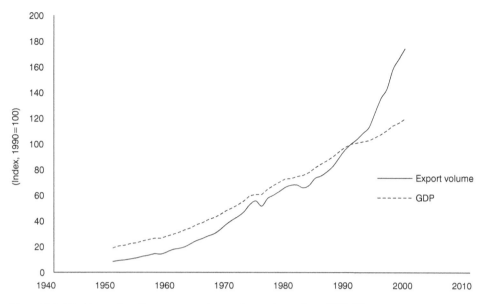

Figure 29.1 World merchandise exports and gross domestic product, 1950–99

Source: International Trade Statistics 2000, WTO, Table II.1

Although effective tariff rates fell from their height in 1932–33, the disaster of the Great Depression was soon followed by World War II and all the major trading economies were decimated, with the exception of the United States.

In contrast to the abysmal record of trade during the interwar era and during World War II, the growth in world trade in the second half of the twentieth century was astounding. However, as Krugman (1995) observes, much of the growth in trade was just recovering what was lost through protectionism and war which followed the first wave of globalization 50 years earlier. Krugman (1995: 331) identifies the first wave as starting in 1859 and lasting until 1913, noting that it was not until sometime between 1973 and 1985 that U.S. trade as a share of GDP finally passed its previous 1913 peak.

The value of world trade grew about 8 percent a year during the 1950s and 1960s according to the WTO, compared to average world GDP growth of 5 percent in that period. Thereafter, trade volumes grew 63 percent in the 1970s, 40 percent in the 1980s and 74 percent in the 1990s. All told, between 1950 and 2000, trade volumes increased by almost 2000 percent. Of course GDP was growing at that time as well, so it is striking to compare trade growth to production growth during that period as well (see Figure 29.1). Trade growth outstripped GDP growth for all but seven years during this period, so that world trade increased 3.7 times as much as world GDP.

Not only the rising volume of trade, but also its changing composition was a hallmark of trade in the latter part of the twentieth century (see Figure 29.2). The merchandise traded was increasingly composed of more manufactured goods relative to raw materials. Furthermore, the manufactured final goods were increasingly complicated and more likely to be traded as intermediate products in their production process. As will be discussed in more detail below, the splitting up of the value chain of a final product, and its production in several countries goes a long way toward explaining why trade has grown so much more than GDP, and why falling trade barriers have such a magnified effect on trade volumes (Yi 2003).

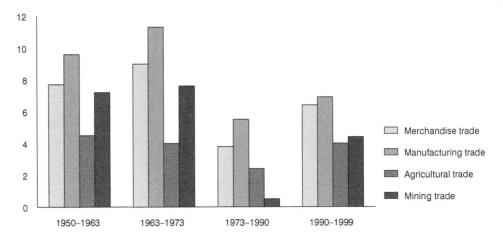

Figure 29.2 Trade by major product group (annual average percentage change in volume)

Source: International Trade Statistics 2000, WTO, Chart II.1

At first glance, the main cause for trade growth seems obvious, namely, barriers to trade fell. But there are the questions as to which barriers fell and how much of their fall can be attributed to GATT/WTO. Barriers to trade are both natural (such as physical distance) and political. The effects of natural barriers have declined due to advances in technology, and while they will make up an important component of the fall in overall barriers, the fall in the cost of physical barriers cannot be attributed to trade institutions. The political barriers seem more likely candidates to be attributable to GATT/WTO, but there is still some question of how much tariff reduction and how much trade growth is due to GATT/WTO membership. A related phenomenon is the rise of the preferential trade agreements (PTAs), bilateral trade agreements which have risen in tandem with GATT/WTO, especially in the last quarter of the century. The expansion of PTAs to encompass 40 percent of world trade (Winters 2011) raises many similar questions about their role in trade expansion and a host of other questions related to whether or not they impede or encourage further trade liberalization. This chapter focuses on explaining the roles of the above in the expansion of world trade.

Theories to explain increased trade: reduced barriers

As noted in Feenstra (1998), there are four possible explanations for why trade has risen: trade liberalization, lower transportation costs, income convergence[1] and growth, and vertical specialization. Baier and Bergstrand (2001) propose to estimate the relative importance of a subset of these factors using a data set that includes bilateral trade flows among sixteen OECD countries in the periods 1958–1960 and 1986–1988. They estimate that of the 148 percent increase in trade, approximately 100 percentage points were due to income growth, about 38 percentage points were due to lower trade barriers, and about 12 percentage points were due to reduced transportation costs. For their sample, there is little evidence of income convergence as an explanation for the growth in trade, though given their sample of OECD countries, there is too little variation to establish the importance of this variable. Each of these factors is discussed below, in addition to two other determinants of trade that were beyond the scope of the Baier and Bergstrand (2001) study: vertical specialization and reduced communication costs.

Anderson and van Wincoop (2004) survey the various costs of trade: tariffs, nontariff barriers, and transportation costs both within and between countries. Transportation costs in their estimation include shipping/freight costs, "border barriers" such as currency, information, and contract/insecurity barriers. As we will discuss below, the costs of many of these barriers have been significantly reduced over the last fifty years, but Anderson and van Wincoop note that trade costs (from foreign production point to domestic consumption point) still represent a 170 percent tax equivalent. The 170 percent "tax" can be divided into 44 percent "border costs," 21 percent transportation costs, and 55 percent wholesale and retail distribution costs[2] (Anderson and van Wincoop 2004: 692). For the purpose of this chapter, the declines in the first two costs are of the most interest for explaining international trade.

Institutional changes and the growth of trade: trade liberalization and the decline of border barriers

GATT/WTO

The Bretton Woods Conference of 1944 intended the creation of three institutions of international economic integration: the International Monetary Fund (IMF), the World Bank, and the International Trade Organization (ITO). However, because the U.S. did not ratify the ITO's charter, this third institution of international economic integration never came into being. Instead, in 1947 the world's largest trading countries signed the General Agreement on Tariffs and Trade (GATT). There were then eight rounds of tariff negotiations between 1948 and 1994, and the last round resulted in the creation, at long last, of the World Trade Organization. Henceforth, this institutional framework will be referred to as GATT/WTO.

There are three characteristics of GATT negotiations that have been credited with the institution's success: multilateralism, nondiscrimination, and reciprocity. Multilateralism refers to the negotiations bringing all GATT members together in rounds, rather than piecemeal negotiations between country pairs. Nondiscrimination, or the Most Favored Nation principle, refers to the requirement that each country must extend its lowest tariff rate, i.e., that tariff rate offered to its "most favored" nation, to *all* signatories of GATT. Reciprocity refers to negotiating the mutual lowering of tariffs, with the idea that what production advantage a country loses by reducing its tariff on foreign goods, will be gained in its export sector when the other countries lower their trade barriers. It should be noted that the principles of nondiscrimination and reciprocity largely apply only to negotiations among larger economies.[3]

These principles were primarily time-saving devices intended to increase transparency. Furthermore, according to Bagwell and Staiger (1999), the principles play a role in eliminating a prisoner's dilemma that resulted from the terms of trade externality (where a large economy can gain from protectionism by depressing the terms of trade for its imported goods). Specifically, the authors assert that there are real terms of trade considerations that lead countries to engage in partial equilibrium optimal tariff setting. They demonstrate that the reciprocity principle of GATT ("We lower tariffs on your exports if you lower them on ours") leads to efficient tariffs – tariffs that maximize national income (Bagwell and Staiger 1999). Broda, Limão and Weinstein (2008) find empirical support for Bagwell and Staiger's work. They find evidence that fifteen countries set trade policy according to market power. Specifically, the more market power a country had, the more protectionist its policy, so that GATT/WTO membership resulted in lower tariffs. Furthermore, they find that a country is less likely to display market power in commodities, and more likely in differentiated goods, so that in a world where trade is increasingly in differentiated products, the existence of WTO to mediate trade disputes would seem even more important.

Krugman (1997) makes a more political economy argument for the benefits of GATT/WTO: governments have the misguided mercantilist attitude that imports impoverish and exports will enrich a country, so GATT/WTO works within this misperception "not to protect us from unfair foreign competition, but to protect us from ourselves" (Krugman 1997: 118). Reciprocity creates the perception of a "win" when the other country reduces barriers on the home country's exports to compensate for the "loss" of reducing protection against imports from the other country.

Tariffs indeed have fallen dramatically in the post-WWII period. From 60 percent deflation-adjusted tariffs under Smoot–Hawley, the average U.S. tariff rate fell to single digits by the 1970s. During the period of GATT negotiations, from 1947–1992, U.S. tariffs fell from around 20 percent down to 5 percent. It would seem that GATT/WTO has been very successful. Indeed, according to the WTO,

> GATT was provisional with a limited field of action, but its success over 47 years in promoting and securing the liberalization of much of world trade is incontestable. Continual reductions in tariffs alone helped spur very high rates of world trade growth during the 1950s and 1960s — around 8 percent a year on average.[4]

However, a large body of literature questions exactly what role GATT/WTO played in reducing tariff rates.

On the surface, since the whole point of GATT/WTO is to liberalize trade, the correlation between the expansion of GATT/WTO and the fall in tariff rates would seem so obviously causal that no one questioned the relationship until recently and with surprising results. Rose (2004a) finds that there is no evidence that GATT/WTO increases trade, and furthermore, Rose (2004b) finds that WTO members do not have more liberal trade policy using 68 different measures of trade policy and trade liberalization. His argument is fairly convincing, if by sheer volume of evidence alone. He considers a wide variety of measures – using both cross-sectional (members versus non-members) and time-series (to determine if liberalization occurs with a lag) data. Grouping countries according to characteristics, such as levels of development, he finds only one measure of liberalization that seems to be consistent with WTO membership: increased freedom according to the Heritage Foundation's index.

Not surprisingly, given the conventional wisdom that GATT/WTO has been responsible for trade liberalization, the responses to Rose's findings have been numerous. But while the responses have given a more nuanced interpretation to Rose's results, they have not overturned them. For example, Subramanian and Wei (2007) respond that there is an explanation for Rose's finding in that WTO rules are not applied evenly: some goods are largely exempt (agriculture) and some countries were exempt from reciprocity requirements (developing countries). They find that once these "asymmetries" were accounted for, GATT/WTO has significantly increased trade (imports). However, GATT/WTO did not promote trade if a country was not a member, if it was developing and came in before the Uruguay Round which ran from 1986–1994, or if a good was exempted or produced primarily by developing countries. Another response, by Broda, Limão and Weinstein (2008) finds evidence of lower tariffs promoting trade for goods in which the importer has market power *with* GATT/WTO, providing support for the idea that this trade institution does play some role in trade liberalization.

Perhaps membership in GATT/WTO is endogenous and therefore a reflection of more fundamental institutional changes: what does explain the fall in tariffs? It is hard to ignore the political economy explanations of protectionism and attribute the fall in tariffs to governments abandoning special interest politics and moving to maximize national income, so perhaps some change in what is traded can help explain broader political support for trade liberalization. Grossman and Rossi-Hansberg (2008) model vertical specialization/ trade in tasks and show that reduction in costs of trading can lead to gains to all factors of production, so there is not the distributional conflict from trade in tasks that more typical trade generates. Outlined below is the argument that much of the increased trade is due to vertical specialization, so the resistance to trade liberalization may have declined as there are fewer factors of production that lose from trade and, therefore, fewer protests.

Preferential trading agreements

Preferential trading agreements (PTAs) are intended to enhance trade among signatories by reducing trade barriers between those countries. A free trade agreement (FTA) is the extreme: tariffs are reduced to zero. A customs union is a preferential trading agreement that is a FTA with common external tariffs toward non-member states. As noted in Baier and Bergstrand (2004), in 1996, 289 of 1431 (about 20 percent) of all possible trading country-pairs were in a FTA. Winters (2011) notes that almost every country in the world is in at least one FTA and 40 percent of world trade moves through some sort of PTA. The explosion in the late twentieth century is interesting for two reasons: first, it raises questions about whether the move to regional free trade is welfare improving, and second, it raises questions about what impact growing regionalism will have on multilateralism.

The discussion of the welfare effects of PTAs is much more complicated than the unambiguous benefits of moving to multilateral free trade. First, beginning with Viner's observations in 1950, and using his language, there is a real debate on whether FTAs are trade creating (welfare improving) or trade diverting (welfare reducing). The question is empirical: theory establishes that FTAs can be good or bad for a member country depending on a number of characteristics of the country pair entering into a FTA relative to each other and relative to the world. Still, some explanation of why the question is too complicated to be answered by theory is in order.

The basic intuition of Viner (1950) was that FTAs, and hence PTAs, have a decidedly ambiguous effect on member country welfare (it gets even more complicated when third country non-member welfare is included). Say country C is the lowest-cost producer of a good, charging P_c. Country B is the lower-cost producer, charging P_b, and country A is the high-cost producer, charging P_a, such that $P_c < P_b < P_a$. Initially, country A has a tariff t protecting the industry such that $t > P_b - P_c$, imports from country C, and receives tariff revenue. Then countries A and B form a FTA so that only the imports from country C face the tariff such that $P_b < P_c + t < P_a$. Trade has been *created* since country A will import more than before the FTA, with all the associated welfare benefits of increase trade. However trade will also be *diverted*, since the low cost producer is no longer supplying the good, and country A has lost the tariff revenue that it earned before the FTA was established, which reduces welfare. It may certainly be the case that the costs of trade diversion outweigh the benefits of trade creation, making member countries worse off.

Adding necessary real world complications to Viner's insight does not reduce the ambiguity of the welfare effects. With the added complication that the PTA is large such that its external tariffs can affect terms of trade with non-members, it is more likely to be welfare improving for members, but welfare reducing for nonmembers (Winters 2011). Greater differences in comparative advantage between member countries tend to increase trade creation, while the similarity of the combined comparative advantage of the FTA with the rest of the world tends to reduce diversion.

With the added complication of imperfect competition, the analysis is further clouded by gains from exploiting economies of scale and gains from variety weighed against the losses from trade diversion with lost tariff revenues (Krueger 1999). The literature on the impact of PTAs on member and nonmember welfare effects has grown faster than the phenomenon itself, with the current consensus being that whether PTAs are welfare improving or worsening for both member countries and the rest of the world is dependent on so many factors that it is nearly impossible to make generalizations about the welfare effects of PTAs.

Another branch of literature that has grown with the increase in PTAs addresses the question of whether or not the proliferation of PTAs will help or hinder the move toward multilateral opening of trade. And again the literature comes to no consensus, since the discussion moves beyond considerations simply of net welfare gain or loss to include the political economy of who gains or loses from trade liberalization within each country and the theory of the second best.

The camps have drawn on colorful names to describe the different conclusions various models reach: PTAs are stumbling blocks or building blocks (Bhagwati), friends or foes (Winters), bad bilateralism (Krugman) presumably countered with good multilateralism. As with the question of whether PTAs are welfare improving or not, the question of whether they hinder or promote multilateralism will have to be answered empirically in future research.

As a final note on the fall of political barriers to trade, some mention must be made of the "new" (post-WTO) protectionism: dumping accusations. Staiger and Wolak (1994) demonstrate that just the threat of protectionism due to antidumping investigation acts as a significant damper on trade. In the U.S. an ongoing antidumping investigation in the industry for a given product is estimated to have reduced trade in that product by 17 percent on average, so there remain significant political barriers, even when one measure of those barriers, namely tariffs, have fallen significantly.

Technological changes

In addition to the political barriers to trade, there are the more prosaic "natural" barriers: it is costly to move goods from one point to another, and more so when the two points lie in different countries.

Transportation costs and quality

Hummels (2007) has done the definitive work on transportation costs in international trade in the last half of the twentieth century. He notes that three big changes have occurred in international transportation since World War II: Jets, container shipping, and a change in the types of goods shipped. These three developments have had an impact on the quality and quantity of shipments. There has been a dramatic increase in air transport as measured by share of value of goods shipped and miles shipped, largely due to the change in the composition of the goods we now ship (lightweight, expensive electronics versus heavy, inexpensive raw materials) and due to the decline in the marginal cost of an additional air mile shipped. However, the share of goods transported by air remains relatively small compared to the share shipped by sea. By one measure, the cost of transport by ship did not decline significantly in the post-World War II period. Gains in efficiency due to containerization (see discussion of Levinson (2006) below) were balanced with the dramatic increases in cost of fuel in the 1970s. And although the fall in fuel prices in the mid-1980s did subsequently reduce ocean shipping costs in particular, Hummels (2007) speculates that there are unmeasured quality improvements from containerization (increased speed, increased efficiency/reduced uncertainty) that have aided the rapid increase in trade, rather than a large decline in shipping costs per ton.

Levinson (2006) describes the revolution of container shipping which began in the mid-1950s and dramatically decreased the labor portion of shipping costs. Because of the high start-up costs and fixed costs of capital, it took a while to catch on, but there has been a dramatic shift to the use of containers from the labor-intensive, non-standardized shipping, which is clear evidence of cost effectiveness. Levinson makes a convincing qualitative argument that the move to container shipping drastically reduced the cost of shipping, relative to what it would have been otherwise. The increased fuel costs of the 1970s and early 1980s certainly put upward pressure on transportation costs, but without the downward pressure on costs from containerization, the impact on trade of the oil shock would have been significantly negative. Although Levinson deems that the "revolution" was over by the early 1980s, he notes that the effects have been much longer-lived as the volume of sea freight shipped in containers increased 400 percent over the last two decades of the century. Low-cost container shipping allowed for trade in low-cost products around the world, which would have been impossible otherwise (Levinson 2006: 271).

There is some question of why distance between two countries matters so much in determining trade volumes between them. Clearly distance relates to transportation costs, but there is increasing evidence that even more so it is a proxy for information costs. Interestingly, the evidence for the importance of information costs in trade comes from the research on cross-border equity flows by Portes and Rey (2005). They use a gravity model[5] to explain asset trade and make a strong case that distance proxies for information costs as well: financial assets are nearly costless to "transport." Furthermore, when other variables that more closely represent information flows (as related to financial assets), like telephone communication or foreign bank branches in the country, are included in the model they are all statistically significant. When they estimate the same model using trade data rather than financial data, they find similar effects. Their results are robust to including the usual language/border/shared colonial history variables that often appear in the gravity model of trade. This confirms the importance of the second set of technological advances used to explain increased trade volumes: improved communication technology.

Communication costs and quality

The cost of communication is important to trade in final goods because these goods must be marketed, distributed and adapted to match the export market, which is costly, and even more so if gathering information about the foreign market is costly. As noted in Krugman (1995), distance matters, as seen in gravity model estimations, perhaps because it is correlated with the degree of contact between consumers and producers, and between manager and factory, among others. Not only have technological changes reduced the time it takes to move a quantity of goods, but they have also reduced the time required to communicate a quantity of information.

Freund and Weinhold (2004) test a model of imperfect competition and segmented markets for which there are fixed costs of entry into an export market. They hypothesize that

357

the internet, by reducing the fixed costs of entry (specifically the costs of finding information on new markets, costs of advertising) contributes to export growth. Their data cover host sites by country for 56 countries in the period 1995–1999 (during which time the mean number of country host sites went from about 30,000 to over 260,000). They find that between 1997 and 1999 a 10 percentage point increase in host sites leads to export growth of 0.2 percent – a significant amount given the very rapid growth of host sites over this time period.

Like Portes and Rey (2005), Freund and Weinhold (2002) look at the "transportation costs" of something costless to transport to make inferences on what the true transportation costs are for goods. Specifically, they consider the impact of the internet on trade in services. This consideration is nontrivial. On the one hand the relationship would seem an obvious one as the electronic transmission of data would make the "transportation" of many services costless. The study is particularly interesting in that it gives a way to explore how much distance proxies for other "transportation" costs such as differences in language, culture, and legal systems that are not as easily overcome by the costless transfer of data. Using U.S. bilateral service trade with 31 countries, they find that a 10 percent increase in internet host sites results in a 1.7 percent increase in exports to the U.S. and a 1.1 percent increase in imports from the U.S. They do not include intrafirm trade in services, noting that this omission of approximately one-third of U.S. trade in services biases downward their estimates of the role of the internet in trade in services. This is important to note because one aspect of the increase of trade as a share of GDP is growth in vertical specialization and intrafirm trade in goods, which is attributable in part to lower communication costs. This relationship should also carry over to intrafirm trade in services, and hence is another contributor to the increase in vertical specialization detailed below.

Networks and migration

Another change in the postwar period that explains some increase in trade is the rise in migration. Unlike trade policy, migration policy has become more restrictive in OECD countries, and yet there has been a significant increase in migration, especially to developed countries. According to the UN, since 1990 migrants have made up about 3 percent of world population, but the share of migrants in developed country populations has grown substantially from 7.2 percent in 1990 to 8.7 percent in 2000, and 10.3 percent in 2010.[6]

In his seminal work, Gould (1994) proposes that immigration increases trade not only by creating domestic markets for foreign goods, but by reducing information and other transaction costs associated with international trade. These transaction costs include anything from language barriers to understanding of foreign market preferences, regulations, or contracting mechanisms. His empirical analysis finds that immigrants have a greater impact on exports than imports, and more of an impact on consumer goods (which tend to be more differentiated) than on producer goods.

Rauch (1999) extends his more micro-oriented research (Rauch 1996) on the effect of networks on trade to a macro model. Specifically, he uses the gravity model to determine if historical (colonial) and cultural (language) links have different impacts on trade in different types of goods. Specifically, he hypothesizes that, compared to homogenous goods, trade in differentiated products which do not have an organized exchange or reference price will be more sensitive to the presence of networks needed to address the problem of imperfect information. Given that the growth in trade (as measured by value) has been primarily in differentiated (manufactured) products, this is an important consideration. Using data for 63 countries in 1970, 1980, and 1990, he finds evidence that networks are also important for *both* homogenous and differentiated goods, though he does not find much support that "links" between countries have a significantly different impact on differentiated goods compared to homogenous goods.[7]

Summary: the decline of barriers

The barriers to trade have fallen precipitously in the post-war period, but there are two important caveats. First, barriers to trade remain a significant tax on trade. Anderson and van Winccop (2004: 723) estimate a 44 percent border barrier "tax" due to trade policy restrictions (8 percent), language differences (7 percent), currency differences (14 percent) and information and security costs (9 percent).[8] The other important caveat is that, without further understanding of how the composition of trade has changed, it is difficult to justify the rapid growth in trade volumes using just the declines in barriers.

Income convergence

According to the trade models of monopolistic competition as summarized by Helpman and Krugman (1985), income convergence can explain increased trade. Helpman (1987) in particular develops the testable implications of the theory of monopolistic competition and trade: size convergence between countries and increased size (as a share of world GDP) both lead to an increase in trade as a share of GDP. As countries with similar income levels will demand similar types of goods, the theory predicts that increased similarity will lead to increased trade (as a share of GDP) of differentiated products between countries. In addressing the question of whether the increase in trade relative to GDP since World War II is due to greater size similarity between countries (income convergence) there are two papers of particular note.

Hummels and Levinsohn (1995) turn to the data of trade between 26 OECD countries during the period 1961–1983. They explain 98 percent of trade using a model that only contains fixed effects and a measure of income similarity between country pairs, offering initial support for the theory of Helpman (1987). However, when the same estimating equation is used to explain trade for non-OECD countries for which the monopolistic competition model clearly would not apply, income similarities still explain up to 67 percent of trade. They conclude that while increased income similarities may explain increased trade, the theoretical underpinnings of monopolistic competitions are not found in the data.

Debaere (2005) adapts the estimating equations to better reflect Helpman's testable implications (regarding size convergence between countries and increased size – as a share of world GDP – both leading to an increase in trade as a share of GDP) and changes the estimation techniques to deal better with the vagaries of the data. He also finds that both convergence and larger size relative to the world economy explain increased trade/GDP among OECD countries. However, when he looks at non-OECD countries, increased trade is explained by larger GDP, not convergence, offering support for the suitability of using income convergence between OECD countries to explain some of the growth in trade. Still, the final explanation considered, vertical specialization, is arguably more compelling.

Vertical specialization

Our concept of trade often involves the increasingly outmoded idea of final goods being imported and exported. The growth in what Hummels et al. (2001) term "vertical specialization"' has been the greatest change in trade patterns in the late twentieth century. Hummels et al. (2001) define vertical specialization as occurring when the production of a final good can be broken down into multiple, sequential stages, which occur in different countries so that the intermediate goods cross international borders, possibly multiple times, before becoming the final product – which then may be exported itself. Using input–output tables of countries contributing 82 percent of world exports, they find that the vertical specialization share of exports rose by about 40 percent between 1970 and 1995 (from 18 percent to 25 percent). Another, slightly less exact measure of the expansion of vertical specialization is to note that intermediate good trade has grown faster than trade in final goods, so that by the end of the twentieth century, intermediate goods represented 30 percent of world trade in manufacturing according to Yeats (1998). The fall in trade barriers has made this expansion of vertical specialization possible. But then again, vertical specialization explains why the fall in trade barriers has had a magnified impact on trade.

Fall in trade barriers and the expansion of vertical specialization

Vertical specialization allows efficiency gains and cost savings from comparative advantage realized across *multiple stages* of the production process. But as noted by McLaren (2000), vertical specialization also promotes efficiency gains by making more efficient organizational forms possible. McLaren uses a transaction costs model to demonstrate that increased openness (lower transportation costs, lower tariffs, etc.) will lead to vertical specialization as input suppliers are no longer locked into supplying local firms and, therefore, no longer require costly contracts to incur the sunk costs of specializing in a particular input. Hanson, Mataloni, and Slaughter (2005) using data on intrafirm trade, note that while higher trade costs make foreign direct investment (FDI)[9] a more attractive option (produce close to the market rather than export to the market), their data also indicate that higher trade costs change how goods are produced as firms try to reduce their use of imported inputs. Their findings that intrafirm trade is indeed sensitive to trade costs support the theoretical model in Yi (2003) outlined below. Specifically, they find evidence that multinationals decide between horizontal and vertical foreign direct investment, with increased vertical FDI occurring in countries with lower trade costs and lower labor costs.

The importance of the improvement in communication and transportation is highlighted in Grossman and Rossi-Hansberg (2008) which models "trade in tasks." The production process is broken down into small pieces of value added or tasks which are then performed in different countries according to their comparative advantage/differences in factor cost. It is hard to imagine such trade in tasks occurring in a world without reliable communications or with uncertainty that intermediate goods would be delivered in a timely manner. Finally, one reason for the growth in vertical specialization may be because the type of final product being traded lends itself to segmentation. As mentioned in the introduction, we trade manufactured goods with many parts, versus commodities of a century ago.

Vertical specialization and trade expansion

Vertical specialization explains how we see magnified effects of reduced trade barriers on international trade volumes. One of the "mysteries" of the growth in trade is that it is so much greater than the fall in transportation, communication, and tariff costs, given reasonable assumptions about elasticities of substitution. As Yi (2003: 53) notes, tariffs on manufactured goods have fallen 11 percentage points while trade has grown by 340 percent in the same period. Furthermore, in the final years of the twentieth century, trade was increasingly sensitive to tariff barriers, so there is a nonlinear relationship between trade and tariffs. Yi explains this phenomenon by modeling a final good that crosses borders (as intermediate goods) numerous times in its production process, gaining value added in each country, so that lower tariffs (and by extension other trade costs) have a compounded effect. Trade expansion is explained both by falling barriers and by a change in the relationship between barriers and trade volumes due to vertical specialization.

Conclusions

A few conclusions are clear: trade has risen as the world economy has grown and as barriers have fallen since the end of World War II. Much of the fall in barriers is attributable in one form or another to technological advance. Whether it is faster jets to transport the goods, faster communication to aid in both production and distribution, or the very fact that the goods we consume are high-tech manufactured goods that lend themselves to multiple, separable production stages, technology is central to globalization. The role institutional changes have played is considerably less clear. On the one hand, the dramatic fall in tariffs could be deemed an institutional change that has promoted trade. But the impact of actual international institutions, such as GATT/WTO and preferential trading agreements, is much less clear in the data, though still largely accepted by conventional wisdom.

Notes

1 Inasmuch as income level determines the types of goods in a country's consumption bundle, countries with similar income levels produce and consume similar, though differentiated, products. Therefore, it is predicted that income convergence between two countries can lead to higher trade volumes as their demand becomes more similar.

2 Note that these costs are "compounding": $1 + 1.70 \approx 1.44 \times 1.21 \times 1.55$.

3 See the discussion in Subramanian and Wei (2007) on the exclusion of developing economies from these principles.

4 www.wto.org/english/thewto_e/whatis_e/tif_e/fact4_e.htm

5 The gravity model, first introduced by Tinbergen (1962), is the workhorse model for predicting bilateral trade flows between countries i and j, V_{ij}, as a function of country sizes as measured by GDP, Y_i and Y_j, their distance from one another, D_{ij}, and various other factors that impede or promote trade, Z_n, $n = 1 \ldots N$:

$$V_{ij} = \beta_0 Y_i^{\beta_1} Y_j^{\beta_2} D_{ij}^{\beta_3} \left(\prod_{n=1}^{N} Z_n^{\gamma_{(n}} \right)$$

$\beta1$ is the elasticity of trade with respect to changes in the income of country one, $\beta2$ is the elasticity of trade with respect to changes in the income of country two, $\beta3$ is the elasticity of trade with respect to changes in the distance between countries who trade, etc.

6 http://esa.un.org/migprofiles

7 For other important works on the relationship between immigration and trade see Combes et al. (2005), Head and Ries (1998), and Rauch and Trindade (2002). For the impact of immigration on foreign direct investment see Javorcik et al. (2011).

8 Note that these costs are "compounding": $1.44 \approx 1.08 \times 1.07 \times 1.14 \times 1.09$.

9 FDI entails the acquisition of a controlling share of a foreign company or building a new facility in the foreign country that is headquartered in the home country.

References

Anderson, J.E. and van Wincoop, E. (2004) 'Trade costs', *Journal of Economic Literature*, 42: 691–751.

Bagwell, K. and Staiger, R.W. (1998) 'Will preferential agreements undermine the multilateral trading system?' *Economic Journal*, 108: 1162–82.

Baier, S.L. and Bergstrand, J.H. (2001) 'The growth of world trade: tariffs, transport costs, and income similarity', *Journal of International Economics*, 53: 1–27.

Baier, S.L. and Bergstrand, J.H. (2004) 'On the economic determinants of free trade agreements', *Journal of International Economics*, 64: 29–63.

Broda, C., Limão, N. and Weinstein, D.E. (2008) 'Optimal tariffs and market power: the evidence', *American Economic Review*, 98: 2032–65.

Combes, P., Lafourcade, M., and Mayer, T. (2005) 'The trade-creating effects of business and social networks: evidence from France', *Journal of International Economics*, 66: 1–29.

Debaere, P. (2005) 'Monopolistic competition and trade, revisited: testing the model without testing for gravity', *Journal of International Economics*, 66: 249–66.

Feenstra, R.C. (1998) 'Integration of trade and disintegration of production in the global economy', *Journal of Economic Perspectives*, 12: 31–50.

Freund, C. and Weinhold, D. (2002) 'The internet and international trade in services', *American Economic Review*, 92: 236–40.

Freund, C. and Weinhold, D. (2004) 'The effect of the internet on international trade', *Journal of International Economics*, 62: 171–89.

Gould, D.M. (1994) 'Immigrant links to the home country: empirical implications for U.S. bilateral trade flows', *Review of Economics and Statistics*, 76: 302–16.

Grossman, G.M. and Rossi-Hansberg, E. (2008) 'Trading tasks: a simple theory of offshoring', *American Economic Review*, 98: 1978–97.

Hanson, G.H., Mataloni, R.J., Jr. and Slaughter, M.J. (2005) 'Vertical production networks in multinational firms', *Review of Economics and Statistics*, 87: 664–78.

Head, K. and Ries, J. (1998) 'Immigration and trade creation: econometric evidence from Canada', *Canadian Journal of Economics*, 31: 47–62.

Helpman, E. (1987) 'Imperfect competition and international trade: evidence from fourteen industrial countries', *Journal of the Japanese and International Economies*, 1: 62–81.

Helpman, E. and Krugman, P. (1985) *Market Structure and Foreign Trade*, Cambridge, MA: MIT Press.

Hummels, D. (2007) 'Transportation costs and international trade in the second era of globalization', *Journal of Economic Perspectives*, 21: 131–54.

Hummels, D. and Levinsohn, J. (1995) 'Monopolistic competition and international trade: reconsidering the evidence', *Quarterly Journal of Economics*, 110: 799–836.

Hummels, D., Ishii, J. and Yi, K. (2001) 'The nature and growth of vertical specialization in world trade', *Journal of International Economics*, 54: 75–96.

Irwin, D.A. (1998) 'The Smoot–Hawley Tariff: a quantitative assessment', *Review of Economics and Statistics*, 80: 326–334.

Javorcik, B., Ozden, C., Spatareanu, M. and Neagu, C. (2011) 'Migrant networks and foreign direct investment', *Journal of Development Economics*, 94: 231–41

Krueger, A.O. (1999) 'Are preferential trading agreements trade liberalizing or protectionist?', *Journal of Economic Perspectives*, 13: 105–24.

Krugman, P. (1995) 'Growing world trade: causes and consequences', *Brookings Papers on Economic Activity*, 1995: 327–77.

Krugman, P. (1997) 'What should trade negotiators negotiate about?', *Journal of Economic Literature*, 35: 113–20.

Levinson, M. (2006) *The Box: How the Shipping Container Made the World Smaller and the World Economy Bigger*, Princeton, NJ: Princeton University Press.

McLaren, J. (2000) 'Globalization and vertical structure', *American Economic Review*, 90: 1239–54.

Portes, R. and Rey, H. (2005) 'The determinants of cross-border equity flows', *Journal of International Economics*, 65: 269–96.

Rauch, J.E. (1996) 'Trade and search: social capital, sogo shosha, and spillovers', National Bureau of Economic Research, Working Paper No. 5618.

Rauch, J.E. (1999) 'Networks versus markets in international trade', *Journal of International Economics*, 48: 7–35.

Rauch, J.E. and Trindade, V. (2002) 'Ethnic Chinese networks in international trade', *Review of Economics and Statistics*, 84: 116–30.

Rose, A.K. (2004a) 'Do we really know that the WTO increases trade?', *American Economic Review*, 94: 98–114

Rose, A.K. (2004b) 'Do WTO members have more liberal trade policy', *Journal of International Economics*, 63: 209–35.

Staiger, R.W. and Wolak, F.A. (1994) 'Measuring industry specific protection: antidumping in the United States', National Bureau of Economic Research, Working Paper No. 4696.

Subramanian, A. and Wei, S. (2007) 'The WTO promotes trade, strongly but unevenly', *Journal of International Economics*, 72: 151–75.

Tinbergen, J. (1962) *Shaping the World Economy,* New York: The Twentieth Century Fund.

Viner, J. (1950) *The Custom Union Issue,* New York: Carnegie Endowment for International Peace.

Winters, L.A. (2011) 'Preferential trading agreements: friend or foe', in K.W. Bagwell and P.C. Mavroidis (eds.) *Preferential Trade Agreements: A Law and Economics Analysis,* New York: Cambridge University Press.

Yeats, A. (1998) 'Just how big is global production sharing', World Bank Policy Research Working Paper No. 1871.

Yi, K. (2003) 'Can vertical specialization explain the growth of world trade?', *Journal of Political Economy*, 111: 52–102.

PART IV

The contemporary era

30

WORLD
HYPERINFLATIONS

Steve H. Hanke and Nicholas Krus

> We too must bring into our science a strict order and discipline, which we are still
> far from having…by a disorderly and ambiguous terminology we are led into the
> most palpable mistakes and misunderstandings – all these failings are of so frequent
> occurrence in our science that they almost seem to be characteristic of its style.
>
> (Eugen von Böhm-Bawerk 1891: 382–83)

Regardless of how far the study of economics has advanced, the disorderly and ambiguous
terminology cited by Eugen von Böhm-Bawerk over a century ago still exists. For example,
Friedrich Hayek complained about the kaleidoscope of definitions surrounding the word
"capital" (1941). Fritz Machlup also emphasized this point in *Economic Semantics* (1991),
with a call for clarity in definition. It is only after analysts – armed with first principles –
develop definitions and classification systems that data can be properly collected, sorted, and
analyzed, in a way that can be replicated.

This chapter supplies what has been long overdue in the study of hyperinflation – a table
that contains all 56 hyperinflation episodes, including several which had previously gone
unreported.[1] The hyperinflation table (Table 30.1) is compiled in a systematic and uniform
way. Most importantly, it meets the replicability test. It utilizes clean and consistent inflation
metrics, indicates the start and end dates of each episode, identifies the month of peak
hyperinflation, and signifies the currency that was in circulation, as well as the method used
to calculate inflation rates.

The literature on hyperinflation is replete with ad hoc definitions, vague, ill-defined
terminology, and a lack of concern for clear, uniform metrics. In consequence, sloppy
reasoning is all too common. Although Peter Bernholz (2003) has provided the most
comprehensive list of hyperinflation episodes available (30 cases), he does not follow a precise,
consistent definition, and misses almost half of the cases we report in this chapter. Without a
complete list of hyperinflation episodes in the scholarly literature, many people simply rely
on Wikipedia and the unreliable information contained therein (e.g. Fischer 2010). To fill
the void in the academic literature, we set out to construct a new, comprehensive table of the
world's hyperinflation episodes.

The arduous data compilation process

We soon learned why no such table exists. We frequently found leads suggesting new episodes, only to discover that the proper documentation of their source was lacking. Even in cases in which we thought replication would be straightforward, it was not.

Despite the fall of communism having occurred over two decades ago, the Soviet-Bloc countries were a particular source of frustration – the data had seemingly been lost in time. After scouring the Library of Congress and the Joint World Bank–IMF Library in Washington D.C., as well as a variety of online databases, we finally came across a series of World Bank publications that ostensibly contained the requisite information.[2] But, much of the information was not presented in a usable form. It was not uniform, and its dimensions were not always defined. For example, we did not know whether the numerical values represented year-over-year changes, monthly changes, or a price index. To put the raw data into shape, analysis and considerable effort were required.

The challenges we faced with the Soviet Bloc were compounded, as we looked to the Balkan States and began to investigate hyperinflation episodes of the 1990s. In particular, Bosnia and Herzegovina, and the Republika Srpska posed the most difficult problems. The Socialist Federal Republic of Yugoslavia had a history of very high inflation, punctuated by episodes of hyperinflation. Prior to its collapse, it circulated the Yugoslav dinar. But, shortly after Bosnia and Herzegovina declared its independence from Yugoslavia in 1992, there were five currencies circulating in the region: the German mark, the Croatian kuna, and three separate dinars issued by Bosnia and Herzegovina (BH), the Republika Srpska (RS), and the Federal Republic of Yugoslavia (Brown et al. 1996).

From what data were initially available, we knew that Yugoslavia had experienced hyperinflation, and that Croatia had not (CNB 2012). Because the BH dinar and the RS dinar were both initially pegged to the Yugoslav dinar, and based on the annual inflation data that were available, we knew that the Republika Srpska and Bosnia and Herzegovina had experienced hyperinflation (Brown et al. 1996). We then began our search for monthly data. For months, we pored over reports from the International Monetary Fund (IMF), the World Bank, the U.S. government, the Central Bank of Bosnia and Herzegovina, and Bosnia and Herzegovina's Federal Office of Statistics (FZS), and we were still unable to find the monthly data. We also consulted numerous officials from local and international agencies, but, by all accounts, the information had simply not survived the war.[3]

Finally, in the eleventh hour, we obtained the essential data for both the Republika Srpska and Bosnia and Herzegovina.[4] As can be seen in the table, Bosnia and Herzegovina's peak month of inflation occurred in June 1992, with a monthly rate of 322 percent. The Republika Srpska experienced its peak monthly inflation rate of 297,000,000 percent in January 1994.

In another case, we were able to overcome data deficiencies in a different way. We knew that the Free City of Danzig engineered a currency reform in 1923, following inflationary developments similar to those that had visited Germany. Suspecting that this currency reform was enacted in response to a case of hyperinflation, and lacking inflation data, we were forced to employ creative methods to estimate Danzig's inflation rate.

In 1923, Danzig was considered an independent "Free City", under the protection of the League of Nations. However, it did not issue its own domestic currency, but instead circulated the German papiermark. How could we estimate the inflation rate for such a small, relatively unknown city-state, which had adopted another country's currency as its own, and for which no inflation data existed? From past experience (Hanke and Kwok 2009), we knew that purchasing power parity (PPP) could overcome such an obstacle. The theory states that the ratio of the price level between two countries is equivalent to their exchange rate. But, did PPP hold for the case of Danzig? In short, yes. As Jacob Frenkel (1976) showed – with Germany's hyperinflation during the same time period – as inflation accelerates towards hyperinflation, theory becomes reality.[5]

Accordingly, exchange-rate data held the key to discovering the missing inflation rate. Since Danzig circulated the German papiermark, it had an exchange rate of one with Germany.[6] The price level in Danzig, therefore, was equivalent to that of Germany, placing the Free City of Danzig into the hyperinflation club, with a peak monthly inflation rate of 2,440 percent in September 1923.

Some "missing" cases were easier to find. We discovered the data for the Democratic Republic of Congo's August 1998 hyperinflation using the IMF's International Financial Statistics database – one readily available to most economists. Surprisingly, these data had gone unnoticed and ignored in the major works on hyperinflation.

Another largely unreported hyperinflation episode occurred in the Philippines, during World War II. In 1942, during its occupation of what was then the Commonwealth of the Philippines, Japan replaced the Philippine peso with Japanese war notes. These notes were dubbed "Mickey Mouse money", and their over-issuance eventually resulted in a hyperinflation that peaked in January 1944. It should be noted that the U.S. Army, under orders from General Douglas MacArthur, did add a relatively small amount of fuel to the Philippine hyperinflation fire by surreptitiously distributing counterfeit Japanese war notes to Philippine guerilla troops (Hartendorp 1958).

As our search for hyperinflation episodes drew to an end, we checked our work, and one figure in particular caught our attention. In October 2009, when we first obtained data for Azerbaijan, the International Financial Statistics database listed a peak monthly inflation rate of 118 percent. But, as of November 2011, this statistic had been changed to 327 percent. We inquired as to the reason for this change. The IMF informed us that the number should have been kept at 118 percent, thanked us for bringing this issue to their attention, and corrected the entry. This incident attests to the fact that simple clerical errors can lead to misleading results, particularly when the erroneous number is nearly three times the size of the true number.

Construction of the table

One of the biggest problems encountered when discussing hyperinflation is the extreme size of the monthly inflation rates. For example, in July 1946, Hungary had a monthly inflation rate of 4.19×10^{16} percent. Physicist Richard Feynman, a master of communication, provided the following analogy to help his readers grasp the size of the minute particles he studied, "If an apple was magnified to the size of the earth, then the atoms in the apple would be approximately the size of the original apple" (Feynman et al. 1995: 5). Feynman's analogy highlights the "size problem" one encounters in the study of atomic theory. Similarly, in the study of hyperinflation, it is difficult to comprehend the size of the "large" numbers represented by monthly inflation rates.

In an effort to overcome this size problem, we included two metrics that help put hyperinflation into perspective: the equivalent daily inflation rate and the time required for prices to double. Following Feynman's analogy, as atoms are to apples, equivalent daily inflation rates are to monthly inflation rates. Thus, by making these calculations, we can more easily grasp the magnitude of Hungary's world-record hyperinflation; during its peak month, July 1946, the equivalent daily inflation rate was roughly 207 percent, with prices doubling every 15 hours.

To ensure uniformity in the table, we then determined which price index to use as our primary inflation measure. We ultimately chose to use consumer price indices, as they best reflect price changes experienced by the final consumer. If consumer prices were not available, we utilized a wholesale price index, even though these prices are once removed from the final consumer.

During periods of extreme hyperinflation, however, conventional price indices are sometimes not available. In these cases, it is necessary to utilize proxies to determine monthly inflation rates. Greece's inflation rate, for example, was calculated by measuring the rise in the drachma price of the gold sovereign, and France's was derived using changes in exchange rates. For the case of Zimbabwe, the official consumer price index ended in July 2008. This date is often incorrectly cited as the peak month of its hyperinflation (Koech 2011); when, in fact, Zimbabwe's peak inflation occurred three and a half months later. As Hanke and Kwok (2009) determined – by calculating the changes in the exchange rate implied by the prices of a stock that traded simultaneously on stock exchanges in Harare and London – Zimbabwe's hyperinflation actually peaked in mid-November 2008, with a monthly rate over 30 million times higher than the final inflation rate reported by the government.

For clarity, it was also necessary to indicate the currency in circulation, because several countries that experienced hyperinflation were "dollarized". For example, the rapidly depreciating Russian ruble circulated throughout many of the post-Soviet countries in 1992. Accordingly, in places like Ukraine and Moldova, hyperinflation occurred even though these countries did not issue a domestic currency.

Additionally, in the case of the world's first hyperinflation, that of France, there were two separate currencies in circulation in 1796, the mandat and the assignat. But, in reading the literature, you wouldn't know it. Many experts incorrectly claim the peak of France's hyperinflation was associated with the rapidly depreciating assignat (e.g. Cagan 1987, Végh 1995, Bernholz 1995). But, it was the even more rapidly depreciating mandat (not the assignat) which set the record, generating a monthly inflation rate of 304 percent in mid-August 1796. Unfortunately, when it comes to currencies and exchange-rate regimes, errors like this are all too common, as factoids often come to replace facts (White and Schuler 2009, Hanke 2002).

The definition of hyperinflation

The literature on hyperinflation is riddled with a variety of definitions, and more often than not, they are vague and ill-defined. In search of a cornerstone for our definition of hyperinflation, we began with Philip Cagan's (1956) widely accepted definition: a price-level increase of at least 50 percent per month.

Under Cagan's definition, an episode of hyperinflation starts when there is a month in which the price level increases by at least 50 percent. When the monthly inflation rate drops below 50 percent and stays there for at least one year, the episode is said to end.[7] However, even Cagan does not strictly adhere to his own definition. For example, in addition to making several errors in his hyperinflation table (1956: 26), Cagan selectively excludes Germany's 1920 case of hyperinflation, presumably because of its short duration (one month).[8]

We chose to follow Cagan's definition strictly. In the Hyperinflation Table, we can see the implications of this in the Chinese and Taiwanese episodes of hyperinflation. Whereas these cases are typically considered to be single periods of hyperinflation, under our definition, the episodes qualify as two and three separate instances, respectively.

The hyperinflation table

Hyperinflation is an economic malady that arises under extreme conditions: war, political mismanagement, and the transition from a command to market-based economy – to name a few. In each of these circumstances, there are barriers to the recording and publication of reliable inflation statistics. As we discovered over the course of our investigation, overcoming these barriers was an arduous and painstaking process. In light of this, it is little wonder that no one has been able to fully and accurately document every case of hyperinflation.

After years of disorder in the study of hyperinflation, we can now, with Table 30.1, the hyperinflation table, finally let the data speak for themselves.

Acknowledgments

The authors wish to thank Alex Kwok and Wyatt Larkin for their comments.

Notes

1 If we were to include our estimate for the 2009–11 case of hyperinflation in North Korea, the total number of hyperinflation episodes would increase to 57. However, as explained in the notes to the table, the available North Korean data did not meet our minimum quality standards. Accordingly, we omitted this episode from the table.

2 See the footnotes to the table for the references to these publications.

3 The authors contacted many of Steve Hanke's former colleagues in the region in an effort to obtain data. Hanke was a personal economic adviser to Živko Pregl, the vice president of the Socialist Federal Rebuplic of Yugoslavia, from 1990 to June 1991. Hanke later served as a special advisor to the U.S. Government on the establishment of Bosnia and Herzegovina's currency board (see Hanke and Schuler 1991, Hanke 1996/7).

4 The authors would like to thank Dr. Mladen Ivanić and Prof. Simeun Vilendecic for their assistance in providing the monthly inflation data for the Republika Srpska. The authors would also like to thank Prof. Shirley Gedeon and Prof. Dzenan Djonlagic for their assistance in providing the monthly inflation rates for Bosnia and Herzegovina.

5 The validity of purchasing power parity has also been shown and explained for other countries with very high inflation or hyperinflation (McNown and Wallace 1989, Hanke and Kwok 2009).

6 Danzig also circulated a negligable amount of "emergency mark currency" (Loveday 1924).

7 For example, if the monthly inflation rate for July is 50 percent, and the next twelve months are marked by monthly inflation rates below 50 percent, then the end date of the episode would be July.

8 Cagan (1956) failed to report the correct end dates for Austria's and Germany's hyperinflation episodes. His table (1956: 26) also contains errors for the start date, end date, and peak month of inflation during the Russia/USSR hyperinflation of the early 1920s. Cagan's analysis of Greece's hyperinflation in 1941 also illustrates his inconsistency in applying his own methodology. If Cagan were to have strictly applied his definition to the data he used, the Greek episode would qualify as two separate cases. That said, by utilizing a different, more accurate data set (see note 7 to the table), we determined that Greece experienced a single episode of hyperinflation, from 1941–45.

Table 30.1 The hyperinflation table

Location	Start date	End date	Month with highest inflation rate	Highest monthly inflation rate	Equivalent daily inflation rate	Time required for prices to double	Currency	Type of price index
Hungary[1]	Aug. 1945	Jul. 1946	Jul. 1946	4.19×10^{16}%	207%	15.0 hours	Pengő	Consumer
Zimbabwe[2]	Mar. 2007	Mid-Nov. 2008	Mid-Nov. 2008	7.96×10^{10}%	98.0%	24.7 hours	Dollar	Implied Exchange Rate★
Yugoslavia[3]	Apr. 1992	Jan. 1994	Jan. 1994	313,000,000%	64.6%	1.41 days	Dinar	Consumer
Republika Srpska[†4]	Apr. 1992	Jan. 1994	Jan. 1994	297,000,000%	64.3%	1.41 days	Dinar	Consumer
Germany[5]	Aug. 1922	Dec. 1923	Oct. 1923	29,500%	20.9%	3.70 days	Papiermark	Wholesale
Greece[6]	May 1941	Dec. 1945	Oct. 1944	13,800%	17.9%	4.27 days	Drachma	Exchange Rate‡
China[7]	Oct. 1947	Mid-May 1949	Apr. 1949	5,070%	14.1%	5.34 days	Yuan	Wholesale for Shanghai
Free City of Danzig[8]	Aug. 1922	Mid-Oct. 1923	Sep. 1923	2,440%	11.4%	6.52 days	German Papiermark	Exchange Rate★★
Armenia[9]	Oct. 1993	Dec. 1994	Nov. 1993	438%	5.77%	12.5 days	Dram & Russian Ruble	Consumer
Turkmenistan[††10]	Jan. 1992	Nov. 1993	Nov. 1993	429%	5.71%	12.7 days	Manat	Consumer
Taiwan[11]	Aug. 1945	Sep. 1945	Aug. 1945	399%	5.50%	13.1 days	Yen	Wholesale for Taipei
Peru[12]	Jul. 1990	Aug. 1990	Aug. 1990	397%	5.49%	13.1 days	Inti	Consumer
Bosnia and Herzegovina[13]	Apr. 1992	Jun. 1993	Jun. 1992	322%	4.92%	14.6 days	Dinar	Consumer
France[14]	May 1795	Nov. 1796	Mid-Aug. 1796	304%	4.77%	15.1 days	Mandat	Exchange Rate
China[15]	Jul. 1943	Aug. 1945	Jun. 1945	302%	4.75%	15.2 days	Yuan	Wholesale for Shanghai
Ukraine[16]	Jan. 1992	Nov. 1994	Jan. 1992	285%	4.60%	15.6 days	Russian Ruble	Consumer
Poland[17]	Jan. 1923	Jan. 1924	Oct. 1923	275%	4.50%	16.0 days	Marka	Wholesale
Nicaragua[18]	Jun. 1986	Mar. 1991	Mar. 1991	261%	4.37%	16.4 days	Córdoba	Consumer
Congo (Zaire)[19]	Nov. 1993	Sep. 1994	Nov. 1993	250%	4.26%	16.8 days	Zaïre	Consumer
Russia[††20]	Jan. 1992	Jan. 1992	Jan. 1992	245%	4.22%	17.0 days	Ruble	Consumer
Bulgaria[21]	Feb. 1997	Feb. 1997	Feb. 1997	242%	4.19%	17.1 days	Lev	Consumer
Moldova[22]	Jan. 1992	Dec. 1993	Jan. 1992	240%	4.16%	17.2 days	Russian Ruble	Consumer
Russia/USSR [23]	Jan. 1922	Feb. 1924	Feb. 1924	212%	3.86%	18.5 days	Ruble	Consumer
Georgia[24]	Sep. 1993	Sep. 1994	Sep. 1994	211%	3.86%	18.6 days	Coupon	Consumer
Tajikistan[††25]	Jan. 1992	Oct. 1993	Jan. 1992	201%	3.74%	19.1 days	Russian Ruble	Consumer
Georgia[26]	Mar. 1992	Apr. 1992	Mar. 1992	198%	3.70%	19.3 days	Russian Ruble	Consumer

Country	Start Date	End Date	Month of Highest Inflation	Highest Monthly Inflation Rate	Equivalent Daily Inflation Rate	Time Required for Prices to Double	Currency	Type of Price Index
Argentina[27]	May 1989	Mar. 1990	Jul. 1989	197%	3.69%	19.4 days	Austral	Consumer
Bolivia[28]	Apr. 1984	Sep. 1985	Feb. 1985	183%	3.53%	20.3 days	Boliviano	Consumer
Belarus††[29]	Jan. 1992	Feb. 1992	Jan. 1992	159%	3.22%	22.2 days	Russian Ruble	Consumer
Kyrgyzstan††[30]	Jan. 1992	Jan. 1992	Jan. 1992	157%	3.20%	22.3 days	Russian Ruble	Consumer
Kazakhstan††[31]	Jan. 1992	Jan. 1992	Jan. 1992	141%	2.97%	24.0 days	Russian Ruble	Consumer
Austria[32]	Oct. 1921	Sep. 1922	Aug. 1922	129%	2.80%	25.5 days	Crown	Consumer
Bulgaria[33]	Feb. 1991	Mar. 1991	Feb. 1991	123%	2.71%	26.3 days	Lev	Consumer
Uzbekistan††[34]	Jan. 1992	Feb. 1992	Jan. 1992	118%	2.64%	27.0 days	Russian Ruble	Consumer
Azerbaijan[35]	Jan. 1992	Dec. 1994	Jan. 1992	118%	2.63%	27.0 days	Russian Ruble	Consumer
Congo (Zaire)[36]	Oct. 1991	Sep. 1992	Nov. 1991	114%	2.57%	27.7 days	Zaïre	Consumer
Peru[37]	Sep. 1988	Sep. 1988	Sep. 1988	114%	2.57%	27.7 days	Inti	Consumer
Taiwan[38]	Oct. 1948	May 1949	Oct. 1948	108%	2.46%	28.9 days	Taipi	Wholesale for Taipei
Hungary[39]	Mar. 1923	Feb. 1924	Jul. 1923	97.9%	2.30%	30.9 days	Crown	Consumer
Chile[40]	Oct. 1973	Oct. 1973	Oct. 1973	87.6%	2.12%	33.5 days	Escudo	Consumer
Estonia††[41]	Jan. 1992	Feb. 1992	Jan. 1992	87.2%	2.11%	33.6 days	Russian Ruble	Consumer
Angola[42]	Dec. 1994	May 1996	May 1996	84.1%	2.06%	34.5 days	Kwanza	Consumer
Brazil[43]	Dec. 1989	Mar. 1990	Mar. 1990	82.4%	2.02%	35.1 days	Cruzado & Cruzeiro	Consumer
Dem. Rep. of Congo[44]	Aug. 1998	Aug. 1998	Aug. 1998	78.5%	1.95%	36.4 days	Franc	Consumer
Poland[45]	Oct. 1989	Jan. 1990	Jan. 1990	77.3%	1.93%	36.8 days	Zloty	Consumer
Armenia††[46]	Jan. 1992	Feb. 1992	Jan. 1992	73.1%	1.85%	38.4 days	Russian Ruble	Wholesale
Tajikistan[47]	Oct. 1995	Nov. 1995	Nov. 1995	65.2%	1.69%	42.0 days	Tajikistani Ruble	Wholesale
Latvia[48]	Jan. 1992	Jan. 1992	Jan. 1992	64.4%	1.67%	42.4 days	Russian Ruble	Consumer
Turkmenistan††[49]	Nov. 1995	Jan. 1996	Jan. 1996	62.5%	1.63%	43.4 days	Manat	Consumer
Philippines[50]	Jan. 1944	Dec. 1944	Jan. 1944	60.0%	1.58%	44.9 days	Japanese War Notes	Consumer
Yugoslavia[51]	Sep. 1989	Dec. 1989	Dec. 1989	59.7%	1.57%	45.1 days	Dinar	Consumer
Germany[52]	Jan. 1920	Jan. 1920	Jan. 1920	56.9%	1.51%	46.8 days	Papiermark	Wholesale
Kazakhstan[53]	Nov. 1993	Nov. 1993	Nov. 1993	55.5%	1.48%	47.8 days	Tenge & Russian Ruble	Consumer
Lithuania[54]	Jan. 1992	Jan. 1992	Jan. 1992	54.0%	1.45%	48.8 days	Russian Ruble	Consumer
Belarus[55]	Aug. 1994	Aug. 1994	Aug. 1994	53.4%	1.44%	49.3 days	Belarusian Ruble	Consumer
Taiwan[56]	Feb. 1947	Feb. 1947	Feb. 1947	50.8%	1.38%	51.4 days	Taipi	Wholesale for Taipei

Notes to Table 30.1

When a country experiences periods of hyperinflation that are broken up by 12 or more consecutive months with a monthly inflation rate below 50%, the periods are defined as separate episodes of hyperinflation.

The currency listed in the chart is the one that, in a particular location, is associated with the highest monthly rate of inflation. The currency may not have been the only one that was in circulation, in that location, during the episode.

* We are aware of one other case of hyperinflation: North Korea. We reached this conclusion after calculating inflation rates using data from the foreign exchange black market, and also by observing changes in the price of rice. Based on our estimates, this episode of hyperinflation most likely occurred from December 2009 to mid-January 2011. Using black-market exchange-rate data, and calculations based on purchasing power parity, we determined that the North Korean hyperinflation peaked in early March 2010, with a monthly rate of 496% (implying a 6.13% daily inflation rate and a price-doubling time of 11.8 days). When we used rice price data, we calculated the peak month to be mid-January 2010, with a monthly rate of 348% (implying a 5.12% daily inflation rate and a price-doubling time of 14.1 days). All of these data were obtained August 13, 2012 from Daily NK, an online newspaper that focuses on issues relating to North Korea (http://www.dailynk.com/english/market.php). We also acknowledge that our investigation was aided by reports from Good Friends USA, a Korean-American advocacy and research organization, as well as from Marcus Noland at the Peterson Institute for International Economics.

† The authors calculated Zimbabwe's inflation rate, from August to November 2008, using changes in the price of the stock, Old Mutual, which was traded both on the Harare and London stock exchanges. The stock prices yielded an implied exchange rate for Zimbabwe dollars, under purchasing power parity.

† The Republika Srpska is a Serb-majority, semi-autonomous entity within Bosnia and Herzegovina. From 1992 until early 1994, the National Bank of Republika Srpska issued its own unique currency, the Republika Srpska dinar.

‡ Greece's inflation rate was estimated by calculating the drachma/gold sovereign exchange rate.

§ The peak monthly inflation rate listed for China in the table differs from that presented in one of the authors' previous pieces on hyperinflation (Hanke and Kwok 2009). This revision is based on new data from a number of sources, which were recently obtained from the Library of Congress in Washington, D.C.

** We calculated the Free City of Danzig's inflation rate using German inflation data, since the German papiermark was in circulation in Danzig during this time. It is worth noting that Germany and Danzig experienced different peak months of hyperinflation. This is because the last full month in which the German papiermark circulated in the Free City of Danzig was September 1923. Germany continued to circulate the papiermark beyond this point, and subsequently experienced its peak month of hyperinflation (October 1923).

†† The data for many of the post-Soviet countries were only available in the World Bank's *Statistical Handbook: States of the Former USSR*. In this publication, the authors stated that the data should be viewed with an extra degree of caution because the statistics were taken from the corresponding official internal government source and not independently reviewed by the World Bank. However, these statistics are official and are the only source of data available for the corresponding time periods for each country.

1. Nogaro, B. (1948) 'Hungary's Recent Monetary Crisis and Its Theoretical Meaning', *American Economic Review*, 38 (4): 526–42.
2. Hanke, S.H. and Kwok, A.K.F. (2009) 'On the Measurement of Zimbabwe's Hyperinflation', *Cato Journal*, 29 (2): 353–64.
3. a) Hanke, S.H. (1999) 'Yugoslavia Destroyed Its Own Economy', *Wall Street Journal*, April 28, p. A18.
   b) Petrovic´, P., Bogetic´, Z. and Vujoševic´, Z. (1999) 'The Yugoslav Hyperinflation of 1992–1994: Causes, Dynamics, and Money Supply Process', *Journal of Comparative Economics*, 27 (2): 335–53.
   c) Rostowski, J. (1998) *Macroeconomic Instability in Post-Communist Countries*, New York: Clarendon Press.
4. a) Republika Srpska Institute of Statistics, Announcements 19/92 (p. 801), 20/92 (p. 825), 1/93 (p. 31), 2/93 (p. 54), 3/93 (p. 83), 4/93 (p. 155), 7/93 (p. 299), 16/93 (p. 848), 19/93 (p. 790), 20/93 (p. 808), 23/93 (p. 948), 1/94 (p. 29), 9/94 (p. 345), 17/94 (p. 608), 22/94 (p. 710), 23/94 (p. 717), 26/94

(p. 768), 27/94 (p. 784), 30/94 (p. 840), 1/95 (p. 7), Banja Luka: Official Gazette.

b) Vilendecic, S. (2008) *Banking in Republika Srpska in the Late XX and early XXI Century*, Banja Luka: Besjeda.

5. Sargent, T.J. (1986) *Rational Expectations and Inflation*, New York: Harper & Row.
6. Makinen, G.E. (1986) 'The Greek hyperinflation and stabilization of 1943–1946', *Journal of Economic History*, 46 (3): 795–805.
7. Chang, K. (1958) *The Inflationary Spiral, The Experience in China, 1939–1950*, New York: The Technology Press of Massachusetts Institute of Technology and John Wiley and Sons.
8. Sargent, T.J. (1986) *Rational Expectations and Inflation*, New York: Harper & Row.
9. IMF 'International Financial Statistics (IFS)', Washington, D.C.: International Monetary Fund, accessed October 2009. http://elibrary-data.imf.org/.
10. World Bank (1996) *Statistical Handbook: States of the Former USSR*, Washington, D.C.: World Bank.
11. Liu, F.C. (1970) *Essays on Monetary Development in Taiwan*, Taipei, Taiwan: China Committee for Publication Aid and Prize Awards.
12. IMF 'International Financial Statistics (IFS)', Washington, D.C.: International Monetary Fund, accessed October 2009. http://elibrary-data.imf.org/.
13. Kreso, S. (1997) *Novac Bosne i Hercegovine: Od BHD do Novog Novca BiH*, Sarajevo: Jez.
14. White, E.N. (1991) 'Measuring the French Revolution's inflation: the Tableaux de dépreciation', *Histoire & Mesure*, 6 (3): 245–74.
15. Young, A. (1965) *China's Wartime Finance and Inflation, 1937–1945*, Cambridge, MA: Harvard University Press.
16. State Statistics Committee of Ukraine. 'Consumer Price Indices', accessed May 2012. http://www.ukrstat.gov.ua/.
17. Sargent, T.J. (1981) 'The Ends of Four Big Inflations', working paper, Federal Reserve Bank of Minneapolis, 158.
18. IMF 'International Financial Statistics (IFS)', Washington, D.C.: International Monetary Fund, accessed October 2009. http://elibrary-data.imf.org/.
19. Beaugrand, P. (1997) 'Zaire's Hyperinflation, 1990–96', working paper, International Monetary Fund, April, 97/50.
20. World Bank (1993) *Statistical Handbook: States of the Former USSR*, Washington, D.C.: World Bank.
21. IMF 'International Financial Statistics (IFS)', Washington, D.C.: International Monetary Fund, accessed October 2009. http://elibrary-data.imf.org/.
22. National Bureau of Statistics of the Republic of Moldova. 'Consumer Price Indices', accessed May 2012. http://www.statistica.md.
23. Bernholz, P. (1996) 'Currency substitution during hyperinflation in the Soviet Union 1922–1924', *Journal of European Economic History*, 25 (2): 297–323.
24. IMF 'International Financial Statistics (IFS)', Washington, D.C.: International Monetary Fund, accessed November 2011. http://elibrary-data.imf.org/.
25. World Bank (1993) *Statistical Handbook: States of the Former USSR*, Washington, D.C.: World Bank.
26. Wang, J.Y. (1999) 'The Georgian hyperinflation and stabilization', working paper, International Monetary Fund, May, 99/65.
27. IMF 'International Financial Statistics (IFS)', Washington, D.C.: International Monetary Fund, accessed October 2009. http://elibrary-data.imf.org/.
28. IMF 'International Financial Statistics (IFS)', Washington, D.C.: International Monetary Fund, accessed October 2009. http://elibrary-data.imf.org/.
29. World Bank (1994) *Statistical Handbook: States of the Former USSR*, Washington, D.C.: World Bank.
30. World Bank (1994) *Statistical Handbook: States of the Former USSR*, Washington, D.C.: World Bank.
31. World Bank (1994) *Statistical Handbook: States of the Former USSR*, Washington, D.C.: World Bank.
32. Sargent, T.J. (1981) 'The ends of four big inflations', working paper, Federal Reserve Bank of Minneapolis, 158.
33. IMF 'International Financial Statistics (IFS)', Washington, D.C.: International Monetary Fund, accessed October 2009. http://elibrary-data.imf.org/.

34. World Bank (1993) *Statistical Handbook: States of the Former USSR*, Washington, D.C.: World Bank.

35. IMF 'International Financial Statistics (IFS)', Washington, D.C.: International Monetary Fund, accessed April 2012. http://elibrary-data.imf.org/.

36. IMF 'International Financial Statistics (IFS)', Washington, D.C.: International Monetary Fund, accessed October 2009. http://elibrary-data.imf.org/.

37. IMF 'International Financial Statistics (IFS)', Washington, D.C.: International Monetary Fund, accessed November 2009. http://elibrary-data.imf.org/.

38. Liu, F.C. (1970) *Essays on Monetary Development in Taiwan*, Taipei, Taiwan: China Committee for Publication Aid and Prize Awards.

39. Sargent, T.J. (1981) 'The ends of four big inflations', working paper, Federal Reserve Bank of Minneapolis, 158.

40. IMF (1973–1974) 'International Financial Statistics (IFS)', Washington, D.C.: International Monetary Fund.

41. World Bank.(1993) *Statistical Handbook: States of the Former USSR*, Washington, D.C.: World Bank.

42. IMF 'International Financial Statistics (IFS)', Washington, D.C.: International Monetary Fund, accessed November 2009. http://elibrary-data.imf.org/.

43. IMF 'International Financial Statistics (IFS)', Washington, D.C.: International Monetary Fund, accessed October 2009. http://elibrary-data.imf.org/.

44. IMF 'International Financial Statistics (IFS)', Washington, D.C.: International Monetary Fund, accessed November 2011. http://elibrary-data.imf.org/.

45. IMF 'International Financial Statistics (IFS)', Washington, D.C.: International Monetary Fund, accessed October 2009. http://elibrary-data.imf.org/.

46. World Bank (1996) *Statistical Handbook: States of the Former USSR*, Washington, D.C.: World Bank.

47. IMF 'International Financial Statistics (IFS)', Washington, D.C.: International Monetary Fund, accessed October 2009. http://elibrary-data.imf.org/.

48. Central Statistical Bureau of Latvia. 'Consumer Price Indices', accessed May 2012. http://data.csb.gov.lv/.

49. World Bank (1996) *Statistical Handbook: States of the Former USSR*, Washington, D.C.: World Bank.

50. a) Hartendorp, A. (1958) History of Industry and Trade of the Philippines, Manila: American Chamber of Commerce on the Philippines, Inc. b) Sicat, G. (2003) 'The Philippine economy during the Japanese occupation, 1941–1945', discussion paper, University of the Philippines School of Economics, 0307, November.

51. IMF (1990–1992) 'International Financial Statistics (IFS)', Washington, D.C.: International Monetary Fund.

52. Sargent, T.J. (1986) *Rational Expectations and Inflation*, New York: Harper & Row.

53. IMF 'International Financial Statistics (IFS)', Washington, D.C.: International Monetary Fund, accessed October 2009. http://elibrary-data.imf.org/.

54. Lithuania Department of Statistics. 'Consumer Price Index (CPI) and Price Changes', accessed May 2012. http://www.stat.gov.lt.

55. IMF 'International Financial Statistics (IFS)', Washington, D.C.: International Monetary Fund, accessed November 2011. http://elibrary-data.imf.org/.

56. Liu, F.C. (1970) *Essays on Monetary Development in Taiwan*, Taipei, Taiwan: China Committee for Publication Aid and Prize Awards.

References

Bernholz, P. (1995) 'Currency competition, inflation, Gresham's Law and exchange rate', in P. Siklos (ed.) *Great Inflations of the 20th Century: Theories, Policies, and Evidence*, Brookfield, VT: Edward Elgar.

Bernholz, P. (2003) *Monetary Regimes and Inflation*, Northampton, MA.: Edward Elgar.

Böhm-Bawerk, E. (1891) 'The Austrian economists', *The Annals of the American Academy of Political and Social Science*, 1: 361–84.

Brown, S., Marrese, M., Odenius, J., Zanello, A., Krelove, R. and Brooks, R. (1996) *Bosnia and Herzegovina: Recent Economic Developments*, IMF Staff Country Report no. 96/104, Washington, D.C.: International Monetary Fund.

Cagan, P. (1956) 'The monetary dynamics of hyperinflation', in M. Friedman (ed.) *Studies in the Quantity Theory of Money*, Chicago, IL: University of Chicago Press.

Cagan, P. (1987) 'Hyperinflation', in J. Eatwell, M. Milgate and P. Newman (eds.) *The New Palgrave: A Dictionary of Economics*, 2 (3), London: Macmillan.

CNB (n.d) 'Nonfinancial statistics: consumer price and producer indices', Republic of Croatia: Croatian National Bank, accessed July 2012. http://www.hnb.hr/statistika/estatistika.htm.

Feynman, R., Leighton, R. and Sands, M. (1995) *Six Easy Pieces: Essentials of Physics Explained by Its Most Brilliant Teacher*, Reading, MA: Addison-Wesley.

Fischer, W. (2010) *German Hyperinflation 1922/23: A Law and Economics Approach*, Lohmar, Germany: Eul Verlag.

Frenkel, J.A. (1976) 'A monetary approach to the exchange rate: doctrinal aspects and empirical evidence', *Scandinavian Journal of Economics*, 78: 200–24.

Hanke, S.H. (1996/7) 'A field report from Sarajevo and Pale', *Central Banking*, 7 (3), Winter.

Hanke, S.H. (2002) 'On dollarization and currency boards: error and deception', *The Journal of Policy Reform*, 5(4): 203–22.

Hanke, S.H. and Kwok, A.K.F. (2009) 'On the measurement of Zimbabwe's hyperinflation', *Cato Journal*, 29 (2): 353–64.

Hanke, S.H. and Schuler, K. (1991) *Monetary Reform and the Development of a Yugoslav Market Economy.*, London: Center for Research Into Communist Economics. Also published in Serbo-Croatian in 1991 by the Ekonomski Institute Beograd.

Hartendorp, A. (1958) *History of Industry and Trade of the Philippines*, Manila: American Chamber of Commerce on the Philippines, Inc.

Hayek, F. (1941) *The Pure Theory of Capital*, London: Macmillan.

Koech, J. (2011) 'Hyperinflation in Zimbabwe', *Globalization and Monetary Policy Institute Annual Report*, Dallas, TX: Federal Reserve Bank of Dallas.

Loveday, A. (1924) 'Note on Danzig currency reform', *League of Nations Report: Financial Committee*, Geneva, 19 January.

Machlup, F. (1991) *Economic Semantics*, New Brunswick, NJ: Transaction Publishers.

McNown, R. and Wallace, M. (1989) 'National price levels, purchasing power parity, and cointegration: A test of four high inflation economies', *Journal of International Money and Finance*, 8: 533–45.

Végh, C. (1995) 'Stopping high inflation: an analytical overview', in P. Siklos (ed.) *Great Inflations of the 20th Century: Theories, Policies, and Evidence*, Brookfield, VT: Edward Elgar.

White, M. and Schuler, K. (2009) 'Retrospectives: who said "Debauch the currency": Keynes or Lenin?', *Journal of Economic Perspectives*, 23 (2): 213–22.

31

THE FINANCIAL CRISIS OF 2007–2009

Gary Gorton and Andrew Metrick

Introduction

The financial crisis of 2007–2009 was the event which was not supposed to happen, but it did. Few economists thought that the U.S. economy would ever experience a systemic financial crisis again. Or that it would turn into a global crisis. But, the crisis, which began in August of 2007, developed into the worst crisis in the U.S. since the Great Depression. It has been unprecedented in its depth and scope.

Though unobserved by those not on trading floors, the crisis was started by a bank panic, a run on short-term money market instruments, in particular sale and repurchase agreements and asset-backed commercial paper. These markets had become so large that the refusals of investors to renew the short-term debt meant that large financial firms had to try to raise the cash by selling assets. Asset prices plummeted. The entire U.S. financial system was in danger of meltdown. Federal Reserve Chairman Ben Bernanke reported that of the thirteen "most important financial institutions in the United States, 12 were at risk of failure within a period of a week or two."[1] The resulting loss of confidence, concerns about liquidity and the solvency of counterparties, led to cash hoarding and cutbacks in bank lending. Credit markets froze, real investment sharply declined, and millions became unemployed.

The recession in the United States spread around the world. It appeared for a time that a new Great Depression was going to occur, but central banks engaged in extraordinary efforts to stabilize the economy. Events were momentous. And, as of this writing, recovery has been weak at best.

Table 31.1 shows the global nature of the recession. The top panel shows that the 2007–2009 recession was much worse than the average post-World War II recession, not surprising since the other recessions did not have systemic financial crises. The bottom panel compares the U.S. crisis-related declines to those of other countries. Notably, the U.S. suffered steeper declines in investment and employment.

For comparison purposes, in the United States during the worst years of the Great Depression between 1929 and 1933, employment fell about 25 percent and output fell about 30 percent. The 2007–2009 financial crisis recession ranks as one of the worst in recent U.S. history, but it was not as severe as the Great Depression and the recession of 1937–38. The crisis of 2007–2009 did not become as bad as the Great Depression likely due to extraordinary

Table 31.1 The 2007–2009 recession in perspective: changes in per capita variables for each peak-to-trough episode

	Output	Consumption	Investment	Employment	Hours
U.S. postwar recessions vs. 2007–2009 recession (percentage change)					
Average postwar recessions	−4.4	−2.1	−17.8	−3.8	−3.2
2007–2009 recession (2007 Q4–2009 Q3)	−7.2	−5.4	−33.5	−6.7	−8.7
2007–2009 recession, U.S. vs. other high income countries★					
United States	−7.2	−5.4	−33.5	−6.7	−8.7
Canada	−8.6	−4.6	−14.1	−3.3	–
France	−6.6	−3.4	−12.6	−1.1	–
Germany	−7.2	−2.9	−10.2	0.1	–
Italy	−9.8	−6.6	−19.6	−3.0	–
Japan	−8.9	−3.6	−19.0	−1.6	–
United Kingdom	−9.8	−7.7	−22.9	−2.9	–
Average other high-income countries	−8.5	−4.8	−16.4	−2.0	–

Source: Ohanian (2010)

actions taken by the Federal Reserve. To stem the crisis, the Federal Reserve lent a total of $1.1 trillion to various financial firms. Four banks—Bank of America, CitiGroup, Royal Bank of Scotland, and Barclays Group—borrowed $233 billion. These Federal Reserve programs were in addition to the U.S. government's Troubled Asset Relief Program (TARP), which allowed the U.S. Treasury to insure or buy up to $700 billion of troubled assets. Further, there was the American Recovery and Reinvestment Act of 2009 of about $800 billion (GAO 2011: 132). The Federal Reserve actions may well have prevented the crisis from equaling or exceeding the Great Depression.

The financial crisis of 2007–2009 is difficult to understand because the bank run was not visible publicly. And the markets and financial instruments involved were not widely understood. The run happened in over-the-counter markets when firms and institutional investors ran on some financial intermediaries. Academic economists had not studied the markets and institutions that were at the core of the crisis, and so they were uninformed. Bank regulators were unaware of the transformation of the banking system and so they too were caught unaware. Into the resulting vacuum came many popular narratives of what happened, some highlighting problems that, while not at the essence of the problem, are important. Other narratives emerged that reflect populist anger and little else. Understanding the crisis of 2007–2009 is imperative in order to keep such an event from happening again, at least for a significant period of time.

What has to be explained to understand what happened?

To understand what happened it is important to be clear about what has to be explained.

First, the subprime mortgage shock which triggered the crisis was not large. The crisis was connected to subprime mortgages, a relatively new kind of mortgage that was designed to make home ownership available to lower-income people, but which depended on house prices rising for its efficacy (Gorton 2010). When house prices stopped rising, there were expected losses on these mortgages, many of which had been securitized.[2] But, subprime was not large enough to explain the crisis. At the time of the crisis there were about $1.2 trillion of subprime mortgages outstanding, about 80 percent of which had been securitized. Even if every single one of those mortgages defaulted with no recovery at all, it would not explain the magnitude of the crisis. Furthermore, the losses on subprime mortgages have not, in fact, been large. Park (2011) examines trustee reports on February 2010 for 88.6 percent of the notional amount of subprime bonds issued between 2004 and 2007. She calculates the realized principal losses on the $1.9 trillion of originally AAA/Aaa-rated subprime bonds issued between 2004 and 2007 to be 17 basis points as of February 2011. The same point is made by the Financial Crisis Inquiry Commission (FCIC) Report (2011: 228–29) by looking at the ratings on subprime mortgages. The FCIC notes that:

> Overall, for 2005 to 2007 vintage tranches of mortgage-backed securities originally rated triple-A, despite the mass downgrades, only about 10% of Alt-A and 4% of subprime securities had been "materially impaired"—meaning that losses were imminent or had already been suffered—by the end of 2009.

So, if the shock was not large, how did we get a crisis?

Second, at the onset of the crisis all bond prices fell (spreads rose), not just subprime-related bonds. In particular, the prices of all manner of asset-backed securities fell. Why did the prices of, say, AAA/Aaa credit card asset-backed securities nose-dive when this asset class has nothing to do with subprime mortgages, and did not experience losses? Moreover, the prices of other securities falling closely tracked measures of the deterioration of bank counterparty risk, rather than track prices of subprime mortgages. Financial institutions' counterparty risk is usually measured by looking at LIBOR (the London Interbank Offered Rate), the rate at which large financial institutions lend to each other, minus the rate on the overnight index swap (OIS), which is taken as the riskless rate. So, LIBOR minus OIS (LIB – OIS) measures the risk premium in the interbank market. Figure 31.1 shows this measure of counterparty risk (LIB – OIS) together with the spreads on three categories of AAA/Aaa asset-backed securities—student loans, credit card receivables, and auto loans (so, auto loans minus OIS, for example). Spreads on subprime did not follow this pattern, but rose continuously from January 2007 (Gorton and Metrick 2012). The measure of interbank counterparty risk and the spreads on non-subprime bonds moved together, but they did not move with subprime spreads.

Finally, any explanation of the financial crisis confronts another issue, namely, the question of whether the crisis of 2007–2009 was special, an unlucky convergence of a number of unique factors. Or, was it at root fundamentally similar to all the financial crises that have repeatedly occurred throughout the history of market economies internationally? This question is especially important for policy considerations.

The evidence discussed here can be summarized as follows. The crisis of 2007–2009 was triggered by a bank run in the (unregulated) wholesale financial markets, where non-financial firms and institutional investors do their banking with financial intermediaries. There was a bank run by institutional investors and firms on investment banks, which had been providing a deposit-like bank product to institutional investors and non-financial firms, namely, sale and repurchase agreements. Also, asset-backed commercial paper was another bank instrument that suffered runs.[3] These markets had become very large over the previous thirty years. In fact, they were so large, that in the face of the bank run, it was not possible

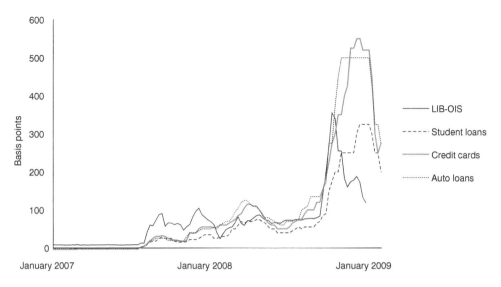

Figure 31.1 Spreads on non-subprime-related AAA/Aaa asset-backed securities and counterparty risk

Source: Gorton and Metrick (2012)

for the financial system to honor the claims for cash. Too much cash was demanded. This is what Chairman Bernanke was noting when he said that 12 of the 13 largest financial firms were on the verge of insolvency.

Like other bank runs in history, this one was not irrational. Bank runs are not irrational. The problem is that there, in fact, is reason to fear counterparties' defaults, even if in the end very few firms are in fact insolvent. There is a problem with the banks and so there is a run. It is not the other way around. Previous banking panics occurred when public information arrived that there was a coming recession, when a leading indicator of recessions was above a threshold (see Gorton 1988).

The wholesale banking system that had grown over the last thirty years provided a transaction product for institutions, very similar to demand deposits, namely sale and repurchase agreements (repo). Repo works as follows: an institutional investor, say a bond fund, deposits $100 million with an investment bank overnight. The fund will earn interest overnight on the deposit. To ensure the safety of this deposit, the investment bank will provide $100 million of bonds as collateral. So, the fund will earn, say, 3 percent per annum overnight, and the bond (which the fund has taken possession of) earns, say, 6 percent. But the 6 percent accrues to the bank. So, like traditional banking the bank is earning a spread, the difference between 6 and 3 percent. Note that to conduct this banking business the bank needs to hold bonds, which it can finance via repo.

Banks produce debt; that is, their output is debt. The debt is used for storing value over short intervals, and it can be used in transactions. In order for bank debt to be used in transactions, it must be unquestionably worth par. In other words, it needs to have the property that counterparties need not perform due diligence on the debt when it is offered in payment. Prior to deposit insurance hundreds of millions of dollars of checks were exchanged at par without questions being asked. In the repo market, every morning hundreds of billions of dollars of repo would be renewed without any depositor seriously looking at the collateral. Banks aim to produce this kind of transaction product.

But, repo, like demand deposits before deposit insurance, was vulnerable, in the sense that information about a coming recession can make depositors worry. Concerns such as this led to a demand for the comfort of cash. As Ben Bernanke (2010: 3) put it:

> Should the safety of their investments come into question, it is easier and safer to withdraw funds—"run on the bank"—than to invest time and resources to evaluate in detail whether their investment is, in fact, safe.

The build-up to the crisis

Sale and repurchase agreements (repo) have been in existence for many decades; repo is not a new product. What is new are the changes that have occurred in the financial sector of the economy which created a demand for repo and changes that resulted in the creation of or supply of private collateral for use in repo. These changes are at the root of the growth of this alternative wholesale banking system. First, the growth of institutional investors or institutional cash pools created a demand for a bank product to use as interest-earning money. And second, the decline of the traditional model of banking led to securitization, the creation of asset-backed bonds.

In the last thirty years a number of forces caused asset markets to become dominated by very large institutional investors. Pozsar (2011) identifies three forces. The first is globalization. Large global corporations now manage corporate cash pools centrally. Second, asset management firms and pension funds have grown very large, and they have centralized the liquidity management of mutual funds, hedge funds, and separate accounts into large pools. Finally, derivatives-based investment strategies involve overlaying synthetic investments, that is cash is held in near-riskless investments and risk is taken using derivatives, rather than buying risky cash bonds. These pools of cash are typically $1 billion or more.

This growth of institutional cash pools resulted in a demand for liquidity; in particular, the investors have a demand for insured deposit alternatives. But, the demands of these funds for "safe" assets far exceeded the available safe assets, U.S. Treasury bonds. Pozsar (2011: 3) estimates

> that between 2003 and 2008, institutional cash pools' demand for insured deposit alternatives exceeded the outstanding amount of short-term government guaranteed instruments *not* held by foreign official investors by a cumulative of at least $1.5 trillion; the 'shadow' banking system rose to fill this gap. (emphasis in the original)

The shortfall was filled largely by asset-backed securities. In the 1980s, the traditional banking model became less profitable in the face of competition from money market mutual funds and junk bonds. Securitization, the sale of loan pools to special-purpose vehicles that finance the purchase of the loan pools via issuance of asset-backed securities in the capital markets, was an important response. The growth of securitization was explosive. The private-label securitization market grew from under $500 billion in issuance in 1990 to over $2 trillion in issuance in 2006, the year before the crisis.

The shadow or wholesale banking system was the coming together of the demands for insured deposit alternatives by the institutional cash pools and the creation of asset-backed securities via securitization. In order to supply repo, the investment banks (or dealer banks) had to hold securities that could be used as collateral for repo. These repo banks were broker-dealer banks, the old investment banks, and the largest of the commercial banks, as well as many foreign banks. Officially, these U.S. banks are broker-dealers, "dealer banks" for short, not regulated depository institutions.[4] These are firms that were often in the press: Goldman Sachs, Lehman Brothers, Bear Stearns, Citibank, Morgan Stanley, and so on.

It is hard to say how large this shadow banking system had become prior to the crisis. There are no official data measuring the overall size of this market. Various estimates suggest that it was around $10 trillion, the same size as total assets in the U.S. commercial banking sector (Hördahl and King 2008). The fact is, however, that we do not know for sure. The European repo market is viewed as being much smaller than the U.S. market. According to the International Capital Markets Association European Repo Market Survey, the European repo market was EUR 4.87 trillion ($3.5 trillion) in June 2009, having peaked at EUR 6.78 trillion ($5.1 trillion) in June 2007, a fall of 31 percent. Asset-backed commercial paper (ABCP) was also large, but nowhere near as large as repo. ABCP peaked at about $1.2 trillion in July 2007.

One way to see the growth of the shadow banking system is to look at the growth of the total assets of the U.S. dealer banks, the "banks" which specialized in repo banking. Looking at U.S. Flow of Funds data, the ratio of the total assets of the dealer banks to the total assets of the commercial banks grew from 6.3 percent to about 30 percent from 1990 until 2006, just before the crisis, an increase of 376 percent. And, the Security and Exchange Commission filings of Goldman Sachs, Merrill Lynch, Morgan Stanley, Lehman Brothers and Bears Stearns shows that these five former investment banks together had financial assets worth $1.4 trillion of which 48 percent were pledged as collateral at the end of 2006. In other words, there was a very large repo banking system that had developed over a fairly long period of time. The repo banks needed to hold assets to be able to supply collateral to repo depositors. Repo banking is a depository banking system.

The shadow banking system is genuine. It serves a real economic function. But it was vulnerable in the same way that uninsured depository banking systems were vulnerable. And the vulnerability of a banking system peaks following a credit boom. Credit booms often precede financial crises. In fact, the one variable that is most robust in predicting the likelihood of a systemic financial crisis is the growth in credit prior to the crisis (Schularick and Taylor 2012). In the case of the U.S. in the recent crisis, the credit boom took the form of an increase in the issuance of asset-backed securities, particularly mortgage-backed securities. This is visible in Figure 31.2, which shows the increasing amounts of outstanding debt of various types in the U.S. economy prior to the crisis.

A credit boom means that firms and households are borrowing substantially more in the economy. What are they spending this money on? Many people were buying homes. In the U.S., housing prices were rising so fast that many thought home prices should be best described as a bubble. Reinhart and Rogoff (2008) show that house price increases are coincident with many credit booms which precede financial crises.

Thus, the stage was set. The changes in the economy over a decades' long period had resulted in a very large wholesale banking system based on short-term, uninsured, debt instruments that were vulnerable to being run. There was a coincident credit boom and house price increases, a build-up of fragility, a sensitivity to a shock. The shock did not need to be large.

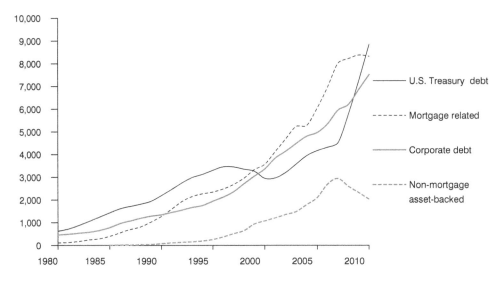

Figure 31.2 Outstanding U.S. bond market debt, $ billions

Source: SIFMA, based on U.S. Treasury Department, Federal Reserve System, Federal agencies, Dealogic, Thomson Reuters, Bloomberg, and Loan Performance

The panic

The bank run began in August 2007, after months of problems in the subprime mortgage market. During the first half of 2007 a number of subprime originators had failed and prices of subprime-related securities had been deteriorating.

The bank run first took the form of an increase in repo haircuts or of a refusal to renew the repo at all. A repo "haircut" corresponds to a demand by a depositor for over-collateralization. For example, suppose a bond that was completely financed by borrowing in the repo market is subsequently only 90 percent financed. In that case, there is said to be a 10 percent repo haircut. Concretely, this means that there is a withdrawal of 10 percent, the amount that the borrowing bank now has to fund in some other way.

Here's an example. Let's suppose that an institutional investor deposits $100 million overnight in a repo and receives bonds with a market value of $100 million as collateral. The bank pays a 3 percent repo rate and the bank receives 6 percent on the bond collateral, even though the institutional investor has taken possession of the bonds. In this case, the repo deposit is financing 100 percent of the bond. The next day the nervous institutional investor only deposits $90 million overnight (he takes $10 million back), but asks for the full $100 million collateral. Now the bank has to come up with $10 million dollars from some other source in order to finance the bonds. In this case the institutional investor has withdrawn $10 million from the bank. It is a 10 percent haircut.

If there is no new funding forthcoming, the borrowing bank must sell assets to meet the demands for cash. When many firms are forced to deleverage in this way—all selling assets at the same time— there are fire sale prices, prices below the value of the assets. This happens because there are not enough buyers to buy this volume of assets. This is what happened. By September 2009, repo transactions by the primary dealers (the banks that are eligible to trade with the Federal Reserve) had fallen by about 50 percent from the level of activity prior to Lehman's bankruptcy. The *Financial Times* reported that "Overall repo activity in the U.S. during the first six months of this year has fallen to levels not seen since 2003."

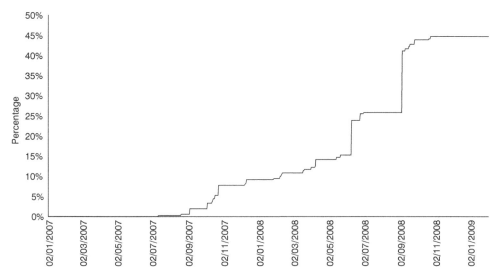

Figure 31.3 Average haircuts (on nine asset classes)

Source: Gorton and Metrick (2012)

Haircuts continued to rise during the crisis, with the largest increases following the bankruptcy of Lehman Brothers. This is shown in Figure 31.3, which plots the average haircut on nine asset classes, two categories of corporate bonds and seven categories of structured products (Gorton and Metrick 2012). The figure is consistent with a spiral downwards of prices, causing haircuts to rise, more assets to be sold, a further decline in prices, and so on.

Since haircuts are withdrawals from the repo banking system, these firms were forced to sell assets (because no one would invest new money in these firms). And, they chose to sell the specific assets that would raise the most money. To raise the most money you would want to sell valuable assets, AAA/Aaa assets that were unrelated to subprime. But, all the dealer banks did the same thing, they sold the same assets. This explains Figure 31.1.

To get a sense of the scale involved, consider a back-of-the envelope calculation. Suppose the repo market was $10 trillion and haircuts rose from, say, zero to thirty percent. That would be a withdrawal of $3 trillion from the shadow banking system.

Real effects from the crisis

The resulting loss of confidence in counterparties, concern over liquidity and solvency in the financial sector, particularly after Lehman Brothers failed, resulted in cash hoarding and a decline in the supply of credit. Of course, in a recession the demand for credit goes down, but the financial crisis exacerbates the recession by also reducing the supply of credit even further.

Ivashina and Scharfstein (2010) look at syndicated loans, a market which has evolved over the last thirty years much like the shadow banking system. The syndicated loan market has become the main portal for large corporations to get loans. Lending via this market was 47 percent lower in the fourth quarter of 2008 than in the prior quarter and 79 percent lower than at the peak of the credit boom, which was the second quarter of 2007. Syndicated lending fell, but commercial and industrial loans reported by the U.S. regulated banking sector rose by about $100 billion from September to mid-October 2008. But, Ivashina and

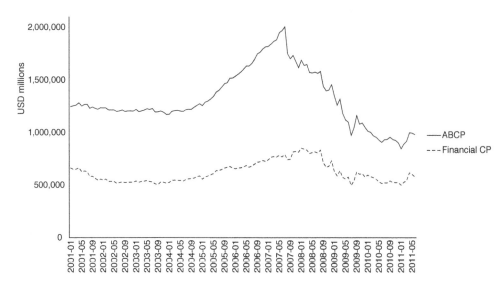

Figure 31.4 Financial and asset-backed commercial paper outstanding (seasonally adjusted)

Source: Federal Reserve System

Scharfstein show that this increase was not due to an increase in *new* loans. In fact, this was another run on the banks, as corporate borrowers drew down existing credit lines, that is, credit lines that had been negotiated prior to the crisis. Their main point, however, is that banks that were more vulnerable to a run, those that were to a greater extent financed by short-term debt other than insured deposits, cut their syndicated lending by more. So, the supply of credit was reduced by fragile banks.

The reduction in the supply of credit had real effects. Campello, Graham and Harvey (2010) surveyed 1,050 chief financial officers in 39 countries in North America, Europe and Asia in December 2008 asking whether they were financially constrained during the crisis. Among other questions, the survey asks whether a firm's operations are "not affected," "somewhat affected," or "very affected" by the turmoil in the credit markets. Firms that described themselves as "somewhat affected" or "very affected" were then further probed with questions concerning the nature of the effects, e.g., higher costs of external funds or limitations on credit. For U.S. firms, 244 indicated that they were unaffected by credit constraints, 210 indicated that they were somewhat affected, and 115 said they were very affected. (In Europe, the numbers respectively were 92, 71, and 26; and in Asia, the numbers were 147, 112, and 24.)

While all firms cut back on expenditure and dividend payments and saw their cash holdings and the number of employees decline, the constrained firms contracted these policies much more, in a very noticeable (and statistically significant) way. For example, unconstrained firms reduced the number of their employees by 2.7 percent on average, while constrained firms reduced the number of their employees by almost 11 percent. With respect to investment during the crisis, 86 percent of constrained U.S. firms reported that they bypassed attractive investments, compared to 44 percent of unconstrained firms.

What are the constraints that firms face? Eighty-one percent of the very affected firms reported that they experienced less access to credit; 20 percent cited problems with lines of credit. Thirteen percent of the constrained firms said that they drew down on their credit lines to have cash in the future. And 17 percent drew down their credit lines as a precaution, compared to 6 percent of the unconstrained firms. In other words, it seems that the reductions in credit that Ivashina and Scharfstein (2010) reported in their study of banks led directly to and resulted in the constraints studied by Campello, Graham and Harvey (2010).

The policy responses

The sudden and deep deterioration of the financial markets, and then the real economy, called forth some extraordinary policy responses, including monetary policy, central bank lending programs, bailouts, and fiscal stimulus programs. These are discussed by the Bank for International Settlements (2009) in Chapter VI of its *79th Annual Report*, the International Monetary Fund (2009) in Chapter 3 of the *Global Stability Report*, GAO (2011), and Cecchetti (2009), among others.

Central banks created many new and innovative programs to address the immediate funding needs of financial intermediaries, particularly after Lehman Brothers' failure. Governments also took action to prevent the collapse of the financial sector. In the U.S., Congress passed the Emergency Economic Stabilization Act of 2008 which authorized the creation of the Troubled Asset Relief Program (TARP) and allocated $700 billion for that purpose. This came to be commonly viewed as a bailout of the financial system.

The Federal Reserve System adopted a number of lending facilities, each with a different purpose and aimed at a different group of affected firms. In total the loans from the Federal Reserve System reached $1.1 trillion (GAO 2011).

Finally, the U.S. Congress passed a stimulus bill, the American Recovery and Reinvestment Act of 2009, which included about $800 billion.

It is too early for a full evaluation of these policies. This is a task that will occupy economists for some time. For some early evidence, we turn to IMF (2009), which classified 153 policy actions across thirteen major economies into five groups: interest rate cuts, liquidity support, recapitalizations, asset purchases, and liability guarantees. The IMF then performed event studies on the announcement effects of these actions of various measures of economic and financial stress. Overall, they found a mixed record of short-term success for most types of policy actions. The best results were found for two types of actions: first, liquidity support actions—mostly looser lending terms by central banks—which were effective prior to the bankruptcy of Lehman; second, recapitalizations of financial institutions—either through equity or subordinated debt—which were effective following the bankruptcy of Lehman.

Conclusion

The Financial Crisis of 2007–2009 was a watershed event in modern economic history. As the largest financial crisis and global recession since the Great Depression, the effects of this event are still felt strongly as of this writing. In many ways, the crisis followed the script of previous crises: a large build up of leverage throughout the economy, a sharp increase in housing prices, and a run on short-term debt. The novelty of this crisis was that the run did not take place in the traditional banking sector, but rather in the newly evolving wholesale or "shadow" banking sector formed at the nexus of securitization, money market mutual funds, commercial paper, and repurchase agreements. With this crisis, we have learned that old maladies can be present with new kinds of carriers, a challenge for policymakers and economists that remains unmet.

Notes

1 *Financial Crisis Inquiry Commission Report* (2011: 354).
2 Securitization means the pools of the mortgages had been sold into the capital markets via bonds linked to the pools.
3 Asset-backed commercial paper is short-term debt with a maturity of between 1 and 180 days issued by a special-purpose vehicle (a legal entity, a kind of robot bank) which uses the funds to buy asset-backed securities.
4 A dealer bank or broker-dealer operates as a securities dealer by underwriting and trading publicly registered securities. "Investment banks" are dealer banks that do not have any depository function.

References

Bank for International Settlements (2009) *79th Annual Report*, Basel: BIS.

Bernanke, B. (2010) 'Statement by Ben S. Bernanke, Chairman, Board of Governors of the Federal Reserve System, before the Financial Crisis Inquiry Commission', September 2, 2011, Washington D.C.

Campello, M., Graham, J. and Harvey, C. (2010) 'The real effects of financial constraints: evidence from a financial crisis', *Journal of Financial Economics*, 97: 470–87.

Cecchetti, S. (2009) 'Crisis and responses: the Federal Reserve in the early stages of the financial crisis', *Journal of Economic Perspectives*, 23: 51–75.

Financial Crisis Inquiry Commission (2011*) Report*, New York: Public Affairs.

GAO (United States Government Accountability Office) (2011) 'Federal Reserve System: opportunities exist to strengthen policies and processes for managing emergency assistance', GAO-11–696.

Gorton, G. (1988) 'Banking panics and business cycles', *Oxford Economic Papers*, 40: 751–81.

Gorton, G. (2010) *Slapped by the Invisible Hand: The Panic of 2007*, Oxford: Oxford University Press.

Gorton, G. and Metrick, A. (2012) 'Securitized banking and the run on repo', *Journal of Financial Economics*, 104: 425–51.

Hördahl, P. and King, M. (2008) 'Developments in repo markets during the financial turmoil', Bank for International Settlements, *Quarterly Review* (December), 37–53.

International Monetary Fund (2009) *Global Stability Report*, Washington, DC: IMF.

Ivashina, V. and Scharfstein, D. (2010) 'Bank lending during the financial crisis of 2008', *Journal of Financial Economics*, 97: 319–38.

Ohanian, L. (2010) 'The economic crisis from a neoclassical perspective', *Journal of Economic Perspectives*, 24: 45–66.

Park, S. (2011) 'The size of the subprime shock', Korea Advanced Institute of Science and Technology, working paper.

Pozsar, Z. (2011) 'Institutional cash pools and Triffin dilemma of the U.S. banking system', IMF Working Paper, WP/11/190.

Reinhart, C. and Rogoff, K. (2008) 'Is the 2007 U.S. sub-prime financial crisis so different: an international historical comparison', *American Economic Review*, 98: 339–44.

Schularick, M. and Taylor, A. (2012) 'Credit booms gone bust: monetary policy, leverage cycles and financial crises, 1870–2008', *American Economic Review*, 102: 1029–61.

32

MONETARY POLICY IN 2008 AND BEYOND[1]

W. Douglas McMillin

The financial crisis that began in 2007 led to serious impairment of the functioning of financial markets worldwide and contributed significantly to the recession of 2008–2009 experienced by the world's major economies. Monetary policymakers responded initially in a conventional way by cutting interest rate targets and by making borrowing from existing lending facilities more attractive, but, as the crisis intensified and the recession deepened, monetary policy makers began to employ more unconventional tactics. This chapter discusses the monetary policy actions undertaken by major central banks during the crisis and some of the implications of the crisis for post-crisis monetary policy.

Central bank response

Channels of monetary policy and policy tools

Before discussing central bank responses to the crisis, it is useful to briefly describe how the effects of monetary policy are transmitted to the economy and the policy tools of central banks. Monetary policymakers set a target for a short-term (often overnight) interest rate like the federal funds rate and then use open market operations (the purchase and sale of securities) to adjust the volume of reserves in the banking system and move the actual value of the short-term rate to the target level. As described in the liquidity-premium hypothesis of the term structure of interest rates, longer-term interest rates are averages of current and expected future short-term interest rates plus a liquidity premium that reflects the higher interest rate risk of the longer-term security. A decrease in the short-term interest rate, especially a decrease that is expected to persist for some time, leads to a decrease in longer-term interest rates that in turn leads to an increase in consumer durables and investment spending. Chung et al. (2011) estimated that in the U.S. for the 1987–2007 period a 100 basis point (1 percent point) cut in the federal funds rate was associated with a 25 basis point (BP) decline in the yield on 10-year Treasury bonds. Further, a decrease in interest rates leads to a depreciation of the foreign exchange value of the domestic currency and an increase in the prices of assets like stocks, land, and houses; these changes reinforce the interest rate induced increase in spending.

Open market operations (OMO) are the most important monetary policy tool. When the central bank buys (sells) securities from (to) the public, it credits (debits) the reserve account at the central bank of the seller's (purchaser's) bank, thereby increasing (decreasing) banking system reserves. Most OMO involve repurchase agreements (repos) and reverse repurchase agreements (reverse repos) and hence result in temporary changes in reserves. In a repo (reverse repo), the central bank buys (sells) securities from (to) a counterparty with the agreement that it will sell (purchase) the securities back to (from) the counterparty at a specified price after a specified period of time, usually a very short period of time, and banking system reserves rise (fall). In essence the repo (reverse repo) is a short-term loan to (from) the counterparty. When a central bank wants to change the volume of reserves for an extended period of time, it may engage in outright purchases or sales, i.e. transactions with no agreement to reverse the initial transaction.

Central banks typically also have standing facilities—a lending facility at which banks can borrow from the central bank at a penalty rate that is a mark-up over the policy rate target and a deposit facility at which banks can earn interest on their reserves at an interest rate that is usually a "mark-down" from the policy rate target. A borrowing bank must pledge collateral, usually high-quality collateral, in excess of the value of the loan to obtain the loan. Since the standing facility rates are normally tied to the target for the policy rate, when the policy rate target is changed, so are the standing facility rates. Thus, most changes in the standing facility rates provide no independent information about central bank policy. However, there are circumstances in which this is not the case. For example, a reduction in the mark-up of the lending rate over the policy rate target would tend to encourage banks to borrow more from the central bank. Payment of interest on reserves allows the central bank to change the equilibrium value of the policy rate when the volume of reserves in the system is sufficiently large relative to the demand for reserves so that the equilibrium policy rate equals the interest rate on reserves. In this case, if the central bank wanted to raise the policy rate, it could raise the interest rate on reserves and the actual policy rate would follow. Prior to the crisis, the European Central Bank (ECB) and the Bank of England (BoE) had both lending and deposit facilities. The Federal Reserve (Fed) had only a lending facility, but, as the crisis progressed, the Fed prevailed upon Congress to accelerate the implementation of a previously authorized deposit facility, and, in October 2008, the Fed's deposit facility opened.

Credit easing and quantitative easing

As the financial crisis began to unfold and economies moved toward recession, central banks reacted in their normal way and cut their policy rate targets (and hence the rates at their standing facilities) in a series of steps. As the crisis progressed and financial institutions' demand for liquidity rose, central banks responded in their role as "lender of last resort" by supplying more liquidity to the financial system in both standard and innovative ways.

Central bank policy innovations can be broadly categorized as credit easing and quantitative easing policies. Credit easing (CE) involves changing the composition of the central bank's balance sheet without expanding its size. More conventional assets like holdings of short-term Treasury securities and short-term loans to banks are replaced with more unconventional assets like longer-term loans to banks and other financial institutions, longer-term securities, and non-Treasury securities to include private securities. The goal is to enhance the operation of financial markets by increasing liquidity and providing support to particular markets and particular types of financial institutions by changing the mix of assets held by the central bank. Of course, this also increases the risk faced by the central bank—interest rate risk rises as the share of longer-term securities held increases, and default risk rises as the share of private securities rises. In pure credit easing, the effect on reserves of increased loans to financial institutions or the purchase of non-traditional securities is sterilized (offset) by open market sales of the traditional securities held, or by reducing short-term loans while expanding longer term loans.

Quantitative easing (QE) refers to a policy of expanding the size of the balance sheet without changing its composition, and this is achieved by increasing the volume of open market purchases. This leads to concomitant increases of banking system reserves and the monetary base. This could lead to a significant increase in the money supply if banks use the additional reserves to expand loans and/or buy securities. If the money supply rises, the public would find itself holding excess money balances and could use these excess money balances to purchase other assets—both financial and real, thereby bidding up their prices and reducing their yields. During and after the recent crisis, most of the additional reserves created by QE were held as excess reserves, and the money supply rose by a much smaller percentage than did total reserves and the monetary base.[2]

Does a relatively small increase in the money supply mean QE is necessarily ineffective? Joyce et al. (2010) discuss several ways QE might be effective in reducing yields and raising asset prices even if the money supply does not rise significantly, and these channels provide the rationale for QE by the Fed and the BoE. Joyce et al. note that QE may serve as a signal that the central bank thinks economic activity will be depressed for a good while and that the policy rate will remain at a low level for an extended period of time, thereby reducing expectations of the level of future short-term interest rates and hence reducing long-term interest rates (macro-policy news channel). Since short-term rates are very likely to be close to zero when QE is begun, QE is likely to be implemented through the purchase of longer-term bonds which, by significantly reducing the supply of long-term bonds to the public, should reduce yields on these bonds and thereby trigger a shift by investors into other assets like stocks or real assets (portfolio rebalancing channel). If the central bank becomes a significant buyer in the dysfunctional financial markets, market functioning and liquidity improves, and the liquidity premium on securities traded in the market falls as does the yield (liquidity premium channel). Finally, if QE is expected to help stabilize macroeconomic activity at normal levels, the risk of bankruptcy would be expected to fall as would the risk premium on securities issued by firms. This would in turn reduce the level of interest rates (macro risk premium channel).

Prior to September 2008, when turmoil in financial markets increased substantially, the innovative central bank policies can be characterized as mainly CE. After September 2008, the innovative policies are best characterized as a blend of CE and QE, especially for the Fed and BoE. There were a number of significant disruptions to financial markets in September 2008, including the failure of the investment banking firm Lehman Brothers. The crisis deepened after September 2008, and, as the turmoil in financial markets increased, interbank loans fell significantly, and the demand for liquidity rose substantially.

Monetary policy actions

Figure 32.1 plots the policy rate targets for the Fed, the ECB, and the BoE from January 2007 until April 2011. The first vertical line marks the month of August 2007, the beginning of the crisis, and the second vertical line marks the month of September 2008 when turmoil in financial markets increased substantially. Note that these central banks all reduced their target interest rates substantially. The Fed reduced its target for the fed funds rate in September

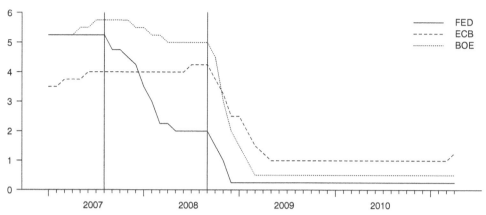

Figure 32.1 Central banks' policy target rates, 2007–2011

2007 as a preemptory move to counter the expected future effects of the financial crisis on the economy. As the financial crisis worsened and the economy moved into recession, the Fed continued to aggressively cut its target funds rate until it established a target range of 0–0.25 percent in December 2008. The BoE raised its policy rate target twice in 2007 because of concerns about inflation, but it began cutting its policy rate target in December 2007 and over time reduced its target rate to 0.5 percent in March 2009. The ECB did not change its target rate until July 2008 when it raised it in response to rising inflation stemming from adverse supply shocks. The ECB's first cut in the policy rate came as part of the unprecedented coordinated cut in policy rates in October 2008 by a number of central banks including the Fed and the BoE. Thereafter the ECB continued to reduce its policy rate until it hit 1 percent in April 2009. As these central banks cut their policy rate targets, following normal procedure, they also reduced the rates on their standing facilities. It can be argued that all three central banks essentially reduced their policy rate targets to the zero lower bound below which the policy rates can't be reduced further. Although the ECB reduced its target rate only to 1 percent, effectively it hit the zero lower bound since the ECB allowed the rate on overnight lending among banks (the EONIA rate) to fall to the rate paid on deposits (0.25 percent).

In addition to cutting the Fed funds rate target, the Fed also tried to manage market expectations about future values of the fed funds rate and hence maximize the effects of its policy rate cuts on long-term interest rates by adding language (forward-guidance) to its policy statements indicating that the funds rate would be held at exceptionally low levels for an extended period of time. Neither the ECB nor the BoE used explicit forward guidance; both indicated they preferred the public to draw their own inferences about future values of the policy rate from central bank communications about policy actions and forecasts of economic activity.

Liquidity provision

As noted earlier, as the crisis progressed and the demand for liquidity grew, in their role as "lender of last resort" central banks provided substantial amounts of liquidity in both standard and innovative ways. In essence, the provision of liquidity by central banks substituted for the intermediation that took place in normally operating markets. The Fed was the most innovative and set up a number of new facilities to supplement its regular liquidity-providing facilities. For the most part, the innovative actions of the ECB and the BoE took place within their normal frameworks for monetary policy. As noted by Lenza et al. (2010), before the crisis the Fed dealt with a smaller number of counterparties than did the ECB, and the ECB also accepted a wider range of collateral including asset-backed securities than did the Fed or the BoE. The new Fed facilities allowed the Fed to deal with a broader range of counterparties and to accept a wider range of collateral than before the crisis. Further, as Bean (2011) notes, relative to the BoE, the broader range of new facilities of the Fed also reflects the greater variety of non-bank financial institutions in the U.S. compared to the UK.

The actions of the central banks to provide liquidity to the system are outlined next, starting with the Fed. To encourage borrowing from the discount window, as the Fed cut its policy target rate, it also reduced the spread between the lending rate and the target fed funds rate and lengthened the maturity of discount window loans from overnight to 30 days and then to 90 days. To further encourage borrowing by reducing the stigma normally associated with borrowing from the discount window, the Fed introduced a temporary lending facility (the term auction facility) which auctioned funds to banks for 28 or 84 days. The competitively determined rate at this facility was typically below the lending (primary credit) rate.

Under authority granted in section 13(3) of the Federal Reserve Act (which allows the Fed, in unusual and exigent circumstances, to lend to individuals, partnerships, and corporations that are unable to obtain adequate credit), the Fed extended lending beyond banks to other financial market participants. The Fed set up separate facilities to make loans of funds and Treasury securities to primary government security dealers, to improve the functioning of the commercial paper (CP) market, to stem the outflow of funds from money market mutual funds, and to provide support to asset-backed securities markets. In addition, the Fed used its emergency authority to provide support to specific financial firms. Further, the Fed engaged in currency swaps with other central banks in which dollars were provided in exchange for other currencies so that the other central banks could make dollar-denominated loans to banks in their countries.

By establishing the new facilities, the Fed increased the number of counterparties and the range of collateral accepted for loans, and the risk carried on the Fed's balance sheet rose substantially. However, Fleming and Klagge (2011) noted that the net earnings to the Fed from the new facilities was about $13 billion over the 2007–09 period and that thus far there have been no credit losses on the new facilities. Formal evaluation of the effectiveness of the new facilities has just begun. In a study of the auction facility for loans from the Fed, McAndrews, Sarkar and Wang (2008) and Christensen, Lopez and Rudebusch (2009) found a significant beneficial effect of this facility whereas Taylor and Williams (2009) and Thornton (2010) found no effect. Campbell et al. (2011) found that the facility designed to improve the functioning of markets for asset-backed securities did so, and Duygan-Bump et al. (2010) found that one of the facilities designed to improve the functioning of the commercial paper market significantly reduced the outflow of funds from money market mutual funds that held a high share of securities eligible for this facility.

As it cut its policy rate target, the ECB also reduced the spread between its lending rate and the policy rate target. After the crisis began, the ECB allowed banks, through the execution of repos, to obtain as much overnight liquidity as desired at the then-prevailing target policy rate. Subsequently, it introduced supplemental repos with terms of three and six months while simultaneously reducing the volume of repos with shorter terms to maturity. During 2007, most of the liquidity provided came from repos rather than from its lending facility, and this remained true throughout the crisis. The range of counterparties was extended, and in December 2007, the ECB engaged in currency swaps with the Fed. Beginning in October 2008, the ECB introduced "enhanced credit support." The ECB allowed financial institutions to obtain the full amount of liquidity they wanted at the policy rate, broadened the range of collateral accepted for repos to include less liquid assets, and further extended the list of counterparties. The ECB also expressed intent to provide more funding through six-month maturity repos and later introduced repos with one year maturity. In May 2009, it announced its intent to purchase €60 billion in covered bonds[3] in order to help restore functioning in this important market. Casual empiricism suggests that these efforts were important in stabilizing financial markets (interest rate spreads fell and stock and bond markets improved), and Lenza et al. (2010) found empirical evidence that the enhanced credit support policy had substantial effects on interest rates and loans and, with a delayed effect, on real economic activity. They also examined the effects of unconventional policy by the Fed and the BoE and found that these policies were also stabilizing.

The BoE also greatly extended its provision of liquidity to the system. It cut the spread between its lending rate and its policy rate target as an inducement to borrow. In December 2007, the BoE began to offer a larger volume of extended term repos and broadened the range of collateral for these repos to include residential mortgage-backed securities (MBS) and covered bonds. Later the collateral was further broadened to include commercial MBS and corporate bonds. The BoE also established a currency swap facility with the Fed and established a temporary facility to allow banks to exchange temporarily illiquid MBS and other securities for UK government treasury-bills, which enhanced the liquidity of the borrower's balance sheet. In October 2008, the BoE established a permanent facility with the same function as the temporary facility. The BoE also expanded the range of its counterparties to include a larger set of banks. As before, casual empiricism suggests these liquidity-supplying efforts helped stabilize financial markets.

Balance sheets and quantitative easing

Figure 32.2 plots the evolution of these central banks' balance sheets as measured by the volume of assets from January 2007–April 2011. The size of each balance sheet is normalized to be 1 in January 2007. Prior to September 2008, there was virtually no change (Fed) or relatively little change (ECB and BoE) in the balance sheets, but, beginning in October 2008, there were particularly large increases in the balance sheets of the Fed and BoE and a much more modest but still substantial increase for the ECB. Prior to September 2008, the central banks sterilized the effects of the additional liquidity provided. The Fed did this by open market sales of Treasury bills, and the Treasury helped by selling supplemental Treasury securities to the public and depositing the proceeds in its account at the Fed, a procedure that drained reserves from the banking system. The ECB did this by reducing short-term repos at the same time it was engaging in longer-term repos, and the BoE did this by engaging in open market sales and the sale of a new instrument—Bank of England bills (a non-monetary liability of the BoE with a maturity of one week)—to the public.

After September 2008, sterilization ended, and the size of the balance sheets and reserves rose. The increase in the size of the balance sheets of the Fed and the BoE was accelerated by the adoption of QE, which, as implemented, was simply open market purchases of longer-term securities. The ECB did not engage in quantitative easing to any extent, although it did begin to purchase covered bonds in order to enhance the functioning of that market. A key reason the ECB did not engage in QE was that the size of its balance sheet at the beginning of the crisis was much larger than that of either the Fed or the ECB. Both the Fed

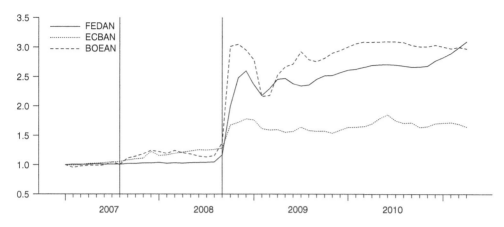

Figure 32.2 Central banks' total assets, 2007–2011

and BoE made clear that a major purpose of QE was to reduce longer-term interest rates by significantly reducing the supply of longer-term bonds to the public. Thus, QE was seen as a way of providing more stimulus to spending at a time when the zero lower bound had been hit and policy rates couldn't be lowered further.

In November 2008, the Fed announced it would begin to purchase securities issued by Fannie Mae, Freddie Mac, and the Federal Home Loan Banks and MBS securities issued by Fannie Mae, Freddie Mac, and Ginnie Mae, and longer-term Treasury securities were later added to the list. This first round of long-term security purchases (QE1) ended in the first quarter of 2010 and resulted in the purchase of $1.75 trillion in long-term securities of which $1.25 trillion were MBS, $200 billion were agency securities, and $300 billion were Treasury securities. These purchases represented about 22 percent of the outstanding stock of these securities at the beginning of QE1. Initially the Fed did not replace maturing securities purchased under QE1, which meant that its balance sheet began to shrink in size. In August 2010, it announced that it would replace maturing securities with longer-term U.S. Treasury securities, thereby maintaining the size of the Fed's balance sheet and hence the effects of QE on interest rates and asset prices. In November 2010, in response to continuing weak economic activity and concern that underlying inflation was trending lower, the Fed announced that it would purchase another $600 billion of longer-term U.S. Treasury securities by the middle of 2011 (QE2). Note that both QE1 and QE2 changed not only the size of the balance sheet but also its composition, so there are elements of both credit and quantitative easing in these programs. These programs also increased the risk level of the Fed's balance sheet since interest rate risk rises as the proportion of longer-term securities on the balance sheet rises.

The BoE began its program of QE in March 2009 with the express intent of increasing nominal demand sufficiently to hit the BoE's inflation target of 2 percent over the medium term. Earlier the BoE had been authorized, and had begun, to purchase £50 billion in corporate securities (CP and bonds) in order to improve the functioning of these markets, but these purchases were funded by Treasury bills issued by the government and not by reserve creation. In March 2009, however, the range of securities was expanded to include government longer-term bonds (gilts), and the security purchases were paid for by reserve creation. Under its QE program, the BoE purchased £200 billion in securities, of which £198 billion were gilts (20 percent of non-government holding of gilts). The level of risk of the

BoE's balance sheet rose, although, unlike the Fed, the government indemnified the BoE for any losses on the securities it acquired through QE and through its earlier purchases of corporate securities.

As noted earlier, the intent of QE was to lower longer-term interest rates, and, based on an evaluation of several studies of the effect of QE in the U.S., Chung et al. (2011) estimated that QE1 reduced longer-term interest rates by about 50 BP.[4] Based on their estimates of the effect of a change in the federal funds rate on long-term rates, Chung et al. (2011) argued the effect of QE1 on long-term yields was approximately equal to a 2 percent point cut in the Fed funds rate. If we simply scale down the estimated 50 BP decline in long-term rates from QE1 for the size of QE2 relative to QE1, QE2 would be expected to have an approximate 17 BP effect on long-term rates (equivalent to an approximate 0.7 percent decrease in the fed funds rate). Consistent with this, Krishnamurthy and Vissing-Jorgensen (2011) found smaller interest rate effects for QE2 than for QE1. They also found significant increases in expected inflation as a result of both QE1 and QE2 thereby suggesting that the effects of these programs on real interest rates were larger than the effect on nominal interest rates and that these programs helped guard against deflation. Joyce et al. (2010) estimated that QE in the U.K. reduced longer-term interest rates by 50–100 BP across bonds with maturities of 5–25 years, but found the effects were concentrated on longer-term securities.

Thus, most studies for both the U.S. and the UK suggest significant effects of QE on longer-term interest rates. With regard to measures of economic activity like real GDP, inflation, the unemployment rate, stock prices, and the exchange rate, Chung et al. (2011) estimated the effects of QE1 and QE2 on economic activity in the U.S. to be the equivalent of a 3 percent point cut in the Fed funds rate. The studies to date mainly suggest beneficial effects of QE, but not everyone is convinced of the efficacy of QE. See, for example, Cochrane (2011) who expressed concerns about the methodology of studies of the effects of QE and noted that interest rates rose subsequent to the November announcement of QE2 and that yields on five-year maturity bonds that were the focus of QE2 did not decline relative to yields on bonds of other maturities.

Exit from QE and other crisis policies

Even if QE has been successful in stimulating aggregate demand and thereby helping move the economy toward normalcy, is there a longer run danger to QE? As we have noted, since QE involves the large-scale purchase of securities, reserves rise significantly. Normally, this would also generate a significant increase in the money supply. However, in the recent crisis, most of the increase in reserves has been held as excess reserves by banks and hence haven't been used by banks to extend loans or buy securities. Over time, loan demand should begin to revive and banks are likely to use their excess reserves to extend loans. There is thus the potential for a massive increase in the money supply as this happens with a consequent threat to price stability. For example, Chari (2010) noted that if the reserve-to-deposit ratio returned to its level before the crisis, that the broadly-measured money supply would increase about 50-fold. Central banks are, of course, aware of this possibility and have thought about and discussed exit strategies from QE as the economy recovers.

At the April 2011 FOMC meeting the Fed made clear (FOMC 2011) that it wants to reduce the size of its balance sheet and return to its pre-crisis framework in which the Fed sets a target for the Fed funds rate and holds only Treasury securities. Most participants in the meeting saw increases in the target funds rate as the preferred tool for tightening monetary policy as the economy expands. An important question is how to move the actual funds rate to a higher target. One possibility is to simply engage in open market sales of securities purchased during QE—either outright sales of U.S. government securities and MBS or continual roll-over of reverse repos. The Fed is concerned, however, given the enormous volume of reserves in the system, that the scale of open market operations required to decrease reserves enough to raise the funds rate would have to be so large that bond markets would be disrupted and the recovery threatened. Consequently, most participants in the FOMC meeting believed that asset sales should be put on a largely predetermined and preannounced path, although the pace might be adjusted if there were substantial changes in economic activity. The initial step in the reduction of its holdings of securities would be to stop reinvestment of the principal on maturing securities.

If open market sales are to be done only slowly over time, how then might a higher target funds rate be achieved? The preferred option is to raise the interest rate on reserves enough to induce banks to continue holding large volumes of excess reserves while reserves are being slowly drained from the system through open market sales. This process could be facilitated by use of the newly established term deposit facility in which the Fed offers term deposits (deposits with a specific maturity date) to financial institutions that are eligible to earn interest on their reserves at the Fed. Reserves shifted to term deposits are no longer classified as reserves, so as banks take out term deposits at the Fed, reserves in the system fall. The interest rate the Fed pays on term deposits will, of course, be greater than the interest rate on reserves, and changes in the interest rate paid on term deposits will affect the volume of reserves.

The temporary liquidity facilities set up by the Fed have expired. The Fed will continue to pay interest on reserves, but this was a policy change that would have been implemented in October 2011 even if there had been no crisis.

Like the Fed, the BoE has made clear that when it begins to tighten monetary policy it will first raise the target for its policy rate and then begin sales of securities acquired through QE. Fisher (2010) noted that the decision about the pace of security sales will depend on the outlook for inflation, but care will be taken not to unduly disrupt the operation of the gilt market. To that end, it will coordinate its sales with the government's debt management office. With regard to its other programs, the last security swaps under its temporary facility expired in January 2012, and that facility was then closed. The permanent security swap facility will remain in place. The BoE does not expect its balance sheet to return to its pre-crisis level since it expects banks will want to hold more reserves than pre-crisis and because the range of banks that can hold reserve accounts was expanded during the crisis.

Unlike the Fed and the BoE, although the ECB bought a relatively small volume of covered bonds, it did not buy substantial volumes of securities and hence doesn't face the problem of how to divest itself of securities bought in the crisis. Instead, most of its liquidity provision took the form of longer-term repos that are self-extinguishing. As noted in ECB (2010), the unconventional measures will be phased out in order to avoid disruptions to financial markets. However, the emergence of the European sovereign debt crisis in 2011 has led the ECB to delay the phase out.

Implications of the crisis for central banks

The crisis and subsequent implementation of unconventional monetary policy by major central banks has raised a number of questions about monetary policy and its implementation. Mishkin (2011) discusses in detail the principles that guided monetary policy before the crisis and how the crisis might change monetary policy strategy, and the proper conduct of monetary policy in light of the crisis has been discussed by others as well. This chapter can only briefly touch on some of the issues about monetary policy that will no doubt be debated intensely for some time to come.

One issue is how central banks should respond to asset price movements. Should central banks respond only indirectly to asset prices to the extent that asset prices affect aggregate demand, or should central banks try to identify emerging asset price bubbles and "lean against" the rise in asset prices? If a bubble has developed, should the central bank proactively pop the bubble or should it clean up after a bubble pops on its own? Proponents of direct response argue that the bursting of asset price bubbles, especially those that are fueled by significant credit creation, can generate prolonged recessions, so it is better to try to deflate a bubble before it gets too big and bursts on its own. Opponents note that it is often difficult to identify asset price bubbles, since if fundamental determinants of asset prices have changed significantly, then substantial changes in asset prices are warranted. They also note that monetary policy is a "blunt tool" for dealing with an asset price bubble since an increase in the policy rate affects not only the asset whose price is "bubbling" but also the prices of other assets as well as consumption and investment spending. Some argue that it would be better to use macro-prudential regulation like changes in capital requirements, changes in loan-to-value ratios, and more stringent collateral requirements for lending than monetary policy to address emerging bubbles. Issing (2011) notes that before the current crisis, central banks followed the "Jackson Hole Consensus": don't target asset prices, don't try to prick a bubble and "mop-up" after a bubble bursts. Both Issing (2011) and Mishkin (2011) note that this consensus is being rethought. Mishkin points out that it is much easier to identify a credit-driven bubble than one that stems from irrational exuberance, and both Issing and Mishkin suggest that monitoring of credit market conditions will very likely become an essential part of the monetary and regulatory processes.

Prior to the recent crisis, most regulation of financial institutions was micro-prudential in nature, i.e. the focus was on the health of the individual institution and less attention was paid to the interconnections among institutions and hence the possibility that problems at one institution would be transmitted to others connected to it. The crisis revealed this to be an inadequate regulatory strategy, and macro-prudential regulation that aims to reduce systemic risks in the financial system is now considered essential. A key question is whether central banks should be the macro-prudential regulator or whether this task should reside in another institution. Proponents of a separate regulator stress enhanced accountability since a separate regulator has a well-defined mission. They also note that vesting authority in a single institution responsible for both monetary and regulatory policy may create too powerful an institution, and regulatory responsibility, especially for systemically important institutions, might end up politicizing monetary policy. Proponents of central banks serving as the macro-prudential regulator argue that information obtained from regulation about the financial health and interconnections among institutions is useful in conducting normal monetary policy and in serving as lender of last resort. These proponents note that information sharing among different government agencies is typically less than perfect so it is better to have one institution perform both functions. For a more detailed discussion, see Blinder (2010) and Mishkin (2011).

A third issue is the appropriate target rate of inflation. The major central banks have an explicit or implicit target of 2 percent or slightly less. As noted earlier, the major central banks essentially hit the zero lower bound for their policy rate during the crisis and hence had no further scope for lowering the policy rate. Consequently, they had to rely solely on unconventional policy at this point. Blanchard, Dell'Ariccia and Mauro (2010) argue that if central banks would raise their explicit or implicit target to 4 percent, then they would have more scope for normal monetary policy and would be less likely to hit the zero lower bound. A higher inflation target means higher expected inflation and higher nominal interest rates and hence more leeway for the central bank to reduce policy rates in a crisis. This is a very controversial proposal, and opponents point out that the costs of increasing the inflation target as well as the benefits must be considered. They worry that raising the target inflation rate would reduce the hard-earned credibility of central banks as inflation fighters (Issing 2011), and they argue that history suggests it is much more difficult to stabilize prices when inflation is above 3 percent than when it is below 3 percent (Mishkin 2011). They also note the costs of higher inflation are continual, but the benefits of higher inflation for monetary policy implementation are realized only when the zero lower bound is reached. Since it is rare for central banks to hit the zero lower bound, the benefits won't be realized very often but the costs are ever present.[5]

Conclusion

After the onset of financial crisis in 2007, monetary policymakers faced significant challenges. Financial markets were in turmoil, normal credit flows were significantly disrupted, and economies moved into recession. Central banks sharply reduced their policy rates, effectively reaching the zero lower bound, and responded in an aggressive way to improve the functioning of financial markets. As "lenders of last resort," central banks provided liquidity to financial market participants who were having difficulty replenishing their funding through normal market channels and extended the maturity of their lending in light of the extensive and ongoing nature of the crisis. Existing operational facilities were used but the Fed and, to a lesser extent, the BoE set up new lending facilities, and the Fed used emergency powers to provide assistance to particular financial firms. Further, the Fed and the BoE engaged in quantitative easing to help revive specific markets and to lower longer-term interest rates and raise asset prices. In their crisis response, central banks demonstrated flexibility and a willingness to innovate, and cooperated to help each other. Key elements of cooperation included the establishment of reciprocal currency swaps, the coordinated policy rate cut in October 2008 after the crisis began to worsen, and the general discussion and sharing of information about policies and the state of financial markets and economic activity. The bulk of the evidence to date suggests that the actions of central banks mitigated the effects of the crisis and fostered recovery.

As a consequence of the liquidity provision and monetary policy easing, the size of the balance sheets of the major central banks rose substantially after September 2008, and reserves and the monetary base rose sharply, although the money supply expanded by a much smaller magnitude since most of the reserves created were held idle by banks. Over time as financial markets return to normal, liquidity provision designed to enhance market functioning will naturally decrease and this will help shrink the balance sheets back towards normal levels. However, the central banks that engaged in quantitative easing are developing "exit strategies" that will help them shrink their balance sheets back towards a more normal size.

The crisis and central bank responses have stimulated discussion of the appropriate way to implement monetary policy and the role of central banks in both micro-prudential and macro-prudential regulation. An important lesson from the crisis is that central banks, whether they are the ultimate micro- or macro-prudential regulator or not, must pay more attention to the level of systemic risk in formulating policy and to how their monetary policies might affect the degree of systemic risk. Accordingly, central banks have begun the task of identifying indicators of the level of systemic risk and have begun the discussion of how this information will be used in monetary policy decisions.

Notes

1 A more detailed version of this chapter is available at http://bus.lsu.edu/McMillin/Working_Papers/monpolcrisis.pdf
2 There are several explanations for this including a recession-induced reduction in the demand for loans, the payment of interest on reserves, an increase in banks' perception of the riskiness of loans, and uncertainty about the specifics of increased capital and leverage regulation that will be imposed as a result of the crisis.
3 Covered bonds are securitized bonds similar to a mortgage-backed security except the assets "covered" by the bond are retained on the balance sheet of the issuer.
4 However, the earlier studies suggest there is a good bit of uncertainty about the true size of the effect of QE1 on interest rates.
5 Another issue is whether price level targeting would be superior to the (explicit or implicit) flexible inflation targeting practiced by many central banks. There are arguments pro and con for price level targeting over inflation targeting; see, for example, Walsh (2010) and Mishkin (2011).

References

Bean, C. (2011) 'Lessons on unconventional monetary policy from the United Kingdom', speech at US Monetary Policy Forum, New York, Feb. 25.

Blanchard, O., Dell'Ariccia, G. and Mauro, P. (2010) 'Rethinking monetary policy', IMF Staff Position Note, Washington, DC: IMF.

Blinder, A.S. (2010) 'How central should the central bank be?', *Journal of Economic Literature*, 48: 123–33.

Campbell, S., Covitz, D., Nelson, W. and Pence K. (2011) 'Securitization markets and central banking: an evaluation of the Term Asset-Backed Securities Loan Facility', Federal Reserve Board Finance and Economics Discussion Series No. 2011–16.

Chari, V.V. (2010) 'Thoughts on the Federal Reserve system's exit strategy', Federal Reserve Bank of Minneapolis Economic Policy Paper 10–1.

Christensen, J.H.E., Lopez, J.A. and Rudebusch, G.D. (2009) 'Do central bank liquidity facilities affect interbank lending rates?', Federal Reserve Bank of San Francisco Working Paper 2009–13.

Chung, H., Laforte, J-P., Reifschneider, D., and Williams, J.C. (2011) 'Have we underestimated the likelihood and severity of zero lower bound events?', Federal Reserve Bank of San Francisco Working Paper 2011–01.

Cochrane, J.H. (2011) 'Inside the black box: Hamilton, Wu, and QE2', Comments at NBER Monetary Economics Progam meeting, March 4, 2011.

Duygan-Bump, B., Parkinson, P.M., Rosengren, E.S., Suarez, G.A. and Willen, P.S. (2010) 'How effective were the Federal Reserve emergency liquidity facilities? Evidence from the asset-backed commercial paper money market mutual fund liquidity facility', Federal Reserve Bank of Boston Working Paper No. QAU10–3.

ECB (2010) *European Central Bank Monthly Bulletin*, October, Frankfurt: ECB.

Fisher, P. (2010) 'An unconventional journey: the Bank of England's asset purchase programme', speech to contacts of the Bank's Agency for the South-West, Stonehouse Court, Gloucestershire, October 11.

Fleming, M.J. and Klagge, N.J. (2011) 'Income effects of Federal Reserve liquidity facilities', *Federal Reserve Bank of New York Current Issues*, 17, No. 1.

FOMC (2011) Minutes of the Federal Reserve Open Market Committee, April 26–27.

Issing, O. (2011) 'Lessons for monetary policy: what should the consensus be?' IMF Working Paper.

Joyce, M., Lasaosa, A., Stevens, I. and Tong, M. (2010) 'The financial market impact of quantitative easing', Bank of England Working Paper No. 393.

Krishnamurthy, A. and Vissing-Jorgensen, A. (2011) 'The effects of quantitative easing on interest rates', Brooking Papers on Economic Activity.

Lenza, M., Pill, H. and Reichlin, L. (2010) 'Monetary policy in exceptional times', European Central Bank Working Paper No. 1253.

McAndrews, J., Sarkar, A., and Wang, Z. (2008) 'The effect of the Term Auction Facility on the London Inter-Bank Offered Rate', Federal Reserve Bank of New York Staff Report No. 335.

Mishkin, F.S. (2011) 'Monetary policy strategy: lessons from the crisis', NBER Working Paper 16755.

Taylor, J.B. and Williams, J.C. (2009) 'A black swan in the money market', *American Economic Journal: Macroeconomics*, 1: 58–83.

Thornton, D.L. (2010) 'The effectiveness of unconventional monetary policy: the Term Auction Facility', Federal Reserve Bank of St. Louis Working Paper 2010–044A, October.

Walsh, C.E. (2010) 'Post-crisis monetary policy strategies: panel discussion', 8th *Journées* of the Banque de France Foundation.

33

RETAIL INNOVATIONS IN AMERICAN ECONOMIC HISTORY

The rise of mass-market merchandisers

Art Carden

Introduction

Retail changed in the twentieth century as small, independent retailers gave way to national chains of massive general merchandise stores. In the late twentieth century, the retail sector was at the front of American economic change. This has been especially true of general merchandise retailers and Walmart specifically. In the twentieth century, the U.S. economy shifted toward services and away from agriculture and manufacturing. The late twentieth century saw a continuing structural shift away from independent single-establishment retailers ("mom-and-pop" stores) and toward national discount chains operating large stores that deliver broad arrays of goods to multiple markets.[1]

Retail has surpassed manufacturing as the leading sector in American economic growth (Campbell 2009: 262), and the transition to a service economy has occurred in spite of the view that the service sector consists largely of low-productivity, low-wage, dead-end "McJobs" (Triplett and Bosworth 2004: 1). The rise of mass-market retailers illustrates an important point that has emerged in the literature on economic history and New Institutional Economics largely following Douglass C. North's (1968) study of productivity changes in ocean shipping: technological improvements matter, but organizational changes, institutional changes, and market development might be more important. Information technology has increased retail productivity, but the rise of mass-market merchandisers is part of longer-run trends in retail explained by combinations of economies of scale and scope (Chandler 1977, 1990, Basker et al. 2012) and "economies of density" (Holmes 2011) that include "economies in advertising and in transactions" (Kim 1999: 95).

Any discussion of late twentieth century retail and the rise of mass-market merchandisers is also inevitably a story about Walmart Stores, Inc. Walmart is no monopoly, but it dwarfs its competition and (again) appeared in the number one slot in the 2011 Fortune 500. Walmart is famous for its use of computerized inventory tracking, extensive automation through its distribution network, and the Walmart Satellite Network, which was completed in 1987 and is the largest private network in the U.S. (Walmart Stores 2011). Technology has played a role, but mass-market merchandisers are the product of much more than scanners and satellites. Modern mass-market, discount merchandising is rooted in trends that predate World War II.

Retail and the changing American economy before World War II

Well before chains, mass merchandisers, department stores, and mail-order houses, consumers bought from small merchants dealing mostly in local goods. Peddlers wandered the countryside hawking their wares, and small, independent retailers distributed limited selections (Vance and Scott 1994: 16–17). After the Civil War, there were three major retailing innovations: department stores, chain stores, and mail-order houses (Vance and Scott 1994: 17–21). Department stores offered an early form of one-stop shopping with posted prices, no haggling, generous return policies, and various amenities (Vance and Scott 1994: 18). Aided in part by cheap or free rural postal service, mail-order houses brought a cornucopia of new goods to rural customers (Vedder and Cox 2006: 38, Chandler 1977: 233). Chains emerged for several reasons and would draw major political fire in the early twentieth century.

The economic rationales for chain stores are straightforward.[2] First, falling transportation costs make it easier to manage several stores over a broader area. Second, an increasingly mobile population increases the value of a credible brand name (Kim 1999, 2001). Third, chain stores allow an organization with several outlets to spread risk across a geographically diversified portfolio of outlets. The first national retail chain was the Great Atlantic and Pacific Tea Company (A&P), which had been founded in 1859 as Gilman and Hartford's in New York City (Hicks 2007: 7). Its operations were still confined to New York City by 1865, but it had a footprint that stretched from Norfolk, Virginia to St. Paul, Minnesota by 1880 and a coast-to-coast presence by 1900 (Chandler 1977: 234). By 1930, A&P had 15,500 locations (Hicks 2007: 8), and chain stores "accounted for almost 40 percent of retail grocery sales" (Ross 1986: 125).

Improvements in transportation infrastructure made layers of middlemen redundant, and population growth encouraged specialization throughout the supply chain (Vance and Scott 1994: 16–17). The development of the automobile and home-based refrigeration as well as innovations at the store level like self-service and the cash-and-carry model lowered prices (Neumann 2011: 4). In response to pressure from innovative supermarkets, firms like A&P and Kroger "closed many of their small clerk-service stores and replaced them with fewer— but much larger—stores, which were located on major thoroughfares for the convenience of automobile drivers" (Vance and Scott 1994: 22).

A recurring theme in the history of retail trade is the conviction that consumers' demand curves for many goods are highly elastic. This leads to innovations along the supply chain that allow firms to earn profits by selling high volumes at very low profit margins. This was evident in the nineteenth century just as it was in the late twentieth (Chandler 1977: 227). Competition and innovation in retail and wholesale lowered the costs of transporting goods and transmitting information; it also increased the quality both of the goods on offer and the price information to which people across the supply chain responded (Chandler 1977: 209–10, 215–19).

Retail also evolved in response to changing transaction costs. Chandler (1990: 29) writes that both "wholesalers and retailers were organized specifically to exploit the economies of scale and scope," but Kim (1999, 2001) argues that multi-unit firms developed in response to transaction costs associated with larger markets. Small single-unit manufacturers and small single-unit retailers had created a market for wholesalers, for example, because arranging trades between small retailers and small manufacturers would have been prohibitively costly without the coordinating actions of middlemen (Kim 2001). Increasing urbanization and larger markets replaced repeated interactions between small retailers and the consumers they served with more anonymous trade. This made advertising and branding advantageous sources of credible commitment, which encouraged the rise of multi-unit firms (Kim 1999: 95, 97, Kim 2001). Brand names developed as market signals that reduced asymmetric information problems, and retailers had incentives to integrate backward into the manufacture of private-label brands because this better aligned incentives along all parts of the supply chain—particularly between those who did the manufacturing and those who did the selling (Kim 1999: 97, Kim 2001). In 1929, small chains purchased less directly from manufacturers than did large firms (Kim 2001: 316). Legal innovations also mattered as 1905 legislation protected trademarks and therefore made them clearer signals of quality (Kim 2001: 310–11).

Retail competition has always been a contentious political and social issue. Some viewed the chains as a type of colonization of the South, Midwest, and West by northeastern business interests (Schragger 2005: 117). Opposition became so bad that Sears, Roebuck would ship wares in unmarked wrappers to pacify customers fearing social sanction (Ryant 1973: 208). Moussalli and Flesher (2002) record how Mississippi used sales taxes and licensing regulations to punish competitors for in-state retailers. Many states passed laws aimed at restricting competition from chain stores; Moussalli and Flesher (2002: 1202) write that Mississippi's 1930 chain store tax was enacted "to hobble the chains, not collect revenue." Ross (1986: 127, 136) points out that state anti-chain laws burdened grocery chains in particular and reduced competition.

The political economy of the political war on chains is straightforward. Firms used governments at various levels to protect them from competition, but this was also undergirded by a "producerist" ideology (Schragger 2005: 10, Hicks 2007: 17). With the exigencies of the war, the development of a Washington, DC lobbying organization (the American Retail Federation), a new source of support in labor unions who had just signed "a series of collective bargaining agreements with A&P" (Lebhar 1963: 192–93, Ross 1986: 127), and another new source of support in farmers who came to accept chains when they saw that chains "helped dispose of a number of bumper crops without depressing prices" (Ross 1986: 127), the war on chains ultimately ended. This worked to the long-run benefit of American consumers and set the stage for the retailing innovations and trends of the post-World War II era.

Retail and the changing American economy since World War II

After World War II, the population grew substantially, but the number of retailers and the number of retail establishments grew more slowly than population (Jarmin et al. 2009: 239). The number of single-location retailers fell between the late 1950s and the late 1990s, "the number of chain store locations more than double[d]," and chain store employment passed employment in single-unit firms in 1977 (Jarmin et al. 2009: 239–240, 249). Pre-war farmers had warmed to chain stores because of their ability to move product, and manufacturers warmed to the discount store for the same reason (Vance and Scott 1994: 25). As Hicks (2007: 12) writes, "(c)onsumers today buy more goods and services than their grandparents but spend a declining share of their income on retail goods." The retail share of total personal income declined gently between 1929 and the end of the twentieth century before the transition from Standard Industrial Classifications (SIC) to North American Industrial Classifications (NAICS) altered the way retail is defined[3] (Hicks 2007: 12), and retail trade sales stayed roughly constant at 8 percent of national income between 1960 and 2004 (Vedder and Cox 2006: 48).

Vance and Scott (1994: 24) call discount merchandising "(t)he most important retailing development of the post-World War II era." The trend has been away from small, single-unit retailers and toward chain stores operating larger establishments, and the discount retail sector has gotten more concentrated over time (Jia 2008: 1268). The modern discount store did not spring fully formed from the mind of Sam Walton. Discounting "emerged from the fringe of American retailing" in the 1950s (Vance and Scott 1994: 24–25), and Walton borrowed liberally from other innovators like Martin Chase, Sol Price, and Harry Cunningham. Chase's Ann & Hope store was successful because of "a reputation for integrity and a liberal return policy" (Vedder and Cox 2006: 49). Price founded Fed-Mart and Price Club, which later became part of Costco (Vedder and Cox 2006: 49). Cunningham fundamentally changed S.S. Kresge during his tenure as CEO; he opened the first Kmart in 1962 (Vedder and Cox 2006: 49). Rising incomes among people who had typically been poor also worked to the advantage of discounters because many of these who now had more money were not used to and were not willing to pay for department store amenities and service (Vance and Scott 1994: 25).

Through the 1960s, established firms and other upstarts experimented with discounting. Kmart, for example, opened 100,000 square foot stores in suburban locations with the specific goal of "surround(ing) a city" and standardized its store layouts in the late 1960s (Vance and Scott 1994: 31–32). Woolworth's Woolco stores were even larger, with 115,000–180,000 square feet, and J.C. Penney's 180,000 square foot Treasure Island stores combined discount operations with supermarkets (Vance and Scott 1994: 32–33). Target started in Minneapolis and "specialized in relatively high-quality, higher-price merchandise" (Vance and Scott 1994: 33). Minneapolis-based Gamble-Skogmo opened 20,000–40,000 square foot Tempo Discount Center stores in small towns, and both Woolworth and Fed-Mart experimented with smaller stores in smaller cities and towns (Vance and Scott 1994: 34).

Changes in the structure of the retail sector—which included eating and drinking establishments in addition to stores before the switch from SIC to NAICS—in the late twentieth century have been examined in detail by Foster et al. (2006) and Jarmin et al. (2009). Foster et al. (2006: 748) attribute 14 percent labor productivity growth in the retail trade sector over the 1990s to entry by larger, more-efficient establishments and exit by smaller, less-efficient establishments rather than across-the-board increases in productivity at all establishments. In particular, they argue that entry by high-productivity establishments that are part of national chains and exit by low-productivity single-unit establishments drove retail labor productivity gains in the 1990s (Foster et al. 2006: 749). Citing the findings of Doms et al. (2004), Jarmin et al. (2009: 242) make two observations about information technology investments in retail. First, "large firms account for nearly all the investment in IT in the retail sector." Second, "IT improves the productivity of large firms more than it does for small firms."

The trend across the entire retail sector has been away from small mom-and-pop businesses and toward local, regional, and national chains. Jarmin et al. (2009: 240) note that in 1963, the percentage of retail establishments operated by chains was 20.2 percent while it was 35 percent in 2000. Within the general merchandise sector, independent retailers are "disappearing from many markets" (Jarmin et al. 2009: 260–61). Jarmin et al. (2009: 237–8) argue specifically that "the rise of technologically sophisticated national retail chains like Wal-Mart, Toys-R-Us, and Home Depot is simply part of the larger trend—underway for some time—towards larger scale retail firms" (Jarmin et al. 2009: 238).[4]

Using Census Bureau Enterprise Statistics and Company Statistics data, Kim (1999: 80) points out that in 1958, multi-unit retailers accounted for 2.8 percent of firms, 10.8 percent of establishments, and 40.2 percent of employees in their sector. These percentages increased to 6 percent, 32.3 percent, and 58.8 percent respectively in 1987 (Kim 1999: 80). In the general merchandise sector, multi-unit retailers accounted for 2.2 percent of firms, 14.4 percent of establishments, and 80.3 percent of employees in 1958; these percentages increased to 7.6 percent, 78.6 percent, and 97.3 percent respectively in 1987 (Kim 1999: 80).

Since 1977, general merchandisers have grown more rapidly than more specialized retailers; further, the general merchandisers adding the most stores also had larger increases in their selection (Basker et al. 2012). Specifically, they offer broader arrays of goods rather than deeper selections within categories. Basker et al. (2012) report that the percentage of general-merchandise stores with floor space in excess of 50,000 square feet increased from 53.7 percent in 1977 to 61.5 percent in 2007. In the discount sector specifically, the trend has been toward consolidation into national chains. According to Jia (2008: 1268), 49.3 percent of discount stores representing 41.4 percent of sales were operated by the 39 largest discount chains in 1977 while "the top 30 chains controlled about 94 percent of total stores and sales" twenty years later, in 1997. In the general merchandise sector, the number of county markets served by single-unit firms, local chains, and regional chains decreased between 1977 and 2000 while it increased for national chains (Jarmin et al. 2009: 256).

Technology mattered, but it was not a magic bullet. Holmes (2001: 709) argues that the use of bar codes meant more deliveries, more precision in inventory management, and larger stores. Basker (2011a) argues that while the adoption of barcode scanners led to a 4.5 percent productivity increase for firms that installed them by 1982, these productivity increases were largely offset by setup costs. Market conditions and complementary technologies also matter. Lagakos (2009), for example, argues that cars increase observed retail productivity. What matters is not the technology *per se*, but how it is deployed. Lewis (2004: 95) points out that the productivity increase was accompanied by retailers and wholesalers adopting information technology that had been in use for decades.

Economies of scale, economies of scope, and economies of density have combined to transform the retail sector. Kim (1999: 95) attributes the rise of multi-unit firms to "economies in advertising and transactions," and Holmes (2011) argues that Walmarts located near one another and near distribution centers present the company with an ultimately-favorable tradeoff between cost-reducing economies of density and possible sales cannibalization by closely-located stores. The distinguishing fact about general merchandisers is the interaction between cost-lowering factors like trade liberalization, organizational changes, and better information technology and a demand-pull from consumers' preferences for one-stop shopping (Basker et al. 2012). The Walmart effect might run even deeper: in a study of DVD sales, Chiou (2009: 306ff) argues that the average shopper would still prefer Walmart even holding distance, price, and one-stop shopping convenience constant.

Walmart

Walmart's size alone warrants studying its effects.

(Emek Basker 2007: 178)

A growing body of literature considers Walmart, the iconic and ubiquitous "face of twenty-first-century-capitalism," to borrow from the title of Lichtenstein (2006). The company's reach is considerable. Basker (2007:178) points out that

By the end of 2005, 46 percent of Americans lived within five miles of the nearest Wal-Mart or Sam's Club store, and 88 percent lived within 15 miles of the nearest store; and Wal-Mart accounted for nearly 9 percent of all retail workers in the United States. Because the chain has a presence in so many markets, virtually all other retailers compete head-to-head with Wal-Mart: 67 percent of all retail stores in the United States are located within five miles of a Wal-Mart.

The newness of this literature is evident in the fact that so many of the papers are of relatively recent vintage. Approximately one-third of the papers cited by Basker (2007) were working papers, as were many of the studies cited in books by Hicks (2007) and Vedder and Cox (2006). Walmart passed Kmart in 1991 to become the country's largest retailer (Jia 2008: 1269), and it has held the top position in the Fortune 500 eight times between 2002 and 2011. Its first appearance in the top spot, in 2002, was the first time a service firm had held the position (Lewis 2004: 92), and the 2011 Forbes 400 list of the richest Americans included four Walmart fortunes in its top ten. In 1987, Walmart had a 44 percent productivity advantage over other general merchandisers; this increased to 48 percent in 1995 as Walmart tripled its market share (Lewis 2004: 92–93). According to Lewis (2004: 91), competitors faced a stark choice: either catch up with Walmart, or go out of business. Walmart became the largest corporation in the United States by building an organization that moves massive quantities of merchandise at razor-thin profit margins that have hovered between 3 and 4 percent for most of the company's history, as indicated by Figure 33.1.

The Walmart controversy stems from the company's effects on employment opportunities, incomes, and incumbent businesses. Estimates of the employment effect vary: Basker (2005a) argues that the long-run effect of Walmart's entry on a county labor market is a net increase of fifty retail jobs that is offset by a reduction of some twenty wholesale jobs. Neumark et

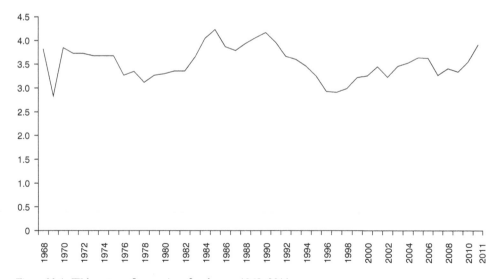

Figure 33.1. Walmart profit margins, fiscal years 1968–2011

Sources: Vedder and Cox (2006: 55, 57, 59, 61) and Walmart annual reports. Profit margin calculated as after-tax profits divided by sales. An accounting change lowered Walmart's after-tax profits in 1975. Financial reports for a given year are revised from report to report; the latest available data are used where possible

al. (2008), by contrast, estimate that each new job at Walmart displaces 1.4 retail jobs that would have otherwise emerged in Walmart's absence. In aggregate, this is a small effect on retail employment: Neumark et al. (2008: 428) point out that their estimate implies that the increase in retail employment between 1961 and 2004 would have been 279 percent rather than 271 percent in Walmart's absence.

Their estimate of a negative effect on retail employment notwithstanding, Neumark et al. (2008: 428) "suspect that there are not aggregate employment effects, at least in the longer run, as labor shifts to other uses." Their suspicion is consistent with the findings of Sobel and Dean (2008), who explore the relationship between Walmart expansion and small business at the state level and find that Walmart does not affect "the overall size, growth, or profitability of the U.S. small business sector" (Sobel and Dean 2008: 691).

Entry by Walmart and other "big box" retailers has unwelcome implications for competitors. Haltiwanger et al. (2010) estimate negative effects of big box retailers on employment at smaller businesses in the same narrowly defined sector and in close geographic proximity in the Washington, DC area, are largely due to market exit by competing establishments. Basker (2005a: 180) estimates that four small establishments (defined as establishments with 20 or fewer employees) close within five years of Walmart's entry, and 0.7 medium establishments (20–99 employees) close in the second year after Walmart enters a market. Sobel and Dean (2008) argue that the process of "creative destruction" might work at a more aggregated level than the county. Using state-level data, they find no statistically significant effect of Walmart penetration on several measures of the small business sector, specifically the self-employment rate, the number of establishments with one to four employees normalized by population, the number of establishments with five to nine employees normalized by population, growth rates in self-employment and the number of small establishments, and small business bankruptcy rates. Jia (2008: 1307) attributes "37–55 percent of the net change in the number of small discount stores and 34–41 percent of the net change in the number of all discount stores" to Walmart's expansion between 1987 and 1997.

A 2005 Global Insight study commissioned by Walmart and overseen by an independent panel suggested that a new Walmart would create, on net, 137 jobs in the short term and 97 jobs in the long term (Global Insight 2005: 2). Studying Pennsylvania counties, Hicks (2005, discussed by Vedder and Cox 2006: 110) found that the company led to a net increase of 50 new jobs with a 40 percent reduction in job turnover. Hicks (2007: 93–94) uses data from Indiana to estimate that Walmart increases rural retail employment from 3.4 percent to 4.8 percent after correcting for endogeneity. After correcting for endogeneity of urban Walmart entry, Hicks argues that Walmart leads to a 1.2 percent increase in employment but points out that this estimate is statistically insignificant.

Basker (2007) estimates that between 1982 and 2002, sales per worker grew by 35.3 percent while sales per worker at Walmart grew by 54.5 percent; subtracting Walmart would cut growth in sales per worker in general retailing between 1982 to 2002 to 18.5 percent (Basker 2007: 182–3). In short, Walmart accounts for just less than half of general merchandise productivity growth between 1982 and 2002 (Basker 2007: 182). Using data from the Bureau of Labor Statistics, Vedder and Cox (2006: 134) report that average annual productivity growth within the retail sector between 1987 and 2004 breaks down as follows: 0.2 percent among grocery stores, 1.3 percent among department stores, 2.3 percent among gas stations, 2.8 percent among auto dealers, and 7.6 percent among big box retailers.

Other firms and sectors grew in part by adopting Walmart's best practices like the "big box" retail format, the company's policy of "Every Day Low Prices," and managerial innovations throughout the corporate hierarchy (McKinsey 2001). Retailers and wholesalers that have increased their productivity have done so in large part by imitating Walmart's best practices (McKinsey 2001). One of Target's top officials, for example, claimed that his company is "the world's premier student of Walmart" (McKinsey 2001: 11, quoted in Basker 2007: 191). The McKinsey Global Institute reported that wholesale trade was still labor-intensive throughout the 1990s; only 25 percent of warehouse operations were automated as late as 2001 (McKinsey 2001).

Walmart's most obvious effect on the retail sector comes through its policy of "Every Day Low Prices." Basker (2005b) and Basker and Noel (2009) estimate that Walmart has a substantial price advantage over competitors with the effect being that prices among incumbent competitors fall after Walmart entry. Hausman and Leibtag (2007: 1147) argue that the compensating variation from big box retailers' effect on prices leads to welfare increases of some 25 percent of total food expenditure for people who enjoy the direct and indirect effects of big box stores. Further, they argue (Hausman and Leibtag 2009) that the Consumer Price Index is over-estimated because it fails to account properly for price effects of supercenters, mass merchandisers, and club stores. Evaluating estimates of the price effects of big box retailers and adjusting for foreign sales, Vedder and Cox (2006: 18–19) argue that "the annual American-derived welfare gains are probably still in excess of $65 billion, or about $225 for every American, or $900 for a typical family of four."

Walmart's shoppers tend to be average for the country as a whole but poorer than those who patronize some of Walmart's prominent competitors. Walmart shoppers have an average household income of approximately $40,000-$45,000; by comparison, Target shoppers have an average income of $60,000 and Costco shoppers average $74,000 (Basker 2007: 187). Poorer people also tend to shop at Walmart; summarizing Pew Center survey data, Basker (2007: 187) puts the fraction of people below $20,000 in annual earnings who shop at Walmart "regularly" at 53 percent, and the fraction of people above $50,000 in annual earnings who are regular Walmart shoppers at 33 percent.

Zhu et al. (2009) point out that Kmart and Walmart locate in similar markets while Target is a "niche" discounter. Basker (2011b) estimates the income elasticity of demand for goods at Target and goods at Walmart generally and finds that the income elasticity of demand for Target is approximately 0.8 or 0.9, while the income elasticity of demand for goods at Walmart is –0.5 at most with a "realistic" estimate being around –0.7. This suggests that a one percent reduction in personal disposable income will actually increase Walmart's revenues and decrease Target's revenues.

In spite of criticisms of Walmart's labor practices, Jason Furman (2005) called Walmart a "progressive success story" because of its impact on prices. He notes that if the 2005 Global Insight estimate of annual average household savings of $2,329 is accurate, the annual Walmart-related consumer savings of $263 billion dwarfs Walmart-generated reductions in retail wages of $4.7 billion estimated by Dube et al. (2005).[5] Hicks (2007: 82) notes that reductions in nominal retail wages are likely offset by larger price reductions, which translates into higher real wages. Courtemanche and Carden's (2011a) estimate of $177 per household in savings attributable to the effects of Walmart Supercenters in 2002 multiplied by the 105,401,101 households in the 2000 census yields household savings of $18.7 billion, which is still substantially higher than Dube et al.'s estimate of lost wages.

Hausman and Leibtag (2007: 25) argue that the compensating variation—i.e., welfare increase—attributable to supercenters, mass merchandisers, and club stores is some 25 percent of food expenditures. Since poorer households spend more of their income on food, the effect (as a percentage of income) is higher toward the bottom of the income distribution (Furman 2005: 2–3). Hausman and Leibtag (2007: 1172, 1174) further argue that compensating variation from access to non-traditional retailers is higher at lower income levels, which would make the effect even more progressive.

Courtemanche and Carden (2011a: 165) argue that the expansion of Walmart Supercenters explains approximately 10.5 percent of the increase in obesity in the United States since the late 1980s. This could be mostly due to the effect of Walmart Supercenters on food prices (Courtemanche and Carden 2011a: 177–8). They use estimates from Basker and Noel (2009) and Hausman and Leibtag (2007) to construct a back-of-the-envelope estimate of household savings from the direct and indirect effects of Super Walmart and arrive at a calculation of $177 per household, some 5.6 percent of which is offset by additional obesity-related health costs (Courtemanche and Carden 2011a: 174, 179). Another back-of-the-envelope calculation by Vedder and Cox (2006: 135) puts the social saving from the big box revolution at some 5 percent of gross domestic product, which they note is comparable to the social saving attributable to railroads in the nineteenth century.

Courtemanche and Carden (2011b) find that while Sam's Club does not affect grocery prices among incumbent retailers, Costco actually leads to a slight increase in prices across a number of categories of some 1.4 percent on average in the short run, and 2.7 percent in the long run. The effect is largest for items where the brand is not specified, which suggests that incumbents might be competing with Costco by improving the quality first of the goods on offer and second of the overall shopping experience.

Matsa (2011) argues that this is one of the ways firms respond to Walmart entry, with one specific aspect of the quality of a shopping experience being inventory control. Having goods on hand is an important element of a satisfactory shopping experience. Stockouts— when firms don't have goods they carry on the shelves or in inventory—make customers angry. Grocers lose $6–$12 billion because of stockouts each year (Matsa 2011: 1540). Matsa argues that competitive pressure from Walmart causes better inventory management with an average reduction in stockouts of 10 percent after Walmart entry (Matsa 2011: 1542). There are pronounced effects on prices and stockout rates in low-income areas after Walmart enters; as Matsa writes, "Walmart's format most appeals to low-income consumers, and these consumers also appear to be the biggest beneficiaries of Walmart's competitive effects on other stores" (Matsa (2011: 1543). Glandon and Jaremski (2011) argue that a firm increases the frequency of its sales—particularly on popular items—as its stores get closer to Walmart.

Walmart is the most visible face of the global economy. Walmart and other chains have provided entrée for imports from less developed countries, and "Walmart handles 6.5 percent of U.S. retail sales but accounts for over 15 percent of U.S. imports of consumer goods from China" (Basker and Van 2010: 414). Basker and Van (2010: 414) estimate that the

> disproportionate growth of large retailers between 1997 and 2002 is associated with approximately one-third of the overall growth in consumer-goods imports, half of the growth in consumer-goods imports from China, and nearly three-quarters of the growth from Mexico.

The anti-chain movement of the early twentieth century has its modern incarnation in the public debate about Walmart. Approximately 19 percent of survey respondents said that Walmart is bad for the community while 24 percent said "Wal-Mart was bad for the country" (Basker 2007: 178). Slater (2004: xi) reports that Walmart was defending itself against "some 6,649 lawsuits as of September 2003." Walmart's explicit and active opposition to labor unions has earned it a substantial number of political enemies. The company's role as a conduit for goods from less-developed countries earns it the contempt of labor unions in manufacturing, competition from Walmart makes it more difficult for unions that represent grocery workers to demand higher wages and generous benefits, and adding only half of Walmart's 2.1 million employees to the Union of Food and Commercial Workers (UFCW) or the Service Employees International Union (SEIU) would nearly double the size of the UFCW or increase the size of the SEIU by 50 percent.

Walmart has a complex relationship with governments at various levels. On one hand, the company has made use of government subsidies and special tax treatment (Mattera and Purinton 2004). In 2005, Walmart supported an increase in the minimum wage and in 2009 joined with the SEIU and the Center for American Progress to call for employer mandates for health coverage.[6] At the same time, some states and localities are working to make Walmart entry prohibitively onerous through laws imposing special taxes and requirements on firms with certain size characteristics; these laws appear to target Walmart specifically (Hicks 2007: 267ff).

Walmart (or simply commerce in general) might also affect quality-of-life indicators that are not narrowly "economic." A popular claim is that chains decimate local businesses and leave towns stripped of important social and institutional capital (Lebhar 1963: 159–60). With respect to Walmart, this received some empirical support from Goetz and Rupasingha (2006), but Carden et al. (2009a) argue that across a range of indicators assembled for Putnam's (2000) study of social capital, Walmart has no identifiable effect. Carden et al. (2009b) show that this is also true for measures of political, social, and cultural values, while Carden and Courtemanche (2009) argue that Walmart increases participation in some leisure activities, including those for which the equipment can be purchased at Walmart and "high culture" activities—specifically classical music concerts and trips to art galleries.

Conclusion

The rise of mass-market merchandisers in the late twentieth century has been but one in a series of episodes in which the U.S. economy has transformed itself through a process of creative destruction. The retail sector has been transformed: it delivers goods to consumers with a combination of quantity, price, and promptness that would have been unthinkable in the earlier twentieth century.

One firm—Walmart—towers above the rest. The crusade against Walmart echoes the crusade against chain stores in the early twentieth century, and the threat Walmart poses to the unionized service sector suggests first that unions are right to be concerned and second that criticism is unlikely to abate.

It is tempting to credit scanners and satellites for a structural earthquake in the retail sector, but managerial and organizational innovation in the face of changing market conditions was extremely important. This echoes Douglass C. North's (1968) explanation of the sources of productivity change in ocean shipping as the product of institutions, organization, and market development rather than technology, and Kim's explanation of the rise of multi-unit firms as a response to "economies in advertising and in transactions" (Kim 1999: 95).

Several trends are apparent in late-twentieth century retail. First, retail outlets have become larger. Second, chains have become increasingly important while single-establishment firms have become less important. Third, prices have fallen while the assortment available to the average consumer has increased dramatically. The savings and productivity advances made possible by mass-market merchandisers testify to the importance of these changes. The research in this area is still relatively young, and the retail sector continues to change. Time will tell just what mass-market merchandisers have meant, and will mean, for the evolution of the structure of the American economy.

Acknowledgments

This chapter is drawn in part from remarks made at a number of institutions and seminars. Emek Basker, Barry P. Bosworth, Charles Courtemanche, Michael J. Hicks, Jack Triplett, and session participants at the 2010 Southern Economic Association meetings and the American Institute for Economic Research provided valuable comments. Barry P. Bosworth was kind enough to share data on industry contributions to multifactor productivity that I used in an earlier version. I also benefited from a conversation with Sarah Estelle. Sameer Warraich, Julia Clapper, and Julie Doub provided research assistance at various stages. Julie Doub, Linda Gibson, and Rachel Smith proofread the manuscript. This research was supported by Faculty Development Endowment Grants from Rhodes College in 2010 and 2011, and a Visiting Research Fellowship at the American Institute for Economic Research in 2011.

Notes

1 See Jarmin et al. (2009) for a summary of retail trends.
2 These are adapted from and elaborated on by Hicks (2007: 8–9).
3 SIC denotes the Standard Industrial Classification System, which U.S. statistical agencies used to classify business establishments until it was replaced by the North American Industrial Classification System in 1997. See www.census.gov/eos/www/naics/ for more information. Accessed March 29, 2012.
4 Census Bureau data sets on firms—like the Longitudinal Business Database used by Jarmin et al. (2009) as well as County Business Patterns and other data sets—come with an important caveat: they only count firms with paid employees and not independent contractors or sole proprietors without paid employees. I thank Emek Basker for emphasizing this.
5 Dube et al. (2007) put the figure at $4.5 billion.
6 http://www.americanprogress.org/pressroom/releases/2009/06/Walmart_hc.html, accessed May 27, 2011.

References

Basker, E. (2005a) 'Job creation or destruction? Labor-market effects of Wal-Mart expansion', *Review of Economics and Statistics,* 87: 174–83.
Basker, E. (2005b) 'Selling a cheaper mousetrap: Wal-Mart's effect on retail prices', *Journal of Urban Economics,* 58: 203–29.
Basker, E. (2007) 'The causes and consequences of Wal-Mart's growth', *Journal of Economic Perspectives,* 21: 177–98.
Basker, E. (2011a) 'Raising the barcode scanner: technology and productivity in the retail sector', Working Paper, University of Missouri.
Basker, E. (2011b) 'Does Wal-Mart sell inferior goods?', *Economic Inquiry,* 49: 973–81.
Basker, E. and Noel, M. (2009) 'The evolving food chain: competitive effects of Wal-Mart's entry into the supermarket industry', *Journal of Economics and Management Strategy,* 18: 977–1009.
Basker, E. and Van, P.H. (2010) 'Imports "R" Us: retail chains as platforms for developing-country imports', *American Economic Review Papers and Proceedings,* 100: 414–18.
Basker, E., Klimek, S. and Van, P.H. (2012) 'Supersize it: the growth of retail chains and the rise of the "big box" format', *Journal of Economics and Management Strategy,* 21: 541–82.
Campbell, J.R. (2009) 'Comment on Jarmin, Klimek, and Miranda', in T. Dunne, J.B. Jensen and M.J. Roberts (eds.) *Producer Dynamics: New Evidence from Micro Data,* Chicago, IL: University of Chicago Press.
Carden, A. and Courtemanche, C. (2009) 'Wal-Mart, leisure, and culture', *Contemporary Economic Policy,* 27: 450–61.
Carden, A., Courtemanche, C. and Meiners, J. (2009a) 'Does Wal-Mart reduce social capital?', *Public Choice,* 138: 109–36.

Carden, A., Courtemanche, C. and Meiners, J. (2009b) 'Painting the town red? Wal-Mart and values', *Business and Politics,* 11 (Article 5).

Chandler, A.D. (1977) *The Visible Hand: The Managerial Revolution in American Business*, Cambridge, MA: Belknap Press of Harvard University Press.

Chandler, A.D. (1990) *Scale and Scope: The Dynamics of Industrial Capitalism*, Cambridge, MA: Belknap Press of Harvard University Press.

Chiou, L. (2009) 'Empirical analysis of competition between Wal-Mart and other retail channels', *Journal of Economics and Management Strategy,* 18: 285–322.

Courtemanche, C. and Carden, A. (2011a) 'Supersizing supercenters? The impact of Walmart supercenters on body mass index and obesity', *Journal of Urban Economics,* 69: 165–81.

Courtemanche, C. and Carden, A. (2011b) 'Competing with Costco and Sam's Club: warehouse club entry and grocery prices', NBER Working Paper 17220.

Doms, M.E., Jarmin, R.S. and Klimek, S.D. (2004) 'Information technology investment and firm performance in U.S. retail trade', *Economics of Innovation and New Technology,* 13: 595–613.

Dube, A., Eidlin, B. and Lester, B. (2005) 'The impact of Wal-Mart growth on earnings throughout the retail sector in urban and rural counties', Working Paper, University of California-Berkeley Institute of Industrial Relations.

Dube, A., Lester, T.W. and Eidlin, B. (2007) 'A downward push: the impact of Wal-Mart stores on retail wages and benefits', UC Berkeley Center for Labor Research and Education Research Brief.

Foster, L., Haltiwanger, J. and Krizan, C.J. (2006) 'Market selection, reallocation, and restructuring in the U.S. retail trade sector in the 1990s', *Review of Economics and Statistics,* 88: 748–58.

Furman, J. (2005) 'Wal-Mart: a progressive success story', Online: http://www.americanprogress.org/kf/walmart_progressive.pdf, accessed May 24, 2011.

Glandon, P.J. and Jaremski, M. (2011) 'Sales and firm entry: the case of Wal-Mart', Working Paper, Vanderbilt University.

Global Insight (2005) 'The economic impact of Wal-Mart', Online: http://www.ihsglobalinsight.com/publicDownload/genericContent/11–03–05_walmart.pdf, accessed August 30, 2011.

Goetz, S.J. and Rupasingha, A. (2006) 'Wal-Mart and social capital', *American Journal of Agricultural Economics,* 88: 1304–10.

Haltiwanger, J., Jarmin, R. and Krizan, C.J. (2010) 'Mom-and-pop meet big-box: complements or substitutes?', *Journal of Urban Economics,* 67: 116–34.

Hausman, J. and Leibtag, E. (2007) 'Consumer benefits from increased competition in shopping outlets: measuring the effect of Wal-Mart', *Journal of Applied Econometrics,* 22: 1157–77.

Hausman, J. and Leibtag, E. (2009) 'CPI bias from supercenters: does the BLS know that Wal-Mart exists?', in W.E. Diewert, J.S. Greenlees and C.R. Hulten (eds.) *Price Index Concepts and Measurement*, Chicago, IL: University of Chicago Press.

Hicks, M.J. (2005) 'What do quarterly workforce dynamics tell us about Wal-Mart? Evidence from New Stores in Pennsylvania', Unpublished Paper, Ball State University.

Hicks, M.J. (2007) *The Local Economic Impact of Wal-Mart*, Youngstown, NY: Cambria Press.

Holmes, T.J. (2001) 'Bar codes lead to frequent deliveries and superstores', *RAND Journal of Economics,* 32: 708–25.

Holmes, T.J. (2011) 'The diffusion of Wal-Mart and economies of density', *Econometrica,* 79: 253–302.

Jarmin, R.S., Klimek, S.D. and Miranda, J. (2009) 'The role of retail chains: national, regional, and industry results', in T. Dunne, J.B. Jensen and M.J. Roberts (eds.) *Producer Dynamics: New Evidence from Micro Data*, Chicago: University of Chicago Press.

Jia, P. (2008) 'What happens when Wal-Mart comes to town: an empirical analysis of the discount retailing industry', *Econometrica,* 76: 1263–1316.

Kim, S. (1999) 'The growth of modern business enterprises in the twentieth century', *Research in Economic History,* 19: 75–110.

Kim, S. (2001) 'Markets and multiunit firms from an American historical perspective', *Advances in Strategic Management,* 18.

Lagakos, D. (2009) 'Superstores or mom and pops? Technology adoption and productivity differences in retail trade', Federal Reserve Bank of Minneapolis Research Department Staff Report 428.

Lebhar, G.M. (1963) *Chain Stores in America 1859–1962*, New York: Chain Store Publishing Corporation.

Lewis, W.W. (2004) *The Power of Productivity*, Chicago, IL: University of Chicago Press.

Lichtenstein, N. (ed.) 2006 *Wal-Mart: The Face of Twenty-First-Century Capitalism*, New York: New Press.

Matsa, D. (2011) 'Competition and product quality in the supermarket industry', *Quarterly Journal of Economics,* 126: 1539–91.

Mattera, P. and Purinton, A. (2004) 'Shopping for subsidies: how Wal-Mart uses taxpayer money to finance its never-ending growth', Online: http://www.goodjobsfirst.org/sites/default/files/docs/pdf/wmtstudy.pdf. Accessed May 27, 2011.

McKinsey Global Institute. (2001) *U.S. Productivity Growth 1995–2000: Understanding the Contribution of Information Technology Relative to Other Factors*, Washington, DC: McKinsey Global Institute.

Moussalli, S.D. and Flesher, T. (2002) 'Taxing outsiders in Mississippi', *State Tax Notes,* 24: 1197–1205.

Neumann, T.C. (2011) 'Competition among early 20th century retailers: could the lack of a retail industrial revolution been caused by a lack of competition?', Working Paper, University of California, Merced.

Neumark, D., Zhang, J. and Ciccarella, S. (2008) 'The effects of Wal-Mart on local labor markets', *Journal of Urban Economics,* 63: 405–30.

North, D.C. (1968) 'Sources of productivity change in ocean shipping, 1600–1850', *Journal of Political Economy,* 76: 953–70.

Putnam, R. (2000) *Bowling Alone: The Collapse and Revival of American Community,* New York: Simon and Schuster.

Ross, T.W. (1986) 'Store wars: the chain tax movement', *Journal of Law and Economics,* 29: 125–37.

Ryant, C.G. (1973) 'The South and the movement against chain stores', *Journal of Southern History,* 39: 207–22.

Schragger, R.C. (2005) 'The anti-chain store movement, localist ideology, and the remnants of the progressive constitution, 1920–1940', *Iowa Law Review,* 90: 101–84.

Slater, R. (2004) *The Wal-Mart Triumph: Inside the World's #1 Company,* New York: Portfolio.

Sobel, R. and Dean, A. (2008) 'Has Wal-Mart buried mom and pop? The impact of Wal-Mart on self employment and small establishments in the United States', *Economic Inquiry,* 46: 676–95.

Triplett, J.E. and Bosworth, B.P. (2004) *Productivity in the U.S. Services Sector: New Sources of Economic Growth,* Washington, DC: Brookings Institution Press.

Vance, S.S. and Scott, R.V. (1994) *Wal-Mart: A History of Sam Walton's Retail Phenomenon,* New York: Twayne Publishers.

Vedder, R. and Cox, W. (2006) *The Wal-Mart Revolution: How Big-Box Stores Benefit Consumers, Workers, and the Economy,* Washington DC: AEI Press.

Walmart Stores (2011) History Timeline. http://walmartstores.com/aboutus/7603.aspx. Accessed May 27, 2011.

Zhu, T., Singh, V. and Manuszak, M.D. (2009) 'Market structure and competition in the retail discount industry', *Journal of Marketing Research,* 46: 453–66.

34

GOVERNMENT BAILOUTS

Robert E. Wright

A bailout occurs when a government provides aid to (bails out) a financially distressed entity (business, industry, or government).[1] "Bailing out" evokes three relevant emergency-related metaphors: emptying water from a sinking boat, parachuting from a doomed aircraft, and getting out of jail. Government bailouts (hereafter simply bailouts) are a subset of government resource transfers called subsidies or, when directed to big businesses, corporate welfare (Adams and Brock 1987: 75; Glasberg and Skidmore 1997: 2–3; McGee 2008: 9). They can be differentiated from disaster relief, or aid designed to counteract distress caused by natural or manmade forces clearly outside of the resource recipient's control (Auerswald et al. 2006).[2] Some bailouts are complete, entailing no losses to creditors, employees, managers, owners, or other stakeholders. Others protect only uninsured creditors or other preferred stakeholders (Kaufman 2004). Some bailouts are systemic while others aid only a specific entity or entities.

Bailout resource transfers can take numerous forms, including: asset purchases, cash, contract flexibility (e.g., allowing costs overruns or relaxing performance standards), criminal prosecution immunity, (subsidized) insurance, contract process manipulation (e.g., no bid), (unwarranted) deregulation, liability forgiveness, loans and loan guarantees, market power creation (e.g., cartelization), (compensated) nationalization, physical infrastructure (e.g., manufacturing plants), regulatory forbearance, (unwarranted) research grants, stock purchases, tariffs and other forms of protection from foreign competition, tax breaks, and welfare policies (Pierce 1983: 363–64; Adams and Brock 1987: 66–80; Glasberg and Skidmore 1997: 4; Gup 2004: 38–43; Rosas 2009: 6–8).

Governments and resource recipients justify bailouts by asserting that the expected costs of not bailing out a distressed entity exceed expected bailout costs (Forman 1981: 46; Freeman and Mendelowitz 1982: 448; Adams and Brock 1987: 63–65; Stern and Feldman 2004: xi–xii; McGee 2008: 2). Failure to bail out a distressed entity, they typically claim, will decrease economic output and employment, increase stress on government budgets by decreasing tax receipts and increasing social safety net expenditures, and induce the extinction of culturally, economically, and/or strategically important services, companies, or industries. Failure to bail out will also create so-called knock on or contagion effects that may cause the failure of stable institutions and thereby spread distress across industrial sectors and national borders (Adams and Brock 1987: 68; Gup 2004: 43–44; Stern and Feldman 2004: 44–47).

Bailout decisions, however, are not based on precise cost–benefit analyses because the net costs of bailouts are difficult to assess (Webel, Labonte and Weiss 2009: 2, 7–8), even *ex post* (Stern and Feldman 2004: 23; Reinhart and Rogoff 2009: 163–64, 224; Rosas 2009: 3), a point discussed in more detail below. Some experts think that the risk of system-wide contagion is low, especially if the distressed entity is not a depository institution (Benston 1999: 8), but others believe contagion highly likely. The net costs of government cash grants, securities purchases, and loan guarantees are difficult to calculate because they involve assumptions about risk-adjusted returns and the opportunity costs of government funds. More indirect forms of aid are difficult to identify, let alone precisely quantify (Webel, Labonte and Weiss 2009: 2–3).

Bailouts have had a long, checkered history in the United States (Wright 2010), Canada (Gordon 1981, Trebilock et al. 1985), Mexico (Shull 2010: 13), Japan (Yabushita and Inoue 1993; Yokohama 2007), Europe – where the first recorded bailout occurred in 33 A.D. (Rosas 2009: 2) – and elsewhere (Gup 2004: 43; Shull 2010: 12–13). Some bailouts have clearly been salutary. Others exposed well-meaning but bungling government agencies. Still others appear to have been "bad" bailouts implemented by bureaucrats, for bureaucrats (Benston 1999: 33, 53–55; Stern and Feldman 2004: 43–44, 52–59; Shull 2010: 15; Skeel 2010: 11–12), or that unduly aided powerful special interests – a large corporation, influential industry, or potent combination of smaller interests[3] – at the expense of taxpayers[4] (Glasberg and Skidmore 1997: 138–40; McGee 2008: 7–8).

Bailout results vary partly because representative governments typically concede less to special interests than authoritarian governments do (Rosas 2009: 8–11), ostensibly because they are more responsive to taxpayers and the bailed out entity's rivals (Gordon 1981: 153). Democracies countenance bad bailouts because their largest cost, increased moral hazard (post contractual asymmetric information),[5] is difficult to quantify precisely. Belief that bailouts greatly increase moral hazard is strong because economists suspect that entities that expect to receive a bailout if they encounter difficulties will be inclined to earn higher profits by assuming higher levels of risk (Stern and Feldman 2004: 23–24; Mishkin 2006, 2007: 48). Bankers who expect a bailout, for example, will benefit by building riskier loan portfolios and insured depositors will benefit by reducing their monitoring efforts (Benston 1999: 32). U.S. history strongly suggests that most types of bailouts do, in fact, increase future risk taking.

Before the Great Depression, the U.S. government minimized bailout expectations by providing emergency aid on only a handful of occasions (Perkins 1994: 249–50; Cowen 2000: 153–59, 178 n. 96; Leathers and Raines 2004: 4–5; Kamensky 2008; Ventrudo 2009; Shull 2010: 12). Most important were the actions of Treasury Secretary Alexander Hamilton, who in 1792 teamed up with the first Bank of the United States (1791–1811) to squelch a financial panic (Sylla, Wright and Cowen 2009), and Nicholas Biddle, who in 1825 as president of the second Bank of the United States (1816–1836) successfully prevented a financial crisis from spreading to America from Britain. Both of those system-wide bailouts followed the Hamilton–Bagehot Rule. According to Hamilton (and later Walter Bagehot, founding editor of *The Economist* magazine, who until recently had received exclusive credit for developing the Rule), central banks should act as a lender of last resort (LLR) during financial panics by lending at a penalty rate to any entity that could post "what in ordinary times is reckoned a good security" (Bagehot 1873/1962: 97). Such actions stop panic and contagion by reassuring solvent (assets greater than liabilities) but temporarily illiquid (insufficient cash) firms that they can borrow from the LLR regardless of money market conditions. The Rule also prevents losses to taxpayers by requiring ample collateral and minimizes moral hazard by allowing entities that assumed excessive risks to fail and their creditors to suffer losses (Wright 2010: 21–23; Rosas 2009: 4–7, 171–77). It is analogous to allowing a house fire to rage while preventing the conflagration from spreading to nearby buildings (Acharya et al. 2010: 135).

Despite the success of the Hamilton–Bagehot Rule, the government opted not to use it for the better part of a century. Between the demise of the second Bank in 1836 and the opening of the Federal Reserve (Fed) in November 1914,[6] the Treasury did little to act as a LLR during financial panics beyond depositing some of its funds in money center banks (Bruner and Carr 2007: 136). Private alternatives, including bank clearinghouses and investment bankers (e.g., J.P. Morgan in 1907), filled some of the void (Leathers and Raines 2004: 18–19; Bruner and Carr 2007) but Bagehot (1873/1962: 162) considered the "American system … faulty" in both "its very essence and principle." Most Americans, however, did not consider bailouts in "the general interest" of the LLR function sanctioned by the U.S. Constitution. Several state constitutions even explicitly forbade state governments from lending to, or guaranteeing the debts of, individuals or businesses (Smith 1853/1966: 260). Finally, many Americans considered waves of commercial bankruptcies salutary. They argued:

> As one after another goes down, there is one less engaged in the scramble for money, and the survivors experience the same sort of relief as men in a crowd do when some of them faint and are carried out.
>
> (Smith 1853/1966: 245)

That is not to argue, however, that laissez-faire ideology dominated early American political economy. Nineteenth-century U.S. governments transferred significant resources to specific enterprises and industries. Most of those transfers – copyrights, corporate charters, patents and other monopoly rights; land grants to railroads and settlers; tariffs – were general subsidies, not bailouts. Early state governments subsidized private transportation corporations such as toll bridges, canals, turnpikes, and railroads, and some of the aid could be considered bailouts because it went to distressed firms (Mason and Schiffman 2004: 49–50). Some emergency payments of cash (or securities purchases), however, are better described as disaster relief because they were made to repair damage caused by floods or other natural catastrophes (Wright forthcoming; Moss 2002). After the Civil War, government takeovers of privately-owned transportation corporations became increasingly frequent but few could be considered bailouts because stockholders received little or no compensation as the improvements escheated to some level of municipal government (Wright forthcoming). The postbellum federal government continued to subsidize railroads with land grants and other concessions and manufacturers with tariffs but few of its actions could be considered bailouts, which were politically anathema and, in an age of dynamite-throwing anarchists, potentially physically dangerous for recipients (Gage 2009).

In the twentieth century, however, government bailout activity increased dramatically due to the tremendous stresses caused by both World Wars, the Cold War, the Great Depression, and the demise of fixed exchange rates. Bailout expectations initially proved sticky (resistant to change) but by the early twenty-first century a feedback cycle was clearly in place: more bailouts increased bailout expectations which induced more risk-taking which increased the number and severity of crises and hence the need for more bailouts. That cycle began to develop, slowly, as early as World War I. The War Finance Corporation (WFC, 1918–1929) was more of a general subsidy program than a bailout vehicle per se (Rosenfield 1985: 355) but it did incidentally aid distressed companies. Moreover, it set a precedent for the Reconstruction Finance Corporation (RFC) (Leathers and Raines 2004: 19–20). The RFC (1932–1957) at first made loans only to distressed financial institutions and railroads but the government soon allowed it to lend to distressed municipal governments and manufacturers (Leathers and Raines 2004: 21–26; Mason and Schiffman 2004; Levitin 2010: 54). Many New Deal programs can be interpreted as attempts to bail out specific groups, including depositors (FDIC), farmers (AAA), financiers (SEC), homeowners (HOLC), and various other entities through cartelization, price supports, and other anti-competitive measures (NRA) as well as direct transfers (Mahoney 2001; Shlaes 2007).

Although unprecedented in scale and scope, New Deal bailouts were seen as aberrations and hence did not radically increase bailout expectations. Moreover, the RFC essentially followed the Hamilton–Bagehot Rule because it lent at a penalty rate and under stringent collateral valuation rules (Leathers and Raines 2004: 23). According to a late New Deal monograph on government corporations like the WFC and RFC, "the protection of government credit cannot be implied." In other words, "unless a positive guaranty is included in the act," the Treasury could not be held responsible for the debts of *government-owned and operated* corporations, much less private businesses (McDiarmid 1938: 65–66, 216). By the 1980s, however, investors believed that the bonds of government-sponsored enterprises (GSEs) like Fannie Mae and Freddie Mac were de facto backed by the full credit of the U.S. Treasury even though Congress had not authorized an explicit guarantee. Just thirty years later, many lenders believed that taxpayers would reimburse them if any foreign government or large private corporation, financial or not, defaulted, and leading experts on central banking publicly wondered if "monetary policymakers might be tempted to 'follow the markets' slavishly, essentially delivering the monetary policy that the markets expect or demand" (Blinder 2004).

The sea change in sentiment occurred because during and after World War II the government became an increasingly potent economic force (Higgs 1987). Under Bretton Woods, the Fed began actively managing the money supply (or interest rates). American governments at all levels stepped up the direct regulation of prices (during the war, during the Nixon administration, and with rent controls and minimum wage laws) and increasingly attempted to mandate specific economic outcomes (Moss 2002). The public and private sectors became so "completely intertwined" that "no clear distinction" between them could be made (Reich 1982: 878). In 1970, the government awarded Penn Central Railroad $125 million in loan guarantees while it was in bankruptcy because it considered the company a public utility that provided rail service rather than a private business (Rosenfield 1985: 355). Shortly thereafter, the troubled Conrail received $3 billion in aid for essentially the same reason (Freeman and Mendelowitz 1982: 452; Rosenfield 1985: 356).

Perhaps the most important example of the melding of government and business interests, however, was the "military-industrial complex" that emerged from World War II and matured during the Cold War. Close ties between the Pentagon and its arms manufacturers created a cadre of mismanaged defense contractor firms that believed that "if adversity strikes" they could "count on government bailouts" (Adams and Adams, 1972: 284). Some defense contractor bailouts were done quietly through the award of major contracts of dubious necessity, some as aid to foreign allies like Iran (Kurth 1973: 43–46), some as contractual modifications favorable to the distressed firm (Ramey and Erlewine 1954), and some as new, comfortably-padded contracts (Higgs 1993: 40). A few, like the government's $250 million loan guarantee for Lockheed in 1971, were explicit and justified on the grounds of employment and national defense (Kurth 1973: 36–37; Freeman and Mendelowitz 1982: 451–52).

Senator William Proxmire warned Treasury Secretary John Connally that "Lockheed's bailout ... is not a subsidy ... it is the beginning of a welfare program for large corporations" (Jasinowski 1973: 8). He was right that an important corner had been turned (Adams and Brock 1987). Lockheed and other bailouts, including the "special tax relief" extended to the American Motor Corporation in 1967 and large loan guarantees and import restrictions provided to dying steel companies in the 1970s, prompted Chrysler to ask for federal assistance when it faced bankruptcy in the late 1970s (Freeman and Mendelowitz 1982: 447, 451; Rosenfield 1985: 355–56; Adams and Brock 1987: 66). Chrysler chairman Lee Iacocca justified his aid request by arguing that "free enterprise died a while back" (Rosenfield 1985: 353) and that the bailout was "amply precedented" (Adams and Brock 1987: 65). Although Chrysler's case was arguably much weaker than those of previous bailout recipients, the government relented, ostensibly because the scorn of unemployed workers would be more powerful at the ballot box than the gratitude of those taking the new jobs that would have been created eventually if Chrysler was shuttered (Freeman and Mendelowitz 1982: 451–53; Rosenfield 1985: 354; Adams and Brock 1987: 65; Bickley 2008: 2).

Chrysler's aid package, worth an unprecedented $3.5 billion (Rosenfield 1985: 353), further pried opened the lid of a "Pandora's box" of bailouts (Hoffman 1980: 871; Rosenfield 1985: 356). Increasingly un-sticky expectations about the government's willingness to provide emergency assistance induced yet other troubled firms to seek government bailouts and they of course "cited the Chrysler bailout as a plausible reason why they ought to have one" (Hoffman 1980: 869). A wave of bailout requests, some successful, ensued. For example, manufacturers of TRIS, a flame-retardant chemical banned from use in children's sleepwear after its carcinogenic properties were discovered, successfully lobbied for federal funds in late 1982 (Garmon 1983: 22; Painter 1984: 1073–74). In 1984, the government bailed out forest product companies that had bid too much for timber cutting rights (Mattey 1990). Soon after, Dennis Carney, the president of a bailed out steel firm, claimed that "you can't win the game with free enterprise anymore" (Rosenfield 1985: 357), and Wharton professor Edward Herman sneered that the government had birthed a form of "crybaby capitalism" that rewarded the most vocal complainants (Rosenfield 1985: 354). By the mid-1990s, the federal government had bailed out over 400 non-financial corporations (Glasberg and Skidmore 1997: 3, 138) and its support of distressed defense contractors continued (Weber 2001). The number and size of sovereign (e.g. Latin American debt crises) and municipal government bailouts (e.g. loan guarantees to New York City in 1975 and 1978) also increased in the 1970s, 1980s, and 1990s (Adams and Brock 1987: 65–66; Reinhart and Rogoff 2009; Webel, Labonte and Weiss 2009: 8).

After a long postwar lull during which only a handful of very small banks failed, inflation, technological change, and overly ambitious deregulation began to take its toll in the 1970s and 1980s. Unsurprisingly, bank bailouts increased in number and size, mostly in the form of FDIC purchase and assumption agreements and Federal Reserve LLR actions (e.g., Union Bank in 1971, Bank of the Commonwealth in 1972, Franklin National in 1974, and First Pennsylvania Bank in 1979) (Sprague 1986: 35–106; Shull 2010: 6–7). Those bailouts overwhelmed the effect of "two potential bailouts that never happened," Penn Square and Seafirst (Sprague 1986: 107–45), increasing the bailout expectations of bankers and inducing them to "take riskier actions than if government intervention was unlikely" (Shapiro 1982: 730). By the early 1980s, bankers had substituted expensive equity with low-cost "implicit insurance provided by government bailout activities" (Kane 1980: 360). The bailouts, most of which left even uninsured depositors unscathed, also greatly reduced large depositors' incentives to monitor their banks (Shull 2010: 7).

In the 1980s and early 1990s, the trickle of bank failures became a torrent. The entire savings and loan (S&L) industry collapsed, Continental Illinois failed (Sprague 1986: 149–99), the Bank of New England reeled under bad real-estate loans, and Citibank wavered on the brink of insolvency. All received bailouts, ranging from regulatory forbearance to Fed discounts to FDIC guarantees of uninsured deposits to the purchase of underperforming assets by a taxpayer-funded "bad bank," the Resolution Trust Corporation (RTC) (Benston 1999: 78; Murphy and Webel 2009: 7). In 1987, the Farm Credit System, a GSE, also received a $4 billion bailout (Nickerson and Phillips 2004; Hill 2010). In all, over $150 billion (some 2 percent of GDP) was redistributed (Stern and Feldman 2004: 23–24).

New legislation (Financial Institutions Reform, Recovery, and Enforcement Act – FIRREA in 1989 and Federal Deposit Insurance Corporation Improvement Act – FDICIA in 1991) attempted to limit future bailouts by reducing regulators' discretion about when and how to resolve failed banks (Shull 2010: 8). The government also refused to bail out junk bond giant Drexel Burnham in 1990 (2010: 477–81) and both MJK Clearing and Superior Bank in 2001 (Stern and Feldman 2004: xi–xii; Gup 2004: 43). Those exceptions and the new laws, however, did little to decrease market participants' belief that the government intended to follow a policy of "too big to fail" (TBTF). Beginning with the 1984 bailout of Continental Illinois, policymakers explicitly[7] promised free, unconditional aid to the eleven (and later a deliberately ambiguous number of the) largest banks (later, financial institutions of any sort) under the supposition that they were too big, important, or interconnected to be allowed to remain insolvent (Sprague 1986: 259). "The assumption that big banks will not be allowed to fail … contributed to imprudent lending" (Rosenfield 1985: 357), as did the erosion of economic incentives, especially the franchise value of financial institutions, that had traditionally limited risk-taking (Stern and Feldman 2004: 24–26, 149–58).

At the same time, market participants learned that they could maintain high levels of risk regardless of their size or the macroeconomic climate because if the entire financial system encountered difficulties the Fed stood ready to provide ample, timely, and inexpensive aid. Instead of following the Hamilton–Bagehot Rule as it traditionally had at least given lip service to (Meltzer 2003: 75–76, 113–14, 125–26, 730–31), at the outset of crises the Fed under Alan Greenspan increased market liquidity by purchasing bonds in the open market and lowering interest rates for banks, both the overnight bank-to-bank target rate and the rate it charged at its own discount window (Axilrod 2009: 162, 169–70; Hetzel 2008: 227–33; Mishkin 2007: 48; Norberg 2009: 14). Relaxation of the Hamilton–Bagehot Rule increased moral hazard and risk-taking at all banks (Bordo and Schwartz 1999: 8–9) and TBTF policy induced financial institutions to grow large as quickly as possible to receive the free insurance (Kaufman 2009). In 1987, the Greenspan Fed stopped a stock market rout by supporting banks that lent to distressed broker-dealers. In 1997 and 1998 it lowered interest rates in response to the Asian financial crisis, the Russian default, and the failure of Long-Term Capital Management, the sale of which Greenspan brokered and implicitly guaranteed (Axilrod 2009: 146–50; Hetzel 2008: 206–26). The Fed also injected cash into the economy in late 1999 to prevent panic in the event of Y2K-related problems and did so again in the wake of the terrorist attacks in September 2001. More dubiously, the Fed lowered interest rates for a considerable period to buffer the economy, and investors, from the bursting of the dotcom bubble in early 2000 (Levitin 2010: 53). In addition to increasing confidence in the existence of a so-called "Greenspan put," long periods of low real interest rates invited increased leverage and other forms of risk-taking implicated in the subprime mortgage crisis of 2007 (Woods 2009: 25–29).

Under Greenspan's successor as Fed chairman, economist Ben Bernanke, the Fed also reduced interest rates when trouble struck, eventually lowering nominal overnight rates to zero and keeping them there into 2012 while also indicating they intended to have them remain there until 2014. As the intractability of the subprime mortgage crisis became increasingly apparent, the Fed invoked its emergency authority under section 13–3 of the Federal Reserve Act (which granted it broad powers during "unusual and exigent circumstances") to implement an unprecedented array of novel policies, most of which did not impose large direct burdens on taxpayers (Congleton 2010: 30). The rescue of investment bank Bear Stearns in March 2008, however, exposed taxpayers to up to $29 billion in losses and effectively extended TBTF expectations to all large financial institutions (Jickling 2008).

In September 2008, the new Federal Housing Finance Agency took troubled GSE mortgage lenders Fannie Mae and Freddie Mac into conservatorship and the Treasury explicitly guaranteed some $5 trillion of their debt in exchange for a 79.9 percent stake in the companies, effectively (re)nationalizing them (Congleton 2010: 18). Shortly thereafter, Lehman Brothers failed, triggering a run on money market mutual funds that the Treasury and FDIC stopped by guaranteeing that investors would not lose money. Soon after that AIG, a large, shaky financial conglomerate, received from the Fed an $85 billion line of credit, at a penalty rate of interest, again in exchange for a 79.9 percent stake in the company (Webel, Labonte and Weiss 2009: 4–5). The Treasury later purchased $40 billion in AIG preferred stock via the Troubled Assets Relief Program (TARP) enacted in early October as part of the Emergency Economic Stabilization Act (Congleton 2010: 21–22). Despite early indications that the $700 billion of TARP funds would be used to purchase bad assets, most of the appropriation funded the purchase of the preferred stock of troubled financial institutions by the Treasury, which apparently decided it would leave the technically difficult and politically dangerous process of defining and pricing "toxic" assets to the Fed (Norberg 2009: 118–19; Congleton 2010: 23–24, 30–31).

Also in early October 2008, the Fed opened a Commercial Paper Funding Facility that bought hundreds of billions of short-term bonds directly from non-financial businesses. The FDIC liquidated the enormous failed thrift Washington Mutual but the government pushed the "assisted purchases" of Wachovia by Wells Fargo and Merrill Lynch by Bank of America, which in January 2009 itself received a massive and complex bailout (Webel, Labonte and Weiss 2009: 3–4). In November 2008, Citigroup was also bailed out by the Fed, Treasury, and FDIC (Jickling 2008; Graham 2010: 119–21). In November, the Fed introduced TALF (Term Asset-Backed Securities Loan Facility) to reinvigorate the market for asset backed securities composed of student, auto, credit card, and home equity loans (Agarwal et al. 2010).

In the American Recovery and Reinvestment Act of 2009, the new Obama administration authorized an additional $800 billion of expenditures, including some $200 billion for cash-strapped state governments, and various Keynesian stimulus programs (Congleton 2010: 28–29). It also bailed out two major automakers, GM and Chrysler. In addition to their finance wings receiving billions in TARP funds (Webel, Labonte and Weiss 2009), both auto giants continued to operate despite filing for bankruptcy because of U.S. government loan guarantees and capital infusions worth over $50 billion (Canis et al. 2009: 20; Congleton 2010: 25–26). The government justified the intervention by claiming that shuttering both companies would have reduced real GDP by 1 percent and increased unemployment by one million people (Canis et al. 2009: 31–33).

Proponents of the 2007–09 bailouts argued that a depression was imminent (Graham 2010: 119; Congleton 2010: 16, 27, 35). Chairman Bernanke claimed that if bailouts were not implemented "we may not have an economy on Monday" (Norberg 2009: 99–100), even though experts familiar with his work on the causes of the Great Depression of 1929–33 (Bernanke 2000) – namely deflation brought on by strict adherence to the gold standard, widespread unit banking, high trade barriers, and a relatively inflexible wage structure – believed otherwise (Labonte 2009). Ironically, the apparently unduly (Woods 2009: 49–50) pessimistic sentiments emanating from key policy figures probably worsened the crisis by further frightening investors. The uncertainty fostered by frequent changes in policy also negatively impacted businesses (Congleton 2010: 19, 23–24 n.22; Woods 2009: 54).

The recent bailout wave has raised important questions (Tarr 2009). Not much work has been done on bailout ethics, but one leading business ethicist argues that most types of bailouts are unethical (McGee 2008). Most critics question the fairness, effectiveness, and/or overall effects of bailouts, particularly those that do not follow the Hamilton–Bagehot Rule (Rosas 2009: 171; Rosenfield 1985: 356–57). A bailout, noted Freeman and Mendelowitz (1982: 444):

> is seen as costly because society is being asked to subsidize that which the marketplace has specifically rejected, and unfair because the government provides windfalls to a privileged group of creditors, stockholders, and employees associated with the failing firm.

Numerous observers note that bailouts redistribute wealth "from the poor to the rich" (Mahmud 2010), effectively socializing risk while allowing profits to remain largely private (Adams and Brock 1987: 80; Rosenfield 1985: 357; Wright 2010: 18). As Rosenfield (1985: 358) put it, bankers appear:

> free to make marginal loans in good times and to keep the profits, but they can be confident that the federal government will prevent these marginal loans from becoming outright losses when recession strikes.

Bailout incidence (analogous to tax incidence, the entities ultimately receiving aid) is not, however, always clear cut. Bailouts of governments by the IMF and World Bank, for example, primarily benefit the distressed governments' creditors, typically large institutional investors, banks (Roubini and Setser 2004; Stiglitz 2002: 201–05), and cronies (Faccio, Masulis and McConnell 2005). Similarly, Chairman Bernanke claimed with some justification that AIG's bailout accrued to consumers' retirement accounts and insurance policies as well as to banks (Levitin 2010: 63–64). Obscure incidence and the case-by-case nature of bailout policies create perceptions of favoritism, some well-founded (Faccio, Masulis, and McConnell 2005). Proponents retort that ad hoc policies restrict bailouts to a few exceptional cases (Schultze 1983: 11), a point that suggests that case-by-case discretion may at times block "good" bailouts. Americans may dislike bailouts so much, for example, that the government may not implement one even if it is warranted (expected benefits clearly exceed expected costs) for fear of a political backlash (Rosas 2009: 9–10; Levitin 2010: 58–61).

Of course, as mentioned above, the net costs of bailouts are much disputed and never precise, even after the fact (McGee 2008: 5). The total gross costs of the most recent bailouts will not be known for some years and early estimates vary by *trillions* of dollars (Tarr 2009: 3–4; Congleton 2010: 19, 27). Moreover, the bailouts' benefits will always be a matter of conjecture because we can never know for certain what would have transpired in their absence. Unemployment, for example, doubled to 10 percent during the 2007–09 crisis but Chairman Bernanke claimed that it could have hit 25 percent if aid had been withheld (Congleton 2010: 35 n.41).

Econometricians have used comparative statistical techniques to try to parse out the economic effects of bailouts but a consensus has yet to emerge due to the enormous complexity of the problem. Some studies find that bailouts increase the stability of bailed out firms and their creditors (see, e.g., Faff, Parwada and Tan 2010) and that Fed programs like TALF helped reduce risk spreads and increase liquidity (Agarwal et al. 2010). But most such studies do not attempt to assess the fiscal costs of bailout packages, the bailouts' longer term consequences, or their effects on specific groups (McGee 2008: 2–3). Bailouts, for example, advantage sunset over sunrise industries because the former enjoy considerably more political clout (Walters 1983: 31). RFC loans did not restore railroads to economic or financial health and probably hastened their long-term decline (Mason and Schiffman 2004). The failure of Continental Illinois, scholars now believe, would *not* have caused a significant ripple effect among its creditors. More generally, many episodes of apparent contagion were actually the well-justified withdrawal of support from shaky institutions, not blind panics that indiscriminately ruined solid companies (Stern and Feldman 2004: 48–49).

In addition, Bordo and Schwartz (1999: ii) found, after accounting for the self-selection problem and controlling for other important variables, that "participation in an IMF program has a significant and negative effect on member countries' real growth." And Rosas and Jensen (2010: 134) concluded from a statistical examination of a large, global sample of late-twentieth-century cases that bank bailouts on average do not improve macroeconomic conditions, a major problem given that the fiscal costs alone of bank bailouts typically range from around 2 percent (U.S. during S&L crisis; Norway in 1987) to 50 percent (Argentina in the early 1980s and Indonesia in 1997) of GDP (Honohan and Klingebiel 2000; Reinhart and Rogoff 2009: 164; Rosas 2009: 2–3). Rosas found that, on average, democracies implement less costly and more economically justified bailouts than authoritarian regimes do (2009: 5, 172–73).

If Rosas is correct, the United States and other democracies should seek to break the bailout-expectation cycle. Academics including Ayotte and Skeel (2010), Balleisen and Moss (2010), Graham (2010), Hillinger (2010), Hoenig, Morris and Spong (2009), Shull (2010), Jackson (2009), Stern and Feldman (2004), Wilmarth (2010), Wright (2008, 2010), and numerous others have made proposals ranging from radical restructuring of the financial system and/or its regulatory apparatus to more modest reforms like increased use of bankruptcy laws and debtor-in-possession (DIP) financing to liquidate hopelessly insolvent institutions and restructure salvageable ones. To date, however, few have been adopted despite the criticism heaped upon the U.S. government's first major post-crisis financial reform attempt, the Dodd–Frank Wall Street Reform and Consumer Protection Act of July 2010 (Acharya et al. 2010; Black 2011; Skeel 2010). Future crises and bailouts, therefore, can be expected.

Notes

1 For so-called stock bailouts, see Metzer (1968). For the long-term (relational) contract adjustments known as bailouts, see Ramey and Erlewine (1954). Other meanings can be traced via the *Oxford English Dictionary*.

2 Application of those definitions requires some discretion. For instance, some observers consider the loan guarantees (and some direct loans) extended to the airline industry after the September 2001 terrorist attacks as a bailout (Gup 2004: 36–39; Webel, Labonte and Weiss 2009: 8) because the airlines were partly responsible for the success of the attacks and because they were already in financial trouble. Others place most blame for the attacks and the airlines' woes on the government and hence see the aid as more closely akin to disaster relief. The difficulty is compounded by the incentive of entities to appear closer to the relief than the bailout end of the spectrum (Mattey 1990: 10–14). General Motors (GM) and Chrysler, for example, claimed that they were victims of the financial crisis of 2008–09, which made borrowing and raising capital more expensive, and the ensuing deep recession, which decimated new car sales (Canis et al. 2009: 1–2). Other famous examples include the San Francisco (1906) and Kanto (1923) earthquakes, both of which helped to cause financial panics (1907 in the U.S. and 1927 in Japan) (Odell and Weidenmier 2002; Yabushita and Inoue 1993: 394).

3 Bailout lobbying often creates seemingly odd bedfellows, as when the NAACP backed the Chrysler bailout (Adams and Brock 1987: 65; Levitin 2010: 65–66).

4 Money for government bailouts comes mostly from the Treasury, which is funded by taxpayers, and the Federal Reserve, which is self-funded through the expansion of its monetary liabilities (notes and deposits). Taxpayers suffer, however, when the Fed's profits decline because it credits the Treasury with its profits (net of dividends to member banks). In addition, excessive money creation stimulates inflation, which essentially taxes all domestic holders of dollars, and depreciation, which taxes unhedged holders of dollars abroad. Relatively small amounts come from the FDIC, which is funded by prudent banks (through their insurance premiums) and taxpayers (Benston 1999: 6–8; Ennis 2009; Webel, Labonte, and Weiss 2009).

5 Moral hazard occurs when one party to a contract uses superior information to extract resources from the other party. Arson of an insured building is a classic example. Agency problems, such as employee slacking or executive embezzlement, are also examples of moral hazard.

6 The Fed was chartered in 1913 but took almost a year to organize and begin operations (Meltzer 2003: 72–82).

7 TBTF had long been implicit (Sprague 1986: 242–44; Gup 2004: 30–32), even in the bailout of non-financial companies (Adams and Brock 1987) like railroads (Mason and Schiffman 2004), as it is easier to justify the bailout of larger, and hence ostensibly more important, entities.

References

Acharya, V.V., Cooley, T.F., Richardson, M.P. and Walter, I. (eds.) (2010) *Regulating Wall Street: The Dodd–Frank Act and the New Architecture of Global Finance*. Hoboken, NJ: John Wiley & Sons.

Adams, A. and Adams, J.A. (1972) 'The military-industrial complex: a market structure analysis', *American Economic Review*, 62: 279–87.

Adams, W.A. and Brock, J.W. (1987) 'Corporate size and the bailout factor', *Journal of Economic Issues*, 21: 61–85.

Agarwal, S., Barrett, J., Cun, C. and De Nardi, M. (2010) 'The asset-backed securities markets, the crisis, and TALF', *Federal Reserve Bank of Chicago Economic Perspectives*, 4: 101–15.

Auerswald, P.E., Branscomb, L.M., La Porte, T.M. and Michel-Kerjan, E.O. (eds.) (2006) *Seeds of Disaster, Roots of Response: How Private Action Can Reduce Public Vulnerability*. New York: Cambridge University Press.

Axilrod, S.H. (2009) *Inside the Fed: Monetary Policy and Its Management, Martin through Greenspan to Bernanke*. Cambridge, MA: MIT Press.

Ayotte, K. and Skeel, D.A. (2010) 'Bankruptcy or bailouts?', *Journal of Corporation Law*, 35: 469–98.

Bagehot, W. (1873/1962) *Lombard Street: A Description of the Money Market*. Homewood, IL: Richard D. Irwin.

Balleisen, E.J. and Moss, D.A. (eds.) (2010) *Governments and Markets: Toward a New Theory of Regulation*. New York: Cambridge University Press.

Benston, G.J. (1999) *Regulating Financial Markets: A Critique and Some Proposals*. Washington, DC: AEI Press.

Bernanke, B.S. (2000) *Essays on the Great Depression*. Princeton, NJ: Princeton University Press.

Bickley, J.M. (2008) 'Chrysler Corporation Loan Guarantee Act of 1979: background, provisions, and cost', Congressional Research Service, R40005.

Black, W.K. (2011) 'Still banking on fraud', *Dollars & Sense* (Jan./Feb.), 20–25.

Blinder, A.S. (2004) *The Quiet Revolution: Central Banking Goes Modern*. New Haven, CT: Yale University Press.

Bordo, M.D. and Schwartz, A. (1999) 'Measuring real economic effects of bailouts: historical perspectives on how countries in financial distress have fared with and without bailouts', Carnegie Rochester Conference on Public Policy, November, 19–20.

Bruner, R.F. and Carr, S.D. (2007) *The Panic of 1907: Lessons Learned from the Market's Perfect Storm*. Hoboken, NJ: John Wiley & Sons.

Canis, B., Bickley, J.M., Chaikind, H., Pettit, C.A., Purcell, P., Rapaport, C. and Shorter, G. (2009) 'U.S. motor vehicle industry: federal financial assistance and restructuring', Congressional Research Service, R40003.

Congleton, J.D. (2010) 'More on the bailouts of 2008–10: the politics, effects, and limits of crisis insurance', SSRN working paper, 1709482.

Cowen, D.J. (2000) *The Origins and Economic Impact of the First Bank of the United States, 1791–1797*. New York: Garland Publishing.

Ennis, H.M. (2009) 'Avoiding the inflation tax', *International Economic Review*, 50: 607–25.

Faccio, M., Masulis, R. and McConnell, J.J. (2005) 'Political connections and corporate bailouts', SSRN Working Paper.

Faff, R.W., Parwada, J.T. and Tan, K. (2010) 'Were bank bailouts effective during the 2007–2009 financial crisis?: evidence from contagion risk in the global hedge fund industry', SSRN Working Paper 1493004.

Forman, R. (1981) 'History inside business', *Public Historian*, 3: 40–61.

Freeman, B.M. and Mendelowitz, A.I. (1982) 'Program in search of a policy: the Chrysler loan guarantee', *Journal of Policy Analysis and Management*, 1: 443–53.

Gage, B. (2009) *The Day Wall Street Exploded: A Story of America in Its First Age of Terror*. New York: Oxford University Press.

Garmon, L. (1983) 'Government rescues TRIS-pajama makers', *Science News,* 123: 22.

Glasberg, D.S. and Skidmore, D. (1997) *Corporate Welfare Policy and the Welfare State: Bank Deregulation and the Savings and Loan Bailout*. New York: Aldine De Gruyter.

Gordon, M. (1981) *Government in Business*. Montreal: C.D. Howe Institute.

Graham, A. (2010) 'Bringing to heel the elephants in the economy: the case for ending "too big to fail"', *Pierce Law Review*, 8: 117–55.

Gup, B. (2004) 'What does too big to fail mean?', in B. Gup (ed.) *Too Big To Fail: Policies and Practices in Government Bailouts*. Westport, CT: Praeger.

Hetzel, R.L. (2008) *The Monetary Policy of the Federal Reserve: A History*. New York: Cambridge University Press.

Higgs, R. (1987) *Crisis and Leviathan: Critical Episodes in the Growth of American Government*. New York: Oxford University Press.

Higgs, R. (1993) 'How military mobilization hurts the economy', in D.N. McCloskey (ed.) *Second Thoughts: Myths and Morals of U.S. Economic History*. New York: Oxford University Press.

Hill, J.A. (2010) 'Bailouts and credit-cycles: Fannie, Freddie, and the farm credit system', *Wisconsin Law Review*, 2010, 1: 1–77.

Hillinger, C. (2010) 'The crisis and beyond: thinking outside the box', *Economics: The Open-Access, Open Assessment E-Journal*. www.economics-ejournal.org/economics/journalarticles/2010-23

Hoening, T.M., Morris, C.S. and Spong, K. (2009) 'The Kansas City plan', in K.E. Scott, G.P. Shultz and J.B. Taylor (eds.) *Ending Government Bailouts As We Know Them*. Stanford, CA.: Hoover Institution Press.

Hoffman, A.C. (1980) 'The rise of economic power: some consequences and policy implications', *American Journal of Agricultural Economics,* 62: 866–72.

Honohan, P. and Klingebiel, D. (2000) 'Controlling the fiscal costs of banking crises', World Bank Policy Research Working Paper No. 2441.

Jackson, T.H. (2009) 'Chapter 11F: A proposal for the use of bankruptcy to resolve financial institutions', in K.E. Scott, G.P. Shultz and J.B. Taylor (eds.) *Ending Government Bailouts As We Know Them*. Stanford, CA: Hoover Institution Press.

Jasinowski, J.J. (1973) 'The great fiscal unknown: subsidies', *American Journal of Economics and Sociology*, 32: 1–16.

Jickling, M. (2008) 'Containing financial crisis', Congress Research Service, RL 34412.

Kamensky, J. (2008) *The Exchange Artist: A Tale of High-Flying Speculation and America's First Banking Collapse*. New York: Viking.

Kane, E.J. (1980) 'Accelerating inflation, technological innovation, and the decreasing effectiveness of banking regulation', *Journal of Finance*, 36: 355–67.

Kaufman, G.H. (2004) 'Too big to fail in U.S. banking: quo vadis?', in B. Gup (ed.) *Too Big To Fail: Policies and Practices in Government Bailouts*. Westport, CT: Praeger.

Kaufman, H. (2009) *The Road to Financial Reformation: Warnings, Consequences, Reforms*. Hoboken, NJ: John Wiley & Sons, Inc.

Kurth, J.R. (1973) 'Why we buy the weapons we do', *Foreign Policy*, 11:33–56.

Labonte, M. (2009) 'U.S. economy in recession: similarities to and differences from the past', Congressional Research Service, R40198.

Leathers, C.G. and Raines, J.P. (2004) 'Some historical perspectives on "too big to fail" policies', in B. Gup (ed.) *Too Big To Fail: Policies and Practices in Government Bailouts*. Westport, CT: Praeger.

Levitin, A.J. (2010) 'In defense of bailouts', Business, Economics and Policy Working Paper Series Research Paper No. 1548787.

Mahmud, T. (2010) 'Is it Greek or déjà vu all over again?: neoliberalism, and winners and losers of international debt crises', *Loyola University Chicago Law Journal*, 42: 629–712.

Mahoney, P.G. (2001) 'The political economy of the Securities Act of 1933', *Journal of Legal Studies*, 30: 1–31.

Mason, J.R. and Schiffman, D.A. (2004) 'Too-big-to-fail, government bailouts, and managerial incentives: the case of reconstruction finance corporation assistance to the railroad industry during the Great Depression', in B. Gup (ed.) *Too Big To Fail: Policies and Practices in Government Bailouts*. Westport, CT: Praeger.

Mattey, J.P. (1990) *The Timber Bubble That Burst: Government Policy and the Bailout of 1984*. New York: Oxford University Press.

McDiarmid, J. (1938) *Government Corporations and Federal Funds*. Chicago, IL: University of Chicago Press.

McGee, R.W. (2008) 'An ethical analysis of corporate bailouts', SSRN Working Paper 1304754.

Meltzer, A.H. (2003) *A History of the Federal Reserve, Volume I, 1913–1951*. Chicago, IL: University of Chicago Press.

Metzer, P.A. (1968) 'The impact of Section 306 upon convertible preferred stock issued in a corporate reorganization', *University of Pennsylvania Law Review*, 116: 755–98.

Mishkin, F. (2006) 'How big a problem is too big to fail?: A review of Gary Stern and Ron Feldman's *Too Big to Fail: The Hazards of Bank Bailouts*', *Journal of Economic Literature*, 44: 988–1004.

Mishkin, F. (2007) *Monetary Policy Strategy*. Cambridge: MIT Press.

Moss, D.A. (2002) *When All Else Fails: Government as the Ultimate Risk Manager*. Cambridge, MA: Harvard University Press.

Murphy, E.V. and Webel, B. (2009) 'Financial market intervention', Congressional Research Service RS22963.

Nickerson, D. and Phillips, R.J. (2004) 'The federal home loan bank system and the farm credit system: historic parallels and implications for systemic risk', in B. Gup (ed.) *Too Big To Fail: Policies and Practices in Government Bailouts*. Westport, CT: Praeger.

Norberg, J. (2009) *Financial Fiasco: How America's Infatuation with Homeownership and Easy Money Created the Economic Crisis*. Washington, DC: Cato Institute.

Odell, K.A. and Weidenmier, M. (2002) 'Real shock, monetary aftershock: the San Francisco earthquake and the panic of 1907', NBER Working Paper No. 9176.

Painter, C.M.E. (1984) 'Tort creditor priority in the secured credit system: asbestos times, the worst of times', *Stanford Law Review*, 36: 1045–85.

Perkins, E. (1994) *American Public Finance and Financial Services, 1700–1815*. Columbus, OH: Ohio State University Press.

Pierce, R.J. (1983) 'Reconsidering the roles of regulation and competition in the natural gas industry', *Harvard Law Review*, 97: 345–85.

Ramey, J.T. and Erlewine, J.A. (1954) 'Mistakes and bailouts of suppliers under government contracts and subcontracts: a study of doctrine, practice and adhesions', *Cornell Law Quarterly*, 39: 634–88.

Reich, R.B. (1982) 'Making industrial policy', *Foreign Affairs*, 60: 852–81.

Reinhart, C.M. and Rogoff, K.S. (2009) *This Time Is Different: Eight Centuries of Financial Folly*. Princeton, NJ: Princeton University Press.

Rosas, G. (2009) *Curbing Bailouts: Bank Crises and Democratic Accountability in Comparative Perspective*. Ann Arbor, MI: University of Michigan Press.

Rosas, G. and Jensen, N.M. (2010) 'After the storm: the long-run impact of bank bailouts', in R.E. Wright (ed.) *Bailouts: Public Money, Private Profit*. New York: Columbia University Press.

Rosenfield, H.N. (1985) 'The free enterprise system', *The Antioch Review*, 43: 352–63.

Roubini, N. and Setser, B. (2004) *Bailouts or Bail-Ins: Responding to Financial Crises in Emerging Markets*. New York: Peterson Institute.

Schultze, C.L. (1983) 'Industrial policy: a dissent', *The Brookings Review*, 2: 3–12.

Shapiro, A.C. (1982) 'Risk in international banking', *Journal of Finance and Quantitative Analysis*, 17: 727–39,

Shlaes, A. (2007) *The Forgotten Man: A New History of the Great Depression*. New York: Harper.

Shull, B. (2010) 'Too big to fail in financial crisis: motives, countermeasures, and prospects', Levy Economics Institute Working Paper No. 601.

Skeel, D.A. (2010) 'The new financial deal: understanding the Dodd–Frank Act and its (unintended) consequences', Institute for Law and Economics Working Paper No. 10–21.

Smith, E.P. (1853/1966) *A Manual of Political Economy*. New York: George P. Putnam & Co.

Sprague, I.H. (1986) *Bailout: An Insider's Account of Bank Failures and Rescues*. New York: Basic Books.

Stern, G.H. and Feldman, R.J. (2004) *Too Big to Fail: The Hazards of Bank Bailouts*. Washington, D.C.: Brookings Institution Press.

Stiglitz, J.E. (2002) *Globalization and Its Discontents*. New York: W.W. Norton.

Sylla, R.E., Wright, R.E. and Cowen, D.J. (2009) 'Alexander Hamilton, central banker: crisis management during the U.S. financial panic of 1792', *Business History Review*, 83: 61–86.

Tarr, D.G. (2009) 'Bailouts and deficits or haircuts: how to restore U.S. financial market stability', SSRN working paper 1401555.

Trebilock, M., Chandler, M., Gunderson, M., Halpern, P. and Quinn, J. (1985) *The Political Economy of Business Bailouts* (2 vols.). Toronto: Ontario Economic Council.

Ventrudo, M. (2009) 'The Bank of Columbia: toxic assets in the federal period', *Financial History*, 95: 24–27.

Walters, R.S. (1983) 'America's declining industrial competitiveness: protectionism, the marketplace, and the state', *PS: Political Science and Politics*, 16: 25–33.

Webel, B., Labonte, M. and Weiss, N.E. (2009) 'The cost of government financial interventions, past and present', Congressional Research Service R22956.

Weber, R. (2001) *Swords Into Dow Shares: Governing the Decline of the Military-Industrial Complex*. New York: Westview Press.

Wilmarth, A.E. (2010) 'Reforming financial regulation to address the too-big-to-fail problem', *Brooklyn Journal of International Law*, 35: 707–83.

Woods, T.E. (2009) *Meltdown: A Free-Market Look at Why the Stock Market Collapsed, the Economy Tanked, and Government Bailouts Will Make Things Worse*. Washington, DC: Regnery Publishing.

Wright, R.E. (2008) 'How to incentivize the financial system', *Central Banking*, 19: 65–67.

Wright, R.E. (2010) 'Hybrid failures and bailouts: social costs, private profits', in R.E. Wright (ed.) *Bailouts: Public Money, Private Profit*. New York: Columbia University Press.

Wright, R.E. (forthcoming) 'Private and government investment in the transportation age, 1780–1860', manuscript Augustana College.

Yabushita, S. and Inoue, A. (1993) 'The stability of the Japanese banking system: a historical perspective', *Journal of the Japanese and International Economies*, 7: 387–407.

Yokohama, K. (2007) 'Too big to fail: the panic of 1927', SSRN Working Paper 980879.

35

GOVERNMENT DEBT, ENTITLEMENTS, AND THE ECONOMY

John J. Seater

Introduction

Governments have been borrowing from the public since time immemorial, but until the end of the seventeenth century, borrowing was infrequent and of negligible size relative to the economy. Over the last 50 or 60 years, there has been an unprecedented reliance by many countries' governments on debt finance for central government expenditures. Over the same few decades, both the amount and nature of central government expenditures changed. Total spending grew because of the emergence and growth of major social spending programs, which themselves are in effect an implicit form of debt. Until recent times, there has been little obvious effect of government debt on countries' economies. However, the recent, unprecedented peacetime growth of debt and the future taxes that it implies may lead to a departure from the historical lack of association between debt and economic activity.

History of government debt

Until the last 50 or 60 years, governments generally undertook major borrowing only to finance wars. Persistent "central government" fiscal activity of any kind was mostly absent in Europe until the Hundred Years War (1337–1453). During that war, royal taxes became a permanent phenomenon because the war lasted so long (Daileader 2007). Subsequently, central governments still borrowed to pay for wars, repaying the creditors in the subsequent peace time. As Europe moved into the seventeenth century, two simultaneous developments increased the importance of debt as an element of government finance: (1) the mercantilist/ colonial era with its expansion of both commercial and political empires and (2) the development of modern capital markets. The first fueled a demand for large loans to finance temporary expenditures for colonial wars and other expansionist activities. The second made the loans available. Over most of the last three centuries, national governments continued the pattern of borrowing principally to finance wars and then repaying the loans in times of peace. Social spending programs of any consequence did not exist, and when they did begin to emerge around the beginning of the nineteenth century, they were funded with taxes, not debt. In modern times, however, governments began borrowing regularly to finance non-military activities. They also began adding to the national debt in an implicit way through spending promises implicit in various modern social welfare programs. This chapter will examine first the history of explicit debt (i.e., actual paper obligations issued by the government with stated terms of repayment) and then the history of implicit debt.

Government debt

Government debt comprises the outstanding stock of bonds, notes, and bills issued by the government. Short of default, those instruments constitute binding contracts between the government and its creditors, committing the government to repay the loans at a specific time in the future with a specific rule for determining the amount of interest payment. Figures 35.1–35.13 show the ratio of total government debt to GDP for the several countries over long time spans.[1] Measuring debt as a fraction of GDP is better for most purposes than just measuring the debt itself for two reasons. First, it automatically adjusts for price changes. Because both the numerator and the denominator are measured in dollar terms, the dollar units cancel and leave a pure fraction. Second, it adjusts for economic growth. A debt of $1 billion means much less to the U.S. today with its $15 trillion economy than in 1800 when U.S. GDP was only $520 million in current dollars. The economic implications of the debt do not depend on its absolute size but on its size relative to the economy. For these two reasons, most of the discussion below will be in terms of debt/GDP ratios.

A good place to start is with the debt histories of the Netherlands, Sweden, the United Kingdom, and the United States. We have very long time series for those four countries, and over the available sample periods none of those countries has defaulted on their national debt. Several major features of these data stand out. The first is the effect of war on a country's debt-to-GDP ratio. For now, ignore the behavior of those four countries' debt-to-GDP ratios after 1950. The post-1950 era is discussed below. National debt for the three European countries was high around 1800. For both the Netherlands and the United Kingdom, the ratio of debt to GDP peaked at a little over 250 percent; i.e., at some point the outstanding national debt was more than two and a half times as large as the gross domestic product. In both cases, the large values reflected spending on wars. The Netherlands engaged in major wars from about 1600 with Spain, through the seventeenth and eighteenth centuries with France and Britain, and ending with the Belgian revolution of 1830–31. Similarly, over the period 1692–1820 the United Kingdom engaged in major wars with France, Prussia, Russia, and Spain, as well as in a host of smaller wars with a host of other countries. Wars of both the Netherlands and the United Kingdom continued after 1830 or so but were greatly diminished in intensity and demand on the countries' treasuries. As a result of this pattern of spending, the debt/GDP ratio fluctuated with particular wars but trended upward until about 1840. After that, both wartime spending and the debt/GDP ratio trended down until the two World Wars. The United Kingdom's debt/GDP ratio shot up during World War I, started falling after the war ended, shot up again during World War II, and then fell over the next 40 years or so until about 1990. The pattern for the Netherlands is similar, except that there was little growth in the debt/GDP ratio during World War I because the Netherlands remained neutral during that war and suffered little effect of it. Sweden's debt/GDP ratio before 1950 was always much lower than the ratios for the Netherlands and the United Kingdom, never exceeding 55 percent over that period. Nonetheless, it has the same time pattern as the debt/GDP ratios for the Netherlands and the United Kingdom and for the same reasons. From 1700 to 1820, Sweden engaged in wars with Denmark, Finland, France, Norway, Russia, Prussia, and the United Kingdom, and during that time Sweden's debt was high. As Sweden's war activities petered out in the early nineteenth century, its debt/GDP ratio fell. It stayed low until the beginning of World War II. Even though Sweden remained neutral in that war, it greatly increased its defense expenditures in response to the conflicts all around it. Finally, the debt/GDP ratio for the United States follows the same overall pattern. Before 1980, US debt was a relatively small fraction of GDP, going up in wars and then back down in peace time. The U.S. came into existence in its modern form with the ratification of the U.S. Constitution in 1789. The country still had a large outstanding stock of debt left from the Revolutionary War. That debt fell over time as it was paid down until the War of 1812, when the debt/GDP ratio rose again. The debt then fell and nearly reached zero under President Andrew Jackson, the only time over the past 200 years that a major economy has had no outstanding central government debt. A small amount of debt was issued to finance the Mexican–American war over 1846–48. That debt was paid down over the next decade. The debt/GDP ratio then rose abruptly with the outbreak of the Civil War in 1861. After the war's end in 1865, the debt/GDP ratio gradually fell. It rose again during World War I and then skyrocketed during World War II to an historic high of about 120 percent of GDP. The debt/GDP ratio was so high at the end of World War II that the need for revenue during the Korean War and the Vietnam War did not reverse its downward trend.

Barro (1979) offers a theory of public debt that suggests a straightforward interpretation of these debt histories. Barro's theory is that countries at any particular moment have a desired "normal" amount of government activity, which can be measured as the ratio of government spending to GDP, called the expenditure ratio. Like everyone else, the government has a lifetime budget constraint requiring it ultimately to finance its expenditures with taxes. If there were no fluctuations in government spending or economic activity, Barro's theory implies that governments would finance all their spending with taxes. Debt comes into the picture precisely because there are fluctuations. Both the numerator and the denominator of the expenditure ratio can change temporarily in response to unexpected events. The numerator can go up because of wars. The government can finance the extra expenditure either by raising the tax rate temporarily or by borrowing. Alternatively, the denominator of the expenditure ratio can go down because of recessions. In that case, the original tax collections being used to finance government spending become a larger share of the now-lower output. The government can prevent the tax share of output from rising by temporarily reducing tax collections and replacing the lost revenue by borrowing. What should the government do?

The answer comes from a well-known result in the economics of public finance. All real-world taxes involve economic distortions because all real-world taxes are levied as a fraction of the value of some economic activity. For example, consider a worker earning a wage w, and suppose the government uses a proportional income tax with a tax rate of τ. Then each hour, the worker earns a gross wage of w, pays the government τw in tax, and keeps $(1 - \tau)$ w for himself. That means, if the worker puts in another hour on the job, he nets only $(1 - \tau) w$, not w. In effect, from the worker's point of view, his wage is effectively $(1 - \tau) w$ rather than w. The worker's employer sees it differently. What the worker pays in tax is of no concern to the employer. All he cares about is that he is paying the worker an hourly wage of w. Thus the employer and the worker have different views on what the wage is, and that difference unavoidably creates a misallocation of resources and a concomitant net social loss of welfare. In a famous article, Harberger (1964) showed that the size of the social loss is proportional to the square of the tax rate. For example, doubling the tax rate quadruples the social loss due to economic inefficiencies engendered by the tax. Squaring is a convex function, and convex functions have the property that the function evaluated at the average of two values (such as a low tax rate τ_L and a high rate τ_H) will be lower than the average of the function's values at each tax rate. That is,

$$\text{Loss}\left(\frac{\tau_L + \tau_H}{2}\right) < \frac{\text{Loss}(\tau_L) + \text{Loss}(\tau_H)}{2}$$

That in turn means that the government can minimize the social loss arising from the tax system by keeping the tax rate constant at the average tax rate $(\tau_L + \tau_H) / 2$ rather than allowing the tax rate to fluctuate as expenditure or the tax base fluctuate in response to the vagaries of transitory shocks. As a result, the best thing for the government to do when a war or a recession breaks out is to leave the tax law alone and issue debt to cover the temporary deviation of required revenue from what the existing tax law will produce. Once normal times have returned, the debt can be repaid.

Barro's theory implies that government debt will go up when the ratio of spending to GDP is unusually high for whatever reason, and will fall when that ratio is unusually low. Historically, the most important reason for fluctuations in the expenditure ratio has been war. As we have seen, most of the big increases in the debt/GDP ratio in the four countries examined above came during wars, and the decreases came during times of peace. The debt/GDP ratio behaves as if the government does use debt to prevent taxes from fluctuating wildly in response to transitory events.

The remaining countries shown in Figures 35.1–35.13 generally have shorter sample periods available, so for them attention must be confined to the nineteenth century and later. There is a wide variety of countries shown here, from some that were among the very first to develop in the mercantilist age and the Industrial Revolution to others that only recently have begun sustained economic development. Nonetheless, we see the same pattern as with the previous four countries. Those countries that engaged in either of the World Wars show increases in the debt/GDP ratio during the wars and decreases thereafter. Other wars mattered, too. For example, Spain engaged in several wars after 1860, the most important of which were the Ten Years' War in Cuba (1868–1878), the Philippine Revolution (1896–1898), the Spanish–American War (1898), and the Spanish Civil War (1936–1939). Even though wartime data sometimes are missing for many countries, the sketchy data we have shows the usual wartime/peacetime pattern.

Historically, wars have been by far the most important cause of large movements in the debt/GDP ratio before 1950. The other major cause has been cyclical fluctuations in GDP. In particular, during recessions, the debt/GDP ratio rises as GDP falls. Such movements typically are dwarfed by wars because the vast majority of recessions are small deviations from trend, whereas war spending often is a large increase over normal spending. However, a clear example of the effect of cyclical downturns on the debt/GDP ratio is the increase in the US debt/GDP ratio in the early years of the Great Depression. In 1933, output was 73 percent of what it had been in 1929. The corresponding increase in the debt/GDP ratio is obvious in Figure 35.13. A less obvious example of the same thing is the large drop in Italy's debt/GDP ratio immediately after World War II. Italy's real GDP had been depressed by the war but recovered somewhat as soon as the war ended. More important was a bout of high inflation that raised nominal GDP without changing the nominal value of the outstanding debt. Both the growth in real GDP and the inflation increased the denominator of the debt/GDP ratio without changing the numerator, thus dropping the ratio. A similar pair of events explain the sharp drop in Brazil's debt/GDP ratio over the period 1939–1951 when the ratio fell from 650 percent to 32 percent.

It is clear from the debt histories shown in Figures 35.1–35.13 that countries can sustain quite high debt/GDP ratios. The debt/GDP ratio for the United Kingdom exceeded 250 percent in 1820 and was over 100 percent for the full century from 1760 to 1860. The

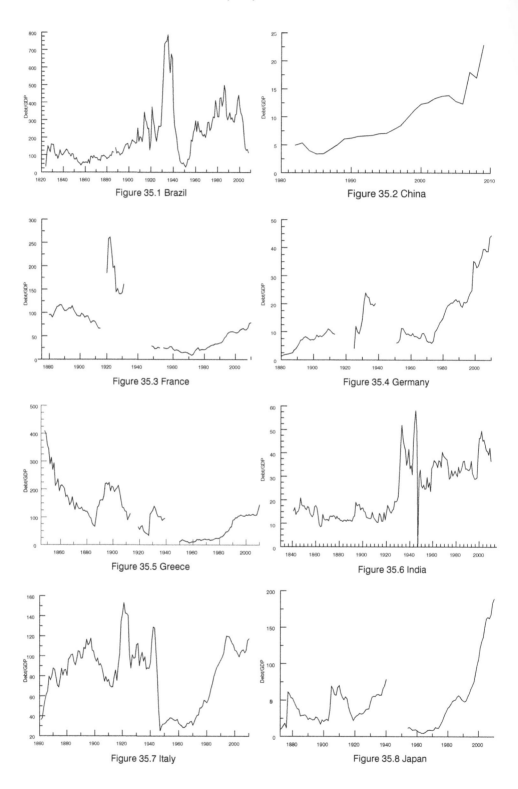

Figure 35.1 Brazil

Figure 35.2 China

Figure 35.3 France

Figure 35.4 Germany

Figure 35.5 Greece

Figure 35.6 India

Figure 35.7 Italy

Figure 35.8 Japan

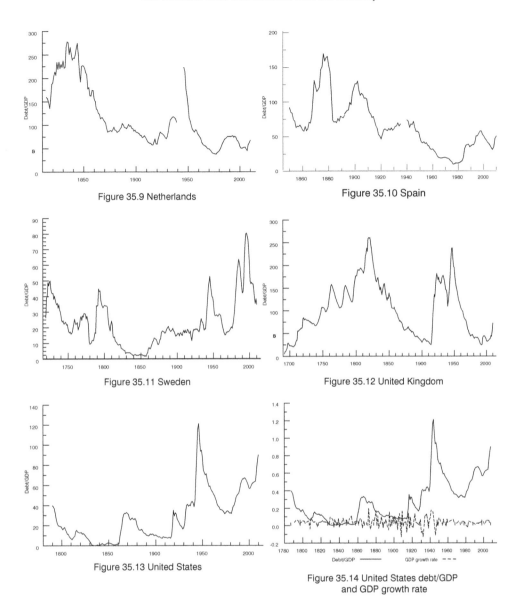

Figure 35.9 Netherlands

Figure 35.10 Spain

Figure 35.11 Sweden

Figure 35.12 United Kingdom

Figure 35.13 United States

Figure 35.14 United States debt/GDP
and GDP growth rate

ratio nearly reached 250 percent again during World War II. The debt/GDP ratio for the Netherlands was above 250 percent for much of the time between 1830 and 1845. It is interesting to contrast those high numbers with debt/GDP ratios of 144 percent, 117 percent, and a mere 48 percent for Greece, Italy, and Spain in 2010, when there was much concern over the possibility of sovereign defaults in those countries. Brazil's debt/GDP ratio exceeded 200 percent most of the time from 1908 through 1942 and all of the time from 1958 through 2004. Indeed, Brazil's ratio exceeded 500 percent from 1931 through 1939 and 300 percent every year but two from 1976 through 2002. Brazil's maximum debt/GDP ratio was 783.9 percent in 1935.

The debt/GDP ratio in every country in Figures 35.1–35.13 underwent a change in behavior somewhere between 1950 and 1980, usually between 1970 and 1980. For those thirteen countries, the debt/GDP ratio began rising as if there were either a small war or a substantial recession that persisted for twenty or thirty years, even though there was neither. All countries experienced recessions throughout the period after 1950, but the recessions did not last for two or three decades. Most of the countries in the sample engaged in no wars. In other words, at some point after 1950, each country's debt/GDP ratio began to show wartime or recession-like behavior during a time of both overall peace and overall prosperity. Some countries, such as Australia and Russia, do not show the same behavior, but enough do that there seems to be a substantial positive co-movement across countries, something that is unprecedented in the historical records. Apparently there was a change in the way countries conducted their fiscal affairs. This phenomenon has not been noted previously, much less studied, and it is unclear what caused it. For example, in all democratic countries, the growth in the debt/GDP ratio is uncorrelated with the political party running the government.

A large increase in the debt/GDP ratio during a time of both peace and prosperity is important because of its implications for future spending and taxes. Wars and recessions are temporary events. When they happen, temporary budget deficits increase the debt/GDP ratio. When normal times return, the temporary deficits disappear, and the debt/GDP ratio falls from its temporary high. The situation is quite different when the debt/GDP ratio rises in times of peace and prosperity because there is nothing obviously temporary about the deficits that are driving up the ratio. The increased debt eventually must be repaid, along with the interest on it, but there is no automatic future economic event to make that happen. Governments that accumulate high debt relative to GDP in normal economic times are committing themselves to one of three possibilities: substantially lower future expenditures than used to be normal, substantially higher taxes than used to be normal, or a default on the debt, which is just a type of tax aimed specifically at the government's creditors.[2] At the time of this writing, that was exactly the situation most of Europe found itself in, with Portugal, Italy, Ireland, Greece, and Spain all teetering on the edge of either a major default on their debt or an enormous and socially disruptive realignment of their tax, spending, and monetary policies. Other countries, including Belgium, France, and the United States, were not as immediately threatened but faced the same problems. All governments face a lifetime resource constraint, according to which the present value of spending, including debt repayment, must be matched by the present value of tax collections. The constraint is the economic equivalent of the conservation of mass and energy. It is an identity, guaranteed to bind. Many governments apparently did not understand that and found themselves facing completely predictable unpleasant choices regarding spending and taxation.

Social spending: entitlements as implicit debt

In economics and finance, the term "debt" implies the existence of an explicit loan contract that specifies the terms of repayment. That is the kind of debt this chapter has discussed so far. Debt in that sense is a promise by one party to repay money borrowed from another party, backed up by force of law. What should one make of political promises to provide benefits at some future time or under some particular circumstances? On the one hand, there are explicit promises to make payments under specific conditions, but on the other hand there is no legal authority guaranteeing that those promises will be kept. The absence of a guarantee of repayment in fact is not as decisive a difference as it may seem. Formal debt does not guarantee repayment because there always is the possibility of default due either to bankruptcy or to inflation. The difference between formal debt and political promises seems more a matter of degree than of kind. To use financial terminology, political promises are merely riskier expected future payments than are the payments associated with formal

Table 35.1 Early social spending

| | Year | Percent of GNP | |
		Poor relief	Public education
Belgium	1820	1.03	
	1850	0.28	0.38
England & Wales	1776	1.59	0
	1820–1821	2.66	0
	1850	1.07	0.07
France	1833	0.63	0.13
Netherlands	1790	1.70	
	1822	1.36	
	1850	1.38	0.29
Sweden	1829	0.02	
United States	1850	0.13	0.33
All other countries	1776–1815	≈0	≈0

Source: Table 1.1, Lindert (2004)

debt instruments. With that perspective, we now examine the historical behavior of social spending or, as it often is called, entitlement spending.

Social spending comprises many components. Tables 35.1 and 35.2, taken from Lindert (2004), show the growth of social spending in several countries since the early nineteenth century.

For all the countries shown, the history is roughly the same: social spending grew slowly before World War II and then rapidly after it. The first social spending programs were for poor relief. Those were in place in several countries by the early nineteenth century and in England by the late eighteenth century. Around the middle of the nineteenth century, countries began public education programs. Around 1880, new types of social programs began to appear: health care subsidies, pension subsidies, unemployment compensation, and housing subsidies, usually in that order. The first countries to institute those types of programs were Australia, Denmark, New Zealand, Norway, Sweden, and the United Kingdom. Other countries followed over the next 70 years or so. Table 35.2 shows that social spending increased, often very rapidly, in all developed countries.

Table 35.3 shows the composition of social spending for 21 OECD countries in 1995. Associated with these new expenditures were promises of still more expenditures in the future. When countries adopted these programs, they did not merely pay benefits to the existing population. They also promised to pay the same kinds of benefits to future generations. The spending programs carry an implicit promise to make specific payments in the future, so it seems reasonable to treat entitlements as an implicit public debt. The size of that debt can only be estimated because there are no printed bonds attesting to the amount to be paid. By any estimate, the implied debt is huge. For the U.S., Tanner (2011) estimates that at the beginning of 2011 the value of the future expenditures promised by the federal retirement (Social Security) and health care (Medicare and Medicaid) programs was at least $45 trillion and perhaps as much as $104 trillion. The ambiguity arises from uncertainties about the path of Medicare expenditures. The amount of federal debt in the hands of the public at the beginning of 2011 was far smaller, only $9.6 trillion. U.S. GDP at the time was

Table 35.2 Social transfers in 21 OECD countries' percentages of GDP

	1880	1890	1900	1910	1920	1930	1960	1970	1980	1990	1995
Australia	0	0	0	1.12	1.66	2.11	7.39	7.37	10.90	13.57	14.84
Austria	0	0	0	0	0	1.20	15.88	18.90	23.43	24.54	21.39
Belgium	0.17	0.22	0.26	0.43	0.52	0.56	13.14	19.26	22.45	23.11	27.13
Canada	0	0	0	0	0.06	0.31	9.12	11.80	12.91	17.38	18.09
Denmark	0.96	1.11	1.41	1.75	2.71	3.11	12.26	19.13	26.44	26.97	30.86
Finland	0.66	0.76	0.78	0.90	0.85	2.97	8.81	13.56	18.32	24.66	31.65
France	0.46	0.54	0.57	0.81	0.64	1.05	13.42	16.68	22.95	23.70	26.93
Germany	0.50	0.53	0.59	–	–	4.82	18.10	19.53	20.42	19.85	24.92
Greece	0	0	0	0	0	0.07	10.44	9.03	8.67	13.95	14.43
Ireland						3.74	8.70	11.89	16.20	18.05	18.30
Italy	0	0	0	0	0	0.08	13.10	16.94	17.10	21.34	23.71
Japan	0.05	0.11	0.17	0.18	0.18	0.21	4.05	5.72	10.48	11.57	12.24
Netherlands	0.29	0.30	0.39	0.39	0.99	1.03	11.70	22.45	26.94	27.59	25.70
New Zealand	0.17	0.39	1.09	1.35	1.84	2.43	10.37	9.22	16.22	22.12	18.64
Norway	1.07	0.95	1.24	1.18	1.09	2.39	7.85	16.13	18.50	26.44	27.55
Portugal	0	0	0	0	0	0	–	–	10.10	12.62	15.23
Spain	0	0	0	0.02	0.04	0.07	–	–	12.97	17.01	19.01
Sweden	0.72	0.85	0.85	1.03	1.14	2.59	10.83	16.76	29.78	32.18	33.01
Switzerland	–	–	–	–	–	1.17	4.92	8.49	14.33	–	18.87
UK	0.86	0.83	1.00	1.38	1.39	2.24	10.21	13.20	16.94	18.05	22.52
USA	0.29	0.45	0.55	0.56	0.70	0.56	7.26	10.38	11.43	11.68	13.67
Median	0.29	0.39	0.55	0.69	0.78	1.66	10.41	14.84	21.36	24.00	22.52

Source: Table 1.2, Lindert (2004)

$14.5 trillion. Not only does the debt implicit in entitlement programs dwarf the official debt, it also dwarfs the US economy. Presumably the same is true for other countries with large social spending programs, such as those shown in Tables 35.2 and 35.3.

Measurement Issues

Measuring the amount of government debt is not as simple as one might think. Obviously measuring the present value of promised future social spending involves some estimation because there are no securities or other documents specifying the schedule of future payments, and there is no legal commitment behind the promises. However, measuring just traditional debt (outstanding government bonds, notes, and bills) is not completely straightforward, either. The simplest measure of government debt is the sum of all the individual outstanding government securities. That number often is reported in newspaper accounts and political debates, but it must be adjusted for inflation, interest rate changes, who holds the debt, and the size of the economy, to be as informative as possible.

The usual number for the size of the debt reported in the press is the nominal par value of government securities. The nominal value is the price in dollars that the securities would fetch on the open market. That value is fixed at the time the debt is issued (except for the very small fraction of "inflation protected" securities). Consequently, if general prices rise because

Table 35.3 Types of social spending in 21 OECD countries in 1995 percent of GDP

	Public pensions and disability	Unem- ployment compensa- tion	Public welfare	Public health	Public housing and other	Total social transfers	Public education
Australia	4.1	1.3	3.4	5.8	0.3	14.8	4.5
Austria	10.5	1.4	2.8	6.3	0.4	21.4	5.3
Belgium	12.2	2.8	3.7	7.8	0.6	27.1	5.0
Canada	5.2	1.3	1.4	7.1	3.1	18.1	5.8
Denmark	11.6	4.6	6.0	6.2	2.4	30.9	6.5
Finland	14.2	4.0	5.8	6.5	1.1	31.6	6.6
France	10.9	1.8	3.9	8.9	1.4	26.9	5.8
Germany	10.3	2.4	3.4	8.1	0.8	24.9	4.5
Greece	9.6	0.4	0.4	3.9	0.1	14.4	3.7
Ireland	4.7	2.7	3.4	6.2	1.3	18.3	4.7
Italy	15.2	0.9	1.7	6.0	0.0	23.7	4.5
Japan	5.3	0.4	0.5	5.8	0.2	12.2	3.6
Netherlands	10.4	3.1	2.5	8.7	1.0	25.7	4.6
New Zealand	6.4	1.1	2.9	7.4	0.8	18.6	5.3
Norway	12.4	1.1	5.1	7.8	1.1	27.6	6.8
Portugal	6.7	1.0	1.8	5.6	0.1	15.2	5.4
Spain	9.8	2.5	1.2	6.8	0.2	20.4	4.8
Sweden	14.8	2.3	6.2	7.5	2.2	33.0	6.6
Switzerland	6.7	1.1	1.5	8.2	1.3	18.9	5.5
UK	10.6	0.9	2.8	6.1	2.1	22.5	4.6
USA	5.2	0.3	0.8	6.7	0.6	13.7	5.0

Source: Table 7.1, Lindert (2004)

of inflation, the real value of the debt (the number of goods that the nominal debt can buy) goes down. Real, not nominal, values are what matter because people are interested in how many goods they can buy with the wealth that their bonds represent, which is precisely what the real value measures. Adjusting official debt and deficit figures for inflation can make a big difference to measurements of the debt's size. For example, for 1947, the official statistics report a federal surplus of $6.6 billion. However, inflation that year was nearly 15 percent; this inflation reduced the value of the huge outstanding debt by about $11.4 billion. That reduction was equivalent to an additional surplus because it reduced the real value of what the federal government owed its creditors. The true surplus was about $18 billion, nearly three times the official figure. Similarly, the official federal deficit was positive every year of the 1970s, whereas the inflation-corrected deficit was negative (i.e., there was a real surplus) in exactly half those years.

The par value of the debt is the face value of the debt, which is fixed. The market value of the debt is what the debt sells for in the open market. The market value changes inversely with market interest rates and can be quite different from the par value. Unfortunately, market values for the total outstanding government debt are not readily available.

Still another measurement issue concerns total central government debt versus debt in the hands of the public. The numbers usually reported in the press and often elsewhere are the value of total debt. Some of that total, however, may be entirely internal to the government.

One agency may borrow from another. That kind of behavior has been a common occurrence in the United States, where federal agencies with more revenue than they needed in a given year would lend the surplus to other federal agencies. The loans take the form of federal debt assigned as a credit to the lending agency and a liability to the borrowing agency. That internal federal debt is included in total federal debt. However, internal debt is merely a bookkeeping device that implies no future taxes. One agency's liability is another agency's credit, and the two cancel. An example may be helpful.

Suppose the federal government plans to spend $100 billion for national defense. In the absence of any other revenue source, Congress would impose a tax of $100 billion to pay for the expenditure. For ease of discussion, suppose the tax used is the personal income tax. Suppose also that the Social Security system is obliged this year to pay out $200 billion in benefits to retirees, which it obtains from the Social Security tax. In the absence of any other consideration, U.S. taxpayers have a total tax bill of $300 billion – $100 billion to pay for national defense and $200 billion to pay for Social Security benefits.

Now suppose that this year happens to be a boom year for the economy, and as a result the Social Security tax raises $210 billion in revenue. The Social Security system thus has $10 billion more in revenue than it has in expenditures. What does it do with the extra money? It lends it to the U.S. Treasury by buying Treasury bonds. By law, when Social Security revenues exceed expenditures, the excess is invested in special non-marketable U.S. Government bonds. As a result, in the example under discussion, Congress only needs to raise $90 billion from the personal income tax, and so it reduces taxes to that amount. U.S. taxpayers *still* have a total tax bill of $300 billion, but it is distributed across the two types of tax differently than when there was no intra-government loan. So in the year that the special government bonds are issued, taxpayers see no change in their tax payments compared to what those payments would have been without the special bonds. What happens when the special bonds are repaid?

To keep the example simple, suppose the special government bonds sold to the Social Security system have a maturity of one year and carry an interest rate of 10 percent. Suppose also that in the second year national defense spending is $150 billion and Social Security benefits are $210 billion. In the absence of the bonds, the government would have to collect $150 billion from the personal income tax and $210 billion from the Social Security tax. Taxpayers thus would have a total tax bill of $360 billion. However, with the bonds, the Treasury must repay the money it borrowed from the Social Security system last year plus interest. That payment is $11 billion, comprising $10 billion in principal and $1 billion in interest. To cover all its expenditures, the Treasury needs $161 billion in revenue from the personal income tax: $150 billion for national defense and $11 billion to repay its loan from the Social Security system. Now consider the Social Security system. It needs $210 billion to pay this year's Social Security benefits. However, it has $11 billion in receipts from the Treasury, so it needs to collect only $199 billion from the Social Security tax. Taxpayers thus must pay $161 billion in personal income tax and $199 billion in Social Security tax for a total tax payment of $360 billion, which is exactly the same as if the internal government debt didn't exist. The two possible scenarios are identical in terms of how much taxpayers end up paying the government and in terms of the effects on taxpayers' incentives to undertake economic activity.

The foregoing example shows that the government as a whole cannot raise revenue by issuing internal debt. What one department receives for the sale of the debt is matched by what another department paid. Internal debt implies no net taxes on the public. That's why for economic analysis the internal debt should be ignored and only the external debt or "debt in the hands of the public" should be included.

As with adjustments discussed above, accounting for internal government debt can make a big difference to the economically relevant quantity of debt outstanding. For example, at the beginning of 2012, total federal debt was about the same size as the US gross domestic product, so the debt/GDP ratio was about 100 percent. However, fully one-third of that debt was internal. When the internal debt is subtracted, the ratio of the remaining debt "in the hands of the public" to GDP was about 67 percent.

Finally, as mentioned earlier, for most purposes the value of the outstanding debt should be measured as a fraction of the economy, which is why our earlier discussion dealt with the debt/GDP ratio.

In trying to understand the behavior of government debt of the last two centuries, the important adjustments are for inflation and the size of the economy. The other two – measuring market value rather than par value and adjusting for internal debt – do not alter the major movements of debt over long periods. Fortunately, adjusting for inflation and the size of the economy is easy. Data for nominal debt and nominal GDP are readily available, and all one needs to do is divide one by the other to get the real debt/GDP ratio.

Economic effects

There is little evidence that "normal" levels of debt in themselves have much effect on economic activity. Figure 35.14, for example, shows the debt/GDP ratio and the growth rate of real GDP for the United States.[3]

There is no apparent correlation. A large body of empirical work has found no robust relation between debt on the one hand and a host of important variables on the other, including the level of output, the growth rate of output, consumption, unemployment, investment, interest rates, and inflation. See Seater (1993) and Ricciuti (2003) for surveys of the literature. There are effects of the level of government spending and the structure of the tax system used to pay for it, but the timing of taxes – which is what debt affects – seems not to have had any appreciable effect on anything of importance. That lack of effect is consistent with the Ricardian Equivalence Hypothesis that all households taken as a whole do not treat government debt as net wealth because households take into account the future taxes implied by the debt. However, Ricardian Equivalence requires that taxes be lump-sum in nature, which they never are in any developed economy. The consistency of the data with Ricardian Equivalence thus must be due to some other hitherto undiscovered explanation. What might that be?

To begin to answer that question, let's consider the channels through which government debt can affect the economy. There are two: wealth effects and the timing of distorting taxes.

The idea behind the wealth effect is that government can reduce current taxes by issuing debt. The reduction in taxes makes households feel wealthier, which induces them to increase aggregate demand. There are many slips twixt cup and lip in that story, too many to discuss here, but the one addressed by Ricardian Equivalence is that households are rational and forward-looking, will recognize the future taxes implied by the current debt, and so not feel any wealthier at all when the government substitutes debt for current taxes. As with any bond, government debt carries an explicit promise to repay the lender at some specific future time. To make those repayments, the government ultimately will have to raise future taxes beyond what it otherwise will need to pay for its other activities. A simple example illustrates. Suppose the government buys $1 trillion worth of goods and services every year and pays for them entirely by collecting taxes. The government's budget is balanced because revenue equals expenditure. Suppose that the government decides to keep its expenditures the same but change the way it finances them. In the first year, the government reduces taxes by $100 billion and replaces the lost revenue by selling $100 billion worth of bonds that mature in one year and carry an interest rate of 10 percent a year. In the second year, the bonds mature, and the government pays the $100 billion principal and the $10 billion of interest. Taxes in the first year are $100 billion lower, and the government runs a deficit of that amount. In the second year, however, taxes must be $110 billion higher, and the government runs a surplus. In the first year, the collection of citizens give the same total amount of revenue to the government as they did when they paid only taxes, but now $100 billion of the total payment is in the form of a loan that will be repaid in the second year with $10 billion in interest. On that account, people may feel richer because they seem to be paying less in total taxes over the two periods. This year, they pay $900 billion in taxes and $100 billion in loans, for the same $1 trillion total that they were paying before the government decided to issue debt. Next year, however, it seems they will be better off than before. They will pay $1 trillion in taxes but they will receive $110 billion in repayment of their first-year loan. Their net payment in the second year will be only $890 billion. This may seem like a good deal, but it will not turn out that way. When the second year arrives, people will find that their net payment is $1 trillion, just as if the debt never had been issued. To pay the $110 billion in principal and interest, the government must come up with an extra $110 billion in revenue, so it must raise taxes by that amount. Those extra taxes exactly cancel the payment of the principal and interest! The government gives with one hand and takes away with the other. The net result is that people don't really get back the $100 billion they lent the government or the $10 billion in interest on it, and the loan is equivalent to having paid the $100 billion in taxes in the first year. The same result holds from any maturity of debt, whether it is a one-year bond, as in the previous example, a ten-year bond or even a perpetuity. There is a lot of evidence that people are forward-looking in planning their consumption expenditures and work effort, and there is no reason to think they fail to account for taxes when they are figuring their future incomes. The wealth effect of public debt thus seems doubtful, and the data do not support its existence.[4]

The second channel through which debt can affect the economy is by altering the timing of the economic distortions inherent in any realistic tax system. Taxes in the real world take some fraction of the "tax base" and give it to the government. The problem with real-world taxes is that they have positive marginal tax rates. Without loss of generality, we can keep the discussion simple by restricting attention to income taxes. The marginal income tax rate reduces the marginal rate of return from any economic activity and thus distorts incentives to work, invest, borrow, and lend. Government debt rearranges the timing of tax collections. It therefore also rearranges the incentive effects associated with those taxes and so will affect the timing of people's economic decisions and have real effects on the economy. The disincentive effects are stronger if people do not know what the new timing of tax collections will be after debt is issued. Even if a newly-issued government bond says it will be repaid in 10 years, the government may avoid collecting the taxes to repay the debt by rolling over the debt, i.e., by issuing new debt to replace the maturing debt. As a result, no one really knows when the government will collect the taxes to repay the outstanding debt.

It appears that government behaves as if it understands the incentive effects involved (Lindert 2004, Alexander and Seater 2012). When expenditures are a large share of GDP and thus require taxing away a large fraction of GDP, governments typically reduce the distortions in the tax law by broadening the tax base and making tax less progressive with lower marginal tax rates. Thus the average tax rate goes up, but the marginal rate rises little or even falls. To see how that can happen, consider the following simple but surprisingly accurate formula for the progressive income tax:

$$t = aY^b$$

where T is tax revenue, Y is taxable income (the *tax base*), and a and b are constants determined by the tax law. If $b > 1$, the tax is progressive. The marginal tax rate (MTR) is

$$\text{MTR} = \frac{dT}{dY} = baY^{b-1}$$

which is positive. Because the government has two parameters at its disposal, it can simultaneously increase T and reduce MTR by moving a and b in opposite directions. Such changes in the tax structure could largely nullify the rearrangement of tax distortions that would be caused by replacing current taxes with debt. An example will illustrate how this works.

Begin by setting up a baseline by considering the case where the government finances all expenditures with taxes, issuing no bonds. Suppose the government needs $10 billion in revenue. Let $Y = 100$, $a = 0.04$, and $b = 1.2$. Then solving the above expressions gives $T = 10$ and MTR $= 0.12$. Now suppose the government decides to sell bonds in the first period to reduce taxes by $1 billion. The bonds have a maturity of one year and carry an interest rate of 10 percent. The government will repay the bonds and the interest in the second period. Suppose that in doing all this the government wants to keep the marginal tax rate at 0.12. In the first period the government needs $9 billion in tax revenue. A little algebra shows that, to collect that amount of revenue and also keep the marginal tax rate at 0.12, the government must set $a = 0.019$ and $b = 1.333$. In the second period, the government must repay the debt plus the interest on it and also must collect revenue to pay for its regular expense of $10 billion. The debt plus interest amounts to $1.1 billion, so the government needs to collect a total of $11.1 billion in taxes while keeping the marginal tax rate at 0.12. Again, a little algebra shows that the government must set $a = 0.077$ and $b = 1.08$. Thus when the government needs less tax revenue, it chooses a low value for a and a high value for b, and does just the opposite when it needs more revenue. This simple example shows how the values of a and b can be played off against each other to achieve any combination of average tax rate T/Y and marginal tax rate MTR.

The historical evidence shows that what governments generally have done with taxes is manipulate a and b so that the marginal tax rate is low when the average tax rate is high and vice versa. Lindert (2004) presents a large amount of cross-country evidence that countries with high tax burdens also have relatively low marginal tax rates. Alexander and Seater (2012) present evidence that over the life of the personal income tax in the U.S., a and b have moved in opposite directions. That kind of behavior reduces one kind of economic impact of the tax law (either a high average tax rate or a high marginal tax rate) when the other impact is large. Playing off the two kinds of effects against each other may explain why the data generally are consistent with Ricardian Equivalence, as discussed above. When the government reduces current taxes by borrowing today, it effectively promises higher taxes in the future. Apparently when governments actually do that, they also increase the marginal tax rate today and reduce it in the future, easing one burden to offset an increase in the other.

We must conclude on a note of caution, however. Over recent decades, as we have seen, governments have driven up debt/GDP ratios and simultaneously have increased social spending and the debt implicit in it. The total debt, explicit plus implicit, now is huge, several times GDP in many countries. It may well be impossible for the government to meet those obligations by raising taxes. The tax increases may have to be so large that both a and b must be increased substantially, leading to large increases in both kinds of economic impacts discussed above: the total tax burden and the marginal tax rate. That situation is unprecedented among the developed economies of the world, so we have little experience on which to base predictions of how it will play out. Past binge-and-default cycles in countries such as Argentina and Brazil are not encouraging. Reinhart and Rogoff (2009), in an exhaustive study, find that huge increases in debt/GDP ratios of the type we have seen recently in much of the world usually are associated with subsequent severe economic downturns and defaults on government debt.

Notes

1 Data are from Carmen M. Reinhart's web page: http://www.carmenreinhart.com/data/browse-by-topic/topics/9/
2 Inflation, an option frequently used by deeply indebted governments, is a type of tax that falls on those who own debt with interest rates that were fixed before the inflation started. Because it falls on those who hold nominal debt, it can be regarded as a method of gradually defaulting on the debt.
3 Data on debt-to-GDP ratio is from Carmen M. Reinhart. See footnote 1. Real GDP growth rates are computed from the data on the level of real GDP in Carter et al. (2006) and the U.S. Department of Commerce's "National Economic Accounts."
4 There are many minor qualifications to the foregoing discussion, but they do not affect the final conclusion of no convincing evidence in favor of an important wealth effect of government debt. See Seater (1993) and Ricciuti (2003) for detailed discussion.

References

Alexander, M. Erin and John J. Seater. (2012) "The nonlinear federal income tax," working paper, North Carolina State University.
Barro, Robert J. (1979) "On the determination of the public debt," *Journal of Political Economy* 87: 940–71.
Carter, Susan B., Scott Sigmund Gartner, Michael R. Haines, Alan L. Olmstead, Richard Sutch, and Gavin Wright. (2006) *Historical Statistics of the United States: Earliest Times to the Present,* New York: Cambridge University Press.
Daileader, Philip (2007) *The Late Middle Ages*, Chantilly, VA: The Teaching Company.
Harberger, Arnold C. (1964) "The measurement of waste," *American Economic Review* 54: 58–76.
Lindert, Peter H. (2004) *Growing Public: Social Spending and Economic Growth Since the Eighteenth Century*, New York: Cambridge University Press.
Reinhart, Carmen M. (n.d.) "Debt-to-GDP Ratios," http://www.carmenreinhart.com/data/browse-by-topic/topics/9/
Reinhart, Carmen M. and Kenneth S. Rogoff. (2009) *This Time Is Different: Eight Centuries of Financial Folly*, Princeton, NJ: Princeton University Press.
Ricciuti, Roberto (2003) "Assessing Ricardian equivalence," *Journal of Economic Surveys* 17: 55–78.
Seater, John J. (1993) "Ricardian equivalence," *Journal of Economic Literature* 31: 142–90.
Tanner, Michael (2011) "Bankrupt: entitlements and the federal budget," *Policy Analysis* #673, Washington, DC: Cato Institute.
U.S. Department of Commerce (n.d) "National Economic Accounts", http://www.bea.gov/national/

INDEX

Note numbers follow page numbers with an *n*.

Printed and bound by CPI Group (UK) Ltd, Croydon, CR0 4YY

08/05/2025

01864335-0004